# fourth edition

# JAZZ STYLES
## history & analysis

## MARK C. GRIDLEY

*Heidelberg College*
*Tiffin, Ohio 44883*

**prentice hall**   englewood cliffs, new jersey 07632

Library of Congress Cataloging-in-Publication Data

Gridley, Mark C.
    Jazz styles : history & analysis /Mark C. Gridley.--4th ed.
     442 p.   cm.
    Includes bibliographical references and index.
    ISBN 0-13-508458-X (1 cassette), 0-13-507963-2 (2 cassettes)
    1. Jazz--Analysis, appreciation. 2. Style. Musical. 3. Jazz
musicians. I. Title.
ML3506.G74  1991                                        90-19473
781.65--dc20                                               CIP
                                                           MN

Editorial/production supervision and interior design: Arthur Maisel and Jordan Ochs
Cover design: Pat McCarty
Prepress buyer: Herb Klein
Manufacturing buyer: Dave Dickey

Portions of pages 68–74 originally appeared in *Jazz Educators Journal*, Vol. XVI (1984), No. 3, pp 71–72, as "Why is Louis Armstrong So Important?" Portions of pages 324–332 originally appeared in *Popular Music and Society*, Vol. IX (1983), No. 2, pp. 27–34, as "Clarifying Labels: Jazz, Rock, Funk and Jazz-Rock." Portions of pages 40–49 originally appeared in *The Black Perspective in Music*, Vol. 12 (1984), No. 1, pp. 44–56, as "Towards Identification of African Traits in Early Jazz." Portions of pages 166–172 originally appeared in *Popular Music and Society*, Vol. IX (1984), No. 4, pp. 41–45, as "Why Have Modern Jazz Combos Been Less Popular Than Swing Big Bands?" Portions of pages of 195–199 originally appeared in *Tracking: Popular Music Studies*, Vol. 2 (1990), Issue 2, pp. 8–16, as "Clarifying Labels: Cool Jazz, West Coast and Hard Bop." All of the above are reproduced here by permission of their respective editors. The "(Meet the) Flintstones Theme" is used on the JAZZ STYLES CASSETTE by permission of Barbera-Hanna Music (copyright 1960 and 1967), composed by William Hanna, Joseph Barbera and Hoyt Curtin. Reproduction and performance without permission of Barbera-Hanna Music is forbidden.

 ©1991, 1988, 1985, 1978 by Prentice-Hall, Inc.
A Division of Simon & Schuster
Englewood Cliffs, New Jersey 07632

Printed in the United States of America

10  9  8  7  6  5  4  3

ISBN   0-13-508458-X        with 1 cassette

ISBN   0-13-507963-2        with 2 cassettes

Prentice-Hall International (UK) Limited, *London*
Prentice-Hall of Australia Pty. Limited, *Sydney*
Prentice-Hall Canada Inc., *Toronto*
Prentice-Hall Hispanoamericana, S.A., *Mexico*
Prentice-Hall of India Private Limited, *New Delhi*
Prentice-Hall of Japan, Inc., *Tokyo*
Simon & Schuster Asia Pte. Ltd., *Singapore*
Editora Prentice-Hall do Brasil, Ltda., *Rio de Janeiro*

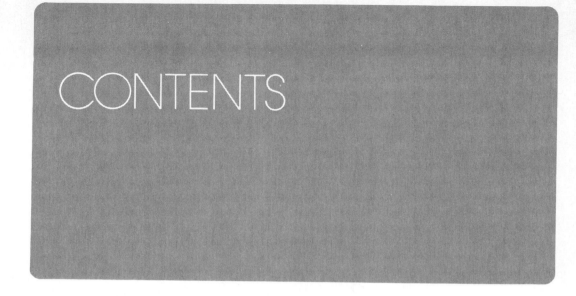

# CONTENTS

# APPENDIX

# TABLES & ILLUSTRATIONS

## TABLES

## SPECIAL BOXED FEATURES

## LINE DRAWINGS AND INSTRUMENT PHOTOS

## MUSICIAN PHOTOS

# PREFACE

The purpose of this text is to help listeners increase their appreciation and enjoyment of jazz. The book and its accompanying JAZZ STYLES CASSETTE give readers a peek into how jazz musicians put together performances and how methods have differed from style to style. There is discussion of how jazz originated, and the JAZZ CLASSICS CASSETTE offers examples of the earliest recordings as well as many major styles that developed later. A variety of styles are described in ways that should help the reader get more out of listening to them. Styles are presented in roughly chronological order, and the historically minded reader can use that order to examine major currents in the history of jazz, though the book was intended as a description of the styles themselves rather than a decade-by-decade chronicle of the changing jazz scene.

This text was designed as a smorgasbord of selections so readers would have a flexible reference source. Chapters can be skipped without doing serious damage to an introductory course in jazz appreciation or a single-semester course in jazz history. Numerous deletions and rearrangements in this book's contents have supplied workable sequences for hundreds of jazz courses since the first edition appeared in 1978.

Because of space limitations, this book deals almost exclusively with American instrumental jazz, and coverage is neither comprehensive nor encyclopedic. For more comprehensive coverage, see "Supplementary Reading" (pages 406–411), the books that are footnoted throughout the text, and the discussions, bibliographies, and discographies that appear in the author's teacher's manuals available from Prentice Hall and from the International Association of Jazz Educators. With space limitations in mind, however, the book was designed to devote proportionally more pages to music that developed since 1940, especially the past thirty years. Because, since the first jazz recordings were not made until 1917, about two-thirds of recorded jazz history has occurred since 1940, and this is music that occupies the lion's share of available recording, nightclub, and concert fare encountered by today's readers. Much of the music discussed here in reference to the 1960s—John Coltrane and Chick Corea for instance—provided foundations for the dominant styles of the 1970s, 80s, and 90s, just as much discussed here in reference to the 1930s—such as Count Basie and Lester Young for instance—provided foundations for the dominant styles of the 1940s and 50s.

No technical knowledge of music is required to understand the contents of this book, and the text's vocabulary has proven to be comprehensible for high school students as well as college students. Past editions have been used effectively in high schools and community colleges as well as in universities. Many instructors have successfully taught their courses from this book without devoting any attention to technical terms. Other instructors have used the "Elements of Music" appendix (pages 358–90) at the beginning of their course to introduce basic technical concepts before discussing selected jazz styles.

Though the book was originally conceived as a text for non-musicians, previous editions have also been used as the basic text in jazz history courses for music majors. This occurred because of the "For Musicians" appendix (pages 415–31) that provides notations illustrating basic musical principles (chord changes, modes, comping, walking bass, ride rhythms, etc.) and because the book is especially concerned with detailing the ways styles sound and how they can be differentiated in terms of preferred instruments, tone quality, melody, harmony, rhythm, and approaches to improvisation. Supplements of musical notation are referenced in footnotes throughout the text as well as in "Technical References" (pages 410–11) and "Sources for Notated Jazz Solos" (pages 412–14).

**How To Use This Book** With the JAZZ STYLES CASSETTE and the addition of the new JAZZ CLASSICS CASSETTE, this text can serve as the core of a self-paced course of study in which the reader/listener becomes familiar with the sights and sounds of jazz, separate from the presentations made by the instructor. Technical concepts that otherwise require lecture/demonstrations by professional musicians can be learned by pairing the cassette with the accompanying text pages. The contents of the JAZZ STYLES CASSETTE can be used as reinforcement of lecture/demonstrations performed by the instructor because they provide a handy source of review materials for study outside of class. Some professors have required that their students learn the contents of the JAZZ STYLES CASSETTE outside of class, presenting additional styles in the class time they saved in not having to cover those topics on the cassette. No matter what approach is taken to using this textbook and its cassettes, every individual and class is encouraged to listen to as much jazz, both recorded and live, as possible. **The book will be an effective guide only if reading is accompanied by extensive listening.**

This book was originally conceived in an omnibus format whose organization was intended to provide a flexible reference for learning about jazz. The next five paragraphs outline approaches that have proven successful in colleges and universities where previous editions of this book have been required.

The text provides the essentials for a course in UNDERSTANDING JAZZ if it is accompanied by a well-chosen collection of records (the footnoted albums provide a good start) and several carefully conceived, in-class demonstrations by musicians. For those demonstrations, many instructors follow the guidelines described in "Getting the Most From a Drumming Demonstration and Live Rhythm Section" in *How To Teach Jazz History* (Mark C. Gridley, NAJE Press, 1984; available from the International Association of Jazz Educators, Box 724, Manhattan, Kansas

66502; phone 913–776–8744). They also use the strategies that are demonstrated in "Teaching Jazz History to Nonmusicians" and "Where's the Melody" (1984 NAJE Convention Cassettes #37 and 38, available from Mark Records, 10815 Bodine Road, Clarence, NY 14031; phone 716–759–2600). Previous editions of the text have been used in this way at several colleges, with these chapters providing the keys: Elements of Music Appendix (pages 358–391), chapter 2 (What is Jazz?), chapter 3 (Appreciating Jazz Improvisation), and chapter 4 (Origins of Jazz). Much emphasis was placed on the listening guides that appear throughout the text. Instructors usually supplemented that material with selected portions of styles chapters. The portions that give readers the greatest insight into how jazz is made are the nonbiographical units that appear at the beginnings of chapters 5, 6, 9, 14, and 16.

The text provides the essentials for a historically organized INTRODUCTION TO JAZZ STYLES. Again, a basic collection of records is essential. The skeleton of the course is contained in the "styles" chapters: chapter 5 (Early Jazz), chapter 6 (Swing), chapter 9 (Bop), chapter 10 (Cool), chapter 11 (Hard Bop), chapter 14 (Avant-Garde/Free Jazz), and chapter 16 (Jazz/Rock). Instructors frequently preface their styles sequence with appendix materials and the introductory chapters, and they frequently select more specialized chapters to use as supplements (the chapters devoted to Duke Ellington and Miles Davis, for instance).

The text provides the essentials for a course concerned primarily with MAJOR FIGURES IN JAZZ: Louis Armstrong (covered in chapter 5), Duke Ellington (chapter 7), Charlie Parker/Dizzy Gillespie (chapter 9), Miles Davis (chapters 12 and 16), and John Coltrane (chapter 13). For those who wish to explore more than just the top five or six figures, the text also includes substantial coverage of such other giants as Jelly Roll Morton (chapter 5), Earl Hines (chapter 5), Count Basie (chapter 8), Lester Young (chapter 8), Lennie Tristano (chapter 10), Ornette Coleman (chapter 14), Charles Mingus (chapter 14), Bill Evans (chapter 15), Sun Ra (chapter 14), and Stan Kenton (chapter 10), to name just a few.

For a course in THE HISTORY OF JAZZ, the text can be used intact, though minor juggling of contents can make the final five chapters more chronological. The main treatment of Miles Davis (chapter 12) runs from the 1950s to 1970; so the instructor may wish to postpone coverage of its second half until John Coltrane (chapter 13) and Bill Evans (chapter 15) have been covered. Similarly, the instructor may wish to postpone the final two thirds of chapter 15 until the 1970s have been covered, because the bulk of its material overlaps the same span, and then spills into the 1980s with its updates on Herbie Hancock and Chick Corea. The coverage of Charles Mingus in chapter 14 runs from the 1940s to the 1970s, as does that of Sun Ra. The end of chapter 14 (Art Ensemble of Chicago, Anthony Braxton, World Saxophone Quartet) overlaps the same time period as jazz-rock (chapter 16).

This text has also been used in courses called "American Music," "Contemporary Music," "Twentieth Century Music," "Popular Music in America," "Afro-American Music," and "Black Music." The last third of the text is used in many courses called "Rock," "The History of Rock and Roll," and "Jazz/Rock Foundations." The "Elements of Music" appendix is used in numerous music appreciation courses. The

"For Musicians" appendix is used in many courses in "jazz theory" and "Introduction to Jazz Styles," "Jazz Survey," and "Jazz Perspectives." At least one professor requires the text to be read by students in courses called "jazz trumpet," "jazz trombone," "jazz saxophone," "jazz piano," "jazz bass," and "jazz drums."

A number of professors have said that this book has too much information in it, and, in particular, that it is impossible for them to cover some chapters, such as Ellington and Coltrane, in a single-semester college course. These professors are correct. However, if they are unduly frustrated by this, they are overlooking two considerations. First is that **this book, like most good textbooks, is intended to be merely a resource, not a rigid syllabus for a particular course. It was never intended to be studied line by line, cover to cover by novice listeners in a single-semester jazz appreciation course.** The second consideration is that part of **a teacher's job is to make judicious choices from the assortment of information offered in a textbook and then guide students to a comprehensible sampling that is suitable for them.** Students are often confused and frustrated in courses where professors do not routinely follow a detailed syllabus that tells what pages, terms, and musicians the students are expected to learn. Textbooks tend to be overwhelming when students assume that they must learn everything in them. Helpful teachers tell their students what not to be overly concerned with. A few examples will clarify this. Whereas some teachers consider sideman names to be superfluous, others believe that familiarity with every musician in the Ellington chapter is essential for a minimum understanding of the music. Whereas some teachers feel that to know Coltrane was an important post-Parker saxophonist is sufficient, other teachers consider an appreciation of Coltrane's McCoy Tyner-Jimmy Garrison-Elvin Jones rhythm section also to be essential. And some teachers want students to remember not only that Coltrane had roots in the style of Lester Young, but also that Coltrane influenced such current giants as David Liebman and Michael Brecker. Some teachers believe that a basic introduction to jazz involves learning to discriminate soprano from tenor saxophone timbre. Other teachers feel that such a skill exceeds reasonable expectations for nonmusician students. Whereas some teachers feel that students should be able to recognize the sound of a 12-bar blues before receiving a passing grade in an introductory course, other teachers are more concerned that their students remember the birthplaces of famous musicians. Some teachers believe that an immersion in the sounds of jazz is sufficient and students need not acquire knowledge about how it is made. Regardless of a teacher's philosophy of education, students benefit from being told what that philosophy is, and they welcome knowing what pages to read and what they will be expected to remember from those pages.

Here is an example of the flexibility that the book recently offered to a professor who was willing to glean relevant material from the resources in the text rather than assuming the course must rigidly follow the book page by page. For a one-semester course in jazz and rock that students took as a music appreciation elective, the instructor first introduced some "how to listen" ideas, by way of in-class demonstrations of instruments and analysis of song forms (as explained in the Elements of Music Appendix and chapter 3). Then an African retentions sequence (as explained in chapter 4) was presented, moving smoothly to jazz-rock, because jazz-rock has more Africanisms than other jazz styles have and because the course title was "Jazz and Rock." Both instructor and students were already familiar with Spyro Gyra, so that style became a good jumping-off place, and they analyzed one of their favorite recordings by that band. Joe Zawinul's "Birdland" was another handy point of departure because the students had heard the popular Manhattan Transfer version and could connect it to the Count Basie riff band style they heard in "One O'Clock Jump." (These are now found together at the beginning of the new JAZZ CLASSICS CASSETTE.) Then an assortment of pop music was presented (James Brown, Ray Charles, the Jacksons, and various Motown recording artists), and its African connections were outlined via chapter 4 (Origins of Jazz) and chapter 16 (Jazz-Rock). The explanations for African connections and origins of jazz/rock were keyed to the chart of parallel streams that appears in chapter 16. Much of the sequence was done according to suggestions found in the "Demonstrating African Connections" chapter of my *How To Teach Jazz History* (NAJE Press, 1984). Then, for the remainder of the course, a few key jazz styles such as swing and bop were introduced, and discussion was offered for only a few absolutely essential figures (Louis Armstrong, Duke Ellington, Count Basie, Charlie Parker, Dizzy Gillespie, Miles Davis, and John Coltrane).

**CHANGES IN THIS FOURTH EDITION**

Most all the essential facts and style analyses in the third edition were retained in this fourth edition for the convenience of professors who used the third edition and wish to continue teaching with similar course content, format, and exams. Consistent with this rationale, most changes were minor. We added 16 new listening guides, but dropped only the "Take the 'A' Train" guide and the brief profiles of Frank Teschemacher, Artie Shaw, Herschel Evans, Buck Clayton, Lucky Thompson, and Don Ellis. Most changes consisted of updating, rephrasing to increase clarity of exposition, adding summaries, taking album titles and musician names that students had found distracting and relegating them to footnotes, adding footnotes to announce recently released LPs and CDs containing cited performances.

Surveys showed that most students did not have convenient access to the *Smithsonian Collection of Classic Jazz*, and a number of schools and professors themselves lacked the collection. Surveys also showed that few professors had the essential albums which comprised the "Small Basic Collection" listed in previous editions of *Jazz Styles*. So the two-cassette version of this new edition of *Jazz Styles: History and Analysis* comes with a sampling of classic jazz recordings that have been selected to give the broadest scope that could be represented on a single cassette tape—*The Jazz Classics Cassette*. It contains at least one example of original music for each chapter, and this includes music for most of the listening guides that appeared in past editions. For the convenience of schools where adequate access to the SCCJ exists, most of the *Jazz Classics Cassette* contents were chosen intentionally to not duplicate the SCCJ. "West End Blues," "Lester Leaps In," "Taxi War Dance," and "Shaw Nuff" are the only duplications. The JAZZ CLASSICS CASSETTE's "Harlem Airshaft" cannot be found in the revised SCCJ, and its "Cottontail" cannot be found in the original SCCJ. In addition, the JAZZ CLASSICS CAS-SETTE contains many important players and styles that are not represented in either version of SCCJ. *It can therefore serve equally well as a supplement instead of a substitute for the SCCJ.*

Though almost all the material was retained from the third edition, some of it now appears in a different place because professors said they wanted the chronology of styles to be more obvious, and they wanted it organized within fewer chapters. Here is a guide to these changes:

1) Now combined in a single chapter 14 (1960s and 70s Avant-Garde and "Free" Jazz) are the contents from the third edition's chapters on Charles Mingus (chapter 14), Free Jazz (chapter 13: Ornette Coleman, Cecil Taylor, Don Cherry and Albert Ayler), and the Second Chicago School (chapter 16: Sun Ra, AACM, Art Ensemble of Chicago, Anthony Braxton, and the World Saxophone Quartet).
2) The content of the third edition's chapter 18 (Wayne Shorter, Ron Carter and Tony Williams) has been combined with a rewritten chapter 12 (Miles Davis).
3) The third edition's chapter 17 (John Coltrane) is now chapter 13.
4) The third edition's chapter 19 (Twenty Years of Jazz, Rock and American Popular Music) is now chapter 16, and it has a new title: Jazz-Rock Fusion.
5) The third edition's chapter 20 (Big Bands) has been redistributed: Woody Herman is now in chapter 9 (bop), Stan Kenton is in chapter 10 (cool), Maynard Ferguson and Thad Jones-Mel Lewis are now in chapter 11 (hard bop).

Students said they felt the chapter summaries were very valuable in previous editions, and they wanted more. So now all chapters have numbered summary statements. Several professors mentioned wanting more about the way jazz styles have been received by the public and how they fit in with the rest of American music. Therefore new sections about "Popular Appeal" have been added, and "Popular Appeal" sections from previous editions have been updated. For the same reasons, sections about New Age Music and Pat Metheny are introduced for the first time.

Professors said they wanted enlarged bibliographies. So now each chapter has more extensive footnoting of jazz books, and very few sources are now cited only in the "Supplementary Reading" section of the appendix. Surveys showed that more and more schools were developing jazz majors in their music departments and requiring *Jazz Styles* as the textbook for their student musicians to use as a reference. This new edition accordingly has added extensive footnoting of technical references such as books of transcribed jazz improvisation and analyses of jazz styles.

A few professors said that they wanted more discussion about how jazz originated. So this edition has an entirely rewritten unit on the Origins of Jazz (chapter 4) that includes most of what was in previous editions, plus more obvious chronology and more about the brass band and dance band music that started jazz.

The Cool Jazz, Hard Bop, and Miles Davis chapters have been entirely rewritten in response to student requests for more generalizations about style characteristics and less detail. Fewer tune titles and sidemen names were included in this edition, and illustrations and documentations for main points were more frequently relegated to footnotes.

For the convenience of professors who teach jazz history instrument by instrument, the swing, bop, hard bop, and West Coast sections in this new edition have been organized more by instruments. This entailed breaking down "rhythm section" units into separate "piano," "bass," and "drum" units. It also meant adding guitar and trombone units to the West Coast coverage.

The JAZZ STYLES CASSETTE was created because instructors said that frequently they were unable to bring musicians to class for lecture/demonstrations, yet students had said that chapter 3 ("Appreciating Jazz Improvisation") was difficult to understand without help from the instructor and in-class demonstrations by musicians. So the cassette was devised to help readers practice matching the sounds with the text descriptions, and the cassette contents were keyed to the book's photos and sketches, some of which were changed for greater clarity and accuracy. (If the book you are reading now did not come with that cassette shrink-wrapped to it, ask for your money back, and get a book that does have the cassette.) It has been improved and updated for this fourth edition of the texbook according to comments from students and professors. Another reason for the cassette was that students said a single demonstration in class was not sufficient for learning such concepts as pitch bends and blue notes, chord progressions, comping, walking bass, ride rhythms, or for learning the distinctions between alto sax and tenor sax, trumpet and fluegelhorn, muted trumpet and unmuted trumpet, double-time and half-time, flute and clarinet, soprano sax and clarinet, snare drum and bass drum, etc. These are distinctions that not all professors require students to make. All these comparisons were made available, however, because surveys showed that most professors require students to learn at least a few such discriminations. For example, the chord progression for the 12-bar blues is taught almost universally in jazz appreciation and jazz history classes.

Because teachers said they did not know how to find jazz videos, page 432 now has names, addresses and phone numbers of distributors. Because first-time instructors said they wanted guidance in organizing their courses, a new chapter in the teachers' manual was based on interviews with first-time instructors, and it outlines pitfalls to avoid, grading schemes, syllabi, and sources for getting materials in a hurry.

To keep instructors current with what important records and CDs are available, the discography of the teacher's manual was expanded and updated, with names and addresses of distributors attached. Phone numbers for some of the distributors were added, especially where 24 hr/day ordering service is available.

**ACKNOWLEDGMENTS**  A large number of musicians, journalists, teachers, and other jazz fans have taken time out of their own busy schedules to generously share their observations with me. I am deeply grateful for their kindness. The continual fine tuning of this book and its supplements would not be possible otherwise.

As with the first three editions, Harvey Pekar and Chuck Braman unselfishly continued to supply me with new ideas that improved this book. There is material in almost every chapter that reflects the research and thinking of Pekar, and I will always be grateful for his contributions and the influence he has had on my thinking. Braman once again contributed valuable new ideas for content, format, and phrasing in this new edition.

Joel Simpson and Victor Schonfield devoted months of their spare time to combing the entire second edition, line by line, and making numerous suggestions, Schonfield identifying errors of historical fact and potentially misconstrued meanings, Simpson spotting infelicities of phrasing and offering many structural improvements. Morris Holbrook also supplied a detailed list of impressions and identified rough spots for me. Some of their changes were incorporated in the third edition, and many more were incorporated in this new fourth edition. Changes in every chapter have resulted from their concerted efforts. Holbrook critiqued several drafts of the newly rewritten cool jazz chapter, and allowed me to include some of his own personal observations and phrasing. Chuck Braman's, Jon Goldman's, and Harvey Pekar's ideas are also reflected in rewrites of the sections about cool jazz and hard bop. Braman also critiqued the rewrites on Miles Davis and John Coltrane. Karl Koenig performed a line by line critique of the Origins of Jazz and Early Jazz chapters of the second edition, as well as commenting on later chapters. He supplied an almost endless stream of documents and interpretations about the origins of jazz, critiqued several drafts of my current rewrite, then allowed me to paraphrase his unpublished writings in chapter 4 of this new edition. My rewrites of this material in the third and fourth editions also reflect the influence of Wallace Rave, Scott Deveaux, Lawrence Gushee, David Such, Liz Sesler, and Fred Starr.

I also received assistance for preparation of expansions and revisions in this fourth edition from Dave Berger, Bill Dobbins, Pat Pace, Bob Belden, Ernie Krivda, John Klayman, Gary Aprile, Frank Butrey, Chris Hovan, Dan Poletta, Rick Helzer, Gunnar Biggs, Mike Lee, Fred Sharp, Dick Lurie, Carl Woideck, Stanley Dance, Helen Oakley Dance, Alden Ashforth, Steven Lasker, Michael Cox, Mal Barron, Anita Clark, Maureen Ferguson, Gary Carner, Richard Salvucci, Billy Barnard, Karen Knowlton, Charles Colbert, Chas Baker, Bruce Kennan, Paul Ferguson, Chuck Ventrella, Pete Neff, Dan Levinson, George Judy, Richard Sudhalter, and Theodore Dennis Brown.

I am deeply indebted to these individuals for their sterling copy editing: Ed Huddleston, Chuck Braman, Jenifer Stepien, Holly Kuppinger, Robert Derwae, and Brian Sheridan.

Preparation of this edition was far easier than earlier editions because of the efficient computer services provided by Chris Yannella and Dave Cradle.

Bill Anderson updated and proofread all the footnotes, particularly the discographical entries for the text and the expanded discography that appears in the teachers manual. He also made valuable suggestions regarding text content and put me in touch with his students so that I could learn first-hand where the rough spots were and what students need in a jazz appreciation course. Anderson and John Richmond have continued to keep me abreast of reference materials and to loan and tape rare albums and lend me historical documents. They have also continued the error correction procedures that they began in 1973. Pat McCarty, Anita Clark,

# SUPPLEMENTS FOR USING THIS BOOK

Several sources of additional material have been prepared to supplement study of this edition of *Jazz Styles: History and Analysis*. The JAZZ STYLES CASSETTE contains 90 minutes of audio demonstrations for instrument sounds (guitar vs. banjo, trumpet vs. fluegelhorn, clarinet vs. soprano sax, ride cymbal vs. crash cymbal, etc.), and musical concepts (blue notes, swing eighth-note patterns, A-A-B-A song form, 12 bar blues chord changes, etc.). The cassette illustrates the contents of the Elements of Music appendix and Chapter 3: "Appreciating Jazz Improvisation." There are 171 audio demonstrations, and the cassette should have come shrink-wrapped to the book you are now reading. The JAZZ CLASSICS CASSETTE contains 26 selections of historic jazz recordings, at least one for each chapter, totalling 90 minutes of music and narration (Louis Armstrong, Lester Young, Charlie Parker, Miles Davis, John Coltrane, etc.). The pieces match the listening guides which appear in this textbook. Very few of these recordings are in the *Smithsonian Collection of Classic Jazz.* * Therefore the JAZZ CLASSICS CASSETTE can serve as a substitute or a supplement to SCCJ. It is available in the two-cassette edition of this book.**

*(SCCJ), a compilation of historic recordings, available on LP, cassette, and CD from Smithsonian Books & Recordings, P.O. Box 2071, Colchester, Vermont 05449-9988; 1-800-336-5221. Note that there are two editions of the SCCJ which are not identical. This book refers specifically to the "revised SCCJ" in cases where there are differences between the two editions.

**Regarding Format of Footnoted Information About Recordings.** The footnotes citing recordings are designed to provide the information necessary for obtaining the examples discussed in the text and/or to note further recordings by the artist discussed. They tell the reissue currently available or the most recently available packaging of past recording. The currently available format is also indicated. Note that many LPs are being discontinued in favor of CDs or cassettes. So, even if available as this book went to press, they may not be available much longer. Also given is information concerning alternate titles, original issue numbers, and year of recording. The development of the compact disc has influenced the availability of jazz recordings. In addition, CDs have appealed to libraries and teachers because of their convenience of storage, access to individual selections, and the ability to locate given passages in a selection by the timer control. They are also less subject to deterioration of sound quality (which is generally superior to begin with). Because many libraries and stores are moving to CDs exclusively, this book provides the information on CD availability for many cited recordings, and it lists LPs only when a CD is not yet available.

# chapter 1
# INTRODUCTION

The term "jazz" indicates many different kinds of American music. There are small groups and big bands that present jazz as serious music in concert halls. There is jazz in the Dixieland music of the Roaring Twenties. Jazz can be heard in some of the "easy listening" fare that is offered on the radio. There is jazz in some of the dance music we hear at the disco. Pianists include jazz in their music for our night clubs and restaurants. Jazz is so interesting that it is played and analyzed in hundreds of universities and conservatories. Jazz bands exist in almost every high school and college. Jazz has been imitated by musicians on every continent, and today there is no city without it. It has influenced the development of new styles in popular music and the work of symphonic composers. Jazz is so resilient that all the old styles have persisted, and new styles are continuously being developed. In fact, jazz is regarded as a fine art, not just a passing fad. In this book and its accompanying cassette, we will learn about a wide variety of jazz styles that have captivated listeners all over the world.

What makes jazz unique is not just its provocative rhythms but its insistence that performers create their parts as they play them. Each jazz performance represents an original and spontaneous creation because all jazz contains improvisation. Today jazz stands out as the most developed improvisational music in the world. Part of the engaging vitality we hear in jazz comes from the spontaneity of its improvisation. What is so exciting about jazz is that the musicians are *creating* in our very presence, and taking us along with them, involving us in the action of making up fresh sounds. This is akin to the impossible situation of seeing a finished painting as we watch the artist apply paint to the canvas, *at the same time* as we watch one manufacturer produce the canvas and another manufacturer produce the paints themselves!

We can reap intellectual rewards from jazz. We can begin to follow the inventive thinking of the musician at the actual moment he is improvising the music. We

1

automatically tune into the way he develops his phrases, and we can begin noticing the moment-to-moment changes that his accompanists make. The more attentive we become, the more we can appreciate the beauties of different chord sounds and the complementary splashes of drums and cymbals. The more skilled we become as listeners, the more pleasure we will extract from these sounds. And this is all possible without being musicians ourselves!

Many of these aspects are not available to us immediately. But most are accessible after we exert some effort to find out what is going on. Jazz offers a set of pleasures that deepen with understanding. Though some work is required of the listener, the rewards are guaranteed—you will delight in the surprises that jazz improvisations offer.

There are good reasons for learning about jazz history, too. The more styles you study, the more favorites you are likely to discover. And you will learn more about African and European music since jazz began as an amalgam of both. By studying the history of jazz, you will learn principles of stylistic evolution that apply to all art forms, not just jazz. Studying jazz can lead you to related styles that you will enjoy, too. The better you become at listening to jazz, the more you will derive from listening to all forms of music.

As you explore the musical relationships between styles, you will discover a remarkable continuity. Some developments occurred so smoothly that contemporary observers were actually unaware of them until they had already happened. Here are some other ideas to keep in mind while you study jazz history. First of all, the central figures did not create their innovations entirely by themselves. Rather, their work reflects the influence of other players, as well as chance occurrences that were combined, modified, and developed in original ways. A stream of styles might emanate from the talent and persistent hard work of a few musicians who devised the freshest approaches. However, jazz history cannot accurately be described as a single stream evolving from Dixieland directly to swing, and from swing directly to bop and so forth. Nor can approaches used in playing a given instrument be traced to a narrow line of innovators, each of whom is the sole influence on the next—a prominent saxophonist from the 1930s influencing his successor in the 1940s, who in turn influenced another successor in the 1950s, for example. There is no neat line of succession, with each subsequent style rendering the previous ones obsolete. Ordinarily, many different styles of jazz coexist, no matter which ones are in vogue with any particular market segments.

Jazz includes a loose collection of many streams. Styles come about in many diverse ways: Offshoots of some streams form streams of their own; sometimes streams remix; sometimes they consolidate by imitation of a particularly distinctive innovator. But, more often, styles come from gradual overlapping of approaches and a host of influences that even the players themselves are frequently unaware of. Most of all, we must remember that jazz history cannot be accurately considered the series of "reactions," as though musicians collectively became angry and then suddenly fought the style by "inventing" another to oppose it, as historians are so fond of believing. The truth is that most musicians simply find their own favorite way of playing. Often it is an existing style they like which they modify to suit their tastes and capabilities; sometimes they combine different approaches until the proportions please them. Many players stick with that style for good; others change their styles when they become bored with what they are doing. But the changes are evident only gradually because it takes so much work to develop a style and then to master it well enough to perform in public.

Before continuing with your study of this book and cassette, glance at the following list of terms. Then if you find any of them unfamiliar, you might find it helpful to study pages 358–391 before you proceed with the next chapter.

| | |
|---|---|
| atonal | minor |
| blue note | mode |
| blues poetry | octave |
| bluesy quality | orchestration |
| bridge | polyrhythm |
| chord | polytonal |
| chord progression | quarter note |
| chord voicing | rhythm |
| chorus | scale |
| chromatic | scoring |
| dotted eighth note | sixteen-bar blues |
| dotted eighth-sixteenth figure | sixteenth note |
| eighth note | staccato |
| eighth note triplet | swing eighth note |
| fifth | syncopation |
| flat fifth | tempo |
| flat seventh | thirty-two-bar forms |
| flat third | tonal |
| fourth | tone center |
| intonation | tone color |
| key | turnaround |
| legato | twelve-bar blues progression |
| major | verse |
| measure | voicing in fourths |
| meter | waltz |

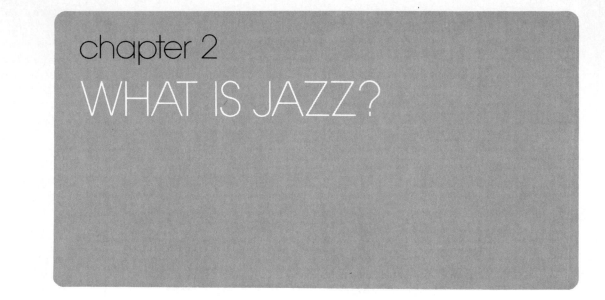

# chapter 2
# WHAT IS JAZZ?

A variety of meanings have been attached to the word "jazz," and definitions of jazz tend to be controversial. When listening to jazz, not everyone focuses on the same aspects. So it is no surprise that people cannot agree about how to define the music. It seems an impossible dilema because even when people do focus on the same aspects, they don't use the same words to describe what they hear. The existence of many distinctly different jazz styles also makes it difficult to arrive at an adequate definition. When people attempt to define jazz, they usually have in mind the styles they know, not necessarily the entire range of music that has been called jazz. Another barrier to adequate definition is that jazz is usually played first and only written down later, if at all. This makes it much more difficult to discuss than sounds which derive from written music and can be examined on paper. But despite all these problems, there are two elements that most jazz styles have in common—improvisation and jazz swing feeling.

**IMPROVISATION**  To improvise is to compose and perform simultaneously. A great deal of improvised music is spontaneous, unrehearsed, not written down beforehand. This is roughly parallel to extemporaneous speech, in which you talk "off the cuff," using words and phrases you have used before but using them now in a new way, new order, and without rehearsal or memorization. Instead of saying "improvise," many people say *ad lib*, *ride*, or *jam*. Some of the vitality associated with jazz may be due to the spontaneity of improvisation. Jazz musicians are so conscious of spontaneity and originality that they try never to improvise in a given context the same way twice. Several versions of a tune played by a soloist during the same recording session may be entirely different from each other because of this.

For most people, improvisation is an essential element of jazz, and musicians occasionally say "jazz" when they mean "improvise." For example, in a music publisher's brochure describing big band arrangements, a note might be included saying, "only the tenor saxophone part requires jazz." Or a musician's contractor might phone a player requesting that he play "jazz trumpet chair" in a big band, meaning the player will be the only musician in the trumpet section required to improvise.

The inexperienced listener may have difficulty in differentiating what has been written or memorized beforehand from what is being improvised. One clue is that if a performance sounds improvised, it quite often is. The problem with using that clue, however, is that the best improvisations are so well constructed that they sound almost like written melodies. Many jazz fans solve the problem by knowing that in most performances when the melody of the piece itself ends, what follows is improvised. It is all improvised until that same melody begins again. In the case of large jazz ensembles where the players sit down in front of music stands containing written arrangements, the audience knows that a player is improvising when he stands up alone and solos. Otherwise the music is coming from the prewritten parts. And, of course, any lines played by several players in unison must have been prepared beforehand. Note that even though improvisation is the big emphasis in jazz, not everything is spontaneous. Most jazz bands use arrangements of some sort. In the next chapter, we will examine a few of the common practices that indicate what parts in a jazz performance are usually worked out in advance.

## SWING FEELING

Next we are going to consider different views regarding what jazz is. Some of the views allow music which bears no jazz swing feeling to be called jazz. Some views allow nonimprovised music to be called jazz. As a foundation for describing jazz swing feeling, let's discuss a few elements which contribute to swing feeling in performances of both jazz and non-jazz styles.

If music makes you want to dance, clap your hands, or tap your feet, it has the effect we call a swinging feeling. This effect can be created by almost any kind of music, not just jazz. Music that keeps a relatively steady beat and is performed with great spirit seems buoyant. In that sense, many non-jazz performances can be described as swinging. But to specify the unique ways in which an effective jazz performance swings, we must outline both the general characteristics of swinging and those characteristics specific to jazz swing feeling.

Swing is a rhythmic phenomenon which is the sum of several easily defined factors and a few subtle, almost indefinable factors. This is solely a rhythmic concept. Musicians can play out of tune with each other yet still swing. For the sake of our discussion here, note also that the term swing should not be confused with its use as a label for an era in American popular music that began during the 1930s and continued until the late 1940s (swing era, swing bands, King of Swing, etc.). It is also not to be confused with its occasional use as a synonym for jazz itself.

## Swing in the General Sense

One of the easily defined factors causing swing feeling is **constant tempo**. This helps us distinguish it from symphonic music because the adherence to steady tempo is much less rigid there. In jazz, a steady beat is nearly always maintained. Constant tempo brings a certain momentum to music, and this momentum is essential to swing feeling. Much of the excitement in jazz comes from players tugging against this foundation with slight anticipations and delays.

Another easily defined element of swing feeling is **cohesive group sound**. This is achieved when every member's playing is precisely synchronized with that of every other member. The different members need not be playing the same rhythms in unison, but each player must execute the rhythms of his part with great precision in relation to the beat and the sounds of the other instruments. A group cannot swing if its members are not playing closely together.

Saying that a performance swings means that the group is keeping a steady tempo and its rhythmic parts are synchronized. But to call music swinging also indicates that the performance features a rhythmic lilt. This is a property that is genuine but is very difficult to define. It is also sometimes referred to as a good rhythmic groove. In fact, verbs derived from the nouns "swing" and "groove" are commonly applied to the sound of jazz: "The band is swinging tonight." "That pianist is really grooving." To a certain extent, swinging simply denotes pleasure. A swinging performance is like a swinging party. Both are very enjoyable.

The **spirit** with which a group plays contributes to swing feeling. Jazz has a reputation for being highly spirited music. In fact, the word "jazzy" is sometimes used instead of the word "spirited." To "jazz up" and to "liven up" are often used interchangeably, and "jazzy" clothes are gaudy or extroverted clothes.

Music that swings, then, is characterized by constant tempo, cohesive playing, and is performed with rhythmic lilt and spirit. Listeners may be inclined to describe a good performance of any kind of music as swinging if it conveys a feeling of life and energy that compels the listener to respond. This description of swinging applies not only to jazz, but also to lilting performances of polkas, waltzes, flamenco music, Gypsy music, marches, bluegrass, rock, and classical music. This general sense of swing can describe the feeling achieved by a good performance of almost any music that bears constant tempo, cohesive group sound, lilt, and spirit.

## Swing in the Jazz Sense

For music to swing in the way peculiar to jazz, the above characteristics are necessary but not sufficient. Jazz requires additional properties before it can swing in the way that is identified with it. One important element in jazz swing feeling is the **preponderance of syncopated rhythmic figures** (see pages 360–362 for detailed explanation). Syncopation often takes the form of accenting notes that occur just before or just after a beat. In this way, you might wish to think of syncopation as being off-beat accenting, or the occurrence of stress where it is least expected. Jazz swing feeling requires precisely such off-beat accents. The tension generated by members of a band tugging at opposite sides of the beat is essential to jazz swing feeling. Playing slightly after the beat can lend music a soulful or laid back feeling, and syncopations are especially good at providing this property. Jazz musicians exaggerate this tendency more than classical musicians do, and, if a classical musician were presented with a written syncopation, he would play it slightly earlier than would a jazz musician. Because rhythm is a matter of timing, we must remember that a player's degree of jazz swing feeling is tied to the success with which he times his syncopations. This means that when a player's quality of swing feeling is appraised, tone quality, note selection, and melodic imagination are all secondary to his sense of timing.

Another factor contributing to the special kind of swing feeling found in jazz is called the **swing eighth note pattern**, a concept that is difficult to explain in a brief introduction and best described in the appendix for nonmusicians on pages 363–364. If you have not already read that section, you might find it useful to study now.

One more component of jazz swing feeling, this one suggested by jazz historian Harvey Pekar, is not actually a rhythmic element. It is the continuous rising and falling motion or the alternation of more and less activity in a jazz line that provides **alternation of tension and relaxation**.

Swing in the jazz sense is composed of the elements that comprise swing in the general sense (constant tempo, cohesive playing, rhythmic lilt, and spirit) plus the elements of syncopation, swing eighth-note patterns, and the continuous alternation of tension and relaxation. As with swing in the general sense, jazz swing feeling exists in the ear of the beholder. **Listeners disagree about whether a given performance swings** at all, and, if so, how much. Note also that **there are several different types of jazz swing feeling**.

**DEFINING JAZZ: FOUR VIEWS\***

1) For many people, music need only **be associated with the jazz tradition** to be called jazz. Defining jazz in this way is circular. According to this approach, jazz can be anything that anyone ever called "jazz." In other words, the meaning of the term resides in the use to which the term has been put. To know what jazz is, we have to go by how the word is used. Many individuals say that jazz cannot be defined. They just use the term, and then whatever they used it for becomes its meaning. So if someone calls a particular kind of music jazz, then that particular kind of music really *is* jazz. In fact, some people apply the term to almost any music that displays characteristics that have ever been associated with anything ever called jazz. For example, music might be called jazz just because it has a bluesy flavor, or just because it uses instruments that have been associated with jazz, such as saxophones and drums, or just because it has "jazzy rhythms," or just because it displays manipulations of pitch and tone quality that are associated with jazz (see chapter 4 for discussion of buzzings, roughnesses, blue notes, drops, doits, scoops, smears, and bends). This means that a given performance might fall into the jazz category even though it uses no improvisation and projects no swing feeling. When people use the term that loosely, they rarely distinguish between jazz and other kinds of music to which we might best apply the term "jazz-like."

2) For many other people, a performance need only **project jazz swing feeling** in order to be called jazz. These people tend to say, "Jazz is a feeling more than anything else," or "Jazz is not *what* you play but *how* you play it."

3) For some people, a performance need only **be improvised** in order to qualify as jazz. Note, however, that if we define jazz this way, we overlook characteristics that can distinguish jazz from other kinds of music that also employ improvisation, such as rock, and the music of India and Africa.

\* For a lengthy examination of these issues, see "Three Approaches to Defining Jazz" by Mark Gridley, Robert Maxham and Robert Hoff, in the *Musical Quarterly* Vol. 73, No. 4, 1989, pg. 513–531.

4)   Probably the most common definition for jazz requires that a performance **contain improvisation and project jazz swing feeling**.

Much music can be sorted according to the two categories of swing feeling (the general sense and the jazz sense) and the four approaches to defining jazz. The next few paragraphs illustrate these definitional approaches by highlighting kinds of music in which one or more of the critical elements are absent.

**Applications of the Four Definitions**

If we adhere to our fourth definition of jazz (must be improvised and project jazz swing feeling), then what can be said about "jazz" performances in which the music doesn't seem to be improvised? For example, there are historically significant solos on alternate versions of the same record that differ very little from each other, thus suggesting that the later versions are not improvised, even if the first one was. Some concert music written and performed by famous jazz musicians also falls into this category. If we define jazz rigidly and insist that *some* improvisation is *always* required, then such performances can *not* be jazz. This may seem to be a ludicrous conclusion in the case of pieces by bandleaders well known for performing jazz, but it is both logical and useful. In fact, a category for such works already exists: *swinging concert music.* And this term not only saves the marriage of jazz and improvisation, but it also creates a category for a musical tradition that, though *deriving* from jazz, might be kept *separate.*

Yet for those of us who would be outraged to find someone calling our favorite "jazz" solo or "jazz" concert work anything other than jazz, our first definition (association with the jazz tradition) is most appropriate because it would allow such improvisationless performances to be called jazz.

Our fourth definition (must be improvised and swing) is useful because it *excludes* music that does not swing and that jazz musicians do not ordinarily consider jazz, such as George Gershwin's symphonic piece "Rhapsody in Blue." This distinguishes it for those people who would consider the piece to be jazz merely because it has bluesy melodies and jazzy rhythms—see the first definition. Controversy surrounds our fourth definition because it excludes some music that is called jazz by most listeners. Among the troublesome examples are a) pieces you will study in the chapter called "1960s and 70s Avant Garde" because they do not project jazz swing feeling, b) some of the concert music you will study in the chapter on Duke Ellington because it is neither swinging nor largely improvised (for instance "Transblucency" in the JAZZ CLASSICS CASSETTE), and c) Manhattan Transfer's vocal recreations of jazz instrumentals, because the singers are not improvising.[1]

We could also apply this reasoning to classifying the very popular piano solos of George Winston. Most jazz musicians agree that Winston does not swing, and

---

[1]By our first definition (association with elements in the jazz tradition) and our second definition (jazz swing feeling), Manhattan Transfer's first recording of Joe Zawinul's "Birdland" would qualify as jazz because of its jazzy rhythms and swing feeling. However, Weather Report's original version of "Birdland" would qualify more clearly because of its improvisation and swing feeling (fourth definition) and because of its use of saxophone (an element associated with the jazz tradition, a criterion of our first definition).

Winston himself refuses to call his music jazz. However, his albums are often found in the jazz bins of record stores, and many listeners call him a jazz pianist. Winston's music qualifies as jazz by our third definition (must be improvised), but not by our second (must swing) or our fourth (must swing and be improvised). Perhaps his music could be considered jazz in the same flexible sense of the term that is outlined in our first definition. This is the flexible sense that allows people to consider "jazz" the music in the famous movie with Al Jolson called *The Jazz Singer*, even though it is about a vaudeville singer who neither improvises nor swings.

**IS JAZZ POPULAR?** *  Now that we have considered a few definitions of jazz, let's examine five ways to answer the question of whether it is popular music.

1) If "popular" means that something is liked by a large portion of the population, jazz does not qualify as popular music because jazz represents only about three percent of radio airplay and record sales.

2) If "popular" means "of the common people," jazz does not qualify as popular music. Unlike most folk musicians and blues players, jazz musicians represent a highly versatile and specially trained elite whose level of sophistication is not common to the population at large. We will learn more about this in the next chapter.

3) Some jazz is "popular music" in the sense that it is functional music or "utilitarian" because it constitutes dance music, film music, and party music. But for the most part, jazz fits none of those qualifications. It is not *primarily* utilitarian in nature. Instead, it is appreciated for its esthetic and intellectual rewards, and it is approached with some effort.

4) Some jazz can be considered "popular music" because it possesses an easy accessibility. But much jazz, especially the post-1930s styles, does not qualify in this way because it requires a cultivated taste.

5) The term "jazz" was once applied so loosely that it denoted syncopated popular music as a whole. We can find illustrations for this in the 1920s, when Al Jolson's movie about a vaudeville singer was titled *The Jazz Singer*. The confusion was furthered by the Neil Diamond remake of that movie. We must also remember that fiction writer F. Scott Fitzgerald dubbed the 1920s "The Jazz Age." So today many people think jazz is only music of "The Roaring Twenties," with musicians playing in speak-easies and wearing red-and-white striped clothing. Partly because of that situation, the term "jazz" is still frequently confused with popular music as a whole, long after it began acquiring a much narrower meaning. For instance, today many people still lump jazz with rock, and vice versa. Even now some people use the term "jazz" to designate almost every popular style that is not "classical"

---

* For a more detailed documentation of these points, see "Is Jazz Popular Music?" by Mark C. Gridley, in *The Instrumentalist,* March, 1987, Volume 41, Issue 8, 19–22, 25–26, 85.

music. I have heard the word jazz applied to the folk music of Peter, Paul & Mary, the folk-rock of Bob Dylan, the popular singing of Isaac Hayes, the written piano music of George Gershwin, and the minimalist compositions of Philip Glass and Steve Reich. And I have been told that when Guy Lombardo first came to America he considered his music to be "jazz." This last case is especially odd because most musicians consider "Lombardo" a label that designates music as being very unlike jazz. That even Lombardo called his music "jazz" illustrates how loosely the term has been used, and it shows how jazz could be viewed as "popular music" if Lombardo's tremendously popular band sound were an example of it.

In summary, much jazz fails to qualify as popular music by any of the above definitions of the term "popular." It warrants the label of "art music." But to be prepared for arguments, we must remember that some jazz is popular music according to some conceptions of "popular music," and some jazz is popular music according to all of the above conceptions.

## CHAPTER SUMMARY

1)  Jazz involves improvisation and swing feeling.

2)  Though most jazz groups use arrangments of some sort, a substantial portion of each performance is spontaneous.

3)  Swing feeling is achieved by spirited performances of many different kinds of music which employ steady tempo.

4)  Jazz swing feeling is like swing feeling in the general sense but with the additional elements of syncopation, swing eighth-notes, and a continuous rise and fall of tension.

5)  Some people use the term jazz very loosely, applying it to anything they ever heard called jazz or anything that reminds them of anything they think it is.

6)  For some people jazz is a feeling more than anything else, jazz swing feeling.

7)  Some people believe that improvisation is the central requirement of jazz.

8)  Most of what is called jazz contains improvisation and swing feeling.

9)  Jazz is "popular music" the extent to which people use it as party music, film music, and dance music.

10) Jazz is not particularly popular by comparison with most other kinds of music, as evidenced by its three-percent market share.

11) For most people, jazz is a cultivated taste and not easily accessible. This makes it art music rather than popular music.

# chapter 3
# APPRECIATING JAZZ IMPROVISATION

Much pleasure can be derived from listening to jazz improvisation. But it can also be a demanding task. With knowledge and practice, however, it becomes easier as it becomes more and more rewarding. So this chapter suggests general ways to listen. It can also help to keep in mind some of what the improviser knows. So this chapter describes unwritten rules that musicians follow, what to expect in terms of formats for chord progressions and tune construction, roles of different instruments in a jazz combo, and the alternatives available to the improviser.

**This book means little without the actual music it describes.** You are doing yourself a disservice if you plan to read the book as you might read a textbook about economics or history. **This book is a guide intended to make jazz more comprehensible by improving your listening skills. Your primary learning will come from hearing the music,** not just from reading about it. For the information in this book to be meaningful, stop reading, and listen carefully to a good example of the music after you have finished about every five paragraphs. Choose your listening materials from records and CDs cited in footnotes and in references to the JAZZ CLASSICS CASSETTE. If your library is not adequate, the Guide to Record Buying can help you find these materials (see page 392). It will also be beneficial to study the JAZZ STYLES CASSETTE and pages 358 to 391 before beginning this chapter. Throughout your study of the book, you might also return to the JAZZ STYLES CASSETTE once in a while because the more jazz you hear, the more meaningful the demonstrations will be, and the more familiar the demonstrations, the more you will recognize in the jazz you hear. In addition, so much is demonstrated on the JAZZ STYLES CASSETTE that you will not absorb it all the first time you listen to it, anyway. (Don't listen to the entire cassette at a single sitting. It is much more effective if you space your listening sessions over several days.)

**LISTENING**
**TECHNIQUES**

Before reading the description of instrument roles which follows, get a record or tape made between the middle 1950s and the late 1960s, on which only horn (sax, trumpet, or trombone), piano, bass, and drums are playing. It is important to find a recording on which the bassist and drummer are clearly audible. If you do not already have or know about a record that meets these criteria, glance at the following list of suggestions:

1) Anything Sonny Stitt recorded after 1969.
2) Miles Davis albums made for Columbia, entitled *E.S.P.*, *Sorcerer*, *Someday My Prince Will Come*, *Kind of Blue*, *Basic Miles*, *Milestones*.
3) Sonny Rollins's "Blue 7" (in SCCJ).
4) Sonny Rollins's "Pent-Up House" (in SCCJ).
5) Miles Davis's "So What" (in SCCJ).
6) Any Dexter Gordon records made for Blue Note.

First listen to a selection as you normally would. Then listen an additional four times to that same selection: *first*, concentrate on every sound but drums and cymbals; *second*, listen carefully to the soloist and bassist; *third*, ignore the soloists

**Figure 3.1.** Possible visualizations of tone perceptions.

Sforzando crescendo

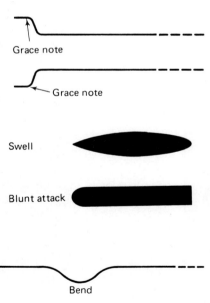

Grace note

Grace note

Swell

Blunt attack

Bend

Trill

Splat

and listen only to the piano, bass, and drums; and *fourth*, ignore everything except the interaction between the chords the pianist is playing and notes of soloists. Finally, listen four more times, each time concentrating on a single performer.

You may find it helpful to **hum the original tune to yourself while listening to the improvisations which are based on its chord changes.** Synchronize the beginning of your humming with the beginning of a solo improvisation and maintain the same tempo as the performer. (This technique is demonstrated on the JAZZ STYLES CASSETTE, side 1.) You might hear snatches of the original tune embedded in the improvisation, and you will begin to hear the chords in the accompaniment more clearly. You will also become aware of two compositions based on the same chord changes: the original tune and the improvised melody.

**Try to imagine a graph of the solo line.** The horizontal dimension of the graph represents the passage of time. The vertical dimension represents highness and lowness of pitch. Your graph can be embellished by colored shapes and textures representing the accompanying sounds of piano chords, drums, cymbals, bass, and so on. The solo line itself can include all the ornamentations soloists employ: scoops, bends, shakes, doits, drops, smears, trills, vibrato, changes in tone color, changes in sharpness of attack, and changes in loudness (see Figure 3.1 and the line drawings in the next chapter for examples).

You might be able to **imagine layers of sound, one on top of another, all moving forward in time, each layer representing the sound of a different instrument.** Once you become skilled in visualizing separate sounds, you will begin to observe relationships between those sounds. That, together with hearing chords change in the accompaniment, is an important step toward appreciating the interaction between musicians which is so essential to jazz.

**Hearing the improvised lines of a jazz soloist as melodies in themselves should help you enjoy much jazz.** On the other hand, some music of Sun Ra, Cecil Taylor, and post-1968 Miles Davis is especially accessible to listeners who are attuned to variations in mood, interesting tone colors, and rhythms because in that music there is less emphasis on clear-cut melody and accompaniment. Sometimes the mood alone may be the single most prominent aspect. Most jazz, however, can be appreciated for a combination of all those aspects.

**Try listening to every note in a soloist's improvisation.** You might not be able to detect each note in fast passages, especially those of saxophonist John Coltrane or pianist Oscar Peterson. But with repeated listening and close concentration, you should eventually be able to hear every note. Do not be discouraged if this proves difficult for you. Even professional musicians require repeated listenings before they can account for every note in some improvisations. Just remember that your ears will get better and better if they are given proper exposure to the music.

## CHORD PROGRESSIONS AND TUNE CONSTRUCTION

To improvise is to compose and perform simultaneously. Jazz musicians make up their music as they go along. Much of this chapter outlines the unwritten rules that are so well known by jazz musicians that they automatically guide the spontaneous piecing together of performances in bands of musicians who do not know each other and have not had a chance to rehearse.

Most jazz is guided by the musicians agreeing beforehand to maintain a given tempo, key, and progression of accompaniment chords. They then invent and play their own melodies and accompaniments in a way that is compatible with those chords. Frequently, the agreed-upon harmonies are borrowed from a familiar melody, and the melody itself is played before and after the improvisations. This is easy because jazz musicians tend to know many of the same tunes in the same keys. Though the original melody is often kept in mind by the improvisers to help them keep their place while improvising over the progression of chords, rarely are the improvised lines actually variations on the original melody. The improvised melodies and the original melody have only a progression of accompaniment chords in common. (Listen to the JAZZ STYLES CASSETTE for explanation and demonstration.) Performances are facilitated because standard chord changes for these tunes are followed, and traditions regarding the sequence of melody and improvisations are adhered to. In the next few paragraphs, we will examine those traditions.

When a jazz group plays a twelve-bar blues, the melody of the piece is usually played twice by everyone. Then the soloists improvise over the progression of chords in its accompaniment. **One complete twelve-bar progression of chords is called a chorus.** (All this is explained on pages 377–388 and demonstrated on the JAZZ STYLES CASSETTE, side 1.) Each soloist ordinarily improvises for several choruses. When one soloist ends an improvisation, another soloist takes over. The chords continue to progress in an unvarying cycle, even if a musician misses an entrance or overlaps into someone else's chorus. In that way, the whole group stays together. That particular twelve-bar progression of chords and the tempo at which it is played are the glue that holds the music together. After all the solos are taken, the group concludes by playing the melody to the piece twice more.

Some tunes are written in the form of four sections of eight measures a piece. (This is demonstrated on the JAZZ STYLES CASSETTE, at the end of side 1. The concept of "measure," also known as "bar," is explained on pages 359–361.) This is called a thirty-two bar form. The most common arrangement for such pieces has one section called the A section and another called the B section, also known as the bridge, release, inside, second strain, or channel. The A section is played twice in succession. Then the B section is inserted, followed by the A section again. The sequence is **A-A-B-A,** and thousands of tunes composed during the 1920s, 30s, 40s, and 50s were organized in such a format. You might recall the format if you hum the melody to the Christmas carol "Deck the Halls." The same format is used for "Cottontail" (in the JAZZ CLASSICS CASSETTE).[1] When jazz musicians play an A-A-B-A tune, they usually play its melody once before and once after the solo

---

[1]A few of the thirty-two bar A-A-B-A pieces found in SCCJ are "Body and Soul" (done once by Coleman Hawkins and once by Benny Goodman), "I Got Rhythm" (done by Don Byas and Slam Stewart), "Lester Leaps In" and "Taxi War Dance" (by Count Basie with Lester Young), "I Can't Believe That You're In Love With Me" (Benny Carter), "Willow Weep For Me" (Art Tatum), "The Man I Love" (Coleman Hawkins), "Moten Swing" (Bennie Moten), and "Smoke Gets in Your Eyes" (Thelonious Monk). If you do not have access to SCCJ, and you do not have examples of any thirty-two bar A-A-B-A compositions listed on page 380, dig through your record collection and look for a copy of "Honeysuckle Rose," "Undecided," "Moose the Mooch," "Roseland Shuffle," "Jumpin' at the Woodside," "Off Minor," "There Is No Greater Love," "Polka Dots and Moonbeams," "Stompin' at the Savoy,"

improvisations. Each solo adheres to the tune's chord progression so that a repeating sequence of A-A-B-A is followed over and over again without interruption. The cycle continues A-A-B-A-A-A-B-A-A-A-B-A, etc. What musicians signify by the term **chorus** is one playing through of the progression of accompaniment chords. A solo's duration is determined by how many choruses the soloist improvises. The soloist ends on the thirty-second measure (the twelfth measure if a blues progession) of some chorus and is immediately followed by another soloist who starts on the first measure of the next chorus. If a soloist stops improvising in the middle of a chorus—usually at the end of an eight-measure section—another player immediately takes up where the previous player left off, and the A-A-B-A form continues unchanged in its cycle.

Soloists sometimes trade eight-measure sections with each other. One musician improvises on the first eight measures, another on the second eight, and so on. This is called *trading eights.* The same thing is done with four-measure sections and is called *trading fours.* (Listen to the fourth chorus of "Lester Leaps In" in the JAZZ CLASSICS CASSETTE or SCCJ. Pianist Count Basie and tenor saxophonist Lester Young trade fours within the tune's thirty-two bar A-A-B-A construction.)

In jazz styles of the 1940s and 50s, it is common for drummers to trade fours or eights with the rest of the group. A soloist, accompanied by the rhythm section, plays for four (or eight) bars, and then the entire band drops out while the drummer improvises alone for the same number of bars. This pattern repeats over and over so that various soloists are trading fours (or eights) with the drummer. The form of the tune and its tempo are maintained throughout that sequence, even though no chords or melodies are played during the drum solos. Adherence to that format allows the entire band to begin playing again, precisely after four (or eight) measures because each musician is silently counting the beats and thinking of the chords that are progressing while he is not playing.

When you are listening to improvisations and trying to detect the form of an underlying chord progression, look out for three different manipulations which might throw off your counting. First is an **absence of steady tempo**. This is not commonly found in jazz, but introductions and endings sometimes employ it, and ballad melodies sometimes receive this treatment the first time they are played. (Miles Davis uses it for the beginning melody statement on his famous 1964 recording of "My Funny Valentine.") Jazz musicians use the term **rubato** to indicate the absence of steadiness in tempo.[2]

---

"Give Me the Simple Life," or Mel Torme's "Christmas Song" ("Chestnuts roasting on an open fire . . ."). Note that the format followed by musicians recording these tunes might not be identical to the routine described above, but at least their solos will probably adhere to the chord progression of the tune. It should not take much time or thought to determine how the musicians are handling the form. Just listen for such musical landmarks as turnarounds and bridges as described on pages 386–387 and in the JAZZ STYLES CASSETTE.

[2]Classical musicians, however, call that practice "free rhythmic style," and they reserve the term rubato for designating the situation in which the tempo remains steady but part of the time originally occupied by some notes is robbed from them and used to extend the sound of other notes. In other words, classical musicians use the term rubato to indicate that a passage is not played exactly as written and that the relative durations of the notes are rearranged at the discretion of the performer.

Aside from the infrequent occurrence of rubato, a passage within an improvisation might sound as though its tempo increased simply because of an increased amount of activity. Or, a passage might sound as though the tempo is decreasing simply because of a decreased amount of activity. Most of these situations can be deceiving because each chord is in effect exactly the same amount of time as it was when it accompanied the theme statement at the beginning of the piece, and the chords change at the same rate. **Only the density of musical activity is changing**, not the tempo for the passage of the chords that guide improvisation. It is often difficult to differentiate a true rubato, in the jazz sense of the term, from an alteration in density (what you might call "pseudo rubato"), and some performers, notably post-1960 stylists, use both techniques. But it should not be too difficult to learn to detect two other manipulations: double-timing and half-timing.

When a member of a band starts playing as though the tempo were twice as fast, double the tempo that had been in effect immediately before, the musician is said to be **double-timing**. This results from doubling the rate of notes without doubling the passage of chords or the amount of time each chord is in effect. (Listen to Coleman Hawkins depart from the ballad tempo feeling of the melody in his "Body and Soul" in SCCJ or Charlie Parker similarly doubling the pace of notes on "Embraceable You" in SCCJ.) To create double-time feeling, a soloist might switch from improvising eighth notes to improvising sixteenth notes. A bassist, for example, can create double-time feeling by playing eighth notes where he would ordinarily play quarter notes so that he plays two notes on each beat instead of playing only one, and his walking bass pattern might now best be characterized as "running bass." The result of this practice is a feeling that the tempo has doubled, even though there is no difference in the amount of time each chord's harmony is in effect. This can deceive the listener who is trying to keep track of the relation between the improvised solo line and the underlying chord progression because twice as many sounds now occur on each beat, even though the tempo at which the chords pass has not changed. The solution for the listener is to concentrate harder on humming the original melody to himself while the improvisation occurs and to tap his foot at the original tempo to help keep his place in the same manner used before the piece seemed to double its pace. (This is demonstrated on the JAZZ STYLES CASSETTE, side 2.)

The opposite of double-timing is **half-timing**. In half-timing, we halve the number of notes that are played without halving the rate at which the chords change. The tempo remains the same, but the note values become twice as long, so that the tempo seems to be slower, half as fast as the absolute rate at which chords are passing. As with double-timing, the chords remain in effect for the same amount of time, regardless of the pace that is perceived. (Listen to the JAZZ STYLES CASSETTE, side 2.)

Half-timing is rare, but double-timing is quite common. During the 1950s and 60s, improvisations on ballads were often played in double-time. After the piece's melody was played once in its original tempo, solo improvisations followed, nearly always in double-time, as though the improvisers wanted to swing hard and were impatient with the slowness of the original tempo. Chords progressed in these performances at the same absolute rate during solos as during the tune itself, but the improvisations seemed twice as fast as the tune.

Double-timing is also common in Latin American jazz because the beat in that music is usually subdivided into eighth notes instead of quarter notes. Rock music of the 1960s is often in double-time, and some is actually in quadruple-time. **In quadruple-time the beat is sounded in four equal parts (sixteenth notes).** Young dancers during the early 1960s often requested "fast music" when in fact they did not want up-tempo performances at all. They wanted rock in a double-time or quadruple-time feel. To the dancers, it was fast.

Another manipulation that often leads the listener to believe mistakenly that the tempo has changed is the **stop-time solo break.** Its name "stop-time" implies that the tempo stops when all group members except the soloist stop playing. Actually, however, the tempo and constant passage of chords is maintained, but since everyone except the soloist has stopped playing, we perceive the tempo as suspended (or "the time has stopped"). (On "Lester Leaps In," on the JAZZ CLASSICS CASSETTE, listen to the third chorus.)

Stop-time solo breaks are especially effective as springboards for solo choruses. Often, groups finish the opening melody statement with a two-measure break for the first soloist. Many tunes end with a long note held for one or two measures, and this "empty space" in the melody furnishes a good opportunity for a solo break. In other words, a combo might stop playing during the last two measures of a thirty-two-bar tune, giving the soloist a two-measure break to launch his improvisation. If the piece is a twelve-bar blues, the solo break takes place in the eleventh and twelfth measures. (This is demonstrated on the JAZZ STYLES CASSETTE at the end of side 1.)

**Beginning and Ending a Piece**

Other standard alternatives are also available to aid unrehearsed performances. For example, **introductions** are optional. But if a piece is to include one, the performers have at least four stock alternatives:

1) Use the final four or eight measures of the tune, and let the rhythm section rework and play it without the hornmen.

2) Have the rhythm section improvise a common four- or eight-measure progression and, at the same time, a line compatible with it. (Listen to Count Basie's four-measure introduction to "Lester Leaps In" in the JAZZ CLASSICS CASSETTE or SCCJ.)

3) Use an introduction that the entire group knows (from a famous recording of the tune, for example) thus including the hornmen in addition to the rhythm section.

4) Let the rhythm section play a one-, two-, or four-bar figure (called a vamp) over and over until the hornmen feel like starting the tune.

**Endings** are handled in similar ways. A few of the standard alternatives include:

1) End immediately at the end of the melody itself, with no extra notes.

2) Improvise a *ritard* for the last three or four bars, and then sustain the final chord. (Listen to the ending used by Louis Armstrong and Earl Hines on "Weather Bird" in SCCJ.)

3) Sustain a chord or rest while a soloist takes a *cadenza* (an improvisation out of context), then follow it with a final, sustained chord.

4) Repeat the last four bars of the tune, thus creating a tag, and then sustain the tune's final chord.

5) Use a well-known ending.

6) Let the rhythm section play a vamp followed by a final chord.

7) Have the rhythm section improvise some common progression and end with it.

Once a progression has begun, its chords and its tempo remain in charge of the situation. Even strangers can play with each other and be instantly compatible. Musicians from different eras can also play with each other without much conflict because the tempo and chord progression hold things together.

**Exceptions to the Rules**

Although the tune is usually played as written, before and after the improvised solos, **jazz performers occasionally omit the melody statement.** For example, the 1945 Don Byas-Slam Stewart recording of "I Got Rhythm" (in SCCJ) does not have a return to the melody at the end. Charlie Parker does not completely state the melody in either of his 1947 Dial recordings of "Embraceable You" (in SCCJ). Coleman Hawkins departs considerably from completing an opening melody statement in his 1939 recording of "Body and Soul" (in SCCJ) and never states the melody at the end, either. Miles Davis once recorded a twelve-bar blues improvisation without a melody and, quite understandably, called it "No Line." (Other examples can be found throughout the JAZZ STYLES CASSETTE.)

**During the 1960s and 70s, much jazz departed from the tradition of improvising within fixed chord progressions and preset chorus lengths.** Ornette Coleman and Cecil Taylor popularized such practices. (Listen to the excerpts of Coleman's *Free Jazz* album and Taylor's *Unit Structures* album in SCCJ.) Such music is often called "free jazz" because improvisers are free from the requirement to follow preset chord changes.

Beginning in the 1960s, **John Coltrane and his disciples recorded pieces whose melodies had chord progressions in their accompaniment but whose improvisations were not based on those progressions.** These improvisations were accompanied by extensively repeated, two-chord patterns. Coltrane's improvisations on "My Favorite Things" exemplify this approach.

**SKILLS POSSESSED BY THE IMPROVISER**

Spontaneous music is not totally spontaneous creation. Extensive preparation is required. Before a musician can improvise coherent lines with jazz feeling, he must undergo much training. Some is formal, but most is informal. Jazz players spend years practicing their instruments and learning tunes and the chord changes that accompany them.

**Near-effortless command of an instrument** is the constant goal of a jazz player, because the ability to play any musical idea that comes to mind, and to play it immediately, is related to instrumental proficiency. It is not unusual for a player to practice by himself for more than two hours a day, and some average four hours a day, five to six days per week. In other words, they play every spare minute. In addition to practicing scales and exercises, the jazz musician invents, collects, and develops phrases he might later use during improvisation. He tries out rhythmic variations of his favorite phrases. He practices to achieve fluency in different keys, in different registers of his instrument, and in different tempos and rhythmic styles.

To adequately respond to the harmonies produced by accompanists, **a jazz improviser must be well acquainted with harmony.** So, because the piano keyboard provides a means for seeing and hearing relationships between melody and harmony at the same time, **most jazz soloists know the piano well.**

To respond in a split second to his accompanists, the improvising soloist must have **an extremely quick and keen ear for pitch and rhythm.** This ability also helps him imagine a note or phrase and immediately play it. Jazz musicians are so quick to perceive and respond to subtle nuances in style and group direction that they can usually play a respectable performance the first time they work with an unfamiliar group.

**Most jazz musicians have remarkably good memories for sounds.** The average jazz improviser is able to hear a note or phrase once and then remember it and accurately play it back. In fact, you can often hear an improviser incorporate phrases from the solo that immediately preceded his.

A jazz musician has to **remember hundreds of tunes and chord progressions.** He must be as familiar with pop tunes and jazz standards as he is with his native language, perhaps more so. The convenience of knowing many of the same tunes helps musicians play together without rehearsal.

Another helpful skill is that of **recognizing chord progressions** quickly. Many jazz musicians can play a tune from memory after hearing it only a few times, and they often improvise solos compatible with the tune's chord progression after hearing it only once or twice.

Even though improvisation is their primary skill, most jazz musicians can also read music. Basically, **the skills of reading and writing music** can be described as four levels:

1) The **ability to read music** accurately if allowed to practice or look it over ahead of time. Many people call that "reading music."

2) The ability to play a piece of music correctly the first time it is seen. This is called "**sight-reading.**" Musicians simply term this skill "reading." When musicians say someone "reads," they usually mean he is capable of sight reading. This skill is possessed by all symphony orchestra musicians and by most jazz musicians, but, it is not a common skill among pop singers or rock or country and western musicians. The ability to sight read saves rehearsal time because it is easier to learn a new piece by reading it than by trial and error ("by ear"). Some people go so far as to say that a player "is not a real musician unless he reads music." I do not agree. Many players who are both instrumentally proficient and compositionally creative are unable to read music.

3) The **ability to make up an original tune and correctly notate it**: "writing music" or "composing." Actually the act of making up a tune is "composing"; notation is more specialized. But the term "writing music" usually refers to the process of making up a tune, and not necessarily to writing it down for musicians to play. Many people who are said to write music actually cannot write down their ideas. In other words, there are composers who cannot read or write music. Pop singers and rock musicians often make up songs and then pay a skilled musician to write them down for copyright, sales, and publication. (The singers and rock musicians usually teach songs to each other by ear instead of placing sheet music in front of each other.)

4) The highest level of music reading and writing is **the ability to listen to someone else's music and then correctly notate it**. This skill is possessed by people who write down jazz solos they hear on records.

During the 1950s and 60s, it was rare to find rock groups or country groups who could quickly notate their own work or sight read someone else's. Some pop singers can read music, but most are unable to sight read. But it is common for jazz musicians to both compose and notate their own tunes. **Nearly all jazz improvisers are also composers.** Most jazz musicians occasionally write down their improvisations in the form of tunes. Few of the tunes become famous in jazz history, but all serve as vehicles for improvisation. Some jazz players have written every tune on every album they have recorded. It is not unusual to find a jazz saxophonist or pianist who has written more than one hundred original tunes. Though many of them never write a memorable tune, some become so good at writing that they are more important to jazz as tune writers or band arrangers than as improvising players.

**INSTRUMENT ROLES**  What follows is a general description of some instrument roles that developed during the 1930s and 40s. These roles have become standardized, although the roles have not been strictly maintained because, since the 1960s, certain jazz groups have made innovations in the use of instruments.

Jazz is partly an ensemble art. The soloist and rhythm section combine to form an ensemble which attempts to play as a single unit, though the parts of that unit are described here in terms of separate roles. The rhythm section usually consists of string bass or electric bass guitar (see Figure 3.2), drums (see Figure 3.3), and an instrument which plays chords, such as a piano or guitar.[3] The *rhythm section* is a group of players, improvising together, who both accompany and inspire the soloist. They provide a springboard for his lines and can make or break his effectiveness.

---

[3]An organ can be substituted for both the bass and chord instrument because bass lines can be played on the organ by means of foot pedals. But in spite of this advantage, most jazz organists actually play bass lines with the left hand, using the foot pedals for assistance. This technique restricts the organist to a single hand for playing chords and, consequently, no extra hand for chording behind right-hand solos. The poor pianos and poor sound systems often furnished by night clubs compel many groups to carry their own portable electric piano or electric organ. Carrying an organ has the additional advantage of saving salary for a musician, the bassist, because an organist can supply bass lines together with chords.

The following discussion is intended to clarify the role of each instrument in the rhythm section.

**Bass**  The bassist plucks one note per beat with occasional embellishments added (listen to Miroslav Vitous play this way on "Steps" in the JAZZ CLASSICS CASSETTE, and see p. 426 for notations of typical bass lines). Many bassists pluck the second and fourth notes of each measure harder than the first and third, thus contributing to the creation of a swing feeling. The bassist keeps the beat and gives buoyancy and a low-register component to the group sound. This style of playing is called **walking bass.** The notes played by the bass are chosen from important notes of the chord progression or from notes compatible with these chords (demonstrated on side 1 of the JAZZ STYLES CASSETTE). The bass clarifies a chord progression by playing its most important notes. Good walking bass lines make musical sense by themselves. In fact, some soloists consider walking bass to be the single most essential sound in the rhythm section. They would play without drums or chording instrument before they would play without walking bass. (Listen to the JAZZ STYLES CASSETTE, side 1, for examples of a jazz combo without bass.)

**Figure 3.2.** Jimmy Blanton, Jaco Pastorius. String bass, also known as acoustic bass, bass viol, or upright bass (left). Electric bass guitar, also known as Fender bass or electric bass (right). Though it looks like a guitar, the electric bass can be differentiated from the solid body electric guitar by having four instead of six tuning pegs, one for each string. (*Blanton photo courtesy of Frank Driggs, Pastorius photo courtesy of Randy Norfus*)

Some bassists employ a variety of techniques in their work. Occasionally a bassist will pluck two strings at the same time. That is called a **double stop**. Or he might strum his four strings as though his bass were a guitar. In symphony orchestras, the bass sound is usually extracted by a bow drawn across the strings in the manner of a saw cutting through wood. This technique is called **arco**, not to be confused with plucking, which is also known as **pizzicato** ("pitts-a-cah-toe"). Though most jazz bassists are capable of it, they do not use the bow very often. (Listen to the JAZZ STYLES CASSETTE, side 1 for demonstration of arco contrasted with pizzicato.)

Some bassists fill in silences with musical remarks, almost as though they were talking with the rest of the group (sometimes called "broken time"). In some post-1960 groups, these musical remarks have become more important than the beat. The role of the bassist has changed, and now he is often involved in musical conversations as intricate as those typically carried on among trumpet, trombone, and clarinet during Dixieland jam sessions. (Listen to Scott LaFaro play "Solar" in the JAZZ CLASSICS CASSETTE.) After the 1950s, bassists also played melody more often than they traditionally had. Note also that their accompaniment rhythms became more varied now that they were freed from playing exclusively walking style.

**Piano**    The pianist plays chords in a syncopated fashion, providing harmonies and rhythms which complement and support the soloist. These chords are usually played in the middle of the piano keyboard, a pitch range that is easy to hear (see pages 424–425 for notations of typical piano accompaniments). What the pianist does underneath a soloist is called **comping** (accompanying or **complementing**). The pianist uses both hands to play the chorded rhythms behind a soloist. However, **when taking his own solo, he uses his left hand to comp while his right hand plays melodic lines.** (For a demonstration, listen to the JAZZ STYLES CASSETTE, side 2, and listen Chick Corea comp for himself in his "Steps" on the JAZZ CLASSICS CASSETTE.)

Comping is an improvised activity intended to enhance the solo line. Sometimes it inspires the soloist, suggesting chords and rhythms for use in his improvisation. Comping also involves responding instantaneously to changes in direction taken by a soloist. When the soloist's line suggests a particular sequence of chords, the pianist must follow suit even if that progression is not standard for the piece and was not discussed ahead of time. The pianist must be inventive when he comps, without getting in the soloist's way. That is a difficult task, requiring a great deal of discretion. Sometimes the pianist may drop out if he feels that the soloist would sound better without piano accompaniment. Comping must not clash with the work of the bassist or conflict with the drummer's kicks and prods. Ideally, the pianist and drummer will kick and prod the soloist in some integrated fashion. The members of the rhythm section are providing an accompaniment for the ever-changing melodic and rhythmic directions of the soloist's improvisation. They also underscore rhythms in written melodies and ensemble figures.

**Drums**    The drummer uses his right hand to play rhythms which provide both regular pulse and swing feeling just as the bass often does. The drummer plays these rhythms on

Ride cymbal

High-hat
(sock cymbal)

Crash cymbal

*louder, splashier, shorter accents*

*chick*

Snare drum

Large tom-tom

Small
tom-tom

Bass drum

**Figure 3.3.** Audience view of drum set.

the *ride cymbal*, which is suspended to his right over the drum set (see Figure 3.4). These rhythms are called **ride rhythms**. Occasionally they consist of one stroke per beat *(ching, ching, ching, ching)*, played in unison with the walking bass, but they are usually more complicated, for example, *ching chick a ching chick a ching chick a ching* OR *ching ching ching chick a ching* OR *ching chick a ching chick a ching chick a chick a ching*, etc. (See page 430 for notations.) The drummer may play ride rhythms on other parts of his set, too. In fact, before the ride cymbal came into common use, ride rhythms were played on the snare drum and high-hat cymbals. Note also that the drummer might play ride rhythms on another cymbal suspended to his left, and that the drummer's right hand is not limited to playing the ride cymbal. He can use it on any part of his set, but the ride cymbal gets more of its attention.

The drummer's left hand is free to accent and color the group sound by striking his *snare drum*, on a stand close to his lap (see Figure 3.4 and listen to demonstration on the JAZZ STYLES CASSETTE, side 1). The sounds made by striking the snare drum are often called "fills" because they fill in a musical gap left by the soloist. The snare drum has a crisp, crackling sound. The *crash cymbal* is often struck by the right hand, after a fill, while ride rhythms are interrupted. The crash cymbal is chosen for its tone color and the quickness with which its sound disappears. The ride cymbal is chosen for its tone color and the quality of its "ping." Its sound generally sustains longer than that of a crash cymbal (this comparison is demonstrated on the

right arm

left arm

large tom-tom

snare drum

high-hat (sock cymbal)

ride cymbal

crash cymbal

small tom-tom

bass drum

**Figure 3.4.** Drums.

JAZZ STYLES CASSETTE, side 1). In addition to "fills," the snare drum is used to provide an undercurrent of activity that seems to be "chattering" while the band is playing. (Listen to Roy Haynes play in this way on "Steps" in the JAZZ CLASSICS CASSETTE.) The *small tom tom*, suspended over the bass drum, and the *large tom tom*, sitting on the floor to the player's right, are also available for accent and coloration (demonstrated on the JAZZ STYLES CASSETTE, side 1).

Accentuating the swing feeling achieved by the bassist's emphasis of the second and fourth beats in each measure, the drummer plays those same beats by pressing his left foot on a pedal which closes two cymbals together making a "chick" sound. This apparatus is called a *high-hat* or *sock cymbal* (see Figure 3.5 and listen to the JAZZ STYLES CASSETTE). The high-hat will produce a "chick" sound if the pedal is depressed and held in closed position for a second. It can then be opened and closed again for another "chick" sound. A "ching" sound can be achieved by bringing the cymbals together just long enough for them to strike each other, and

**Figure 3.5.** Open high-hat, closed high-hat (demonstrated on JAZZ STYLES CASSETTE, side 1).

Sticks    Brushes    Mallets

**Figure 3.6.** Sticks, brushes, mallets (demonstrated on JAZZ STYLES CASSETTE, side 1).

then releasing them to resonate. All this is done by means of the high-hat's foot pedal. The high-hat can also be sounded by being struck with sticks, wire brushes, or mallets, all of which produce different sounds (see Figure 3.6). The high-hat cymbals can be struck when they are closed or open. Each cymbal in the unit can also be struck independently. Any part of any cymbal can be struck; each part produces a different sound (demonstrated on the JAZZ STYLES CASSETTE, side 1).

The drummer uses his right foot to press a pedal which, in turn, causes a mallet to strike the *bass drum* (see Figure 3.7). The drummer sometimes plays the bass drum lightly on all four beats of each measure, and he also uses it for accents.

A drummer can be recognized on a record by the particular instruments he plays and the characteristic ways in which he strikes them. No two drummers have the same cymbal sound, and each drummer has his own personal way of tuning the drums and cymbals. By means of adjustment bolts, drummers tighten the plastic or animal hide striking surfaces (drumheads). In addition, some drummers attach gauze and tape to their drumheads to deaden the sound. They tune cymbals by critical placement of tape on the underside. To produce a "sizzle" sound, they often

**Figure 3.7.** Bass drum—foot pedal.

drill holes in a cymbal and attach rivets that vibrate against the cymbal when the cymbal is struck; another technique, one which does not require drilling, is to hang a large key chain across the top of the cymbal which bounces when the cymbal is struck.

Cymbals on a bandstand often appear old and dirty. Very few drummers polish their cymbals because the sound of the cymbal will be changed if any part of its surface is removed, whether it be dirt, corrosion, or the brass itself. Many drummers actually let new cymbals age to provide a desired tone quality.

Even though they come in various brands, thicknesses, and diameters, there is not enough standardization to guarantee perfect cymbals for every drummer. No two are alike, even among the same make and model. Drummers spend years searching for cymbals which give them the particular sound they desire. Many drummers collect cymbals, using certain ones for certain jobs, depending on the sound required. When required to play on someone else's drum set, a jazz drummer often removes its cymbals and uses his own.

The drummer can create a huge variety of sounds, depending on what drum or cymbal he strikes, how hard he strikes it, and what part of the surface is struck. Striking the center of the cymbal creates a sound different from that produced by striking half-way out to the edge which, in turn, is unlike striking the edge itself. The sound also varies according to what means are used to initiate it: sticks, wire brushes, mallets, and bare hands all produce different effects. (Listen to drummer Max Roach on Charlie Parker's "Ko Ko" in SCCJ. Roach plays snare drum with wire brushes for the introduction then switches to playing ride cymbal with a drum stick for accompanying the solos. Roach can also be heard contributing spontaneous interjections by striking his snare drum with a drum stick and by striking the bass drum with a mallet that is mounted on a foot pedal.)

What has just been summarized is the basic drum set (also known as a "drum kit" or a "set of traps"). However, most drummers also carry additional instruments such as extra cymbals, tom toms, and Latin American percussion instruments. Until the 1960s, many drummers also had a cowbell (without its clapper) and a wood block (demonstrated on the JAZZ STYLES CASSETTE, side 1).

The public often considers drummers merely to be timekeepers for a band. Though this is true in some bands, throughout jazz history, drummers have also added sounds and rhythms that make music more colorful and exciting. Many of these colorful sounds do make the tempo explicit. However, the point here is that much jazz percussion work does not consist merely of timekeeping patterns. It consists of decoration for the band's sound. In other words, **the drummer acts as a colorist in addition to acting as a timekeeper**. In fact, some bands have employed drummers exclusively for coloristic playing instead of timekeeping. Instead of "drummer," the designation "percussionist" is frequently used to describe that role. (Listen to Dom Um Romao play in this manner on "Surucucu" in the JAZZ CLASSICS CASSETTE.)

The drummer not only keeps time and colors the group sound, but **kicks and prods the soloist** in ways that relate to rhythms the pianist and bassist are using. The jazz drummer plays figures that underscore rhythms in the band arrangements. By the mid-1960s, the conception of jazz drumming changed so much that the sounds made by drummers in some groups were in the forefront as much as melody instruments. The amount of interplay between drummers and other group members began to equal the amount of interplay previously expected only among the front-line instruments (trumpet, clarinet, and trombone) that were simultaneously improvising in Dixieland jam sessions. (Listen to Elvin Jones play in this style on "The Promise" in the JAZZ CLASSICS CASSETTE.)[4] In addition, **by his own playing, a drummer can control the loudness level, sound texture, and mood of a combo's performance, much as a conductor does with a symphony orchestra.** (Listen to Tony Williams play in this manner on "Masqualero" in the JAZZ CLASSICS CASSETTE.)[5]

The 1970s saw a large number of combos using two or more drummers.[6] In some performances, all the drummers would function as colorists. However, in most performances, one player would be explicitly stating the beats on a standard drum set while the other colored the group sound using auxiliary percussion instruments.

**Soloist**     The improvising soloist learns to be aware of a number of important events. Although he cannot possibly be conscious of all of them all the time, he does manage to respond intuitively to most of them. Much successful jazz improvisation is largely the result of ultra-high-speed intuition. Here are **a few things the improvising soloist tries to do:**

1) *Remember the chord changes common to the tune he is playing.*[7]
2) *Create phrases compatible with the chord changes.*[8]
3) *Edit* his work so that each improvisation represents a clear musical statement.

[4]Listen to the John Coltrane albums *Live at Birdland* MCA/Impulse 33109, CD/LP; and *Sun Ship* MCA 29028 (Impulse 9211), 1965; or the Miles Davis albums *Miles Smiles* CBS 9401, LP, 1966; and *Filles de Kilimanjaro* CBS 9750, LP, 1968.

[5]Listen to the drumming on "Masqualero" in the Miles Davis album *Sorcerer* CBS 9532, LP, 1967, on the JAZZ CLASSICS CASSETTE.

[6]Listen to the Weather Report albums called *I Sing the Body Electric*, CBS 31352, LP, 1971–72; *Black Market*, CBS 34099, LP, 1976; and *Sweetnighter*, CBS 32210, LP, 1973; or the Miles Davis albums called *Live-Evil*, CBS 30954, LP, 1970; and *On the Corner*, CBS 31906, LP, 1972.

[7]Occasionally, when the improviser is at a jam session or sitting in with a strange group, he may not know the chord progressions of the tune being played. He might know the melody, but be unsure of some of the progressions. Or he might be requested to play a tune he once knew but whose progressions he has forgotten. In these cases, he listens to the rhythm section and determines the chord changes while he improvises. He can usually guess some of the progressions because he knows certain patterns which recur in hundreds of tunes. He can also determine the chords by listening to other soloists use them. Note, however, that he cannot always predict the chord progressions the rhythm section will play because a tune can be harmonized in many ways which are unlike each other. This practice of altering chord progressions, **reharmonization,** is very common in jazz.

[8]The concept of compatibility is very broad. Both the particular style and the individual player determine what notes are compatible with the chord changes. For example, some notes that are compatible for modern jazz of the 1940s are not compatible for jazz of the 1920s.

4)   *Think ahead* so that the phrases will fit together well.

5)   *Remember what he has played* so that self-duplication does not occur.

6)   *Swing* with the tempo of the piece. When it is said that the rhythm section keeps time for the band, you might assume that constant tempo would not be maintained without a rhythm section, but that is not the case at all. Much jazz was originally dance music, so you might say that the rhythm section was keeping time to make the beat obvious for dancing. The improvising soloist, as well as all the other players, keeps time to himself. The ability to keep perfect time enables a soloist to swing without a rhythm section or in spite of a bad one.

7)   *Respond to the rhythmic figures of his accompanists* so that a healthy interaction will occur instead of a monologue.

8)   Keep loudness at a level which will *project* out beyond the sound of the band to the audience.

9)   *Play in tune and with the desired tone quality.*

10)  *Remember how long he has been soloing* so that he can stop before he uses up the time left for other soloists.

11)  *Play in the mood of the piece.*

12)  *Create something personal and original.*

This last point requires some clarification. An improviser's lines are not totally original in each and every performance. There are recurring themes in the improvisations of every jazz musician. In fact, these very themes combine with the player's own unique tone qualities and rhythmic feeling to help us identify the player's style. Using recurring themes is an accepted practice. Aspiring jazz musicians are advised to collect favorite "licks," those very themes and fragments which will later recur in their music and help us identify them. Most improvisers tend to play bits and pieces of lines they have played before, melodic figures they have practiced, and pet phrases of other improvisers. An improviser may actually play portions of a solo he remembers from another musician's recording. Sometimes an improviser will quote snatches of a pop tune or a classical piece. The bits and pieces that constitute a solo may not themselves be original, but the way in which they are combined often is.[9]

[9]To understand the mechanics of a sound that a musical model produces and the phrases that he prefers, developing jazz musicians usually analyze, memorize, and then imitate the model's work. Once the player has mastered the techniques required to produce whatever sounds and phrases he wants, he usually develops variations of the learned imitations and mixes them with his own original ideas. The process of artistic development starting with imitation is not exclusive to jazz musicians. It has been employed by painters, writers, and composers for centuries. It may seem curious to the outsider, but the musician's practice of analyzing, memorizing, and imitating is not usually viewed as plagiarism (stealing another's idea and calling it your own), but rather as a necessary first step in the elaborate training process which jazz musicians undergo. If, however, the player never moves beyond the imitation phase and ends up living out his career sounding much like his model, he frequently elicits the dismay of music critics and, to a lesser extent, the disappointment of fellow

Jazz improvisations can be very intimate, personal creations. This is especially obvious when a soloist uses his instrument almost as an extension or substitute for his own voice. This is apparent when drummers can be seen mouthing their rhythmic figures. It is also evident when pianists and guitarists can be heard humming the lines they are playing. Pianists Keith Jarrett and Oscar Peterson are known for this, often to the distraction of their listeners. Guitarist George Benson has intentionally incorporated such tendencies into his style. He sings the same notes he is playing on guitar, and makes certain that the audience hears the mixture of his voice and his guitar. The result is a unique and compelling sound that he adds to recordings that otherwise feature just his guitar alone or voice alone.

**ALTERNATIVES AVAILABLE TO THE IMPROVISER**

Describing what an improvising soloist does must take into account the actual playing situation. Let us examine a few alternatives suggested by three different situations: playing alone, playing with chord instruments, and playing according to chord changes and constant tempo. The following descriptions are separated only for the sake of clarity. The rules listed in each category are not binding, and they are not necessarily exclusive to that category. The player probably never thinks in these terms, either. He responds intuitively to the requirements of each situation. Consider these three situations as groups of requirements that build upon each other in the order presented here. In other words, the rules increase as the number of players increases and as the adherence to musical forms and roles increases. The first situation is what has become known as "free jazz," whereas the third situation typifies improvisatory practices employed from the 1930s through many current styles of jazz.

If he is playing alone and not required to follow chord changes or keep time, he is free to play anything that comes to mind:

1) He can organize his notes in a melodic sequence or
2) just place them in a haphazard way.
3) He can use notes common to a single key,
4) switch keys occasionally, or
5) play in no key at all.
6) He can group his notes in a way that implies a tempo, or
7) use no tempo of any sort, either stated or implied.
8) He can play loudly or softly at will.

---

musicians. But there are exceptions to this. Some players may be so proficient or play with such beauty that they earn admiration despite their failure to develop beyond the imitation stage. Sometimes imitation itself leads to innovation. For instance, tenor saxophonist Lester Young produced a tone quality that was unusual and highly influential for its time, partly because he was imitating the playing of Frankie Trumbauer, whose instrument was the smaller C-Melody saxophone. Almost as important to jazz history as Young was trumpeter Roy Eldridge, who created an innovative style by imitating jazz saxophonists instead of trumpeters.

If he is playing with chord instruments (piano, guitar, etc.), but not necessarily improvising on a tune or chord changes:

1) He must play notes which are compatible and in tune with the other sounds.

2) His notes should not make the ensemble sound cluttered—they must have clarity and balance.

3) He must sequence his notes so that they fit with what preceded them and what is likely to follow. This means paying attention to both the construction of his own line and its relationship to the lines of the other performers.

4) He must adjust the loudness of his playing in response to the group sound, though he might suddenly play louder or softer for the sake of contrast.

5) He might play melodically with such strength that he surfaces to the forefront of the ensemble sound, or

6) he might choose, at any moment, to play notes and rhythms which are subsidiary to those of another group member. Those sounds might help create an ensemble texture instead of a solo line.

If an improviser is playing according to chord changes and constant tempo:

1) His lines must reflect the direction set by the chord progression.[10]

2) He must maintain the tempo of the piece, and

3) swing in that tempo, letting the steadiness of tempo give momentum to his improvisation.

## CHAPTER SUMMARY

1) Unwritten rules are followed that enable jazz improvisers to piece together respectable performances without rehearsal.

2) Musicians know many of the same tunes, and they follow common practices when performing tunes having 12-bar blues and 32-bar A-A-B-A construction.

3) Jazz musicians play the melody before and after they play improvisations that are guided by a cycle of repetitions of its accompaniment.

---

[10]Though jazz musicians in this situation usually play notes that fit with the underlying chords, improvisers are free to initiate lines that deviate from an otherwise strictly defined chord progression. But if the line is to sound good, the improviser's accompanists must listen and instantly follow suit. Frequently a hornman initiates the deviation and the pianist responds with appropriate chords. Or a pianist can suggest alterations in harmony by what he plays. Then the hornman picks up the direction, and the ensemble works together with the alteration. Soloists can also play notes which are incompatible with the underlying chords, while the rhythm section maintains the preset progression. This is called playing "against the changes" or playing "outside," and it is used effectively by some soloists, including many of the saxophonists who soloed on Miles Davis records during the 1970s and 80s.

4) It sometimes sounds like the musicians are playing twice as fast (double-time) when they double the density of their activity or half as fast (half-time) when they halve the density of their activity, even though accompaniment chords change at the same rate throughout the performance of a given piece.

5) Jazz musicians are thoroughly trained in methods of playing their instruments, reading and writing music, and they know so many tunes and chord progressions that they can instantaneously respond to the notes each other plays when improvising.

6) Walking bass style involves playing notes that serve to keep time for the band as well as outlining the chord progression being followed by the improvisers.

7) The jazz drummer uses snare drum, bass drum, ride cymbal, and high-hat cymbals to keep time for the band as well as contribute kicks and prods that communicate with the improvising soloist.

8) Comping is the accompaniment style in which the pianist feeds chords to the improvising soloist in a flexible and syncopated way.

9) The improvising soloist keeps many considerations in mind while performing—chord progressions, logical and original construction of the solo, communication with accompanists, etc.

A jazz combo performing at a New York night club in 1953: bass viol (Charles Mingus), drums (Roy Haynes), piano (Thelonious Monk), and saxophone (Charlie Parker). (*Photo by Bob Parent, courtesy of Don Parent*)

# chapter 4
# ORIGINS OF JAZZ

Jazz originated in blends of folk music, popular music, and light classical music that were current near the beginning of the twentieth century, especially in New Orleans.[1] Several different processes contributed to the birth of jazz: (1) the creation of new kinds of music by black Americans, such as ragtime and blues, (2) the expansion of improvisation within European and African traditions, (3) performance of established kinds of music in ways that involved (a) varying the pitches of given tones, (b) using rough and varied timbres, (c) anticipating and delaying selected notes to syncopate the phrases (sometimes termed "ragging"), and (d) articulating in a more slurred manner, with accents placed in a way that pushes and enlivens the way the notes move.

Jazz has several characteristics in common with African music. Let's consider some history in order to appreciate why this is so. When African slaves were brought to the United States, they were not allowed to bring musical instruments. Moreover, villages and families of Africans were so thoroughly separated that many groups of slaves in America did not even have a single language in common. But they did bring their own musical tastes and a tradition of musical practices. This may explain why European musical material could sound different when played in the New World by musicians of African ancestry. For example, some slaves modified European church hymns, folk songs, and dance music to fit their own tastes and traditions. Their children followed suit, and in this way preferences were retained across generations. In other words, jazz did not derive its similarities to African music from direct contact with African music. It acquired these characteristics secondhand, through other music that developed by contact with African musical practices in the New World. Keep in mind also that there is much about jazz that has nothing to do with African music.

---

[1]See the instructor's resource manual for bibliography, discography, and a lengthy discussion of the controversies.

**WHY DID JAZZ ORIGINATE IN NEW ORLEANS?**

Before analyzing the features of jazz in greater depth, let's first examine the setting in which it was born. We will begin with the history of ethnic diversity in New Orleans. The next two paragraphs are paraphrased from the work of James Haskins in his book *The Creoles of Color of New Orleans* (Crowell, 1975).

**Ethnic Diversity and Creoles of Color**

France began building New Orleans in 1718, and 147 black slaves were brought there in 1719. There were free blacks there as early as 1722. In the 1750s, France and Spain fought a war against Prussia together and signed a treaty in 1763, with France giving the territory of Louisiana to Spain as a gift. But Spanish rule was not firmly established until 1769, and despite Spanish rule, the language and customs there remained primarily French. However, significant social patterns can be traced back to that period of Spanish rule. At that time, marriage between the different ethnic groups in Louisiana occurred more frequently. Furthermore, the Spanish freed many slaves, thereby increasing the number of free blacks (there were 1,147 by 1789), and under Spanish rule, **free people of color began to be regarded as a class that was separate from the whites and the slaves, with status closer to that of whites.** Many light-skinned women of color became mistresses to white men and were set up as second families to the men in separate houses. This was common where there were more white men than white women. Sex between blacks and whites prior to the mid-1800s led to a mixing of African and European traditions. The offspring from some of these unions, whose ancestry was part African and part French, were called *Creoles of Color*, or Creoles, for short. Creoles were not referred to as Negro. That term was reserved for blacks who had little or no white blood. Strictly speaking, however, Creole originally meant people speaking Spanish and French who were born in the New World. This included French and Spanish Americans who were white, not just those of mixed lineage, to whom the term was later applied in a manner similar to mulatto, which means half black and half white.

In 1801, Spain ceded Louisiana back to France, but Spain continued to rule the territory until the United States bought it from France in 1803. Another event affected New Orleans Creoles at about this time. A slave revolt in Haiti (from 1791 to 1804) against the white French and the Creole planters caused many free people of color from Haiti to move to New Orleans after, in 1809, being forced out of Cuba, where they had been given refuge. By 1810, the number of free people of color living in New Orleans had increased to 5,000, making them the majority ethnic group there. A sharp separation existed between the two groups of New Orleans residents who had African ancestry. Creoles of Color were mostly well-educated, successful people—businessmen, physicians, landowners, and skilled craftsmen. They spoke French. Many owned slaves, and often required their slaves to speak French, too. Children in Creole families often received high-quality musical training, some even traveling to Paris for study at a conservatory. The Creoles maintained a resident symphony orchestra, and supported an opera house. This reinforced the intensely musical orientation of New Orleans, a city that had three opera houses, far more than any other American city of comparable size. Many of the Creoles lived downtown in the area of New Orleans today known as the French

Quarter. Negroes lived in a racially mixed neighborhood, a large portion of which was uptown, and they worked primarily as house servants and unskilled laborers. The small white American population reacted to their own minority status with fear. They began enacting laws and continued enacting laws for about 100 years which, little by little, eroded the favored status of the Creoles and eventually placed them in the same position as Negroes. The process was slow. As late as 1830, Creole families owned almost 2,500 slaves and continued to prosper in business. However, by the mid-1840s, life became sufficiently uncomfortable for the Creoles that many left New Orleans.

**The Blues**    The vocal music of the uptown blacks in New Orleans included Afro-American work songs, devised to ease the burden of laborers, and Afro-American religious music that was a compromise between European church music and African vocal style. Another kind of black vocal music was the cry of the street vendor, a kind of music which capitalized on expressive variations in pitch and voice quality (heard in the first selection on the JAZZ CLASSICS CASSETTE). By the first decade of the twentieth century, these sounds had evolved into another kind of music that was initially an unaccompanied solo vocal style but finally developed into using guitar or banjo as accompaniment. The chords in this accompaniment were originally almost incidental to the melodic line—whatever chords the singer could play. The progression of chords was simple. Sometimes only two or three different chords were used in an entire song. Lyrics and melody lines were also simple, with brief pauses between phrases and much repetition. This was the form of music we now call *the blues*. (See pages 374–379 for explanation. Listen to the JAZZ STYLES CASSETTE for demonstration of the chord progression. For an early vocal example, listen to Robert Johnson sing "Hellhound on My Trail" in SCCJ. For a modern-day instrumental example, listen to "Frame for the Blues" in the JAZZ CLASSICS CASSETTE.)

The bit of history we have just outlined bears on our quest for the roots of jazz because Creoles wholeheartedly embraced European music, whereas some music played by Negroes retained aspects of African musical practices. Though many Negro musicians received musical training, their music was generally less refined than that of the Creoles. It may have included improvisation, but we do not know. In summary, many European concert traditions were absorbed and maintained by Creole music, and some African traditions were preserved in Negro music. No doubt, the French and Creoles blessed New Orleans with a strong musical tradition. By comparison with residents in other regions, they took the pleasures of music and dance more seriously.

**The Need For Live Music**    To help us appreciate the setting in which jazz emerged, historian-musicologist Karl Koenig encourages us to envision life at the beginning of the twentieth century. Let's follow his observations, paraphrased in the next five paragraphs from his writings.

To understand the effects of living in an age without the electronic devices we now possess, imagine trying to amuse yourself on a night in the New Orleans area. You could not listen to any radio or television programs, records, or tapes. You could not call anyone on the telephone or visit movie theaters or video arcades. Candle-light would be needed for reading. However, you could go to the town park or square, which would be illuminated by gas lamps. There you could buy flavored ices from a vendor, exchange pleasantries with your neighbors, and take a walk in the moonlight. You could also listen and dance to the local band. In other words, there almost had to be music, *live* music. A town without a band was a very dull place to be. The social and fraternal organizations knew this, as did the newspapers and commercial establishments. Therefore sponsorship was provided for most of the local bands by churches (mostly Catholic), social and benevolent clubs, fraternal clubs (Elks, Masons, etc.), fire departments, townships, undertakers, and plantation owners.[2]

**Brass Bands**    The band was present at almost every social activity, most of which took place outdoors: picnics, sporting events, political speeches, or dramatic presentations at the town hall, and dances in the open-air pavilions—the dance was the main social activity of the nineteenth century. The band played before the event and for the dance which followed. So that the music could be heard in outdoor settings, a large brass band was used. In the narrowest sense, a "brass band" has only brass instruments and percussion. The early Louisiana bands, though dominated by brass, also included a clarinet and later a saxophone (both of which are known as "wood-winds," even when not constructed entirely of wood; see photographs on page 88). They also had a bass drum, a cymbal, and a snare drum. When the activity was held indoors, a large band was not needed. Thus emerged the smaller "string band," often composed of cornet, violin, guitar, bass, and piano.

There had been bands in the New Orleans area long before the Civil War. Then, during the war, occupation by Union troops had exposed the city to many more. About thirty different regimental bands of the occupational forces were stationed in and around New Orleans. They were very conspicuous, playing not only for the many military ceremonies but also for concerts of patriotic and popular music. Their presence was an additional impetus for the band tradition in New Orleans.

**Ragtime**    By the end of the 1800s, **ragtime** was very popular in New Orleans. The word "rag" is a noun identifying a compositional form that borrowed its construction from European military music and borrowed some of its rhythms from Afro-American banjo music. The word "rag" is also a verb: "to rag" is to alter the rhythms in a piece of music in order to lend it a distinctive syncopated or ragged-time feeling. "Rag-time" is a label ordinarily used to describe a kind of written piano music that first appeared in the 1890s and was associated with the popular compositions of Scott

[2]Though the plantation system of labor was nonexistent in name, the plantations still operated with hired labor. And most of the plantations hired bandmasters/teachers to in-struct these hired hands and to form bands. Many early jazz musicians received their musical training there.

Scott Joplin
"Maple Leaf Rag"
off of a roll

Scott Joplin. (*Photo courtesy of New York Public Library*)

Joplin (1868–1917). (Listen to Joplin's "Maple Leaf Rag" in SCCJ.) The label has also been used to identify an entire era of music, not exclusively written piano music. For example, between the 1890s and the 1920s, there were ragtime bands, ragtime singers, ragtime banjo players, in addition to ragtime pianists. Many of the musicians we classify today as "jazz musicians" called themselves "ragtime" musicians, and some scholars consider ragtime to have been the first jazz style. However, because ragtime was improvised only to a limited extent, and its capacity for evoking jazz swing feeling was also limited, ragtime fails to qualify as jazz by the definition of jazz that requires the music to swing and be improvised. Ragtime was a precursor of jazz. It popularized using accents before and after the beat instead of always directly on it. Jazz musicians play "around" the beat partly because ragtime made the practice popular.

**Combining Influences**

During the 1890s, there were bands in almost every small town and settlement in Southern Louisiana, and their music reflected several influences. It combined march music and ragtime, two styles that were interrelated. John Philip Sousa had included ragtime pieces in his band concerts, and ragtime pianists often performed

Sousa marches in a ragtime style. Another significant force was music of the Mexican bands that visited New Orleans. Musicians from these bands settled in and around New Orleans, and some became music teachers. Their music was respected and enjoyed so much that it influenced the styles in which New Orleans trumpeters played.

Band music influenced jazz quite directly. By the beginning of the twentieth century, New Orleanians were accustomed to hearing brass bands such as Sousa's and Arthur Pryor's, having already heard Patrick Gilmore's military bands of the Gulf Coast Command. Dances held in the middle 1800s were often provided with music by the military marching band that was stationed in the region. The march form was sometimes modified and used as dance music in New Orleans, and later a popular dance called the "two-step" was done to march-like music. Moreover, the relative organization and duration of various themes in ragtime pieces is similar to the arrangement found in marches. Roles of various instruments were transferred from marching band to jazz band. For instance, clarinets in early jazz bands often adapted the flute and piccolo parts from march arrangements. In the typical marching drum part, the bass drum played on beats one and three, while the snare drum, with its sharper sound, played on beats two and four. In early jazz there is a correspondingly heavy emphasis on beats two and four (see pages 360–361 for more explanation). (Listen to the "Dixie Jazz Band One-Step" in the JAZZ CLASSICS CASSETTE, and note its similarity to march music.)

**Party Atmosphere**    Other factors besides the brass band movement made New Orleans an ideal setting for the birth of jazz. New Orleans was a center for commerce because of its nearness to the mouth of the Mississippi River, a flourishing trade route for America, the Caribbean, and Europe. Because the city was a seaport, it catered to travelers from all over the world, and New Orleans maintained a cosmopolitan party atmosphere. There were numerous taverns and dance halls. One aspect of the entertainment it provided was a famous brothel district known as Storyville. It took its name from an alderman (city councilman), Sidney Story, who drafted legislation that sectioned off a portion of the town in 1897 and limited prostitution to that area. **The reason the party atmosphere of New Orleans is important to the beginning of jazz is that it generated so much work for musicians. This, together with the tremendous need for brass bands, was so intense that the consequent demands for fresh material caused musicians to stretch the styles, and to blend, salvage, and continuously revise odd assortments of approaches and material into what ultimately became jazz.** Karl Koenig has offered this as the key explanation for the origin of jazz.

**Dance Music**    Now let's delve a bit more deeply into what probably occurred at the time jazz was born. Ordinarily jazz is thought to have derived from blues and rags that were popular in New Orleans. However, only a few pieces in the repertory of New Orleans brass bands were rags, and—at least between 1905 and 1915—twelve-bar blues pieces were nowhere near as common as we would expect if we designated these groups as "jazz" bands. In other words, our current notion of "jazz repertory" is not really reflected in the music of the first jazz musicians.

Unlike most of today's jazz, the earliest jazz was intended mostly for dancing, not just for listening. The music's beat, form, and spirit interested the dancers the most. The evolution of new dances and the overall popularity of dancing was a big factor in the evolution of jazz. Dancers were not necessarily impressed by the wonders of collective improvisation or the inspirations of well-crafted solo improvisations. They responded more to new jazz rhythms. The musicians who performed the first jazz have said that their repertory was constructed primarily to accompany dances such as the mazurka, schottische, quadrille, and one-step. These musicians, whom today we call "jazz players," were not hired specifically to play jazz.

At the beginning of the twentieth century, New Orleans parade bands and dance bands shared the same musicians and much of the same repertory. It was almost as though the musicians walked directly from the street parade into the dance hall, often putting down a brass instrument and picking up a violin. The performing groups accompanying dances were termed "string bands" or "orchestras"—violin, guitar, bass viol, and one or two wind instruments, played by the same musicians who had paraded with trumpet and trombone. To satisfy the demands of dancers, these musicians often amalgamated music from different sources. Sometimes they ended up creating new sounds that were very compelling rhythmically. These approaches became the core of jazz style, and their manner of playing led to the idea that jazz is not *what* you play, but *how* you play it. In other words, **jazz was an outgrowth of treatments for many kinds of music being played on the demand of dancers.** Today we call these same musicians "jazz musicians," and their music "New Orleans jazz" or "Dixieland," though some people reserve the term "Dixieland" solely for the music of white bands. **Because their audiences liked ragtime so much, the musicians adapted repertory from many sources, often syncopating ("ragging") otherwise unsyncopated pieces, often lending rhythmic vitality to pieces that lacked it.**

**In parades as well as dance halls, small bands were trying to perform music originally written for large bands. Their compromises led to what became standard Dixieland style and instrumentation. In trying to fill out the sound, more activity was required of each player, and musicians accordingly improvised parts to order. They got in the habit of improvising, and as jazz evolved, this habit evolved from a necessity into a choice.** In essence, the musicians in New Orleans were drawing upon a diverse exchange of materials and making original combinations to please people who had a taste for special kinds of musical excitement. Jazz originated directly in the instrumentation, repertory, and musical practices of brass bands and string bands that were active before the 1920s.

## WHY DID JAZZ EMERGE NEAR THE TURN OF THE CENTURY?

There are several factors that might explain why jazz emerged when it did. One is that the intensity of musical activity in New Orleans was especially high at the beginning of the twentieth century. Karl Koenig has noted that the evolution of jazz coincides with the zenith of popularity for the brass concert band in America. Koenig reminds us that this was a very fertile time because there was so much work for musicians, there were so many bands, plenty of motivation to play varied styles, and almost all the musicians listened to each other's music. Also, because of the popularity of the ragtime style, there was incentive to "rag" music from non-rag sources. This resulted in improvising syncopations in the performance of compositions that did not necessarily bear much syncopation. Similarly, as the twentieth century began, the popularity of blues encouraged musicians to play band instruments in a bluesy way even when not playing a blues piece. This was especially common in music for a dance called the "slow drag."

Another factor is the cumulative effect of social and legal changes in Louisiana that gradually resulted in Creoles being consigned to the same low status the Negroes had. Remember that between the beginning of the 1800s and the beginning of the 1900s, distinctions between "pure" and "mixed" ancestry were more and more ignored. All citizens with any African ancestry were consigned to the same category. Creoles were forced to give up the status they had attained during the 1700s. They had to assume the status of Negroes and mix socially and occupationally with Negroes. Though the Creoles resented this, jazz was the ultimate benefactor because this readjustment further facilitated the blending of European traditions (as represented by the Creoles) with African traditions (as represented by the Negroes).

**An African Heritage of Musical Tastes**

Before beginning a more detailed examination of jazz elements, we must consider some important qualifications regarding the mixing of styles when Afro-American ragtime and blues began affecting the performance of other kinds of music. Preferences are learned, not genetic. Preferences for certain African techniques were indeed passed down from generation to generation by imitation and instruction. But slaves also learned European music that was available. For example, by the mid-1800s, there were highly accomplished concert artists in the European style who had slavery backgrounds. (Conversely, by the 1920s, there were highly accomplished jazz musicians whose backgrounds were strictly European and white.) It is not reasonable to expect all music played by blacks to sound African. No one inherits desires for music of any particular region; there is no "racial unconscious" that is transmitted genetically. Remember that in New Orleans, most black and especially Creole musicians played European types of dance music such as mazurkas, waltzes, polkas, and quadrilles. They had to, or they would not be hired. The fact that these New Orleans musicians had African ancestry was irrelevant to the music they played. So, as you consider the next few pages of analysis, keep in mind that (1) when we speak of African traditions, we are referring only to tastes for particular ways of making music, (2) these tastes were conveyed more by American Negro culture than by Creole culture, (3) the opportunity to alter established styles, and thereby season to taste, was capitalized upon by Afro-Americans in such a highly creative way that the result was ragtime, blues, jazz, rock, and funk music; but (4) many Americans of African descent never had such preferences, and many whites did. Incidentally, by the 1980s, Afro-American musical styles had become the most popular in the world not just among people of African descent, but among all races in every geographic region.

**WHAT IS AFRICAN AND WHAT IS EUROPEAN ABOUT JAZZ?**

Most innovators in jazz have been black musicians, and, until recently, a disproportionately high percentage of jazz musicians were black. Those are two reasons that lead us to ask whether jazz contains characteristics of African music that might have filtered into it through the Afro-American culture that produced so many of its practitioners. The question is impossible to answer, however, because African music and European music have so many elements in common and because both were available as models when jazz was forming. But it remains interesting to consider the possibilities. So now we are going to examine some features of jazz, keeping in mind African and European sources.

**Improvisation**    The first feature of jazz we are going to examine is improvisation, the practice of **spontaneously varying individual parts.** It has been an important element of music since the beginning of time, and only recently in history was it difficult to find in European concert music. Improvisation characterizes some African music and much jazz. Musicologists are uncertain about the extent to which Afro-American music retained improvisatory traditions from African music. Let's first look at improvisation in music of cultures that contributed slaves to the New World. For instance, in the Ghanaian drum ensemble, the lead drummer is in charge of giving signals. His part is more variable than any of the others, and therefore it might be regarded as improvised. In the Mandinka drum ensemble, the senior player has leeway to improvise more than the others, but all members are allowed to slightly vary their parts as they play. Some African singing in leader-and-chorus format allows spontaneous variations in the part of the leader, as in "Hunter's Dance" in the JAZZ CLASSICS CASSETTE. To keep this in perspective we must note, however, that these practices come nowhere near the extent of improvisation that is found today in jazz. In the West African singing and the Afro-American blues singing that evolved from it, improvisations did not consist of inventing elaborate melody lines as eventually came to be common for jazz improvisers. Instead, these singers chan-neled their creativity into altering the sound of a single sustained tone, varying the timing, pitch, and timbre at the beginning and ending of it. They also improvised by toying with the rhythms of melodies. Tones would be started a bit earlier or later, or a given tone might be repeated several times in succession instead of being sung only once. Similarly, a tone might be started, then softened, and then pushed again by an abrupt increase in volume before it was allowed to end. Sometimes whole phrases would be placed differently in relation to the underlying beat, a technique known as *rhythmic displacement.* (These practices are evident in the samples of vocal music at the beginning of the JAZZ CLASSICS CASSETTE.) Incidentally, these techniques are still evident in performances of gospel music by Afro-American singers and in gospel-influenced styles of pop music, such as the singing of Aretha Franklin and James Brown.

The reason we discuss singing at this point in a textbook about instrumental jazz is that the vocal practices described here are thought to have influenced the styles used by jazz musicians who played trumpet, trombone, clarinet, and saxophone. (This is demonstrated in the playing of Miles Davis that directly follows the cry of the Afro-American street vendor at the beginning of the JAZZ CLASSICS CAS-SETTE.) Individual creativity and unorthodox means for learning how to play have also been suggested as roots of pitch and timbre improvisation in horn work. Some musicologists believe that demand for live music was so great in New Orleans that many unpolished amateurs were called upon to perform as professionals, and the incomplete mastery these players had over their instruments gave us the collec-tion of raw, unorthodox sounds we now associate with New Orleans jazz. Imitation of singing style, however, is the most popular explanation among musicologists. In addition, some musicologists believe the spirit of improvisation and the stress on individuality in jazz stem from African traditions. But these traits are also found in America within non-African folk music as well. So a striving for individuality among jazz musicians could be, but is not necessarily or exclusively, an extension of African preferences, or what has been called "the black esthetic."

Now let's consider what European music could have contributed to the origins of improvisation in jazz. In America there was already a well-developed European tradition for improvising by the time jazz had begun. Improvised ornaments were common in pre-twentieth-century concert music, and they have long been common in folk music and popular music. And, within informal American music prior to the emergence of jazz, there are precedents for improvisation in the form of musicians making spontaneously varied entrances or singers starting notes whenever they feel like it rather than in unison with the others. This is termed *heterophony*, sounding to our ears like ensemble "sloppiness." It is also notable that improvised variations were common parts of solo recital format for some keyboard artists. During the 1800s, concert pianists often improvised within the encore number of their program. And there existed a French and German keyboard tradition for improvisation called *preluding.* Some early American musicians were even required to possess the skill of improvising a piece on demand, using phrases supplied by their audience. So it is clear that the practice of making up music as you go along is precedented in both West African and European music, and both of these traditions could have influenced the use of improvisation in jazz.

Now consider the use of improvisation among New Orleans musicians at the beginning of the twentieth century. At least as late as 1923, the improvisational creativity of the players was directed primarily at piecing together band routines. Some ensemble routines were spontaneously devised during performances, thereby qualifying as improvised. Published arrangements, known among musicians as "stocks," often provided the skeleton. For the first few run-throughs, many of the parts were not fixed. Trombone counterlines, clarinet obbligatos, and trumpet variations of the melody were sometimes invented and performed spontaneously. Accompaniments were improvised and varied by the more adventurous and creative of the players. After a suitable set of parts had been worked out, the musicians frequently remained relatively loyal to them. A striving for improvisation was not as central to a jazz esthetic as it has become. The extent to which new melodies were freshly improvised during performance was limited. There was, however, a striving for personalization and individualization which did not require improvisation, at least in the sense that the term is used here. Though the seeds were planted in New Orleans, it is possible that the kind and the extent of jazz improvisation known today did not first emerge there.[3]

---

[3]The players may have done much without referring to written scores. However, the absence of notation in these situations should not be taken as evidence of improvisation any more than we would consider "improvised" the music of today's wedding bands and lounge acts that sometimes play fresh routines and do so without notation. Research by Karl Koenig has shown that most of the early New Orleans jazz musicians could read music well enough to work out the notes and fingerings, though they could not necessarily sight read fast. Some could not read music, however, and most chose not to read pieces once they had been learned.

By the late 1920s, these improvisational tendencies had expanded to the extent of improvisation we ordinarily expect from most jazz today. Unfortunately, we will never know why this change occurred. But several possible reasons are: 1) boredom with fixed routines, 2) a need to learn new material without recourse to sheet music, 3) increased interest in bravura solo excursions and emergence of the "star" system of players, 4) a continuation of European and/or African traditions for spontaneous alteration, 5) an unbridled creativity, 6) longer dances, necessitating stretching out the numbers, in turn leading to solos that give other hornmen time to rest their lips, 7) a combination of these reasons.

**Syncopation**

Next let's consider **syncopation,** another prominent feature of jazz. Syncopation is a rhythmic phenomenon most easily understood as the occurrence of accents that are not directly on a main beat. (For more explanation of this technical concept, study pages 360–365. To hear the difference between unsyncopated and syncopated playing, listen to the piano comping demonstrations on the JAZZ STYLES CASSETTE, side 2.) Syncopation is common in both African and European music, though Africa is especially known for highly syncopated music. Some syncopation in jazz is thought to derive from Afro-American banjo music and ragtime, and some is thought to stem from the heterophony that we discussed above. The taste for syncopation that exists among jazz musicians might stem, in part, from musical preferences for *rhythmic contrast*, which musicologist Olly Wilson has shown to prevail among much African and Afro-American music.

**Harmony**

A third feature of jazz is **harmony.** Though harmony is found in African music, the chord progressions that we find in jazz are not common to native African music. European music provided chord progressions of the type that jazz uses. (For explanation of chord progressions, see pages 372–384. To hear demonstrations, listen to side 1 of the JAZZ STYLES CASSETTE.)

**Instruments**

A fourth feature of jazz is the choice of instruments. Where did the earliest jazz groups derive their **instrumentation?** The European brass band provided the model that included trumpet, trombone, clarinet, saxophone, and tuba. These groups played music that was common repertory for concert bands and parade bands of nineteenth-century America. The black and the white fraternal bands that were plentiful in New Orleans at the beginning of the twentieth century used brass band instrumentation, and they played marches and pop tunes for parades, picnics, dances, and funerals. The region of Africa that supplied slaves for the New World did not have musical instruments that closely resembled the trumpet, clarinet, trombone, or saxophone.

What about drums? The drums of West Africa can be found in some modern jazz groups. The drums used in the earliest jazz, however, were European, brass band drums (see illustrations in the previous chapter). The wood block and cowbell, two other percussion instruments used in the manner of drums, have been heard in jazz since the earliest recordings. (Listen to wood block in the JAZZ STYLES CASSETTE, and in "Dixie Jazz Band One-Step" on the JAZZ CLASSICS CASSETTE.)

They are thought to have African ancestry, though China and Turkey have also contributed forerunners for many similar instruments used in the New World. (Incidentally, the way the ride cymbal is used in jazz is very similar to the way West African musicians play their atoke or karinyan, a slender, iron instrument, technically classed as a clapperless bell.)

What about stringed instruments? The earliest jazz bands frequently employed banjo (see Fig. 4.1), an Afro-American instrument that descended from the African halam. And they also employed guitar, which has a European ancestry. The bass viol (see illustration in the preceding chapter) was also common in early jazz, and it too came from Europe.

**Role of Percussion**  A fifth feature of jazz is the **prominent role of percussion.** Most jazz groups include a drummer who plays a set of assorted instruments and provides almost continuous timekeeping sounds as well as generating musical excitement. (Listen to side 1 of JAZZ STYLES CASSETTE, and see preceding chapter for illustrations and discussion.) Essentially, by adding a drummer to a string band, you have an early jazz band. Dancing to quadrilles, for example, did not require percussion. So historically, drums were an important addition to dance bands that lent them a "jazz sound." Drums are very important in much African music, too. And percussion is important in brass band music of European traditions as well as in European folk dance music such as Irish.

**Figure 4.1. Guitar and banjo (note that the guitar has six tuning pegs, one for each string, and the banjo has four). Guitars appear in a variety of shapes. The one pictured here is a guitar used in early jazz. Electric guitars are usually solid slabs of wood with electronic attachments embedded. Basically, a banjo is a drum with a guitar-like neck and strings. The banjo commonly used in early jazz had four strings, but some banjos have as many as nine strings.**

A feature related to the role of percussion in jazz is playing melodic instruments in highly rhythmic or percussive ways. Nonpercussion instruments are used in these ways in many other kinds of music, too. But the extent to which melodic instruments are used this way is outstanding in jazz. It resembles the way melody instruments are employed in Africa, a tendency Olly Wilson has termed *rhythmization.*

**Roughenings, Buzzes and Ringings**

A sixth feature of jazz is the presence of **rough sounds, buzzes, and ringings.** For instance, jazz drummers sometimes place a key chain atop the ride cymbal to create a sustained hiss or ringing sound. Some drummers insert rivets in a cymbal so that the vibration of the rivets against the cymbal creates a sizzle sound. Many jazz saxophonists cultivate a rasping tone quality. Saxophonist John Coltrane produced a wide range of sound qualities, from smooth to guttural, from full to shrieking. In the JAZZ CLASSICS CASSETTE, you can hear raw tone qualities of soloists on Duke Ellington's "Harlem Airshaft" and the gruff tone quality of saxophonist Ben Webster on "Cottontail." Compare this with the occasionally rough quality in the singer's voice on "One Day." In the JAZZ CLASSICS CASSETTE, you can hear jazz trumpeters and trombonists play in a rough "growl" style—trumpeter Cootie Williams at the beginning of "Cottontail," and trombonist Joe Nanton on "Harlem Airshaft." Other evidence of a preoccupation for rough sounds and buzzes is the jazz brassman's preoccupation with the tone-altering potential of mutes. (For details, see page 390, and listen to side 2 of the JAZZ STYLES CASSETTE, then listen to Joe Oliver's muted trumpet solo on "Dippermouth Blues" and Cootie Williams's on Ellington's "Concerto for Cootie" in SCCJ.) Preferences for these kinds of sounds are thought to derive from African musical tastes and African traditions for improvising on tone quality.

**Repetition of Brief Patterns**

A seventh feature of jazz is the **extensive repetition of brief patterns.** Musicians use the term *ostinato* (from the Italian word meaning "obstinate") to describe the brief, repetitive patterns we are discussing. Ostinato is common in many different kinds of music, but it is particularly common in African music and jazz. One example is the ride rhythm. You can hear it in the West African "Hunter's Dance" at the beginning of the JAZZ CLASSICS CASSETTE. For examples in jazz, listen to side 1 of the JAZZ STYLES CASSETTE. (See page 430 for musical notations.) Another example of extensive repetition is the style of figure played by the left hand of the boogie-woogie pianist. (Listen to Meade Lux Lewis play "Honky Tonk Train" in SCCJ.) Other examples can be found in brief, repetitive bass figures common to jazz/rock fusion, as in recordings by Herbie Hancock and Weather Report from the 1970s and 80s. There is extensive repetition of short phrases called *riffs* in some jazz styles of the 1930s and 40s as well as in jazz-rock of the 1970s and 80s. Both of these are illustrated at the beginning of the JAZZ CLASSICS CASSETTE—the riff band style in Count Basie's "One O'Clock Jump" and the jazz-rock in Weather Report's "Birdland." These characteristics came from accompaniment rhythms in folk music and march music that were popular in America at the same time. Some came from ragtime and military drumming. The use of these musical devices contributes to swing feeling. The effect of these devices in African music is so similar to their effect in jazz that musicologists believe a taste for this effect was retained in Afro-American culture, and it ultimately caused these practices to emerge in jazz. Though scholars are not unanimous about this, most consider jazz swing feeling to be an African or an Afro-American contribution to jazz.

**Polyrhythms**

An eighth feature of jazz is **the practice of sounding different rhythms at the same time**. In particular is the sounding of some rhythms that have a basis of two pulses while sounding other rhythms that have a basis of three pulses. The combination is called a **polyrhythm**. It contributes to the swing feeling and rhythmic excitement of jazz because it creates tensions within the listener who can neither resist following either division of pulses nor can reconcile the two. (See pages 359 and 365 for more explanation, and listen for moments of such rhythmic conflict in John Coltrane's "The Promise" on the JAZZ CLASSICS CASSETTE and in James P. Johnson's "Carolina Shout" in SCCJ.)

   Much of the polyrhythmic construction in jazz comes from the inventiveness of the musicians, not necessarily from the imitation of pre-existing models. We know this to be true, for example, in some work by drummers Max Roach and Elvin Jones. (Listen to Jones on "The Promise" in the JAZZ CLASSICS CASSETTE.) But some polyrhythms in early jazz are thought to be borrowed from combinations of rhythms found in ragtime. Note that polyrhythms are employed in European folk music and concert music that were present in America before jazz originated. And they are prominent in African music. If derived from ragtime, these polyrhythms in jazz have a partly African ancestry because ragtime has roots in an Afro-American banjo tradition. Olly Wilson believes jazz musicians's preference for polyrhythmic construction reflects a tradition retained from African preference for rhythmic contrast. However, we must not overlook its long use in European music, too, even though it seems somewhat less prominent there than in African music.

**The Ways Tones are Decorated**

A ninth feature of jazz is the assortment of **ways in which tones are decorated.** Some of these came to us by way of practices in European classical, opera, and folk music. Some came by way of West African practices. Some originated in the New World from blending and expanding European and African tendencies. We have already discussed a preference for rough timbres (our seventh feature of jazz). Now let's examine alterations of pitch. Study side 2 of the JAZZ STYLES CASSETTE to understand what is meant by "tonal inflection," "embellishment," "pitch bending," and "pitch manipulation." Listen until you can identify the occurrence of no vibrato, slow vibrato, fast vibrato, terminal vibrato, drop, scoop, smear, and doit. The first six minutes of the JAZZ CLASSICS CASSETTE have plenty of examples, such as the street vendor letting pitch fall at the end of his notes, the male singer on "One Day" who creatively toys with the pitches at the beginnings of his notes, the clarinetist on "Dixie Jazz Band One-Step" who smears the pitches at the end of his notes, Miles Davis using his horn to imitate the street vendor (from the "Porgy and Bess" opera) by placing pitch bends in the middle of his notes, etc. Listen to this music while you keep in mind the dimensions of sound that can be altered at will by the jazz improviser: duration, intensity, pitch (vibrato is a steady alternation of pitch), quality (roughness, for example), attack (how a note begins), and decay (how a note ends). Listen to the examples on the JAZZ CLASSICS CASSETTE several times. They go by quickly, but you will notice more and more decorations of tones each time you listen.

*Louis Armstrong*

*Bichet: foot*

To understand vibrato, imagine a sustained tone as a straight line.

Now imagine the pitch of that tone oscillating, that is, becoming alternately higher and lower. The up and down motion of the line represents the slight changes in pitch which constitute vibrato.

We often tend to take vibrato for granted, because it can be almost imperceptible. But if you listen carefully to sustained tones in the work of most singers, violinists, saxophonists, trombonists, and trumpeters, you will hear it.

Vibrato can be present or absent, fast or slow, regular or irregular. Many jazz singers and some jazz instrumentalists tend to start vibrato slowly and then increase its rate so that it is fastest at the end of the note.

This contrasts with the practice of musicians in symphony orchestras who tend to maintain an even rate of vibrato through a tone's complete duration. They employ different rates of vibrato for different styles of composition, however, and many use no vibrato at all.

Vibrato is considered an expressive device. It can also be a prime characteristic for differentiating styles. Early jazz players tended to use much quicker vibratos than modern jazz players. The fast vibrato was undoubtedly a characteristic contributing to the popular description of early jazz as "hot," while modern jazz of the 1940s and 50s with its slower vibrato was "cool." During the 1960s and 70s, many jazz saxophonists employed faster vibrato than was common during the 1940s and 50s. Saxophonists of the 1980s often used a regular rate of vibrato, rather than increasing it near the end of the tone. If you compare music from these periods, you will notice distinct differences in feeling, partly due to the vibrato rate.

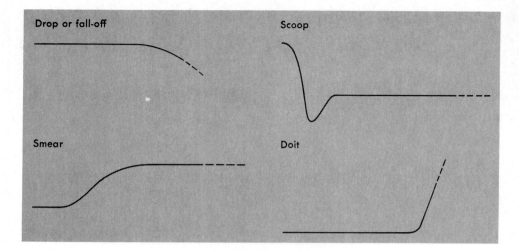

**Blue Notes**

A tenth feature of jazz is the **blue note.** This is a concept best understood by listening to the examples on the JAZZ STYLES CASSETTE and studying the full discussion that appears on page 371. A rough idea of what the term means can be gained by imagining the piano keyboard to represent the entire selection of pitches which musicians are allowed to draw upon. Then imagine how notes would sound if drawn from finer gradations of pitch, as though produced by piano keys existing in the cracks between the ordinary arrangement of keys. The notes that come out from "between the cracks" are blue notes. European music's pitch system, as represented by the piano's seven white keys and five black keys, does not provide all the intervals needed by West African music. Thus, sometimes when Africans performed European-style music, they sang using their own intervals. The sound of these intervals in reference to our ear's expectations was "blue." This is the area of musical performance we call "intonation." This manner of toying with the pitch of notes is an expressive device that has become a jazz tradition, and, though not used by all jazz musicians—they are impossible for pianists—blue notes are common in jazz horn playing. Some of these pitches, which in formal European music would constitute "playing out of tune" or being "off-key," are common in jazz. They are not ordinarily considered mistakes or the result of incomplete mastery of the musician's instrument. That such "out-of-tune" playing is prominent in so many styles of jazz reflects an esthetic of pitch flexibility more than any player's lack of ability to play "in tune." In other words, the kind of out-of-tune playing found in jazz is usually intentional, and it is used as a central element of the art. This might represent a retention of African or Afro-American musical practices, though such "neutral" pitches, as they are technically termed, were not exclusive to African traditions. They were also present in Anglo-American and Scotch-Irish folk music that was heard in early America.

### Listening Guide for Street Cries

"Street Cries of Charleston" (male street vendor)
"Fishermen, Strawberry, and Devil Crab" (trumpet solo)

Available on the JAZZ CLASSICS CASSETTE, side one; originally in "Street Cries of Charleston" on *The Riverside History of Classic Jazz* (reissued by Fantasy as Riverside RB–005) and Miles Davis—*Porgy and Bess* (originally Columbia CL 1274/CS 8085; reissued on LP and CD as CBS 40647).

This comparison illustrates traditions for expressive inflections of pitch in both Afro-American vocal and jazz instrumental styles. First is the call of an Afro-American street vendor advertising the blackberries he is trying to sell. This recording was made early in the twentieth century in Charleston, South Carolina. Second is an excerpt from a piece called "Fishermen, Strawberry and Devil Crab" in an instrumental version that Miles Davis made in 1958 of George Gershwin's opera, "Porgy and Bess." The opera was inspired by Afro-American life in Charleston, including Gershwin's own scores for the musical sounds of vendors pitching their wares. As a jazz trumpeter, Davis is distinguished for his uniquely personal, very expressive tone qualities and inflections of pitch. His mastery of this tradition is conspicuous here.

Musicologists generally believe that approaches to pitch and timbre among jazz horn players are not a direct imitation of African singing. They stem instead from imitating wide-ranging, imaginative sounds found in New World vocal idioms such as Negro field hollers, work songs, cries of street vendors, and the blues. The bluesy manipulations of pitch that are found in jazz horn work stem, in part, from imitating approaches to singing that were devised in the New World by blacks, as demonstrated in the first minute of the JAZZ CLASSICS CASSETTE. In New Orleans, the most bluesy interpretations of dance music were frequently associated with black musicians.[4] Some of this was perpetuated in the humorous, novelty effects ("hokum" style) used by minstrel show musicians. The tendency to playfully vary the sounds of instruments might stem in part from African traditions. However, similar musical traditions also existed in other ethnic groups in New Orleans at the same time. So these practices do not necessarily reflect exclusively Afro-American sources.

[4]You might be able to detect blue notes in the Joe Oliver cornet solo on "Dippermouth Blues" in SCCJ. There are many Rex Stewart cornet solos which use blue notes on Duke Ellington records from the 1930s and 40s. His "Boy Meets Horn" is the most famous example. Modern trumpeter Miles Davis is also particularly known for using blue notes. Listen to "Strawberries" on his *Porgy and Bess* album, excerpted in the JAZZ CLASSICS CASSETTE, or "Solea" on his *Sketches of Spain* album. During the 1970s, Don Ellis played on a specially made trumpet that, by the addition of an extra valve, could produce quarter tones, those "notes in the cracks." Ordinarily, trumpeters had achieved the same sound by depressing their trumpet key halfway, thereby leaving a cocked valve. The Ellis trumpet managed the same effect, but much more reliably.

**Call and Response**

An eleventh feature of jazz is **call-and-response format**. One member or one section of the band offers a musical phrase that is roughly analogous to a question, and another member or section of the band follows it with a new phrase that is roughly analogous to an answer. (Listen to the "call" of the bassist and the "response" of the horns in the theme statement of "So What" by Miles Davis in SCCJ.) This is not as common as most of the other features we have discussed, though it receives considerable attention in accounts by most musicologists when they are describing jazz and African music. (There is overlapping call and response in the four excerpts that are sequenced together at the beginning of the JAZZ CLASSICS CASSETTE— West African, American Gospel, Count Basie riff style, and Weather Report jazz-rock fusion.) It can be found in some styles of band arrangements (as in "Taxi War Dance," "Lester Leaps In," and "Cottontail" on the JAZZ CLASSICS CASSETTE). However, it is not necessarily a distinguishing feature of improvised combo jazz. What many believe to be a call-and-response kind of communication among group members is in many instances just solo and accompaniment in which the accompaniment follows its own patterns more than it spontaneously generates fresh responses to an improvising soloist. This is revealed when we examine recordings in which the solo line is missing, and we discover comping that is almost identical to that which occurs in the presence of improvised solo lines. Also remember that comping ordinarily derives from a repertory of learned patterns (see pages 424 and 425), not necessarily from a spur-of-the-moment response that is evoked by the call of another musician's sound. (Prior to the Bill Evans Trio of 1961, heard on "Solar" in the JAZZ CLASSICS CASSETTE, there was far less spontaneous interaction among rhythm section members and far less between accompanists and soloists than observers ordinarily believed.) In general, improvised lines are much more a "response" to the challenges of the chord progressions and the player's own ingenuity than to any "call" of another musician.

Some commentators have applied "call and response" to describe the function of the phrases that instrumentalists play to fill in a singer's pauses within the twelve-bar blues (for example, in Bessie Smith's blues pieces in SCCJ). However, careful listening reveals that the fills are not necessarily "responses" to the singer's phrases. They merely arrive in sequence with them. Often they are just improvised lines inspired only by the player's own imagination. They frequently originate more from attempts to reconcile horn lines with the underlying chord progressions than from attempts to establish a musical dialog with the singer. The term "call and response" is therefore not an appropriate designation.

Responsorial singing is a pervasive trait of African music, and it is common in European-derived church music found in America. Call-and-response patterns can be found in classical music and in folk music of many ethnic groups present in America. In summary, call-and-response format can be found in some jazz, and the model for it could reflect any or all of several available sources.

*[handwritten margin note: Bessie Smith "Hard Working Man" w/ Louis Armstrong clarinet]*

**Listening Guide for Afro-American Sequence
on Side One of the JAZZ CLASSICS CASSETTE**

**"Hunter's Dance," a West African folk number
"One Day," an American gospel singing number
"One O' Clock Jump," a swing-era riff band number
"Birdland," a jazz-rock fusion number**

These four pieces illustrate several properties that are common to West African music, Afro-American gospel music, swing-era riff-band style, and jazz-rock fusion. Each piece demonstrates extensive repetition of brief patterns, much syncopation, an overlapping call and response format, and the capacity to evoke swing feeling in the listener. By the strictest definition, none of these truly qualifies as jazz because not much is improvised. The third and fourth pieces are usually called jazz, though, because they are played by jazz bands and because they swing.

Though call and response format is common in many kinds of music, not just African and Afro-American styles, the format in which the response overlaps the call is particularly noticeable in African and Afro-American music. The following examples therefore illustrate *overlapping* call and response format, not merely call and response.

"Hunter's Dance" is popular peasant music made by the people of Mali, also known as the Malinke people. To obtain this music, in 1952 ethnomusicologist Gilbert Rouget journeyed to Karala, a relatively isolated native village in the West African country of Guinea. The recording features a six-string harp-lute (dozo-konu), the voice of the man who plays it, a women's chorus accompanying him, a wooden whistle (fere), and a metal scraper (karinyan), which is a small tube of wrought iron that is slit down the middle. The karinyan is held in the left hand and struck with a nail held in the right hand, playing a rhythm similar to the jazz drummer's ride rhythm. ("Hunter's Dance" was originally on *Musique D' Afrique Occidentale*, a French record album, Vogue LVLX 193, later reissued in the U.S. on *Anthology of Music of Black Africa*, Everest 3254/3.)

When listening to "Hunter's Dance," notice that the rhythms of the different parts are carefully calculated to achieve a provocative effect that is peculiarly African. Also notice how the music's excitement increases as the performance evolves and more layers of activity are added.

| *Elapsed Time* | |
|---|---|
| | repeating bass figure, obtained by plucking the strings of the dozo-kuno; accompanied by a repeating rhythm on the metallic sounding karinyan. |
| 15″ | melody sung by the male voice |
| 20″ | response sung by women's chorus |
| 23″ | Before the response is complete, the male voice begins to sing again (thus the expression "overlapping call and response"). |
| 27″ | Women's chorus responds again. |
| 28″ | Whistle sounds. |
| 30″ | Male voice returns. |

"One Day" was recorded in 1951 by the Angelic Gospel Singers (four women), the Dixie Hummingbirds (five men), and a pianist (reissued in an album compilation *The Gospel Sound*, Columbia G 31086).

As in all the pieces of this Afro-American sequence, the music's excitement increases over the course of the performance as more parts are layered on top of each other, each part's rhythms tugging at the others's in a provocative way. Tremendous spirit and exhuberance are projected by this music. Ultimately the music sounds almost like it is going to break apart in wild abandon.

Here are a few highlights. The intensity and momentum are unrelenting, and they occur without the assistance of any bass or drums. Though highly rhythmic piano accompaniment is in the background, the manner in which the singers produce their rhythms is so compelling that they could probably swing without any accompaniment at all. Male voice is in the foreground, though its sound eases in and out of the sounds of background singers answering its phrases. Notice the tendency of the male lead singer to smear up into the pitch of the main notes. This gliding through the pitch range is a very expressive device he uses expertly. Also note the raspy timbre the male singer uses for one of his phrases. This is a preference that is also common to West African singers and musicians. The entrances of the lead singer are highly syncopated, and these syncopations are timed to evoke maximum swing feeling and rhythmic conflict. The responsorial chorus provides the repeating riff in this selection. Notice that the call and response pattern doubles in rate near the end, and finally a woman's voice soars high over the proceedings as one more element to tug at the beat and generate excitement. (A similar device is used at the end of "Birdland.")

"One O'Clock Jump" recorded in 1942 by the Count Basie big band. This is a riff-band piece from the swing era. The original 1937 version of it was a big hit. Excerpted here are the ninth and tenth choruses in twelve-bar blues form. Several different riffs are played against each other at the same time by different sections of the band: trombones, trumpets, and saxophones. This illustrates the principle of antiphony, literally "against sounds." Saxes play a syncopated figure, as though answering the trombone phrase. Trumpets play a different riff that is also syncopated, as though on the opposite end of a see-saw from the trombones. A timekeeping foundation is provided by piano, rhythm guitar, walking bass, and the drummer using sticks to play ride rhythms on opening and closing high hat. The overlapping of these parts generates rhythmic excitement.

"Birdland" by Weather Report, recorded in 1977 on Oberheim Polyphonic Synthesizer (Joe Zawinul), soprano sax (Wayne Shorter), bass guitar (Jaco Pastorius), drums (Alex Acuna), and tambourine (Manolo Badrena); originally on *Heavy Weather*, Columbia 34418 (reissued on CD with same number).

"Birdland" is in a style called jazz-rock fusion. This performance is excerpted from Weather Report's best-selling recording, a discoteque hit. For many years this piece continued to be copied and re-arranged by numerous ensembles, including the singing group Manhattan Transfer. Excerpted here is the chorus of the piece, the melody of which is played by sax, synthesizer, bass guitar, and voice. The chords in the accompaniment are provided by the synthesizer. Percussion accompaniment includes hand claps on beats #2 and #4, tambourine providing steady eighth notes, and the sound of open high-hat cymbal struck with drum stick on upbeats, snapped shut on downbeats. In addition to doubling the melody, bass guitar fills in the gaps between the notes and phrases of the melody. A high-pitched male voice (bass guitarist Jaco Pastorius) sustains tones over the ensemble sound, offering a countermelody.

## CHAPTER SUMMARY

1) Jazz originated in New Orleans around the beginning of the twentieth century.

2) New Orleans was the ideal site for the birth of jazz because it was an intensely musical city with a history of rich ethnic diversity, especially French and African.

3) Jazz emerged when brass bands were at a zenith of popularity and ragtime was in such high demand that brass bands and string bands were improvising rag-like syncopations into their pieces to please dancers.

4) Afro-American forms of music such as the blues and ragtime blended with European dance music and church music.

5) Jazz has features that reflect African musical tastes that were retained in Afro-American music—improvisation, syncopation, rough timbres, extensive repetition of brief patterns, polyrhythms, and call and response format.

6) Jazz reflects European music's instruments, chord progressions, and improvisation.

7) Blending of European and African practices resulted in blue notes and various decorations of a note by altering its pitch.

Joe "King" Oliver's Creole Jazz Band, 1923: Baby Dodds (drums), Honore Dutrey (trombone), Oliver (cornet), Louis Armstrong (cornet), Bill Johnson (bass viol), Johnny Dodds (clarinet), Lil Hardin (piano). (*Photo courtesy of The Cleveland Press Collection/ Cleveland State University Archives*)

# chapter 5
# EARLY JAZZ:
# COMBO JAZZ PRIOR
# TO THE MIDDLE 1930s

Early jazz musicians often began improvising by embellishing the melodies of pop tunes. As jazz evolved across the 1920s, the embellishments sometimes became as good as and more important to a performance than the tunes themselves. In some performances of the 1930s, all that remained was the original tune's spirit and chord progressions. What is today called improvising was referred to by early jazz musicians as "messin' around," embellishing, "jassing," or "jazzing up."

Early jazz differs from its ragtime, blues, and brass band roots in several important respects:

1) Much of each performance was improvised.
2) Rhythmic feeling was looser and more relaxed, thus anticipating jazz swing feeling.
3) It generated much of its own repertory of compositions.
4) The collective improvisation created a more complex musical product than was typical in ragtime, blues, or marching band music.
5) There was more vitality and variety in jazz than there had been in ragtime, blues and brass band music.

Combo jazz began in New Orleans, and that city contributed several soloists of far-reaching significance. The best known were trumpeter Louis Armstrong and clarinetist-saxophonist Sidney Bechet. Jelly Roll Morton was the most significant composer-arranger from New Orleans, and his finest recordings were made during the 1920s in Chicago. New combinations of musicians in Chicago also made several other figures important: Pittsburgh-born pianist Earl Hines; and Bix Beiderbecke, a Davenport, Iowa-born cornetist. Chicago was additionally the home of "The Austin High Gang," which, together with The New Orleans Rhythm Kings, created a white

**53**

**TABLE 5.1.  A Few of the Many Early Jazz Musicians**

| Trumpet | Violin | Piano |
|---|---|---|
| Buddy Bolden | Joe Venuti | James P. Johnson |
| Freddie Keppard | | Fate Marable |
| Joe "King" Oliver | **Clarinet and** | Jelly Roll Morton |
| Louis Armstrong | **Saxophone** | Willie "The Lion" Smith |
| Wingy Manone | Johnny Dodds | Fats Waller |
| Red Nichols | Sidney Bechet | Lil Hardin Armstrong |
| Bix Beiderbecke | Jimmie Noone | Pete Johnson |
| Tommy Ladnier | Frank Teschemacher | Clarence Williams |
| Henry "Red" Allen | Benny Goodman | Meade Lux Lewis |
| Joe Smith | Albert Nicholas | Albert Ammons |
| Bubber Miley | Barney Bigard | Cripple Clarence Lofton |
| Charlie Teagarden | Omer Simeon | Cow Cow Davenport |
| Jabbo Smith | Alphonse Picou | Elmer Schoebel |
| Nick LaRocca | Mezz Mezzrow | Pinetop Smith |
| Paul Mares | Jimmy Strong | Jimmy Yancey |
| George Mitchell | Sidney Arodin | Earl Hines |
| Sidney DeParis | Darnell Howard | Frank Signorelli |
| Muggsy Spanier | Leon Rappolo | Fletcher Henderson |
| Phil Napoleon | Buster Bailey | Joe Sullivan |
| Wild Bill Davidson | Don Redman | Jimmy Blythe |
| Mutt Carey | Bud Freeman | Henry Ragas |
| | Floyd Towne | |
| **Trombone** | Coleman Hawkins | **Guitar and Banjo** |
| Kid Ory | Jimmy Dorsey | Lonnie Johnson |
| J. C. Higginbotham | Hilton Jefferson | Johnny St. Cyr |
| Miff Mole | Stomp Evans | Elmer Snowden |
| Jack Teagarden | Charlie Holmes | Eddie Lang |
| Fred Robinson | Larry Shields | Eddie Condon |
| Charlie Green | Pee Wee Russell | |
| Jimmy Harrison | Adrian Rollini | **Drums** |
| Charlie Irvis | Don Murray | |
| Joe "Tricky Sam" | Tony Parenti | Baby Dodds |
| Nanton | Izzy Friedman | Papa Jack Laine |
| George Brunis | Min Leibrook | Paul Barbarin |
| Bill Rank | Cecil Scott | Zutty Singleton |
| Tommy Dorsey | Frankie Trumbauer | Sonny Greer |
| Glenn Miller | Edmond Hall | Dave Tough |
| Wilbur DeParis | Gene Sedric | George Wettling |
| Eddie Edwards | George Lewis | Ben Pollack |
| Honore Dutrey | | Andrew Hilaire |
| | **Bass** | Chauncey Morehouse |
| **Composer—Arranger** | | Gene Krupa |
| Jelly Roll Morton | Pops Foster | Vic Berton |
| Kid Ory | Wellman Braud | Ray Bauduc |
| W. C. Handy | John Lindsay | Tony Sbarbaro |
| Clarence Williams | | |
| Fats Waller | | |

parallel of the New Orleans combo style that today is called "Dixieland." Another important part of early jazz was an East Coast piano tradition that evolved partly from New Jersey-born James P. Johnson and continued through Fats Waller to Count Basie. Let's examine these styles now.

It was in Chicago that many black New Orleans musicians were first recorded in the early 1920s. What is usually referred to as New Orleans style is not the music that was played between 1900 and 1920 in New Orleans—we have never heard that music because it was not recorded—but rather the music recorded by New Orleans musicians in Chicago during the 1920s. According to interviews and a few early records, the earliest forms of jazz were characterized by collective improvisation, with all group members playing at the same time. These early bands featured choruses in which every player was simultaneously creating phrases which complemented every other player. For many listeners, the greatest appeal of early jazz is the activity of several horn lines sounding simultaneously without clashing. Roles developed whereby a clarinet would play multi-noted figures ornamenting a trumpet lead, and a trombone would play simpler figures outlining the chord notes, filling in low harmony, and creating lower pitched motion. This followed the roles these instruments had served in brass band music.

The style of the black Chicago musicians, most of whom were from New Orleans, evolved away from a strictly collective approach in favor of a style which featured more improvised solos. The skills of the improviser who was required to solo dramatically differed from those of the improviser who was required to blend with the collectively improvised phrases of other players. The delicate balance and sensitive interplay in collective improvisation which characterized the earliest form of jazz receded during the Chicago period of the New Orleans players. However, musicians of subsequent eras who played Dixieland tried to recapture the essence of those special skills which make successful collective improvisation possible.

Though much jazz developed in New Orleans, it was not until New Orleans jazz musicians traveled to Chicago and New York that the music was recorded. **The Original Dixieland Jazz Band** made the first recordings. This was a collection of white New Orleans musicians who organized a band in Chicago during 1916 and played in New York in 1917. They used cornet, clarinet, trombone, piano, and drums. Under the leadership of cornetist **Nick LaRocca** (1889–1961), the band recorded its first 78 r.p.m. record in 1917. They played "Livery Stable Blues" on one side and "Dixie Jazz Band One-Step" on the other. It garnered phenomenally high sales, international fame, and numerous imitators. Even during the 1980s, musicians were forming Dixieland jazz bands in the style of this group. (Listen to their "Dixie Jazz Band One-Step" in the JAZZ CLASSICS CASSETTE. It is the first jazz record ever made.)[1]

---

[1]*The Original Dixieland Jazz Band*, RCA LPV-547. For more about this band, and this period of jazz history, see *Jazz Masters of New Orleans* by Martin Williams (Macmillan, 1970; reprinted by DaCapo), *Hear Me Talkin' to Ya* by Nat Shapiro and Nat Hentoff (Rinehart, 1955; reprinted by Dover), *Really the Blues* by Mezz Mezzrow (Random House, 1946; reprinted by Anchor), *Early Jazz* by Gunther Schuller (Oxford, 1968), *The Essential Jazz Records, Vol. 1: Ragtime to Swing* by Max Harrison, Charles Fox, and Eric Thacker (Mansell, 1984; reprinted by DaCapo).

### Listening Guide for "Dixie Jazz Band One-Step"

Recorded February 26, 1917, by Nick LaRocca (cornet), Larry Shields (clarinet), Eddie Edwards (trombone), Henry Ragas (piano), and Tony Spargo (drums); available in the JAZZ CLASSICS CASSETTE, Side One.

This record was made in New York by a group of white New Orleans musicians who had come together in Chicago the preceding year. They called themselves the Original Dixieland Jass Band (ODJB). "Dixie Jazz Band One-Step" (also known as "Original Dixieland One-Step") was on the reverse side of "Livery Stable Blues," one of the most popular discs in the first decade of recorded jazz. The piece heard here originated from a combination of ideas contributed by all the band members, though ragtime composer Joe Jordan wrote its third theme, and the sheet music for this piece lists bandleader Nick LaRocca as composer. Worldwide sales of the record it was on are said to have reached about a million copies by the late 1930s.

This is the first instrumental jazz recording ever released, and music by the ODJB has continued to influence musicians, partly because this band made the first jazz records. However, there is controversy about what to call the music. First, the name for the style, as well as the piece itself, was originally "jass," not jazz. Second, the music on this recording might not qualify as jazz if we define jazz as music that has improvisation and swing feeling. We don't know whether any of the music was freshly improvised for this particular recording session, but we do know that most of the ODJB's music was worked out in advance, despite the spontaneity of its sound. For instance, the embellishments were recreated almost intact for most performances, though they are likely to have been improvised when this arrangement was first devised. Regarding its quality of swing, the feeling of this music does not have the easy rise and fall of tensions that we associate with swing feeling of later jazz. However, the ODJB's music is loaded with syncopations that evolved from ragtime, and it is highly spirited.

The roles that the different instruments assume on this recording were associated with what is known today as New Orleans, Chicago, or Dixieland style jazz. We can consider this record to be an example of music that was popular in New Orleans during this period because most of the fashions heard here were already common in New Orleans ragtime bands by 1917. So even though it was the first to be recorded, the ODJB was not necessarily the first or "The Original" band of its kind, as its name implies.

Though it often sounds as if a larger band is playing, this performance was constructed by only five instruments: cornet, clarinet, trombone, piano, and drums. The clarinet is most evident, and the piano is least evident, almost inaudible. The cornet and trombone sounds frequently blend so closely that you may have difficulty distinguishing them, though many trombone smears are conspicuous. As was typical for New Orleans drummers of the period, Spargo frequently switches instruments. At various moments he can be heard playing snare drum, wood block, and cowbell. He uses the cymbal sparingly, and a cymbal crash usually signifies a climactic moment in the music, as it does in nonjazz idioms.

To prepare yourself for following the various activities in this piece, it may help to keep three things in mind. First, the music goes by very fast. So you will need to count "1234 1234 . . ." almost as fast as you can to keep your place by counting beats. Second, you'll hear more each time you replay the recording. So don't get frustrated if it sounds like a blur the first time you listen to it. Third, the arrangement contains only three brief themes, and they are frequently repeated. So once you become acquainted with them, you will know almost all that is necessary for following this arrangement.

Many of the different sounds are so close in their pitch range and rhythm that they blend together and disguise each other. But the more often you listen, the more distinct they will become. Your search for the separate instruments might resemble peering at a trick sketch on a comic book or cereal box. (Remember trying to identify a tiger hidden in jungle ferns where overlapping lines camouflaged its contours?) Repeated listening also allows you to get swept up in the excitement of this music. Then you can appreciate why this band was so popular.

You may find it helpful to think of the performance as a loud party in which people are talking to each other very energetically, sometimes agreeing, sometimes disagreeing, often interrupting each other. Once in a while an interrupter gets everyone's attention, and they stop to hear what he has to say. But they almost immediately return to chattering boisterously among themselves. Sometimes as one person speaks, others shout out their agreement with him, and a running commentary is happening most of the time.

To help get your counting synchronized with the music, note that the first two sounds in the performance indicate the first two beats. There is no sound on beat three or beat four. The musicians count these unsounded beats silently to themselves so they can restart their playing together on the first of the next group of four beats (henceforth termed "a measure"). Then the pattern repeats. This goes by very fast, but it is a dependable indication of the tempo for the entire piece. The third measure is occupied by a smear from the trombone that starts high, goes low, then goes back up high again, finishing on the first beat of the next measure.

The ODJB's roots in the brass band tradition are reflected in this piece's opening. The rhythm of the first four-measure sequence is called a "roll-off," a device usually played by a parade band's drummer to prepare musicians to march. Its effect is dramatic, as in a call to arms. The band stands at attention during the roll-off, then begins to march. By listening closely, you can hear the drummer playing the roll-off pattern underneath the horns. His rhythm is the same as theirs. The trombone smear in the third measure coincides with a drum roll. Like other march-style popular music of this period, this piece was also used to accompany a dance, in this case the dance was called the one-step.

The form of the performance is A - A' - B - B' - A - A' - B - B' C - C' - C - C' - C - C'.

Terms to learn from the JAZZ STYLES CASSETTE before listening: eighth notes, stop-time, bass drum, snare drum, wood block, trombone smears, clarinet, and trumpet.

*Elapsed Time*

## FIRST THEME  (The "A" Section)

| | | | |
|---|---|---|---|
| *First Measure:* | bang . . . . . . bang . . . . . . . silence . . . . . . . silence | | |
| *numbered beats:* | 1 . . . . . . . . . 2 . . . . . . . . . .3 . . . . . . . . . .4 | | |
| *Second Measure:* | bang . . . . . . bang . . . . . . . silence . . . . . . . silence | | |
| | 1 . . . . . . . . . 2 . . . . . . . . . .3 . . . . . . . . . .4 | | |
| *Third Measure:* | trombone smear . . . . . . . . . . . . . . . . . . . . . . | | |
| | 1 . . . . . . . . . 2 . . . . . . . . . .3 . . . . . . . . . .4 | | |
| *Fourth Measure:* | smear ends . . . silence . . . . . . crash | | |
| | 1 . . . . . . . . . 2 . . . . . . . . . .3 . . . . . . . . . .4 | | |

0' 03"

*Fifth, Sixth, Seventh, and Eighth Measures:*

Band plays a new theme, with the clarinet playing around the cornet and trombone parts. The drummer plays a military snare drum rhythm as a counteractivity to the rhythms of the horn lines.

0' 07"

## REPEAT OF THE FIRST THEME  (A', 8 measures)

We call this section A' ("ay-prime") because it is the same as A, but the end differs.

*Elapsed Time*

**0' 15"**

### SECOND THEME (B, 8 measures)

In the final two beats of A', the trombone begins to slide up until he reaches the first beat of the second theme, called "B." The entire band joins him on that beat. Then every instrument but clarinet immediately goes silent, and all we hear is clarinet slurring from note to note during beats 2, 3, and 4. This continues through another measure and is called a "stop-time." Then the clarinetist is joined by his bandmates, all playing different lines for an additional six measures (24 beats).

**0' 23"**

### REPEAT OF SECOND THEME (B'; "bee-prime," 8 measures)

The beginning of this eight-measure section resembles the beginning of the preceding section, but the music goes in a different direction for its final four measures, conveying a more resolved quality than the first B. For that reason we designate this strain as B' rather than B.

**0' 30"**

### A-A'-B-B' (32 measures)

This repetition occurs with only a few alterations. Follow the listening guide from the beginning.

**1' 00"**

### THIRD THEME (C, 16 measures)

"That Teasin' Rag" composed by Joe Jordan

Trombone exchanges with clarinet in a call-and-response fashion, playfully trading descending smears; "clickety-clacking" of the drummer's sticks sound military rhythms on the wood block for the first eight measures, then alternately striking wood block and cowbell.

Trombone plays descending smears in unison with piano as a "call." Cornet and clarinet harmonize a bobbing little figure of eighth notes as a "response." This section ends with the horn parts going in different directions. A robust, authoritative trombone part emerges with a repeating figure near the end. Intensity builds and it culminates with a high-pitched, descending clarinet smear.

**1' 16"**

### C' (16 measures)

Note: Every other time C occurs, it ends differently. So these alternate renditions are designated C' ("see-prime").

First beat is played by the drummer striking his cymbal for a crash. Then he plays wood block and cowbell. The trombone briefly carries a melody of its own in the final eight measures, using a style similar to tuba parts in march arrangements. The cornet chimes in with a sustained tone on an offbeat in the second to last measure.

**1' 32"**

### C (16 measures)

Drummer begins this section emphasizing his cowbell and uses wood block less than before. Notice the descending trombone smears. A quick, high-pitched clarinet smear ends this section.

**1' 48"**

### C' (16 measures)

Drummer begins the section with a cymbal crash, then plays patterns on wood block. He interrupts his pattern during the middle of this section and strikes the bass drum twice in succession.

*Elapsed Time*

2' 03"

**C** (16 measures)

If you listen closely during the last half of this section, you will hear the piano pounding out bass patterns. This section ends with a descending clarinet smear played more hurriedly than in the first C.

2' 18"

**C'** (16 measures)

*Final Eight Measures*

2' 26"

Drummer is playing snare drum instead of wood block and cowbell. Then he ties up the piece with a cymbal crash.

Joe Oliver's **Creole Jazz Band** was an all-star New Orleans group which, at various times, had most of the best black New Orleans jazz musicians in Chicago. Trumpeter **Joe Oliver** (1885–1938) had worked with several New Orleans bands, then moved to Chicago in 1918, worked with several more bands, and finally formed one of his own. A group of recordings made under Oliver's leadership in 1923 are often cited as the first recording of black New Orleans combo jazz. Aside from accompaniments for singers, however, a band led by New Orleans-born trombonist Kid Ory had been the first black jazz combo to have its playing issued on record.[2] This chapter devotes considerable space to the styles of three sidemen in Oliver's band: trumpeter Louis Armstrong, clarinetist Johnny Dodds, and drummer Warren "Baby" Dodds. (Listen to their "Dippermouth Blues" in SCCJ.)

Chicago was the center for a very active jazz scene during the 1920s. Musicians there can be described in terms of three main categories. One was the transplanted New Orleans black musicians. Another contained their white New Orleans counterparts, among whom were the New Orleans Rhythm Kings (Friar's Society Orchestra).[3] These two groups of musicians, in turn, were influencing a third group of younger white musicians, many of whom were Chicago natives. This young white community developed what was called **The Chicago Style,** or **The Chicago School.** Its music was modeled on the New Orleans style, but sounded more hurried. Several of these musicians (Jimmy McPartland, Frank Teschemacher, and Bud Freeman) had attended the same Chicago high school, Austin High. They subsequently earned the name of *The Austin High Gang,* though their "gang" included Dave Tough, who attended Wayne High. In addition to the Austin High Gang, the white Chicago scene included other notables (see Table 5.2.).

Eventually the Chicago musicians and the transplanted New Orleans musicians mixed with New York musicians. By the late 1920s, a strong New York scene had also developed. Key performers in the early combo jazz of New York included trumpeter Red Nichols, trombonist Miff Mole, and violinist Joe Venuti. Most of the original Chicagoans had moved to New York by the 1930s.

[2] *Louis Armstrong & King Oliver*, Milestone 47017, LP set, 1923–24; *King Oliver's Jazz Band*, Smithsonian 2001, LP set, 1923; Ory's recordings from 1922 are in *Steppin' on the Gas, Rags to Jazz, 1913–1927*, New World 269, LP anthology. For more about Oliver, see *King Oliver* by Laurie Wright (Storyville, 1987).
[3] *The New Orleans Rhythm Kings*, Milestone 47020, LP set, 1922–23

**TABLE 5.2. The New Orleans and Chicago Jazz Styles—Representative Musicians**

| New Orleans | | Chicago |
|---|---|---|
| Joe "King" Oliver | Zutty Singleton | Muggsy Spanier |
| Bunk Johnson | Johnny St. Cyr | Jimmy McPartland |
| Freddie Keppard | Lonnie Johnson | (Austin High School) |
| Buddy Bolden | Omer Simeon | Frank Teschemacher |
| Louis Armstrong | Jelly Roll Morton | (Austin High School) |
| Sidney Bechet | Honore Dutrey | Dave Tough |
| Jimmie Noone | Albert Nicholas | Bud Freeman |
| Kid Ory | Barney Bigard | (Austin High School) |
| Baby Dodds | George Brunies | Joe Sullivan |
| Johnny Dodds | Leon Roppolo (Rappolo) | Mezz Mezzrow |
| | | Eddie Condon |
| | | Gene Krupa |

Early jazz has been identified by many labels which lack standard use. Certain labels have definite meanings for some jazz scholars and musicians, though they are not uniformly applied by everyone. Chicago jazz and New Orleans jazz are two of these terms. Ragtime, gut bucket, barrelhouse, Dixieland, classic jazz, and traditional jazz are others. These terms tend to be applied to solo piano styles and combo jazz, to include both black and white musicians, and to refer to music produced by old New Orleans and Chicago veterans as well as revivalist groups. As though this is not already confusing enough, note that the terms "ragtime" and "jazz" have frequently been used to encompass all popular music of the period instead of designating just the jazz-related styles discussed here. And the problem has worsened because novelist F. Scott Fitzgerald dubbed the 1920s "The Jazz Age," and numerous other writers adopted the term in a way that indiscriminantly confused what we today call jazz with almost all the syncopated music that was popular in that decade.

**Piano**     We know that jazz piano styles were evolving in places other than New Orleans prior to 1920. In fact, many outstanding jazz pianists of the 1920s were from the East Coast. Many of them played unaccompanied. Early jazz piano styles evolved from ragtime. Playing ragtime did not always necessitate reading or memorizing written music. Once the style had been absorbed, skilled pianists appeared who could improvise original rags as well as embellish pre-written ones. One jazz piano style with roots in ragtime is known as *stride style*. Stride piano playing uses percussive, striding, left-hand figures in which low bass notes alternate with mid-range chords, while the right hand plays melodies and embellishments in a very energetic fashion. This is demonstrated in piecemeal fashion on the JAZZ STYLES CASSETTE, side 2, and illustrated by one of its founders in James P. Johnson's "You've Got To Be Modernistic" on the JAZZ CLASSICS CASSETTE.[4]

*"raggish"*

Jelly Roll Morton (1890–1941) was a pianist, composer-arranger, and bandleader from New Orleans. Some historians consider him to be one of the first jazz pianists as well as the first jazz composer. Morton was capable of performing in both the ragtime style and the jazz style. He perfected rhythmic techniques that altered the character of eighth-note lines so that they swung. Pianist-historian James Dapogny, has pointed out that Morton used long-short, long-short patterns in playing eighth notes (see page 364 for explanation) and that Morton alternated intensities of eighth notes so that they gave the impression of strong-weak, strong-weak. These tendencies, plus a reduction in adornment, helped lend Morton's playing a lighter and more swinging feeling than was borne by ragtime.

Morton's piano style was quite involved. He often played two or three lines at a time, much in the manner of a band. It was as though trumpet parts, clarinet parts, and trombone parts were being heard coming from a piano! Morton's playing featured a variety of themes and much activity within a single piece, using stop-time solo breaks (explained on JAZZ STYLES CASSETTE) in the same manner as horns in a combo. Morton mixed ragtime with less formal, more blues-oriented New Orleans styles (listen to "Maple Leaf Rag" in SCCJ).

The best-known of Morton's several bands were a series of recording groups in Chicago called the Red Hot Peppers. The imagination of Morton's compositions and arrangements that is evident on those recordings remains respected by jazz composers and scholars. Morton employed many of the same New Orleans-born musicians shared by other black Chicago groups. However, under Morton's leadership, the resulting sounds were unusually well-organized, though they retained the spirit of music made by less tightly run bands. (Listen to his "Black Bottom Stomp" in SCCJ.)

In summary, Jelly Roll Morton is historically notable because:

1) He was possibly the first jazz composer.
2) He contributed a body of original compositions, several of which became well-known in rearranged form by other bands—"Wolverine Blues," "Milenburg Joys," "Wild Man Blues," "King Porter Stomp".
3) He introduced arranging practices in his small-group performances that came to be imitated during early stages in the history of big bands.

---

[4]Stride style left-hand consists of playing a bass note on the first and third beats and a mid-range chord on the second and fourth beats of each measure. Listen to a dissected example on JAZZ STYLES CASSETTE, side 2. Together, the two hands produced music which you might imagine as a small orchestra with a driving rhythm section. This style is very demanding for the pianist. Listen to James P. Johnson's "You've Got to Be Modernistic" on the JAZZ CLASSICS CASSETTE.

[5]For more about Morton, see *Mister Jelly Lord* by Alan Lomax (University of California Press, 1973), and listen to Jelly Roll Morton *The Pearls*, RCA Bluebird 6588, LP. His "Mamanita" and "The Pearls" are in *Jazz Piano*, Smithsonian 39, LP, CD, cassette.

Jelly Roll Morton and his Red Hot Peppers, one of the first groups to masterfully combine improvisation and well-developed compositions without losing the spirit of New Orleans jazz. (*Left to right*): Andrew Hilaire (drums), Kid Ory (trombone), George Mitchell (trumpet), John Lindsay (bass), Morton (piano), Johnny St. Cyr (banjo), Omer Simeon (clarinet). Pictured here in 1926. (Photo supplied by Duncan Schiedt.) Listen to JAZZ STYLES CASSETTE, side 2, to hear trombone pictured here.

 4) He was one of the first jazz musicians to blend composition with improvisation in an elaborate and balanced way that still conveyed the kind of excitement that had typified collectively improvised jazz. In this way, Morton anticipated similar contributions by Duke Ellington, Charlie Mingus, and Sun Ra.

▷ 5) He recorded piano solos that were well-organized, forcefully executed musical statements with horn-like lines in them.

▷ 6) He helped bridge the gap between ragtime piano style and jazz piano style by loosening ragtime's rhythmic feeling and decreasing its embellishments. (See page 412 for information on how to get James Dapogny's transcriptions and analyses of Jelly Roll Morton solos.)

**Earl Hines** (1903–1983) was born in Pittsburgh. He moved to Chicago in 1924, bringing an assortment of different jazz techniques together in the form of one

"Weather Bird"
+ Louis Armstrong
1928
- piano is forcefull, staccatto

catchy style. Hines's playing had enormous influence during the late 1920s when he recorded with Louis Armstrong and also through his recording of unaccompanied solo improvisations. (Listen to Hines on Louis Armstrong's "West End Blues" in the JAZZ CLASSICS CASSETTE.) This impact extended during the 1930s by way of radio broadcasts and tours with his own big band, which was based at the Grand Terrace Ballroom in Chicago. He led the band there from 1928 to 1939, and musicians as far away as Kansas and Texas heard his broadcasts. The Hines style affected Teddy Wilson, Nat Cole, and Art Tatum, who themselves became major influences. Hines was also responsible for a portion of the Fats Waller-derived style of Count Basie. And because Hines was a primary influence on Billy Kyle, who in turn influenced Bud Powell, Hines can be said to have affected Powell, the single most imitated pianist in modern jazz of the 1950s.

The physical force Hines employs to strike the piano keys is so great that his music sometimes sounds as though the piano is shouting. (Hines is known to have accidentally broken the large, very strong, bass strings on pianos by sheer force in his left-hand playing. Most people could not break those strings even by smashing a fist down on the piano's bass keys.) Even when Hines plays in a flowery way, a roughness remains in his sound. Rarely is anything sustained, and nearly everything has a punching quality. These properties combine with his method of phrasing to lend a brassy quality to the sound of the piano. Because his right-hand lines sometimes sound like jazz trumpet playing, **the Hines approach earned the title of trumpet-style or horn-like.** His piano lines even seem to breathe at the moments a trumpeter would breathe and contain phrases and rhythms that are ordinarily preferred by trumpeters rather than pianists. This manner stems partly from Hines having originally begun his musical training with the goal of becoming a trumpeter instead of a pianist. And it stems from what Hines did to overcome the piano's inability to be heard over loud band instruments (long before electronic amplification came to the aid of jazz pianists). He played very hard, phrased like a trumpeter and began doubling his right-hand melody lines in octaves (demonstrated on JAZZ STYLES CASSETTE, side 2, and by Hines on Armstrong's recording of "West End Blues" in the JAZZ CLASSICS CASSETTE).

The Hines style is the one most commonly associated with the term "trumpet-style," despite Jelly Roll Morton's having previously improvised piano passages in the manner of band instruments. This approach is historically significant because, by playing more as a horn and less in the standard piano styles, Hines paved the way for modern jazz pianists who solo with essentially the same conception that is used by jazz trumpeters and saxophonists. It is less flowery and more direct. It is less classically pianistic and more swinging. The Hines approach is more flexible than the rigidly structured ragtime and stride approaches, and, because of this, Hines had greater capacity for conveying a broad assortment of musical feelings.

Earl Hines is known for a sturdy sense of tempo which persists relentlessly despite the many interruptions in melodic flow that he makes. This sense of tempo, plus his insistently percussive attack and varied syncopations, make Hines one of the most rhythmically compelling jazz pianists. (Listen to Hines on Armstrong's recording of "Weather Bird" in SCCJ.)

Hines was prone to introducing new and often jarring ideas into his solos in midflight, departing on tangents, the source of which was understood only by him. Instead of maintaining a smooth flow and consistent texture from the beginning of a piece to its end, he filled his work with surprises. In the middle of a piece, he would frequently stop a pattern, cease left-hand accompaniment, employing both hands to seemingly leap all over the keyboard before resuming any repeating pattern. On any of his unaccompanied piano solos, such as "Stowaway," "Caution Blues," "Blues in Thirds," "57 Varieties,"[6] or "Down Among the Sheltering Palms," he pulls a multitude of techniques into play, sometimes all in a single piece (explained and demonstrated on JAZZ STYLES CASSETTE, side 2):

*Earl Hines*

1) stride style  *left - right ; bass note - chord*
2) walking tenths (the two outside fingers of the left hand moving in scale-wise fashion, simultaneously sounding tones of about a ten-step interval apart)
3) horn-like lines  *like a trumpet*
4) flowery embellishments
5) octave voicing
6) tremolo
7) stop-time solo breaks for the right hand
8) brief double-time figures
9) off-balance left-hand rhythms which are highly syncopated, seeming to come out of nowhere

Later these techniques prominently appeared in the playing of several generations of jazz pianists. Some historians believe that Hines was the single most pervasive influence on pianists of the swing era in the 1930s, and a few consider him to be the most influential of all jazz pianists. He did not come up with most of these techniques himself, but he combined them in a way that was absorbed by others.

One of the best known products of the stride piano style was New York-born **Fats Waller** (1904–1943).[7] Though his jazz contributions have been overlooked because of his reputation as a popular entertainer, Waller played with excellent technique and a bouncing swing feeling which he used to create countless lighthearted and joyful performances. Aspects of Waller's style were continued in the playing of pianist-bandleader Count Basie. Waller wrote hundreds of tunes, the most familiar of which are "Ain't Misbehavin'," "Honeysuckle Rose," "Squeeze Me," and "Jitterbug Waltz." During the 1970s, an entire Broadway revue was devoted to music

[6]*Louis Armstrong & Earl Hines 1928*, Smithsonian 2002, LP set; *Louis Armstrong Vol. 4: "Louis Armstrong & Earl Hines,"* CBS 45142, CD/LP. "Blues in Thirds," "Chimes in Blues," and "Fifty-Seven Varieties" are in *Jazz Piano*, Smithsonian 39, LP, CD and cassette. See Stanley Dance's *The World of Earl Hines* (Scribner, 1975; reprinted by DaCapo). See pages 263–291 in Gunther Schuller's *The Swing Era*, Oxford, 1989. See Richard Hadlock's *Jazz Masters of the Twenties*, Macmillan, 1965; reprinted by DaCapo.

[7]Fats Waller *Piano Solos 1929–1941*, RCA Bluebird AXM2-5518, LP set. See Ed Kirkeby's biography, *Ain't Misbehavin'* (Dodd, Mead, 1966).

associated with Waller. This immensely successful show was called "Ain't Misbehavin'," and it revived interest in Waller's work. (Listen to his "I Ain't Got Nobody" in SCCJ.)

In addition to ragtime and stride styles, early jazz pianists developed **boogie woogie**. A prime characteristic of boogie woogie is the subdivision of each beat in the left-hand figures so that, in a measure of four beats, there are actually eight pulses ("eight to the bar"). These left-hand patterns surfaced around 1912 in southern pianists. If you hear a record of boogie woogie, you will have no trouble recognizing it immediately because it has been revived so many times that it has become a well-known and popular jazz piano style. Pianist Pinetop Smith actually entitled one of his tunes "Boogie Woogie," and his rendition was a hit record in 1929. An adaptation of it became an even bigger hit record in 1938 and again in 1943 for trombonist Tommy Dorsey's big band. The leading boogie woogie pianists include Pete Johnson, Albert Ammons, Cow Cow Davenport, and Meade Lux Lewis (listen to Lewis's "Honky Tonk Train Blues" in SCCJ). Popular pianist Jerry Lee Lewis developed much of his style from this concept. Note that some uses of the word "boogie" during the 1970s and 80s do not fit the meaning described here.

**James P. Johnson** (1894–1955) was born in New Jersey and is part of an East Coast jazz piano tradition that was developing at about the same time as combo jazz was developing in New Orleans. He was the most respected and influential of

*"You've got to be Mordernistic'*
*"razz"*
*- stride style*

James P. Johnson, father of stride piano, pictured here in 1921 at age 27. (Photo courtesy of Frank Driggs)

Composed and performed by pianist James P. Johnson, recorded January 21, 1930; available on the JAZZ CLASSICS CASSETTE, Side One.

James P. Johnson was among the two or three most significant pianists in the first thirty years of jazz. This recording documents one of his meatiest and most spirited performances. The virtuoso technique, staggering strength and richness displayed on this recording help us understand why an entire generation of stride-style pianists were so impressed. (For demonstration of stride style, listen to Side Two of the JAZZ STYLES CASSETTE.)

Pay particular attention to the stride-bass style played by Johnson's left hand almost relentlessly in this performance. The tremendous momentum of the piece is partly due to the locomotive-like power of Johnson's left-hand work and partly due to his percussive forcefulness in playing the highly syncopated right-hand parts.

Johnson worked out in advance most of what is heard here, though he varied it somewhat from performance to performance, as was the practice for pianists at that time. The choruses of the trio section contain the most improvisation, and Johnson's renditions of the first and second strains contain the least.

*Elapsed Time*

## INTRODUCTION

*Four Measures*

0' 04"

**FIRST SECTION** (technically termed "first strain")

16 measures (A-A'-A-B, four measures in each section)

0' 20"

**REPEAT OF FIRST STRAIN,** with some modifications

16 measures (A-A'-A-B, four measures in each section)

0' 34"

**SECOND STRAIN**

16 measures (A-A-B-A, four measures in each section)
The striding left-hand figures are sporadic.
Notice the syncopation and tricky interaction of the right and left hands in the B-section.

0' 48"

**REPEAT OF SECOND STRAIN,** with modifications

16 measures (A-A-B-A, four measures in each section)
To appreciate how rhythmically complicated the B-section is, notice how much easier it is to count "1234 2234 3234 . . ." when you are listening to the other sections.

1' 05"

**FIRST STRAIN** (16 measures)

The melody is played an octave higher than before.
The striding left-hand part resumes.

1' 19"

**INTRODUCTION TO TRIO SECTION** (four measures)

This new group of sections is termed a "trio" because it is like the central section of a march, and such sections used to be written in three-part harmony.

1' 23"

In each 16-measure chorus of this trio, Johnson selects a melodic idea and varies it. Some of the choruses center about syncopated riffs in the manner that became common for swing era band arrangements, a device that is central to the pieces in the Afro-American Retentions Sequence at the beginning of this cassette. And, like its effect there, the riff style here also evokes a lilting, buoyant feeling. This is some of the first piano music to "swing" in the jazz sense of the term.

| Elapsed Time | |
| --- | --- |

**THE "TRIO" SECTION**

1' 23"

*First Chorus of Trio*

Johnson repeats a single riff six times.

1' 40"

*Second Chorus of Trio*

Johnson toys with a figure that involves firmly striking two adjacent piano keys in the high register of the piano and letting the resulting dissonance ring. These piano keys represent the "major third" and "minor third" steps of the scale, which when crushed together approximate a "blue pitch," as demonstrated on the JAZZ STYLES CASSETTE.

1' 53"

*Third Chorus*

Johnson's melody for this chorus is played in the bass range.

2' 09"

*Fourth Chorus*

This chorus is the most rag-like of all Johnson's choruses.

2' 24"

*Fifth Chorus*

The melody of this chorus is like the first strain.

2' 40"

*Sixth Chorus*

Johnson bases the first eight measures on one riff, the second eight measures on another.

2' 54"

*Seventh Chorus*

Johnson plays his right-hand chords more frequently, thereby giving the illusion that the tempo has increased.

pianists who smoothed the transition from ragtime to jazz. One of the first jazz musicians to broadcast on the radio, Johnson was already a prominent figure by the time jazz began to be recorded. In 1914 he wrote "Carolina Shout," and then, when he recorded a version of it in 1921, the style behind his reputation was documented for posterity (listen to it in SCCJ). Though stride style was played by other pre-1920s pianists also, Johnson is usually referred to as "the father of stride piano" because his own brand of stride style did the most to spread this approach. (Listen to JAZZ STYLES CASSETTE, side 2, for an example of stride style left hand playing.) According to Johnson's biographers, Dick Wellstood and Willa Rouder, Johnson dispensed with the stiff rhythms, the broken-chord melodies and march-like bass of ragtime, while contributing a fluidity, a harmonic sophistication, and an attention to chord voicings. He perfected an orchestral approach to jazz piano playing, as though he were a one-man band. Many musicians feel that he was never surpassed in this style. (Listen to his "You've Got To Be Modernistic" in the JAZZ CLASSICS CASSETTE.) At a time when informal competitions among solo pianists were common in New York, Johnson is said to have won more contests than anyone else. His speed, precision, dexterity, and imagination amazed musicians. The force and swing of his pianistic feats are legendary. Most pianists who emerged during the 1920s, such as Art Tatum and Duke Ellington, cite Johnson as an influence on them.

James P. Johnson is known to jazz musicians primarily as an innovative stride pianist, but much of his living was made from work as composer/conductor/pianist for stage shows, and accompanist for singers. Johnson wrote 230 popular tunes, 19 symphonic works, as well as scoring 11 musicals for the stage. In fact, the famous piece "The Charleston" was written by Johnson for a stage show called "Runnin' Wild," that was popular in 1923. So in appreciating Johnson's status in American music, we need to remember that only one aspect of his career was central to jazz history. Since so much of his time was occupied writing nonjazz works, he was not very visible in the jazz scene for some years. His jazz stature was eclipsed during the 1930s by the attention given to other players. For this reason, he has not been given his proper due, even though he continued to record jazz during the 1940s.[8]

**Trumpet**

Trumpeter **Louis Armstrong** (1901–1971) is often called the "father of jazz." In fact, musicians often refer to him as "Pops." No list of jazz greats omits him, and most start with him. Born in New Orleans, he left in 1922 upon the invitation of Joe Oliver, who had already established a New Orleans band in Chicago. The band's best known piece "Dippermouth Blues" derives its title from another Armstrong nickname, a reference to his mouth being as large as a dipper. A third nickname, Satchmo, is a variation on the same idea: Satchel Mouth.

Although some of Armstrong's 1940s and 50s recordings are outstanding, his most significant are the innovative series of recordings made in 1927 and 1928, billed as "Louis Armstrong and His Hot Five" (or "Hot Seven").[9] Some of them included his colleagues from New Orleans, trombonist Kid Ory and clarinetist Johnny Dodds. Armstrong's earliest appearances on record displayed him involved primarily with collective improvisation, as in his 1924 playing with Clarence Williams on "Cake Walkin' Babies From Home" (in SCCJ). But on his Hot Five and Hot Seven recordings of 1925–28, Armstrong's dramatic solo style was showcased more than his collective improvisation skills. The music that he documented in those recordings became a model for the swing era that followed.

Louis Armstrong appeared in about fifty movies and sang in most of his post-1930 performances. For instance, his vocal rendition of the theme song from the Broadway musical "Hello, Dolly" was #1 for one week on the popularity charts, putting him ahead of the phenomenally popular singing group called The Beatles, and it was #5 on the year-end popularity chart. With the success of the 1988 revival

[8]See biography *James P. Johnson: A Case of Mistaken Identity* by Scott E. Brown and Robert Hilbert (Scarecrow, 1986).

[9]Listen to "Struttin' With Some Barbecue" and "Hotter Than That" in SCCJ, and see Scott Reeves's analysis of the solo on "Hotter Than That" in his book *Creative Improvisation* (Prentice-Hall, 1989). Gunther Schuller provides transcriptions and analyses for several of Armstrong's best solos of the 1920s in his book *Early Jazz* (Oxford, 1968). More from this period can be heard in this series of Armstrong albums: *Hot Fives & Sevens, Vol. 1*, CBS 44049, CD/LP, 1925–26; *Vol. 2*, CBS 44253, CD/LP, 1926–27; *Vol. 3*, CBS 44422, CD/LP, 1927–28; *Vol. 4*, CBS 45142, CD/LP. Gunther Schuller provides transcriptions and analyses for several Armstrong solos of the 1930s and 40s on pages 158–197 in his book *The Swing Era* (Oxford, 1989). For more about Armstrong's life, see *Louis* by Max Jones and John Chilton (Little, Brown, 1971; reprinted by Da Capo) or Armstrong's autobiography, *Satchmo: My Life in New Orleans* (Prentice-Hall, 1954).

**Listening Guide for "West End Blues"**

Composed by Joe Oliver; recorded June 6, 1928 in Chicago by Louis Armstrong (trumpet and vocal), Jimmy Strong (clarinet), Fred Robinson (trombone), Earl Hines (piano), Mancy Cara (banjo), and Zutty Singleton (drums); available on the JAZZ CLASSICS CASSETTE, side one, and SCCJ (reissued on CD as *Volume IV: Louis Armstrong and Earl Hines*, Columbia CK 45142; also on CD in the Revised SCCJ).

Terms to know from the JAZZ STYLES CASSETTE before using this listening guide: ride rhythm, legato, staccato, pitch smear, tremolo, octave voicing, stride style, double-time, 12-bar blues, chorus, vibrato, banjo, trumpet, trombone, and clarinet.

## INTRODUCTION

The opening phrases in this piece are among the most famous in jazz history. Note the drama in Armstrong's ascent to his highest note, the one he sustains. Then listen to the manner in which he gradually descends to finish with a note that lends a sense of anticipation for what follows. Notice his warm, brassy tone and his sure-footed manner. This introduction is a masterpiece that you might want to hear several times before listening to the rest of the performance.

The idea of a bravura solo style, particularly an unaccompanied solo passage like this, was common in light classical music that was popular in America around 1900. Virtuoso cornet soloists were frequently featured in band concerts at that time. In addition, the trumpet sounds of Mexican bands that visited New Orleans had impressed musicians there. When Louis Armstrong devised this stirring opening, he was drawing, either consciously or unconsciously, from that tradition in light classical music, and he was establishing a tradition in jazz.

*Elapsed Time*

0' 13"    Full band plays a chord.

0' 16"    **FIRST CHORUS** (a 12-bar blues played slowly)

*Melody Played by Armstrong on Trumpet*

Notice Armstrong's firm, deliberate manner and quick vibrato.

Accompaniment includes:

soft, sustained trombone notes (often preceded by a smear of pitch that begins well below the ultimate note);

sustained tones of clarinet, sometimes paralleling the motion of the trumpet line (listen for the clarinet's edgy timbre and fast vibrato);

trombone and clarinet notes together indicating the chords changing underneath the trumpet;

piano chords sounded in unison with banjo chords played staccato on each beat ("chomp chomp chomp chomp . . . ")

0' 50"    **SECOND CHORUS**

*Trombone Solo*

The trombonist uses the high register and many smears of pitch.

Accompaniment includes:

staccato chording from banjo;

tremolo chords from piano;

*Elapsed Time*

slow ride rhythm played by drummer on a hand-held "Bock-a-da-Bock" apparatus that brings together two cymbals that are each about three inches wide; to play them, the drummer cups the apparatus in his hand as in playing spoons.*

1' 25"

### THIRD CHORUS

*Improvised Duet Between Clarinet and Armstrong's Wordless Vocal*

This chorus employs a call-and-response format, with the vocal supplying the responses. It is an early example of "scat" singing. Piano and banjo are chording in a staccato manner on each beat. The duet's last phrase is done in harmony. No percussion instruments are used here or in the next chorus.

2' 00"

### FOURTH CHORUS

*Unaccompanied Piano Improvisation by Earl Hines*

*First Four Measures*

Pianist's left hand is contributing legato chording in stride style while right hand improvises flowery figures.

2' 10"

*Second Four Measures*

Style of playing by right hand switches to brash character and pounds out a double-time figure voiced in octaves. This is the famous "trumpet-style" piano playing of Earl Hines.

2' 23"

*Third Four Measures*

Style returns to flowery character.

2' 33"

### FIFTH CHORUS

*Trumpet Solo*

*First Four Measures*

Sustained high note from trumpet for 16 beats. Accompaniment includes staccato chords from piano on each beat, sustained trombone notes, sustained clarinet notes.

2' 45"

*Second Four Measures*

Trumpet line features double-timing.

2' 55"

*Third Four Measures*

Horns stop playing for 12 beats while piano plays a descending sequence of chords, striking each in bell-like fashion, linking them with a glissando. Piano sustains a chord. Armstrong returns with a long, drawn-out bluesy figure played in a markedly slowed pace. It is accompanied by long tones harmonized by trombone, clarinet, and piano to form three different chords that conclude the piece.

* The Bock-A-Da-Bock cymbal apparatus is pictured as "cymbal tongs" on page 50 of *The Percussionist's Dictionary* by Joseph Adato and George Judy (Belwin-Mills, 1984; available from P.O. Box 21269, Cleveland, Ohio 44121).

Louis Armstrong, possibly the most influential of all jazz musicians, and clearly the most influential trumpeter in pre-modern jazz. Pictured here at age 27, in 1927, the year several of his classic Hot Five and Hot Seven recordings were made. (*Photo courtesy of Frank Driggs*)

of his "What a Wonderful World" (in the movie "Good Morning Viet Nam"), Armstrong demonstrated the longest career on the national singles charts, even outdistancing singers Bing Crosby and Frank Sinatra. (Crosby and Armstrong both had hits during the 1920s.) Understandably then, the post-1930s public knows Armstrong more as an entertainer than as an innovative jazz improviser. Even though they have heard his name, most people are not aware of Armstrong's monumental contributions to the history of jazz.

Armstrong was the most widely imitated jazz improviser prior to the appearance of modern saxophonist Charlie Parker in the 1940s. Armstrong's style is especially easy to detect in three of the most prominent trumpeters of the 1930s and 40s: Oran "Hot Lips" Page, Bunny Berigan, and Buck Clayton. His influence extended not only to trumpeters, but to saxophonists, pianists, guitarists, and trombonists. For instance, Johnny Hodges, the most influential alto saxophonist of the 1930s, credits Armstrong with affecting his sax style. Players within the swing era almost universally cite Armstrong's influence, and segments of his tunes and improvisations continued to be found in the work of such post-swing era innovators as Charlie Parker and Lee Konitz.

Let's examine a few aspects of Armstrong's work that musicians appreciated so much:

*Kind of*

1) Armstrong showed that the New Orleans technique of collective improvisation need not be the only approach to jazz horn work. Intelligently developed solos could be improvised in a stirring manner, and the musical effectiveness of such solos need not depend much on ensemble interaction. In other words, **Armstrong was one of the first great soloists in jazz history**, and, partly because of him, post-Armstrong styles usually stressed solo improvisation instead of group improvisation.

2) Armstrong was one of the first jazz musicians to refine a rhythmic conception that

   a) abandoned the stiffness of ragtime,
   b) employed swing eighth-note patterns,
   c) gracefully syncopated selected rhythmic figures, sometimes staggering the placement of an entire phrase, as though he were playing behind the beat, a technique called "rhythmic displacement." This projected a more relaxed feeling than ragtime and exhibited more variety in the ways that notes seemed to tug at opposite sides of the beat.

      These rhythmic elements combined to produce one of the first jazz styles that could elicit in the listener what is today called "jazz swing feeling." Though none of these elements was entirely new with Armstrong, they were more clearly evident as a finished product in his playing than in the playing of either his predecessors or other trumpeters of the 1920s.

3) Despite the numerous giants who have followed Armstrong in jazz history, few equal him as musical architects. Few had his degree of control over the overall form of a solo. He calmly forged sensible lines that had both the flow of spontaneity and the stamp of finality. His improvisations are well-paced, economical statements. The organization of Armstrong's phrases suggests that he was thinking ahead, yet the phrases manage to sound spontaneous, rather than calculated.

4) He brought a superb sense of drama to jazz solo conception. His pacing was careful, allowing a solo to build tension. His double-time solo breaks were constructed to achieve maximum excitement, and his high-note endings ensured a properly timed peak of intensity and resolution of tension. (Listen to "West End Blues" in the JAZZ CLASSICS CASSETTE, and listen to side 2 of the JAZZ STYLES CASSETTE for explanations of double-time.)

5) During a period when most improvisers were satisfied simply to embellish or paraphrase a tune's melody—and Armstrong himself was a master at both—Armstrong frequently broke away from the melody, and improvised original, melody-like lines that were compatible with the tune's chord progressions. This became the predominant approach for improvisation in the next fifty years of jazz history.

**Distinguishing Cornet From Trumpet**

In the early years of jazz, the cornet was much more widely used than the trumpet. The trumpet's and cornet's tones and ranges are quite similar, and many listeners cannot tell the two instruments apart. Their appearance is also a confusing factor, but one distinguishing feature is the apparent length. The tubing of the cornet, although equal in length to that of the trumpet, is organized so that it looks shorter. Some old jazz cornets are especially compact and stubby.

trumpet

cornet

The prime difference between trumpet and cornet, a difference that is difficult to see, is that the inside of the cornet's tubing is cone-like, whereas the trumpet's is more cylinder-like. The technical term for the inside diameter is bore. So, it is said that cornets have a primarily conical bore and trumpets have a primarily cylindrical bore. Although the instruments are played in almost the same way, their mouthpieces are slightly different. The tone color of the cornet is said to be mellow, and that of the trumpet is said to be more brilliant.

Except for Nat Adderley and Thad Jones, most modern players usually use trumpet instead of cornet. Before 1927 nearly all jazz trumpeters used the cornet. The 1930s and early 40s was a period of transition between the two instruments: every band had a so-called trumpet section, but in at least two famous bands, Duke Ellington's and Fletcher Henderson's, the trumpet section sometimes contained more cornets than trumpets. I prefer to ignore this problem and label most cornetists as trumpeters for the following reasons: (a) most listeners cannot detect the difference in sound; (b) it is often impossible to determine from recording data whether a player was using trumpet or cornet on a particular session; (c) the only player I am fairly certain used cornet exclusively throughout his career was Bix Beiderbecke; and (d) trumpet tone colors in jazz vary across a range far greater than that which separates the most pure of cornet from trumpet tones, and actually encompasses the pure tones of both.

6) Armstrong's command of the trumpet was arguably greater than that of any preceding jazz trumpeter on record, and it became a model to which others aspired. He had an enormous, brassy tone, and remarkable range which, together with his rhythmic and dramatic sense, conveyed a sureness and surging power. Even during the final decades of his career, Armstrong maintained a tone quality that was unusual for its weight, breadth, and richness.

7) Armstrong popularized the musical vocabulary of New Orleans trumpet style and then extended it.

8) Armstrong's tremendously fertile melodic imagination provided jazz with a repertory of phrases and ways of going about constructing improvisations. In other words, he extended the vocabulary for the jazz soloist.

These next two contributions are less central to what made his reputation among jazz instrumentalists, but they remain significant in the broadest sense of jazz history.

9) The Armstrong singing style influenced many popular singers, including Louis Prima, Billie Holiday, and Bing Crosby. In this way, he affected American music beyond the boundaries of jazz. Armstrong's influence was so pervasive that Leslie Gourse titled a book about American jazz singers *Louis' Children*.

10) Armstrong popularized scat singing, a vocal technique in which lyrics are not used. The voice improvises in the manner of a jazz trumpeter or saxophonist. (This technique can be heard in his recordings "West End Blues" in the JAZZ CLASSICS CASSETTE and "Hotter Than That" in SCCJ.) Recent examples of the technique can be found in the work of George Benson, Al Jarreau, and Bobby McFerrin.

**Bix Beiderbecke** (1903–1931) was a great white trumpeter and composer from Iowa. His recordings are important in early jazz, but he fits neatly into neither New Orleans nor Chicago style. He and Armstrong were the leading trumpeters during the late 1920s and early 1930s, and Beiderbecke's style offers an alternative to Armstrong's, though both developed at about the same time.

Beiderbecke first recorded in 1924 with a small group called the Wolverine Orchestra. Beginning in 1927 he became better known as a featured soloist with a much larger group—the famous Paul Whiteman Orchestra. Often considered the first great white jazz improviser, Beiderbecke influenced many trumpeters, the best known of whom were Jimmy McPartland, Red Nichols, and Bobby Hackett.

Beiderbecke was almost as original and creative as Armstrong, but he had less command over his instrument and a bit cooler sound. Beiderbecke's tone was softer, lighter weight, and less brassy than Armstrong's. His rhythmic approach was less aggressive. Like most early jazz players, he did not have pronounced jazz swing feeling when he began performing, but later he developed a swing feeling which approached that of Armstrong. Beiderbecke's attitude differs considerably from Armstrong's. He is less dramatic and more subtle. In contrast to Armstrong's assured, outgoing style, Beiderbecke is quieter and considerably more restrained. He plays more in the instrument's middle register than does Armstrong, who likes high

**TABLE 5.3.  Comparing Louis Armstrong with Bix Beiderbecke**

|  | Armstrong | Beiderbecke |
|---|---|---|
| command of trumpet | virtuoso | solid |
| tone quality | full | bell-like |
|  | hot | warm |
|  | brassy | dry |
| range | wide | moderate |
| improvisatory character | outgoing | reflective |
| rhythmic conception | swinging | closer to ragtime |
| influences | Chris Kelly | Nick LaRocca |
|  | Buddy Petit | Emmett Hardy |
|  | Joe "King" Oliver | ragtime |
| birthplace | New Orleans | Davenport, Iowa |

notes. Beiderbecke also pays more attention to stringing together unusual note choices and acknowledging every passing chord in the progression—something he knew well because he was also a good pianist. In this way, he anticipated trumpeter-guitarist Bobby Hackett, who also made masterful use of chord notes in his improvisations, acknowledging almost every passing chord. This approach brought acclaim to Hackett in his Beiderbecke-like solo on Glenn Miller's famous 1942 recording "String of Pearls." [10] (For comparison with Armstrong, see Table 5.3.)

Beiderbecke is also known as a composer who blended ragtime style with the French Impressionist style of Maurice Ravel and Claude Debussy. His "Flashes," "In the Dark," and "Candlelights" are not well known, but his "In a Mist" has been orchestrated by numerous jazz arrangers, and his own 1927 piano recording of it is especially effective. [11] The piece is distinguished by its use of the whole-tone mode, a sound that was favored by Debussy (see piano keyboard illustration on page 149).

Beiderbecke joined saxophonist **Frankie Trumbauer** (1901–1956) for several landmark recording sessions. Their 1927 recordings of "Singin' the Blues" and "A Good Man Is Hard to Find" represent two of the most relaxed, melodic, and tender

—relaxing

[10]Glenn Miller *Pure Gold*, RCA 3666–2, CD
[11]*The Bix Beiderbecke Story, Vol. 3*, CBS CL 846

performances in early jazz.[12] Trumbauer's instrument was a C-melody saxophone, whose size falls between the alto and the tenor. It is capable of a pale, light-weight tone. Trumbauer was a very precise and melodic soloist who employed a vibrato that was uncommonly slow for early jazz. Tenor saxophonist Lester Young, a significant figure in the beginnings of modern jazz, has said that he modeled his own light, cool tenor saxophone sound on the playing of C-melody saxophonist Trumbauer. Like Trumbauer, Young also used a slower vibrato than his contemporaries. (Listen to Young on "Lester Leaps In" and "Taxi War Dance" on the JAZZ CLASSICS CASSETTE.)

The Trumbauer-Beiderbecke "Singin' the Blues" performance is one of the most heralded recordings in jazz history (listen to it in SCCJ). Many players have memorized the improvisations on it, and the Fletcher Henderson big band twice recorded the piece with a harmonized transcription of Trumbauer's solo. Jazz historians routinely cite Beiderbecke's solo for its advanced use of the tune's harmonies. The notes Beiderbecke chose for his solo go beyond the notes offered by the tune's accompanying chords and reflect a higher level of musical thinking than was common with most other improvisers of the 1920s.

**Clarinet**   Clarinet was more common than saxophone in early jazz, a situation that was reversed in modern jazz. Clarinet usually played countermelodies around the trumpet part. Clarinet solos were not usually as dramatic as the trumpet solos. Eventually, however, clarinetists were able to get away from a conception based on embellishment, and by the late 1930s some early players and many swing era players were capable of dramatic, well-paced solo lines.

**Johnny Dodds** (1892–1940) was one of the leading New Orleans clarinetists who moved to Chicago. Dodds used an edgy tone and fast vibrato. With great confidence, he constructed fluid counterlines that managed an almost relentless activity for recordings by Joe Oliver's band in 1923. He had an aggressive solo style that featured swooping pitch bends that sometimes dwell on a single blue note. Many listeners call the effect of his playing "raw." (A jazz historian once said that some of Dodds's work could "curl your hair!") Listen to his work in the recording of "Dippermouth Blues" by Oliver's band and in "Struttin' With Some Barbecue" by Louis Armstrong's band (in SCCJ).

**Jimmie Noone** (1895–1944) was a more polished player than Johnny Dodds and possessed a greater command of the clarinet. Some consider Noone to be the best New Orleans clarinetist. He had a dark, warm, round tone. He often played jumping staccato lines which had a lot of flash and verve. Noone was a favorite of Benny Goodman, a leading white Chicago clarinetist who went onto become the best known clarinest in the twentieth century. (Noone made an excellent series of recordings in 1928 with pianist Earl Hines. Their "Four or Five Times" is in the revised SCCJ.)

New Orleans clarinetist and soprano saxophonist **Sidney Bechet** (1897–1959) was

---

[12]*Bix Beiderbecke, Vol. 1: Singin' the Blues*, CBS 45450, CD; *The Bix Beiderbecke Story, Vol. 2*, CBS CL 845, LP. See the biography *Bix: Man & Legend* by Sudhalter, R.M., Evans, P.R., & Myatt, W.D. (Schirmer, 1974).

**Figure 5.1.** Clarinet and soprano sax. (*Photo courtesy of the Selmer Company*) To compare the sounds of these instruments, listen to JAZZ STYLES CASSETTE, side 2.

one of the most highly regarded musicians in early jazz (see Figure 5.1 for a comparison of clarinet and soprano sax.). He was one of the first great soloists. In addition to Armstrong, he was one of the first improvisers to display jazz swing feeling. Like Armstrong, he double-timed and created dramatic solos. Bechet had a big, warm tone with a wide, rapid vibrato. He was a very energetic, hard-driving improviser who played with broad imagination and authority. Along with Louis Armstrong, Bechet was among the earliest improvisers to devise a stirringly dramatic way of constructing solos. He and Armstrong cultivated these approaches after they had learned the requirements of collective, nonsolo improvisation which are essential to the New Orleans tradition. (Listen to the New Orleans-style collective improvisation in their playing on "Cake Walkin' Babies From Home" in SCCJ.) In this respect, they introduced a new way for jazz hornmen to be viewed in combo format. Both men eventually became regarded primarily as soloists instead of ensemble players. This helped make jazz into an improvising soloist's art, and, for at least the next four decades of jazz, collective improvisation skills remained almost exclusively the domain of rhythm section musicians, not hornmen.

Bechet exerted his impact on solo conception by mastering the timing of central notes and carefully using extended pitch bends. (See chapter 4 for details.) Though capable of complicated, supercharged solo improvisations, Bechet's most popular solos are quite simple. Those that journalists discuss the most ("Summertime" and "Blue Horizon" in SCCJ) are slow-tempo performances that exemplify meticulous placement of a few carefully chosen notes. The pitches of these notes are bent in manners that have been perceived as being highly sensual. "Blues drenched" is how some writers describe the sounds. The timing of these expressive devices demonstrates the command of restraint necessary for making an emotionally effective climax. This is especially evident in the ornaments Bechet employs to lead up to a central note. The scoop or smear of pitches Bechet uses to introduce a note is essential to the success of his improvisation. The long, swooping lead-in, which carries at its topmost note the precise moment for maximum dramatic effect, became standard in the vocabulary of the saxophone. Swing era saxophonist Johnny Hodges, a Bechet disciple, and contemporary saxophonist John Coltrane, who followed in Hodges's footsteps, used it extensively.[13]

Many of Bechet's solos simply display the reworking of elementary blues phrases. The musical concepts of "bluesy" and "funky" are defined by Bechet's playing. He summarizes the instrumental equivalent of the blues singer. And, in this way, Bechet summarizes what many listeners have come to regard as the essential feeling of New Orleans style: an earthy, warm and full sound. (Listen to Bechet's "Blue Horizon" in SCCJ.)

**Trombone**    In ensemble improvisation, trombonists invented low harmony parts and filled in gaps with devices similar to those played by tuba and trombone in brass band music. With clarinet and trumpet filling out the middle and upper registers, trombone contributed to the combo sound in the lower range. When soloing, early trombonists tended toward a jazz trumpet conception to which they added the trombone's unique capacity for smears and slides. Rarely, however, did they play lines as intricate as those of early jazz trumpeters.

**Kid Ory** (1886–1973) was one of the first notable New Orleans jazz trombonists. His husky tone and assertive presence were an important part of several early jazz combos. He had a hard, cutting tone, and a percussive attack. His work had a boisterous air about it. Ory was also a composer and group leader. His "Muskat Ramble" (later spelled "Muskrat Ramble") became a jazz standard. (Listen to Ory on Louis Armstrong's "Struttin' With Some Barbecue" in SCCJ.)

---

[13]Hodges preferred to preface an important note with a gradual smearing of pitches, whereas Coltrane usually selected a rapid, scale-like sequence to sweep up to that central tone. (Listen to Coltrane play soprano and note his attention to such prefaces to his high notes in "The Promise" on the JAZZ CLASSICS CASSETTE. Listen to the exquisite timing and very sensual results in the Johnny Hodges rendition of "Prelude to a Kiss" in the JAZZ CLASSICS CASSETTE.) Hodges's pre-1940 playing also displayed some of the double-timing and ebullience of Bechet. For an example of Hodges's double-timing, listen to his solo on Duke Ellington's 1940 recording of "In a Mellotone" in the revised SCCJ. For close comparison of the two soprano sax styles, play Bechet's 1938 "Really the Blues" then Hodges's 1938 "Jeep's Blues" and Bechet's 1941 "When It's Sleepy Time Down South" then Hodges's 1938 "Empty Ballroom Blues." (The Hodges numbers are in *Hodge Podge*, Columbia Special Products, JEE 22001, LP, 1938–39. The Bechet numbers are in *The Legendary Sidney Bechet*, RCA Bluebird 6590, CD/LP, 1932–41.) Hodges later slowed down and smoothed out considerably but retained the smoothness of tone and soulful inflections of pitch which he had learned from Bechet. During the 1960s, the soprano sax was resurrected by modern saxophonist John Coltrane, who called one of his compositions "Blues to Bechet." Then during the 1980s, the instrument reached its widest audience in the hands of saxophonist Kenny G, whose records sold millions of copies. Also see Bechet's biography by John Chilton, *Sidney Bechet* (Oxford, 1987).

**Jack Teagarden** (1905–1964) was a trombonist from Texas who paid close attention to producing and maintaining a smooth, full tone which was prettier than that of most other premodern trombonists.[14] His work projected a thoughtful, relaxed quality even though some of his favorite phrases were technically demanding. (Listen to his solos on the Red Nichols band version of "Dinah" in SCCJ-R.) Teagarden's unique feeling and well-formed phrases were an inspiration to the trombonists of modern jazz. His style was possibly as important to jazz trombone history as Armstrong's was to trumpet. His career was long and productive, running from the 1920s until his death in 1964.

**Rhythm Section**   The front line of most early jazz combos included trumpet, clarinet, trombone, and occasionally, saxophone. The rhythm section was made up of several instruments which might include guitar, banjo, tuba, bass saxophone, string bass, piano, and drums. No bands had all these instruments playing at the same time, but most drew some combination from that collection. It was not unusual for early jazz combos to be without string bass, and many early jazz recordings were made without drums. Some groups substituted tuba for string bass, and in many groups the bassists alternated brass bass with string bass. Eventually many tuba players learned to play string bass, and by the late 1930s, most had abandoned the tuba. Some groups used bass saxophone (see Figures 5.2 and 5.3). Groups often included both guitar and

**Figure 5.2.** Baritone saxophone—bass saxophone. Key mechanisms are omitted so that the distinctive differences in the sizes of the instruments and the shapes of the looped necks will be more readily apparent.

**Figure 5.3.** Tuba (Besson, BB♭) (*Photo courtesy of the Selmer Company*)

[14]Jack Teagarden *King of the Blues Trombone*, Columbia Special Products JSN 6044, LP set. For biography, see *Jack Teagarden: The Story of a Jazz Maverick* by Jay D. Smith and Leonard F. Guttridge (Cassell, 1960; reprinted by DaCapo).

Original Dixieland Jass Band (also called Original Dixieland Jazz Band), 1916. Left to right: Tony Spargo [Sbarbaro, Sparbaro] (drums), Eddie Edwards (trombone), Nick La Rocca (trumpet), Alcide Nunez (clarinet), Henry Ragas (piano). (*Photo courtesy of Duncan Schiedt*)

banjo, though some had only one of these. Usually one player alternated between the two instruments. Piano was absent from some recordings and replaced banjo and guitar on others, though usually both piano and banjo or guitar were used.

The banjo and guitar were often strummed all four beats of each measure. The tuba, bass sax, or string bass frequently played on only the first and third of every four beats. That meant they played on only two beats per measure, a style known as "two-beat" rhythm. Prior to 1927, string bass was often bowed instead of plucked. (See chapter 3 for illustration of string bass.) Walking bass and two-beat style in that situation consisted of longer tones than the staccato sound that is ordinarily produced when the bass strings are plucked.[15]

Sometimes the pianist played chords in unison with the guitar or banjo, sometimes embellishments instead. In many groups, the pianist created countermelodies while the front-line instruments were playing melodies and countermelodies of their own. Comping as demonstrated on the JAZZ STYLES CASSETTE was only sporadically heard during this era.

[15]SCCJ provides examples for these techniques. A two-beat style tuba part can be heard in portions of the 1927 "Potato Head Blues" recorded by Louis Armstrong. Walking bass alternating with two-beat style can be heard in the 1926 "Black Bottom Stomp" and "Dead Man Blues" recorded by Jelly Roll Morton, available in SCCJ. A bass saxophone can be heard playing in this rhythm role on the 1927 Trumbauer-Beiderbecke "A Good Man Is Hard to Find" in *The Bix Beiderbecke Story, Vol. 2*, CBS CL 845, LP. See Figure 5.2 for bass saxophone illustration. For more about early bass, see *Pops Foster: The Autobiography of a New Orleans Jazzman* (University of California Press, 1971).

**Drums**   Early jazz drummers are poorly heard on records because early studio equipment was not well-suited to recording drums. At that time, records were made by playing into acoustic recording horns, which looked like the horn that comes out of the phonograph in the famous picture of the Victor dog listening to "His Master's Voice." The small end of the horn was connected to a cutting needle which made grooves in a cylinder or a disc. Any loud sound, especially a blow to the bass drum, could literally knock the needle off the cutting surface. Many recordings during this period consequently represent working bands minus their drummers. Many of the recordings that do employ drummers either omit most drum equipment entirely or muffle it so much that, when combined with terrible recording quality, drum sounds are almost inaudible. We are often left with little more than the clickety clicking sound that is made by drum sticks striking a wood block (a small block of wood that has been hollowed out to increase resonance, demonstrated on JAZZ STYLES CASSETTE, side 1). This was one of the only sounds drummers were ordinarily allowed to produce during the recording sessions in which engineers were afraid of loud sounds. (However, you can detect a number of different rhythm instruments in "Dixie Jazz Band One-Step" in the JAZZ CLASSICS CASSETTE.)[16]

Though this drumming sound described above was particularly convenient in adapting to the restrictions imposed by early recording situations, it represents only one sample in a range of sounds commonly generated by the earliest jazz drummers. Light, staccato sounds were also produced by striking a cowbell or the bass drum's rim (the shell of the instrument, not the drum head that usually receives the blow). These sounds were also employed in some early record dates, but, at that time, aggressive use of the snare drum and bass drum was generally limited to band engagements. A large cymbal or gong was sometimes used to signal a dramatic height in the music, and some jazz combo drummers of the 1920s also had orchestra and theater band experience, and brought some of that orchestral approach to their combo playing. When playing on the light-sounding instruments, however, many of the earliest drummers chose patterns from military drumming and ragtime drumming, not necessarily from orchestral drumming tradition in which the percussionist only embellishes or reinforces other instrumental activity. The 1917-23 drumming heard in recordings uses more military than orchestral concepts. (If you have a keen enough ear, you might be able to detect these military patterns played on snare drum by Tony Sbarbaro with the Original Dixieland Jazz Band in their 1917 "Dixie Jazz Band One-Step" in the JAZZ CLASSICS CASSSETTE.)

Although we do not know exactly how he sounded, we do know what kind of instruments the early jazz drummer played. He did not have a high-hat. He had a floor cymbal apparatus which enabled him to strike a cymbal with a foot pedal, but it did not allow him to achieve the "chick" sound possible with the high-hat. He also

---

[16]Listen to Warren "Baby" Dodds play wood block with Oliver's Creole Jazz Band in their 1923 "Dippermouth Blues" in SCCJ, and listen to Tony Sbarbaro play it in the Original Dixieland Jazz Band's 1920 "Margie" (see footnote 1) or their 1921 "Home Again Blues." See pages 413–414 for information on how to get an illustrated history of premodern drumming. For more about these techniques, see Larry Gara's biography *The Baby Dodds Story* (Contemporary, 1959) and listen to *Footnotes to Jazz, Vol. 1, Dodds*, Folkways FJ 2290, LP, 1946; also available on cassette by special request from Smithsonian Press.

had a bass drum, almost marching band size, two to three times as large as that which became popular during the mid-1960s. A snare drum mounted on a stand and a cymbal suspended above the set were also at his disposal. Wood block and cowbell were attached to the bass drum.

New Orleans drummer **Warren "Baby" Dodds** (1898–1959), brother of clarinetist Johnny Dodds, has been credited with pioneering the use of the ride rhythm. He played it on the snare drum. Later in jazz history, ride rhythms were played on the high-hat. Eventually in the 1950s and 60s, they became the primary timekeeping rhythms, and drummers played them on the ride cymbal. (Listen to JAZZ STYLES CASSETTE, side 1 for demonstrations.)

**Arthur "Zutty" Singleton**  (1898–1975), another leading New Orleans drummer, was among the first to use wire brushes to strike his drums. Brushes did not totally replace sticks, but they offered a lighter, softer sound, as well as the capacity to produce sustained sounds if dragged across and around a drum head or cymbal. Zutty also pioneered the use of bass drum on all four beats of each measure. Many drummers had struck the bass drum primarily on the first and third beats. Singleton can be heard playing brushes on Louis Armstrong's 1928 recordings of "St. James Infirmary" and "Tight Like This." He can be heard playing a suspended cymbal on "Skip the Gutter." And, on "No, Papa, No," Singleton can be heard briefly playing ride rhythms on a cymbal, thereby predating, by about a decade, the sound that was to characterize modern jazz timekeeping style.[17] Singleton influenced George Wettling and Sid Catlett. Catlett played a transitional role in jazz, helping jazz drum conceptions move from early jazz to modern jazz.

There are significant similarites and differences between the roles assumed by the earliest jazz drummers and the roles that jazz drummers assumed later in jazz history. For example, on some of the earliest recordings, horn lines often existed without drum accompaniment. That these lines could exist and often did exist without drum accompaniment is especially important when combined with the observation that, on some of the pieces in which drum lines were present, drum lines constituted an additional instrument line rather than the timekeeping or "swing machine" function that drums provided for some later styles. The earliest jazz drummers could also perform in timekeeping style and often did. However, the point here is an additional one: **the earliest jazz drummers often devised lines of activity bearing rhythmic and melodic contours that were distinctly different from the contours of lines being contributed by their fellow musicians.** The practice of playing an independent line of activity was suppressed in swing, the primary jazz style of the 1930s. It enjoyed a resurgence, however, in bop, the primary modern jazz style of the 1940s. In modern jazz, this independent line of activity has sometimes been termed "chatter," and it provides a layer of boiling sounds that increases the excitement of the combo sound. The use of this activity continued throughout the 1950s and 60s, increasing in density and importance. It has been an accepted practice for all modern drummers of the 1970s and 80s. The rhythms used by the

[17]All these examples can be found *The Louis Armstrong Story* Vol. 3, CBS CL 853; *Louis Armstrong Vol. 4,* CBS 45142, or *Louis Armstrong & Earl Hines,* Smithsonian 2002.

modern drummers were not those of ragtime, but the spirit in which they were played is analogous to the conception shown by the earliest jazz drummers.

Another important comparison can be made between early jazz drumming and later styles. The earliest drummers sometimes changed loudness, rhythm, and/or instrument for each successive soloist. Many of their accompaniment patterns, however, usually remained patterns rather than deriving spontaneously from rhythmic ideas heard in the improvised solo lines they accompanied, as later occurred in modern drumming. Spontaneous interaction between soloist and accompanist was limited.[18]

**Guitar**   During the 1920s, most guitarists confined themselves to timekeeping, or, when they played exposed parts, they used simple, chorded solos. Guitar was generally ignored as a jazz solo voice until the late 1930s, partly because of the limited loudness that guitarists could generate before the electric amplification of the instrument became common. But two significant guitar soloists did record: Philadelphia-born **Eddie Lang** (1902–1933) and New Orleans-born **Lonnie Johnson** (1899–1970). Lang's work can be heard in recordings by violinist Joe Venuti, and in recordings made by the Beiderbecke-Trumbauer team, such as "Singin' the Blues" (in SCCJ). Good examples of Johnson's music exist in combo recordings with Louis Armstrong such as "Hotter than That" (in SCCJ) and a few moments with Duke Ellington such as the 1928 Okeh version of "The Mooche."

The guitar styles developed by Johnson and Lang contrast markedly. Johnson was a bluesier player than Lang. A favorite means for creating the earthy flavor in his work was to let a tone ring while he glided up to desired pitch. Both men were well organized in their solos, but, in his execution, Lang projects an almost classical conception. (It is notable that he was first trained as a classical violinist.) His

[18]The foregoing discussion will be almost meaningless unless you take time and seek examples of the sounds that are described. Listen to the playing of Baby Dodds on "Dippermouth Blues" in SCCJ and that of Zutty Singleton with Louis Armstrong in "West End Blues" in SCCJ. In those examples, Dodds plays wood block and Singleton plays a pair of small, hand-held cymbals. (Wood block is demonstrated on JAZZ STYLES CASSETTE, side 1.) It would also be helpful to sample recordings that are not contained in SCCJ. For instance, Singleton can be heard on other Armstrong recordings of 1928: "My Monday Date" and "Sugar Foot Stomp" (see footnote 17). Dodds is best heard on the recordings that Oliver's Creole Jazz Band made for the Gennett company, not those made for Okeh, which Smithsonian has reissued in their Oliver set. (Oliver's recordings for Gennett are available on *Louis Armstrong & King Oliver*, Milestone 47017, LP.) The 1923 "I'm Going to Wear You Off My Mind" has particularly distinct wood block playing, in which Dodds's accompaniment rhythms show considerable variety, seeming to constitute a response to the rhythms of the solo lines. This might, however, have been worked out ahead and not be purely improvised for this particular recording. Tony Sbarbaro can be heard on the 1917 recording of "Dixie Jazz Band One Step" by the Original Dixieland Jazz Band in the JAZZ CLASSICS CASSETTE. After a passage of snare drum, bass drum, and cymbals, he plays wood block and cow bell. This combination can also be heard in the 1918 recording of "Clarinet Marmalade." Note that most all of Sbarbaro's instruments can be heard in these recordings, despite what has been said about drummers not having entire drum sets in the studio. (The ODJB recordings for Victor were reissued on *The Original Dixieland Jazz Band*, RCA, LPV-547.)

technique was excellent, and his lines were executed more cleanly than Johnson's. Listen to the counterlines which Lang improvises delicately under the horn lines in "Singin' the Blues" (in SCCJ). Their construction and execution is almost like that of classical chamber music. Although both players are historically significant, Lang has been the more influential of the two.

**Popular Appeal**     The earliest jazz had a wide appeal, especially to youthful audiences and particularly to social dancers. This roughly parallels the kind of popularity enjoyed by rock during the 1950s and 60s. But it contrasts dramatically with public response to modern jazz of later eras. Whereas modern jazz recordings rarely penetrated the hit parade, the Original Dixieland Jazz Band had several records hover near the top of the popularity charts, and jazz giants such as Louis Armstrong, Jelly Roll Morton, and Bix Beiderbecke were known to a wide public.

Like much rock and roll of the 1950s, New Orleans and Chicago styles of the 1920s are perceived as happy music. Traditionally they have been used as entertainment to set a mood of cheer and frivolity. Though scholars and musicians often take the music quite seriously, the public associates the sound with images of exciting parties in the "Roaring Twenties." Unlike the solemn view often ascribed to modern styles, the earliest styles are usually perceived as lighthearted and fun, though many of the early classics possess masterful construction and great depth of emotion.

New Orleans and Chicago styles did not just live and die with the 1920s. Their popularity has had its ups and downs since the decade ended, but the music has persisted, because demand for it has remained. For instance, there was a revival of interest in New Orleans combo jazz during the 1940s, and several players who had left music returned to careers in performing. The music at New Orleans's Preservation Hall, since 1962, has been so popular that they have always had to have several bands on hand so that one could be on tour and at least one could be in residence. For many years it has been common to find a few good Dixieland bands in every major U.S. city. In addition, many regions of America sport yearly festivals of traditional jazz.

## CHAPTER SUMMARY

1) The first forms of jazz resulted from blending improvisational approaches to ragtime, blues, spirituals, marches, and popular tunes.

2) The first jazz bands used the instruments of brass bands: trumpet, clarinet, trombone, tuba, drums, and (occasionally) saxophone.

3) The earliest jazz was not recorded. We can only infer how it sounded on the basis of recordings made by New Orleans players after they had moved to Chicago.

4) The first jazz group to record was the Original Dixieland Jazz Band in 1917.

5) Chicago was the jazz center of the world during the 1920s, comprised of
   a) all-star black groups such as Oliver's Creole Jazz Band which had moved from New Orleans,

b) white bands from New Orleans such as the New Orleans Rhythm Kings,

c) Chicago-born imitators of the New Orleans Rhythm Kings such as the Austin High Gang.

6) One of the most historically significant New Orleans natives to first record in Chicago was pianist-composer-bandleader Jelly Roll Morton.

7) Morton was the first great jazz composer. Several of his tunes became standards: "Wolverine Blues," "King Porter Stomp," "Milenburg Joys."

8) Morton devised a piano style that featured horn-like lines and long-short, strong-weak eighth-note patterns that swung more than ragtime.

9) Morton blended New Orleans improvisational approaches with elaborately arranged, prewritten passages.

10) The single player who stands above all others in jazz history is New Orleans-born trumpeter Louis Armstrong.

11) Armstrong possessed a large tone, wider range, and better command of the trumpet than most early players.

12) Armstrong's improvisations were especially well constructed.

13) Armstrong was one of the first combo players to effectively demonstrate solo improvisation instead of retaining the New Orleans tradition of collective improvisation.

14) Armstrong is possibly the most influential of all trumpeters, having been imitated by saxophonists, trombonists, and pianists as well as by trumpeters.

15) Next to Armstrong, Bix Beiderbecke was the most influential brass player of the 1920s, and he was harmonically more advanced than Armstrong.

16) In addition to a cool, thoughtful style, Beiderbecke was a composer in the tradition of French Impressionists Maurice Ravel and Claude Debussy.

17) Soprano saxophonist-clarinetist Sidney Bechet helped move jazz horn conception from collective improvisation techniques to a dramatic solo style.

18) Bechet influenced Johnny Hodges and John Coltrane, especially in the expressive timing of ornamentations which precede important notes.

19) Earl Hines helped take jazz piano conception from a traditionally pianistic orientation to a horn-like conception.

20) Hines influenced numerous other piano greats, including Teddy Wilson, Art Tatum, and Nat Cole.

21) The stride piano tradition of James P. Johnson was continued by Fats Waller, who, in turn, became the principal influence on Count Basie.

22) Waller was an excellent composer who wrote several tunes that have become jazz standards, such as "Honeysuckle Rose," "Ain't Misbehavin'," and "Jitterbug Waltz."

# chapter 6
# SWING:
# THE EARLY 1930s
# TO THE LATE 1940s

With the adoption of swing eighth-note patterns and a looser, less stiff rhythmic feeling, jazz began to swing more. This was a gradual change which began during the late 1920s and continued into the 1940s. Most jazz from this period is called swing music, and, since much of it was played by bands of ten or more men, it is often called the big band era. **Swing was the most popular style in jazz history**, and it attracted millions of dancers. It also produced several excellent big bands. Several soloists with these bands went on to influence the development of modern jazz. Swing differs from early jazz in several ways:

1) The preferred instrumentation for swing was **big band** rather than combo, and greater use of written arrangements therefore occurred during the swing era.

2) **Saxophones** were more common in swing.

3) **Bass viol** appeared more often in swing.

4) **High-hat** cymbals were used more.

5) Collective improvisation was rare in swing.

6) Overall **rhythmic feeling was smoother.**

7) Swing musicians usually showed a **higher level of instrumental proficiency** in terms of speed, agility, tone control, and playing in tune.

**Big Band Instrumentation**  Big bands were made up of ten or more musicians whose instruments fall into three categories: brass, saxophones, and rhythm section. The brass section included trumpets and trombones. Although saxophones are also made of brass, they are technically called woodwinds because they originated from instruments traditionally made of wood (clarinet, flute, and oboe) and are played in the manner of traditional wooden instruments. Because most saxophonists also play clarinet, and both sax and

**TABLE 6.1.  A Few of the Many Swing Style Musicians**

| Composing— Arranging | Saxophone | Clarinet | Vibraharp |
|---|---|---|---|
| Fletcher Henderson | Coleman Hawkins | Benny Goodman | Lionel Hampton |
| Eddie Durham | Johnny Hodges | Artie Shaw | Red Norvo |
| Benny Carter | Benny Carter | Barney Bigard | Adrian Rollini |
| Sy Oliver | Willie Smith | Woody Herman | Tyree Glenn |
| Don Redman | Chu Berry | Buster Bailey | |
| Duke Ellington | Herschel Evans | Jimmy Hamilton | **Bandleaders** |
| Billy Strayhorn | Dick Wilson | | |
| Eddie Sauter | Ben Webster | | Duke Ellington |
| Will Hudson | Lester Young | **Guitar** | Count Basie |
| Budd Johnson | Georgie Auld | | Bennie Moten |
| Edgar Sampson | Don Byas | Django Reinhardt | Benny Carter |
| Jimmy Mundy | Russell Procope | Charlie Christian | Chick Webb |
| Deane Kincaide | Illinois Jacquet | Eddie Durham | Andy Kirk |
| | Hilton Jefferson | Oscar Moore | Jay McShann |
| **Drums** | Tab Smith | Irving Ashby | Cab Calloway |
| | Flip Phillips | Al Casey | Tommy Dorsey |
| Jo Jones | Pete Brown | | Benny Goodman |
| Sid Catlett | Buster Smith | **Piano** | Jimmy Dorsey |
| Chick Webb | Tex Beneke | | Glenn Miller |
| Gene Krupa | Jerry Jerome | Art Tatum | Charlie Barnet |
| Sonny Greer | Boomie Richman | Teddy Wilson | Boyd Raeburn |
| Cozy Cole | Vido Musso | Billy Kyle | Woody Herman |
| Louis Bellson | Ernie Caceres | Mary Lou Williams | Stan Kenton |
| Buddy Rich | Earl Bostic | Milt Buckner | Gene Krupa |
| Dave Tough | Joe Thomas | Count Basie | Artie Shaw |
| Jimmy Crawford | Budd Johnson | Duke Ellington | Fletcher Henderson |
| Ben Thigpen | Jimmy Dorsey | Nat Cole | Lionel Hampton |
| | | Erroll Garner | Bunny Berigan |
| **Trombone** | **Trumpet** | Clyde Hart | Harry James |
| | | Johnny Guarnieri | Earl Hines |
| Lawrence Brown | Roy Eldridge | Jay McShann | Billy Eckstine |
| Dicky Wells | Cootie Williams | Mel Powell | Jimmie Lunceford |
| Trummy Young | Bunny Berigan | Jess Stacy | Luis Russell |
| Jimmy Harrison | Harry James | | Claude Thornhill |
| Benny Morton | Buck Clayton | **Bass** | |
| Vic Dickenson | Charlie Shavers | | |
| Joe "Tricky Sam" Nanton | Frankie Newton | Walter Page | |
| Bill Harris | Henry "Red" Allen | Jimmy Blanton | |
| J. C. Higginbotham | Oran "Hot Lips" Page | John Kirby | |
| Jack Jenney | Harry "Sweets" Edison | Israel Crosby | |
| Tommy Dorsey | Rex Stewart | Wellman Braud | |
| | Harold "Shorty" Baker | Milt Hinton | |
| | Jonah Jones | Slam Stewart | |
| | Taft Jordan | | |
| | Jabbo Smith | | |
| | Herman Autrey | | |

clarinet have cane reeds attached to their mouthpieces, the sax section was often called the "reed section," a label which was retained in later decades even when saxophonists began adding flute, a non-reed instrument.

The alto and tenor saxophones were the most frequently used saxes, and, by the late 1930s, most bands had also adopted the baritone saxophone (see Figure 6.1). The soprano and bass saxophones were not especially common. (To identify the sounds of these instruments, listen to side 2 of the JAZZ STYLES CASSETTE. To hear them playing together, listen to "Harlem Airshaft" and "Cottontail" in the JAZZ CLASSICS CASSETTE.)

The sax section contained from three to five musicians. Saxophonists did not usually play one instrument to the exclusion of the others. Some men, for instance, were required to alternate from clarinet to alto and baritone saxophones. Eventually a section of two altos, two tenors, and a baritone became standard. The leader of the sax section, an alto saxophonist, sat in the middle, with the baritone on one end, tenor on the other. (Listen to the tenor and baritone sax solos on "Cottontail" in the JAZZ CLASSICS CASSETTE.)

**Figure 6.1.** Alto (on left), tenor (on right), and baritone saxophone (lying down). Listen to JAZZ STYLES CASSETTE, side 2 to compare the sounds of these instruments.

The size of the trumpet section varied from two to five men, three being the standard number during the late 1930s and early 40s. The lead trumpeter usually sat in the middle. The trombone section ranged from one to five men, two or three being standard. The lead trombonist was in the center.

The growth of big bands was accompanied by an increase in the use of written arrangements, which had not been necessary with small combos. As bands became bigger, it was more difficult to improvise a respectable performance. Many big bands did succeed in playing without written arrangements, but eventually considerations of convenience and variety forced musicians to learn to read and write arrangements. A newcomer had much less difficulty adapting to a band whose materials consisted of written arrangements rather than memorized routines.

The compositional devices employed in a large portion of the arrangements were simple. Melodies were played by the entire band in unison or in harmony. (Listen to the saxes and trumpets play the melody together in "Cottontail" on the JAZZ CLASSICS CASSETTE.) Then jazz improvisation followed, accompanied both by the rhythm section and by figures scored for other members of the ensemble. (Listen to the bridge of the second and third choruses of "Cottontail" to hear sax improvisation accompanied by rhythm section and brass figures.) The melodies and accompanying figures were passed from one section of the band to another. Saxes might state the A section, brass state the bridge, and so forth. In addition to pop tune melodies, arrangements often contained variations on those themes, some of which were actually as good as improvised solos. (Listen to the sax soli, precisely that kind of variation, in the fifth chorus of "Cottontail.") These were offered as passages for one section of the band to play while another remained silent or accompanied them. Sometimes, portions within the passages were passed back and forth, so that it sounded as though one section of the band posed a question and another section answered it. (Notice that format in the sixth chorus of "Cottontail.") This technique is called question and answer, call and response, or responsorial style. (Listen to the end of "One O'Clock Jump" at the beginning of the JAZZ CLASSICS CASSETTE.)

Short, simple, phrases called riffs were used by some big bands as essential elements of their style. At times, different riffs were assigned to various sections of the band and played against each other. Such antiphonal (an-TIFF-on-ull) activities could swing a band buoyantly and give jazz improvisation a good send-off. Sometimes entire arrangements were based on such riffs. (Listen to Count Basie's "One O'Clock Jump" and "Taxi War Dance" in the JAZZ CLASSICS CASSETTE.)

**The Rhythm Section**

The rhythm section ordinarily contained piano, guitar, bass, and drums. **Rhythm guitar** remained a part of Count Basie's band until guitarist Freddie Green died in 1987, but it had disappeared from most other big bands during the late 40s. Although the banjo had been present in early-style bands, it dropped out of sight during the 1930s. Tuba had preceded string bass in some bands, but had been abandoned by the mid-1930s. Before the guitar and string bass became firmly established, guitarists were often required to alternate guitar and banjo, while bassists were required to alternately play both tuba (also called brass bass) and string bass (also called bass viol or bass fiddle).

The **pianist** in the rhythm section occasionally played melody instead of just chords and embellishments. Comping was not the common accompaniment style during the swing era, though Count Basie did use it. Pianists of the swing era used stride style or played a chord on every beat or every other beat. They did not necessarily improvise new rhythms to flexibly fit those of the solo line, as did their successors in modern jazz.

**Guitar and bass** were usually assigned timekeeping duties. The sound of the guitarist percussively strumming a chord on each beat, known as *rhythm guitar style*, was prominent on most swing era recordings (demonstrated on JAZZ STYLES CASSETTE, side 2). So was the sound of the **bassist** who was playing a note on the first and third of every four beats, *two-beat*, or on every beat, *walking* (demonstrated on the JAZZ STYLES CASSETTE, side 1). Bassists during the swing era remained in the background, auditorily as well as visually. Bass features were very rare until the 1950s and remained relatively infrequent thereafter. In the next chapter, we will mention how Duke Ellington's bassist **Jimmy Blanton** originated melodically-conceived pizzicato bass solos. But bassists in this era were usually felt more than they were heard. Some dancers and attentive listeners might have detected a difference in a band's rhythmic feeling resulting from a weak bassist or the absence of a bassist, but those same listeners would rarely have known the cause for the difference.

When musicians discuss this period, three bassists besides Jimmy Blanton are also mentioned: **Walter Page, Slam Stewart** (1914–1987), and **Milt Hinton** (b. 1910). (For more about Page, see the Count Basie chapter.) Hinton made his reputation playing with Cab Calloway's big band during the 1930s, but he continued to be in demand for a variety of jazz settings through the 1990s. Known for his sure sense of tempo and huge tone, Hinton acquired a nickname of "The Judge" because once he set the tempo for a piece, he was remarkably firm and authoritative in maintaining it.[1] Slam Stewart was a good timekeeper and a responsive accompanist, especially for the melodic flights of pianist Art Tatum, whom he often accompanied. Stewart is best known, however, as an inventive soloist. He is notable for a solo technique in which he bowed his bass while humming the same notes. The combination of voice and bass produced a rough-textured and original tone color. He humorously slid from note to note, but always managed to make a lot of melodic sense. Historically, Stewart's solo playing moved jazz bass a step away from the role of mere time-keeper. (Listen to his solo in the Don Byas rendition of "I Got Rhythm" in SCCJ.)

The majority of drummers who played with big bands during this period tended to limit themselves to making the beat obvious for dancers and lending swing feeling to the band instead of doing as the earliest jazz drummers had done and creating a separate line of rhythmic activity that coexisted with the melodic rhythms of the horns. With the exception of striking cymbals and gongs for dramatically timed effects, many of the big band drummers played lengthy passages without doing much more than stating each beat on the bass drum and reinforcing this with a simple timekeeping pattern played on the snare drum with wire brushes or on a

---

[1]See Hinton's autobiography: *Bass Lines* (Temple, 1988). Listen to his feature numbers with Cab Calloway's big band: "Ebony Silhouette" on *Jammin' for the Jackpot*, New World 217; "Pluckin' the Bass," on *Sixteen Cab Calloway Classics*, CBS (France) 62950. Notice his accompaniment work in Lionel Hampton's band version of "When Lights Are Low" in SCCJ.

closed high-hat with sticks. Sometimes the second and fourth beats of each measure were emphasized by striking the snare drum with sticks. (This rhythm is called a "back beat.") Deviations from these patterns usually constituted simple embellishments of the beat or busy patterns that were quickly played when the horns were pausing between ensemble phrases. Swing drummers tended not to play new and provocative rhythms that ran counter to the horn lines. Listeners had to wait until modern jazz developed during the 1940s before they could hear drummers again offering a parallel line of activity instead of just keeping time. Listeners also had to wait to hear a substantial amount of interaction between improvising soloist and accompanying drummer. For the most part, swing drumming was quite conservative and not very light or swinging. It was not until the late 1930s that a lighter and more graceful sound was heard from big band drummers. And, even then, it was only heard in the few bands that were lucky enough to boast such drummers as Jo Jones or Dave Tough.

Jazz drumming authority Denny Brown has pointed out that the nature of the 1930s big band style restricted the jazz drummer's activity, decreasing the rhythmic freedom that combo drummers had. The riff-based format used by big bands discouraged swing drummers from playing complex rhythmic patterns because such complexity might conflict with the melodic rhythms of the written horn parts. Brown contends that the 1930s swing era originated the idea that a jazz drummer should only be felt, not heard. Exceptions to this rule are notable, however, and **Gene Krupa's** popularity during this period might stem partly from his violating the norm. Brown suggests that Krupa's playing forecast aspects of modern drumming by being heard and by including patterns that responded to horn lines as well as building excitement. Some of Krupa's accompaniments are like solos. In that respect they are a throwback to the methods of the earliest jazz drummers and a contrast to the typical approach of swing drummers.[2]

During the late 1930s, a contrast to the Krupa style was offered by Count Basie's drummer **Jo Jones**. In place of the loud and insistent pounding of the bass drum on each beat that Krupa did, Jones often omitted bass drum playing altogether. In contrast to striking his high-hat while it was closed, Jones continued a ride rhythm on it while it was continuously opening and closing. He let the cymbals ring, thereby making a more sustained and less abrupt sound pattern (demonstrated on the JAZZ STYLES CASSETTE, side 1). This technique, together with an unusually close coordination with the bassist, projected a more flowing feeling than had typified other swing era rhythm section sounds. Jones also gave each beat more equal treatment than his contemporaries had done. The feeling Jones conveyed, and the precision with which he played, evolved into the modern jazz drummer's tendency to play timekeeping rhythms on a suspended cymbal that is now known as the ride cymbal. (It is also notable that Jones steered clear of cowbell and wood block, sounds that today help us identify the corny aspects of premodern jazz drumming. For more, see chapter 3 and listen to side 1 of the JAZZ STYLES CASSETTE. Jones can be heard in "Taxi War Dance" and "Lester Leaps In" on the JAZZ CLASSICS CASSETTE.)

---

[2]See pages 413–414 to get Brown's history of premodern drumming.

**Bandleaders**  Some of the best swing bands were led by Fletcher Henderson, Count Basie, Duke Ellington, Jimmie Lunceford, and Benny Goodman.[3] Following this discussion are entire chapters devoted to Ellington and his musicians and Basie and his musicians. The Henderson and Ellington bands bridged the gap between the styles of early jazz and the swing approach. Each had begun in the early 1920s and grown larger and more sophisticated by the late 1930s.

A very large portion of great early jazz and swing era improvisers worked with pianist-arranger **Fletcher Henderson** (1897–1952) between the early 1920s and late 30s (see Table 6.2). Henderson's was an all-star band. (Get SCCJ, and listen to Henderson's band play Don Redman's arrangement of "The Stampede," featuring saxophonist Coleman Hawkins, then listen to the band play Henderson's arrangement of "Wrappin' It Up.") His style represented one major stream of big band jazz; Ellington's represented another. In his arrangements, Henderson pitted saxes against brass. He also used block voicing, in which the melody is the top voice of a series of chords, and each note in a chord is assigned to a different instrument or combination of instruments. It produced a thicker sound than if the line were not harmonized. Ellington used block voicing too, but he added an assortment of other special techniques that made his sound unique (see next chapter for details). Part of Henderson's arranging reputation resulted from the use of his work by the phenomenally popular band of Benny Goodman.[4]

**Jimmie Lunceford** (1902–1947) led an excellent big band that was noted for its quality of swing feeling and well-disciplined musicianship. The consistency and

[3]Commercial albums of these bands come in and go out of print so fast that it is almost futile to list them here. On the other hand, the Smithsonian Institution carries compilations of them all, and it keeps its products available for a considerable time. Therefore, selections that are available in Smithsonian offerings will often be listed in this book instead of commercially available records that duplicate those selections. The Smithsonian offerings can be obtained by mail and ordered by a toll-free phone number (800-678-2677). All the big bands mentioned in this chapter can be heard in *Big Band Jazz*, Smithsonian 2200, a six-LP set. (Contents are listed in *Teachers Manual & Discography*.) Fletcher Henderson is well represented in *Developing an American Orchestra*, Smithsonian 2006, LP set, 1923–37. Ellington sets which are produced and distributed by Smithsonian are listed at the end of the next chapter. Lesser known big bands can be heard in *Jammin' for the Jackpot*, New World 217, LP anthology. In addition, most important bands and musicians from this era can also be heard in SCCJ, and the Basie and Ellington bands are well represented in the JAZZ CLASSICS CASSETTE. All the pianists mentioned in this chapter, except Milt Buckner, can be heard in *Jazz Piano*, Smithsonian 039, LP, CD, cassette.

[4]Henderson's work can be heard on Goodman's recordings of "King Porter Stomp," "Wrappin' It Up," "Blue Skies," "Sometimes I'm Happy," "Japanese Sandman," and "When Buddah Smiles." For more about his and other important bands of the era, see Gunther Schuller's *The Swing Era* (Oxford, 1989), Stanley Dance's *The World of Swing*, (Scribner, 1974; reprinted by DaCapo), George T. Simon's *The Big Bands* (Collier, 1974), Nathan Pearson's *Goin' to Kansas City* (University of Illinois, 1987), and Nat Shapiro and Nat Hentoff's *The Jazz Makers* (Grove, 1957).

**TABLE 6.2. Musicians Prominent in the Fletcher Henderson Bands**

| Trumpet | Saxophone and Clarinet | Trombone |
| --- | --- | --- |
| Louis Armstrong | | Jimmy Harrison |
| Rex Stewart | Coleman Hawkins | Charlie Green |
| Roy Eldridge | Chu Berry | Dicky Wells |
| Tommy Ladnier | Don Redman | J. C. Higginbotham |
| Cootie Williams | Benny Carter | Benny Morton |
| Joe Smith | Ben Webster | |
| Bobby Stark | Russell Procope | |
| Henry "Red" Allen | Hilton Jefferson | |
| Emmett Berry | Buster Bailey | |
| **Drums** | **Bass and Tuba** | |
| Sid Catlett | John Kirby | |
| Kaiser Marshall | June Cole | |
| | Bobby Escudero | |
| | Israel Crosby | |

*"Don't be That Way"*

*"Seven Come 11"*

balance of sound projected by each section of the band was matched only by their smooth, even swing feeling. Lunceford's band had exciting solo improvisers, and it could generate musical moments of "white heat" (the title of a lively feature number[5]). Its place in jazz history was earned for this special touch and the effect it had on dancers as well as fellow musicians.

During the 1930s and 40s, **Benny Goodman** (1909–1986) led the most well-known big band that was jazz-oriented. His big band had a very hard-driving effect and showcased its leader's swinging, technically impressive clarinet playing. (Listen to Goodman's clarinet solos on Red Nichols's band version of "Dinah" in Revised SCCJ.)[6] His name was so high, so often on the popularity charts that he ranks above all but five other artists making recordings between 1890 and 1954. This means that Goodman was one of the most popular figures in the music industry as a whole, not just in jazz. Today he ranks with Louis Armstrong and Dave Brubeck as one of the best known musicians in all of jazz history. In addition to his impact as a clarinetist, he may be responsible for influencing the course of jazz by the exposure he provided for other outstanding improvisers. His small combos were especially effective for

[5]*Willie Bryant and Jimmie Lunceford and Their Orchestras*, RCA Bluebird AXM2-5502; Listen to "Lunceford Special" in SCCJ or "Organ Grinder Swing" in the Revised SCCJ. A wider sampling is available in "Stratosphere," "Uptown Blues," "Organ Grinder Swing" on *Big Band Jazz*, Smithsonian 2200.

[6]Benny Goodman, *Sing, Sing, Sing*, RCA Bluebird 5630, CD/LP, big band material from 1935–38; *After You've Gone*, RCA Bluebird 5631, CD/LP, small-group material from 1935–37.

Benny Goodman, the best known of all clarinetists and swing era bandleaders. Pictured here in 1936 (standing in front, playing clarinet), Gene Krupa (drums), trumpets (left to right): Nate Kazebier, Pee Wee Erwin, and Chris Griffin; Jess Stacy (piano), Allan Reuss (guitar); reeds (left to right): Hymie Schertzer and Bill DePew (both are playing clarinet, with alto sax in lap), Art Rollini (playing clarinet, with tenor sax in lap), Dick Clark (playing bass clarinet, with tenor sax and clarinet on a stand); trombones (left to right): Red Ballard and Murray McEachern; Harry Goodman (bass). (Photo courtesy of Duncan Scheidt.) Listen to the band play "King Porter Stomp" and "Sing, Sing, Sing" in *Big Band Jazz* (Smithsonian 2200).

bringing wide recognition to such swing era stand-outs as pianist Teddy Wilson, guitarist Charlie Christian, and vibraharpist Lionel Hampton. (Listen to Goodman's trio play "Body and Soul" and his sextet play "I Found a New Baby" in SCCJ.)[7]

[7]Several of the players Goodman spotlighted also led their own swing bands at one time or another:

1) trumpeter Bunny Berigan
2) trumpeter Harry James (1916–1983, who continued to lead big bands for decades after the end of the swing era)
3) trumpeter Cootie Williams (see Duke Ellington chapter for discussion)
4) vibraharpist Lionel Hampton (b. 1909; see page 152 for illustrations of the vibraharp, and listen to his "When Lights Are Low" in SCCJ)
5) drummer Gene Krupa (1909–1973; listen to his "Rockin' Chair" in SCCJ), whose drum solos helped emancipate jazz drummers from their restricted role of being merely timekeepers.

For more about Goodman, see Bruce Crowther's biography *Benny Goodman* (Apollo, 1988), *Benny Goodman: Listen to His Legacy* by D. Russell Connor (Scarecrow, 1988), James Lincoln Collier's biography *Benny Goodman and the Swing Era* (Oxford, 1989), and pages 3–45 in Gunther Schuller's *The Swing Era* (Oxford, 1989).

**Trombone**  Many of the leading trombonists in early jazz were also leading trombonists in the swing era. Their styles became more refined, and they were found more often in big bands than in Dixieland-style combos. Jack Teagarden and Tommy Dorsey were among this group (see preceding chapter for coverage of **Jack Teagarden**). **Tommy Dorsey** (1905–1956) led a tremendously popular series of dance bands during the 1930s, 40s and 50s, as well as co-leading others with his saxophonist brother Jimmy Dorsey.[8] He is best known among musicians because he developed a method of playing trombone which produced an extremely smooth, clear tone. His mastery of the instrument, his consistently polished manner, and his high-register work, became the model for a string of highly skilled trombonists who had glossy tones and meticulous technique. **Lawrence Brown** was another stand-out of the era, but his style is treated in the Ellington chapter because he was known primarily to Ellington fans. The swing era spilled into the decade of the 1940s and produced an important trombonist who did not already have a reputation in early jazz. **Bill Harris** (1916–1973) was probably the most original and influential of the brass soloists featured in the Woody Herman big band of the 1940s. Harris is a transitional figure in the development of modern jazz trombone, emerging before J.J. Johnson. He had a broad, thick tone and quick vibrato which remained for the duration of each tone. Harris played with pronounced authority and employed good high range, by 1940s standards. Harris's well-constructed solos made use of staccato, punching figures in addition to slides and smears.[9]

**Trumpet**  Trumpeter **Roy Eldridge** (1911–1989) was one of the most advanced improvisers of the swing era. (Listen to his work with Benny Carter on "I Can't Believe That You're In Love With Me" in SCCJ.) He is often considered a link between swing and modern jazz. Eldridge had a very aggressive style and unprecedented instrumental proficiency. His imaginative choice of notes and sax-like lines provided continuity in the history of jazz trumpet from the style of Louis Armstrong to the modern approach pioneered by Dizzy Gillespie. Eldridge creatively varied the size, texture, and vibrato of his tone. Sometimes it was clear and warm, at other times brittle and edgy. His high-register playing had a sweeping scope; in that register, his entrances and syncopations were timed with a rhythmic feeling which suggested the modern jazz inflections that replaced early jazz rhythmic style.[10]

**New with Roy Eldridge was the idea that a trumpeter could improvise long, sinewy lines which, though easy to execute on saxophone, do not lend themselves to the mechanics of the trumpet.** Eldridge's influence caused modern trumpeters to

---

[8] *This is Tommy Dorsey, Vol. 1*, RCA VPM 6038; *Vol. 2*, RCA VPM 6064; *The Best of Tommy Dorsey*, MCA2-4074; *Yes Indeed!*, RCA Bluebird 9987, CD/LP, 1939–45.

[9] Harris solos on "Bijou," "Northwest Passage," "Apple Honey," and "Woodchopper's Ball" in Woody Herman—*The Thundering Herds*, CBS 44108, CD/LP, 1945–47.

[10] *All the Cats Join In*, MCA-1355, 1943–46; *Roy Eldridge with the Gene Krupa Orchestra*, CBS 45448, CD, 1940–42. Listen to his blazing 1941 solo on "After You've Gone" with Gene Krupa's band, *Gene Krupa*, Columbia Special Products JCL-753, LP, 1940–47; also on *Little Jazz*, CBS 45275, CD/LP anthology. For transcription and analysis of his solo on "I Can't Believe That Your're in Love With Me" (in SCCJ), see pages 458–60 of Gunther Schuller's *The Swing Era* (Oxford, 1989).

cultivate considerably more instrumental facility and to improvise in more intricate and unpredictable ways than their early jazz counterparts had done. His conception also extended the average phrase length used by improvising trumpeters. Eldridge's influence extended into the 1950s by way of modern trumpeter Dizzy Gillespie, who built his own influential style upon the foundation of Eldridge's bristling high-register work, unorthodox choice of notes, and saxophone style of phrasing. (Listen to Eldridge's solos in Gene Krupa's band version of "Rockin' Chair" in SCCJ.)[11]

One of the most famous swing era trumpeters was **Bunny Berigan** (1908–1942). His 1937 "I Can't Get Started" solo was well loved,[12] and his improvisation in the Tommy Dorsey band's recording of "Marie" was transcribed and included in subsequent arrangements for other bands. Berigan was a very proficient trumpeter with a clear tone and remarkably clean articulation. His relaxed, assured style of playing was characterized by a fullness and consistency of tone from the lowest to the highest registers. Louis Armstrong's influence was evident in Berigan's solo playing.

**Saxophone**  The man generally considered to be the father of jazz tenor saxophone playing is **Coleman Hawkins** (1904–1969). Prior to his arrival on the jazz scene in the 1920s, the saxophone was treated as little more than a novelty instrument. Hawkins's supercharged playing on it brought the horn recognition. His deep-toned, husky command of the tenor set the pace for decades of other saxophonists. Tenor sax became one of the most popular instruments in jazz. In fact, for many people today, tenor saxophone symbolizes jazz. (Listen to his solo on Lionel Hampton's band version of "When Lights Are Low" in SCCJ.)

Hawkins not only had exceptional command over his instrument and an aggressive delivery for his lines, but he also demonstrated more understanding of and interest in chord progressions than most other premodern saxophonists had. His improvisations revealed less attraction to devising new melodies and more attraction to investigating the chord progressions that could be added to a tune's original accompaniment. Though it is not entirely accurate, Hawkins is therefore known primarily as a harmonic improviser rather than a melodic improviser.[13] He devoured complex chord progressions, such as those of "Body and Soul", and he added chords to pieces which did not already have enough harmonic activity for him. (Listen to his 1939 recording of "Body and Soul" in SCCJ.)[14]

Hawkins was a featured soloist with the Fletcher Henderson band from 1923 to

[11]To detect the Eldridge character in Gillespie's earliest playing, listen to Eldridge's solo on the Gene Krupa band recording of "After You've Gone," then listen to Gillespie's playing on the 1940 Cab Calloway recording of "Pickin' the Cabbage" from *Dizzy Gillespie: Development of an American Artist*, Smithsonian 2004.

[12]*The Complete Bunny Berigan, Vol. 1*, RCA Bluebird AXM2-5584, LP set, 1937

[13]Coleman Hawkins *Body and Soul*, RCA Bluebird 5658 (CD) or 5658 (LP), 1939–56; *Classic Tenors*, Doctor Jazz/CBS 38446, CD/LP, 1943

[14]For technical analysis of Hawkins, see pages 426–50 of Gunther Schuller's *The Swing Era* (Oxford, 1988). For transcription and analysis of the Hawkins solo on "Body and Soul," see Stuart Isacoff's *Solos for Jazz Tenor Sax* (Carl Fischer, 1985). Order from Carl Fischer Music Store, 54 Cooper Square, NY, NY 10003. For more about his life, see Burnett James's biography *Coleman Hawkins* (Hippocrene, 1984).

Coleman Hawkins, father of jazz tenor saxophone. Pictured here at age 45 in 1949. (*Photo courtesy of Duncan Schiedt*)

1934. He worked mostly with small groups thereafter. Though primarily associated with the swing era, he was also a respected figure at modern jazz sessions of the 1940s. Despite his lack of the smoothness and fluid swing that typified modern jazz soloists, his skill with difficult chord progressions helped him adjust to newer styles. Hawkins was one of the most intense and consistent saxophone soloists in jazz history. (Listen to his 1943 recording of "The Man I Love" in SCCJ.) A surging energy continued to flow unabated from his horn for decades. His influence was not limited to his swing era contemporaries. Such modern tenor saxophonists as Sonny Rollins and John Coltrane were also influenced by him. **Next to Coltrane and Lester Young (discussed later), Hawkins was the most influential tenor saxophonist in jazz history.**

**Don Byas** (1912–1972) was more advanced than most swing tenor saxophonists and could hold his own with many modern players of the late 1940s. (Listen to his "I Got Rhythm" in SCCJ.) Byas had fire, enviable command of the saxophone, harmonic sophistication, and melodic daring. He loved to double-time and run through every note in each chord. More significant was his tendency to add new chords to a tune, and to use both the original and new chords in his improvisations, a method he derived from pianist Art Tatum. The richness of his lines easily matches that of later saxophonists. Though he had much of the huskiness in tone possessed by Hawkins, Byas swung more easily than Hawkins, perhaps because the ideas that Byas devised were less varied in their rhythms. The style of Byas was widely appreciated by fellow saxophonists, and it became the primary model for two distinguished modern players: Lucky Thompson and Benny Golson.

**Benny Carter** (b. 1907) and Johnny Hodges were the most influential alto saxophonists of the swing era. Hodges will be discussed in the next chapter, but we will briefly examine Carter here. (Listen to Carter's "I Can't Believe That You're In Love With Me" in SCCJ.) The first elements of Carter's playing that usually strike listeners are the precision of his execution and the glow of his tone quality. His sound is rich and luxurious. His solos flow with grace and lightness. There is a striking neatness and order with which Carter plays his eighth notes, very even and well-measured. Carter devised intelligently conceived solos that are oriented in an obvious way to the changing harmonies of his accompaniment. Carter was also a good trumpeter, clarinetist, and a top-notch arranger.[15]

**Piano**  **Art Tatum** (1910–1956) is among the most widely admired pianists in jazz history. (Listen to Tatum's "Willow Weep for Me" and "Too Marvelous For Words" in SCCJ.) Even when compared with all the very fast, imaginative pianists who have emerged since the 1940s, Tatum still stands above with his impressive technical facility and unceasing energy. Tatum was unpredictable, and he frequently interrupted the direction of his own lines. He seemed to indulge his impulses and momentarily pursue musical tangents. His style combines a variety of techniques. He often employed stride-style left hand (demonstrated on JAZZ STYLES CASSETTE, side 2) as well as horn-like lines. Tatum's playing was quite flowery, with long, fast runs which sometimes overlapped each other. He was a master at spontaneously adding and changing chords during his performance of pop tunes. This is termed chord *substitution*. Sometimes Tatum was found to be changing keys several times within a phrase and still managing to gracefully resolve the harmonic motion. (He had an enviable capacity for neatly getting out of precarious positions within the adventure of his improvisations.) Both his chord substitutions and his key changing in mid-solo (today known as "side-slipping") were picked up from him by modern jazz musicians.

Rhythmically Tatum was also very inventive. His left-hand rhythms were full of surprises. He is also known for changing tempo in mid-solo, sometimes leaving the intent listener dangling on an unresolved pattern while Tatum pursues another tangent. His right-hand playing sometimes seemed to throw showers of notes upon the listener. The rhythms in these showers were often odd combinations, not merely strings of eighth notes and sixteenth notes. But despite their complexity, Tatum's runs have been memorized by hundreds of pianists, and they have been used to decorate solos in performances by jazz pianists and popular pianists alike.

[15]*Benny Carter, Jazz Giant*, OJC-167 (Contemporary 7555), CD/LP, 1957–58. For more about Carter, see the biography-discography *Benny Carter: A Life in American Music, Vol. 1 & 2* by Morroe Berger, Edward Berger, and James Patrick (Scarecrow, 1982).

Art Tatum's impact on jazz history was enormous. The fast lines and added chords of Tatum were absorbed by tenor saxophonist Don Byas and modern saxophonist Charlie Parker. Tatum also influenced two highly innovative pianists who played pivotal roles during the early days of modern jazz: Bud Powell and Lennie Tristano (discussed in upcoming chapters). Both Powell and Tristano, in turn, went on to influence numerous pianists of the 1950s who further extended the reach of Tatum's work.[16]

Next to Art Tatum and Earl Hines, **Teddy Wilson** (1912–1986) was probably the most outstanding pianist in the swing era. (Listen to his work with Benny Goodman on "Body and Soul" in SCCJ.) He, too, contributed to the development of modern jazz.[17] **Wilson lightened the sound of jazz piano playing and removed some of the weightiness that was found in piano styles of early jazz and swing. He replaced it with a fleet smoothness and streamlined quality.** Listeners are particularly impressed by the grace and evenness with which Teddy Wilson improvised even the fastest passages. It was as though equal attention were focused on every note, no matter how brief. His work could be dazzling.[18]

Like Tatum, Wilson is often mistaken for the type of pianist who usually plays in cocktail lounges and is therefore referred to as a cocktail pianist. This is partly due to the pleasantness of his style. Both Tatum and Wilson influenced many cocktail pianists but do not themselves fall into this category. Melodic meat, variety, swing, and refinement distinguish Wilson and Tatum from the multitudes of less-gifted pianists who have incorporated aspects of their styles.

Techniques of Earl Hines were especially evident in the early 1940s work of **Nat Cole** (1917–1965) and Erroll Garner. Cole was one of the first pianists to incorporate spare, hornlike lines in his playing. His lines exhibit a lightness that was not typical of the heavy-handed and flowery styles of premodern jazz. Cole also perfected a style of accompanying in which chords are played as brief, syncopated bursts. This eventually became known as comping (demonstrated on JAZZ STYLES CASSETTE, side 1). In 1939, Cole formed a trio comprised of piano, guitar and bass.[19] Most of his hit records of 1943 to 49 were made with that group. The trio featured pleasant chord voicings that had a modern touch. The musicians closely

---

[16]For transcription and analysis of Tatum's "The Man I Love," see John Rodby's *Solos for Jazz Piano* (Carl Fischer, 1989); order from Carl Fischer Music Store, 54 Cooper Square, NY, NY 10003. For how to get Joseph Howard's four-volume analysis of Tatum's style, see page 414. For more analysis of Tatum, see John Mehegan's *Jazz Improvisation, Vol. 3* (Watson-Guptill, 1964) and pages 476–502 of Gunther Schuller's *The Swing Era* (Oxford, 1989).

[17]When Wilson chose to create horn-like lines, he refined the best of Earl Hines. Wilson's work on the 1936 "Blues in C-Sharp Minor" provides an excellent demonstration of his precisely executed, intelligently conceived horn lines. This can be heard in Roy Eldridge—*Little Jazz*, CBS 45275, CD/LP anthology. For analysis of his style, see John Mehegan's *Jazz Improvisation, Vol. 3* (Watson-Guptill, 1964). For a comparison with Tatum's style, see pages 502–13 of Gunther Schuller's *The Swing Era* (Oxford, 1989).

[18]Teddy Wilson, *Statements and Improvisations*, Smithsonian 2005, LP set, 1934–42

[19]*From The Very Beginning*, MCA 2-4020, 2 LP set, 1936, 1940–41; Listen to Cole's trio on "The Man I Love" (1944) and "Blues in My Shower" (1947) in *Jazz Piano*, Smithsonian 039, LP, CD, cassette. For transcriptions and analysis, see pages 816–25 of Gunther Schuller's *The Swing Era* (Oxford, 1989).

coordinated their parts so that much of the rhythm was played in unison by piano and guitar, with bass lines that tightly corresponded. Highly syncopated introductions and endings were devised, and cheerful little interludes often joined the various sections of each composition. Most of each piece was worked out in advance, but there was usually room for well-paced solos whose construction was logical and easy to follow. The overall effect was light and subtle, with a snappy kind of swing feeling.

Nat Cole had a more pervasive influence than most people realize. Modern pianists Oscar Peterson, Bill Evans, and Horace Silver have all cited him as an influence on their own musical thinking. Peterson has said that Cole was the main source of his own jazz piano style and that he aspired to create as tightly knit a trio technique as Cole's. For several years, Peterson led a successful piano-guitar-bass trio that played in a style that was similar to Cole's. Evans has said that he was impressed by the way Cole could take a melodic idea and develop it over the course of an improvisation. (Similar remarks have since been made about the improvisations of Evans.) Cole's piano style received less and less attention after he became one of the most popular singers in recording history, and it is often overlooked because of that.

**Erroll Garner** (1923–1977) is a unique figure in jazz piano history because he does not fit neatly into either the swing era or the bop era and because he originated a relatively unorthodox style. (Listen to "Fantasy on Frankie and Johnny" in SCCJ.) He attained recognition at a time when swing had already peaked and modern jazz had already been launched. His greatest popularity occurred during the 1950s, even though his style was rooted in the swing era of the 1930s. And though Garner had a swing style, he recorded with saxophonist Charlie Parker, who was the most significant figure in the creation of modern jazz, and Garner influenced several important modern pianists, including George Shearing and Ahmad Jamal.[20]

Garner had a simple, swinging, easy-to-follow style, and his piano trio interpretations of popular songs, including his own composition "Misty," made him one of the best known of all jazz musicians to record during the 1950s. The origins of Garner's approach are far flung. The sound of Earl Hines is suggested by Garner's octave-voiced right-hand lines and his pounding approach, though Garner's melodic sense is much simpler than Hines's, and he showed nowhere near the quantity of rhythmic surprises that typified Hines. It is notable that Garner's style evolved over the years, but he never relaxed his eighth-note conception to the streamlined feeling that was employed by modern pianists or by such advanced swing pianists as Teddy Wilson and Nat Cole. Several aspects of Garner's approach have assumed trademark quality for his name. One is that his left hand played a chord on each beat as a rhythm guitarist might, but each one of those chords was played ever so slightly after the beat rather than directly on the beat. Another is a skillful use of loudness changes. (This is a trait that Ahmad Jamal might have learned from

---

[20]For transcription and analysis of Garner's solo on "I'll Remember April," see John Rodby's *Solos for Jazz Piano* (Carl Fischer, 1989. Order from Carl Fischer Music Store, 54 Cooper Square, NY, NY 10003). For more about Garner's life, see James M. Doran's *Erroll Garner, Most Happy Piano* (Scarecrow, 1985).

Garner.) A third prime aspect associated with Garner is a flowery manner that seems to almost drip with its extensive use of tremolo and grace notes.

Some of Garner's playing is richly orchestral, and it is harmonically like music of Claude Debussy and Maurice Ravel, a style called French Impressionism. Garner often voiced his melodies chordally instead of letting melody notes sound by themselves. This has led jazz historian Harvey Pekar to feel that Garner's historical impact may have been to get pianists to think more in terms of chordal playing. Pekar suggests that, through a concern with chordal playing and Impressionism, Garner may have begun a stream of styles which ran from Ahmad Jamal to Red Garland, and from Garland to Bill Evans and McCoy Tyner. Pekar also notes that Garner's regular statement of the beat with his left hand influenced—possibly through Jamal—Red Garland, though Garner played on all four beats whereas Garland punctuated just twice per measure. (See Miles Davis chapter for more on Garland and John Coltrane chapter for more on Tyner.)

**Milt Buckner** (1915–1977) influenced pianists of the 1940s through his use of block chording, or the so-called *locked-hands style* which is a method of voicing a chord and making the top note of it the melody note.[21] Buckner created piano solos that were like the four-, five-, and six-part horn voicings in band arrangements of the 1930s and 40s. It was as though each finger was playing the part that a saxophone would ordinarily play. This is in contrast to a style in which one hand plays a single melodic line while the other occasionally plays chords. In locked-hands style, the pianist uses both hands as though they were locked together, all fingers striking the piano keyboard at the same time. During the late 1940s and early 50s, Lennie Tristano, George Shearing, Ahmad Jamal, Oscar Peterson, and others used this technique, as did Red Garland and Bill Evans in the late 1950s. During the 1960s, many pianists, including McCoy Tyner, made use of block chording. Each pianist's technique of block chording, particularly the voicings, was a distinctive aspect of his style.

To briefly review jazz piano history up to this time, remember that **James P. Johnson**, Willie "The Lion" Smith, and other early pianists **had contributed the stride style. Earl Hines was a pioneer in playing horn-like lines. Meade Lux Lewis**, Pinetop Smith, Cow Cow Davenport, and others **introduced boogie woogie. Tatum had explored reharmonization.** And now **Milt Buckner had added locked-hands style** to the list of alternatives that were available for pianists to select.

**Guitar**   During the swing era, guitar was beginning to be viewed as more than a timekeeping member of the rhythm section. Prior to the emergence of Django Reinhardt, most jazz guitarists had played brief, chorded solos which were technically quite modest by comparison with piano and horn solos. That changed with the appearance of Charlie Christian (1916–1942) and Django Reinhardt. **Charlie Christian** mastered what was then the almost unexplored world of electric guitar. (Listen to Christian with the Benny Goodman sextet on "Blues Sequence From Breakfast Feud" in SCCJ.) His long, swinging, single-note-at-a-time lines gave solo guitar the

[21]Lionel Hampton, *Steppin' Out*, MCA 1315, LP, 1942–44

stature of a jazz horn.[22] Some of his phrasing had the fluid swing and freshness of tenor saxophonist Lester Young (see Chapter 8). Christian is cited as an influence by almost all modern jazz guitarists who matured before the jazz-rock era. His style provided the foundation for that of Wes Montgomery, who was the single most influential jazz guitarist of the 1960s. This extended Christian's impact long past the 1940s and well into the 1980s, particularly by way of George Benson, who was one of many contemporary players to be influenced by Montgomery and who became a significant influence himself.

**Django Reinhardt** (1910–1953) was a Belgian Gypsy guitarist who was based in France, played mostly within Europe, and visited America only once. However, his recordings were available in America, and he was held in high esteem by American guitarists, especially during the swing era. Reinhardt had a technical command of his guitar that rivalled the speed attained by players of less difficult instruments. Reinhardt's playing was ornate and flamboyant, with a prominent vibrato.[23] He combined the spirited flavor of Gypsy music with the equally spirited sound of jazz. (Listen to his 1934 version of "Dinah" in SCCJ-R.) His lines could have the intelligence of a master composer, or they could be merely a sequence of flourishes.

To examine these two important guitarists in more depth, let's contrast their approaches, element by element.

1) Christian's pace within solos was usually steady, whereas Reinhardt's was uneven and marked by sporadic flashiness;

2) Christian's lines were hornlike, whereas Reinhardt's were more pianistic;

3) Most of Christian's recordings were made with amplified hollow-body guitar, whereas most of Reinhardt's were made on unamplified hollow-body guitar;

4) Christian's tone was usually round and soft, whereas Reinhardt's possessed a bite and was often metallic sounding;

5) Christian drew more from blues tradition, whereas Reinhardt drew from Gypsy music and the French Impressionist composers Ravel and Debussy;

6) Christian used long patterns of swing eighth notes, whereas Reinhardt used somewhat jumpier sequences, with interruptions for drawn-out pitch bends;

7) Christian preferred eighth-note lines, whereas Reinhardt often leaned more toward triplet and sixteenth-note lines;

8) Christian used very little vibrato, whereas Reinhardt employed vibrato as a key element in his approach.[24]

[22]Charlie Christian *Genius of the Electric Guitar*, CBS 40846 (CL 652), CD/LP, 1939–41; *Benny Goodman Sextet Featuring Charlie Christian: 1939–41*, CBS 45144, LP/CD.

[23]Django Reinhardt *Parisian Swing*, GNP Crescendo 9002, LP; *Djangologie U.S.A.*, DRG Swing 8420, CD/LP set, 1936–40. For more about his life, see Charles Delaunay's biography *Django Reinhardt* (Cassell, 1961; reprinted by DaCapo).

[24]For transcriptions and analyses of Christian and Reinhardt solos, see Fred Sokolow's *Solos for Jazz Guitar* (Carl Fischer, 1988; available from Carl Fischer Music Store, 54 Cooper Square, NY, NY 10003). For more Reinhardt transcriptions, see Stuart Isacoff's *Django Reinhardt* (Amsco, 1978).

**Popular Appeal**    A number of jazz musicians were well known to the general public during the swing era. For instance, Benny Goodman, Count Basie, and Duke Ellington were as widely known then as rock stars were known during the 1960s and 70s. Though they may have been recognized more as leaders of dance bands than as jazz musicians, they were certainly known by larger slices of the public than knew the jazz giants of subsequent eras. Even some of their soloists were familiar to large segments of the public, not just to the tiny cults that later became the audience for jazz. The big bands employed hundreds of jazz musicians, so it was better than subsequent eras for musicians to find work as performers. Unfortunately, however, most of the jobs with big bands did not include extensive opportunities to improvise because these groups worked largely from written arrangements. Opportunities to improvise were generous in combos, yet steady employment in jazz combos was difficult to find.

Before we can answer the question of whether jazz itself was popular during the swing era, we first need to decide which definition of jazz to use. (Review Chapter 2 for ways to define jazz.) If music is jazz solely by association with the jazz tradition, the swing era was a great period for jazz. And if music is jazz whenever it swings, this era clearly marks a peak for jazz. But if we employ a strict definition and require jazz to be improvised, the matter becomes sticky. In examining the extent of appeal generated by swing style jazz, we need to comment briefly on the style and size of bands, and to make some distinctions between big bands that emphasized improvisation and big bands that did not.

Though big band was the most common group size during the swing era, big band style does not necessarily mean swing style. There were jazz-oriented big bands before and after the swing era, and many of them sounded distinctly unlike swing bands. Nor does big band style necessarily mean jazz style. Ten to sixteen musicians was the standard size of bands that played all kinds of popular music—not just jazz—during the 1930s and 1940s, just as three to eight musicians was the standard size of bands playing all kinds of popular music thereafter. In addition, during the swing era, journalists and musicians drew distinctions between bands that emphasized jazz improvisation and those that did not. For example, the very popular Glenn Miller big band was a swinging group, and it had a handful of hit records that contained brief jazz improvisations. But, the Miller band emphasized pretty arrangements and vocals more than improvised jazz solos. Therefore, despite its swinging qualities, the band was sometimes classified as a *sweet band* (as in the popularity polls conducted by *Down Beat* magazine in 1940 and 1941). This distinguished it from the *hot band* or *swing band* classification that was reserved for bands such as Count Basie's and Duke Ellington's which placed more emphasis on improvised solos.

With these distinctions in mind, note that this textbook discusses only the most jazz-oriented bands and soloists from the 1930s and 40s big band scene. During the swing era, there were many big bands, though most were not primarily concerned with jazz improvisation. Some of the jazz improvisations that historians have heralded were well known by the public. But most were not. In other words, swing fans were far from unanimous in their awareness and appreciation of jazz improvisation. For jazz groups of later eras, improvisation was the primary focus of each performance. But for most big bands of the swing era, even the jazz-oriented ones, improvisation was not necessarily a first priority.

A few other points should be considered before the era is described as a successful period for jazz:

1) A significant portion of swing era hits contained vocals, and many of those that did not have singing were at least based on songs that listeners had previously learned by way of a vocal rendition. This alerts us to consider that *jazz value might not have provided the primary appeal of the pieces. The popularity of those pieces might just reflect the same appeal that songs have had throughout history.*

2) Most of the swing era hits that were jazz-oriented contained only a few solo improvisations, often only one.

3) The amount of improvisation in most swing era hits was small, sometimes being only sixteen measures, rarely more than a thirty-two bar chorus.

4) The construction of improvised solos in most hits was melodically conservative.

The big band sound, the context for the improvisations, and the tunes being improvised upon were certainly popular during the swing era. And some listeners no doubt focused primarily on the improvised solos themselves. But *for a large portion of the public, the improvisations were incidental, perhaps inconsequential, segments of the performances.* Jazz historians, being jazz fans themselves, like to believe that the adulation of the swing big bands was specifically directed at jazz qualities of the music. It is more likely, however, that most fans were more entranced by the overall effect of big band music and its rhythm than by the inspiration and skill with which solo improvisers devised their lines. Traditionally in most kinds of music only a small segment of the audience has been attracted by nuances of form and innovations of method. There may have been no greater love for the qualities of jazz improvisation during the swing era than there was in any other era, though more improvisers were in the public eye than at any other time in jazz history.

Like rock combos since the 1950s, *one of the most important functions for swing bands of the 1930s and 40s was to provide dance music.* Jazz functioned as dance music more during the swing era than it did thereafter. Another similarity with popular rock combos is that swing era big bands usually used elaborate costumes, showy staging, and most of them routinely carried several singers. The visual appeal of the performance, including the personality and good looks of the singers, was a primary attraction for a sizable portion of the audience. Only occasionally during the swing era were jazz musicians given paid opportunities to perform just for listening, as later became customary. In summary, the popular success of jazz bands during the swing era was partly a result of their appeal to the eyes and feet of fans instead of to the ears alone.

# CHAPTER SUMMARY

1)  Swing differs from early jazz in
    a)  greater use of arrangements
    b)  less emphasis on ragtime-like compositions
    c)  rejection of collective improvisation in favor of solo improvisation
    d)  increased use of string bass instead of tuba
    e)  greater swing feeling, achieved by increased use of swing eighth-note patterns
    f)  increased use of high-hat cymbals
    g)  replacement of banjo with guitar
    h)  big band rather than small-group instrumentation
    i)  saxophone becoming the predominant instrument
2)  Important big bands were led by Fletcher Henderson, Duke Ellington, Count Basie, Benny Goodman, and Jimmie Lunceford.
3)  The most influential saxophonists were Coleman Hawkins, Lester Young, Benny Carter, and Johnny Hodges.
4)  The most influential pianists were Art Tatum and Teddy Wilson.
5)  Tatum possessed phenomenal speed and was known for spontaneously changing and increasing chords in pop tune accompaniments.
6)  Wilson was known for his grace and his streamlining of jazz piano style.
7)  Nat Cole influenced modern jazz piano style by reducing left-hand activity and making right-hand lines more horn-like.
8)  Pianist Milt Buckner perfected the technique of harmonizing melody lines in a block-chord "locked-hands" fashion.
9)  Roy Eldridge paved the way for modern jazz trumpeter Dizzy Gillespie by improvising fiery, saxophone-like lines on trumpet.
10) Django Reinhardt and Charlie Christian were the most prominent guitarists of the swing era.

# chapter 7
# DUKE ELLINGTON

Duke Ellington (1899–1974) is one of the most outstanding figures in jazz history. His contributions were threefold: he was significant as a bandleader, a pianist, and a composer-arranger. He led one of the first jazz-oriented big bands, beginning in 1923, and only his death in 1974 ended the band's run. **Ellington's group was the most stable and longest-lived big band in jazz history,** with some musicians remaining for twenty to thirty years at a stretch. His musicians had strong, unique styles of their own; together they made up an all-star unit. Many of their improvisations were so good that they became permanent parts of the band's pieces, as though composed. Ellington so cleverly and imaginatively mixed and matched their work with his that no other band in jazz history could claim the breadth or depth of repertory possessed by this group. Ellington was also a distinctive jazz pianist. His greatest contribution, however, stems from his being **the single most creative and prolific composer-arranger in jazz history.** Ellington wrote far more than two thousand compositions as well as enormous numbers of arrangements and rearrangements for them. He began composing and arranging before 1920 and continued productively until his death. Recording more than any other jazz group, the Ellington band and its leader's compositions can be heard in hundreds of 78 r.p.m. recordings and long-play albums.

**Pianist**  As a piano soloist, during the first three decades of his career Ellington performed often in the stride-style tradition of James P. Johnson. Thereafter, he usually performed in his own original style, which was still quite percussive though much more economical than the stride style. (Listen to his solo in the fourth chorus of "Cottontail" in the JAZZ CLASSICS CASSETTE.) His playing sparkled and popped with unerring swing feeling, and Ellington became distinguished for unusual harmonies and voicings. (Listen to his improvised accompaniments on "Transblucency" in the JAZZ CLASSICS CASSETTE.) As an accompanist, Ellington was highly praised by

**106**

his sidemen for the vitality and imagination he displayed in finding original ways to frame their phrases, always in a spare and complementary manner. His comping was full of spirit, and his timing and taste were near perfect.

**Composer**    Ellington wrote many tunes, often in collaboration with his sidemen. Some of these became popular songs when lyrics were added, and a few were hits when recorded by singers apart from the Ellington band. Among his best-known songs are "I'm Beginning to See the Light," "Solitude," "Mood Indigo," and "Don't Get Around Much Anymore."[1] Nearly all jazz musicians have played at least one Ellington tune during their careers, and many have devoted entire albums to his music, more albums than have honored any other jazz composer. During the 1980s, an entire Broadway revue, "Sophisticated Ladies," was devoted to Ellington's music. Ellington also wrote hundreds of three-minute instrumentals, a few of which we will study in this chapter. (These instrumentals averaged three minutes because that was the standard length of one side of a 78 r.p.m. record.) **Some of his short instrumentals paint musical portraits of famous personalities** such as the great stride pianist Willie "The Lion" Smith ("Portrait of the Lion") and the comedian Bert Williams ("Portrait of Bert Williams"). **Others paint musical pictures of places** such as "Warm Valley" and "Harlem Airshaft," or sensations such as "Transblucency" (both found on the JAZZ CLASSICS CASSETTE).

Ellington also wrote many longer pieces, and **he is widely acclaimed for having taken jazz into the format of "extended works,"** as these longer pieces are termed. (His "Creole Rhapsody" is in SCCJ, and his "Diminuendo in Blue and Crescendo in Blue" is in the revised SCCJ.) His most respected long work is "Black, Brown, and Beige," a fifty-minute tone parallel to the history of the American Negro.[2] Some of his longest works were film scores; a favorite of musicians and critics is his music for "Anatomy of a Murder," the Otto Preminger movie starring Jimmy Stewart.

[1]Not all of Ellington's pieces represent exclusively his own ideas. Often Ellington incorporated or developed a phrase or countermelody he had heard improvised by one of his musicians. Many works were written by Ellington's musicians or in collaboration with them: for instance, with Bubber Miley, "East St. Louis Toodle-o" and "Black and Tan Fantasy"; with Johnny Hodges, "I'm Beginning To See The Light" and "Don't Get Around Much Anymore"; with Ben Webster, "Cottontail"; with Otto Hardwicke and Lawrence Brown, "Sophisticated Lady". Trombonist Juan Tizol wrote "Caravan," "Bakiff," "Conga Brava," and "Perdido," a melody often mistakenly credited to Ellington. Barney Bigard adapted ideas of New Orleans clarinetist Lorenzo Tio and ended up contributing one strain for Ellington's "Mood Indigo." Then, from 1939 until 1967, Ellington worked closely with pianist-composer-arranger **Billy Strayhorn** (1915–1967). The two men collaborated on countless pieces, and their styles were so similar that most listeners and even the band members themselves rarely knew which of them contributed the larger portion of any particular arrangement. (And, upon later listening, sometimes Strayhorn himself could not recognize what aspects of a piece were his and what came from Ellington.) However, "Satin Doll" is thought to be Strayhorn's, and there are several pieces usually credited just to Strayhorn, the most famous of which is "Take the 'A' Train" which replaced "East St. Louis Toodle-o" as the band's theme. Musicians are especially fond of Strayhorn's ballads "Chelsea Bridge" and "Lush Life," the last of which he wrote while still in high school, long before he joined Ellington.

[2]*Black, Brown & Beige*, RCA Bluebird 6641, CD/LP set, 1944–46

*"It don't mean a thing if ain't got that swing"*
- Hodges (sax)
- Ivy

Ellington (piano)
Cootie (trumpet)
Hodges (sax)

*" Concerto for Cootie "
written by D.E.*

Duke Ellington's 1942 band, the mobile laboratory for explorations in varied tone colors and the multilayered weaving of improvisation and composition. *Left to right:* Otto Hardwicke, Juan Tizol, Harold Baker, Ray Nance (directly behind Ellington, who is seated at the piano), Harry Carney (directly behind Betty Roche), Rex Stewart, Johnny Hodges (alto sax), Ben Webster (tenor sax), Chauncey Haughton, Joe "Tricky Sam" Nanton (trombone), Wallace Jones (trumpet), Lawrence Brown (trombone), and Sonny Greer (drums). (*Photo courtesy of Frank Driggs*)

### Arranging Style

*"Harlem Airshift"
Nanton (trombone)
Barney (clarinet)
tape*

One of Ellington's greatest skills as an arranger was that of **capitalizing on the uniquely personal sounds of individual players.** Most arrangers occasionally showcase particular musicians, and in doing so they write parts that are well suited to the performer's talents as well as writing accompaniments that complement those talents. Ellington did this, too; but he also went much further. When writing for a group of instruments, he did not write parts anonymously assigned to the instruments (lead trumpeter, second trumpeter, third trumpter, etc.), as most arrangers do. Ellington instead **wrote parts suited to the peculiar sounds and capabilities of each player in his band** (Cat Anderson, Cootie Williams, Rex Stewart, etc.). Each one of Ellington's musicians had a highly individual sound. So, even when they were not playing solos, their own unique way of sounding each pitch was considered before giving them a particular part to play. For example, if a chord were scored for three trumpets, Ellington remembered the particular tone quality that each of his trumpeters ordinarily produced for each note in that chord, and he distributed the parts of the chord to them to create the overall color he wanted that chord to have

**Listening Guide to "Transblucency: A Blue Fog You Can Almost See Through"**

Composed by Lawrence Brown and Duke Ellington; recorded July 9, 1946; available on the JAZZ CLASSICS CASSETTE, Side One.*

This recording is included to provide a fuller picture of Ellington's talents than what is conveyed by "Cottontail" and "Harlem Airshaft." "Transblucency" exemplifies Ellington's practice of painting musical pictures, in this case the combined impression of translucency and the color blue. The composition was developed from "Blue Light," an earlier Ellington band number containing a twelve-bar blues theme composed by Lawrence Brown, the trombonist who performed it. This piece displays Ellington's imagination for unique blends of tone colors. Here he combines instrumentalized voice (wordless vocal) with instruments drawn from different sections of the band (voicing across sections). The result is a facet of Ellington's repertory that is not hard-driving or wild. It is pretty and might remind you of opera more than jazz.

This performance allows us to explore controversies about how jazz is defined. To call this a "jazz" recording stretches the conventional definition in two ways. First, it demonstrates Ellington's practice of constructing pieces in which the only improvisation of consequence lies in the accompaniment. Second, the piece is unusual because swing feeling is elicited here only by accompaniment rhythms, and only quite subtly.

Unlike most of Ellington's pieces, "Transblucency" does not use his entire band. Though he assigns the melody to his saxes in the fifth chorus, Ellington otherwise dispenses with everyone except clarinetist Jimmy Hamilton, trombonist Lawrence Brown, and bassist Oscar Pettiford. In a few choruses, the voice of Kay Davis is added as an instrument. Piano chording can sometimes be heard faintly in the background.

*Elapsed Time*

## INTRODUCTION

Piano flourishes by Ellington. At the end of the piano phrases, the bass ever so slightly anticipates the down beat of the first chorus by playing a string of triplets.

0' 04"

## FIRST CHORUS

Slow, 12-bar blues. The melody line is harmonized, clarinet on the lowest notes, cup-muted trombone on the middle notes, and voice on the highest notes. Piano occasionally fills in the pauses between phrases and provides counteractivity underneath sustained tones. Pizzicato bass tones provide timekeeping. Note the triplets played just before the first and third beats of selected measures. This bass style is called "decorative-two" because of the four beats in the measure, it emphasizes only two, sometimes decorated by preceding notes. Bass is joined by piano in some of the decorations here.

0' 38"

## SECOND CHORUS

Muted trombone plays the melody, accompanied by bass playing in a decorative-two style. Notice the absence of piano.

0' 47"

*Fifth Measure*

Trombone is joined by voice and clarinet in harmony, and then the three instruments continue together. Bass accompaniment alternates between decorative-two and walking style.

1' 12"

*Twelfth Measure*

A piano flourish introduces the next chorus.

*The score and parts for "Transblucency" are available from King Brand Products; 333 West 52nd St.; Suite 1400; New York, NY 10019.

| Elapsed Time | |
|---|---|
| 1' 14" | **THIRD CHORUS**<br>Clarinet and voice duet, accompanied by walking bass and piano chording. The harmony created by the two sounds, clarinet and voice, occasionally seems to create a third sound. Ellington has assigned pitches so cleverly that their combination has generated additional pitches, technically termed "heterodynes." |
| 1' 47" | *Final Two Measures*<br>As the melody instruments end their phrase, Ellington improvises a melodic little phrase, which he plays twice. |
| 1' 51" | **FOURTH CHORUS**<br>Sax section softly plays the flowing melody in unison while voice provides a countermelody. Piano chording accompanies softly on each beat. |
| 2' 27" | *Twelfth Measure*<br>Piano re-enters percussively, as though splashing bright colors on the subdued portrait. |
| | **ENDING** |
| 2' 35" | Vocal, trombone, and clarinet join piano. |
| 2' 44" | A marching of piano chords, then a high-register piano chord is emphatically sounded. Its ringing concludes the piece, accompanied by a very soft, arco bass note. |

in his arrangement. In addition, sometimes he would have one trumpeter use a mute, another with no mute, and a third player sound his note with an odd tone quality that only he was able to extract from the trumpet. Ellington scored this way for saxes and trombones, too. This is one reason that performances of Ellington's arrangements never sound like Ellington's band when they are played by other musicians.

Another notable skill employed by Ellington is what we call **voicing across sections of the band.** While most arrangers, including Ellington, routinely write passages that pit the sound of one section of the band, such as the saxes, against another section of the band, such as the brasses (as in "Cottontail" on the revised SCCJ), Ellington often wrote passages to be played by combinations of instruments drawn from different sections of the band. The most famous example of this can be heard in his 1930 recording of "Mood Indigo."[3] There he voiced clarinet with muted trumpet and muted trombone, thus combining instruments from three different sections of the band: trumpet section, trombone section, and saxophone section. In his 1940 recording of "Concerto for Cootie" (in SCCJ), he voiced pizzicato bass notes in unison with the horns. This was unusual because bass was primarily assigned to a timekeeping role as a member of the rhythm section and rarely played melody parts. (Listen to JAZZ STYLES CASSETTE, side 1, for examples of pizzicato bass melody lines.)

[3]*Early Duke Ellington*, RCA Bluebird 6852, CD/LP, 1927–34; for technical analyses of Ellington's composing and arranging, see pages 318–57 in Gunther Schuller's *Early Jazz* (Oxford, 1968) and pages 46–157 in his *The Swing Era* (Oxford, 1989).

**Listening Guide for "Cottontail"**

Available on the JAZZ CLASSICS CASSETTE, side 1; on CD in the Revised SCCJ.*

"Cottontail" is Ben Webster's new tune using the chords of Gershwin's "I Got Rhythm." The "melody in harmony" that he wrote for the sax section in the fifth chorus has some of the melodic and rhythmic character of a modern jazz improvisation. It remains one of the band's most famous passages (Ellington wrote the arrangement)—its popularity with musicians rivaling that of Webster's often-quoted solo on this recording. Technically known as a "saxophone soli," when it is performed, the whole sax section traditionally stands up.

| Elapsed Time | | | |
|---|---|---|---|
| | **FIRST CHORUS** | | |
| | A | Melody stated by saxes and trumpets with rhythm accompaniment. |
| 7" | A | Sax and trumpet melody repeated with trombone section figures added to the accompaniment. |
| 15" | B | Saxes ask musical questions, muted trumpet (Cootie Williams) answers them. |
| 25" | **FOUR-MEASURE INTERLUDE** | | |
| | | This consists of a brief conversation between the sax section and brass section with rhythm accompaniment. |
| 29" | **SECOND CHORUS** | | |
| | A-A | Improvised tenor sax solo (Ben Webster) with rhythm accompaniment. |
| 44" | B | Tenor sax talks for a while with the brass section. |
| 53" | A | Brass depart, leaving tenor to continue improvising with rhythm section accompaniment. |
| 1' 00" | **THIRD CHORUS** | | |
| | A-A | Tenor continues improvisation accompanied by rhythm section. |
| 1' 16" | B | Brass return to talk more with tenor sax. |
| 1' 25" | A | Brass depart and tenor finishes his improvisation accompanied by rhythm section. |
| 1' 32" | **FOURTH CHORUS** | | |
| | A-A | Brass play alone, accompanied by rhythm section. |
| 1' 48" | B | Improvised baritone sax solo (Harry Carney) accompanied by rhythm section. |
| 1' 56" | A | Improvised piano solo accompanied by rhythm guitar, bass, and drums. |
| 2' 03" | **FIFTH CHORUS** | | |
| | A-A-B-A | Sax section plays the whole chorus accompanied by rhythm section. |

*The score and parts for "Cottontail" are available from King Brand Products; 333 West 52nd St.; Suite 1400; New York, NY 10019

**Elapsed Time**

**2′ 34″**

| | | |
|---|---|---|
| **SIXTH CHORUS** | | |
| | A-A | Brass section shouts questions and sax section answers, accompanied by rhythm section. |

**2′ 51″**

| | B | Brass section takes over loudly with rhythm section steaming forward. |
|---|---|---|

**2′ 58″**

| | A | Saxes and trumpets play the melody to its end with rhythm section accompaniment and no trombones. |
|---|---|---|

Another unique method employed by Ellington was placing a **wordless vocal** in an arrangement. Sometimes called *instrumentalized voice*, this became identified with Ellington, and he was applauded for its use in his 1927 recording of "Creole Love Call"[4] and his 1946 recording of "Transblucency" (in the JAZZ CLASSICS CASSETTE).[5]

Other unique sounds typical of Ellington originated with his jobs playing for floor shows at New York nightclubs, which wanted exotic "jungle sounds." Partly to satisfy the clubs's demand for exotic sounds, and partly because of his own admiration for New Orleans jazz, he scored for the **growl style** associated with trumpeter Bubber Miley and trombonist Joe "Tricky Sam" Nanton. (For examples, listen to JAZZ STYLES CASSETTE, side 2, the beginning of "Cottontail" in the JAZZ CLASSICS CASSETTE, and "East St. Louis Toodle-o" in SCCJ.) For the same reasons, he liked to use wailing clarinets. He employed unusual voicings for his clarinets, and his musicians played them very intensely. The effect was highly emotional. Years after he finished his work at these floor shows, he continued to employ these exotic sounds, and they contributed to his group's reputation as a "hot band."

**Clarinet**   Clarinetists **Barney Bigard** (1906–1981) and his successor Jimmy Hamilton provided pivotal voices in the Ellington sound. (Listen to JAZZ STYLES CASSETTE, side 2 to familiarize yourself with the sound of the clarinet.) Both men doubled on tenor saxophone in the band, but their best-known contributions were their solo improvisations on clarinet. Bigard was from New Orleans, and he brought the expressive, soulful approach of his hometown music to Ellington's sophisticated conception of big band style. His long, legato lines swooped and darted through the band sound. Some of his best improvisations are found in Ellington's 1940 recording of "Harlem Airshaft" (in the JAZZ CLASSICS CASSETTE). You might also enjoy studying his improvisation on "Clarinet Lament," a 1936 performance that Ellington built around Bigard.[6]

[4]See footnote 3.     [5]See footnote 2.

[6]Get the JAZZ CLASSICS CASSETTE, and listen to Bigard's work while you study the listening guide of "Harlem Airshaft" on the next few pages and/or the written parts and score that is available for musicians, transcribed and distributed by Dave Berger, through King Brand Products; 333 West 52nd St.; Suite 1400; New York, NY 10019. Berger also distributes the score and parts for "Clarinet Lament." Also see Bigard's autobiography, *With Louis and the Duke* (Oxford, 1986).

**Jimmy Hamilton** (b. 1917) is an original improviser with a style that is less intense than Bigard's. His sound is well manicured and lighter than that of most swing era clarinetists. Hamilton's conception is precise and articulate, with a cool, floating quality that suggests modern jazz. Listen to his duet with wordless vocal on "Transblucency" (in the JAZZ CLASSICS CASSETTE) as well as the albums he recorded with Ellington in 1956 for Bethlehem records, or the Columbia albums the band made during the late 1950s.[7]

**Trumpet**     **Bubber Miley** (1903–1932) and **Cootie Williams** (1910–1985) were known for their *growl style of trumpet playing and the unorthodox use of rubber plunger mutes.* (See the illustration on page 390, and listen to side 2 of the JAZZ STYLES CASSETTE, and to the beginning of "Cottontail" on the JAZZ CLASSICS CASSETTE.) Miley was one of Ellington's leading soloists from 1924 to 1929. His style furnished a playful voice for such classic Ellington recordings as the 1927 "Creole Love Call" and "East St. Louis Toodle-o."[8]

Like Bubber Miley, Cootie Williams was also influenced by the bluesy New Orleans style that placed so much emphasis on spontaneously altering the size, shape, and quality of instrument sounds to achieve a vast range of musical effects. Williams was Miley's successor in the Ellington band, serving as Ellington's main trumpet soloist. He played with the band from 1929 to 1940, rejoining in 1962 and remaining until Ellington's death in 1974. Ellington composed his 1936 "Echoes of Harlem" and his 1940 "Concerto for Cootie" to feature Williams. (Listen to "Concerto for Cootie" in SCCJ. You can also hear Williams on "In A Mellotone" in SCCJ.)

Some of Cootie Williams's most inventive playing was captured in Ellington's 1940 recording of "Harlem Airshaft." (Study the listening guide in this chapter while you listen to the piece in the JAZZ CLASSICS CASSETTE.) His work on this number demonstrates his unique mastery of wide-ranging techniques for colorfully altering pitch and tone quality. (See Chapter 4 for explanation and illustrations of tone quality and pitch manipulation techniques, and listen to side 2 of JAZZ STYLES CASSETTE for examples of the doit, smear, drop, and scoop.) Williams is very calculating in the way he reaches notes, but his sound projects a great naturalness rather than cold calculation. His solos on this piece combine a diversity of techniques reminiscent of blues singing with its searing sensuality and peaks of raw excitement. Another Williams asset is a keen sense of rhythm. Sometimes his notes are so well timed and percussively executed that the listener might assume Williams to be a drummer. In these regards, Miley and Williams helped Ellington create a more New Orleans-like sound than was common to other New York bands of the same era. Incidentally, it is no coincidence that Ellington's "jungle style" was

---

[7]*Ellington at Newport*, CBS 40587 (CL 934), CD/LP, 1956; *Festival Session*, CBS 36979, LP, 1959. See *Instructor's Resource Manual & Discography* for more.

[8]Miley co-authored both. Listen to "East St. Louis Toodle-o" in SCCJ. Its title (sometimes spelled "todalo") is pronounced "toad-el-low," to indicate a kind of dance that imitates the low, tired, dragging walk that the term originally referred to; it is not a farewell expression.

developed during the 1920s when New Orleans-born clarinetists Sidney Bechet and Barney Bigard and bassist Wellman Braud all played with the band.

Ellington had distinctive trumpet soloists besides Miley and Williams. But the only one to achieve much fame outside the Ellington band was **Clark Terry** (b. 1920), one of the band's leading brass soloists from 1951 to 1959. One of the first Ellington sidemen to show the influence of modern jazz, Terry invented a unique style that bridged the gap between the swing era approaches and the new bop style of Dizzy Gillespie. He displayed seemingly effortless command over his horn, no matter how fast or intricate a figure he chose to improvise. He had a talkative, swinging style that is easy to recognize, spontaneously unfolding catchy melodic lines and projecting an enthusiasm that seemed to bubble through every note. (See footnote 7.)

Clark Terry also helped popularize the fluegelhorn, a kind of oversized cornet, played in much the same manner as the cornet and trumpet. (See Figure 7.1, and listen to side 2 of JAZZ STYLES CASSETTE.) Most players stress the instrument's naturally soft, dark tone quality, but Terry achieves a brassy edge, combined with a distinct fullness that is round and vibrant. No other brass player sounds like Clark Terry. (A large portion of his solos on Ellington records feature his fluegelhorn, not his trumpet.)

**Figure 7.1.** Listen for the fluegelhorn on side 2 of the JAZZ STYLES CASSETTE, where you will have the opportunity to compare its sound with that of the trumpet.

**TABLE 7.1.  A Few of the Musicians Most Significant to Ellington**

| Clarinet and Saxophones | Trumpet | Trombone |
|---|---|---|
| | Louis Metcalf | Joe "Tricky Sam" Nanton |
| Rudy Jackson | Bubber Miley | Lawrence Brown |
| Barney Bigard | Arthur Whetsol | Juan Tizol |
| Jimmy Hamilton | Cootie Williams | Britt Woodman |
| Russell Procope | Rex Stewart | Quentin "Butter" Jackson |
| Willie Smith | Taft Jordan | Tyree Glenn |
| Otto Hardwicke | Ray Nance | Buster Cooper |
| Johnny Hodges | Willie Cook | |
| Harry Carney | Cat Anderson | **Bass** |
| Ben Webster | Clark Terry | |
| Al Sears | Harold "Shorty" Baker | Wellman Braud |
| Paul Gonsalves | Johnny Coles | Billy Taylor |
| Harold Ashby | Money Johnson | Jimmy Blanton |
| | | Oscar Pettiford |
| **Drums** | **Piano** | Wendell Marshall |
| | | Jimmy Woode |
| Sonny Greer | Duke Ellington | Aaron Bell |
| Louis Bellson | Billy Strayhorn | Ernie Shepard |
| Sam Woodyard | | |
| Rufus Jones | | |

**Saxophone**   Johnny Hodges (1907–1970) was the best known of Ellington's sidemen. He often played position of lead alto, the saxophonist whose parts contain the highest notes (usually the melody notes instead of the harmony notes) and who leads the other saxophonists in timing and interpretation of written sax parts. His solos and his style in leading the sax section were a vital part of the Ellington sound from 1928 until 1970 (with an absence from 1951 to 1955). Nearly every Ellington album features Hodges, and he was such a consistent player that almost all these recordings contain representative examples. Hodges produced such an unusually deep and lush tone that his recorded alto sax has sometimes been mistaken for tenor saxophone, as on "Prelude to a Kiss," in the JAZZ CLASSICS CASSETTE. He is particularly known for a remarkable way of gliding from note to note very gradually and smoothly, almost as if his instrument were equipped with a slide, like a trombone. This technique is called *portamento*, but jazz musicians generally refer to it as *smearing*. Hodges used it to great effect in ballad playing. Ellington wrote numerous pieces to take full advantage of this well-known Hodges approach.[9]

[9]Listen to Hodges play "Passion Flower" in *Jive at Five*, New World 274, LP.

**TABLE 7.2.    A Few of the Many Saxophonists Influenced by Johnny Hodges**

| | | |
|---|---|---|
| Tab Smith | Willie Smith | Woody Herman |
| Louis Jordan | Ben Webster | Eddie Vinson |
| Earl Bostic | Bobby Plater | John Coltrane |
| Johnny Bothwell | Charlie Barnet | Jan Garbarek |

An exquisite sense of timing was crucial to the Hodges style. Hodges was a master of subtlety in tonal inflections, and his syncopations were especially well timed. Pre-1942 Hodges often displayed flashy double-timing like Sidney Bechet, his primary influence. But after the mid-1940s, Hodges tended to lay back very deliberately, no matter what the tempo. Hodges is possibly the **most influential jazz alto saxophonist to come out of the swing era** (see Table 7.2), and he is one of very few jazz saxophonists to ever have hit records. He is particularly known for a romantic approach to ballad playing that has pervaded American music so much that hundreds of saxophonists are imitating it without even knowing who Johnny Hodges was. (His work on "Prelude to a Kiss" typifies that side to his talents.)[10]

Aside from Hodges, Benny Carter was the most widely respected jazz alto saxophonist of the swing era. Perhaps we can learn more about both styles by comparing them. Both players had rich, full-bodied tones, but they had different rhythmic styles. Carter tended to divide the beat precisely and evenly into legato eighth notes. Hodges had a more natural rhythmic feel. The placement of notes in relation to the beat was far less obvious in Hodges's playing. Though Carter and Hodges both imparted a luxurious feel to their playing, Carter was more obvious in his constructions, Hodges more subtle. Hodges had a strikingly original way of placing accents. His manner set him apart from most swing and early jazz players. Despite how imaginative it was, he made it sound easy and natural. Both Hodges and Carter swung easily, but Carter had more of a classical feeling to his rhythmic conception. (Get SCCJ and compare Carter on "I Can't Believe That You're in Love with Me" with Hodges on "In a Mellotone.")

**Harry Carney** (1910–1974) is usually considered the father of the jazz baritone saxophone, which almost puts him in a class with Coleman Hawkins, the father of the jazz tenor saxophone, a soloist who influenced Carney. (Listen to JAZZ STYLES CASSETTE, side 2, to familiarize yourself with differences in sound among alto, tenor, and baritone saxophones. Listen to Carney improvise the bridge of the fourth chorus in "Cottontail" on the JAZZ CLASSICS CASSETTE.) Carney's ensemble

---

[10]Hodges not only influenced premodern players, he also had an impact on such modern saxophonists as Eddie Vinson, John Coltrane, and Eric Dolphy. Listen to Coltrane's recording of "Theme for Ernie," on his *Soultrane* album, Fantasy OJC-021 (Prestige 7142), CD/LP, 1958, in which his ballad style recalls the fullness of sound and timing of ornaments that Hodges refined. Even as recently as the 1970s and 80s, there was a continuation of the Hodges influence: saxophonist Jan Garbarek cited Hodges as a source for his own style.

playing in Ellington's sax section often vied with that of Hodges himself, providing a rock-solid foundation, often as important as that of the band's bassist. Inspired by Carney's playing, Ellington occasionally scored for baritone sax lead. No other baritone saxophonist has been able to match the size and strength of Carney's mammoth, rich sound. He also played clarinet and bass clarinet for Ellington, each of which, in his hands, became a strong, thick-toned voice in the Ellington ensemble. Although primarily an ensemble player, Carney occasionally received feature numbers, including "Serious Serenade," "Frustration," and "Chromatic Love Affair."

Ellington's most outstanding tenor saxophone soloists were **Ben Webster** (1909–1973) and **Paul Gonsalves** (1920–1974). Webster played with the band from 1940 to 1943, then again in 1948 and 1949. Before Webster began full-time in 1940, Ellington had no major tenor sax soloist. But thereafter, he always featured someone in that position, and it was Gonsalves from 1951 to 1974. Though some of Webster's style was inspired by Coleman Hawkins and Johnny Hodges, Webster should not be viewed as derivative. He established his own distinctive approach. Ben Webster's improvisations were frequently so tuneful that the listener might assume they were not improvised, but were prepared for the written arrangement. In fact, the sense of completeness in Webster's phrases has so greatly affected musicians that Webster phrases are sometimes quoted by other improvisers. Webster provided a model for how to play ballads, one trademark of which was delaying, ever so slightly, the delivery of crucial notes in a phrase—sometimes giving the listener a sense of suspense that was resolved when those crucial notes were finally sounded. Webster's playing gives the listener an overall impression of being laid back. Together with his richly textured, breathy tone, and slow, marked vibrato, Webster used his delayed deliveries to create a very sensual effect. Some of his work in this vein resembles the way a crooner delivers the tones of a love song. Consistent with his sense of drama, Webster was known for changing the character of the music within a single solo by transforming his sound from smooth and soothing to hoarse and rasping. Like other Ellington soloists, Webster seemed capable of making his manipulations of tone and timing at least as important as the choice of notes themselves. Sometimes Webster made listeners hear the rush of air in his breath, not just the saxophone tone that it ordinarily energized. Partly because of the carefully marked vibrato that accompanied it, listening to that rush of air by itself could be an intimately moving experience. In fact, Webster's style is often described as romantic.[11] Apart from Coleman Hawkins and Lester Young, Ben Webster was the most influential tenor saxophonist of the swing era, and he influenced saxophonists in eras as far-flung as the 1940s and the 1970s.[12]

[11]After studying "Cottontail" in the JAZZ CLASSICS CASSETTE, a good place to continue acquaintance with Webster is Ellington's *The Blanton-Webster Band*, RCA Bluebird 5659, CD/LP. To sample the rasping side of his musical character, listen to "Raincheck," "Mainstem," and "Blue Serge." For the crooning side, listen to "All Too Soon," and his obbligato behind the muted brass in the second chorus of "I Don't Know What Kind of Blues I've Got."

[12]Webster influenced Charlie Ventura, Paul Gonsalves, Eddie "Lockjaw" Davis, Archie Shepp, Lew Tabackin, Bennie Wallace, and Scott Hamilton, to name a few.

**Paul Gonsalves** (1920–1974) was Ellington's main soloist during the 1950s, 60s, and 70s. He began as a disciple of Ben Webster but also showed hints of the Don Byas approach. Despite these roots, Gonsalves had a unique style, one aspect of which was a very unusual and fluid conception for medium- and up-tempo playing. He had a soft, diffuse tone without edge, but despite the softness of his tone, his playing had an intense urgency to it. Moreover, Gonsalves's choice of notes was so unusual that it is amazing he could deliver them as fluently as he did. And his solos invariably had substance. Though he was relatively unknown to all but Ellington band fans, Gonsalves ranks among the originators in the history of jazz tenor styles. His solos lent Ellington's music an excitement and a modern character without detracting from the warmth and sincerity that had traditionally been such prime traits of the Ellington sound. Gonsalves played with Ellington from 1951 until his death in 1974.[13]

**Trombone**  Trombonist **Joe "Tricky Sam" Nanton** (1904–1946) was **master of the growl style.** From 1926 until 1946, Nanton gave Ellington a provocative sound to use in arrangements. His most common mute was the rubber suction cup from a plumber's plunger, which he used to open and close the bell of the trombone. An additional mute, alternately termed a *pixie mute* or a *buzz mute*, was secured inside the trombone to lend a buzz to the horn's tone. With his plunger and his unorthodox blowing, Nanton came very close to pronouncing words with his trombone ("ya..ya"). (Listen to his work in "Harlem Airshaft" in the JAZZ CLASSICS CASSETTE.)[14]

**Lawrence Brown** (1907–1988) was one of the first trombonists of the swing era to play with a very smooth, large, consistent sound. His tone added a great deal of body to the sound of Ellington's trombone section, and he played with an aggressive solo style. Ellington wrote "Blue Cellophane" and "Golden Cress" as features for Brown. (Listen to his muted work in the JAZZ CLASSICS CASSETTE's "Transblucency," for which Brown himself composed a theme.)

**Drums**  There have been only a few drummers in the long history of the Ellington band: Sonny Greer (1919–51), Louis Bellson (early 1950s), Sam Woodyard (mid-1955 to 1966), and Rufus Jones (1968–73). Others played briefly with the band but remained relatively unknown. Ellington's drummers have performed a relatively unobtrusive role in creating the band's sound. Although all were swinging drummers, none were as historically significant as Jo Jones with Count Basie, Max Roach

[13]Listen to "Take the 'A' Train" on Ellington's 1950 *Hi-Fi Ellington Uptown*, reissued as *Uptown*, CBS 40836 (CL 830), CD/LP, 1950–51 and the Gonsalves solos on *Ellington at Newport, Newport 1958, Cosmic Scene,* and *Festival Session.* Also see footnote 7.

[14]Listen to Nanton's work in SCCJ on "Blue Serge" and "Harlem Airshaft" (also in the JAZZ CLASSICS CASSETTE). For explanation of his methods, see *Plunger Techniques* by Al Grey and Mike Grey (Second Floor Music, 1987), available from Second Floor Music, 130 West 28th Street, NY, NY 10001.

with Charlie Parker, Elvin Jones with John Coltrane, or Tony Williams with Miles Davis. All Ellington drummers were primarily timekeepers, and there are four eras of this role in the band, reflecting Ellington's adapting to the strengths of four different drummers.

The classic tradition of **Sonny Greer** (1903–1982) lasted for more than half of the band's fifty-year history. Ellington's first drummer, Greer used drumming techniques in the manner of early jazz drummers. He kept time on the snare drum with sticks and brushes, often switching instruments for a new chorus or to accompany a new soloist. (Listen to how hard he swings on "Cottontail" in the JAZZ CLASSICS CASSETTE.) During the 1940s, he sometimes moved his timekeeping rhythms to high-hat. And, in a few isolated instances near the end of his tenure with the band, he played ride rhythms on the ride cymbal. Though simple in style and technique, Greer was dramatic in presentation. His equipment included tympani, gongs, vibraphone, and wood blocks. (On the JAZZ STYLES CASSETTE, woodblock is demonstrated in side 1, vibraphone in side 2.) He contributed exceptionally adept accompaniments in "Echoes of Harlem."

A new era began in 1951 when Greer left and **Louis Bellson** (b. 1924) joined Ellington. In his two-year stay, Bellson changed the technique and technology of Ellington drummers. Like a bop drummer, Bellson kept time primarily with his ride cymbal, using his left hand to play musical punctuations on his snare drum. Blessed with enviable technique, he was a precise and tasteful accompanist. Bellson also added a second bass drum and small tom-tom to his drum kit. (See chapter 3 for illustrations.) Ellington took advantage of Bellson's capabilities by giving him solos. The recording of Bellson's solo on his own composition "Skin Deep" in *Hi-Fi Ellington Uptown* furnished a means for demonstrating sound quality in high-fidelity equipment that was just then becoming popular.[15] The piece became a crowd-pleasing part of Ellington's repertory. Bellson's showmanship revitalized the band's appeal when all big bands were experiencing a declining audience size and Ellington was particularly low due to the temporary loss of Lawrence Brown and Johnny Hodges. After Bellson left, his successors on the drum throne were required to perform the often-requested "Skin Deep." They also employed the modern timekeeping techniques that Bellson used.

Replacing Bellson was **Sam Woodyard** (1925–1988), Ellington's drummer of eleven years. Woodyard supplied a special spark to the band. His style was hard-swinging and unrelenting. Woodyard was not complicated or flashy. He simply established a groove, and by playing so hard and so passionately, he musically challenged the band members to swing equally hard. The records Ellington made with Woodyard have an insistence in their swing feeling that is unmatched by his records from any other period. (See footnote 7.) For many Ellington fans and a number of Ellington's musicians themselves, Woodyard was the all-time favorite drummer for the band.

The Bellson-Woodyard contributions to Ellington's style were expanded by **Rufus Jones** (b. 1936) between 1966 and 1973. In addition to fulfilling the tradi-

[15]*Uptown*, CBS 40836 (CL 830), CD/LP, 1950–51

tional duties for his position, Jones was notable for also devising original rhythms to fit music in African, Latin American, and oriental flavors for suites that Ellington composed on his world tours during this era.[16] Jones played rhythms that were new to the Ellington sound, and, as in the earlier years, Ellington incorporated his drummer's ideas.

**Bass**    Over his long career of bandleading, Ellington had several outstanding bassists. (Note Oscar Pettiford's work on "Transblucency" in the JAZZ CLASSICS CASSETTE.) The greatest standout among them was **Jimmy Blanton** (1918–1942), who played with the band from 1939 to 1941. Blanton shattered traditional conceptions of jazz bass playing with his impressive instrumental proficiency and musical imagination. **His cleanly executed melodic solos demonstrated that, in the hands of a virtuoso, the string bass can contribute much more to a band than just timekeeping.** Though Blanton's sound was also a powerful component of Ellington's rhythm section, he is best known for the ways Ellington capitalized on his unique talents. (Listen to how hard his walking swings in "Harlem Airshaft" and "Cottontail" on the JAZZ CLASSICS CASSETTE.) **Ellington spotlighted Blanton in solo roles, and he arranged parts for Blanton's bass that were like horn parts.** Blanton played melody on Ellington's 1940 "Jack the Bear," played in unison with ensemble horn lines in the 1940 "Concerto for Cootie," and soloed on the 1940 "Sepia Panorama."[17] Blanton profoundly shaped the next twenty years of jazz bass styles. For instance, the idea of voicing pizzicato bass with horns was later used in arrangements by Thad Jones, and it became quite common in modern jazz of the 1970s and 80s, especially in jazz-rock fusion bands. Few of the musicians who use the technique today realize that Ellington had been doing it in 1940.[18]

**Listening Guide for "Harlem Air Shaft"**

Available on the JAZZ CLASSICS CASSETTE, side 1; on CD in *The Blanton-Webster Band* (RCA 5659).*

**INTRODUCTION**
*Four Measures*

The brass instruments call in harmonized, sustained tones, and the saxes respond with an active figure. Then, while they are silent, you can hear a full rhythm section sound with prominent rhythm guitar, walking bass, and Sonny Greer using brushes on snare drum for timekeeping. Ellington inserts a brief piano fill.

*The score and parts for "Harlem Air Shaft" are available from King Brand Products; 333 West 52nd St.; Suite 1400; New York, NY 10019.

[16]*Far East Suite*, RCA Bluebird 7640, CD/LP, 1966; *Latin American Suite*, Fantasy 8419, LP, 1968; *Afro-Eurasian Eclipse*, Fantasy 9498, LP, 1971; *The Ellington Suites*, Pablo 2310-762, LP, 1971–72, has "Goutelas" and "Uwis" suites.
[17]These are in *The Blanton-Webster Band*, RCA Bluebird 5659, CD/LP set, 1940–41.
[18]Listen to Blanton's work on "Concerto for Cootie" in SCCJ and on "Pitter Panther Patter" in *Jive at Five*, New World 274.

*Four Measures*

Saxes now have the lead. Listen to their harmony. Notice more piano fills.

*Four Measures*

Now the trombones take the lead for about a measure and a half with the baritone saxophone coming in with a response at the end of that second measure. Trombones instantaneously return for two measures of punching figures. (Ellington called them his "pep section" because of the function these figures served.)

## FIRST CHORUS

(The remainder of the piece follows a repeating, thirty-two bar A-A-B-A form.)

A  Saxes play a simple melody in unison while muted trumpets repeat a more complex background figure in harmony as an answering embellishment.

A  Repeat the above.

B  Saxes take the foreground by playing a harmonized part in the high register, alternating their calling with trombonist Joe "Tricky Sam" Nanton responding in plunger-muted growl style. Then saxes tie it up with a quick, little, low-register figure at the end of the bridge.

A  Repeat of A, but this time, with a tie-it-up figure from the trumpets to get ready for the upcoming stop-time. Sonny Greer ends the figure by striking a cymbal, then quickly grabs it to prevent ringing. (The sound and timing of this technique is effective for closing a musical idea in an abrupt way.)

## SECOND CHORUS

A  *First Four Measures*

The rhythm section stops playing. This creates a four-measure stop-time break. The saxes use it to play a high-register, harmonized part with sustained tones. This evokes a suspended feeling, partly because the rhythm section is no longer stating each beat, and partly because there is suddenly very little movement in the sax sound. Then Sonny Greer uses sticks to play rolls and rim shots, "breaking things up," to enhance the band's transition from the suspension to a rough and tumble trumpet solo by Cootie Williams.

*Second Four Measures*

Cootie Williams opens his trumpet improvisation by percussively stating the same note repeatedly in an off-the-beat fashion. He creates excitement by using the high register and by shaking his tones as they end. Notice the sax activity underneath Williams.

A  Same strategy as for the first A section. Williams continues with more repeated and shaken high notes, and Greer uses cymbal clasp to end this section of the piece.

B  Sax part becomes more intricate, repeating a climbing figure while Williams continues his improvisation against sax lines. Greer's cymbal clasp ends this section, too.

1' 25"        A   Same strategy as for the first and second A sections. Notice how Williams dramatically slides down from his last high note. Listen to Greer's activity. It almost constitutes another line added to those of Williams and the saxes.

1' 35"

## THIRD CHORUS

A   Trombones play a harmonized melody in the foreground while clarinetist Barney Bigard improvises around it, and saxes play yet another series of interjections underneath. Pay attention to Bigard's swoops and the New Orleans flavor of his playing. Imagine having to invent all those lines and colorations to spontaneously embroider the trombone and sax parts without clashing. This is not an ordinary jazz solo.

1' 45"        A   Same formula as for the first A section.

1' 54"        B   Trumpets join trombones to repeat a sustained tone while Bigard continues his improvisation and answers them. Saxes make periodic interjections. Listen to Bigard's shake at the end of the bridge.

2' 04"        A   Same formula as for the first A section. Note Bigard's blue notes. Drummer Sonny Greer becomes louder, striking high-hat while it is in partially opened position.

2' 14"

## FOURTH CHORUS

(Though it starts softly, this chorus gets louder and louder, gradually raising excitement for the climax.)

A   Band softly plays a syncopated, low-register melody while Bigard's solo from the previous chorus overlaps into the first three measures of this one, with him entering clarinet's lower register. Listen to the rhythm guitar and Jimmy Blanton's driving bass sound. They are easier to hear now that the band has quieted down. Cootie Williams begins a muted trumpet solo where Bigard leaves off. Williams starts softly, but, as he proceeds, note how he changes the size and texture of his tone.

2' 23"        A   Pay attention to the finish of his solo in which Williams taps out the last four notes in the manner of a drummer.

2' 33"        B   The arrangement builds excitement by increasing loudness, adding instrumental activity, and going higher in register. The band calls, and Bigard repeatedly climbs out of the ensemble sound in response. The brass sound becomes clearer. Note the relationship between Bigard's improvised figures and the composed ones being played by the rest of the band. It all fits together despite the spontaneity.

2' 43"        A   Saxes call, and the brass answer repeatedly. A high level of excitement is reached. Bigard is improvising throughout the sounds of several written themes. Saxes repeat a new riff of their own. Bigard enters the high register. Brass begin repeating a new riff. The several levels of competing activity threaten to result in chaos by becoming more and more active at the end, but it all is resolved just in time to prevent an explosion. It ends with the brass sustaining a chord and the baritone sax sounding a low note at the finish.

**Diversity of the Ellington Band**

Diversity and breadth characterized Ellington's music. The pieces in Ellington's repertory were filled with variety, and the lack of repetition within each piece is striking. When compared with the arrangements of most swing bands, Ellington's possessed a larger number of different themes and rhythmic figures. Accompanying figures also reflected a greater assortment than was customary. (Listen to "Harlem Airshaft" in the JAZZ CLASSICS CASSETTE, and note the many layers of activity.) In addition, Ellington's overall repertory was also diverse. It was so varied that we can summarize it as a number of separate books:[19]

1) An impressionistic book with arrangements that place more emphasis on orchestral colors and shading than on swinging. Examples from his pre-LP work include "On a Turquoise Cloud" and "Transblucency" (in the JAZZ CLASSICS CASSETTE). From his LP work, examples include portions of *Anatomy of a Murder* and *Paris Blues*.

2) A book of romantic ballads. Examples from his pre-LP work include "Daydream," "Prelude to a Kiss," and "Sophisticated Lady." Examples from his LP work include the albums *Ellington Indigos* and *At the Bal Masque*.

3) An exotic book. Examples from his pre-LP work include "Caravan," "Flaming Sword," and "Bakiff." Examples from his LP work include entire albums such as *Latin American Suite* and *Togo Brava Suite*.

4) A concert book in which each piece is a long work with much less improvisation than was usually found in his music. Examples in his pre-LP work include "Reminiscing in Tempo," "Black, Brown, and Beige," and "Deep South Suite." Examples in his LP work include *Such Sweet Thunder*, *Suite Thursday*, and *A Drum Is a Woman*.

5) A book of concertos in which each piece frames the style of one Ellington sideman. Examples from his pre-LP period include "Clarinet Lament" (Barney Bigard), "Echoes of Harlem" (Cootie Williams), and "Boy Meets Horn" (Rex Stewart). Examples from his LP work include "Cop-Out" (Paul Gonsalves) and "Lonesome Lullaby" (Ray Nance).

6) A book of music for sacred concerts, a context that brought Ellington to present new shows and use choirs, new vocal soloists, organ, and dancers. It inspired writing for different moods, such as that of prayer. It also inspired extensive lyrics (*Duke Ellington's Concert of Sacred Music* and *Second Sacred Concert*).

7) A book of swinging instrumentals, each with jazz solos, catchy ensemble themes, and punching accompaniment figures. These are evident throughout Ellington's career: "Rockin' in Rhythm" from the 1930s, "Main Stem" and "Cottontail" (in the JAZZ CLASSICS CASSETTE) from the 1940s, "Launching Pad" from the 1950s.

The vastness of Duke Ellington's contributions becomes all the more evident when you have explored a few hundred selections and then realize that Ellington

---

[19]See *Instructor's Resource Manual & Discography* for list of albums containing each example.

also composed several operas, a couple of ballets, and about ten musical shows. We should also remember that, though various editions of the band did portray a somewhat different character because of changes in personnel and repertory, the Ellington band never really fell into any fixed category—early jazz, swing, or modern. It was always unique. Ellington created a jazz classification that was practically his own. And, not only did the Duke Ellington band present a very colorful and richly diverse repertory, it maintained creative energy for more than four decades. The influence of Ellington's music was also vast. Other big bands were influenced by his writing style as early as the 1940s.[20] There was an echo of Ellington in the work of several outstanding arrangers of the 1950s and 60s.[21] Revivals of Ellington's work were frequent during the 1980s, and even a few avant-garde bands and composers of this period drew upon Ellington for inspiration.[22] Ellington's piano style influenced a number of players, including the highly individualistic modernists Thelonious Monk and Cecil Taylor.

Johnny Hodges, Duke Ellington's star alto saxophonist, shown here in 1961 at age 55. (*Photo by Lee Tanner*)

[20]Charlie Barnet's and Woody Herman's bands imitated the Ellington band, and many other bandleaders had hits when they recorded Ellington pieces.

[21]Gil Evans, Charles Mingus, George Russell, Clare Fischer, Sun Ra, Lalo Schifrin, Thad Jones, Toshiko Akiyoshi, to name a few.

[22]James Newton, Anthony Davis, The World Saxophone Quartet and others

## CHAPTER SUMMARY

1) Duke Ellington is among the most significant of all figures in jazz history.[23]

2) As a pianist, Ellington derived his approach from the stride style of James P. Johnson, though he also devised an original style with which he set the pace and mood for his pieces and ornamented the solos of his musicians.

3) Ellington was outstanding as a bandleader, maintaining a large ensemble from the early 1920s until his death in 1974, with many musicians remaining for more than twenty years at a stretch.

4) Ellington composed more than two thousand pieces, frequently in collaboration with his musicians.

5) A few of Ellington's pieces became popular songs, such as "Satin Doll," "Mood Indigo," and "I'm Beginning to See the Light."

6) Some of Ellington's pieces represent pioneering efforts in jazz for exceeding the brief time limit that was standard. Among his "extended works" is "Black, Brown and Beige," a tone parallel to the history of the American Negro.

7) As an arranger, Ellington was distinctive for
   a) using a diversity of themes within a single piece
   b) voicing across sections
   c) using wordless vocals
   d) writing parts particularly for the unique capabilities of each musician
   e) mixing improvised parts with prewritten parts

8) From 1939 to 1941, Ellington showcased bassist Jimmy Blanton, who revolutionized traditional concepts of the bassist's role by playing melody lines by himself and with the horn sections of the band.

9) Ellington's most famous saxophonists were Johnny Hodges and Ben Webster.

10) Ellington featured brass players who were masters of the growl style: trumpeter Cootie Williams and trombonist Joe "Tricky Sam" Nanton.

11) During the 1950s, Ellington featured saxophonist Paul Gonsalves and trumpeter Clark Terry.

[23]For more about Ellington's life, see his autobiography, *Music Is My Mistress* (Doubleday, 1973; reprinted by DaCapo), Stanley Dance's *The World of Duke Ellington* (Scribner, 1970), Mercer Ellington's *Duke Ellington In Person* (Houghton-Mifflin, 1978), and James Lincoln Collier's *Duke Ellington* (Oxford, 1987). Often the recorded performances cited in this chapter are not available on in-print, American albums. Pages 395–399 are therefore devoted to helping you find hard-to-locate records, and the *Instructor's Resource Manual* for this text lists numerous Ellington albums, each with sufficiently detailed content annotations to allow the user to track down sources for the performances discussed here. (The manual is available to instructors via Prentice-Hall sales representatives or by writing College Marketing, Prentice-Hall, Englewood Cliffs, NJ 07632. Please use official college letterhead in all correspondence.)

# chapter 8
# THE COUNT BASIE BANDS

Musicians generally agree that the most swinging big band was that of Count Basie (1904–1984). When compared with all others from the swing era, Basie's never seemed out of breath nor the least bit frantic, and it always seemed to swing more. Basie led a big band almost continuously from 1937 until his death. Every edition of the band had at least two players who made important contributions to jazz history, and some editions had four or five.

**Basie the Pianist**

Basie was originally a stride-style pianist who derived much of his inspiration from Fats Waller. (For a demonstration of stride style, listen to the JAZZ STYLES CASSETTE. For examples of Fats Waller, listen to SCCJ.) Basie's touch was unique among jazz pianists. It was very light and extremely precise. His choice of notes was near perfect, and his impeccable sense of timing was equivalent to a good drummer's. In fact, Basie originally began his musical career as a drummer, not a pianist. Succinct and compact statements are hallmarks of Basie's style. When he soloed, he artfully used silence to pace his lines. During the 1930s and 40s, Basie was a prominent soloist with his own bands. After the 1940s, he featured himself less in the band's arrangements, though the sound of his piano playing usually set the mood and tempo for each piece. Often an entire selection went by without the audience hearing more from Basie than his piano introduction and a few "plink plink" interjections.

**Basie's Rhythm Section During the Late 1930s and Early 40s**

Basie led the first rhythm section in jazz history that consistently swung in a smooth, relaxed way. That famous rhythm section consisted of Basie himself (piano), Freddie Green (rhythm guitar), Walter Page (string bass), and Jo Jones (drums). Before reading about their virtues, review the JAZZ STYLES CASSETTE, side 1, to familiarize yourself with the sounds of *walking bass*, *bass drum*, *high-hat cymbals*, *wire brushes*, and *ride rhythms*. Then listen to the final one third of side 2 to familiarize

Count Basie Band, perhaps the best of swing era big bands. Its rhythm section style and the innovative sax style of Lester Young bridged the gap between swing and modern jazz. They are pictured here at the Famous Door, in 1938, with (from left to right): Walter Page (bass), Jo Jones (drums), Freddie Green (guitar), Count Basie (piano), Bennie Morton (trombone), Herschel Evans (tenor sax), Buck Clayton (trumpet with cup mute), Dicky Wells (hidden), Earle Warren (alto sax), Ed Lewis (hidden), Harry "Sweets" Edison (trumpet), Jack Washington (playing alto with his baritone sax at side), Lester Young (tenor sax). (*Photo courtesy of Frank Driggs*)

*"Jumping @ the Woodside"*

*"Lester Leaps In"*
Basie
Lester (t. sax)
— walking bass (top)

yourself with *rhythm guitar*. The virtues of the Basie rhythm section are evident in their "Taxi War Dance" and "Lester Leaps In" on the JAZZ CLASSICS CASSETTE. Listen to it while you read the following outline.

Among the special qualities of the Basie rhythm section were:

1) An excellent sense of tempo.
2) The ability to keep time and swing consistently without using a hard-driving, pressured approach.
3) Quiet, relaxed playing, which conveyed a feeling of ease.
4) Placing a fairly even amount of stress on each beat instead of on every other beat.
5) Emphasis on buoyancy rather than intensity.

**127**

Bassist **Walter Page** (1900–1957) contributed:

1) A supple walking bass sound. (He is considered to be one of the first masters of the walking style.)
2) A strong, articulated sound with life in it, not the dead thud common to many premodern bassists.
3) Playing all four beats evenly.
4) Balancing his sound to mesh smoothly with piano, bass, and guitar.

Guitarist **Freddie Green** (1911–1987) was noted for:

1) His crisp strokes on unamplified guitar that sounded his rhythm chords with unerring steadiness and propulsive swing feeling.
2) His close coordination with bass and drums.

The style of drummer **Jo Jones** (1911–1985) was distinguished for:

1) Precise playing without any stiffness. Jones offered a loose, assured manner.
2) Quieter bass drum playing than was common in the swing era. Jones sometimes omitted bass drum entirely, sometimes using it only for off-beat accents.
3) Quiet use of wire brushes on high-hat.
4) Ride rhythms played on high-hat continuously as the apparatus was opening and closing. Jones let his cymbals ring prominently between strokes, thereby creating a sustained sound that smoothed the timekeeping pattern instead of leaving each stroke as an abrupt sound. Jones also maintained this conception when using sticks to play ride rhythms on a suspended cymbal (also known as a "top cymbal").

The Basie rhythm section was noted for achieving a balance among the sounds of each member. The four parts were so smoothly integrated that one listener was inspired to compare the effect to riding on ball bearings. If you listen carefully to recordings of the band, you will notice that it is unusual for one member to stick out. Guitar, bass, and drums are all carefully controlled to avoid disturbing the evenness and balance of sound.

In Basie's interjections, jazz piano had the bounce, syncopation, and flexibility of what became known as **comping**. Though he did not invent it, Basie is so thoroughly associated with comping that he might as well have. His comping was very sharp and lively. Basie comped so well and with such relaxed swing feeling that he provided the most-used model for it. (To further understand comping, listen to the JAZZ STYLES CASSETTE, middle of side 1, then listen to "Lester Leaps In" on the JAZZ CLASSICS CASSETTE, and ignore the sax solo while focusing solely its piano accompaniment.) To elevate Basie's comping to its proper place in history, note that even by the mid-1940s many excellent jazz pianists had not learned to comp, though Basie had been doing it for over ten years. They continued in the predominant styles

**TABLE 8.1. Musicians of the 1930s Kansas City Scene (birthplaces in parentheses)**

| | |
|---|---|
| Count Basie (New Jersey) pianist-bandleader | Buddy Tate (Texas) saxophonist |
| Gus Johnson (Texas) drummer | Pete Johnson (Missouri) pianist |
| Walter Page (Missouri) bassist-bandleader | Charlie Parker (Kansas) saxophonist-composer |
| Lester Young (Mississippi) saxophonist | Jay McShann (Oklahoma) pianist-bandleader |
| Buck Clayton (Kansas) trumpeter | Budd Johnson (Texas) saxophonist-composer |
| Andy Kirk (Kentucky) bandleader-saxophonist | Hot Lips Page (Texas) trumpeter |
| Herschel Evans (Texas) saxophonist | Jo Jones (Illinois) drummer |
| Eddie Durham (Texas) guitarist-arranger-trombonist | Jesse Stone (Kansas) pianist-arranger-bandleader |
| Buster Smith (Texas) saxophonist | George Lee (Missouri) saxophonist-pianist-bandleader |
| Bennie Moten (Missouri) pianist-bandleader | Harlan Leonard (Missouri) saxophonist-bandleader |
| Mary Lou Williams (Georgia) pianist-composer-arranger | |

of the 1920s and 30s, accompanying by 1) stride style, 2) playing a chord on each beat in the manner of a rhythm guitarist, or 3) playing flowery countermelodies and embellishments. But by the end of the 1940s, the evolution of jazz had been permanently nudged along by Basie's example, and comping had become central to modern jazz.

**Arrangements**   During the 1920s and 30s there was a thriving jazz scene in Kansas City, Missouri.[1] A number of historically significant jazz musicians worked there and are associated with "Kansas City style jazz," though few were born there (see Table 8.1). Their music was not as glossy or elaborate as that of their New York counterparts; it was lighter and more relaxed. This accounts, at least in part, for its exceptional swing feeling.

**Listening Guide for ''Taxi War Dance''**

Available on the JAZZ CLASSICS CASSETTE, side 1; on CD in the Revised SCCJ.

**INTRODUCTION**

*Four Measures*
   Basie's rolling left-hand figure with no bass, rhythm guitar, or drums accompaniment.

[1]For more about Kansas City style, see Nathan Pearson's *Goin' to Kansas City* (University of Illinois Press, 1987), pages 279–317 of Gunther Schuller's *Early Jazz* (Oxford, 1968) and pages 222–262 of Schuller's *The Swing Era* (Oxford, 1989).

| | |
|---|---|
| *Elapsed Time* | |

*Elapsed Time*

**0′ 4″**    *Four Measures*

Trumpets punctuate in unison with piano as a set-up for the piece, all the while trombones are "walking" underneath them, and Jo Jones has begun playing ride rhythms.

**0′ 9″**    **FIRST CHORUS**

A    Tenor saxophonist Lester Young opens his improvisation by quoting the first line of "Ol' Man River." Listen to Freddie Green playing rhythm guitar, Walter Page playing walking bass lines, and Jo Jones playing ride rhythms on opening and closing high-hat. Basie stops his rolling figures and moves to comping.

**0′ 18″**    A    First four bars Basie returns to his rolling piano figures underneath continuation of Young's solo. After that, Basie returns to comping. Note how Young's lines relate to these changes in accompaniment patterns.

**0′ 27″**    B    Continuation of Young with rhythm section accompaniment.

**0′ 37″**    A    Continuation. (This is a good example of Basie's big band functioning as a combo, something they were particularly distinguished for.)

**0′ 46″**    **SECOND CHORUS**

A    *First Two Measures*

A return to the brass figure that originally opened the piece. Basie's rolling piano figure is also included. The walking trombones are missing, however.

**0′ 50″**    *Remaining Six Measures*

Trombonist Dicky Wells improvises a solo. He is very melodic and sounds like he is poking fun. Pay attention to how he bases his solo on simple phrases to be developed by repetitions and slight alterations. Note how clear and logical his lines are.

**0′ 57″**    A    Solo continues with rhythm section accompaniment, again returning to a small combo performance.

**1′ 07″**    B    Continuation.

**1′ 16″**    A    Continuation.

**1′ 25″**    **THIRD CHORUS**

A    *First Four Measures*

Band returns, Basie abandons comping for patterned figures. Trombones call and trumpets respond.

**1′ 30″**    *Second Four Measures*

Tenor saxophonist Buddy Tate begins a solo improvisation. He can be distinguished from Lester Young by having a coarser tone that is darker and has faster vibrato. Tate's execution is less poised and has less swinging rhythmic feeling.

**1′ 35″**    A    Repeat of layout for first A section.

**1′ 44″**    B    Piano solo by Basie. Notice his light touch, use of the piano's upper register, and impeccable timing.

*Elapsed Time*

**1′ 53″**

A *First Four Measures*

Trombones call and trumpets respond.

**1′ 58″**

*Second Four Measures*

Tate solos with a rapid pattern repeated.

**2′ 03″**

**FOURTH CHORUS**

A *First Four Measures*

Basie plays a boogie woogie figure underneath ensemble figures by trumpets and trombones.

**2′ 07″**

*Second Four Measures*

Tenor saxophonist Lester Young returns with a light feeling. He plays an upper register solo.

**2′ 12″**

A *First Four Measures*

Repeat of the pattern used in the first A section, but this time Young enters his solo space early by using a bit of the four-measure lead-in to get started.

**2′ 17″**

*Second Four Measures*

Young completes his solo remaining with upper register tones.

**2′ 21″**

B  Basie solos in the upper register, playing lightly and staccato.

**2′ 31″**

A *First Four Measures*

Trombones call, and the trumpets respond with a simple, syncopated figure which uses alternation of muted and unmuted sound in rapid succession.

**2′ 36″**

*Second Four Measures*

Lester Young improvises by rapidly alternating his tone quality.

**2′ 40″**

**ENDING**

*Two Measures*

Stop-time solo break for Count Basie.

**2′ 43″**

*Two Measures*

Stop-time solo break for Lester Young (this is called "trading two's").

**2′ 45″**

*Two Measures*

Walking bass unaccompanied.

**2′ 47″**

*Two Measures*

Sticks on drums unaccompanied.

*Two Measures*

Brass play a tie-it-up figure, and Jo Jones strikes a cymbal and grabs it abruptly to prevent it from ringing. This technique effectively closes up the sounds and provides a dramatic means for ending a performance.

Kansas City style was not based on the interweaving lines of the collectively improvised New Orleans style. Arrangements in this style were based instead on short musical phrases called *riffs* that are repeated again and again. Riffs serve two functions. Sometimes they are theme statements, and sometimes they are backgrounds for improvised solos. A few of these riffs were written down, but many were created spontaneously during a performance ("off the top of someone's head"), learned by ear, and kept in the heads of the players. Arrangements of this kind are called **head arrangements**, and they are basic to the Kansas city *riff band style*. (Listen to a combo example of the riff style in "Lester Leaps In" on the JAZZ CLASSICS CASSETTE. Follow the Listening Guide provided later in this chapter. For a best-selling big band example of this style, listen to the final strains of "One O'Clock Jump" at the beginning of the JAZZ CLASSICS CASSETTE.)[2]

**Lester Young**

Many of the best jazz trumpeters and saxophonists of the 1930s and 40s played with Count Basie at one time or another. Basie's most notable soloist during this period was tenor saxophonist **Lester Young** (1909–1959). This musician was so good that he was nicknamed "Pres" (or "Prez"), short for president of tenor saxophone players. Young played lines which were fresher and more smoothly swinging than those of any previous improvisers. He paved the way for modern saxophone tone color, vibrato, rhythmic conception, and phrasing. **Young offered a clear alternative to the heavy tone, fast vibrato, and complicated style of Coleman Hawkins.** (See Table 8.3.) Young's light tone, slow vibrato, and loping, buoyant phrases became the model for an entire generation of saxophonists who often copied his solos note for note (see Table 8.4).

To explore Lester Young's improvisatory style, let's compare it with the approach that Coleman Hawkins devised. Often, where Hawkins seems to be chugging, Young seems to be floating. Hawkins makes improvisation sound like hard work, yet Young makes it seem less taxing. Whereas Hawkins accents hard and often directly on main beats, Young is more subtle. Furthermore, Young may tend to accent off-beats and lightly stress portions of beats that make his lines swing with ease. Though Young's playing was not as intricate as Hawkins's, Young's melodic ideas were at least as advanced. But because Young's ideas are so clear and so gracefully stated, the advanced level of his thinking may not be as apparent as for Hawkins's.

[2]Many riff-based pieces that band members at first identified only by numbers were eventually given names and composer credits. Count Basie's "One O'Clock Jump" and "Jumpin' at the Woodside" are best-selling examples (available in the record anthology *Big Band Jazz*, Smithsonian 2200). Listen to this style in "Moten Swing," as recorded by the Bennie Moten band in 1932 and available now in SCCJ. The piece is a thirty-two measure A-A-B-A form that is based on the chord progression to a song called "You're Driving Me Crazy." This recording will also give you a peek into Kansas City jazz history because Count Basie had been a member of both Moten's band and the Blue Devils, led by bassist Walter Page. These two groups eventually fused to become Basie's first Kansas City band.

**TABLE 8.2. A Few of the Many Musicians Who Have Been Important to Basie**

| Trumpet | Saxophone | Composer-Arranger |
|---|---|---|
| Carl Smith | Lester Young | Eddie Durham |
| Hot Lips Page | Herschel Evans | Andy Gibson |
| Buck Clayton | Jack Washington | Dicky Wells |
| Harry "Sweets" Edison | Tab Smith | Buck Clayton |
| Shad Collins | Earle Warren | Buster Harding |
| Emmett Berry | Buddy Tate | Don Redman |
| Clark Terry | Wardell Gray | Jimmy Mundy |
| Thad Jones | Lucky Thompson | Don Kirkpatrick |
| Joe Newman | Don Byas | Ernie Wilkins |
| Al Aarons | Illinois Jacquet | Thad Jones |
| Sonny Cohn | Serge Chaloff | Frank Foster |
| Snooky Young | Paul Gonsalves | Frank Wess |
| Wendell Culley | Eddie "Lockjaw" Davis | Neal Hefti |
|  | Frank Foster | Quincy Jones |
| **Trombone** | Eric Dixon | Benny Carter |
|  | Jimmy Forrest | Billy Byers |
| Dicky Wells | Billy Mitchell | Chico O'Farrill |
| Benny Morton | Frank Wess | Sammy Nestico |
| Vic Dickenson | Marshall Royal | Al Grey |
| Al Grey | Charlie Fowlkes |  |
| Henry Coker | Bobby Plater | **Drums** |
| Curtis Fuller | Paul Quinichette |  |
| Benny Powell |  | Jo Jones |
|  | **Bass** | Shadow Wilson |
|  |  | Gus Johnson |
|  | Walter Page | Sonny Payne |
|  | Eddie Jones | Louis Bellson |
|  | Buddy Catlett | Harold Jones |
|  |  | Butch Miles |
|  |  | Rufus Jones |

(Listen to Young play what he came to consider one of his own best solos: "Taxi War Dance" on the JAZZ CLASSICS CASSETTE.)[3]

Young's approach contrasted with Hawkins's preference for running through the set of notes contained in each chord (musicians call this "arpeggiating"). Instead of playing every note in every chord, as Hawkins often did, Young was more cool and concise. In fact, **Young sometimes purposely ignored the notes in the chords or chose other tones which, when combined with the chord tones, considerably altered the**

---

[3]In the opening to "Taxi War Dance," Young plays notes that purposely clash with the notes of Basie's rolling piano figure, then the harmonic conflict resolves when Basie comes out of the rolling figure. Another clever Young solo is his improvisation on Basie's 1939 "Jive at Five," available in *Jive at Five*, New World 274, a collection found in most in libraries and schools. This particular solo is especially intriguing because it foreshadows the fluffy tone and melodic approach Stan Getz was to display eight years later.

*"Body & Soul"*

**TABLE 8.3.  Comparison of Coleman Hawkins with Lester Young**

|  | Coleman Hawkins | Lester Young |
|---|---|---|
| tone quality | warm | cool |
|  | dark-colored | light-colored |
|  | heavy-weight | light-weight |
|  | full-bodied | hollow |
| rate of vibrato | medium to fast | slow |
| swing feeling | early jazz style | more relaxed and graceful than Hawkins |
| intricacy of solos | much | less than Hawkins |
| tunefulness of improvisations | little | much |
| came to prominence with | Fletcher Henderson (1923–34) | Count Basie (1936–44) |
| influenced | Herschel Evans | Charlie Parker |
|  | Chu Berry | Wardell Gray |
|  | Dick Wilson | Stan Getz |
|  | Ben Webster | Lee Konitz |
|  |  | Sonny Stitt |
|  |  | Woody Herman band's "Four Brothers" sound and West Coast style players (see Table 8.4) |

**effect of both the tone and the chord.** (Musicians refer to such note selections as "color tones" because they have the capacity to alter the "color" of the sound, much as voicing alters the "color" of a chord.). And even when he played a solo using many notes, the result was not as densely packed as a typical Hawkins solo.[4]

Instead of incorporating afterthoughts into his phrases, as Hawkins was prone to do, Young concerned himself with only a core of melodic material. He possessed the virtue of deliberate restraint. He could pace a solo so well that it seemed an integral part of the written arrangement. His gift for inventing new, easily singable melodies while he improvised is unsurpassed in jazz history. Young possessed a musical storytelling talent which surfaced in nearly every improvisation.[5]

[4]For a transcription and analysis of Young's solo on "Lester Leaps In," on the JAZZ CLASSICS CASSETTE, see Scott Reeve's *Creative Jazz Improvisation* (Prentice-Hall, 1989). The solo is nearly all eighth notes, but the sequences are clear despite the number of notes and surprises they contain. They are free of the many twists and turns which typify Hawkins's improvisations. For comments about 251 Lester Young recording sessions and transcriptions of solos from many of them, see *You Got to Be Original, Man!: The Music of Lester Young* by Frank Büchmann-Møller (Greenwood, 1990).

[5]His clarinet solos on the 1938 "I Want a Little Girl!" and "Pagin' the Devil" illustrate his "storytelling" talent quite well. They were recently available on *Lester Young & Friends*, Commodore/Pair 7002, CD/LP. Also outstanding in this regard is his tenor sax solo on the 1939 "Pound Cake," recently available on *The Essential Count Basie, Vol. 1*, CBS 40608, CD/LP.

**TABLE 8.4. A Few of the Many Saxophonists Influenced by Lester Young**

| | | |
|---|---|---|
| Charlie Parker | Zoot Sims | Richie Kamuca |
| Brew Moore | Lee Konitz | Al Cohn |
| Paul Quinichette | Warne Marsh | Jerry Jerome |
| Dave Pell | Dexter Gordon | Don Lamphere |
| Bob Cooper | Gene Ammons | Jimmy Giuffre |
| Bill Perkins | Sonny Stitt | Buddy Collette |
| Wardell Gray | Stan Getz | John Coltrane |
| Allen Eager | Herbie Steward | Hank Mobley |

The advanced level of Young's conception was evident in his easy swing and in his placement of phrases that seemed unhindered by turnarounds and bridges. (Listen to JAZZ STYLES CASSETTE, side 1, for demonstrations of chord progression organization, and see pages 377–388 for more explanation.) Young often transcended the phrasing of many premodern players who had organized lines around the two- and four-bar sequences of chord progressions. The internal logic of his lines took precedence over strict adherence to the underlying harmonies and the way they were blocked out. He improvised long lines which had a fresh, expansive feeling that is quite unlike the crowded feeling that we often get from the improvisations of other soloists.

Young's playing was strongest during the late 1930s, and his first recordings were probably the best of his entire career. When he left Basie in 1940, his tone began to darken, his vibrato quickened, and his crisp execution decreased. He changed his style. His playing seemed to lose energy steadily until his death in 1959. Yet Young's work remained intelligent and swinging during all those later years. In fact, his loyalty to storytelling-type improvisations increased. But after 1940, he seemed unable to jump into his solos with the animation and freshness of his early work.

**Kansas City Five; Jones-Smith, Inc.**

Several classic records were made by small combinations of Basie band members. Variously called the Kansas City Five, Six, or Seven, depending on how many musicians were used, these combos often included the Basie rhythm section plus Lester Young, Buck Clayton, and Dicky Wells. Their 1939 recordings, such as "Dickie's Dream" and "Lester Leaps In," are combo classics which historically rank alongside the recordings of Louis Armstrong's Hot Five and Hot Seven. One set omitted Basie, added Eddie Durham on guitar and featured some of the all-time best playing of Lester Young and trumpeter Buck Clayton ("Good Mornin' Blues," "Pagin' The Devil," "I Want A Little Girl").[6] Another of these combos included drummer Jo Jones and trumpeter Carl Smith and was given the group name Jones-Smith, Inc. The recordings they made in 1936, including "Shoe Shine Boy" and "Lady Be Good," are masterpieces.[7]

[6]recently available on *Lester Young & Friends*, Commodore/Pair 7002, CD/LP
[7]recently available on *The Essential Count Basie, Vol. 1*, CBS 40608, CD/LP. For transcription and analysis of Young's solo on "Lady Be Good," see pages 230–35 of Gunther Schuller's *The Swing Era* (Oxford, 1989).

## Listening Guide for "Lester Leaps In"

Available on the JAZZ CLASSICS CASSETTE, side 1; on CD in the Revised SCCJ. A transcription and analysis of Young's solo is available in *Creative Jazz Improvisation* by Scott Reeves (Prentice-Hall, 1989).

**FOUR-MEASURE PIANO INTRODUCTION**

**FIRST CHORUS**

0' 3"

A-A    Muted trumpet, trombone, and tenor saxophone play a single four-measure melodic figure four times with rhythm section accompaniment (a typical riff band device).

0' 19"

B    Count Basie piano solo, very spare, just indicating the moments during which chords change. He allows plenty of space for us to hear bass and drums.

0' 27"

A    The three horns state original theme (that same riff) two more times.

0' 35"

**SECOND CHORUS**

A-A-B-A    Lester Young tenor sax solo accompanied by drummer Jo Jones playing ride rhythm on opening and closing high-hat. Nice comping by Basie. Walking bass by Page.

1' 06"

**THIRD CHORUS**

A    Young and Basie improvise counterpoint around each other.

1' 14"

A    Rhythm section creates stop-time solo breaks for Young during first six measures. Rhythm section resumes normal timekeeping patterns for last two measures while Young keeps on improvising.

1' 22"

B    Young continues solo with rhythm section accompaniment.

1' 30"

A    Rhythm section creates more stop-times for Young.

1' 37"

**FOURTH CHORUS**

A    Basie solos the first four measures, Young does the second four.

1' 41"

A    Basie solos the first four measures, Young does the second four.

1' 55"

B    Basie solos the first four measures, Young does the second four.

2' 01"

A    Basie solos the first four measures, Young does the second four. (This is called "trading four's.")

2' 09"

**FIFTH CHORUS**

(This chorus uses another typical riff band device.)

A    *First Four Measures*

Ensemble calls, "BOP    BOP    BOP-BOP    BAAH!"

2' 12"

*Second Four Measures*

Young responds with improvisation.

2' 17"

A    *First Four Measures*

Ensemble calls, "BOP    BOP    BOP-BOP    BAAH!"

2' 21"

*Second Four Measures*

Basie responds with improvisation.

2' 25"

B    Basie continues his improvisation.

*Elapsed Time*

2′ 33″

    **A**  *First Four Measures*

        Ensemble calls, "BOP     BOP     BOP-BOP     BAAH!"

2′ 36″

       *Second Four Measures*

        Young responds with improvisation.

2′ 40″

**SIXTH CHORUS**

    **A**  *First Four Measures*

        Ensemble calls, "BOP     BOP     BOP-BOP     BAAH!"

2′ 44″

       *Second Four Measures*

        Basie responds with improvisation.

2′ 49″

    **A**  *First Four Measures*

        Ensemble calls, "BOP     BOP     BOP-BOP     BAAH!"

2′ 53″

       *Second Four Measures*

        Basie responds with improvisation.

2′ 56″

    **B**  Basie continues his improvisation.

3′ 04″

    **A**  Ensemble calls, "BOP     BOP     BOP-BOP     BAAH!"

       Then the band members collectively improvise a closing by simultaneously playing different lines in Dixieland style.

**Basie After the 1940s**

After the 1940s, Basie retained many elements of his rhythm section style. His own piano style remained constant, and guitarist Freddie Green was still with him, playing in the same style he originated. Basie's post-1940s drummers kept time more on the ride cymbal than on the high-hat, and they played far more fills than Jo Jones had. However, his drummers were not performing in contemporary styles after the 1940s. They kept to what worked best for the Basie big band approach.

For thirty years, the Basie band had the unusual distinction of being almost the only big band that swung while playing softly. Some of the music written for the band during the 1950s and 60s capitalized on the band's skill with dynamic contrasts: loud passages which instantaneously get soft; soft passages interrupted momentarily by very loud chords; passages which rise and fall in volume so gradually that one wonders how it is possible. The band maintained precision and balance at a variety of loudness levels, all without losing the unrelenting drive that is expected of jazz performances. Moreover, the band did this without sounding mechanical. In fact, it projected a warm and supple feeling.

Count Basie's band always placed more emphasis on simplicity and swing feeling than on complexity and colorful sounds. Simple, catchy riffs were the rule, even during the 1950s and 60s when sophisticated composers and arrangers were writing for the band. Basie had previously run the band much as an oversized combo, with more emphasis on swinging solo improvisations than fancy arrangements. That approach contrasted with the highly polished, well-arranged style of Jimmie Lunceford and the elaborate embroidery of written music and improvisation that occurred in Duke Ellington's band. However, Basie's emphasis on the oversized combo format decreased somewhat during the 1950s and more so during the 1960s and thereafter. On the other hand, the group achieved a very high level of polish, and it became known as a swinging showcase for glossy ensemble sound like Lunceford's band of twenty years earlier. (See teacher's manual for a discography of this period.)

## CHAPTER SUMMARY

1) Count Basie was a Fats Waller-derived stride pianist who had a light, precise touch, and impeccable sense of tempo.

2) Count Basie's accompaniment style constituted one of the first examples of comping.

3) Count Basie was one of the few pianists to make silence almost as important as the notes he played.

4) The 1937–40 Basie rhythm section helped bridge the gap between pre-modern and modern methods of timekeeping and accompanying.

5) Basie's band played in the Kansas City style, using simple figures called riffs which were played repeatedly atop pop tune and 12-bar blues accompaniments.

6) Tenor saxophonist Lester Young offered a light-toned alternative to the deep, heavy sound of Coleman Hawkins.

7) Young was very melodic and fresh in his improvisations, becoming the major model for hundreds of modern jazz saxophonists.

8) Basie always stressed simplicity and swing instead of complex arrangements, and he retained the same unhurried feeling throughout his bandleading career.

*Note:* To hear Basie performances that are not in SCCJ, see *Big Band Jazz* (Smithsonian 2200) for "One O'Clock Jump," "Jumpin' At The Woodside," "Sent For You Yesterday," "Volcano," "9:20 Special," and "Shiny Stockings." For more about the Basie band and its musicians, see *Good Morning Blues: The Autobiography of Count Basie, As Told to Albert Murray*, published by Random House, 1985 (400 pages); *The World of Count Basie*, by Stanley Dance, published by Scribners, 1980 (399 pages); *Lester Young*, by Lewis Porter, published by Twayne, 1985 (190 pages); *Lester Young*, by Dave Gelly, published by Hippocrene Books, 1984 (94 pages); *Buck Clayton's Jazz World*, by Buck Clayton, published by Oxford Press, 1986 (255 pages); *The Night People*, by Dicky Wells, as told to Stanley Dance, published by Crescendo, 1971 (122 pages); *You Just Fight for Your Life: The Story of Lester Young*, by Frank Büchmann-Møller, published by Praeger, 1990. Also see *Count Basie: A Bio-Discography* by Chris Sheridan, published by Greenwood Press, 1986 (1,376 pages).

# chapter 9

# BOP:
# THE EARLY 1940s
# TO THE MIDDLE 1950s

Modern jazz became a recognizable sound in the 1940s, having grown from roots laid down in the 1930s by saxophonists Coleman Hawkins and Lester Young, pianists Art Tatum and Nat Cole, trumpeter Roy Eldridge, guitarist Charlie Christian, and the Count Basie rhythm section. "Early jazz" and other pre-1940 styles are sometimes referred to as the "classic period." New styles which have emerged since 1940 are classified as modern jazz. The first modern jazz musicians were alto saxophonist Charlie Parker, pianist Thelonious Monk, and trumpeter Dizzy Gillespie. By the middle 1940s, they had inspired a legion of other creative musicians including trumpeter Miles Davis and pianist Bud Powell. By the late 1940s, Parker and Gillespie had also influenced the music used by a number of big bands, including Woody Herman's which will be discussed in this chapter.

Modern jazz did not burst upon the jazz scene suddenly. It developed gradually through the work of swing era musicians. Parker and Gillespie themselves began their careers playing improvisations in a swing era style. They expanded on swing styles and gradually incorporated new techniques; their work eventually became a recognizably different style, though it was still linked to its roots in the swing era. Modern jazz improvisers were also inspired by contemporary classical music, particularly the work of Béla Bartók and Igor Stravinsky. Rather than being a reaction *against* swing styles, modern jazz developed smoothly *from* swing styles.

Bebop (or just "bop") is the name for the first modern jazz style. It was considerably less popular than swing, and it failed to attract dancers. However, it did contribute impressive soloists who gained disciples for decades to follow. The first bop soloists contributed a new vocabulary of musical phrases and distinctive methods of matching improvisation to chord progressions. This became the most substantial system of jazz for the next forty years. Even during the 1980s, musicians frequently evaluated new players according to their ability to play bop. Mastery of this style was considered the foundation for competence as a jazz improviser.

Charlie Parker (alto sax) and Miles Davis (trumpet), two of the most influential men in modern jazz. Parker devised the bop approach, and Davis went on to develop cool, modal, and jazz-rock approaches. Pictured here in 1947 when Parker was 27 and Davis was 21. (*Photo by William P. Gottlieb*)

Bop differed from swing in a number of performance aspects:

1) preferred instrumentation for bop was the small combo instead of big band.
2) Average tempo was faster in bop.
3) Clarinet was rare in bop.
4) Display of instrumental virtuosity was a higher priority for bop players.
5) Rhythm guitar was rare.
6) Less emphasis was placed on arrangements in bop.

Bop differed from swing in a number of stylistic respects:

1) Melodies were more complex in bop.
2) Harmonies were more complex in bop.
3) Accompaniment rhythms were more varied in bop.
4) Comping was more prevalent than stride style and simple, on-the-beat chording.

**TABLE 9.1. A Few of the Many Bop Style Musicians**

**Trumpet**

Dizzy Gillespie
Fats Navarro
Howard McGhee
Miles Davis
Kenny Dorham
Red Rodney
Benny Harris
Sonny Berman
Freddie Webster
Conte Candoli
Clark Terry
Idrees Sulieman
Benny Bailey

**Trombone**

J. J. Johnson
Kai Winding
Bennie Green
Frank Rosolino

**Bass**

Oscar Pettiford
Ray Brown
Tommy Potter
Curly Russell
Nelson Boyd
Al McKibbon
Gene Ramey
Red Callender
Teddy Kotick
Chubby Jackson
Eddie Safranski

**Saxophone**

Charlie Parker
Dexter Gordon
Lucky Thompson
Stan Getz
Wardell Gray
Allen Eager
Herbie Steward
Brew Moore
Gene Ammons

Sonny Stitt
Flip Phillips
James Moody
Charlie Ventura
Zoot Sims
Al Cohn
Ernie Henry
Leo Parker
Sonny Criss
Serge Chaloff
Don Lamphere
Charlie Rouse
Sonny Rollins
Phil Urso
Boots Mussulli

**Vibraharp**

Milt Jackson
Teddy Charles
Terry Gibbs

**Drums**

Kenny Clarke
Max Roach
Joe Harris
Tiny Kahn
Don Lamond
Roy Haynes
Osie Johnson
Denzil Best

**Piano**

Bud Powell
Thelonious Monk
Al Haig
Dodo Marmarosa
Joe Albany
Walter Bishop, Jr.
Duke Jordan
George Shearing
Oscar Peterson
Billy Taylor
Hank Jones

Argonne Thornton
(Sadik Hakim)
Hampton Hawes
John Lewis
Tadd Dameron
Ahmad Jamal

**Guitar**

Arv Garrison
Tal Farlow
Bill DeArango
Jimmy Raney
Johnny Collins
Barry Galbraith
Chuck Wayne
Barney Kessel
Billy Bauer
Johnny Smith

**Composer-Arranger**

Gil Fuller
George Russell
Neal Hefti
Dizzy Gillespie
Charlie Parker
Thelonious Monk
Tadd Dameron
John Lewis
Shorty Rogers
Ralph Burns
Gil Evans
Gerry Mulligan

5) Drummers played their timekeeping rhythms primarily on suspended cymbal, rather than snare drum, high-hat, or bass drum.

6) Bop tunes and chord progressions projected a more unresolved quality.

7) Bop was a more agitated style than swing was.

8) Bop improvisation was more complex because it contained
   a) more themes per solo,
   b) less similarity among themes,
   c) more excursions outside the tune's original key, and
   d) a greater scope of rhythmic development.

9) Surprise was more highly valued in bop.

Bop improvisations were composed mostly of eighth-note and sixteenth-note figures which seemed jumpy, full of twists and turns. The contours of the melodic lines were jagged; there were often large intervals between the notes and abrupt changes of direction. The rhythms in those lines were quick and unpredictable, with more syncopation than any music previously common in Europe or America. (Listen to Gillespie and Parker's "Shaw Nuff" in the JAZZ CLASSICS CASSETTE.) Performers overcame the tendency of premodern improvisers to stop phrases at or before *turnarounds* (see pages 387–388 for explanation of turnarounds). Bop players took a cue from Lester Young and often began phrases in the middle of eight-bar sections, continuing them through the turnarounds, past the traditional barriers of the eighth bar (twelfth bar in the blues). They planned ahead further and mastered the improvisation of extended lines which reflected a tune's underlying chord progression less and less.

For the basis of their lines, bop musicians did more than embellish the melody. They usually departed from the melodies and retained only the chord progressions. Often they enriched a progression by adding new chords. Players of earlier styles might have employed fewer than five or ten chord changes in a twelve-bar blues, but bop players would want more than that number. (See third example under "Chord Progressions for the Twelve-Bar Blues" on page 416.) Jazz musicians call addition of chords *substitution* or reharmonization because, in place of a single chord or a common chord sequence, new chords are substituted. Art Tatum had previously explored reharmonization of melodies and had added chords to existing progressions. Coleman Hawkins had loved to improvise on complicated chord progressions and to invent solo lines whose construction implied that chords had been added to existing progressions. In these ways, Tatum and Hawkins had set the stage for the wide use of these techniques in bop style. Some bop lines implied chords which were not originally in a tune's accompaniment; these lines were sometimes played against a tune's original harmonies to achieve purposely clashing effects. In other cases, the rhythm section would instantaneously change chords and chord progressions to fit the new harmonic directions implied by an improvised line. Bop rhythm sections learned to be quite sensitive and resourceful.

Bop players also altered existing chords, and they often based their lines more on the alterations than on the fundamental tones. So, by comparison with their predecessors, bop musicians not only used more chords, they used richer chords, and they created lines that drew from the enrichments. The most common alteration was the *flatted fifth* (also known as the lowered fifth or raised eleventh). It soon became identified as much with modern jazz as the lowered third and lowered seventh were identified with premodern jazz. Today all three intervals are basic to the character of jazz. (Dizzy Gillespie's 1945 arrangement of "Shaw Nuff" ends on a flatted fifth. Listen to it in the JAZZ CLASSICS CASSETTE or SCCJ, and see pages 369–371 for explanation and keyboard illustration.)

Because bop musicians liked to improvise on difficult chord progressions, they sometimes wrote original progressions themselves. But a more common practice was to improvise on popular song progressions that were challenging. "All the Things You Are" served this purpose. "Cherokee" became a favorite because the progressions in its bridge are unusual.[1]

Bop players often wrote original tunes using the accompaniment chord progressions of popular tunes, and many of these new tunes went without names. The leader just called out the key and the name of the tune which provided the chord progression. In that way, members of the rhythm section could immediately play a tune they might have never previously heard. This technique was not new to bop. It had been used in swing and early jazz. The chord progression for the twelve-bar blues had been used in that way for decades. And Count Basie's recordings of the 1930s are filled with loosely arranged performances in which riffs and improvisations are placed atop the chord progressions of such popular songs as "Lady Be Good," "I Got Rhythm," and "Honeysuckle Rose." This practice provided a common ground for jam sessions because all the participants knew the chord progressions to these popular songs.[2]

**Charlie Parker**    The musician who contributed most to the development of bop was alto saxophonist Charlie Parker (1920–1955). Jazz musicians and historians feel that he is the most important saxophonist in jazz history. Many musicologists consider Parker to be one of the most brilliant musical figures in the twentieth century. Going beyond the

---

[1]Listen to Charlie Parker's solo improvisations on "Ko-Ko" in SCCJ. The piece has no prewritten melody, just an introduction which alternates between brief bits of composed material and improvised trumpet and sax breaks, atop timekeeping by brushes on snare drum. Then, except for an ending constructed of a brief trumpet improvisation and a "tie it up" figure played in unison by trumpet and sax, the entire performance consists of spontaneous improvisations, guided by repetitions of the accompaniment harmonies to "Cherokee," a sixty-four bar A-A-B-A form.

[2]"Indiana," "What Is This Thing Called Love," "Whispering," and "How High the Moon" respectively provided chord progressions for the bop compositions "Donna Lee," "Hot House," "Groovin' High," and Ornithology." The chord progression of George Gershwin's "I Got Rhythm," was used so much that musicians abbreviated "I Got Rhythm chord changes" to "I Got Rhythm changes," which in turn was abbreviated to "rhythm changes" or just "rhythm." Pieces in SCCJ based on rhythm changes include "Shaw Nuff," "Crazeology" (also known as "Little Benny" and "Bud's Bubble"), and the improvisations of Don Byas and Slam Stewart on "I Got Rhythm." "Cottontail" and "Shaw Nuff" on the JAZZ CLASSICS CASSETTE are based on rhythm changes. This progression is demonstrated on the JAZZ STYLES CASSETTE, end of side 1.

**TABLE 9.2. A Few of the Many Saxophonists Influenced by Charlie Parker**

| | |
|---|---|
| Phil Woods | Jackie McLean |
| Charlie Mariano | Cannonball Adderley |
| Sahib Shihab | Eric Dolphy |
| Ernie Henry | John Coltrane |
| Sonny Criss | Sonny Rollins |
| Charlie McPherson | Ornette Coleman |
| Frank Strozier | Albert Ayler |
| Jimmy Heath | Wardell Gray |
| Lou Donaldson | Dexter Gordon |
| Davey Schildkraut | Art Pepper |
| Sonny Stitt | Bud Shank |
| James Moody | Joe Farrell |

advances made by Lester Young, Coleman Hawkins, and Art Tatum, he built an entire system that was conveyed in his improvisations and compositions. The system embodied

1) new ways of selecting notes to be compatible with the accompaniment chords;
2) new ways of accenting notes so that the phrases have a highly syncopated character;
3) methods for adding chords to existing chord progressions and implying additional chords by the selection of notes for the improvised lines.

Charlie Parker astonished other musicians with his tremendous fertility of melodic imagination, unprecedented mastery of the saxophone, and the dizzying pace with which he was able to improvise.[3] Parker's solos were densely packed with ideas. During his improvisations, his mind seemed to be bubbling over with little melodies and paraphrases of melodies. It was as though he had so much energy and enthusiasm that he could not contain himself. This led to interspersing his solos with double-time and quadruple-time figures. Even in ballad renditions, he tended to ornament slow lines with double-time figures. (For a demonstration of double-timing, listen to the JAZZ STYLES CASSETTE, side 2.) In other words, he played fast, and he played a lot of notes. And it is no coincidence that soon after Parker's mid-1940s recordings appeared, there was an increase in the average tempo, an

---

[3]Sample Parker's extraordinary speed and inventiveness in "Ko-Ko" in SCCJ, or "Bird Gets the Worm" in *Bird—Savoy Original Master Takes*, Savoy ZDS 8801, CD set (2201, LP set), 1944–48. "Ko-Ko" is also in *Bebop*, New World 271, LP anthology, part of a record series found in many schools and libraries.

increase in double-timing, and an increase in the average amount of melodic ideas in the improvisations of other modern jazz musicians. Though this trend had already begun during the swing era, it was also partly a function of the new example set by Parker.

Parker's timbre departed from standard swing era models. In place of the lush, sweet tone preferred by Johnny Hodges and Benny Carter, Parker used the dry, biting tone preferred by Kansas City saxophonist Buster Smith, an early model for Parker. Though Parker's tone had considerable fullness, it possessed a lighter color than the tone of Hodges. In place of the pronounced vibrato of Hodges and Carter, Parker used the slower, narrower vibrato preferred by Smith, and Parker was less prone to dwell on a few choice notes than Hodges was. By comparison with Hodges, Parker sounded more hurried. Rather than an easygoing romantic, Parker sounded like a modern composer who was improvising at lightning speed.[4]

Charlie Parker's improvisations were inspired by many sources. An adequate analysis of his techniques is beyond the nontechnical scope of this book, but we should note that Parker used many of the methods that are routinely employed by classical composers.[5] Though we will not be able to identify use of the classical techniques if we do not know them, we might notice other sources for his improvisations because they draw upon familiar material. Parker interspersed his lines with phrases from highly varied sources, ranging from the solos of Louis Armstrong and Lester Young, to the melodies of blues singers and early jazz hornmen, from pop tunes and traditional melodies, to themes from opera and classical music. Listeners

[4]Listen to "Embraceable You" in SCCJ or in *Bebop*, New World 271 (also available with other classic Parker recordings in *The Legendary Dial Masters, Vol. 1 & 2*, Stash STCD 23 & 25, CD, 1946–47). This is based on a thirty-two bar A-B-A-C song by George Gershwin, and it became one of Parker's most acclaimed improvisations. Notice that Parker engages in much quadruple-timing while the rhythm section remains in the accompaniment style of a ballad. Parker's improvisation is rich with ideas that are complex and unpredictable. Compare his dense, multinoted style with that of the Coleman Hawkins solo on "Body and Soul" in SCCJ. Parker and Hawkins were both interested in playing densely packed solos. They also sequenced the notes to indicate every chord that occurred as well as other chords that might fit the progression, even though their accompanists did not necessarily sound all those chords. Both men were doing more than simply double-timing. They were quadruple-timing. It is also notable that even though Parker has the Kansas City tone color and rhythmic swing feeling of Lester Young, he leans more toward the Hawkins preference for complex improvisation than the Young preference for singable melody.

[5]The single best source for learning more about Parker's musical thinking is a massive, in-depth study called *Charlie Parker: Techniques of Improvisation* by Thomas Owens. See page 413 for ordering instructions. Eight Parker solos are transcribed and analyzed in Stuart Isacoff's *Solos for Jazz Alto Saxophone* (Carl Fischer, 1985; available by mail from Carl Fischer Music Store, 54 Cooper Square, NY, NY 10003). Transcriptions and analyses of Parker's solos on Gillespie's 1945 "Shaw Nuff," in the JAZZ CLASSICS CASSETTE, and Parker's own 1953 "Now's the Time" are in Scott Reeves's *Creative Jazz Improvisation* (Prentice-Hall, 1989; available from Jamey Aebersold, P.O. Box 1244, New Albany, IN 47150; phone 800-456-1388). Parker's solo on "Ko-Ko" is transcribed in John Mehegan's *Jazz Improvisation, Vol. 2* (Watson-Guptill, 1962). More transcriptions are in Stan Ayeroff's *Charlie Parker* (Amsco, 1979; available from Aebersold) and Jamey Aebersold and Ken Slone's *Charlie Parker Omnibook* (Atlantic Music, 1978; available from Aebersold).

who are familiar with any of these sources will recognize snatches of them embedded in Parker's improvisations.[6]

Parker wrote a sizable body of tunes, and their character set the flavor for bop as much as his improvisations did. Their phrases were memorized and analyzed by hundreds of jazz soloists. His "Now's the Time," "Billie's Bounce," and "Confirmation" were played at jam sessions for decades after he introduced them. Though not melody-like in the pop tune sense, they were catchy lines in a jazz vein. Most were accompanied by chord progressions borrowed from popular songs. Many used accompaniments of the twelve-bar blues chord progression. This was the musical language of bop.

Parker's impact on jazz was immense. Bop trumpeter Dizzy Gillespie cites Parker as a primary influence on his own style, and bop pianist Bud Powell modelled some of his lines after those of Parker. Methods of improvisation devised by Parker were adopted by numerous saxophonists during the 1940s and 50s (see Table 9.2). Parker's tunes and phrases were even heard in the earliest recordings of Ornette Coleman and Albert Ayler, leaders of the avant-garde in the 1960s. Jazz clubs were named for Parker—Birdland in New York and Birdhouse in Chicago. Parker's melodic inventiveness is so stunning that bop singer Eddie Jefferson performed Parker's "Billie's Bounce" and "Parker's Mood" with lyrics which had been written for the melodies and the improvisations. During the 1970s, a group called Supersax began using five saxes and rhythm section to play harmonized transcriptions of Parker solos. Supersax was able to treat his solos as compositions because catchy ideas are so abundant in Parker's improvisations.

**Dizzy Gillespie**    Louis Armstrong was the jazz trumpet virtuoso of the late 1920s and early 30s. Roy Eldridge held a similar position in the late 30s. But the innovative melodic concepts, high-register playing, and agility achieved by Dizzy Gillespie (b. 1917) were not only phenomenal for the 1940s, but have rarely been matched since. Great instrumental proficiency was necessary for bop improvisation, and Gillespie's awe-inspiring command of the trumpet accounts for only part of his impact. His stirring musical ideas and the blazing force with which they were delivered account for much of his influence. By the time he first recorded with Parker, he had absorbed the saxophone-style lines and excitement of Roy Eldridge's approach and gone beyond to devise his own brand of bop.

Dizzy Gillespie's harmonic skills were startling, and he flaunted them. His phrases were full of surprises and playful changes of direction. He could precariously go in and out of keys within a single phrase, always managing to resolve the unexpected at the next chord. He often zoomed up to the trumpet's high register

---

[6]To detect the influence of Lester Young, listen to Parker's 1940 recordings with Jay Mcshann that were collected on *First Recordings* (Onyx 221, LP) or *Early Bird* (Spotlite 120; import LP). To hear Parker's similarity to Young and to Hawkins, listen to Parker's 1943 recordings, made on tenor sax, collected on *Birth of the Bebop* (Stash ST 260, LP). To hear the similarity to blues singers and early jazz hornmen, listen to "Parker's Mood" (in SCCJ and in *Bebop*, New World 271). For more about Parker, see Robert Reisner's *Bird: The Legend of Charlie Parker* (Citadel, 1962; reprinted by DaCapo).

Dizzy Gillespie invented the first modern approach to jazz trumpet playing, and he pioneered bop compositional style. He is seen here in 1947 at age 30. (*Photo by William P. Gottlieb*)

during the middle of a phrase and still managed to connect the melodic ideas logically. Sometimes he interspersed quotes from non-jazz pieces such as Bizet's opera "Carmen" or the pop tune "We're in the Money." He often used the quote as a point of departure for developing his own phrases. Gillespie often built a line with increasing tension by going higher and higher with syncopated notes played staccato and then coming down with legato lines that resolved the tension. Yet Gillespie's lines made sense even when he played these rapid cascades of notes. His work bristled with excitement.

Like Roy Eldridge, Gillespie would occasionally toy with a single note, playing it again and again, each time in a different way, creating different rhythmic patterns and using changes in loudness and tone color to achieve variety in his sound. One Gillespie method which is especially reminiscent of Eldridge is to make the trumpet tone brittle and then crack it resoundingly in a burst of high notes. Also, like Eldridge, he could channel all his terrific energy into a ballad, using his exceptional skill with harmony, his fertile imagination, and virtuoso technique to mold a unique, personal creation.[7]

[7]A masterpiece of this kind was his 1945 "I Can't Get Started" solo, in SCCJ and *Dizzy Gillespie: The Development of An American Artist,* 1940–46, Smithsonian 2004 (LP set); transcribed and analyzed in Stuart Isacoff's *Solos for Jazz Trumpet* (Carl Fischer, 1985; available by mail from Carl Fischer Music Store, 54 Cooper Square, NY, NY 10003). Smithsonian 2004 also contains "Night in Tunisia," "Salt Peanuts," "Woody 'n' You," as well as Gillespie's solos with the Cab Calloway big band. For more about Gillespie, see his autobiography, *To Be Or Not To Bop* (Doubleday, 1979).

Gillespie exerted sweeping influence on modern jazz. His pet phrases became stock clichés for two generations of jazz trumpeters; these phrases can also be heard in the playing of pianists, guitarists, saxophonists, and trombonists. During the 1940s, he influenced numerous trumpeters.[8] Some of these players had originally derived their styles from premodern sources, but then they incorporated some of Gillespie's devices upon hearing him. Though only a year or two older than several of them, Gillespie influenced them as a classic model rather than a mere contemporary. Though Gillespie did not drastically alter his trumpet style after 1947, he continued to perform regularly and remained active as recently as the 1990s.

Gillespie also made lasting contributions to modern jazz as a composer.[9] His "Groovin' High" and "A Night in Tunisia" became jazz standards that are still played. After being recorded with lyrics, they gained wider audiences in the 1980s. Afro-Cuban music was one of Gillespie's special interests, and he explored it in his big band numbers "Manteca," "Cubano Be," and "Cubano Bop." These pieces are among the earliest appearances of Latin American music in modern jazz.[10]

After co-leading a combo with Charlie Parker and leading a few small bands of his own, Gillespie began a series of bop big bands.[11] He kept his big bands going through most of the late 1940s, then formed others sporadically thereafter. His combos and big bands saw a flow of powerful players, many of whom—Milt Jackson and John Coltrane, for example—went on to lead significant groups of their own.

In summary, Gillespie contributed

1) a model of unparalleled trumpet mastery;
2) a body of original compositions;
3) a string of high quality combos and big bands featuring numerous jazz stars-to-be;
4) the use of Afro-Cuban music in jazz;
5) a new vocabulary of phrases and ways of matching solo notes to accompanying chords.

**Thelonious Monk**    The emphasis of bop was on improvisation, but there were a few outstanding bop composers. Thelonious Monk (1917–1982) was a pianist and composer whose melodies were unorthodox and whose chord progressions severely challenged improvisers. Monk's compositions influenced the flavor of much modern jazz, and his jazz

---

[8]Howard McGhee, Red Rodney, Benny Harris, Conte Candoli, Kenny Dorham, Fats Navarro, Miles Davis, Thad Jones, and Clark Terry are among the many trumpeters affected by Gillespie's style of the 1940s. His influence did not end in the 1940s. Trumpeter Jon Faddis appeared during the 1970s, often quoting Gillespie recordings of the 1940s note for note.

[9]Gillespie wrote "Birks Works," "Emanon," "Groovin' High," "Blue 'n' Boogie," "Salt Peanuts," "Woody'n' You," "Con Alma," "A Night in Tunisia," and other tunes, as well as original compositions and arrangements for his own big bands. See next footnote.

[10]These are on *The Bebop Revolution*, RCA Bluebird 2177, CD 1946–49.

[11]Listen to the Gillespie big band play his "Things to Come" in *Big Band Jazz*, Smithsonian 2200, LP set; *Bebop*, New World 271; or *One Bass Hit*, Musicraft 2010, LP, 1945–46.

Thelonious Monk, the most unique of all bop composers and pianists, photographed in 1947 at age 30. (*Photo by William P. Gottlieb*)

piano style influenced a number of pianists (see Table 9.3). Several musicians have devoted entire albums to his music, and a few touring bands have constructed their repertories primarily from his compositions. Monk's "Straight, No Chaser," "Well, You Needn't," and "'Round Midnight" became jazz standards.

Monk's tunes have a logic and symmetry all their own. Unlike the tunes of many composers, his are so perfectly structured and concise that they cannot withstand tampering. Monk was expert at placing accents in irregular order—his "Rhythm-n-ing" is exceedingly difficult to play properly because of its odd accents. He was especially skilled in ending phrases on the least expected notes, yet making the piece

**TABLE 9.3. A Few of the Many Pianists Influenced by Thelonious Monk**

| | |
|---|---|
| Randy Weston | Misja Mengelberg |
| Herbie Nichols | Anthony Davis |
| Cecil Taylor | Karl Berger |
| Mal Waldron | Chick Corea |
| Andrew Hill | Dollar Brand |
| Bud Powell | Geri Allen |

**Figure 9.1.** Piano keyboard illustration of a whole-tone sequence of the kind Monk was likely to insert in his improvisations.

sound as though those phrase endings had been expected all along—his "Off Minor," for instance. Monk employed simple compositional devices with very original results. His "Straight, No Chaser" involves basically only one idea played again and again, each time in a different part of the measure and with a different ending. The shifting accents reflect a craftsmanship which can produce depth in simplicity. The melody is an ingenious invention set atop the twelve-bar blues chord progression.[12]

As a pianist, Monk was a curious mixture. His use of stride piano techniques suggests Fats Waller. Some of his horn-like lines are reminiscent of Earl Hines. In some voicings, Monk's playing suggests Ellington's, though Monk conveys more blunt starkness. Monk's style also resembles Ellington's in the percussive way both men strike the piano keys, the dark and rough tone quality they extract from the piano, and the way that both men sometimes allow notes to ring long after the keys are struck. Monk also likes the lower register, another Ellington similarity.

Monk's comping was not like conventional bop comping style. Nor was it like the light and bouncing approach that evolved from Count Basie's methods. It resembled more of a declamation than the springy chording provided by most modern pianists. It assumed more the character of a jazz drummer's snare drumming than a

---

[12]"Off Minor" and "Straight, No Chaser" are in *Genius of Modern Music Vol. 1 & 2,* Blue Note 81510/11, 2 CD/LPs; and *The Complete Blue Note Recordings of Thelonious Monk,* Mosaic MR4-101, LP set, 1947–51. Monk rerecorded these tunes for other companies, but the Blue Note renditions are his first versions. Monk's "Misterioso" (found in the SCCJ) is another masterpiece of simplicity. A sequence of unending notes, it has no rests, no sustained tones, just legato eighth notes. These notes are not arranged in the bop manner, either. They are smooth alternations of low and high notes. Pairs of notes in the interval of a sixth, gradually move up and down a scale, never stopping to rest, constantly moving in stepwise fashion, all set atop an accompaniment of the twelve-bar blues. A large portion of Monk's compositions are in thirty-two-bar A-A-B-A form—"Epistrophy" and "'Round Midnight," for example. "'Round Midnight" is one of his most frequently played ballads. Although it is one of Monk's prettiest melodies, it is not at all conventional. Some measures contain four different chords. The tune does not even start on the first beat of the chord progression. It begins on the second beat and fits four notes into the space of that single beat. A Monk solo version of "'Round Midnight" is in *Jazz Piano,* Smithsonian 039, LP, CD, cassette. For more about Monk, see pages 108–144 in *The View from Within* by Orrin Keepnews (Oxford, 1988), and see the accompanying booklets for *Jazz Piano* (Smithsonian 039) and *The Complete Blue Note Recordings of Thelonious Monk* (Mosaic MR4-101).

guitarist's chording. Monk's comping seemed to be setting up spaces framed by resounding punches. Note also that Monk often stopped comping for long passages, leaving the soloist to improvise with only bass and drums accompaniment.

Monk was one of the most original of all jazz improvisers. In fact, his inventions sound so different from other styles that some listeners feel it is misleading to classify his style as swing or bop. They would rather see him in a category of his own. His lines often display jagged contours, and the construction for some of his improvisations is quite playful. For example, he loved to insert a whole-tone scale abruptly into his line (see Figure 9.1). In his harmonies, Monk is particularly known for combinations of tones that clash resoundingly with each other. It has been playfully said that Monk could make an in-tune piano sound out of tune. Combined with an uneven rhythmic style, these harmonic characteristics made his music quite jarring.

Monk's music conveys a sense of unsettling deliberation. He uses notes so sparingly that silence is almost as important as sound. (Listen to his "Bag's Groove" solo on SCCJ.) The agonizing care he devotes to choosing each individual note and rhythm precludes the long, horn-like improvisations that are generated by most other pianists. His music is not smooth. His piano improvisations convey a sense that he is struggling to decide on every note, and then he reaches that decision just barely in time to play it. Nothing is produced casually or routinely. Each phrase is played very emphatically, and with much consideration for its maximum rhythmic effect. Monk's approach is very intense and percussive. He often strikes a note or chord several times in a row, as though knocking on a door. In fact his rhythms are so pronounced and jaunty that his music does not evoke the easy rise and fall of tensions associated with most jazz lines. In the perceptions of many listeners, Monk's music swings, but for others there is insufficient relaxation and grace to allow more than a rudimentary hint of swing feeling.[13]

**Composers**     Pianist **Tadd Dameron** (1917–1965) was one of the foremost composers in bop. His work covered a broad range—from the bop melody "Hot House," to his simple, but catchy line "Good Bait," to a pretty song that he scored for wordless vocal in the manner of Duke Ellington ("Casbah"). His "Hot House," and "Lady Bird" became standards among jazz instrumentalists.[14]

Much of Dameron's most distinctive work appeared in the form of arrangements for medium-sized bands. Dameron was good at getting a big band sound from a smaller group of instruments. His arrangements had voicings with the thick textures

---

[13]Listen to Monk play "Criss Cross," "Evidence," and "I Should Care," in SCCJ. For greater understanding of similarities and differences among pianists discussed here, compare renditions of "Tea for Two" by Art Tatum (*Art Tatum Masterpieces*, MCA2-4019), Bud Powell (*The Genius of Bud Powell*, Verve 827901), and Thelonious Monk (*Criss Cross*, Columbia CS 8838 (CL 2038)). Monk's innovative rhythmic conceptions are summarized in the way he recast the melody. For transcriptions of Monk solos, see *Thelonious Monk* by Stuart Isacoff (Consolidated Music, 1978; available from Jamey Aebersold).

[14]Listen to Dameron's 1948 "Lady Bird" in SCCJ. Miles Davis borrowed its chord progression for his own "Half Nelson." Saxophonist John Coltrane and Dameron recorded an entire album of Dameron tunes in 1956, including the ballads "On a Misty Night" and "Soultrane" (*Mating Call*, OJC-212, LP). In the 1980s, an all-star New York group called Dameronia formed to perform Dameron's compositions and arrangements.

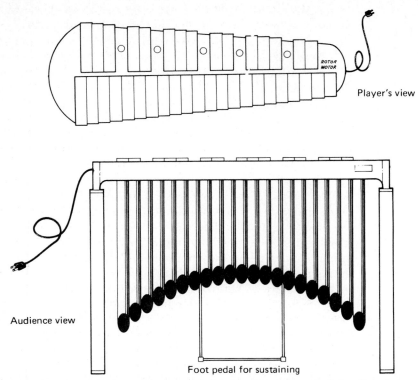

Player's view

Audience view

Foot pedal for sustaining

**Figure 9.2.** Vibraharp. To most people, the vibraharp (also called the vibraphone or vibes) looks like a marimba or a big xylophone with tubes hanging under its keys. The vibraharp is played similarly to the marimba and xylophone, but it is constructed differently. Its keys are metal; those of the xylophone and marimba are wooden. The vibraharp's resonating tubes are like those of the marimba, but each tube contains a disc that twirls by means of an electric motor. The twirling discs enable the sound of ringing keys to project and sustain. The discs give the vibraharp sound a wavering character, an even pulsation called a tremolo. The sound reaches our ears in alternating pulses (wuh . . . wuh . . . wuh . . . ). Tremolo is not to be confused with vibrato. Tremolo is an alternation of loudness, whereas vibrato is an alteration of pitch. Some vibraharps allow the player to control the rate of tremolo by means of a dial attached to the rotor motor. All vibraharps allow the player to start and stop sustaining the sound by means of a foot pedal.

and the rhythmic style of bop piano. Using the strong, clear-toned lead of a trumpeter like Fats Navarro, Dameron would then assign melody notes in a block chord-fashion to alto sax, tenor sax, trombone, and baritone sax. The range of the voicing might encompass three octaves.[15]

Several of the most imaginative writers in bop were associated with the Dizzy

[15]Dameron's Blue Note and Capitol recordings are collected on *The Fabulous Fats Navarro, Vol. 1 & 2*, Blue Note 81531/2, CD/LP, 1947–51. The influence of Dameron's arranging concepts turned up in later work by Benny Golson, Gigi Gryce, and Sun Ra.

Gillespie big band. One was **John Lewis** (b. 1920), who contributed "Two Bass Hit" and "Toccata for Trumpet and Orchestra." He has written hundreds of tunes in a variety of contexts, ranging from ballet music to film scores, with instrumentations ranging from jazz combos to symphony orchestras. (Listen to his "Django" in SCCJ.) A special interest for Lewis is combining classical music with jazz. This idiom is called **Third Stream music.**[16] It usually consists of mixing the instrumentation and forms of classical music with jazz improvisation and jazz swing feeling. The term was coined by Gunther Schuller, a composer whose "Concertino for Jazz Quartet and Orchestra" was written for the Modern Jazz Quartet, Lewis's group.[17]

In 1952, John Lewis and three other musicians from Dizzy Gillespie's bands, formed The Milt Jackson Quartet. After several personnel changes, it became the **Modern Jazz Quartet**—vibraharpist **Milt Jackson** (b. 1923), pianist Lewis, bassist Percy Heath, and drummer Connie Kay. Together they produced a delicate sound that was so polished and dignified that listeners likened it to classical chamber music.[18] A substantial part of this character was due to the style of their vibraharpist. Despite the mechanical and percussive nature of the vibraharp, Jackson managed to extract a warm, gentle sound and project remarkable presence. This was done partly by bluesy melodic figures and a careful regulation of the vibraharp's tremolo speed, emphasizing a particularly slow rate of tremolo (see Figure 9.2). He often adjusted the tremolo rate while playing, just as saxophonists adjust vibrato and blowing pressure for expressive purposes. Jackson's graceful, relaxed style meshed with Lewis's light touch on the piano and his gift for understated melody. The group created a cool kind of bop and became one of the best known bands in modern jazz. Jackson, Lewis, Heath, and Kay played together regularly until the fall of 1974 and then regrouped occasionally thereafter for tours and recordings.[19]

**Bass**   Few bop bassists could approximate the tone quality, agility, or imagination of Duke Ellington's Jimmy Blanton, though most walked effectively underneath the piano and horn parts.[20] Three bop bassists in particular, though, did learn Blanton's

[16]For more about Third Stream, listen to *Mirage*, New World 216, LP anthology; and see pages 114–124 in Gunther Schuller's book *Musings* (Oxford, 1986).

[17]The third stream concept was not new with Lewis or Schuller nor was it unique to their era. The idea of combining jazz and classical music has influenced bandleaders and composers in every era of jazz: Paul Whiteman in the 1920s; Artie Shaw in the 30s; Duke Ellington and John Lewis, beginning in the 40s; and Charles Mingus, Gunther Schuller, Stan Kenton, John Lewis, George Russell, Jimmy Giuffre, Miles Davis, and Gil Evans beginning in the 1950s. The Don Ellis big bands of the 60s and 70s also explored Third Stream techniques.

[18]*The Artistry of the Modern Jazz Quartet*, Prestige 60–016, CD, 1952–56; *Django*, OJC 057, CD/LP, 1953–54.

[19]Jackson is a fluid, clear-thinking improviser with a very fertile imagination. His refinement of bop phrasing is a significant contribution which should not be viewed solely in light of jazz vibraharp. Listen to his work on "Django" in SCCJ, and study its transcription and analysis in Scott Reeves's *Creative Jazz Improvisation* (Prentice-Hall, 1989). Also listen to Jackson's solos on Thelonious Monk's "Evidence" and "Criss Cross" in SCCJ.

[20]Present on more bop sessions than anyone else was Curly Russell (1917–1986). He was not known as a soloist but was widely regarded as accompanist. Tommy Potter (1918–1988) and Al McKibbon (b. 1919) also appeared often in the accompanist role with many important bop groups.

ideas and used them for developing their own styles—**Oscar Pettiford** (1922–1960), **Charles Mingus** (1922–1979), and **Ray Brown** (b. 1926). (For examples of horn-like bass lines, listen to the JAZZ STYLES CASSETTE, side 1.) Pettiford was present at many of the earliest bop sessions, having co-led an important band with Dizzy Gillespie in 1943.[21] The earliest recorded Mingus solos are especially significant because they are among the first on record to go beyond Blanton and incorporate bop melodic concept.[22] And it is not just their historical position and style that is notable, but also their quality. Mingus extracted a large, percussive sound from his bass, and his solos exude strength and sureness. The Mingus improvisations were developed in a compositionally sensible way that was forceful and emphasized every note. Moreover, he continued to evolve new styles for the bass and went on to become one of the top avant-garde composer-bandleaders in the 1950s and 60s. Brown was widely known because he received consistent and extensive exposure in tours and recordings with the very popular Oscar Peterson trios of 1951 to 66. Long viewed as the most swinging modern bassist, he is widely regarded for his big tone, unrelenting drive, and melodic solos.[23]

**Drums**   Jo Jones and Sid Catlett are the swing drummers most frequently cited as influences when bop drummers are interviewed. Jones eliminated bass drum playing in some contexts and recorded some of the earliest examples of flexible interaction between soloist and drummer. (Listen to his work on Benny Goodman's rendition of "I've Found a New Baby" in SCCJ.) Catlett kept time with a more swinging feeling than was common to drummers in the 1930s and was one of the few able to play with bands from both the swing and bop eras. (Listen to Catlett on Dizzy Gillespie's "Shaw Nuff" in the JAZZ CLASSICS CASSETTE.)

The advances made by Jones, Catlett, and others became crystallized in the playing of bop drummers **Kenny Clarke** (1914–1985) and **Max Roach** (b. 1925), who evolved from swing approaches in at least three fundamental respects. First, they **increased the frequency and spontaneity of kicks and prods**, those sounds that deviate from timekeeping rhythms. (When these extra sounds were extracted from the bass drum, they were called "bombs.") Bop drummers were not merely time-keepers. The kicks and prods were means that they developed for spontaneously accenting and coloring solo lines of horns and piano. These sounds served at least two important purposes: a) a kind of communication between the drummer and the solo improvisers they were accompanying; b) "chatter," the assortment of pops and

[21]Listen to Pettiford in a solo role with Coleman Hawkins on his 1943 "The Man I Love" (in SCCJ) and in an accompanying role on Duke Ellington's 1946 "Transblucency" (in the JAZZ CLASSICS CASSETTE). Lucky Thompson gave Pettiford's solos and compositions considerable exposure in a collection reissued as *Dancing Sunbeam*, Impulse 9307 (ABC 111), LP, 1956.

[22]A knowledge of the Parker and Gillespie melodic style is indicated in the Mingus solos on "Mingus Fingers" with Lionel Hampton's band of 1947, on *Jazz in Revolution*, New World 284, LP anthology. For more about Mingus, see chapter 14.

[23]Brown first gained wide recognition when the Gillespie band featured him in its "Two-Bass Hit" of 1947 (in Gillespie's *Dizziest*, RCA Bluebird 5785, LP set). Brown solos on pianist Dodo Marmarosa's "Mellow Mood," of 1946, on *Jazz Piano*, Smithsonian 039, and *Jazz in Revolution*, New World 284, LP anthology.

crashes that provide an energetic layer of activity that increased the excitement of the band sound. (Listen to Roy Haynes accompany Chick Corea on "Steps" in the JAZZ CLASSICS CASSETTE.)

A second advancement was made when **Kenny Clarke and Max Roach took a cue from Jo Jones and altered the manner of timekeeping on the bass drum by playing more gently, "feathering" the bass drum instead of pounding it.** This was a practice that became standard for at least one generation of jazz drummers beyond its originators. However, it is difficult to detect in recordings because not all the drummer's instruments were equally well recorded.

A third advancement occurred in the choice of percussion instrument used for timekeeping. In swing style, tempo had been reinforced by the drummer striking the bass drum and by playing a timekeeping rhythm on snare drum or high-hat. In the bop era, Kenny Clarke and Max Roach extended ways in which Jo Jones and Dave Tough had already been getting away from these devices in the swing era. During the late 1930s, Jones had occasionally played ride rhythms on a single cymbal, as in Count Basie's 1937 recording of "One O'Clock Jump," and Dave Tough had already been playing ride rhythms on a large cymbal that was not part of his high-hat apparatus. (Listen to the JAZZ STYLES CASSETTE for demonstrations, and see page 430 for notations of the rhythms.) Kenny Clarke is generally credited with influencing the widespread adoption of **playing timekeeping rhythms on a cymbal suspended over the drum set.**

Not only the instruments on which timekeeping rhythms were played, but also the way they were executed was different in bop. Modern drummers continued the sustained cymbal sound popularized by Jo Jones. However, they did this on neither the opening and closing high-hat, nor a single cymbal of the high-hat apparatus. They kept time on a large, thick, heavy cymbal which allowed them to extract a "ping" that would sustain until the next "ping." In other words, Jo Jones had smoothed out the manner for playing timekeeping rhythms, and bop drummers extended this to achieve an even more continuous (legato) sound. Bop drummers also emphasized the practice of snapping the high-hat shut sharply on the second and fourth beats of each measure. (For demonstrations, listen to the JAZZ STYLES CASSETTE, side 1.) [24]

**Piano**  Concepts of rhythm section playing did not advance as rapidly as those of solo playing. In fact, some pre-1947 Gillespie and Parker recordings contain bop-style melodies and improvisations which are accompanied by swing-style pianists, bassists, and drummers. However, bop pianists eventually mastered **comping,** a technique of spontaneous chording that flexibly interacts with the improvised solo lines.

[24]Most of this discussion will mean nothing without the sounds it describes. So have a drummer demonstrate all these practices in person for you, and listen to recordings of the drummers mentioned. All can be heard in SCCJ: Jo Jones in Count Basie's "Doggin' Around," "Taxi War Dance," and "Lester Leaps In," and Benny Goodman's "I've Found a New Baby" and "Breakfast Feud;" Sid Catlett in Dizzy Gillespie's "Shaw Nuff;" Kenny Clarke in Miles Davis's "Boplicity" and Tadd Dameron's "Lady Bird;" Roach in Parker's "Klactoveesedstene" and "Ko-Ko" and in Sonny Rollins's "Blue Seven" and "Pent-Up House."

This accompaniment technique had been demonstrated by Count Basie as early as the mid-1930s. (For demonstration examples, listen to the JAZZ STYLES CASSETTE, side 1. For Basie's own comping, listen to "Lester Leaps In" in the JAZZ CLASSICS CASSETTE.) Swing piano styles began to take advantage of the widening use of string bass. Pianists placed less emphasis on the left hand for supplying chorded or single-note bass lines. By the time bop was well underway, pianists had almost entirely abandoned the left hand's bass functions that were so common in stride, boogie woogie, and swing piano; a new left-hand style evolved which was to characterize jazz piano for several decades.

**Bud Powell** (1924–1966) is the most imitated of all bop pianists. Powell crafted his approach from Art Tatum's, with other borrowings from the styles of Billy Kyle and Nat Cole. Atop these foundations, Powell incorporated the style and phrases of Charlie Parker and Dizzy Gillespie. The result was one of the first modern jazz piano styles.[25]

Powell de-emphasized the activity of the left hand, thereby departing from the stride tradition and the "chomp, chomp, chomp, chomp" style of chording used by many swing pianists. This served to lighten the way pianists had begun playing, even more than the streamlining introduced by Teddy Wilson and Nat Cole. In place of the striding left-hand figures, **Powell's left hand inserted brief, sporadically placed two- and three-note chords that reduced his statement of harmony to the barest minimum.** Sometimes the chords sustained for a few beats. Sometimes there was no left-hand sound at all. This comping style became the standard means that modern pianists used to suggest the chords underlying their own solo lines. This development was almost as significant within the history of solo piano conception as the emergence of comping had been for rhythm section pianists who were accompanying horn solos. In other words, **the breakthrough that Count Basie had made in lightening the manner in which a pianist supplied chords and support for an improvising soloist was paralleled by the way Powell lightened the manner in which a pianist accompanied his own solo lines.**

In his prime (prior to the mid-1950s), Powell had the speed and dexterity to create piano solos that almost matched the high-powered inventions of Parker and Gillespie. He mastered the erratically syncopated rhythms of bop and charged through his solos with terrific force. He employed the horn-like lines of Earl Hines

[25]Powell also contributed several original compositions to bop: "Tempus Fugit," "Parisian Thoroughfare," "Celia," "Dance of the Infidels," and "Hallucinations," which is also known as "Budo." Listen to Powell's 1947 rendition of "Somebody Loves Me" in SCCJ, his 1951 rendition of "Night in Tunisia" in SCCJ-R, his 1949 "Tempus Fugit," 1953 "Polkadots and Moonbeams," 1951 "Un Poco Loco" in *Jazz Piano*, Smithsonian 039, and get *The Complete Bud Powell Blue Note Recordings: 1949–1958*, Mosaic MR5-116. See John Rodby's transcription and analysis of "Un Poco Loco" from Blue Note 1577 in his *Solos for Jazz Piano* (Carl Fischer, 1989). For more transcribed solos, see Clifford Jay Safane's *Bud Powell* (Consolidated Music, 1978; available from Jamey Aebersold). See John Mehegan's transcription of Powell's solo on "Nice Work If You Can Get It" (*The Bud Powell Trio Plays*, Roulette CDP 7339022 (Roost 2224), CD, 1947–53) in *Jazz Improvisation, Vol. 2* (Watson-Guptill, 1962) and his analysis of Powell's concepts in *Jazz Improvisation, Vol. 3* (Watson-Guptill, 1964).

and Nat Cole plus the florid ideas of Art Tatum. **Powell was the model for hundreds of pianists during the 1940s and 50s, as James P. Johnson had been during the 1920s and Earl Hines had been after Johnson.**

Though Powell lived until 1966, he was only sporadically active throughout most of his career. Of the other excellent players, another favorite of bandleaders was pianist **Al Haig** (1924–1982). Traveling with some of the top groups, including Parker's and Stan Getz's, Haig was a very sought-after pianist and made numerous recordings. His flowing solos and tasteful comping made him a top figure on the bop scene. Haig never seemed at a loss for ideas. His touch was light and clean. In some ways he resembled Teddy Wilson. Haig could play hard, driving pieces or slow, pretty ballads. On occasion he could be quite flowery, but usually he was a very direct, swinging player. (Listen to Haig on Dizzy Gillespie's "Shaw Nuff" in the JAZZ CLASSICS CASSETTE.)

Two bop pianists who found much larger audiences than Haig or Powell were **George Shearing** (b. 1919) and Oscar Peterson. Peterson's reputation was established in a trio format with bass and guitar or drums, whereas Shearing became known primarily for the group sound he perfected: soft, polished ensemble statements voiced for piano, guitar, vibraharp, bass, and drums. Shearing has probably the cleanest, lightest piano sound in bop. His music sounds so refined that it has been called "polite bop." In addition to playing single-note lines and octave-voiced lines, he helped popularize the locked-hands style heard in Milt Buckner's playing of the mid-1940s, though Shearing's voicings differ from Buckner's. Shearing brought a very sophisticated harmonic conception to jazz piano. In his combo, Shearing often arranged his pieces so that each note of the melody was harmonized by his right hand on the piano, and played in unison with the vibraharp while the guitar played it one octave below with Shearing's left hand sounding the same note on the piano. Bass and drums underscored critical figures and kept time. Individual solos followed, framed by ensemble fills and endings, all well rehearsed and precisely performed. Everything swung and was well controlled.[26]

**Oscar Peterson** (b. 1925) is one of the most widely envied pianists in jazz history. His extraordinary pianistic facility and endurance enable him to take tempos so fast that bassists and drummers can barely keep up with him. Peterson's ballad style is full and orchestral. He sweeps the entire keyboard with a command which amazes other pianists. Peterson has a distinctive style originating from the approaches of Nat Cole, Bud Powell, and Art Tatum. He also has incorporated the funky, gospel-flavored figures popularized by Horace Silver. Peterson has probably generated more swing feeling than any other jazz pianist from the bop era, and his concert and club date recordings are filled with sizzling renditions of pop tunes and jazz standards. He has been one of the most popular pianists in jazz, and his trios, particularly those with bassist Ray Brown, attained the status of a jazz institution. Many

---

[26]An excellent sampler for Shearing is *Lullaby of Birdland*, Verve 827977 (MGM), LP set, 1949–54. Note that Shearing also achieved a successful integration of Latin American elements and bop. Armando Peraza played auxiliary percussion with him from 1954 until 1964. For an interview with Shearing, see *The Great Jazz Pianists* by Len Lyons (Quill, 1983). For a technical discussion of Shearing's techniques, see John Mehegan's *Jazz Improvisation*, *Vol.3* (Watson-Guptill, 1964).

pianists count Peterson among their first influences. Peterson has remained a formidable force on the modern jazz scene since the late 1940s. His surging power and vitality never seemed the least bit diminished.[27]

**Clarinet**  The clarinet has not been an important instrument in modern jazz. One of the most popular instruments during the swing era, it became one of the least popular during the bop era. Only a handful of clarinetists attempted to play bop on the instrument, and none of them gained appreciable recognition.[28]

**Guitar**  Guitar disappeared as a member of the rhythm section during the bop era, but it returned as a solo instrument. Though bop was first pioneered as a style on saxophone and trumpet, it was soon assimilated by players of other instruments. Guitarists were among the last to learn bop style, and they did not improvise with the originality of Parker and Gillespie. Jimmy Raney and Tal Farlow were the most outstanding bop guitarists, and they were more visible during the late 1940s and early 50s than during the developmental period of the mid-40s.[29]

**Trumpet**  Dizzy Gillespie was the leading trumpeter at the beginning of the bop era. But by the late 1940s, Miles Davis and Fats Navarro were so good at the new style that they also had imitators. When Charlie Parker and Gillespie separated, **Miles Davis** became Parker's new trumpeter. Davis and Parker recorded together from 1945 to 1948, and sporadically after that time.[30] In these recordings, Davis displayed elements of both Gillespie's and Parker's styles, though he used a lighter, softer tone and played less in the high register than Gillespie. (See Miles Davis chapter for more.) Even as early as 1945, Davis was important as an original and gifted improviser. Evidence of this is found in his combo recordings with Parker and the impact they had on the styles of trumpeters Shorty Rogers, Chet Baker, and Jack Sheldon. (See next chapter for more.)

[27]A sample of Peterson's hottest playing is in live recordings collected from tours with the *Jazz at the Philharmonic: The Oscar Peterson Trio Set*, Verve 825099, LP, 1952–53. Also listen to Oscar Peterson's 1952 studio rendition of "Night and Day" in *Jazz Piano*, Smithsonian 039. See John Mehegan's transcription of Peterson's solo on "I've Got the World on a String" in *Jazz Improvisation, Vol. 2* (Watson-Guptill, 1962) and "Joy Spring" in *Jazz Improvisation, Vol. 4* (Watson-Guptill, 1965). See John Rodby's transcription and analysis of Peterson's solo on "All the Things You Are" from Mercury 8923 in his *Jazz Solos for Piano* (Carl Fischer, 1989). For more about Peterson, see *The Great Jazz Pianists* by Len Lyons (Quill, 1983).

[28]Tony Scott, Stan Hasselgard, and Buddy DeFranco played bop on the clarinet, but their efforts did not catch on. Listen to DeFranco on "No Figs" in the JAZZ CLASSICS CASSETTE.

[29]Other bop guitarists became known during the 1950s and 60s; among them were Kenny Burrell, Wes Montgomery, Grant Green, and Pat Martino. Raney and Farlow remained excellent performers during the 1980s.

[30]Counting alternate takes and recordings for both Savoy and Dial record companies, Davis recorded more than one hundred selections with Parker. For transcriptions and analyses of Davis solos from this period on "Klactoveesedstene" and "Bird of Paradise," see Stuart Isacoff's *Solos for Jazz Trumpet* (Carl Fischer, 1985; order from Carl Fischer Music Store, 54 Cooper Square, NY, NY 10003).

**Listening Guide for "Shaw Nuff"**

Composed by Dizzy Gillespie and Charlie Parker; Recorded May 11, 1945 by Dizzy Gillespie (trumpet), Charlie Parker (alto sax), Al Haig (piano), Curley Russell (bass), and Sid Catlett (drums); available on the JAZZ CLASSICS CASSETTE, Side One; SCCJ, and *Bebop* (New World 271); available on CD in the Revised SCCJ.

This is one of the earliest bop recordings. It presents Charlie Parker and Dizzy Gillespie in top form. Their work is guided by the chord progression of "I Got Rhythm" in a 32-bar A-A-B-A format. This is similar to the progression of chords used in the accompaniment for "(Meet The) The Flintstones," demonstrated on the JAZZ STYLES CASSETTE, as well as "Cottontail" and "Lester Leaps In" on the JAZZ CLASSICS CASSETTE. The organization of this particular performance will be easier to detect if you have already learned the strategy for keeping your place by counting beats, as explained on page 381, and the A-A-B-A accompaniment pattern, as presented on the JAZZ STYLES CASSETTE.

The sound of bop is often incomprehensible to listeners the first few times they hear it. The contours of the phrases are jagged with unexpected accents and frequent changes of direction. The improvisers pack their solos with many different melodic ideas in rapid succession. Because of this, audiences often perceive the music as chaotic. But bop becomes more comprehensible as it becomes more familiar, and we can easily familiarize ourselves with it by replaying the recordings. Just as a foreign language becomes less forbidding as we begin to recognize its words, bop becomes more comprehensible as we begin to recognize its standard accompaniment devices and we begin to partition the solo improvisations according to those markers. After listening only a few times to a piece, we can begin to recognize phrases and follow the contours of the solos.

Here are some clues for detecting patterns in this performance of "Shaw Nuff." Keep in mind that the tempo is very fast. You will need to count "1234 1234" rapidly if you wish to follow the form of the piece by keeping track of beats. If you get lost, don't despair. Just wait and restart your counting when you hear a new soloist begin. Following the form of jazz pieces is much like watching a merry-go-round because we can jump on when the same part comes around again. Sandwiched between an introduction and an ending, the main melody for "Shaw Nuff" and all its solo improvisations follow the same 32-bar A-A-B-A form. With the beginning and ending melody statements and three solo choruses, that form occurs five consecutive times, four opportunities to catch up if we get lost. And you needn't wait for the same position in the chorus to come round again if you lose your place. Just listen for the beginning of a bridge; it sounds different from repetitions of the A-section. In addition, your familiarity with the "I Got Rhythm" chord progression will guide you.

You might want to begin getting a feeling for the tempo while you listen to the introduction. However, that section is the most rhythmically complicated of the piece, so you might find it easier to determine tempo from the middle sections of the performance.

The final eight-measure section of the introduction has the horns playing in unison. The horn line emphasizes off-beats, and it contains sudden starts and stops. It is a typically syncopated bop line. In the sixth measure of this section, the horns play the first note of the scale for the piece. Then they play it again an octave higher. Finally they end their phrase by dwelling on a note which is the famous "flatted fifth" step of that scale. (For an explanation and keyboard illustration of this interval, see page 371.) This interval became identified with bop, and it is also used to end the piece. Incidentally, Gillespie has said that they played flat fifths "just to be weird." This is consistent with the playful nature of Gillespie's style; and their flat fifth has a teasing effect here because of the abrupt way it is inserted and because the horns don't resolve the tension it generates. After that note, everyone but the pianist stops playing. This provides a stop-time break in which the pianist improvises a line of eighth notes that fill the remaining eight beats (two measures) of the introduction. When all the musicians resume, we hear the main melody of the piece played in unison by the trumpet and saxophone.*

Terms to learn from the JAZZ STYLES CASSETTE before you attempt to use this listening guide: alto sax, trumpet, ride rhythm, high-hat, bass drum, stop-time, A-A-B-A song form, comping, walking bass, staccato, and syncopation.

| Elapsed Time | |
|---|---|

### INTRODUCTION (24 measures long)

*First Eight Measures*

A two-measure pattern played four times by piano, bass and drums.

0' 07"    *Second Eight Measures*

A four-measure phrase played twice in harmony by trumpet and alto saxophone. The end of the second playing differs from the first.

Accompaniment includes sustained piano chords played on the down beat of each measure. Bass is playing a note on every beat with a relentless driving quality. Drummer is playing ride rhythms on opening and closing high-hat.

0' 13"    *Third Eight Measures*

Horns play a line in unison that contains several interruptions, emphasizes off-beats and is accompanied only by drums (no piano or bass). They stop with the sixth measure and let the pianist play alone for the final eight beats, as a transition to the first chorus.

0' 19"    ### FIRST CHORUS (A-A-B-A)
A

Melody is played in unison and octaves by trumpet and sax, accompanied by piano comping, walking bass, and drummer playing ride rhythms with high-hat snapping shut sharply every other beat.

0' 26"    A

0' 33"    B

0' 40"    A

0' 46"    ### SECOND CHORUS (A-A-B-A)

*Charlie Parker Alto Saxophone Improvisation**

Parker constructs his line mostly out of eighth notes, in smoothly rising and falling contours. Comping is sparse.

0' 53"    *Second A-section*

Note how Parker rests briefly before launching the bridge section of his solo.

1' 00"    *Bridge*

Parker tosses ascending and descending phrases. Piano chords are begun on down beats and sustained eight beats. Parker's transition into the last A-section is seamless.

* A written transcription of the Charlie Parker improvisation from this recording is in *Creative Jazz Improvisation* by Scott Reeves (Prentice-Hall, 1989).

*Elapsed Time*

**1' 07"**

*Last A-section*

Piano chording goes back to staccato style and uses more varied rhythms than in the bridge.

**1' 14"**

### THIRD CHORUS (A-A-B-A)

*Dizzy Gillespie Trumpet Improvisation*

**A-A**

Gillespie begins dramatically by running up to a high note and decorating it with a fall-off. This exuberance is a trademark of his style. That opening figure is all the more striking because he leaves nine beats of silence after it. Then he plays a stream of eighth notes until the last measure of the first A-section. Like Parker, he also rests briefly during the eighth bar of each section. In the second A-section, Gillespie unfolds another long line comprised mostly of eighth notes, and then he rests in the eighth measure. The piano chords accompanying him change every two to four beats, and they are played mostly in a staccato manner.

**1' 27"**

*Bridge*

Gillespie begins by playing three high notes very loudly and firmly. Each piano chord lasts eight beats, and Haig strikes them on the first beat of the measure and lets them ring. Then he returns to supplying a more staccato and syncopated chording after the seventh measure of the bridge. Gillespie fills the final four measures of the bridge with a long string of eighth notes.

**1' 33"**

**A**

Gillespie bases the first twelve beats of his line entirely on triplets, that is, three notes on each beat. After that, he returns to playing long strings of eighth notes.

**1' 40"**

### FOURTH CHORUS (A-A-B-A)

*Al Haig Piano Improvisation*

Haig depends mostly on eighth notes to construct his improvisation with his right hand. He accompanies himself with chords played by his left hand. Notice how the rhythms in his lines are similar to Parker's. Haig was one of the first pianists to learn bop style. Accompaniment includes walking bass and ride rhythms on cymbals. The drummer drops "bombs" in the fourth, eighth, tenth, and thirteenth measures. Bombs are more frequent in the bridge.

**2' 07"**

### FIFTH CHORUS (A-A-B-A)

#### Same as FIRST CHORUS (Melody)

Accompaniment includes more bass drum "bombs" than in first chorus.

**2' 34"**

### ENDING

Same 24-measure form as the **INTRODUCTION.** This differs slightly from the way the introduction ends because after the "call" from the horns playing a sustained flat fifth, the "response" from the piano is not a string of eighth notes but a quick whole-tone scale. (See Figure 9.1 for instructions on playing a whole-tone scale. Then play the numbered piano keys in reverse order to approximate the final sound on this recording.)

The trumpeter most often mentioned as a match for Gillespie was **Fats Navarro** (1923–1950). The tremendous high range, speed, and instrumental proficiency of Gillespie were almost equalled by Navarro. In addition to that, he had a fuller, brassier tone which he used more smoothly than Gillespie. His tone was a bit clearer and more even; Navarro was not prone to alter his tone size or color as did Gillespie and Roy Eldridge. However, Navarro did not have the rhythmic imagination and daring of Gillespie. Navarro used vibrato more than Gillespie and Davis did, and this element became an essential aspect in the style of Clifford Brown, Navarro's influential disciple. Brown went on to spread the Navarro style directly to far more trumpeters than Navarro did himself.[31]

**Trombone**   Bop style was so instrumentally demanding that it is surprising the style could be played on so difficult an instrument as the slide trombone. But there were several trombonists in the earliest days of bop, and a number of outstanding masters had emerged by the 1950s (see next chapter for details). **J. J. Johnson** (b. 1924) is the musician most prominently identified with playing bop on the trombone, though he rarely improvised lines that were as complicated as Parker's or Gillespie's. Johnson's lines were often simple and tune-like. Many of his solos are quite singable. Incidentally, this gift for melody was not restricted to jazz improvisation. Johnson was very active as a composer. His jazz albums from the 1950s and 60s are filled with originals he penned, and he spent most of the 1970s writing and arranging music for movies and television instead of playing jazz.

J. J. Johnson departed from several traditions of jazz trombone playing by having an unprecedented command over the instrument and by

1) using very little vibrato
2) producing a smooth, consistent sound rather than the guttural tone quality that many premodern trombonists favored; Johnson attacked each note cleanly and maintained consistent size and quality throughout its duration.
3) avoiding the dependence on wide, drawn-out slurs and rips which typified many early players. When Johnson used inflections at all, they were clipped, and they ornamented his main tones in a well-manicured way.
4) playing with a rhythmic regularity and evenness that lent his music a bounce and a smooth swing feeling, especially evident in his eighth-note lines.

Many earlier players had given their trombones a highly extroverted role in jazz by using a choppy melodic style, rough tone, and extensive pitch inflections. Johnson, on the other hand, brought subtlety to the instrument's role and increased its politeness. Consistent with this stance, Johnson's choice of mute was not the rubber plunger favored by growl-style players. It was a cup mute that made his already

---

[31]Listen to Navarro on Tadd Dameron's 1948 recording of "Lady Bird" in SCCJ. For a wider sampling, get *The Fabulous Fats Navarro, Vol. 1 & 2*, Blue Note 81531/32, CD/LP, 1947–50 or *Fat Girl*, Savoy 2216, LP set, 1946–47. See pages 412–13 for information on how to get Miles Davis, Fats Navarro, and Clifford Brown solo transcriptions and analyses by David Baker.

dark, subdued sound even more gentle and clean. (For an example of this sound, listen to the JAZZ STYLES CASSETTE, side 2.) Johnson narrowed the emotional range of the jazz trombone while taking on the quick pace and increased complexity of bop. In other words, he streamlined jazz trombone conception.[32]

**Tenor Saxophone**

Bop tenor saxophonists drew their styles from two primary sources: Lester Young and Charlie Parker, and several secondary sources including Coleman Hawkins, Don Byas, and others. Some preferred to play the phrases of Lester Young almost unmodified, while others simply adopted the phrases of alto saxophonist Charlie Parker and played them on tenor sax. The most original players mixed several sources with their own ideas.[33]

**Dexter Gordon** (1923–1990) was the first tenor saxophonist to be recognized as a bop player. He is one of the least stereotyped bop tenor saxophonists. Though some of his melodic ideas recalled Lester Young, Gordon's tone was deep, dark, and full, not light or hollow like Young's. He used the entire range of the tenor but had a special love for its low register. Although his style was quite aggressive, his work conveyed great ease. There was a sense of authority and majesty about his work. Perhaps the most melodic of all bop tenors, he was known for his well-paced solo improvisations that are logical, soulful, and muscular. He used a large variety of melodic devices to create his lines. His phrase lengths and rhythms were varied, and he combined bop clichés with his own inventions. Gordon loved to quote from pop tunes and bugle calls. More than any other bop tenor, Gordon was known for developing his solos by making firm statements and following through on them. This tendency increased in his playing during the 1960s and 70s. In his later years, he offered phrase after phrase of complete musical ideas, well rounded and meaty. Gordon was a favorite player for many tenor saxophonists who were later called *hard bop*. Gordon had a strong recording career from the 1940s into the 1980s and his playing displayed depth and swing for over four decades. (Listen to his "Bikini" in SCCJ.)[34]

[32]Listen to *The Eminent J.J. Johnson, Vol. 1 & 2*, Blue Note 81505/6, CD/LP, 1953–55 and *Trombone Master*, CBS 44443, CD/LP, 1958–60. For more about Johnson, see David Baker's *J.J. Johnson Trombone* (Shattinger, 1979) and pages 137–49 in Ira Gitler's *Jazz Masters of the Forties* (Macmillan, 1966; reprinted by DaCapo). For transcriptions of Johnson's own favorite improvisations, see John Leisenring and Hunt Butler's *J.J. Johnson Solos: 13 Personal Favorites* (Jamey Aebersold, 1989).

[33]It is possible to classify bop tenor saxophonists in several ways, including the relative portions of Lester Young's and Charlie Parker's styles that are detectable. The easiest approach lies in the dimension of tone. Bop tenor saxophonists preferred light-weight, light-colored tones or heavy-weight, dark-colored tones. There are gradations within these categories, of course, but it might be helpful to first describe players in terms of the two extremes, and then form your own descriptions to increase and refine your perceptions. The light-toned players include Stan Getz, Herbie Steward, Allen Eager, Brew Moore, and several players of a somewhat later style (West Coast): Buddy Collette, Bill Perkins, Bob Cooper, Richie Kamuca, and others. The heavy-toned players include Dexter Gordon, Gene Ammons, Lucky Thompson, Wardell Gray, Sonny Stitt, and others.

[34]Listen to Dexter Gordon's *Master Takes*, Savoy 1154, LP, 1945–47. For more about Gordon, see Stan Britt's *Dexter Gordon: A Musical Biography* (DaCapo, 1989) and Ira Gitler's *Jazz Masters of the Forties* (Macmillan, 1966; reprinted by DaCapo).

For flowing, powerfully swinging solos, few modern saxophonists could compete with **Sonny Stitt** (1924–1982). His instrumental speed and precision awed other players. His notes were played with a lilt and crispness, the evenness of which was ·unmatched. Stitt's playing had a consistently logical construction and rarely lacked continuity. During the late 1940s and early 50s, Stitt was second only to Charlie Parker as the leading bop alto saxophonist, and his recordings with Bud Powell placed him in the highest rank of bop tenor saxophonists.[35] Stitt was not as much of an originator as Dexter Gordon, but he influenced and inspired many modern saxophonists with his own style.[36] **Stitt inspired many players partly because he had enviable command over the saxophone, playing with great ease, and an unusually high level of precision and consistency, and partly because he systematized a set of patterns which characterized bop approaches to improvisation. These patterns became formula for countless players in the mainstream of modern jazz.** It was much easier to learn these patterns than to learn the less predictable and rhythmically more complex inventions of Parker. In essence, Stitt formalized a mixture of Parker, Lester Young, and his own ideas into a homogeneous method that satisfactorily handled the entire range of tempos and common bop chord progressions.

**Stan Getz** (b. 1927) was one of the most distinctive tenor saxophonists to emerge during the 1940s. He did not rely as heavily on Lester Young's style as most other bop tenor saxophonists did, though he modelled his tone quality after Young's. He did not rely exclusively on Parker's and Gillespie's favorite phrases. He developed an original melodic and rhythmic vocabulary instead. His phrasing and accenting were less varied and syncopated than Parker's or Gillespie's. Getz played in a style that is rhythmically more like Lester Young's than Parker's style. At times, pre-twentieth century classical music seems to have influenced him more than bop.[37] Getz did not usually sound as relaxed as Dexter Gordon, but he was just as melodic. His improvisations were less like bop melodies than like melodies in classical music. Some were quite pretty. That aspect of his style fit well with his light, fluffy tone and graceful approach to the sax. Some historians believe his roots in swing era style are more evident than his bop roots. Many listeners categorize the Getz style as *cool jazz*, not bop. (See the next chapter for more about cool jazz.)

[35]Though he made more than one hundred albums under his own name, Stitt recorded some of his best solos under the leadership of others, including Dizzy Gillespie ("Eternal Triangle" on *Sonny Side Up*, Verve 825674, CD, 1957), Bud Powell ("All God's Chillun" on Sonny Stitt's *Bud's Blues*, OJC-009, LP, 1949–50), and Gene Ammons ("Blues Up and Down" on Gene Ammons/Sonny Stitt's *Prime Cuts*, Verve 2V6S-8812 (MGV 8426), LP set, 1961). For transcriptions of his solos on the albums *Stittsville*, *Sonny Side Up*, and *Soul Electricity*, see Gary Keller's *Sonny Stitt: Improvised Tenor Saxophone Solos* (Studio PR, 1985; available from Aebersold).

[36]Frank Foster, George Coleman, Joe Henderson, and John Coltrane are among the saxophonists who have cited Stitt as an influence. Stitt provided the main model for the mid-1950s style of Coltrane. See chapter 13 for more about this.

[37]Briefly in 1946, Getz performed in a bop style like Dexter Gordon's that is detectable in Getz's "Opus De Bop," "And the Angels Swing," "Running Water," and "Don't Worry About Me" on *Opus De Bop* (Savoy 1105, LP). Before and after that, he favored an original style that reflected a variant on Lester Young's style devised by Herbie Steward, Getz's bandmate in the Woody Herman group. Listen to Getz in Lennie Tristano's "No Figs" on the JAZZ CLASSICS CASSETTE. Then compare Getz with his bandmates in Woody Herman's "Four Brothers" on the JAZZ CLASSICS CASSETTE.

Stan Getz, one of the original "Four Brothers," the most distinctive of the "cool style" tenor saxophonists, and a pioneer of bossa nova. Pictured here in 1967 at age 40. (*Photo by Lee Tanner*)

Stan Getz was one of the few bop musicians to become popular with the general public. One of the prettiest pieces the Woody Herman big band recorded was "Summer Sequence" by Ralph Burns. It was rearranged several times during the late 1940s. One segment often lifted out was "Early Autumn," a feature for Getz.[38] Other Getz hits also took the form of slow, pretty pieces. His 1952 "Moonlight in Vermont" with guitarist Johnny Smith was quite popular. His 1962 "Desafinado" with guitarist Charlie Byrd was a major event in the popularization of *bossa nova*, a cross between Brazilian music and jazz. His 1964 recording of "Girl From Ipanema," with its vocal by Astrud Gilberto, became one of the best-selling records in jazz history.[39] During the 1980s, Getz was playing as well as in the 1940s, with remarkable verve and imagination. Moreover, he was hiring accompanists who reflected styles several generations removed from bop. Getz remained an outstanding figure in the saxophone world.

[38]Woody Herman—*Early Autumn*, Capitol 11034, LP, 1948–50; *Thundering Herds*, CBS 44108, CD/LP, 1945–47. For more about Herman, see pages 86–110 in Gene Lees's *Meet Me at Jim & Andy's* (Oxford, 1988) and Herman's own *Woodchopper's Ball* (Dutton, 1990).

[39]*Jazz Samba*, Verve 810061 (MGV-8432), CD, 1962; *Getz/Gilberto*, Verve 810048 (MGV 8545), CD, 1964. Do not let this discussion's emphasis on Getz's slow, pretty pieces lead you to overlook his exciting medium- and up-tempo style: *Stan Getz at Storyville*, Vogue 600093, CD, 1951 (also issued on Roost and Roulette); and *Stan Getz and J.J. Johnson at the Opera House*, Verve 831272, CD, 1957.

**Big Bands**   A number of big bands were influenced by bop during the 1940s. Though most played primarily in swing era styles, a few had substantial libraries of bop style arrangements.[40] The most outstanding was led by Dizzy Gillespie, whom we have already discussed. A swing style clarinetist-saxophonist named **Woody Herman** (1913–1987) led one of the best known bop-influenced big bands, a favorite among musicians. Toward the end of the 1940s, Herman employed a number of outstanding modern soloists and composer-arrangers (see footnote 38). His most historically significant personnel featured four saxophonists who all had roots in the style of Lester Young and were then assimilating bop styles—the baritone saxophonist Serge Chaloff and the tenor saxophonists Stan Getz, Zoot Sims, and Herbie Steward. (Listen to Chaloff and Getz on Lennie Tristano's "No Figs" in the JAZZ CLASSICS CASSETTE.) Though often considered part of "cool jazz" that was identified somewhat later, they were at an early peak of their creativity during the late 1940s when bop was in full bloom. Because there were four of them and because Jimmy Giuffre wrote a feature number for them called "Four Brothers," this particular Herman band has historically gone by the name of "The Four Brothers Band." (Listen to "Four Brothers" in the JAZZ CLASSICS CASSETTE while you study the listening guide.)

The Four Brothers Band was only one of many high points in Woody Herman's career. In 1939 his band had recorded "Woodchoppers Ball," a riff-based twelve-measure blues that became a big hit. Herman also had a number of other hit records during the swing era, many as a vocalist. Then he not only survived the decline of big bands, but he spent the rest of his life leading a steady stream of excellent bands that often featured distinctive modern players whose styles were far removed from the swing styles—there were John Coltrane disciples among his saxophonists of the 1970s and 80s. Throughout their history, his bands steered clear of ambitious and exotic orchestral conceptions. They always retained a looseness that was identified with Herman's band style. Herman liked his music to be swinging and direct. In fact, he edited out any passages in his men's pieces that he considered elaborate or unswinging. Herman deserves credit for his staying power as well as his allegiance to a simple and unpretentious big band style. Known for diversity and adaptability, Herman's "herds" (as they have been affectionately called) were long a dependable mainstay on the jazz scene.

**Popular Appeal**   With the advent of bop, the status of jazz began to resemble that of classical chamber music more than that of American popular music. It became an art music in the sense that its performance required highly sophisticated skills and it was appreciated by only a relatively small elite. Jazz had always required special skills because of its demand for so much spontaneous creativity, and, as far as American popular music went, it had long been in the elite. Yet bop crystallized those tendencies, removed jazz even further from the mainstream of American popular music,

[40]For bop and bop-influenced big bands, listen to Dizzy Gillespie's *Dizziest*, RCA Bluebird 5785, LP set, 1946–49; *Jazz in Revolution*, New World 284, LP anthology; *Big Band Jazz*, Smithsonian 2200, LP set; *Mirage*, New World 216, LP anthology; and see footnotes in the next chapter for Stan Kenton.

**Listening Guide for "Four Brothers"**

Composed and arranged by Jimmy Giuffre; *Recorded December 27, 1947 by the Woody Herman big band (five trumpets, three trombones, four saxophones, rhythm guitar, piano, bass, and drums); available on the JAZZ CLASSICS CASSETTE, Side One; also on LP and CD in *Big Band Jazz* (Smithsonian), and *Woody Herman: The Thundering Herds, 1945–1947* (CBS CJ 44108).

"Four Brothers" remained one of the most frequently requested numbers in Woody Herman's repertory since its first recording was released. Swing style and bop style are both evident in this arrangement. Lester Young's approach had helped spawn the evolution from swing to bop, and it is echoed here in the saxophone improvisations as well as the composed melody lines. Most of the improvised solos here differ sufficiently from swing style to be regarded as bop. Listeners also perceive this music as bop-flavored because some of the written syncopations were chosen from the favorite rhythms of Dizzy Gillespie and Charlie Parker.

There is no introduction. The performance begins directly on the first A-section of a thirty-two bar A-A-B-A form. The pace is rapid. So if you wish to keep your place by counting beats, be prepared to count "1234 2234 . . . " quickly. To identify the beats, you might synchronize your counting with the notes of the walking bass line or the ride cymbal.

*Elapsed Time*

**FIRST CHORUS** (32 measures)

|  |  |  |
|---|---|---|
|  | A | Three tenors and one baritone saxophone (the "four brothers") state the theme in harmony. Their line is almost all eighth notes. Accompaniment comes from rhythm guitar, piano, bass, and drums. Brass figures punctuate the pauses when the saxophonists take a breath. |
| 0' 08" | A | Same as first A-section, except for the ending that prefaces the bridge. |
| 0' 17" | B | New theme played by same saxophonists. Brass punctuations fill the pauses. |
| 0' 26" | A | Same as first A-section. |

**SECOND CHORUS**

|  |  |  |
|---|---|---|
| 0' 35" | A-A | Improvised solo by tenor saxophonist Zoot Sims. |
|  |  | Piano, guitar, bass, and drums accompany lightly. Brass punctuate sparingly. |
| 0' 53" | B | Improvised solo by baritone saxophonist Serge Chaloff. |
| 1' 02" | A | Chaloff continues. |

**THIRD CHORUS**

|  |  |  |
|---|---|---|
| 1' 10" | A-A | Improvised tenor saxophone solo by Herbie Steward. |
|  |  | Sustained saxophone harmonies provide a soft background. |
| 1' 27" | B | Improvised tenor saxophone solo by Stan Getz. |
|  |  | Trombones and saxes accompany with notes that are mostly two beats long. |
| 1' 36" | A | Getz continues his solo. |
|  |  | Final four measures have sustained trombone and baritone saxophone harmonies sounding softly in the background. That background indicates the progression of chords guiding the improvisation. Each chord lasts two beats. |

* The score and parts for this performance are available as item #7009276 from Hal Leonard Publishers, 7777 West Bluemound Road, Milwaukee, WI 53213.

| | |
|---|---|
| *Elapsed Time* | |
| 1' 44" | **FOURTH CHORUS** |
| | **A** Trumpets play a new figure in the upper register. Saxes answer them with a fresh line in unison that extends to the end of the *A-section*. Brass "kicks" fill in the pauses. Drum fills are scattered throughout. |
| 1' 53" | **A** Trumpets play their figure from the preceding A-section an octave higher. Saxes answer with a new unison line that extends to the eighth measure. Trumpets play a "tie-it-up" figure in the final measures. |
| 2' 02" | **B** Woody Herman clarinet solo. Notice his full, rich tone and his bent pitch ornaments. His choice of solo notes clearly delineates the movement of chords. |
| | Accompaniment includes the saxes softly playing mid-register chords on the off-beats, providing a syncopated rhythm underneath the clarinet solo. Sharply executed, staccato punctuations come from loud brass and snare drum. |
| 2' 11" | **A** Trumpets and trombones play a loud, syncopated phrase in unison with the snare drum. Saxes answer with a phrase of mostly eighth notes that extends almost to the end of the A-section. |
| 2' 20" | **FIFTH CHORUS** |
| | **A** Saxes and brasses play a simple "shout" figure loudly in harmony. This adds to the excitement because it is the first time the saxes and brasses have played a figure together. Drummer fills in the pauses. |
| 2' 29" | **A** Repeat of A. |
| 2' 36" | **B** Saxes play a syncopated figure in harmony. |
| 2' 47" | **A** Repeat of A |
| 2' 55" | **ENDING** |
| | *Two Measures* |
| | Stop-time solo improvisation by Getz, answered by a "kick" from the brass and rhythm section. |
| 2' 58" | *Two Measures* |
| | Stop-time solo improvisation by Sims, answered by a "kick" from the brass and rhythm section. |
| 3' 00" | *Two Measures* |
| | Stop-time solo improvisation by Steward, answered by a "kick" from the brass and rhythm section. |
| 3' 02" | *Two Measures* |
| | Stop-time solo improvisation by Chaloff, answered by two "kicks" from the brass and rhythm section. |
| 3' 04" | *Four Measures* |
| | Stop-time with saxes playing a long, pre-written string of eighth notes in harmony. |
| 3' 10" | *Four Measures* |
| | Entire band plays a chord. Brasses continue sustaining it while saxes play a bluesy figure that departs from tempo. Then saxes sustain their final note to rejoin the brasses. Snare drum fills finish the piece. |

and turned it into a fine art music. It is important to note, however, that like all jazz styles, bop had fans who could not follow every note and chord, but loved it anyway. Most jazz appeals to thousands of fans who like its sound but who lack understanding of its structure and historical significance. The fans of jazz proportionally include far more musicians than the fans of pop, rock, and country music, but even musician-fans do not technically understand what every improviser does. Musicians do have a greater appreciation for the underlying complexities of music, but that appreciation must be coupled with an attraction to the sound before they will spend time and money to hear it. *Knowledge of musical techniques will increase a listener's appreciation for the music, but no understanding is necessary for a listener to enjoy jazz—modern jazz or any other style.*

Bop was not nearly as popular as swing had been. When Charlie Parker died in 1955, he was an obscure figure compared to Benny Goodman, whose name was a household word. And yet Parker was musically a more significant force in jazz than Goodman. Several swing records sold more than a million copies, yet no bop instrumentals ever came close to that mark of popularity. There are several possible explanations for this. Many of them not only touch the differences between swing and bop, but they also constitute observations which help explain the historically low popularity of jazz as a whole.

One account for why bop was less popular than swing is that bop players presented a more serious appearance, one that was perhaps less inviting to all but the most devoted jazz fans. **Bop did not have as much visual appeal as swing.** Most swing bands carried singers, and many also carried dancers and showy staging. Bop combos, on the other hand, rarely carried singers, dancers, or showy staging. To appreciate modern jazz, people had to listen instead of watch.

Another factor affecting bop popularity is that, by comparison with swing, **bop had a scarcity of singers.** The bop listener was rarely offered song lyrics or the good looks and personality of the singer delivering them. More than ever before, jazz fans now had to follow melodies that had no words. This made jazz more abstract and less enjoyable. Singers have traditionally been more popular than instrumentalists. Perhaps people like music with lyrics more than they like purely instrumental music because when someone sings a song, it is as though the singer is talking directly to you. This occurs because lyrics are in a language that is common for both the performer and the listener. Jazz instrumentals, on the other hand, are in a language that is known to only a tiny portion of the listening public. In addition to offering familiarity in the form of words, vocals also offer familiarity in the sound source itself. The human voice produces a sound that is far more familiar to listeners than that of any instrument. And, because of this greater familiarity, music made with the voice can be expected to achieve greater popularity than music made with instruments.

Listeners have historically shown that they like relatively uncomplicated music. Furthermore, they like music to be fairly predictable. They especially like themes that they can sing along with, remember, and hum by themselves. **In comparison to swing, bop is neither uncomplicated nor predictable, and the written melodies in many bop performances are difficult to follow.** A sizable percentage of bop tunes are so complicated that, even if listeners became familiar with them, it is unlikely that they could sing along with them.

It is essential to note that when we say "bop is complicated and unpredictable," we are talking about accompaniment styles as well as solo styles. The point is important when explaining popularity because relatively simple accompaniments backed even the most complicated swing era improvisations. Piano, guitar, bass, and drum parts were relatively simple, and they followed fairly predictable patterns that were quite steady. On the other hand, rhythm section accompaniment in bop style was less regular and therefore less predictable. Then as the 1940s progressed, drummers began to break up their timekeeping patterns and cultivate more and more musical surprises. Therefore the decreasing popularity that was associated with the development of jazz styles during the 1940s might be explained partly by the increasing complexity of solo improvisations and the decreasing predictability of accompaniment rhythms.

Danceability was another problem for bop. **People chose not to dance to bop.** Bop combos sometimes played for dances, but they were invited to do this far less often than they were hired to play strictly for listening. This is curious. People could have danced to bop. It had a steady beat and great rhythmic vitality. But somehow, this was not enough. Here are a few ideas that might account for this situation:

1) Perhaps bop's faster tempos scared away some dancers.
2) Perhaps the beat was not stated simply enough. It had to be made extremely obvious as it was in most swing band performances.
3) Perhaps arrangements provided insufficient repetition to make dancers feel comfortable.
4) Perhaps dancers wanted singable melodies in their ears before they felt like dancing.

The next four explanations are all part of the idea that **jazz improvisation is too abstract for the average listener** to enjoy. First, most bop melodies and improvisation resembled little or nothing that the average listener had heard before. (Listen to Dizzy Gillespie's "Shaw Nuff" in the JAZZ CLASSICS CASSETTE, and ask yourself what common popular music it suggests to you.) **The less familiar a piece sounds, the more abstract it is to the listener.** It is harder to follow when it does not resemble a familiar pattern. The harder it is to follow, the more abstract the listener perceives it to be. And, as a rule, the more abstract something is, the less popularity it receives.

A second aspect of bop that makes it abstract is that the **relation between an improvisation and a tune's original melody is almost nonexistent.** This could upset the listener who expected jazz improvisation to simply consist of variation on a familiar theme, in the manner that singers toy with melodies or the manner in which some popular instrumentalists "interpret" current songs. This problem could be especially acute to the listener who asks "Where is the melody?" and who must be told that, in jazz, the improvisation itself is the melody. Nonthematic improvisation had been done in jazz at least as early as the 1920s by Louis Armstrong and Sidney Bechet. But it was more abundant and more drastic in bop.

Jazz scholar Harvey Pekar has suggested a third aspect of bop that makes it abstract. He observes that **it is extremely difficult for the inexperienced listener to follow the relationship between improvised lines and chord changes in a typical bop performance.** His argument implies that listeners expect to hear particular relationships between notes in a solo line and the notes in the accompanying chord, and that listeners will notice the presence or absence of these expected relationships. As support for this argument, we find that Charlie Parker and Dizzy Gillespie are especially known for stretching the conventional ties between solo notes and accompanying notes and that Parker and Gillespie were less popular than their predecessors. In other words, the relationship between melody notes and accompaniment notes sounded unfamiliar to those who heard bop, and that lack of familiarity decreased the amount of popularity that bop had.

A fourth element of abstractness that might account for bop's low popularity is the **relative absence of formal packaging for improvisation and the greater length and amount of solo improvisations.** To begin appreciating this, first note that the most common size for jazz groups during the swing era was the ten to sixteen piece big band, but that the most common size for bop was the four to six piece combo. Also note that big bands, no matter what the era, tend to use more elaborate arrangements than combos use. Arrangement style that typified swing era big band performances used simple riffs to frame improvisations. The riffs accompanied improvisations, and they occurred before and after improvisations. They also interrupted long improvisations, thereby providing reference points which were especially effective for those listeners who might otherwise be overwhelmed by the newness and unpredictability offered in a jazz improvisation. In the swing format, then, improvisations were made somewhat comprehensible because the listener was required to cope only briefly with the unexpected. The riffs that accompanied the improvisations were simple and familiar, and there was a return to familiar material after each improvisation. (Listen to Count Basie's "Taxi War Dance," and compare it with Dizzy Gillespie's "Shaw Nuff" in the JAZZ CLASSICS CASSETTE.) In the bop format, on the other hand, musicians usually preset only the introduction, the theme, and the ending. Sandwiched between the theme and the ending was uninterrupted solo after solo. In other words, the amount of improvisation was less and the arrangement was more in swing era big bands than in bop combos. When improvisation must stand by itself because accompaniment is minimal, it is more difficult to grasp than when it is frequently interrupted and framed by familiar material. Bop was accordingly less popular than swing.

Another packaging asset available in swing format is that big bands use much of the same music in live performances as in broadcasts and recordings. This is because using written arrangements allows reproducibility that a dependence upon improvisation does not allow. Remember that both the accompaniments and the solos are improvised fresh in every bop combo performance, but preset arrangements provide most of the accompaniment in swing big band performances. This is relevant to popularity because the listener who had been exposed to the music ahead of time would find greater familiarity (hence, less abstractness) in a swing performance than in a bop performance of the same tune by the same musicians. The smaller amount of repetition in the bop performance would therefore present greater listening difficulty and, hence, less popularity for bop than for swing.

There is at least one problem with these explanations, however. They require that we assume jazz fans actually follow every note in the improvisations. Yet a sizable portion of swing fans probably follow only the prewritten parts, and a sizable portion of bop fans probably grasp only the overall feeling of the music.

Further support for these arguments comes when we look at those few bop combos that did achieve commercial success: the George Shearing Quintet, the Modern Jazz Quartet, and the Charlie Ventura Boptet. All three groups used formats that frequently interspersed tightly arranged and well-rehearsed ensemble statements among the improvisations. All offered a greater proportion of simpler, more singable melodies than most other bop combos used. All played many well-known songs. The Boptet had the additional asset of singers Jackie Cain and Roy Kral, and the Modern Jazz Quartet generally produced improvisations that were simpler and easier to follow than those ordinarily found in other bop combos. Two points are being made here. First, despite the generally low popularity of bop, there were a few groups and a few records that did become commercial successes. Second, the music within those successes has some of the same features we have outlined for explaining the popularity of swing. In addition, note that Charlie Parker's best-selling records were those he made of well-known songs with prewritten orchestral accompaniments, and the greatest hits for Stan Getz have been recordings of singable themes such as "Moonlight in Vermont," "Desafinado," and "Girl From Ipanema." As a final consideration, combine these two observations: first, that the Getz recording of "Girl From Ipanema" contains a vocal, and, second, that it represents the largest selling record in the Getz career.

After considering the preceding arguments, you can see that differences in **the amount of popularity enjoyed by different styles of music can be partly explained by differences in performance practices and differences between the ways each style treats basic elements of music.** In comparing the relative popularity of bop with swing, these performance practices are relevant: appearance, amount of improvisation, repetition, the amount of packaging for improvisation, and presence of words in the music. The musical elements of melody, harmony, and rhythm are also treated differently in the two styles. Bop offered higher, faster, more complex playing. Bop featured more variety of rhythms in melody lines and in accompaniments. Bop used richer chords, more chord changes, and a more elaborate relationship between the notes of the melody and the notes of the accompanying chords. Throughout jazz history the differences between jazz and popular music have echoed the same differences that are listed here between bop and swing. Therefore, because jazz has traditionally been less popular than most other forms of American music, its low popularity is probably due, in part, to these same differences in performance practice and use of musical elements.

Modern jazz continued the jazz tradition of influencing American popular music and symphonic music, but it seemed to carve its own sturdy path for musicians and a small audience of nonmusicians. Bop became parent for a series of other modern styles which were also less popular than swing. Jazz did not regain its popularity until the 1970s when a jazz-rock fusion brought millions of new fans.

## CHAPTER SUMMARY

1) Bop differed from swing by using smaller bands, richer chords, more chord changes, faster playing with more surprises and drier, more biting tone qualities.

2) The originators of bop were alto saxophonist Charlie Parker, trumpeter Dizzy Gillespie, and pianist Thelonious Monk.

3) Parker wrote numerous tunes based on popular song and twelve-bar blues chord progressions that became standard repertory for generations of jazz musicians.

4) Gillespie devised a very unorthodox trumpet style and led a string of combos and big bands.

5) Monk played piano in a very spare manner that was filled with unusual rhythms and harmonies, and he wrote tunes that were difficult because of their odd accents and chord progressions.

6) The ideas of Tatum, Parker, and Gillespie appeared in the piano style of Bud Powell who was widely imitated and who significantly altered jazz piano style by reducing the activity of the left hand.

7) Tenor saxophonist Dexter Gordon extended the deep, dark-toned, swing era style and mixed it with bop approaches and his own unique gift for lyricism.

8) Tenor saxophonist Stan Getz blended Lester Young, bop, and classical music to create an original style and became the most popular player on his instrument.

9) Pianists John Lewis and Tadd Dameron were important bop composers, and Lewis continued writing for the Modern Jazz Quartet long after the bop era.

10) The MJQ's vibraharpist Milt Jackson devised a warm, swinging style by way of a slow tremolo rate, intelligently constructed bop lines, relaxed delivery, and funky melodic figures.

11) Bop drummers differed from swing drummers by increasing the frequency and spontaneity of kicks and prods, feathering the bass drum instead of pounding it, playing timekeeping rhythms on a suspended cymbal, and snapping the high-hat shut sharply on the second and fourth beats.

12) Bop styles and their offshoots were less popular than swing styles because they used fewer popular tunes, they had fewer singers, less predictability and more complicated solos and accompaniments.

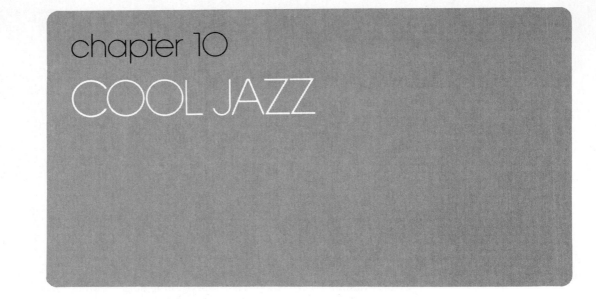

# chapter 10
# COOL JAZZ

Names for jazz styles usually come from journalists and fans, not from the musicians themselves. One of the least specific of these labels is "cool jazz." This term has not been embraced by jazz musicians. In fact, some players have been annoyed to hear it used to describe their music because it suggested that their playing conveyed a lack of passion and that they were emotionally detached from their work. Despite this, "cool jazz" is a widely used designation, and we will borrow it in this chapter to describe several significant jazz styles.

Journalists and record companies did use the term "cool jazz" extensively when they gave a disproportionate amount of attention to the output of white musicians based in California during the 1950s. But the label has not been limited to the work of musicians who belong to any particular race or geographic region. Generally **"cool jazz" has been used to describe music containing sounds that are not loud and tone qualities that are not rough or brassy.** You might find this especially apt for describing the sound of the Modern Jazz Quartet, which was discussed in the preceding chapter. The adjective "cool" has also been used to describe the music of Lester Young and musicians who were influenced by Young and Count Basie. One prominent example is saxophonist Stan Getz. Listeners also apply "cool" to the music that trumpeter-bandleader Miles Davis made before 1960.

Some historians separate cool jazz from bop, and much of the music that is mentioned in the second half of this chapter is indeed simpler, softer, and more melodic than the improvisations of Charlie Parker and Dizzy Gillespie. What has been called "cool jazz" also displays somewhat greater emphasis on countermelodies and preset arrangements. Note, however, that **a substantial amount of music called "cool" is not distinguishable from bop.** A solution to this labeling dilemma might be to use "cool bop" to designate some of the softer, less agitated variants because listeners do tend to perceive some of this music as subdued and understated, even if its rhythms, harmonies, and melodic contours derive from bop.

**174**

**Listening Guide for "No Figs"**

Composed and arranged by Lennie Tristano; Recorded January 10, 1950 by Buddy DeFranco (clarinet), Lee Konitz (alto sax), Stan Getz (tenor sax), Serge Chaloff (baritone sax), Billy Bauer (guitar), Lennie Tristano (piano), Eddie Safranski (bass), Max Roach (drums); available on the JAZZ CLASSICS CASSETTE, Side One; also on LP and CD as *The Bebop Era* (CBS CJ 40972).

With the exception of Tristano, Konitz, and Bauer, these musicians did not usually work together. This recording combined performers who had received the highest number of votes in various categories (' best pianist,' "best alto saxophonist," etc.) of a popularity poll run in 1949 by the jazz magazine *Metronome*.

"No Figs" is included as an example of cool jazz, particularly the unique modern styles of composer-pianist Lennie Tristano and his best known student, Lee Konitz. A number of different styles have been called "cool," but Tristano's was one of the first. His was also among the few modern styles not closely tied to bop. This selection was chosen because it is one of the only recordings that brings together Tristano, Konitz, and the eminent tenor saxophonist Stan Getz. We heard Getz in Woody Herman's "Four Brothers," a performance that combined the influence of Lester Young and bop. Getz has been tagged variously as "cool" or "bop," though his style is so unique that it deserves a category of its own. Coincidentally "No Figs" also features baritone saxophonist Serge Chaloff, another one of the original "four brothers." (Like Chaloff, the remaining soloists here, clarinetist Buddy DeFranco and trombonist Kai Winding, are not ordinarily classified as "cool." Most jazz historians classify them as bop.)

The performance begins with clarinet, alto sax, tenor sax, baritone sax, and guitar, accompanied by piano comping, walking bass, and drums. Guitar is used here as a melody instrument instead of providing chordal accompaniment. The drummer is using brushes to play timekeeping rhythms on the snare drum while snapping shut his high-hat sharply on the second and fourth beats of each measure. His close coordination with walking bass provides a steady and buoyant foundation.

"No Figs" is loosely based on the chord progression of "Indiana," with a form that can be described roughly as thirty-two bar A-B-A-C. (We could describe it as A-B-A-B' because the second "B" repeats portions of the first "B" but "C" is used here for the sake of simplicity.) This performance is comprised of four choruses. No soloist plays for an entire chorus, and Konitz solos only during the last eight measures of the first chorus. The opening theme statement runs through the first three eight-bar sections of "Indiana"'s form, designated here as A, B, and A. Then the improvisation by Konitz occupies the fourth section, C. Getz and Winding split a chorus. Then DeFranco and Chaloff split another. Tristano solos for the first half of the fourth chorus, and then the theme and ending occupy the second half.

*Elapsed Time*

**THEME**  (A-B-A of the "Indiana" chord progression)

A butterfly-like effect is created by complicated lines of triplets and sixteenth notes played in various harmonies and unisons by clarinet, alto sax, tenor sax, baritone sax, guitar, and piano. Notice how instrument sounds appear, disappear, and reappear in different combinations, some in harmony, some in unison. After the initial flurry of notes, a simpler line emerges with longer notes, less harmony, more *unisons and octaves. Then the butterfly-like effect returns, followed again by the simpler line.*

0' 29"  **LEE KONITZ ALTO SAX IMPROVISATION**  (the 8-measure C-section)

Konitz confines himself to the upper register of his instrument. Notice his soft tone and legato phrasing. He begins his solo in a very smooth manner, using mostly eighth notes. Then he bases his phrases on triplets and ends his solo with a crisp burst of sixteenth-notes.

*Elapsed Time*

To appreciate how much jazz alto saxophone timbres vary, contrast the Konitz sound here with the Johnny Hodges sound on "Prelude to a Kiss."

0' 43"   **STAN GETZ TENOR SAX IMPROVISATION** (16 measures, A-B)

Getz's improvisation exemplifies his own light and graceful approach. His solo has a lyric singing quality. This improvisation is filled with pretty melodies, though the fluidity is occasionally interrupted with bursts of notes forming phrases that mimick the Tristano-Konitz style.

Like Konitz, Getz also stays in the upper register. This makes his tone sound like Konitz's even more than would be expected from their mutual allegiance to Lester Young's lightweight, dry timbre. Notice that Getz's solo contains a larger variety of rhythms than Konitz used.

To appreciate how much tenor saxophone timbres vary, contrast the Getz sound here with Ben Webster's on "Cottontail" and John Coltrane's on "Flamenco Sketches."

1' 03"   **KAI WINDING TROMBONE IMPROVISATION** (16 measures, A-C)

1' 25"   **BUDDY DeFRANCO CLARINET IMPROVISATION** (16 measures, A-B)

1' 47"   **SERGE CHALOFF BARITONE SAX IMPROVISATION** (16 measures, A-C)

2' 08"   **LENNIE TRISTANO PIANO IMPROVISATION** (16 measures, A-B)

Almost all of Tristano's solo is in quadruple-time and has the same character as the introduction that he wrote for this piece. He accents the final note of each phrase ending. Most of his notes are harmonized, making his line sound as though played in locked-hands style.

2' 29"   **THEME** (8 measures, A)

2' 42"   **ENDING** (8 measures, C)

The line is in quadruple time, first by the piano alone, then joined by saxes, guitar, and clarinet, with the low-pitched sound of the baritone sax becoming prominent at the end. No bass or drums.

Here is one more example of how involved the labeling can get: The music of pianist-bandleader George Shearing, which was discussed in the preceding chapter and is considered "cool" by some and "bop" by others, has sometimes been termed "polite bop."

**Lennie Tristano and Lee Konitz**

Lennie Tristano (1919–1978) was a pianist, composer, and bandleader who **created a modern jazz alternative to bop** during the late 1940s. At that time, it was the most substantial alternative available. Though rarely a public performer since then, he impressed his students so much that they carried on his style. (Listen to Tristano's "No Figs" in the JAZZ CLASSICS CASSETTE, "Crosscurrent" in SCCJ, or "Subconscious Lee" in SCCJ-R.)

In devising a style of his own, Lennie Tristano began by learning the work of the great masters. Art Tatum and Lester Young were particularly important influences. In developing his pianistic facility, Tristano learned how to play Art Tatum runs that were difficult and impressive. Another piano playing technique Tristano perfected was improvising in the locked-hands style, a technique we first encoun-

A photograph of the January 10, 1950 recording session that produced "No Figs," heard on the JAZZ CLASSICS CASSETTE, Side One. Pete Rugolo conducts, and pianist-composer Lennie Tristano plays with the all-stars. Getz, Konitz, Bauer and Tristano are often tagged "cool jazz" style. The remaining musicians are more closely tied to bop style. (Gillespie's solo is not heard on the cassette version of this performance.) (*Photo by Herman Leonard, courtesy of Bob Asen*)

tered when studying the swing era and Milt Buckner. The composer J. S. Bach was also very important to him. Tristano regarded Bach so highly that he required his students to practice inventions composed by Bach and to perfect the skill of improvising in that style. He treated the music of Lester Young with similar reverence, requiring his students to learn Young's solo improvisations by carefully listening to recordings.

Tristano's music differed from bop in many ways. The pet phrases of Charlie Parker and Dizzy Gillespie did not find their way into his improvisations, though his work was equally complex, with several chord changes sometimes occurring in a single measure. Tristano favored long phrases, and his lines were less erratic than those of Parker and Gillespie. The contours of Tristano lines were smoother and less jumpy, and his choice of notes was original. Tristano's lines often seemed composed of notes that were a step or a half-step away from the notes in the chords, creating an unresolved feeling. Moreover, his lines were not melodic in the pop-tune sense or the bop sense, and his phrases did not swing in the customary bop manner. Instead, his impact tended to be very tight, on top of the beat, with less pronounced syncopation and rhythmic variety than Parker or Gillespie used. Tristano's improvisations were characterized by long strings of uninterrupted eighth notes, interspersed with patches of cleanly executed sixteenth notes. Some recalled Tatum's lines, without as much lightness and bounce. The result was a high-density, virtuosic piano sound, with almost no relaxation of the tension that was built up. Tristano's playing was almost severe in its intensity.

Most of Tristano's output is historically significant, and two performances—"Intuition" and "Digression"—are particularly precedent-setting.[1] As part of their training process during the mid-1940s, Tristano and his musicians had practiced improvising collectively without preset melodies, tempo, meter, or chord progressions (see pages 358–74 for explanations of these terms). Then, in 1949, they allowed a sample of this to be recorded. Though much of it conveyed a feeling of steady tempo and consistent key, these performances were truly free of preset form. In other words, **Tristano and his colleagues recorded collectively improvised "free" jazz, long before Ornette Coleman and Cecil Taylor were to become famous for it.**

Tristano made very few recordings during his career—the equivalent of about seven albums. His records remain collector's items because they did not sell well and are accordingly rare. His force on the jazz scene was partly felt through the teaching that was his primary occupation from 1951 to his death in 1978. Jazz insiders are familiar with his work and accord him significant respect, but most players after the 1950s perceived him as an underground figure or are altogether unaware of him. He influenced a number of excellent jazz musicians,[2] but like Tristano himself, most of them also remain unknown to the majority of jazz musicians and fans. Bill Evans and Cecil Taylor are well-known exceptions, and the Tristano legacy continued because Evans, in turn, influenced Herbie Hancock and Keith Jarrett.[3]

Tristano's most talented students during the 1940s were alto saxophonist **Lee Konitz** (b. 1927), tenor saxophonist Warne Marsh (1927–1987), and guitarist Billy Bauer. Together with bass and drums, Tristano joined his students and made recordings which still dazzle other musicians. (Listen to "Crosscurrent" in SCCJ and "Subconscious Lee" in SCCJ-R.)

In the late 1940s, the Lee Konitz saxophone style constituted a new sound in jazz. Konitz's command of the alto saxophone astonished fellow musicians.[4] In fact, players often argued about whether it was Konitz or Parker who had the most speed

---

[1]*Crosscurrents*, Capitol 11060; *Requiem*, Atlantic SD 2-7003, LP set, contains intact reissue of *Lennie Tristano*, Atlantic 1224, and *The New Tristano* Atlantic 1357.

[2]Tristano influenced pianists Ronnie Ball, Sal Mosca, Clare Fischer, Alan Broadbent, Wally Cirillo, and Connie Crothers, saxophonists John LaPorta, Teo Macero, and Ted Brown, and trumpeters Don Ferrara and Cy Touff. For more about Tristano and Konitz, see pages 226–261 in Ira Gitler's *Jazz Masters of the Forties* (Macmillan, 1966; reprinted by DaCapo).

[3]To hear the resemblance between Tristano and Evans, compare almost any Tristano piano solos with what Evans recorded with George Russell, for example "All About Rosie," in the anthology *Jazz Compositions*, Columbia PC 3702, or the solo on "Oleo" on the Evans album *Everybody Digs Bill Evans*, Fantasy OJC-068 (Riverside 1129), CD/LP. For a continuation of the Tristano legacy, listen to Hancock's solos on "Dolores" and "Gingerbread Boy" on the Miles Davis album *Miles Smiles*, CBS 9401, and Jarrett's solos on "Shades of Jazz" in his album *Shades*, Impulse 9322. For the resemblance between Tristano and Cecil Taylor, listen to Tristano's "Descent into the Maelstrom," Inner City IC 6002, recorded in 1953, then to anything Taylor recorded after 1960.

[4]Listen to "Marshmallow" or "Ice Cream Konitz" on the Konitz album *Subconscious-Lee*, Fantasy OJC 186 (Prestige 7004), LP. Some of the best Konitz solos are in *Konitz Meets Mulligan*, Pacific Jazz 46847, CD. See footnote 10.

and agility. These two saxophonists out-distanced all others. In addition, it is historically important to remember that **Konitz developed and maintained his own Tristano-inspired style at a time when most other young alto saxophonists were imitating Charlie Parker.** The Konitz style was almost totally unrelated to Parker's.[5] Konitz played with a dry, airy tone that was soft in texture and light in weight. He employed a slow vibrato and preferred to use the alto saxophone's high register instead of its deeper tones. His sound is the alto saxophone equivalent to Lester Young's sound on tenor. This was a historic departure from the warm, syrupy lushness of alto saxophonists Benny Carter and Johnny Hodges. It also departed from the biting, bittersweet sound of Charlie Parker. Unlike Parker, Konitz was not inclined to sprinkle his improvisations with quotes from pop tunes. Konitz also differed from Parker in rhythm and articulation, rarely using staccato, and his syncopations were less plentiful than Parker's. Almost all his lines were legato and not percussive at all. The effect of the Konitz style was called "cool." (Listen to Konitz solo on "No Figs" in the JAZZ CLASSICS CASSETTE. Compare it with Parker's solo on "Shaw Nuff" and Hodges's on "Prelude to a Kiss.")

During the late 1940s and early 1950s, most of Konitz's solo work consisted of lines in the style of Tristano's densely packed piano improvisations. Then during the middle 1950s, especially after 1954, Konitz gradually changed his style. The most obvious difference was that he slowed his playing. He also employed a larger variety of ways to construct his phrases. He made more frequent use of silence, and occasionally he imparted a bluesy flavor to his work. His manner lost some of its snap and freshness as well as speed and agility. With his new style, Konitz occasionally performed on tenor instead of alto saxophone, and he was not as fleet.[6] Listeners who knew only his earlier work often found this style difficult to recognize as belonging to Konitz. He toured and recorded for many years after changing his style, thereby giving jazz fans an extended exposure to this additional sound. With this alternative, Konitz became an influence on new generations of saxophonists in the 1970s and 80s.

**Birth of the Cool**    In 1949 and 1950, trumpeter Miles Davis organized recording sessions of a nine-piece band that has become known as the Miles Davis Nonet or the Birth of the Cool Band.[7] The group was created by abbreviating the Claude Thornhill big band.[8] In addition to Davis, the nonet included Lee Konitz, who had been a member of the Thornhill band, and baritone saxophonist Gerry Mulligan, who had played and arranged for Thornhill. These three hornmen all employed relatively light weight tone qualities and preferred a subdued effect. Though the nonet employed a standard rhythm section of piano, bass, and drums, a departure from custom was made in filling out the instrumentation with French horn and tuba. No tenor saxophone or guitar was used, though a trombone was included. (Listen to "Boplicity" in SCCJ.)

[5]Konitz, in turn, influenced Bud Shank, Lennie Niehaus, and Art Pepper, among others, during the 1950s, then Anthony Braxton and Bob Mover, among others, during the 1970s.

[6]*Ideal Scene*, Soul Note 1119

[7]*The Birth of the Cool*, Capitol 16168 (T762), LP, 92862, CD.

[8]Miles Davis asked arranger Gil Evans to provide the smallest instrumentation that could produce or approximate the sound of the Thornhill big band. Listen to the original on *The Memorable Claude Thornhill*, CBS 32906

## WEST COAST STYLE OF THE 1950s

The sound and feeling of the Birth of The Cool sessions was similar to work by several groups of predominantly white jazz musicians centered in Los Angeles during the 1950s. The influence of Lee Konitz and Miles Davis was evident there in saxophone and trumpet styles, respectively, while arrangers sometimes put together bands that placed tuba and French horn in melodic roles, as in the Birth of The Cool band. Though much of this music was indistinguishable from bop, some performances felt more like the Count Basie-Lester Young combo recordings of the 1930s than the Charlie Parker-Dizzy Gillespie collaborations of the 1940s. Some of the music was especially subdued and understated, precisely those qualities that journalists associated with Lester Young and the term "cool jazz." Frequently the music featured solo improvisations that were smoother and more tune-like than bop improvisations. In addition, more emphasis was placed on composition and arrangement.

There were a number of other jazz styles flourishing in California at this time, but journalists specified only this particular group of styles as "West Coast Jazz." Journalists and record companies neglected the other styles, accidentally conveying the impression that cool was almost the only style of significance occurring in California during the 1950s. Rather than using the blanket term "West Coast Jazz," they could have done better by choosing a more specific designation such as "West Coast Cool Jazz." They also could have acknowledged that some of the playing by even the coolest of these musicians was hard swinging and hot. This textbook uses "West Coast" to designate only the musicians who played this particular collection of cool jazz styles because jazz historians usually mean a West Coast brand of cool jazz when they say "West Coast Style."[9]

Many of the musicians associated with West Coast cool jazz first came to the Los Angeles area in big bands. Several such groups had disbanded there during the demise of the big band boom in the 1940s. The most notable of these were led by Stan Kenton and Woody Herman (see Table 10.2). Some of their musicians settled in California to earn livelihoods in the commercial music industry, especially in the studios that developed there to satisfy the need for background music in films. After settling, many of these players sporadically returned to those big bands for tours and recordings. Eventually the television industry also employed a considerable number of these men. Commercial music provided their livelihoods, and jazz became a part-time occupation for all but a tiny few.

---

[9]The term "West Coast Style" will not be used here to indicate the entire variety of jazz styles that were active on the West Coast during the 1950s, such as bebop, hard bop, Dixieland, swing, and free jazz. For a more complete picture, see Robert Gordon's book *Jazz West Coast* (Quartet Books, 1986), William F. Lee's book *Stan Kenton: Artistry in Rhythm* (Creative Press of Los Angeles, 1980), Red Callender's autobiography *Unfinished Dream* (Quartet Books, 1985), Barry McRae's *Jazz Cataclysm* (A. S. Barnes, 1967; reprinted by DaCapo), Joe Goldberg's *Jazz Masters of the Fifties* (Macmillan, 1965, reprinted by DaCapo), and the album *Black California*, Savoy 2215, LP, 1942–1952. The absence of discussion for the fine musicians who performed these other styles should not be taken as a rejection of their work, but only as an indication that a brief text such as this cannot do justice to all jazz styles in all regions in all periods.

**TABLE 10.1. A Few Of The Many West Coast Style Musicians Of The 1950s**

| Trumpet | Piano |
|---|---|
| Chet Baker | Hampton Hawes |
| Conte Candoli | Claude Williamson |
| Jack Sheldon | Russ Freeman |
| Shorty Rogers | Pete Jolly |
| Stu Williamson | Vince Guaraldi |
|  | Carl Perkins |
| **Trombone** | Andre Previn |
|  | Dave Brubeck |
| Bob Brookmeyer |  |
| Frank Rosolino | **Bass** |
| Bob Enevoldsen |  |
| Milt Bernhart | Red Mitchell |
|  | Red Callender |
| **Tenor Sax** | Leroy Vinnegar |
|  | Buddy Clark |
| Bill Perkins | Carson Smith |
| Richie Kamuca | Howard Rumsey |
| Bob Cooper | Curtis Counce |
| Jack Montrose | Joe Mondragon |
| Buddy Collette | Monty Budwig |
| Dave Pell |  |
| Bill Holman | **Drums** |
| Jimmy Giuffre |  |
| Zoot Sims | Shelly Manne |
|  | Mel Lewis |
| **Alto Sax** | Stan Levey |
|  | Larry Bunker |
| Art Pepper | Chico Hamilton |
| Bud Shank |  |
| Herb Geller | **Composer-Arrangers** |
| Lennie Niehaus |  |
| Paul Desmond | Gerry Mulligan |
|  | Dave Brubeck |
| **Baritone Sax** | Shorty Rogers |
|  | Dave Pell |
| Gerry Mulligan | John Graas |
| Bob Gordon | Jimmy Giuffre |
|  | Bill Holman |
| **Guitar** | Marty Paich |
|  |  |
| Howard Roberts |  |
| Barney Kessel |  |
| Jim Hall |  |

**Big Bands**  Every style and era in jazz has been represented at least once in a large-ensemble format known as a "big band." Leaders of these bands often offer styles in addition to the one in vogue at the time of their formation, sometimes sampling idioms than span several decades. Pianist-arranger **Stan Kenton** (1912–1979) led the best known

**TABLE 10.2. A Few of the Many West Coast Style Players Who Played With the Woody Herman and Stan Kenton Big Bands. (The two bands used many of the same musicians. Most were white. Most were good sight readers. Most played in similar styles.)**

| Kenton | Herman |
|--------|--------|
| Lee Konitz | Bill Perkins |
| Art Pepper | Richie Kamuca |
| Bud Shank | Shorty Rogers |
| Lennie Niehaus | Jimmy Giuffre |
| Bill Holman | Conte Candoli |
| Richie Kamuca | Stan Levey |
| Conte Candoli | Shelly Manne |
| Jack Sheldon | Red Mitchell |
| Mel Lewis | Stu Williamson |
| Stan Levey | Zoot Sims |
| Shelly Manne | |
| Bob Cooper | |
| Frank Rosolino | |
| Stu Williamson | |
| Milt Bernhart | |
| Zoot Sims | |

succession of big bands in modern jazz, and he presented repertories that spanned several eras and featured numerous styles.[10] Kenton's name first became well known during the 1940s while he was leading a big band in the swing era style. The idioms of his subsequent bands were sometimes labeled "big band bop." At one time, Kenton dubbed his music "progressive jazz." And then, during the 1970s, portions of his repertory tapped jazz-rock. Despite all these labels and shifts in flavor, Kenton's contributions and the styles of his musicians are linked most closely to cool jazz and the West Coast, where he was based for many years and where so many of his musicians settled during the 1940s and 50s (see Tables 10.1 and 10.2). Kenton acknowledged Claude Thornhill, father of the cool style for big band, as a major influence on his own approach to band writing. Kenton's featured musicians drew liberally from the cool jazz styles of Lester Young, Miles Davis, and Lee Konitz; Konitz himself played with the band for more than a year.

Stan Kenton is one of the few jazz musicians to become widely known by the American public after Louis Armstrong, Benny Goodman, and Duke Ellington. However, his name, unlike Ellington's or Armstrong's, represented a huge number of different composers, arrangers and soloists. Kenton created a composing and arranging style which owed much to Claude Thornhill, Fletcher Henderson, and

[10]A favorite among musicians is *New Concepts in Artistry in Rhythm*, Creative World 1002, LP, and Capitol 92865, CD (Capitol T383), 1952, featuring Lee Konitz, Conte Candoli, Frank Rosolino, and Maynard Ferguson, with arrangements by Gerry Mulligan, Johnny Richards, Bill Russo, and Bill Holman.

Benny Carter. He is particularly well known for the arrangements he originated himself, especially in recordings of "Eager Beaver" and "Artisty in Rhythm," his band's theme song.[11] He also developed a piano style, influenced partly by Earl Hines.

Kenton created a distinctive band style that is immediately recognizable. Though he did record ordinary arrangements of numerous pop tunes, and he did turn out a large body of dance music, the most impressive work he presented was nonswinging concert music which vividly exposed rich, modern harmonies. Two and three moving parts were sometimes presented simultaneously. The weighty pieces differ from the dance-band tradition of big band jazz. A classical feeling was common in his music. In fact, the musicianship of his players was very high, with ensemble precision and tuning sometimes approaching the sterling standards of symphony orchestras. Usually performed without vibrato, his brass and saxophone parts had a dry quality that has sometimes been termed "transparent." Some pieces featured trumpet parts which were high-pitched, loud, and often block-voiced as five-note chords. These sounds were combined with saxophone passages written in long strings of sixteenth notes which came up from the low range of the ensemble like fountains or descended like waterfalls.

Though Kenton's performances usually ranged from the softest to the loudest of sounds, Kenton earned a reputation for leading the loudest big band. This was partly due to the preponderance of brass instruments. It was not unusual, for example, to find five trumpets and five trombones in a Kenton band at the same time as Duke Ellington was carrying only four trumpets and three trombones. Additionally, some Kenton trombonists doubled on tuba, and one version of his band carried an entire section of mellophoniums (trumpet-French horn hybrids specially made for Kenton). The saxophone section was occasionally called upon to augment the band's massiveness by employing the unusual combination of two baritone saxophones.

Another trademark of the Kenton band sound was its glossy trombone tones. The ensemble frequently featured harmonized parts for five trombones that were performed very smoothly and lightly, no matter how loud. For more than three decades, Kenton's trombone soloists invariably preferred high-register work, and they graced the beginnings of many tones with long, climbing smears. They used a meticulously controlled vibrato which was initially slow and then quickened dramatically near the tone's end. Their approach was extroverted, but in the well-manicured way of Tommy Dorsey, rather than the rough, guttural way of earlier jazz trombonists.

To help put the Kenton band sound in perspective, a comparison with Count Basie might be helpful. Just as the feeling projected by the Basie band can be described as easygoing and swinging, the feeling projected by the Kenton band can be described as serious and intense, with an emphasis on massiveness. Much of the Kenton repertory is solemn and weighty, essentially twentieth-century concert music scored for trumpets, trombones, and saxophones plus rhythm section. Some of

[11] *The Jazz Compositions of Stan Kenton,* Creative World 1078, LP, 1956; original recordings of these pieces are on *Milestones,* Creative World 1047 (HT 190), LP, 1943.

the material also required French horns, tuba, strings, and Latin American percussion instruments. The band's character was based more on elaborate arrangements than on the simplicity and swing feeling associated with Basie. Remember that the Basie band of the late 1930s functioned much as a big combo, in the sense that solo improvisation was primary, and many of the ensemble backgrounds were almost incidental to the music. Kenton's approach contrasts markedly in that its effect was frequently similar to that of a brass choir, not a big jazz combo. The Kenton bands usually emphasized composition over improvisation. In fact, some solo improvisations were not solos in the conventional sense but embellishments of the ensemble sound. For example, the Kenton band sometimes intentionally overpowered a soloist in a loud ensemble sound, thereby turning the solo line into an ensemble line that was almost indistinct.

It was not as a pianist or composer that Kenton left his greatest mark. His major contributions to jazz history were his skill at public relations and his motivation and talent for finding and leading creative modern musicians and composers. Lying behind this contribution is the important fact that because of his band's great popularity during the 1940s—"Tampico" and "Artistry in Rhythm" were million-sellers, Kenton became financially free enough to invest in musical experiments. He channeled this freedom into hiring relatively unknown writers and commissioning ambitious compositions which had little chance of commercial success.[12] Improvisers had enjoyed these kinds of opportunities throughout jazz history, but composers had not. In addition, Kenton employed hundreds of musicians who may not have otherwise received much exposure. He must also be credited with tenacity and durability. Though he began leading bands in 1941, when the big band era was still flourishing, he continued into the 1960s and 70s, long after big bands went out of fashion. Moreover, he was one of the founders of the college stage band movement, spawning the enormous jazz education establishment. Jazz in schools perpetuated the big band tradition in jazz after regularly touring big bands disappeared from the jazz scene upon the deaths of Kenton, Basie, Ellington, Woody Herman, Buddy Rich, Harry James, and Don Ellis.

**Trumpet**  A number of good trumpeters have been associated with West Coast cool jazz of the 1950s and 60s (see Table 10.1). Chet Baker and Shorty Rogers are probably the best known. Baker has the more impressive recording career as a soloist, while Rogers is better known for his writing and bandleading.

---

[12]For examples, listen to Johnny Richards' *Cuban Fire*, Creative World 1008 (Capitol T 731); Robert Graettinger's *City of Glass and This Modern World*, Creative World 1006 (Capitol T736); Russ Garcia's "Adventures in Emotions" in *Stan Kenton Conducts the Los Angeles Neophonic Orchestra*, Creative World 1013 (Capitol SMAS 2424); Pete Rugolo's "Mirage" and William Russo's "Egdon Heath," in *Mirage*, volume 216 of the New World Recorded Anthology of American Music. Write New World Records, 701 Seventh Avenue, NY, NY 10036, or phone 212-302-0460. As we went to press, most Kenton records were still available by mail from Gene Norman, Suite 4A, 8400 Sunset Blvd., Los Angeles, CA 90069; phone 213-656-2614. In addition, the *Teachers Manual & Discography* for the book you are now reading contains a discography of Kenton albums organized by composer-arrangers who worked for the band. Teachers can get it from Prentice-Hall sales representatives or by writing College Marketing, Prentice-Hall, Inc., Englewood Cliffs, NJ 07632.

When naming "cool jazz" trumpeters, journalists usually list Miles Davis first and **Chet Baker** (1929–1988) next. Unlike most white West Coast players, Baker did not gain his first wide exposure with the big bands of Stan Kenton or Woody Herman. Though he had played briefly with Charlie Parker, his largest initial exposure came from his membership in the Gerry Mulligan quartet of 1952 and 1953.[13] From there, he toured and recorded prolifically with a variety of rhythm sections until his death in 1988.

Baker is widely admired among musicians, regardless of the idiom or era being discussed. His solos swing in an easy manner, and most of his playing projects a mellow mood. His tone quality is soft, not brassy. In fact, during the 1960s he stopped playing the trumpet temporarily and spent some of his career playing the mellower-sounding fluegelhorn (see photo on page 114).[14] As an improviser, Baker had a talent for being able to pick just the right few notes, and to invest isolated notes and phrases with especially affecting tone qualities. Some of Baker's best work conveys a poignant sense of striving to catch something just beyond his reach, a struggle to overcome obstacles. Often, when he finally plays that perfect note, it attains a delicate balance of fragility and triumph. A master at generating long phrases, Baker never seemed at a loss for melodic ideas, and the tuneful quality of his solos made them always sound fresh.

**Shorty Rogers** (b. 1924) is a trumpeter-composer-arranger who was based in Los Angeles during the 1950s and 60s. He had played trumpet and written for the Woody Herman and Stan Kenton bands. With his own combos and big bands, sometimes called the Giants, he produced music that extended writing styles he had developed in his earlier compositions. His recordings of these pieces featured various combinations of the best jazz musicians living in the Los Angeles area at the time.[15] In isolated recordings, he also anticipated developments that later became better known in association with other musicians. Recordings he made with Jimmy Giuffre and vibraharpist Teddy Charles[16] are historically significant because they were the first after Lennie Tristano's "Intuition" and "Digression" to display improvisation not based on prearranged chord progressions. Their 1954 work predated the Ornette Coleman recordings of 1958 and 1959 which launched an entire style centered on the "free jazz" concept. Rogers also recorded pieces in which improvisation was based on modes instead of chord changes (for explanations of modes, see pages 365–368 and 418–423).[17] These predated the 1958 Miles Davis recording of "Milestones" and the Davis *Kind of Blue* album which launched the mode-based improvisatory styles that were popular during the 1960s and 70s. The connection with Davis is especially intriguing because Rogers derived his trumpet style primarily from the 1940s approach of Miles Davis and, like Davis, used fluegelhorn long

---

[13]*The Complete Pacific Jazz and Capitol Recordings of the Original Gerry Mulligan Quartet & Tentette with Chet Baker*, Mosaic MR5-102, LP box. Available only by mail. Address: Mosaic Records, 35 Melrose, Stamford, CT 06902; phone orders: 203-327-7111.

[14]*Smokin' with the Chet Baker Quintet*, Prestige 7449

[15]*Short Stops*, RCA/Bluebird 5917, CD/LP.

[16]Shelley Manne, *"The Three" and "The Two,"* Fantasy/OJC-172 (Contemporary 3584), LP, 1954

[17]Teddy Charles/Shorty Rogers, *Collaboration: West*, OJC-122 (Prestige 7028), LP, 1953

before it became common among trumpeters (see page 114 for illustration of fluegelhorn).

**Saxophone**  Many excellent saxophonists were associated with West Coast cool jazz (see Table 10.1).[18] They are known particularly for maintaining the tone quality and melodic ideas of Lester Young, though some also incorporated the advances of Charlie Parker. Most played with the big bands of Stan Kenton and Woody Herman at one time or another (see Table 10.2).

Saxophonist **Jimmy Giuffre** (b. 1921) was based on the West Coast from 1946 to 1960. Giuffre's output typifies the notion of cool jazz: he produced a soft, diffuse sound on all the instruments he played, and his lines were understated and melodic. Moreover, his mastery of silence and economy in solo construction is comparable to that of Count Basie and Miles Davis. Though beginning as a saxophonist influenced by the Count Basie-Lester Young combo style of the 1930s, he went beyond Lester Young. Additionally he contributed strikingly original compositions and improvisations, many of which he performed on clarinet, with a special emphasis on the instrument's lowest register. Ultimately he must be ranked as one of the most daring composers and improvisers in jazz, and rhythmically he was the most creative of the West Coast musicians. The consistency, intelligence, and coherence of even his most unorthodox lines surpassed all his colleagues. His improvisations sustain a level of originality that is higher than most modern jazz as a whole, not just West Coast jazz or cool jazz. Despite the "cool" demeanor of his work, Giuffre's sounds impart a sense of intellectual intensity and adventure that lends them a character as convincing as the most outstanding bop and post-bop performances, with little of the tentative or easygoing feeling that is conveyed by much other music produced on the West Coast. Unfortunately, except for recognition as composer of the "Four Brothers" piece featured by Woody Herman's band, he is almost universally overlooked by jazz fans as well as historians, and most of his best recordings went out of print, rarely to be reissued.[19]

There were several excellent alto saxophonists associated with the West Coast scene of the 1950s (see Table 10.1), many of whom were prominently featured at one time or another with the big bands of Stan Kenton. All of them used slow

---

[18]Teddy Edwards, Wardell Gray, Dexter Gordon, and Harold Land are a few of the great bop players associated with California. For more about them, see Leonard Feather's *Encyclopedias of Jazz* or Robert Gordon's *Jazz West Coast*.

[19]An outstanding undertaking for Giuffre was a trio he led with trombonist Bob Brookmeyer and Jim Hall during an eighteen-month period in 1958 and 1959 (*Western Suite*, Atlantic 1330). Their music was light and lyrical, but also earthy and rhythmically daring. It featured close, three-way cooperation in the creation of improvised counterlines. The trio generated group improvisations that were very cohesive, original, and swinging (despite the absence of bass and drums). Another standout among Giuffre's endeavors was some music made after he left the West Coast for New York. On and off from 1961 to 1963, Giuffre played clarinet with pianist Paul Bley and bassist Steve Swallow. Their sound had the flavor of twentieth-century classical music approaches, and it sometimes stemmed from improvisation that was free of preset chord progressions (*Free Fall*, Columbia CL 1964 and CS 8764, LP; *Masters of Modern Piano*, Verve VE2-2514, 2 LPs). Subsequent work by Giuffre has preserved his tendency to lean toward experimentation.

vibrato and produced tone qualities that were thin-textured and light in weight, displaying a dryness we ordinarily associate with Lester Young. This contrasts with the weightier, more syrupy tone quality of Coleman Hawkins and Johnny Hodges. Though aware of Charlie Parker's approach to melodic rhythm and phrasing, they seemed to have more in common with Lee Konitz, though none of them demonstrated the richness of melodic inventions we find in either Parker or Konitz. The West Coast cool saxophonists were especially simple in their improvisations. Frequently it sounded as though they were playing swing era solos spiced with a touch of bop flavoring.

The best known of all West Coast altoists was **Paul Desmond** (1924–1977). In surveys among musicians, Desmond ranks among the all-time favorites on his instrument. He is highly regarded for his good taste, melodic continuity, fertile imagination, and accurate intonation. Desmond received his widest exposure with pianist Dave Brubeck's quartets.[20] His quartet improvisations conveyed a sense of openness and clarity. With his soft, light, pure sound, he unfolded line after logical line. Often he created an impression that his playing was effortlessly soaring above its earthbound accompaniments.[21]

Desmond forged an instantly recognizable style that had almost nothing to do with bop—Desmond cited swing era player Pete Brown, not Charlie Parker as his influence. And, though his tone quality closely resembled that of Lee Konitz, Desmond's style should not be considered derived from the Tristano-Konitz alternative to bop, either. By comparison with Konitz, he swung a bit more. Further, instead of drawing upon the complex melodic conception of Lennie Tristano as Konitz did, Desmond had his own fresh ideas, and the melodies he improvised were much less convoluted than those of the Tristano school. Though he sometimes inserted phrases from popular songs, his improvisational material was usually free of cliché, depending instead upon original melodic invention. He was extremely economical, playing far fewer notes per solo than probably any other modern jazz saxophonist. Many of his lines are as simple and lyrical as the best popular songs. Some of his improvisations may remind listeners of themes in the classical music of Tchaikovsky and Rachmaninoff.

Desmond's playing projects a relaxed, lighthearted mood, but the construction of his improvised lines reflects care, intelligence, and inspiration. Desmond sometimes developed musical sequences by taking a phrase and repeating it in a new key to fit the next chord in his accompaniment, each time altering it or putting it in a

[20]Desmond penned the quartet's biggest hit, "Take Five." It sold more than a million copies in 1961 and remained popular through the 1980s. The original is in the album *Time Out*, CBS 40585 (CL 1397), LP/CD, 1959. For more about Desmond, see pages 243–65 in *Meet Me at Jim & Andy's* by Gene Lees (Oxford, 1988).

[21]Desmond was so consistently inspired that almost every Brubeck album offers representative Desmond solos. A standout is *Gone with the Wind*, Columbia CJ 40627 (CL 1347), especially his solo on "Georgia on My Mind." Away from Brubeck, Desmond recorded some very pleasant playing, including an orchestral album in which he paraphrased well-loved popular standards as well as improvising his own new lines: *Late Lament (Desmond Blue)*, RCA Bluebird 5778 (LPM 2438), CD/LP, 1961. His hottest playing on record is cited in the next footnote.

different place relative to the underlying beat. Some of his rhythmic displacements built tension that was finally resolved by a clever turn of phrase, as though he had escaped miraculously from a self-imposed puzzle. Other times he sounded as though he were playing duets with himself, introducing a line, then answering, paraphrasing or mimicking it in a higher or lower register.[22]

**Art Pepper** (1925–1982) is among the best known and most original improvisers to be associated with the Stan Kenton bands and West Coast jazz. He fashioned a raw, plaintive style for the alto saxophone by amalgamating the approaches of Zoot Sims and Lee Konitz. Then, at the latest stage in his career, he also absorbed the influence of post-bop saxophonist John Coltrane. His was probably the hottest style to emerge from cool jazz of the white West Coast scene. In his playing there is more of a cry than was ordinarily found in West Coast cool saxophonists. Another central difference is his sense of urgency and rhythmic variety. Pepper pushed hard on the beat. He favored short, staccato bursts of notes, many of which were grouped in triplets. Sometimes he tore off a double-time figure (a stream of sixteenth notes) in a tight, crisp manner. Pepper used brief, funky phrases that were abruptly stated with searing emotion. In fact, his emotionality is prized by many fans. The emotional range of his playing runs from a joyous swing feeling, particularly evident on medium- and up-tempo pieces, to despondency, for example, on some ballad improvisations in which his playing is so slow it is almost as though he purposely drags to build tension, sounding almost too sad to play the next note.[23]

**Gerry Mulligan** (b. 1927) was the baritone saxophonist and a primary composer-arranger in the Miles Davis nonet sessions of 1949 and 50. (Listen to "Boplicity" in SCCJ. Mulligan contributes the first improvisation.) He also wrote for the big bands of Claude Thornhill and Stan Kenton. Mulligan used a soft, dry, light-weight tone quality whose texture has been likened to tweed cloth. By comparison with bop style, his approach was relatively uncomplicated. Rhythmically, Mulligan's improvisations were more predictable, less jarring than those of Charlie Parker and Dizzy Gillespie. His solos suggested great deliberation rather than wild exhuberance. He rarely double-timed his phrases. The logic behind them was obvious, and usually they were developed quite systematically. Similarly, Mulligan's compositions were neither as complex as Lennie Tristano's nor as agitated as many bop pieces. A few are quite song-like, and they have the same gentle character projected by his improvisations. This trait, combined with his subdued tone quality, qualifies his music for the "cool" label.

In 1952, Mulligan moved to California and launched a series of piano-less quartets consisting of himself on baritone saxophone, another horn, bass, and drums. While on the West Coast, he also produced material with a ten-piece band in the

---

[22]Desmond loved to play in the alto's high range, and he was one of the first jazz altoists to use notes from the extreme high register, the *altissimo* range. Examples are on "Perdido," in Brubeck's *Jazz at Oberlin*, Fantasy OJC-046 (Fantasy 3-245), CD/LP, 1953.

[23]*The Complete Pacific Jazz Small Group Recordings of Art Pepper*, Mosaic MR3-105, LP box, 1956–57; *Modern Art*, Blue Note 46848, CD, 1956, with Russ Freeman (originally on Jazz West); *Intensity*, Contemporary 7607, CD/LP, 1960. Also see Pepper's autobiography, *Straight Life* (Schirmer, 1979).

style of the Miles Davis nonet. Trumpeter Chet Baker was his best-known partner in these undertakings.[24] Though Mulligan was based on the West Coast for only about three years, his music epitomizes what journalists mean by the term "West Coast cool." Without the piano feeding chords to the soloists, Mulligan and Baker found themselves supplying counterlines to each other, some of which became fairly involved and recalled the ensemble interplay heard in the earliest jazz. The absence of piano in Mulligan's groups was partly responsible for a light, simple sound texture. It also afforded an enhanced appreciation for bass playing because chord notes were no longer shared with piano and overshadowed accordingly. Also contributing to this effect was a relatively conservative approach used by his drummers, who played simply and often used brushes instead of sticks. The resulting clarity of sound was part of the cool feeling conveyed by their music. Mulligan maintained his piano-less format long after returning to the New York area, and, more than thirty years later, many jazz fans still considered his music to be "West Coast cool."

**Drums**   West Coast style was not known for adventuresome drumming, in either the accompaniment or solo capacity. However, one of the most novel bands to originate on the West Coast was led by drummer **Chico Hamilton** (b. 1921). Gerry Mulligan had made Hamilton the drummer in his first piano-less quartet. Then Hamilton formed a group of his own without piano, with an instrumentation that was even more unique: guitar, cello, bass, drums, and a hornman who played saxophones, flute, and clarinet. (Flute and cello were especially unusual to find in jazz at this time.) With tightly arranged pieces and excellent musicianship, the quintet created its own jazz style, which often resembled classical chamber music.[25] Its textures were light and pretty, and the arrangements displayed considerable variety. Sometimes several melodies sounded at the same time. This is a technique that had characterized the earliest jazz. With Hamilton's, Mulligan's, and Brubeck's groups using it, the technique had found favor again.

Chico Hamilton was one of the first modern drummers to get away from nearly always playing conventional ride rhythms as the undercurrent for a group sound. Hamilton's imagination is fertile, orchestral, and subtle. He is known for generating unusual and catchy patterns on his drums and maintaining them as consistent accompaniment figures. Instead of depending primarily on the ride cymbal and high-hat sound, Hamilton is just as likely to use a snare drum or tom-tom as the primary voice in his accompaniment pattern. Each piece features a separate rhythm pattern and percussion color. Hamilton's style is a gentle approach to creating unusual rhythmic textures instead of just defining the beat and prodding the soloists. Even when no longer based on the West Coast, Hamilton's groups continued to create a highly original brand of jazz that was full of surprises.

[24]*The Complete Pacific Jazz and Capitol Recordings of the Original Gerry Mulligan Quartet & Tentette with Chet Baker*, Mosaic MR5-102, LP box. Available only by mail. Address: Mosaic Records, 35 Melrose Place, Stamford, CT 06902; phone orders: 203-327-7111.

[25]*Spectacular*, Pacific Jazz 1209, LP, 1955, with Jim Hall and Buddy Collette; *Gong's East*, Discovery 831 (Warner Brothers 1271), 1958, with Eric Dolphy

**Guitar**  Several modern guitarists were associated with the West Coast scene of the 1950s (see Table 10.1). But none have come to be more revered by jazz musicians than **Jim Hall**. When asked to name their favorite guitarist or their biggest influence, numerous modern guitarists mention Jim Hall. Since the mid-1960s, they mention him almost as often as they mention Wes Montgomery. Though much of his reputation has been acquired since he left the Los Angeles area for New York in 1959, many fans were first introduced to Hall through recordings he made with Chico Hamilton in 1955 and 1956 and with Jimmy Giuffre from 1956 to 1960.

Jim Hall extracts a mellow, soft tone from his guitar, and his sound is clear and pure, often bell-like in its resonance. His clean touch, gentle approach, and immaculate sense of pacing set him above almost all other jazz guitarists. There is nothing offhanded about what he offers his listeners. He begins his notes very precisely. The structure of his ideas displays a crystal clarity. He never overloads the listener with flashy acrobatics or a crowded sequence of notes. In his music there is a sense of politeness, yet at the same time there is a forceful continuity of purpose that suggests Hall knows exactly where he is going. He maintains high creative standards, placing great importance on playing only fresh ideas and avoiding well-worn patterns. Yet despite the pressure that this esthetic exerts, Hall's solos are free of the false starts that we would expect. Instead, we are treated to solos that bear an overall form that is often as good as any composed piece. Rather than beginning ideas and leaving them half-finished, Hall nearly always manages to complete each improvised idea, thereby personifying the meticulous composer as improviser. Because of the limitations such a strategy places on an improviser, Hall is possibly the slowest guitar soloist in jazz. This does not mean that he is not able to play fast, flashy lines. It means only that he chooses notes so judiciously that his pace cannot possibly be as brisk as it would be if he were performing prerehearsed patterns. Unlike many bop soloists, Hall does not ordinarily exceed the limits of his thinking and the speed of his fingers. Because he does stay within his capabilities, each note in his improvised lines is presented firmly, with a sureness of swing feeling.[26]

**Piano**  A number of creative jazz pianists were based on the West Coast during the 1950s (see Table 10.1). All contributed substantially to the quality of the West Coast scene, but only **Dave Brubeck** (b. 1920) achieved tremendous international fame. He performed in the San Francisco area during the 1940s and early 1950s. In the period 1955 to 1985, Brubeck ranked second in record sales among all jazz recording artists. During the 1950s and 60s, his name became almost as synonymous with jazz as Louis Armstrong and Duke Ellington had been in the 1930s and 40s. His fame came mostly as a bandleader and composer. Among musicians, he was universally

[26]Among Hall's most famous recordings are two albums of duets he improvised with pianist Bill Evans: *Undercurrent*, Blue Note 90583 (UA 14003), LP/CD, 1962; and *Intermodulation*, Verve 833771 (MGV 8655), LP/CD, 1966. The music is pretty, with much continuity and originality. The austere and thoughtful conceptions of these two musicians are about as free from redundancy and cliché as any jazz recorded. Moreover, even without bass or drums, their music is insistent and swinging. Hall is also featured on several outstanding Paul Desmond albums. *Late Lament (Desmond Blue)*, RCA Bluebird 5778 (LPM 2438), CD/LP, 1961, contains some of his most relaxed and lyrical improvisations.

Dave Brubeck Quartet, one of the few jazz combos to achieve wide public appreciation without singing or including rock. *Left to right:* drummer Joe Morello, bassist Gene Wright, pianist Brubeck, and alto saxophonist Paul Desmond. (*Photo by Bob Parent, courtesy of Don Parent*)

admired as a composer, though he was not as influential as a pianist. During the 1940s he had led a series of small bands in California which employed approaches similar to the 1949–50 Miles Davis nonet, though they began before he ever heard the Davis recordings.[27] Then, from 1951 to 1967, he teamed with California-born alto saxophonist Paul Desmond and led a quartet which, for millions of listeners, provided an introduction to jazz. (Though associated with "West Coast" jazz, Brubeck was not a California resident during the period of his greatest acclaim. His quartet members lived in the New York area.)

The rhythmic feeling in a lot of Brubeck's playing has much in common with classical music. However, Brubeck never was a classical pianist, though after launching his jazz career he briefly studied composition with the world-renowned symphonic composer Darius Milhaud. It remains a widely held misunderstanding that Brubeck was trained primarily in the classics. Perhaps listeners believe this because of the way Brubeck's music sounds. He is one of the few modern pianists

[27] *The Dave Brubeck Octet*, Fantasy OJC-101 (Fantasy 3-239), LP, 1946 and 1948–49

clearly to avoid standard bop melodic conception and rhythmic feeling. He is unusually inventive and depends almost exclusively on original melodic lines, not the phrases that most of his contempories absorbed from the music of Charlie Parker, Dizzy Gillespie, and Bud Powell. Another reason is that much of Brubeck's invention has a distinctly classical flavor. In fact, sometimes he and Desmond improvised duets that sounded like the two-part inventions of J. S. Bach, set atop jazz bass and drums. In other words, Brubeck is a modern jazz musician who does not use the bop language, and, despite his lack of classical piano lessons, he often sounds more like Bach than bop.

That Brubeck's work sounds classical may explain part of his popularity. By comparison with the jumpy, erratic character of bop style, his compositions and improvisations are much easier to follow. They possess a simple and tuneful quality. His creations are orderly, and they project a freshness and clarity that make the listener's job easy. In addition, most of Brubeck's pieces are pretty, and they convey a light and pleasant mood.[28]

Brubeck was rhythmically innovative. His interest in using meters unusual to jazz brought him a great deal of publicity and spawned trends among other jazz musicians. His quartet crafted a number of tunes and improvisations in odd meters such as three, five, and seven (see page 357 to understand what "meter" entails). His albums *Time Out*[29] and *Time Further Out*,[30] which explored those meters, were immensely popular. *Time Out* contained "Take Five," a funky and engaging little theme by Paul Desmond that employed a simple accompaniment rhythm that was extensively repeated in meter of five. Brubeck was also rhythmically innovative in ways outside his adventures with odd meters. For example, he frequently improvised lines, sometimes in locked-hands style, that pitted his own separate rhythm (for example in meter of three) against the pulse that was emanating from bass and drums (for example, in meter of two). By this strategy he was cleverly attempting to generate a provocative tension. However, the clashing rhythms were often not appreciated by those who were expecting the easy swing feeling that was ordinarily produced by other modern jazz pianists. Brubeck's mastery of odd meters led to respect among musicians, however, and it earned him a significant place in jazz history, even in the minds of musicians who were not especially influenced by his piano style.

**Trombone** There are a number of highly talented trombonists associated with the Los Angeles jazz scene of the 1950s and 60s (see Table 10.1). Among many jazz trombonists themselves, **Carl Fontana** (b. 1928) is the favorite trombonist in modern jazz. Though featured with Stan Kenton and Woody Herman, he was not consistently in the Los Angeles area during this period, but we will discuss him here. Trombonists

---

[28]Other musicians have been attracted to Brubeck's tunes "In Your Own Sweet Way" and "The Duke." Miles Davis recorded "In Your Own Sweet Way" on *Workin' with the Miles Davis Quintet*, Fantasy/OJC-296 (Prestige 7166), LP/CD, 1956; and "The Duke" on *Miles Ahead*, CBS 40784 (CL 1041), CD/LP, 1957. For more about Brubeck, see *The Great Jazz Pianists* by Len Lyons (Quill, 1983).

[29]CBS 40585 (CL 1397), LP/CD

[30]CBS 8490 (CL 1690), LP

are awed by his outstanding improvisations and unparalleled command of the instrument. Fontana's solos have more depth and substance than the work of almost all other trombonists. Fontana comes close to improvising with the thought and fluency of a modern jazz saxophonist. Unfortunately, Fontana has made so few recordings that little proof of his prowess exists for listeners who never had the opportunity to see him perform.[31] Perhaps as a result, the best-known trombonists in West Coast jazz are valve trombonist **Bob Brookmeyer** (b. 1929) and slide trombonist **Frank Rosolino** (1926–1978). Paradoxically, neither man truly qualifies as both West Coast and cool.

Brookmeyer lived in Los Angeles only sporadically, though his playing style could be called cool for several reasons. He uses a tone quality that is soft, not rough or brassy. His rhythmic conception is laid back, and his lines are light and melodic. These characteristics combine to sound altogether more like late-1930s Basie style than any bop style. He uses a combination of lip slurs and half-valve effects, and he follows through on all his ideas, never leaving the listener hanging. Most notable for Brookmeyer's relationship to cool jazz is his work as the other horn on numerous tours and recordings with Gerry Mulligan's piano-less quartets, especially after both men left Los Angeles and returned to New York. He also filled a similar role in Jimmy Giuffre's trio with guitarist Jim Hall. And, like such other West Coast notables as Gerry Mulligan, Shorty Rogers, and Chico Hamilton, Brookmeyer has made much of his living as a writer rather than as a performer.[32]

Frank Rosolino was based in Los Angeles throughout a sizable portion of his career, thereby qualifying for the "West Coast" designation. Yet, like Fontana's, his approach was a hot and fast bop style, not cool. Next to Fontana, Rosolino was often judged to possess the most speed and range of any trombonist during his era, and because of this he was one of the most influential trombonists in jazz. Like Fontana, Rosolino had also been a featured soloist with Stan Kenton.[33]

**Popular Appeal**  A few players in the "cool" category are the most popular musicians in modern jazz. Trumpeter Miles Davis and saxophonist Stan Getz were capable of consistently packing nightclubs and concert halls. The George Shearing Quintets and the Modern Jazz Quartet were also successful during the 1950s and 60s. The Dave Brubeck Quartet and the Modern Jazz Quartet were among the first groups in jazz history that were sufficiently popular to tour regularly as concert artists, appearing routinely on college campuses and in recital halls previously devoted to presenting classical musicians. But such acclaim was achieved by only a few nonvocal jazz groups. For instance, Lennie Tristano, Lee Konitz, and Jimmy Giuffre remain

[31]Fontana's first album as a leader is *The Great Fontana*, Uptown 27.28, CD/LP. He also plays solos in the Supersax album *Salt Peanuts*, Capitol ST-11271, and the Stan Kenton album *Cuban Fire*, Creative World 1008.

[32]Brookmeyer's best work has been out of print for ages: his recordings with Jimmy Giuffre and Jim Hall, *Western Suite* and *Travelin' Light*, both made for Atlantic, and his recordings with Clark Terry (*Tonight*) for Mainstream. However, a good recording with Zoot Sims has been reissued: Zoot Sims, *One to Blow On*, Biograph 12062 (Dawn 1102), LP, 1956. Albums he made with Gerry Mulligan occasionally come back into print and are worth waiting for.

[33]See footnote 10.

among the least appreciated players in that same period, despite the wealth of their contributions. So to say that cool jazz had popular appeal is not entirely accurate. Only some recordings by some cool jazz musicians were popular, and only the names of a few cool jazz musicians garnered much notice beyond the usual small audience of musicians and fans.

## CHAPTER SUMMARY

1) "Cool jazz" is a term applied to modern styles that sound subdued because they use light, dry tone qualities, little or no vibrato, low levels of volume, and avoid high notes. Some of this music is more relaxed and melodic than bop.

2) Cool jazz of the 1950s drew upon the styles of Lester Young and Count Basie of the 1930s, Lennie Tristano and Lee Konitz of the 1940s, and the arranging practices of the Claude Thornhill band that provided the model for the Miles Davis Nonet of 1949–50.

3) Much cool jazz is indistinguishable from bop, and a few cool players were already discussed in the bop chapter: Stan Getz, George Shearing, and the Modern Jazz Quartet.

4) Pianist-composer Stan Kenton led a string of innovative big bands, some of which were influenced by Claude Thornhill's style.

5) Kenton's repertory of the 1950s contained ambitious concert works resembling twentieth-century classical music scored for brass, saxes, and rhythm section.

6) "West Coast style" refers to cool jazz played by a predominantly white community of jazz musicians based in the Los Angeles area during the 1950s, many of whom had played with the big bands of Stan Kenton and Woody Herman.

7) Gerry Mulligan, Chico Hamilton, Dave Brubeck, and Shorty Rogers were prominent West Coast bandleaders.

8) Paul Desmond, Art Pepper, Jimmy Giuffre, and Gerry Mulligan were prominent West Coast saxophonists.

9) Chet Baker and Shorty Rogers were prominent West Coast trumpeters.

10) Carl Fontana, Frank Rosolino, and Bob Brookmeyer were prominent West Coast trombonists.

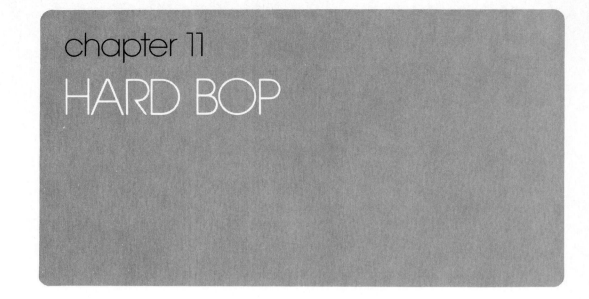

# chapter 11
# HARD BOP

A number of jazz styles emerged during the 1950s and 60s. Most of them, including many of the "cool" styles, were variants on bop. Though musicians tended to refer to all these styles as simply "bop" or "bebop," journalists coined new names based on the differing characteristics of the styles. Unfortunately, the new names, such as hard bop, funky jazz, mainstream, post-bop, and soul jazz, were applied without much consistency, with the result that both the styles and the musicians who played them were often misrepresented. A few popular pieces by key musicians came to be seen as representative of those musicians's overall contribution to jazz, even though the pieces were a small, and in some ways uncharacteristic, fraction of their output. This was especially unfair to such versatile jazz giants as Horace Silver, Cannonball Adderley, and Art Blakey, who were typecast as purveyors of "funky jazz," though today we include them as creators of a broad category called "hard bop." At the same time, the style of their "funky" hits came to be equated with the overall category of hard bop, when it was really only a subcategory.[1]

The small slice of this music that sometimes has been termed "funky jazz" was more popular than any other segment of modern jazz except for a few cool jazz styles, although it was only a minor interest of the most talented modern jazz musicians who played it. The label "funky jazz" was attached most frequently to

[1]For nonfunky examples by these men, listen to Silver's "Ecaroh," in *Art Blakey and The Jazz Messengers*, CBS 37021 (CL897), LP, 1956; "Moon Rays," in SCCJ-R; Cannonball Adderley's *Cannonball & Coltrane (Quintet in Chicago)*, Emarcy 834588 (MG20449) CD, 1959; and the following Art Blakey albums: *A Night at Birdland*, Blue Note 46519/20 (1521/22), CD/LP, 1954; *A Night in Tunisia*, Blue Note 46532 (84049), CD/LP, 1960; *Indestructible*, Blue Note 46429 (84193), CD/LP, 1964; *Buttercorn Lady*, Emarcy 822471 (Limelight 82034), CD, 1966.

**TABLE 11.1.  A Few of the Many Hard Bop Style Musicians**

| Trumpet | Trombone | Piano |
|---|---|---|
| Clifford Brown | J. J. Johnson | Tommy Flanagan |
| Kenny Dorham | Curtis Fuller | Barry Harris |
| Miles Davis | Jimmy Knepper | Cedar Walton |
| Blue Mitchell | Jimmy Cleveland | Duke Pearson |
| Donald Byrd | Frank Rehak | Bobby Timmons |
| Thad Jones | Tom McIntosh | Red Garland |
| Art Farmer | | Wynton Kelly |
| Bill Hardman | **Alto Sax** | Joe Zawinul |
| Joe Gordon | Cannonball Adderley | Junior Mance |
| Carmell Jones | Jackie McLean | Kenny Drew |
| Lee Morgan | Lou Donaldson | Horace Parlan |
| Freddie Hubbard | Gigi Gryce | Les McCann |
| Wilbur Harden | Frank Strozier | Gene Harris |
| Tommy Turrentine | Phil Woods | Ramsey Lewis |
| Benny Bailey | | Horace Silver |
| Booker Little | **Bass** | Elmo Hope |
| Nat Adderley | Paul Chambers | Sonny Clark |
| | Sam Jones | |
| **Baritone Sax** | Doug Watkins | |
| Pepper Adams | Wilbur Ware | **Composer-Arrangers** |
| Cecil Payne | Bob Cranshaw | Horace Silver |
| Nick Brignola | Gene Taylor | Benny Golson |
| | Reggie Workman | Gigi Gryce |
| **Tenor Sax** | Percy Heath | Oliver Nelson |
| Sonny Rollins | Jymie Merritt | Cannonball Adderley |
| John Coltrane | Butch Warren | Nat Adderley |
| Jimmy Heath | Larry Ridley | Wayne Shorter |
| Frank Foster | | Bobby Timmons |
| Clifford Jordan | **Drums** | J. J. Johnson |
| Teddy Edwards | Philly Joe Jones | Jackie McLean |
| Benny Golson | Roy Brooks | Tom McIntosh |
| Billy Mitchell | Louis Hayes | |
| George Coleman | Art Taylor | **Organ** |
| John Gilmore | Roy Haynes | Jimmy Smith |
| Oliver Nelson | Roger Humphries | Jack McDuff |
| Stanley Turrentine | Elvin Jones | Richard "Groove" |
| Junior Cook | Lex Humphries | Holmes |
| Booker Ervin | Max Roach | Don Patterson |
| Joe Henderson | Art Blakey | Jimmy McGriff |
| Wayne Shorter | Mickey Roker | Shirley Scott |
| Hank Mobley | Al Heath | |
| Harold Land | Ben Riley | **Guitar** |
| J. R. Monterose | Jimmy Cobb | Wes Montgomery |
| Tina Brooks | Frankie Dunlop | Kenny Burrell |
| Yusef Lateef | Billy Higgins | Grant Green |

**TABLE 11.2.  Comparing Styles of the 1950s**

|  | West Coast | Hard Bop |
|---|---|---|
| tone color | light | dark |
| tone weight | light | heavy |
| tone texture | soft | raw |
| melodic conception | simple | complex |
| overall character | relaxed | hard-driving |
|  | cool | fiery |
| principal influences | swing and bop | bop |
| sources for alto saxophone styles | Lee Konitz | Charlie Parker |
| sources for trumpet styles | Miles Davis | Dizzy Gillespie |
|  |  | Fats Navarro |
|  |  | Miles Davis |
| sources for tenor saxophone styles | Lester Young | Dexter Gordon |
|  |  | Sonny Stitt |
|  |  | Don Byas |
| sources for arranging practices | Claude Thornhill | Tadd Dameron |
|  | Gil Evans |  |

earthy, blues-drenched, gospelish pieces by Horace Silver and others.[2]  By way of Silver, this bluesy quality influenced a number of players who earned considerable popular attention in the 1960s and 70s. It also influenced hundreds of lesser known pianists and organists performing in taverns and cocktail lounges.[3]

In the rest of this chapter we will examine a stream of styles that coexisted with "funky jazz" and was sometimes performed by the same musicians who included funky pieces in their repertory. This stream of styles has no single, widely accepted name. The terms "post-bop" and "mainstream" were offered by some writers, but

[2]To learn what is meant by "earthy, blues-drenched, gospelish," listen to "One Day" or "Frame for the Blues" in the JAZZ CLASSICS CASSETTE, Avery Parrish's "After Hours" in *Jazz Piano* (Smithsonian 039), Horace Silver's "The Preacher," "Sister Sadie," "Señor Blues," and "Song For My Father," or Bobby Timmons's "Moanin'," Nat Adderley's "Work Song," "Sack o' Woe," "Jive Samba," Joe Zawinul's "Mercy, Mercy, Mercy," or Lee Morgan's "Side-winder." If you do not have access to any of these pieces, look in any good library for the multivolume Recorded Anthology of American Music, prepared by New World Records. In the volume called *Bebop*, NW 271, listen to the funky melody line by Horace Silver called "Stop Time."
[3]Pianists Gene Harris (of The Three Sounds), Ramsey Lewis, and Les McCann, and organists Jimmy Smith, Richard "Groove" Holmes, and Jack McDuff based large parts of their styles on Silver's funky devices and became quite popular as a result. Even the original stylists Bill Evans, McCoy Tyner, and Chick Corea, whose approaches were not primarily funky, demonstrated Silver's influence by making use of his funky devices.

**TABLE 11.3. Two Cities Contributed Many Leading Hard Bop Players**

| Philadelphia | Detroit |
|---|---|
| Clifford Brown | Thad Jones |
| Lee Morgan | Elvin Jones |
| McCoy Tyner | Hank Jones |
| Philly Joe Jones | Barry Harris |
| Jimmy Heath | Charles McPherson |
| Percy Heath | Roland Hanna |
| John Coltrane | Tommy Flanagan |
| Bobby Timmons | Paul Chambers |
| Benny Golson | Ron Carter |
| | Louis Hayes |
| | Yusef Lateef |
| | Kenny Burrell |
| | Donald Byrd |
| | Billy Mitchell |
| | Doug Watkins |
| | Pepper Adams |
| | Curtis Fuller |

they failed to catch on, apparently because they were not sufficiently specific. "Hard bop" is the designation we use in this textbook. The sounds of most styles within this stream often differ little from the sounds of bop. But when they do differ, the following trends frequently can be observed:

1) Improvised lines are somewhat simpler than bop lines.
2) Drummers play with more activity.
3) Tone colors are darker, weightier, and rougher.
4) The forms of the compositions are less frequently identical to pop tune forms, and the chord progressions are more frequently original rather than being borrowed from pop tunes.
5) There is somewhat less of the start-and-stop quality that leaves the listener off balance.
6) There is a hard-driving feeling that pushes relentlessly, with an emphasis on consistent swinging.
7) Piano comping has more variety in rhythms and chord voicings.

These characteristics were first apparent during the early 1950s in the work of trumpeter Clifford Brown and the bands led by drummer Art Blakey.[4] Later the

[4]Listen to Art Blakey's *A Night At Birdland,* Blue Note 46519/20 (1521/22), CD/LP, 1954; and *Complete Blue Note and Pacific Jazz Recordings of Clifford Brown,* Mosaic MR5-104, LP set, 1953–4.

characteristics persisted in the music of subsequent bands which included those same men. It also survived in the music of their associates and disciples (see Tables 11.1, 11.4, and 11.5). The musicians playing with Art Blakey and Horace Silver at any given time worked within this style almost without exception through the 1980s. Some of these characteristics were also evident in bands which departed more drastically from bop traditions, such as the groups led by Miles Davis between 1955 and 1959.[5]

The sounds described here were not exclusive to a particular geographic region. For example, forerunners of hard bop tenor sax styles included Los Angeles-based Dexter Gordon and New York-based Sonny Stitt. Important models for trumpeters included New York-based Miles Davis and Fats Navarro. In addition, Philadelphia and Detroit (see Table 11.3) contributed many vital players, and Indianapolis contributed guitarist Wes Montgomery (discussed later), trumpeter Freddie Hubbard (discussed later), and trombonist Slide Hampton.

A second wave of players can be distinguished within the overall category of hard bop. Much of their music draws upon sources outside hard bop (discussed in later chapters), and it goes beyond hard bop by devising its own stream of styles. These players made their mark in the 1960s and derived their approaches less directly from bop than did those players mentioned above. With the notable exception of saxophonist John Coltrane, who died in 1967, the most prominent among this group were still active through the 1980s and remained models for aspiring jazz musicians to imitate. The outstanding tenor saxophonists in this second wave of hard bop musicians are Joe Henderson (discussed later), and Wayne Shorter (discussed in the next chapter). The top trumpeter is Freddie Hubbard (discussed later). The pianists are McCoy Tyner (see chapter 13), Herbie Hancock, Chick Corea, and Keith Jarrett (all discussed in chapter 15). The drummers are Tony Williams (see next chapter) and Elvin Jones (see chapter 13). You may recognize some of these names grouped here with the 1950s and 60s for other styles that were developed in the 1970s. However, if we recall the versatility that is so common to jazz giants, it should not be difficult to comprehend, for example, Herbie Hancock's contributing significantly to hard bop during the early 1960s and then creating new styles in the jazz-rock fusion genres of the 1970s and 80s.

**Piano**  There were a number of excellent pianists affiliated with hard bop (see Table 11.1). Two of the most prominent were **Tommy Flanagan** (b. 1930) and Horace Silver. Flanagan was influenced primarily by Teddy Wilson, Bud Powell, Art Tatum, and Hank Jones. He had more instrumental proficiency than almost any other hard bop pianist. His touch was very clean, and his lines were well conceived and effortlessly played. Yet in spite of his meticulous attention to technique, Flanagan managed to extract a warm tone from the piano. His tasteful comping, flowing solos, and polite touch provided a perfect complement to trumpeter Miles Davis, saxophonists Sonny

[5]Much of Davis's work is routinely classified as "cool jazz," and this label is not limited to his 1948–50 nonet recordings. It also includes his early 1950s work with Sonny Rollins, Horace Silver, Milt Jackson, and others. Even his 1959 *Kind of Blue* album is tagged "cool jazz" by some, though it more closely fits into the "hard bop" or "modal jazz" category.

Horace Silver. (*Photo by Bill Smith*)

Rollins and John Coltrane, and guitarist Wes Montgomery, whom he accompanied on many of their outstanding albums.[6] Flanagan went on to a long tenure as accompanist for singer Ella Fitzgerald and later remained active as leader of his own groups in the 1980s.

**Horace Silver** (b. 1928) is one of the biggest names in hard bop, a reputation derived mostly from his work as a composer and bandleader. But he also developed an original and substantial piano style. By the 1960s, he had replaced bop's emphasis on long, convoluted lines with his own brief, catchy phrases. Virtuosity is not essential to Silver's style. He almost never double-times. Succinctness and clarity are far higher priorities in his playing than speed and agility. His ideas unfold with a logic that is apparent even to the novice listener. Silver made considerable use of

---

[6]Miles Davis, *Collector's Items*, Fantasy/OJC-071 (P-7044), CD/LP, 1956; Sonny Rollins, *Saxophone Colossus*, OJC-291 (P-7079), CD/LP, 1956; John Coltrane, *Giant Steps*, Atlantic 1311, CD/LP, 1959; Wes Montgomery, *Incredible Jazz Guitar of Wes Montgomery*, OJC-036 (Riverside 320), CD/LP, 1960. Flanagan can also be heard in two selections on *Jazz Piano* (Smithsonian 039) and on Rollins's "Blue Seven" in SCCJ.

**TABLE 11.4. A Few of the Many Horace Silver Sidemen**

| | |
|---|---|
| Blue Mitchell | Junior Cook |
| Art Farmer | Joe Henderson |
| Tom Harrell | Michael Brecker |
| Woody Shaw | Roy Brooks |
| Randy Brecker | Louis Hayes |
| Hank Mobley | Al Foster |
| Bob Berg | Billy Cobham |

silence and employed an exacting deliberation in timing the starting and stopping points of his phrases. His improvised melodic figures are executed in a very forceful, percussive way. His solos are like his tunes—filled with simple ideas that are hummable and easy to remember. It is as though, while improvising, Silver keeps on composing at the same level of creativity and clarity that he maintains in his writing.[7]

As an accompanist, Horace Silver initially drew from bop style. By the late 1950s, however, he had perfected a new style of accompaniment, one in which his figures sounded like prewritten setups for his soloists instead of spontaneous chording that followed the shifting directions taken by the solo improvisations. In this way, the soloists in Silver's bands were supported by backgrounds similar to those in big bands, where written arrangements supply the same accompaniment figures each time the soloist improvises on that piece. This resulted in more continuity in Silver's music than in the music produced by the comparatively informal structure of most modern groups, though these figures were also a restriction, limiting the range of moods an improvising soloist could create. By comparison with traditional bop comping, however, Silver's accompaniment figures gave listeners something to cling to, and this may account for his greater popularity.

Horace Silver was hard bop's most prolific composer. For Blue Note record company alone, he penned almost all the tunes on over twenty-five years worth of his bands' albums. Silver put together arrangements that were generally more elaborate than those of other hard bop groups. They often contained ensemble strains in the middle of a piece, as well as Latin American rhythms and hints of gospel music. Silver often voiced trumpet and tenor saxophone a fourth or fifth apart, an especially successful way to achieve a fullness that made the quintet sound as though it contained more than five musicians. In addition to using this technique, Silver often wrote bass figures and played them on the piano in unison with his bassist. These figures had an engaging quality which expanded the usually limited scope of bop bass lines. It is partly for these reasons that his quintet's identity was

---

[7]For analysis of Silver's piano style, see John Mehegan's *Jazz Improvisation Vol. 3* (Watson-Guptill, 1964).

unlike that of any other bop or hard bop group. In addition, Silver's quintet performances were consistently swinging and polished, and they featured many of the best musicians of the 1950s and 60s (see Table 11.4). Silver remained active in the 1980s and continued to tour and record with bands of similar style and instrumentation.[8]

**Trumpet**  The order of major influences on modern trumpeters begins in the 1940s with Dizzy Gillespie then Miles Davis and Fats Navarro. However, it was the successor to these men who had the greatest impact. His name was **Clifford Brown** (1930–1956), and he drew his style largely from Navarro, with a touch of Davis. Among musicians, Brown is probably the most widely admired trumpeter since the swing era. Brown, however, is not widely known outside the inner circles of modern jazz musicians, and he was documented on recordings from only 1952 to 1956. He did not use the peculiar note choices that typified Gillespie, nor did he convey the intimate moods that distinguished Davis. But, by comparison with Gillespie and Davis, he played at a high level of inspiration and execution more consistently from performance to performance. Brown used a wider, more deliberate vibrato than Gillespie or Davis, something Navarro had occasionally employed. Brown's use of a slow, even, very obvious vibrato may be responsible for its renewed use by jazz trumpeters in the 1950s and 60s. Another distinguishing mark of Brown's style is the overall contour of his solos. Jazz historian Harvey Pekar has observed that Brown's solos are similar to those of Davis in that they jump into the high register less often than Gillespie's and Navarro's, and that the contours of Brown's and Davis's lines are usually smoother than Gillespie's and Navarro's. Because of this, we might regard Brown's solos as cooler than most hard bop, even though his solos are not as simple as the most concise solos of Chet Baker or Miles Davis. It is evident that Brown drew upon previous styles, but he also devised a style that was distinguishable from his sources.

Let's consider several reasons that musicians were so impressed with Clifford Brown's playing. Most prominent was that Brown managed to suggest relaxation in his playing, even when executing intricate melodic figures. This has at least two possible causes: the perfection he achieved in making the trumpet obey his wishes, and his concern with simplifying bop instead of blazing new trails as Parker and Gillespie had. Brown also placed more emphasis on swinging than on trying to throw off the listener with surprise after surprise, as bop soloists often did. Tuneful improvisations were more common for him than for most of his contemporaries.[9] In these respects, Brown's work on trumpet parallels Sonny Stitt's work on saxophone. Brown refined a repertory of phrases and ways of moving gracefully through the

---

[8]Favorites among musicians are the Horace Silver albums *Horacescope*, Blue Note 84042, LP, 1960; *Cape Verdean Blues*, Blue Note 84220, CD/LP, 1965; and *In Pursuit of the 27th Man*, Blue Note 054, LP, 1972.

[9]See pages 412–14 for information on how to get Milton Stewart's book-long analysis of Brown's playing. See David Baker's *The Jazz Style of Clifford Brown: A Musical and Historical Perspective* (Studio PR, 1982; available from Jamey Aebersold). Listen to "Pent-Up House" in SCCJ, and see Scott Reeves's analysis in his *Creative Jazz Improvisation* (Prentice-Hall, 1989).

chord progressions. These techniques, their fluid sensibility, and the easy swing feeling they produced proved accessible to numerous other trumpeters. And, as with Stitt, Brown's contributions were absorbed as stock vocabulary for hard bop players.

Clifford Brown's music projected a joyful spirit. This, together with the lilt and bounce in his lines, was contagious. He could generate long, flowing lines at furious tempos and still maintain the warmth and suppleness of his wide, glowing tone. Most other trumpeters stood in awe of Brown's dazzling speed and agility. Also, he did what is almost impossible at those frantic speeds: he kept his accurate intonation and relaxed swing feeling. His firm command of accurate articulation was unparalleled in modern jazz, and he was able to make meaty phrases come tumbling from his horn, chorus after chorus after chorus. There was an exuberence projected by Brown's music that combined with his assured manner, pretty sound, and fertile imagination to influence an entire generation of modern trumpeters, including Donald Byrd, Bill Hardman, Louis Smith, Lee Morgan, and Carmell Jones.

Miles Davis and Clifford Brown remained models for aspiring trumpeters to imitate long after they first became known among musicians. But by the 1970s, the majority of young trumpeters, including such notables as Woody Shaw and Randy Brecker, were imitating another model: **Freddie Hubbard.** Though his early playing drew from Clifford Brown, Miles Davis, and Chet Baker, Hubbard (b. 1938) had developed his own original approach by the early 1960s. His playing style departed from bop and was compatible with "free jazz" approaches of the 1960s and "jazz-rock" approaches of the 1970s.[10]

A number of characteristics can help us distinguish Hubbard from Brown and Davis. Although he incorporated some Davis methods of manipulating his tone quality and pitch, Hubbard steered clear of the way in which Davis gets away from the beat. Hubbard stuck close to the beat and liked to double-time. In contrast to the solemn and methodical manner of Davis, much of Hubbard's work sounds offhanded and playful. There is a looseness to his fashion that implies great creative freedom and tremendous conceptual flexibility. Instead of following through on every idea, he did not hesitate to interrupt himself if he got a new idea while he was playing an old one. His style bristles with excitement; even his ballad renditions project great verve. Like those of saxophonist John Coltrane, his improvisations exhibit a willingness to spontaneously construct and rework figures from odd combinations of notes and rhythms, not depending on stock bop phrases. In this way he was harmonically daring and impulsive. The richness and range of his imagination combined with his free manner to build a new vocabulary for jazz trumpet style.[11]

Freddie Hubbard is almost universally envied among trumpeters for his outstanding mastery of the instrument. His tone was clear and well focused. His intonation was excellent. His articulation was crisp, and he could improvise coher-

[10]Also, Hubbard was probably the first great brass player to draw heavily from the approach of saxophonist John Coltrane, notably in his use of pentatonic scales, quartal harmony, and chromaticism.

[11]See Stuart Isacoff's *Solos For Jazz Trumpet* (Carl Fischer, 1985) for analyses of Hubbard's solos on "Blue Moon" and "On Green Dolphin Street."

ently at brisk tempos and sound as though he still had plenty of strength and agility in reserve. Like Brown's, Hubbard's sense of time was very precise. Hubbard also mastered a very demanding technique called a lip trill, in which, without changing fingering or shaking the trumpet, he rapidly alternated, in legato manner, intervals of a minor third, moving the bottom note in stepwise fashion. This became a trademark of his highly virtuosic style.[12]

**Drums**    The period in jazz history that produced hard bop also produced several innovative accompaniment styles of jazz drumming. Chico Hamilton has been discussed already in the unit about West Coast style cool jazz. Like Hamilton, several other innovative drummers were also important as bandleaders. Art Blakey and Max Roach are discussed here because their bands, not just their drumming, were at the forefront of hard bop. Philly Joe Jones is also discussed here because his contribution parallels that of Blakey in helping define hard bop accompanying style. Elvin Jones is not discussed until the John Coltrane chapter because, though he performed innovatively during the 1950s, his innovations were most widely showcased with Coltrane in the 1960s.

**Art Blakey** (b. 1919) epitomized the loosening of jazz drumming style, whereby loud, directive intrusions emerged at the forefront of the combo sound. Blakey's playing as an accompanist was so dynamic that for him to solo was almost anticlimactic. He was able to cue and underscore transitions within each piece by the figures he played and the various levels of loudness he used for them. He was often found to be directing the mood and choosing the moments during which it was to rise or fall in tension. His former sidemen have mentioned how he made them aware of pacing their improvisations and trying to build tension and excitement gradually over the course of their solos.[13]

For over thirty years, Art Blakey has been leading quintets and sextets that are clear representatives of the hard bop style. Their music is extremely intense, hard driving, and uncompromising. Their swing feeling is unrelenting and possesses a weightiness that distinguishes it from the "cool jazz" styles that also swing persistently. The list of notables in Blakey's bands is immense (Table 11.5 mentions only a few). These players often received their first wide exposure to jazz fans while they toured and recorded with him. Many of them soon became leaders of their own groups. Ordinarily, Blakey hired individualists who were relatively young but whose playing displayed a high level. Their compositions became Blakey's repertory. The character of those compositions, in turn, became part of the band's character.

---

[12]Though he remained active throughout the 1970s and 80s, Hubbard's playing on albums in the 1960s as a sideman with Herbie Hancock and Eric Dolphy represents some of his most inventive work. Listen to Herbie Hancock's *Empyrean Isles*, Blue Note 84175, CD/LP, 1964; Eric Dolphy's *Out To Lunch*, Blue Note 46524, CD/LP, 1964; and Oliver Nelson's *Blues and The Abstract Truth*, MCA/Impulse 5659 (A-5), CD/LP, 1961.

[13]Listen to Blakey's work with Clifford Brown and Horace Silver from 1954, in which he is engaged in volatile rhythm section drumming years before such activity became common practice: *A Night at Birdland*, Blue Note 46519/20 (1521/22), CD/LP, 1954.

**TABLE 11.5. A Few of the Many Art Blakey Sidemen**

| | |
|---|---|
| Clifford Brown | Junior Mance |
| Donald Byrd | Keith Jarrett |
| Bill Hardman | Curtis Fuller |
| Lee Morgan | Wynton Marsalis |
| Freddie Hubbard | Bobby Timmons |
| Woody Shaw | George Cables |
| Jackie McLean | Reggie Workman |
| Hank Mobley | Jymie Merritt |
| Wayne Shorter | Lou Donaldson |
| Benny Golson | Dave Schnitter |
| Johnny Griffin | Bobby Watson |
| Chuck Mangione | James Williams |
| Horace Silver | Valerie Ponomarev |
| Cedar Walton | Ira Sullivan |

**Max Roach** made his reputation during the bop era and then continued to develop new bands and drumming approaches. He is best and most importantly recognized as the fountainhead of bebop and hard bop drumming styles, more so than Blakey or Philly Joe Jones. Roach is routinely cited for his clean touch and discreet accompanying, and for the fact that, unlike many drummers, he does not flaunt his proficiency. He is known for intelligently developed solos that are often melodic, and a command of the drum set that never overshadows his musical sense. Few modern drummers have escaped his influence. (See chapter 9 for more about his playing.) He continued to lead hard bop-style bands during the 1980s. Roach is singled out for mention again in this chapter because he founded one of the great hard bop bands, a quintet with Clifford Brown, which existed from 1954 until Brown's death in 1956.[14]

**Philly Joe Jones** (1923–1985) was among the most adventurous of rhythm section players in the 1950s. Next to Max Roach, Jones is the most widely cited influence among drummers who emerged during the 1960s. Compared with other drummers, he played more figures, more often, and his activity was more like conversations with his fellow band members. His fills are models of originality and assured execution. They are often as melodic as the horn lines they complement. His work conveyed a constant excitement. His crisp fills on the snare drum, accents on the

---

[14]Some of the tunes they recorded remained favorites among musicians of the 1980s: Brown's "Joy Spring" and "Daahoud." For a sample of the quintet's sound, listen to "Pent-Up House" with saxophonist Sonny Rollins in SCCJ, and "What Is This Thing Called Love?" in the New World Records anthology, *Bebop*, NW 271, or in the album *Clifford Brown & Max Roach*, Emarcy 814645 CD / EXPR-1033, LP (MG 36036), 1954, which features saxophonist Harold Land.

bass drum, and splashes on the cymbal were so well conceived that they became models of how active drummers could be without disturbing the pulse.[15]

**Saxophone**   Cannonball Adderley (1928–1975) was one of the best improvisers to play alto saxophone after Charlie Parker died. In fact, some listeners considered Adderley to be Parker's successor, though Adderley himself felt that to be undeserved praise. In a few respects, Adderley's style is like Parker's: highly fluid, supercharged, and unpredictable. However, Adderley initially derived his style not from Parker but from the swing era styles of Pete Brown and Benny Carter, and his later style demonstrated advances made by John Coltrane. During his creative peak of 1957 to 1959, when he played with Miles Davis and John Coltrane, Adderley's solos were filled with little melodies, and his command over the instrument vied with the virtuosity attained by Parker and Coltrane. Adderley's ability to keep up with Coltrane and sometimes surpass him was an indication of his stunning improvisational prowess.[16]

The tone quality that Cannonball Adderley extracted from the alto saxophone was so deep and full that listeners sometimes mistook it for tenor saxophone. (Listen to side 2 of the JAZZ STYLES CASSETTE to acquaint yourself with the differences between alto and tenor sax sounds. Then listen to "Flamenco Sketches" on the JAZZ CLASSICS CASSETTE, and compare Adderley's sound with Coltrane's.) Together with the vibrato Adderley used, the effect of his tone was warm and glowing. He bent this huge tone with blue notes and wails, thereby creating an earthy, legato style that has been called "blues drenched."[17] Contrasting with the solemn urgency of most hard bop, Adderley's playing conveys a sense of fun. He loved to double-time, and he often incorporated snippets of pop tunes into his lines.[18] A feeling of exhilaration is present when he digs into an improvisation and starts spinning out inspired lines, with their dense activity and ever shifting directions. But Adderley was not entirely bouncy and lighthearted; he could also evoke calm and reflection. For instance, his solos on the Davis album *Kind of Blue* sound quite reflective, and

[15]Listen to side 1 of the JAZZ STYLES CASSETTE to familiarize yourself with the different sounds of instruments in the drum set, and the effects of sticks and brushes. Then listen to Philly Joe Jones's work on "Two Bass Hit" and "Billy Boy," in the Miles Davis album *Milestones*, Columbia CBS 40837 (CL 1193), 1958; "Budo," in *Basic Miles*, Columbia PC 32025, 1955; "Tune-Up," in *Cookin' With the Miles Davis Quintet*, OJC-128 (Prestige 7094), CD/LP, 1956; and "Half Nelson," in *Workin' With the Miles Davis Quintet*, OJC-296 (Prestige 7166), CD/LP, 1956.

[16]His most outstanding solos from this period are found on the Miles Davis album *Milestones*, CBS 40837 (CL 1193), CD/LP, 1958; and a recording of the 1959 Davis group minus Davis, *Cannonball and Coltrane (Quintet in Chicago)*, Emarcy 834588 (MG 20449), CD.

[17]For some of his funkiest playing, listen to "Them Dirty Blues" on his album *Them Dirty Blues*, Landmark 1301 (Riverside 322/1170), CD/LP, 1960.

[18]In the Miles Davis album *Milestones*, Adderley quotes the opening phrases of George Gershwin's "Fascinating Rhythm" in the beginning of his solo on "Milestones," and he transforms the first phrase of Vernon Duke's "I Can't Get Started" on his solo in "Two Bass Hit."

they are among the most original improvisations he recorded. (One of these is in "Flamenco Sketches" on the JAZZ CLASSICS CASSETTE.)[19]

On and off during the 1950s, 60s, and 70s, Cannonball Adderley co-led a series of bands with his brother, cornetist Nat Adderley. The groups enjoyed a large following and continued until Cannonball's death in 1975. Many pieces in the band's repertory constituted what journalists dubbed "funky jazz": "Jive Samba," "Work Song," "Sack o' Woe," and their biggest hit, "Mercy, Mercy, Mercy." Though most of its repertory was swinging music with little dilution of the bop style, the group was best known for its funk hits, "Mercy, Mercy, Mercy," "Walk Tall," and "Country Preacher."

There were many excellent tenor saxophonists in hard bop (see Table 11.1). Although an entire book would be required to do them justice, we will consider four stand-outs: John Coltrane, Sonny Rollins, Joe Henderson, and Wayne Shorter. John Coltrane created an original hard bop style that was documented in recordings he made in the 1950s while with the combo of Miles Davis. (Listen to him on "Flamenco Sketches" in the JAZZ CLASSICS CASSETTE.) We postpone our discussion of Coltrane to a special chapter because of the size and originality of his contributions, his stature in hard bop, his large body of unique compositions, his two other new saxophone styles, and his original ensemble style. In the present chapter, we will briefly discuss Sonny Rollins, who some feel had his creative peak during the 1950s and remains the favorite jazz tenor for many musicians. Then we will examine Joe Henderson, a significant saxophonist-composer-bandleader who was important in new developments during a 1960s and 70s phase of hard bop. In the following chapter, we will evaluate Wayne Shorter, whose contribution to jazz history was threefold: he played hard bop with Art Blakey from 1959 to 1964, devised new approaches to composition and improvisation in the Miles Davis quintet of 1964 to 1969, and developed jazz-rock fusion from 1970 to 1985 with a band called Weather Report.

Next to Stan Getz, **Sonny Rollins** (b. 1930) was the most popular tenor saxophonist of the 1950s. Though he is known today for his originality, Rollins was among the first group of musicians to adopt Charlie Parker's alto sax style for use on tenor.[20] He began recording in 1949, and his name is often mentioned along with Charlie Parker, Sonny Stitt, and John Coltrane when saxophonists themselves list their favorites.

Rollins was widely admired for the way he improvised simple melodic ideas and then developed them, producing solos that possessed integrity and continuity. His

---

[19]See Stuart Isacoff's *Solos For Jazz Alto Sax* (Carl Fischer, 1985) for analyses of Adderley's solos on "On Green Dolphin Street" and "Sack O' Woe." For David Baker's book-long analysis of Adderley's style, write Jamey Aebersold, 1211 Aebersold Drive, New Albany, IN 47150.

[20]To hear the resemblance between Rollins and Parker, listen to Parker play tenor, instead of alto, as he does on "Half Nelson," his 1947 recording (*Bird-Savoy Original Master Takes*, Savoy 8801, CD set (2201 LP set)). Then listen to any records that Rollins made with Bud Powell in 1949, as included in *The Amazing Bud Powell, Vol. 1*, Blue Note 81503, CD; or with Miles Davis in 1951, such as *Dig*, OJC-005 (Prestige 7012), CD/LP.

clarity of mind allowed him to transcend cliché figures, even at the high speeds which ordinarily push saxophonists to use easily fingered patterns instead of original melodic ideas.[21]

During the 1950s, the Rollins timbre was hard, rough, and dry, not as deep or richly textured as Coltrane's. Some listeners called it "brittle." His vibrato was slow and very deliberate. Rollins differed from the majority of bop tenor saxophonists by using staccato phrasing instead of the almost exclusively legato style favored by them. He could manage a blunt attack, move to legato and back again to staccato. His phrases were delivered without ornamentation or any other kind of softening. The overall effect of his playing was abrupt and, though aggressive, it was not necessarily explosive or blistering. Sonny Rollins is a giant in the history of improvisation. He mastered the rhythmic devices necessary to swing, and he swung whenever he wished. But he also purposely deviated from the tempo at times, as if he were inside the beat one moment and ignoring it the next. Rollins treated a piece as though its tempo, chord progressions, and melody were mere toys to be played with. He instantaneously redesigned them from moment to moment without reverence for their original flavor.[22]

Some listeners feel that Rollins's career reached its peak during the 1950s, that he did his most lyrical playing with Miles Davis[23] and his most swinging playing with Clifford Brown.[24] Regardless of whether you agree, there is no question that Rollins's recordings in the 1950s constitute landmarks in the history of tenor saxophone style.[25]

During the 1960s, Rollins streamlined his style[26] and explored less-conventional approaches to improvisation.[27] During the 1970s and 80s, Rollins usually played in

[21]Rollins's fastest, most fluid solos are on "I Know That You Know" and "Eternal Triangle" in Dizzy Gillespie's album *Sunny Side Up*, Verve 825674 (MGV 8262), CD, formerly *The Rollins/Stitt Sessions*, Verve VE2-2505, LP, made in 1957 during a session in which he was prepared to keep up with the lightning-quick playing of fellow saxophonist Sonny Stitt.

[22]Listen to his "Blue Seven" in SCCJ, or "You Don't Know What Love Is," in his *Saxophone Colossus*, Fantasy/OJC-291 (Prestige 7079), CD/LP, 1956. See pages 86–97 in Gunther Schuller's *Musings* (Oxford, 1986) and Scott Reeves' *Creative Jazz Improvisation* (Prentice-Hall, 1989) for analyses of the Rollins solo on "Blue Seven." For David Baker's book-long analysis of the Rollins style, write Jamey Aebersold, 1211 Aebersold Drive, New Albany, IN 47150. For a technical evaluation of the Rollins career, up to 1980, see *Sonny Rollins* by Charles Blancq (Twayne, 1983). Further transcriptions and analyses are in Charley Gerard's *Sonny Rollins* (Consolidated Music, 1980; available from Aebersold).

[23]"Vierd Blues" and "No Line," *Collector's Items*, Fantasy/OJC-071 (Prestige 7044) CD/LP, 1956.

[24]Listen to "Pent-Up House" in SCCJ and *Sonny Rollins Plus Four*, Fantasy/OJC-243 (Prestige 7038), CD/LP, 1956, made under Rollins's own leadership while he was a member of the Clifford Brown-Max Roach Quintet. This is among the few albums Rollins himself has said he is pleased with.

[25]The all-time favorite Rollins album for many musicians and critics is *Saxophone Colossus*, Fantasy/OJC-291 (Prestige 7079), CD/LP, 1956. Also impressive is *A Night at the Village Vanguard (More from the Vanguard)*, Blue Note 46517/18 (475), CD, 1957.

[26]*The Bridge*, reissued as *Sonny Rollins—The Quartets Featuring Jim Hall*, RCA Bluebird 5643 CD/5634 LP (LSP-2527), 1962

[27]*Our Man in Jazz*, RCA LSP 2612

a way that differed significantly from his style of the 1950s and 60s. He adopted a timbre that was broader, coarser, and more guttural. In addition, his playing had less speed and crispness of execution. Some of his lines recalled those of saxophonists associated with the popular music known as rhythm and blues. By contrast with his earlier style, his playing became simpler and funkier. Rollins retained his allegiance to lyricism, but now his roots in Charlie Parker were barely detectable. The tunes he performed were simpler, too, and their accompaniments resembled those common to the popular dance styles called disco, funk, and Latin. Although Rollins occasionally returned to more bop-like playing (as with the Milestone Jazz Stars), his preferred approach during this period remained so simple and funky that it fit perfectly with the style of the Rolling Stones, the popular blues-oriented rock and roll group that used him on one of their recordings.[28] Twenty years after being the top hard bop tenor, Sonny Rollins had mastered a new style and gained a fresh audience.

**Joe Henderson** (b. 1937) is a tenor saxophonist who managed to gain considerable attention among musicians at a time when the mammoth specter of John Coltrane blotted out almost all tenors other than Stan Getz and Sonny Rollins. During the 1970s, Coltrane's was the most widely imitated approach to jazz tenor, with the influence of Michael Brecker slightly overtaking it during the 1980s. Many players of the 1970s and 80s incorporated selected parts of Henderson's approach into their own styles. By comparison with Rollins and Coltrane, however, Henderson influenced far fewer saxophonists seeking to imitate completely a single style model, but his influence is heard almost as frequently in saxophonists exhibiting multiple influences.

Henderson's own origins are not clear. Though he was affected by a number of different models, including Lester Young, and reminds many of Rollins and Coltrane, Henderson reminds some of Junior Cook, a saxophonist known primarily for his recordings with the Horace Silver quintet of 1958 to 64.[29] Like Cook, Henderson capitalized on melodic fragments in a hard, insistent way. However, he was less raw-sounding, more fluid and agile than Cook, with an ability to play extremely quick figures with uncanny accuracy. Some of Henderson's solos sound free of hard bop traditions for solo improvisation. The result is a style that many choose not to call hard bop. Though rarely called "free jazz" either, it is a new approach with a feeling that differs considerably from Parker's and Coltrane's. Henderson has a vocabulary all his own. Rather than playing strings of notes that are all equal, Henderson uses a wide variety of note durations. For example, instead of playing long strings of uninterrupted eighth notes, as other saxophonists usually do, he might combine eighth-notes, triplets, sixteenth-notes, and uneven groupings, which together lend his playing a speech-like effect. He intersperses shakes, trills, and wails in a knife-like way. Henderson often begins his lines with brief figures which he then develops with many transformations, following through on each of his ideas. In many respects, these ideas do not represent a way to navigate through the chord

[28]*Tattoo You*, CBS 40502 (Rolling Stones Records 16052), CD/LP
[29]Compare Cook's work on Blue Mitchell's album *Thing to Do*, Blue Note 84178, CD/LP, 1964, with Henderson's work on the Horace Silver album *Song for My Father*, Blue Note 84185, CD/LP, 1964.

progressions as much as they pose a sound to pit against the rhythm section's activity. He can swing conventionally or intentionally play free of the tempo and develop melodic figures that do not neatly fit with the beats that are passing underneath them. Intense, provocative lines spill from his horn. Some contain syncopated staccato figures, alternating with churning legato phrases. Sometimes he employs well-controlled shrieks. He varies the speed of his vibrato, also. Henderson's playing conveys the impression that he possesses a freedom to think very fast and clearly during the heat of improvising, and to play exactly what he thinks, unhindered by the mechanical limitations of his instrument.[30]

**Trombone**    Though there were first-rate trombone soloists playing in some hard bop groups (see Table 11.1), trombone was unusual to find at all. Note also, that calling any trombonist of the 1950s and 60s a "hard bop trombonist" may not be meaningful because most who played with hard bop bands had styles that differed little from bop. The most prominent trombonist of the period was **J. J. Johnson**, an excellent improviser who had already earned a respected place among bop instrumentalists during the late 1940s and early 1950s (see chapter 9).[31] Johnson was the most visible of all trombonists in the 1950s and 60s, not only because he was an outstanding player but also because he recorded numerous albums as a bandleader. Despite his roots in bop, Johnson streamlined his style during the 1960s and put together bands that made music which felt less rushed than bop. Also, several of the tunes he wrote for these bands had a funky flavor that we tend to associate with hard bop.[32] Another trombonist, **Curtis Fuller** (b. 1934) was an equally impressive improviser, yet most of his career was spent as a sideman. Consequently he never achieved Johnson's high level of recognition.[33]

**Guitar**    Just as there were few guitarists in the bop style of the 1940s, there were few guitarists in the hard bop style of the 1950s. Of these few, the most influential was **Wes Montgomery** (1925–1968). Using his thumb instead of a pick, Montgomery extracted a tone from his guitar that was round and full. Some of his lines are voiced in octaves, a sound that became closely identified with him. (Listen to the JAZZ STYLES CASSETTE, side 2, for examples of guitar lines in octaves, as well as a comparison of sounds extracted by pick and by finger.) Influenced by Charlie Christian, Montgomery played in a style that was relaxed, and melodic. It projected

---

[30]Listen to his work on the Horace Silver album *Cape Verdean Blues*, Blue Note 84220, CD/LP, 1965; "I Have a Dream," on Herbie Hancock's album *The Prisoner*, Blue Note 46845 (84321), CD/LP, 1969; and Henderson's own album *Power to the People*, Milestone 9024, 1969. For transcriptions of solos on Henderson's albums *Page One* and *In 'n Out*, see Don Sickler's *Joe Henderson: Improvised Saxophone Solos* (Studio PR, 1978; available from Aebersold).

[31]See Scott Reeves's *Creative Jazz Improvisation* for analysis of J.J. Johnson's solo on "Aquarius." See David Baker's *J. J. Johnson: Trombone* (Shattinger, 1979; available from Aebersold).

[32]*J.J. Inc.*, CBS 36808 (CL 1606), 1960.

[33]Fuller's work on these albums is representative: John Coltrane, *Blue Trane*, Blue Note 46095 (81577) CD/LP, 1957; Art Farmer-Benny Golson Jazztet, *Meet The Jazztet*, Chess 91550 (Argo 664), 1960; Art Blakey, *Indestructible*, Blue Note 46429 (84193) CD/LP, 1964.

an assured sense of swing and an unhurried, pleasant manner. His playing exudes naturalness, and most listeners perceive the overall effect to be warm and pleasant.

Montgomery systematically developed his solo improvisations in a way that began cool and built tension over several choruses, leading to a climax. Then he would stop altogether or begin the process again. Frequently he began with lines made up of only a single note at a time, then voiced his lines in octaves, then, after a chorus of octaves he concluded with a chorded solo. In this way, he made his sound successively thicker and more exciting in each chorus.

Montgomery's peak of creativity was the late 1950s and early 1960s. He is best known, however, for later recordings made for the Verve and A & M firms. For these popular albums, the studios provided preset orchestral accompaniments, over which Montgomery paraphrased pop tunes and improvised lightly. He played tastefully on these recordings, but his earlier work, available mostly on albums made for Riverside, is a far richer jazz vein.[34]

After Wes Montgomery, the best-known hard bop guitarist is **Kenny Burrell** (b. 1931). Sources for Burrell's style included Charlie Christian, Django Reinhardt, and Oscar Moore.[35] Burrell also drew from bop-style sax and trumpet lines and from the funky melodic figures identified with pianist Horace Silver. Although he is quite versatile, Burrell is particularly well known for his soulful playing on bluesy albums made with organist Jimmy Smith, on which he established a swinging, easygoing mood. Most of these albums featured relatively uncomplicated music that attained considerable popularity.[36]

**Bass**  The instrumental prowess of bassists steadily grew as jazz evolved. Hard bop was marked by further milestones. When young bass players of the period asked, "Who should I be listening to?" the names **Paul Chambers** (1935–1969) and **Sam Jones** (1924–1981) were added to those of Ray Brown and Charles Mingus. Chambers became widely known through the recordings he made with Miles Davis between 1955 and 1963. Sam Jones is best remembered for his work with Cannonball Adderley's groups of 1957 to 1966.[37]

Paul Chambers produced a huge, dark sound on his bass. The notes he chose for walking formed a continuous harmonic complement, and the propulsive way he delivered them played a crucial rhythmic role. (Listen to JAZZ STYLES CASSETTE, Side 1, for demonstrations of bass techniques.) The phrases in his solo improvisations were bop-style and hornlike. These lines were sensible and swinging, possessing melodic and rhythmic richness. Chambers expanded the solo potential of

[34]Listen to his "West Coast Blues" on the Revised-SCCJ and *The Incredible Jazz Guitar of Wes Montgomery*, Fantasy/OJC-036 (R320) CD/LP, 1960. For transcription and analysis of Montgomery's solo on "Four On Six," see Fred Sokolow's *Solos for Jazz Guitar* (Carl Fischer, 1988). Order from Carl Fischer Music Store, 54 Cooper Square, NY, NY 10003.

[35]*Kenny Burrell & John Coltrane*, Fantasy/OJC-300 (NJ 8276), LP, 1957

[36]Jimmy Smith, *Midnight Special*, Blue Note 46399 (84078), CD/LP, 1960

[37]Notice the buoyant, hard-driving accompaniment Sam Jones provides, and listen to his pizzicato solo on "Trouble On My Mind" in the album *Cannonball Adderley in Europe*, Landmark 1307 (Riverside 499), CD/LP, 1962.

jazz bass playing by demonstrating a mastery over his instrument and a compositional approach to improvisation that was not ordinarily associated with the bass.[38]

**Big Bands**   During the late 1950s and through the 1960s, several big bands drew from the sound of hard bop. The three most prominent were led by trumpeters **Maynard Ferguson** (b. 1928), **Gerald Wilson** (b. 1918), and **Thad Jones** (1923–1986). The Jones band was co-led by drummer Mel Lewis, who took over sole leadership when Jones left in 1979. The Ferguson and Wilson bands began during the late 1950s. The Jones-Lewis band was formed in 1965. The groups led by Jones and Wilson were initially founded for the musical enjoyment of free-lance jazz musicians living in New York and Los Angeles, respectively. They began as rehearsal bands (also known as "kicks bands") and rarely performed away from home with their personnel intact. Most of the Jones-Lewis performances took place on Monday nights at a New York nightclub called the Village Vanguard. Of the three bands, only Ferguson's toured widely, sold many records, or became known much outside of relatively small markets.

Many great musicians played with these bands over the years. Ferguson's generally had the youngest and least-known musicians, whereas the earliest Jones-Lewis and Wilson groups were all-star bands. Wilson employed some of the best bop-style musicians to be found outside of New York, several of whom had become known to jazz fans long before they recorded with him. Among the musicians in the Jones-Lewis band, many already had made outstanding jazz records as bandleaders themselves, and, like Jones, a few were pivotal figures from the fertile hard bop scene in Detroit (see Table 11.3)[39] Some of those same men were highly individualistic improvisers who, like Jones himself, had already made significant contributions to the explorative bands of Charles Mingus (see chapter 14).[40]

**Thad Jones** is often ranked as one of the best and most original trumpeters in hard bop. His improvisations were unorthodox and daring.[41] They often contained odd intervals that were not natural to the trumpet and were as difficult as they were unique. Jones was a storehouse of imagination, and Charles Mingus, among others, ranked Jones as a musical genius. He changed his instruments, too; he was one of very few modern trumpeters to frequently perform on cornet, and he also played fluegelhorn extensively (see chapter 7 for illustrations).

The styles of most soloists in the earliest Jones-Lewis band can best be categorized as bop or hard bop. Much of the band's music, however, had a feeling that was lighter than the weighty, solemn intensity that is projected by most hard bop. This was partly due to the style of Jones's compositions, which were often light, playful, and full of surprises. They were filled with silences which served as ventilation.

---

[38]Listen to Chambers introduce the melody line to "So What" with the Miles Davis band in SCCJ. Listen to his solos on John Coltrane's albums *Soultrane*, Fantasy/OJC-021 (P7142), CD/LP, 1958; and *Tranin' In*, Fantasy/OJC-189 (P-7123), CD/LP, 1957.

[39]*Detroit-New York Junction*, Blue Note 1513, LP, 1956; *Presenting Thad Jones-Mel Lewis and the Jazz Orchestra*, Solid State SS18003 (SM17003), 1966.

[40]*Charlie Mingus*, Everest FS 235, LP, 1954

[41]Listen to the Thad Jones solos on Count Basie's album, *Chairman of the Board*, Roulette 52032, 1959.

They stressed soft, staccato phrases produced by sound qualities that were well contained. They also possessed an alternation of funky unison lines with thickly voiced chordal passages. There is a pixie lightness and humor to Jones's melodic rhythms, and he often maintained a suspended feeling by using unconventional accompaniment patterns. He used frequently shifting densities, and occasionally deleted the rhythm section suddenly in the middle of a piece. Although the lines Jones wrote were often very difficult to play, his musicians executed them with finesse. The harmonies he constructed were rarely ordinary; they were rich without sounding muddy or affected. Jones occasionally wrote chords containing eight of the twelve notes in the chromatic scale (as in "Three In One"), a technique that is unusual among big band arrangers. (Sammy Nestico's writing for Count Basie, for example, is typically in four-note chords.) These practices contrast with the ordinary big band arrangers's penchant for massiveness and unceasing sound. Even when his melodies sound almost homespun ("Don't Get Sassy" and "Big Dipper"), they are placed in very thick chord voicings.[42] His melodies show a strong allegiance to the funky, blues tradition ("Big Dipper"), somewhat reminiscent of Horace Silver, though placed in a more elaborate setting. Jones's writing earned him great respect among jazz arrangers, and his pieces found their way into textbooks for jazz composers. He invented such a distinctive arranging style that listeners can often identify it by hearing only a single chord. The Jones arranging style was one of the most original to appear since Duke Ellington's.

The differences between the Jones-Lewis sound and that of other big bands in hard bop were also due partly to approaches employed by the band's bassist, **Richard Davis,** and its drummer, Mel Lewis. Davis contributed concepts to a big band setting that roughly paralleled what Charles Mingus and Scott LaFaro had given to combo settings: In addition to playing walking bass lines, Davis improvised accompaniments containing a great variety of fresh melodic and rhythmic figures that vigorously interacted with the solo and ensemble lines. (This approach was not new for Davis, who was already much admired for his innovative playing in avant-garde combos of the 1960s.) Compatible with the loosening and lightening done by Davis was the light, discreet drumming of **Mel Lewis** (1929–1990), whose style avoided the heavy, aggressive approaches of hard bop. A uniquely flexible accompanist, Lewis is well known for his unerring swing, versatility, and good taste.

Jazz big bands have traditionally been rooted in styles of eras earlier than the one at hand. In addition, solos have been routinely brief and frequently interrupted by screaming ensemble figures. The Jones band stood apart from these traditions. It offered plenty of uncluttered solo space to its improvisers, as well as achieving a flexible interaction between the rhythm section and improvising soloists. During many moments in its performances, the band sounded like an up-to-date modern jazz combo. In this way it recalled Count Basie's big band of the 1930s which often operated as an oversized combo.

**Gerald Wilson** was a respected composer-arranger long before he became identified with his hard bop big band. The Jimmie Lunceford and Duke Ellington bands were among the outstanding groups which had performed his work. In his band of

[42]*Central Park North*, Solid State SS18058, 1969; *Presenting...*, Solid State SS 18003, 1966.

the late 1950s and early 1960s, however, Wilson molded a unique new sound from several sources. He used outstanding hard bop soloists who played with the ferocity and bluesy mood which jazz fans had come to expect from the combos of Art Blakey, Horace Silver, and Cannonball Adderley. He used an original arranging style. It was spare, not intricate. It did not jump around, nor was it light and playful. It was hard and relentless. Each piece created and sustained a consistent mood. Thirdly, he emphasized depth of feeling, and, more often than not, that feeling was dark and serious. By comparison with all other big bands, the Wilson band achieved a groove that more closely resembled hard bop. The moods were funky and earthy, as though Wilson had created a big-band equivalent to the organ/tenor sax combos that were common at inner-city taverns during the 1950s and 60s.[43]

Another unique characteristic of Wilson's sound was a modal flavor. Brief, wailing phrases in a minor key were repeated again and again, over a propelling rhythm. The chords changed slowly, allowing soloists to build their ideas and raise tension over a longer time than bop progressions allowed. Several of the pieces in this genre were compositions Wilson adapted after they had been introduced by Miles Davis ("Milestones," "So What," "Freddie the Freeloader"). Others were Wilson originals ("Moment of Truth," "Viva Tirado") that had the raw ferocity of hard bop as well as a certain exoticism.[44]

Before the hard bop era, **Maynard Ferguson** had already achieved a reputation as trumpeter with big bands led by Charlie Barnet, Boyd Raeburn, and Stan Kenton. His lead trumpet work with Kenton from 1950 to 1952 did much to set the character of the Kenton sound as well as to establish Ferguson's own fame. During the late 1950s, he began a series of his own big bands which prominently featured his high-register trumpet playing. Though these bands continued Kenton's emphasis on loud, flashy brass, they conveyed a different feeling: they swung. In addition, they sounded funkier. (Listen to "Frame for the Blues" in the JAZZ CLASSICS CASSETTE.) The bands had a precise, fast-moving style. Unlike Kenton, Ferguson was not especially experimental. His band belted out driving ensemble passages, in a no nonsense manner, with Ferguson often soaring overhead. Their sound was filled with raw excitement. The band seemed to thrive on fast tempos and loud playing (listen to "Three Foxes," "L-Dopa," "Got The Spirit"). The repertory contained few slow or subdued arrangements.

The Ferguson band's instrumentation also differed from that of other big bands. (See chapter 6 for discussion of big band instrumentation traditions.) Unlike the Ellington, Basie, Wilson, and Jones bands of the same period, Ferguson's were more compact. Rather than the ordinary complement of three to five trombones, Ferguson carried only two. Instead of a sax section with two altos, two tenors, and a baritone, his had one alto, two tenors, and a baritone. Instead of the dark, full-bodied tone qualities associated with Wilson's and Ellington's saxes, Ferguson's had a bright, biting sound that was almost brassy. As the years passed, Ferguson continued to reduce the size of his band, until in the late 1960s, and again in the mid-1980s, he was all the way down to a small combo.

[43]*You Better Believe It*, Pacific Jazz 10097 (PJ34), 1961
[44]*Moment of Truth*, Pacific Jazz 10098 (PJ61), 1962

### Listening Guide for "Frame for the Blues"

Composed and arranged by hard bop trombonist Slide Hampton; recorded May 6, 7 and 8, 1958 in New York City by the Maynard Ferguson big band (four trumpets, two trombones, alto sax, two tenor saxes, baritone sax, piano, bass, and drums); available on the JAZZ CLASSICS CASSETTE, Side One; originally on *Message From Newport* (Roulette 52050), reissued on CD as CDP 7 93272–2.

After the introduction, the piece follows the 12-bar blues form in a very slow tempo. "Frame for the Blues" resembles the simplicity and comfortable feeling of Count Basie's band style and the loud, sleek brass of Stan Kenton's band style. It also has earthier aspects associated with hard bop. Funky, bluesy phrases are abundant in the composition and improvisations. This piece became one of the most requested feature numbers for the Ferguson band of the 1960s. It was so well loved that more than one jazz disc jockey made it his program's theme song.

Terms and sounds to know before using this guide: trumpet, trombone, tenor saxophone, ride rhythm, ride cymbal, snare drum, wire brushes, walking bass, 12-bar blues, fall-off, triplet. All these are explained and demonstrated on the JAZZ STYLES CASSETTE. Learn to keep your place by counting beats in the 12-bar blues by studying the Elements of Music appendix. The appendix also explains what is meant by the term "triplets."

*Elapsed Time*

## INTRODUCTION

The band offers a bluesy call and then sustains the last note of their phrase. Trumpeter Ferguson answers with a bluesy figure played in the extreme high register. He ornaments his sustained tone with a fast shake and then comes down and resolves his line with bluesy, legato figures.

0' 12"   Walking bass begins at the same time as the drummer starts using wire brushes to play timekeeping rhythms on snare drum. Trombones respond with a wailing phrase in their high-register, played with the notes slurred together. Trumpets conclude the introduction with a string of triplets, that is, three notes on each beat.

0' 20"

## FIRST CHORUS

The melody is stated by the entire band in harmony. Accompaniment is provided quietly and discreetly from bass in two-beat style, piano tinkling, and drummer using wire brushes to play timekeeping rhythms on snare drum, while snapping his high-hat closed sharply on the second and fourth beats of each measure.

0' 52"   *Ninth Measure*

Trombones play a legato line in harmony.

0' 54"   *Tenth Measure*

Trombones are joined by the trumpets, descending in a bluesy string of legato triplets.

0' 59"   *Eleventh and Twelfth Measures*

The drummer uses a drum stick on the ride cymbal to play triplets ("123 123 123 123 123 123 123 123"). Pianist plays chords in the same triplet rhythm. This builds excitement in anticipation of the upcoming sax solo. While the baritone saxophone plays a figure that emphasizes the downbeat, the other saxophones play a harmonized figure emphasizing the upbeats.

1' 06"

### SECOND CHORUS

*Tenor Saxophone Improvisation by Carmen Leggio*

Walking bass begins.

After starting his solo, the saxophonist is interrupted by a screaming brass statement consisting of a shake by the trumpet section, a pause, then another shake and a fall-off.

1' 19"

Saxophone solo re-emerges from being swallowed by the brass sounds. It is now accompanied by piano comping, walking bass, and a ride rhythm played on ride cymbal with a drum stick. Sax solo uses many of the bluesy melodic figures that are usually termed "funky." Notice how the saxophonist seems to tell a story with his solo, each note fitting a tuneful structure.

1' 46"

*Eleventh and Twelfth Measures*

While the saxophonist is finishing his improvisation, loud, high-register triplets are played in unison by trumpets, occasionally undergirded by trombone chords on the upbeats and almost inaudible, low-pitched sax tones.

1' 55"

### THIRD CHORUS

*First Eight Measures*

A cymbal crash begins this chorus. Then trumpets and trombones play a harmonized melodic fragment answered by increasingly louder drums and cymbals. Notice how drums underscore the brass rhythms, filling in the pauses and accenting phrase endings.

2' 03"

Trumpets repeat the figure.

2' 06"

While the brass take a breath, they are answered by Ferguson playing a scale-like figure far higher than theirs, then topping off a new chord and ornamenting the end of this phrase with a fall-off.

2' 17"

High-register brass figures go higher and higher with Ferguson.

2' 21"

The rising brass line concludes with Ferguson playing a stratospherically high note to top off the phrase. He ends his note with a brief fall-off.

2' 23"

Fade-out at the ninth measure

During the 1970s and 80s, Ferguson's bands used electric instruments and funk-style accompaniments in the bulk of their performances. Considerable radio airplay was given to some of their pop tune arrangements, particularly their 1970 recording of "MacArthur Park"[45] and their 1972 recording of "Hey, Jude" (a tune by the Beatles, a British singing group). This was a bit of good fortune that little jazz had enjoyed since the 1940s. Ferguson's greatest popularity came with a 1976 recording of the theme song for the immensely popular movie "Rocky." The album it appeared on, *Conquistador*, achieved gold-record status.[46] Following these best-selling pieces, Ferguson mined the same vein by continuing to record television and movie themes, with large amounts of orchestration and small amounts of improvisation.

[45]*M. F. Horn*, CBS 30466, 1970
[46]*Conquistador*, Columbia 34457, 1976

The band also capitalized on the popularity of jazz-rock fusion by recording Herbie Hancock's hit "Chameleon" in 1974 and Joe Zawinul's hit "Birdland" in 1978 (see chapter 16 for more about this style and these particular pieces).

Maynard Ferguson is not ordinarily considered an important hard bop trumpeter. His exceptional command of brass instruments, however, has inspired many musicians of the 1960s, 70s and 80s, partly because his music received such wide exposure and partly because he has an almost freakish mastery of the trumpet that extends throughout its entire range. No register is the least bit awkward for him. His facility takes him to B above double-high C. Significantly, on most nights he does not simply squeal those altissimo-register notes but actually plays them with good intonation and large tone.[47] Most big band high-note artists play few improvised solos, restricting their playing to trumpet-section lead work in order to keep their lips set specifically for those high parts. Ferguson amazes brass players not only by playing high-register lead parts, but also by improvising solos on nearly every tune. In addition to that, his endurance is as phenomenal as his range, and he can switch to trombone or French horn right in the middle of a piece, making an immediate adjustment to it. In fact, he is a master not only of the trumpet but of all the brass instruments, and he plays most of the reed instruments, too.

**Popular Appeal**    Like bop musicians, hard bop musicians found their music to be relatively neglected by the public. Only a few managed to extract steady livelihoods from performing jazz. The historically significant bands of Clifford Brown, Art Blakey, and J. J. Johnson were unknown except to musicians and a small population of fans. During the 1950s, Sonny Rollins and John Coltrane were well known by jazz fans but almost unknown otherwise. The few jazz pieces that found their way onto juke boxes were mostly simple, funky compositions arranged with lots of very repetitive accompaniment rhythms and less improvisation than was found on most hard bop records. Some of these accounted for brief periods of success enjoyed by Cannonball Adderley and Horace Silver, especially during the 1960s and 70s. But the highest record sales went to the organ-guitar-drums and piano-bass-drums groups of Jimmy Smith and Ramsey Lewis, respectively. These are players who musicians and critics do not ordinarily consider to be within the mainstream of jazz developments, though their music helps define funky jazz, and they fit the hard bop designation more closely than they fit any other.

## CHAPTER SUMMARY

1) Hard bop evolved directly from bop during the 1950s, mainly from East Coast and Midwest musicians.

2) When hard bop differs from bop, it is simpler, has more variety in accompaniment patterns, fewer pop tune chord progressions, darker, weightier tone qualities, and more emphasis on hard, unrelenting swinging.

[47]*Message From Newport*, Roulette RE-116 (52012), 1958; *Maynard '62*, Roulette 52083, 1962

3) Funky jazz is a subcategory of hard bop, and it is characterized by bluesy inflections of pitch and gospelish harmonies. Several pieces performed by the bands of Horace Silver and Cannonball Adderley were popular because of their funky qualities and simple, catchy melodies.

4) The most prominent figures in hard bop were pianist-composer Horace Silver, drummer-bandleader Art Blakey, and alto saxophonist-bandleader Cannonball Adderley.

5) The top tenor saxophonists in hard bop were Sonny Rollins, John Coltrane, Wayne Shorter, and Joe Henderson.

6) The top trumpeters in hard bop were Clifford Brown and Freddie Hubbard.

7) Drummers in hard bop were louder and more intrusive than their predecessors. Art Blakey and Philly Joe Jones further emancipated the drummer from the role of mere timekeeper.

8) Hard bop big bands were led by trumpeters Maynard Ferguson, Gerald Wilson, and Thad Jones.

Clifford Brown playing trumpet while Sonny Rollins (tenor sax) looks on, shown here with the Max Roach quintet in 1956. (*Photo by Chuck Stewart*)

# chapter 12
# MILES DAVIS, HIS GROUPS & SIDEMEN

Miles Davis (b. 1926) is a jazz trumpeter and bandleader who has played a pivotal role in the history of modern jazz because he has been deeply involved in recording and promoting several styles well before they became widespread trends. Over a fifty-year period of productivity, Davis has contributed a stylistically diverse body of music, parts of which defined jazz for three different generations of listeners. His recordings have won the near universal admiration of fellow jazz musicians. A significant slice of modern jazz history is documented in Davis-led recording sessions because he gathered the key innovators of the day for his bands. Unlike most artists, Davis never became limited to one particular band style. Among his most important contributions are

**Contributions**

1) Creating an original and substantial trumpet style. This was first evident in recordings he made under Charlie Parker's leadership in the mid-1940s, and it influenced numerous trumpeters of the cool jazz and hard bop idioms (see Table 12.4).

2) Producing a large body of recordings which almost invariably contain distinctive, high-quality performances. His recordings served as textbooks for modern musicians in the way that recordings of Louis Armstrong and Lester Young had served their premodern counterparts.

3) Making a significant change during the 1960s in his original trumpet style. In the 1980s, this variation became the basis for trumpet styles of Wynton Marsalis, Terence Blanchard, and others.

4) Pioneering the "cool jazz" sound by consolidating Claude Thornhill and Gil Evans's orchestration style with the playing styles of Gerry Mulligan, Lee Konitz, and himself on the landmark "Birth of the Cool" recordings of 1949 and 50 (see chapter 10, and listen to "Boplicity" in SCCJ).

**219**

**TABLE 12.1. A Few of the Many Well-Known Saxophonists Who Worked With Miles Davis**

| | | |
|---|---|---|
| Lee Konitz | Bennie Maupin | Wayne Shorter |
| Sonny Rollins | John Coltrane | David Liebman |
| Jackie McLean | Hank Mobley | Steve Grossman |
| Gerry Mulligan | Joe Henderson | Gary Bartz |
| Sonny Stitt | Sam Rivers | Cannonball Adderley |
| Jimmy Heath | George Coleman | Sonny Fortune |

5) Pioneering "modal jazz" on the *Kind of Blue* album in 1959 (listen to "Flamenco Sketches" in the JAZZ CLASSICS CASSETTE).

6) Pioneering the predominant group approaches and individual instrumental styles of the 1980s with his quintet of 1965–68 (listen to "Masqualero" in the JAZZ CLASSICS CASSETTE).

7) Pioneering jazz-rock fusion styles with an amalgamation of elements from "modal jazz," rock, and funk music on his *In a Silent Way* and *Bitches Brew* albums of 1969 (see chapter 16).

Though he did not invent entire jazz idioms himself, Miles Davis organized bands of key innovators at early moments in the development of bop, cool jazz, modal jazz, and jazz-rock fusion (see Tables 12.1, 12.2, and 12.3). Moreover, he invented an original and distinctive trumpet style that fit the sound of each of his bands. Like Duke Ellington's musicians, Davis's often produced the best work of their career while in his bands. (His sidemen speak highly about his help in their own stylistic development and his judicious editing of their music.) There is a feeling of intelligent, well-measured musical creation that pervades most Davis recordings.

**Trumpet Style**   Miles Davis created an unmistakable sound. It is so easily identifiable that we can instantly recognize it even in the crowded mix of a rock record or the background music for a movie. Davis is a uniquely creative thinker who has departed drastically from the traditions of jazz trumpet to give us a sound which seems almost independent of the instrument. It is so personal that to call it "Miles Davis" seems more accurate than to call it "jazz trumpet."

The uniqueness of the Davis style can be divided into at least eight components. The first two are manners of handling the trumpet sound.[1] The most obvious is his

[1]Though original in most respects, Davis did model his sound after Freddie Webster's. To hear this, compare Webster's tone quality, articulation, and overall manner in Sarah Vaughan's recording "You're Not the Kind" on *The Divine Sarah*, Musicraft 504, LP, 1946; with the Davis solo on Charlie Parker's "Now's the Time" from *Bird—Savoy Original Master Takes*, Savoy ZDS 8801, CD set (2201, LP set), 1945. Davis has cited Webster, Clark Terry, Dizzy Gillespie, and others as inspiration for his own style. For transcription and analysis of the Davis solo on "So What" from *Kind of Blue*, also in SCCJ, see *Creative Jazz Improvisation*, by Scott Reeves (Prentice-Hall, 1989; available from Jamey Aebersold, 1211 Aebersold Drive, New Albany, IN 47150). Other Davis solos are transcribed in Stuart Isacoff's *Miles Davis* (Amsco, 1979; available from Aebersold).

**TABLE 12.2. A Few of the Many Well-Known Guitarists Who Worked With Miles Davis**

| | |
|---|---|
| George Benson | John Scofield |
| John McLaughlin | Barry Finnerty |
| Larry Coryell | Mike Stern |

application of alterations in pitch and tone quality to the beginnings and endings of notes (for graphs of such pitch bending ornaments, see page 47; to hear Davis perform them, listen to "Fishermen, Strawberry, and Devil Crab" on the JAZZ CLASSICS CASSETTE, beginning of side one).[2]

A second component of Davis's highly personal style is his frequent use of a Harmon mute without its stem (portrayed on pages 390–391, and heard on "Flamenco Sketches" in the JAZZ CLASSICS CASSETTE). His Harmon-muted solos were amplified by placing the mute directly on the stage microphone (at least until the 1970s, when he attached wireless microphones directly to his horn). This technique resulted in a wispy sound that was delicate and conveyed an intimate mood. By comparison with other modern trumpeters, far more of his output was muted. On many of his albums, more than half of his playing is done through the Harmon mute.[3]

A third component of the Davis style is an unusually skillful timing and dramatic construction of melodic figures. Davis is a master of self-restraint. His placement of silence is at least as significant as his choice of notes, and he often lets several beats pass without playing. During the moments he is not sounding his own notes, the sound of bass, drums, and piano comes through clearly, further enhancing the mood. The effectiveness of this very lean approach also depends on the steadiness of swing feeling and overall musicality of the accompanists. It is significant to recognize that because Davis always hired the best accompanists, the silences in his own solos were filled in a highly musical, well-paced manner.[4] More than most improvisers, Davis conveys the impression that he is editing his solos very carefully while performing them, clarifying his ideas before articulating them. In the same way that Lester Young approached improvisation with the tenor saxophone, Davis pares his thinking down to a bare core of melodic material; and like Young's solos, the best Davis improvisations seem to "tell a story."[5]

[2]All album citations in this chapter that do not have record label and catalog number footnoted are Columbia recordings listed together at the end of the chapter.

[3]Listen to the slowest pieces on *Seven Steps to Heaven*, *Kind of Blue*, or "Summertime" in SCCJ.

[4]An excellent example of this is the "Freddie the Freeloader" solo on *Kind of Blue*.

[5]For examples, listen to his solos on Charlie Parker's recording "Now's The Time" (cited in footnote 1); his own recordings of "The Man I Love" on *Miles Davis & the Modern Jazz Giants*, OJC-347 (Prestige 7150), 1954; "Bags' Groove" on *Bag's Groove*, OJC-245 (Prestige 7109), CD/LP, 1954; "Eighty-One" on *E.S.P.*, 1965; "Sivad" in *Live-Evil*, 1971; or "So What" in SCCJ.

**TABLE 12.3. The Evolution of Modern Jazz Rhythm Section Styles Documented by Miles Davis Recordings**

| | |
|---|---|
| 1950: | Pianist John Lewis, bassist Al McKibbon, drummer Max Roach on *Birth of the Cool.* |
| 1951: | Pianist Walter Bishop, Jr., bassist Tommy Potter, drummer Art Blakey on "Conception"; "Denial"; "Paper Moon." |
| 1956: | Pianist Tommy Flanagan, bassist Paul Chambers, drummer Art Taylor on "No Line"; "Vierd Blues"; "In Your Own Sweet Way." |
| 1955–58: | Pianist Red Garland, bassist Paul Chambers, drummer Philly Joe Jones on *The New Miles Davis Quintet; Steamin'; Cookin'; Workin'; Relaxin'; 'Round About Midnight; Milestones.* |
| 1959–63: | Pianist Wynton Kelly, bassist Paul Chambers, drummer Jimmy Cobb on *Someday My Prince Will Come; In Person at the Blackhawk; Miles Davis at Carnegie Hall.* |
| 1963–68: | Pianist Herbie Hancock, bassist Ron Carter, drummer Tony Williams on many albums, including *My Funny Valentine; Sorcerer; Miles in the Sky; Nefertiti.* |
| 1971: | Pianist Keith Jarrett, bassist Mike Henderson, drummer Jack De-Johnette, percussionist Airto Moreira on "Sivad" from *Live-Evil.* |
| 1969–72: | Groups whose rhythm sections sometimes included two or three keyboards (Miles drew from a pool of pianists which included Joe Zawinul, Chick Corea, Keith Jarrett, Herbie Hancock, Larry Young, Harold Williams, Hermeto Pascoal, Lonnie Liston Smith, and Cedric Lawson). |
| 1970s: | Groups whose rhythm sections sometimes included two or three guitars (Miles drew from a pool of guitarists which included Reggie Lucas, Pete Cosey, David Creamer, Dominique Gaumont, Cornell Dupree). |
| 1970s: | Groups including sitar and tabla. Use of instruments native to India, such as the sitar (a stringed instrument) and tabla (drums), was as unusual in jazz rhythm sections as using two and three keyboards at once. |

A fourth component of the Davis style can be identified by comparing rhythmic conceptions. Most modern trumpeters play swinging lines; but few seem capable of generating lines that are free from a sense of strict tempo and swing feeling, even when they play slow tunes. In the playing of Davis's contemporaries, there is always a very precise subdivision of each beat that rules the passage of notes. Miles Davis distinguished himself not only by his skill in improvising swinging melodic figures,[6]

[6]Listen to "Freddie the Freeloader" on *Kind of Blue*, "Sid's Ahead" on *Milestones*, or "Devil May Care" on *Basic Miles*.

**TABLE 12.4. A Few of the Many Trumpeters Influenced by Miles Davis**

| | | |
|---|---|---|
| Clifford Brown | Stu Williamson | John McNeil |
| Chet Baker | Ted Curson | Terumasa Hino |
| Shorty Rogers | Luis Gasca | Kenny Wheeler |
| Jack Sheldon | Blue Mitchell | Wynton Marsalis |
| Nat Adderley | Lester Bowie | Terence Blanchard |
| Charles Moore | Tom Harrell | Herb Pomeroy |
| Johnny Coles | Randy Brecker | Tim Hagans |
| Eddie Henderson | Mark Isham | Wallace Roney |
| Jim Powell | | |

but also by improvising figures that imply freedom from strict tempo and swing feeling.[7]

A fifth component is an acute sensitivity in paraphrasing melodies. The Davis paraphrases of popular songs are constructed in such fresh and enticing ways that the finished products are almost new melodies.[8]

A sixth component is that Davis is not afraid to play simply. Certainly he does often play bop-style lines that are not simple. But often he constructs solos of very brief, simple phrases. Many of his improvisations on slow pieces and on blues forms are comprised of no more than a few carefully chosen notes that are timed so well and played so expressively that the result is quite dramatic. Sometimes the entire solo is forged from such devices, as in "Solea" on *Sketches of Spain*, "Freddie the Freeloader" on *Kind of Blue*, and "Bitches Brew" on *Bitches Brew*.

A seventh component is the cluster of traits possessed by his tone quality and preference for pitch range. During the 1940s and 50s, Davis played with a tone quality that was lighter, softer, and less brassy than that of most other trumpeters. He used almost no vibrato, favored the trumpet's middle register over its flashier high register, and rarely double-timed. By comparison with the styles of most other modern trumpeters, his was gentle. That trend was reversed, however, on some pieces he recorded during the 1960s, in which he began to reach into the high register more often. This reversal is especially evident in his albums *Miles in Europe* and *"Four" and More*. During the 1970s he developed an even more explosive side to his style, capitalizing on the trumpet's high register, and occasionally including long bursts of notes and splattered tones. He also incorporated electronic echo and "wah-wah" effects into his trumpet tone.[9] Although his later solo work seemed more

[7]As on the final selection of *Kind of Blue*, "Fishermen, Strawberry, and Devil Crab" on *Porgy and Bess*, or the first few measures of "My Funny Valentine" and "Stella By Starlight" on *My Funny Valentine*. For transcription and analysis of the 1964 "My Funny Valentine" solo, see Stuart Isacoff's *Solos for Jazz Trumpet* (Carl Fischer, 1985; available by mail from Carl Fischer Music Store, 54 Cooper Square, NY, NY 10003).

[8]As in his 1956 recording of "It Never Entered My Mind" on *Workin'*, OJC-296 (Prestige 7166); his 1963 recording of "I Fall In Love Too Easily" on *Seven Steps to Heaven*, or "My Funny Valentine" and "Stella By Starlight" on his 1964 album *My Funny Valentine*.

[9]As in *Bitches Brew*, *Live-Evil*, and side one of *Tribute to Jack Johnson*.

outgoing, he never entirely discarded his earlier manners, and his work in the 1980s occasionally displayed all these facets.

An eighth essential component is present in both his trumpet style and the concepts of sound that guided the playing of his bands. Throughout his career, Davis has shown an overriding concern with sound texture. Certainly he has also been interested in melodic and rhythmic aspects of his music. But above all, there has been a recurring creation of a glass-like smoothness of texture, extending from the bottom to the top of the band's sound. This was evident as early as his "Now's the Time" solo of 1945 with Charlie Parker. It characterized his attraction to the Claude Thornhill band sound, which drew heavily upon the concepts of French Impressionist composer Claude Debussy, and emerged in Davis's downsized version of the Thornhill band for his *Birth of the Cool* recordings of 1949 and 50. (Compare Thornhill's "Snowfall" with the Davis nonet's "Moon Dreams.") It was evident in his *Kind of Blue* and *Bitches Brew*, albums in which his own solos were filled with sustained tones that topped off the voicings of distinctly uncluttered accompaniment chords. Consistent with his concern for sound texture, Davis is known for suggesting chord voicings to his pianists and for choosing long notes in his solos that cap the voicings in his accompaniment so well that it sounds like part of an arrangement that presets the sound quality from bottom to top. His concern with texture also dovetails into his attraction to simplicity in the construction of solos. An everchanging line would not provide sufficient sustained tones to mesh with accompaniment chords long enough for listeners to savor as a texture. The Davis concern with texture is also manifested in his retaining arranger Gil Evans as adviser even when he was not directly involved in large-scale recording projects. Apparently Davis felt that it was important to have available the Evans sense of sound quality and balance, even in the work of his small combos. During the jazz-rock fusion period, Davis sometimes used two and three pianists or two and three guitarists playing at the same time, and he hired extra percussionists. Often he told them how actively to play, when to play and when not to play. This reflected the same concern for sound texture that he had shown earlier in other ways.

**The Classic Miles Davis Quintet**

Miles Davis made many of his historically significant recordings as a bandleader for the Prestige record company. Among musicians, the most discussed of these are *Steamin'*, *Cookin'*, *Workin'*, and *Relaxin'*, all recorded in 1956 with tenor saxophonist John Coltrane, pianist Red Garland, bassist Paul Chambers, and drummer "Philly Joe" Jones (for more about Chambers and Jones, see chapter 11).[10] The style and energy of those recording sessions were particularly evident again in *Milestones*, an album he made for Columbia record company in 1958, with the same musicians plus alto saxophonist Cannonball Adderley (discussed more in chapter 11). Though Miles Davis had long been linked with cool jazz, the band on these recordings sounds more like hard bop and later styles. The musicians played with blistering intensity. Their work had an unusual freshness and excitement that combined to

---

[10]*Cookin'*, OJC-128 (Prestige 7094), CD/LP; *Relaxin'*, OJC-190 (Prestige 7129), CD/LP; *Workin'*, OJC-296 (Prestige 7166), CD/LP; *Steamin'*, OJC 391 (Prestige 7200), CD/LP, all 1956.

Cannonball Adderley (alto sax), Paul Chambers (bass), Miles Davis (trumpet), and John Coltrane (tenor saxophone). Each man was a modern jazz giant on his respective instrument, and all were present on the historic *Milestones* and *Kind of Blue* recording sessions. Pictured here at the 1958 Newport Jazz Festival. (*Photo supplied by Frank Driggs*) Listen to "Flamenco Sketches" on the JAZZ CLASSICS CASSETTE to hear the band pictured here.

make these among the most striking performances since the groundbreaking Parker-Gillespie records of ten years earlier. In fact, many musicians and journalists consider these particular Davis albums to be as outstanding as the classic recordings by Louis Armstrong's Hot Five and Hot Seven of the 1920s, the Kansas City Six and Seven (Count Basie-Lester Young) of the 1930s, and the Parker-Gillespie combo of the 1940s.

These recordings marked the first exposure of many jazz fans to tenor saxophonist John Coltrane. Though some journalists considered this particular snapshot of his career merely a development stage, his playing with Davis was so substantial and original that he would still qualify as a jazz giant if he had never moved away from this style and developed his other approaches. (For details, see chapter 13.)

The classic quintet, with the addition of Cannonball Adderley, was responsible for a landmark event in jazz history. With their recording of the "Milestones" selection in 1958, they broke away from the tradition of guiding improvisations solely by chord progressions. Most of the tunes Davis had recorded before 1958 were pop tunes or bop compositions with frequently changing chords in their accompaniment. But instead of using frequently changing chords for their improvisations on

"Milestones," the musicians used two modes (see pages 368–371, and 384–386 for explanations of modes and page 423 for musical notation of the modes used on "Milestones"). The first mode was in effect for sixteen measures, the second mode for another sixteen measures, followed by a return to the first for the final eight measures. The improvisers using this modal format had fewer demands placed on their attention. This represented quite a contrast with the demands placed by frequently changing chords. The players correspondingly had more attention available to devote to piecing together interesting melodies and rhythms. After the *Milestones* album (containing "Milestones") was released, the approach used on "Milestones"—the absence of changing chords—became popular among modern jazz musicians. The momentum of this trend increased upon wide acceptance of mode-based music in the Davis album *Kind of Blue*, recorded in 1959 (discussed later in this chapter and excerpted in "Flamenco Sketches" in the JAZZ CLASSICS CASSETTE). "Milestones" soon took its place in the repertory of standard jam session tunes, next to "Cherokee," "All the Things You Are," "A Night in Tunisia," and numerous pieces based on the twelve-bar blues.

**Collaborations with Gil Evans**

In 1957, Davis renewed his association with arranger **Gil Evans** (1912–1988). Together they had organized the *Birth of the Cool* sessions a decade earlier. This time they put together new works in which Davis was the only soloist with a large band. Evans conducted his own arrangements for groups of brass, woodwinds, string bass, drums, and occasionally harp. The brass section included French horn and tuba in addition to trumpets and trombones. The woodwind section included flutes and clarinets in addition to saxophones; bassoon was added for the *Sketches of Spain* album. The arrangments reflected Evans's prolific imagination and high level of workmanship. With soulful and stirring playing by Davis, these efforts were captured on *Miles Ahead, Porgy and Bess*, and *Sketches of Spain*, three albums which have been surpassed in jazz history only by the best Duke Ellington masterpieces.

*Miles Ahead* was recorded in 1957, with Davis playing fluegelhorn, a previously uncommon instrument to find in jazz (see photo in chapter 7). Although Clark Terry and Shorty Rogers had played it prior to 1957, the Davis recordings provided considerable impetus for its ensuing popularity. By the 1970s, many jazz trumpeters were doubling on fluegelhorn, and arrangers who worked for popular singers and put together nightclub acts were frequently including fluegelhorn parts in their orchestrations.

The program of *Miles Ahead* includes popular tunes and jazz tunes. The pieces are connected by brief interludes which Evans composed specially to bridge the gaps between selections. The contents range from pieces reminiscent of the subtle, unforced swinging of the *Birth of the Cool* recordings, to lush pastels in slow tempo, to moments of brassy excitement. Compared to other big band writing of the 1950s and 60s, its character was more reflective. Here Evans mastered the effective use of shading and contrast of both rhythmic and timbral dimensions. Like Duke Ellington, he freed himself of the formula writing which pitted brasses against saxes. He freely voiced across sections and assigned different parts of a melody to different instruments. Like Ellington, Evans managed to weave improvisations into the framework of a piece without sounding contrived or awkward. The sound of Davis fades into and out of the ensemble gracefully. There are brief passages in which

Davis interpreted pop-tune themes, or in which he improvised on the chord progressions in the arrangements. In either case, the orchestration was perfectly conceived to match the mood and color of the Davis style.

In 1958, Davis recorded George Gershwin's opera *Porgy and Bess*. Gil Evans devised arrangements of sweeping colors and breathtaking drama. Davis reworked the familiar melodies so they acquired a new flavor. (Listen to "Fishermen, Strawberry, and Devil Crab," excerpted on the JAZZ CLASSICS CASSETTE, side 1.)

*Sketches of Spain* was recorded in November 1959 and March 1960. It is nearly a classical album because the music was almost exclusively prewritten, except for "Solea," in which Davis develops a long modal improvisation. Because of Davis's playing, however, this album is not truly classical, but more Third Stream. Joachim Rodrigo's "Concierto de Aranjuez" for guitar and symphony orchestra was rescored by Evans for trumpet and wind orchestra; there are no strings.[11] "Pan Piper," "Saeta," and "Solea" are developments of Spanish folk themes.

Gil Evans had a long career in the field of arranging and bandleading, but he produced no other works that exceed these richly fulfilling and consistently compelling collaborations with Davis. Decades after their first release, *Sketches of Spain*, *Porgy and Bess*, and *Miles Ahead* continue to stand as monumental achievements to combining orchestration and the jazz tradition. They remain among the all-time favorite albums of jazz musicians and music scholars.

**Kind of Blue**     In 1959, Miles Davis recorded one of the best-loved and most historically pivotal albums in modern jazz: *Kind of Blue*. On all but one selection, he used Cannonball Adderley, John Coltrane, pianist Bill Evans, bassist Paul Chambers, and drummer Jimmy Cobb. Bill Evans conceived most of the harmonies, as well as contributing one original composition ("Blue in Green," often mistakenly credited to Davis).[12] One reason the album is so important is that, instead of using a format in which chords change frequently and bear preset durations, the band used formats in which the harmonies of a single chord or mode were in effect for four or more measures (see page 421 for explanatory musical notation). Then the group either preset the durations, as with "So What" (available in SCCJ, the modes of which are notated on page 423), or left the durations up to the spontaneous discretion of the soloist (as in "Flamenco Sketches," in the JAZZ CLASSICS CASSETTE).

The second selection on *Kind of Blue*'s second side was created by an interesting improvisational technique. Instead of playing a melody and improvising on its chord changes, the sextet followed a preset sequence of five modes. Each mode served as the harmonic guide for improvisation as long as a soloist wanted to use it. Then, whenever he wanted a change, he moved to the next mode. Although there were no restrictions on the duration of any mode, the soloists tended to use each mode for an even number of measures. In fact, most soloists used each mode for four measures and then moved to the next. So, in spite of the increased freedom allowed by this techniques, the players usually chose duration patterns which typically occur in conventional jazz improvisation.

[11]This is the same classical piece that inspired Chick Corea's "Spain," which in turn was made popular by a vocal rendition of Al Jarreau.

[12]Listen to "Peace Piece" by Evans on *Everybody Digs Bill Evans*, OJC-068 (Riverside 1129), CD/LP, 1958, recorded four months before *Kind of Blue*.

The second selection on the second side of *Kind of Blue* is known by two different titles because many records were released with the second side's tune titles interchanged. The name that seems to have stuck for the *second* selection is "Flamenco Sketches." Bill Evan's album jacket notes indicate that the piece was supposed to be called "All Blues." But several subsequent Davis versions of second side's *first* selection have been released using the "All Blues" title.

### Listening Guide for "Flamenco Sketches"

Available on the JAZZ CLASSICS CASSETTE, side 2; on CD in *Kind of Blue* (CBS 40579).

**Suggestions for keeping your place while hearing "Flamenco Sketches" and following the modal construction**

1. Remember that the *first* track on the second side of *Kind of Blue* has been labeled "Flamenco Sketches" on many copies of this album. So, if you hear a feeling of "ONE two three Four five six ONE two three Four five six" instead of a very slow "ONE two three four ONE two three four," then you are listening to the wrong selection.

2. To begin synchronizing your counting with the record, notice that the piece starts with a bass note on the fourth beat of a measure that actually precedes the beginning of your counting. If you are to count accurately, you must say "FOUR" when that first note is sounding, then say "One" when the next bass note sounds. That note lasts three beats, so you must continue counting even though there is no clear statement of any beats until the pattern is repeated. In other words, to get you through the introduction and well synchronized with the tempo of the piece, you need to count "FOUR One two three FOUR One two three FOUR." When you say "FOUR One," you are acknowledging the bass notes. When you say "two three," you are acknowledging the middle of the measure, a time when the bass note is still ringing and no clear statement of beats is coming from the musicians. Eventually, you should be able to count "ONE two three four ONE two three four" with or without assistance from the musicians. This will become important later because bassist Paul Chambers sometimes plays figures that purposely delete the simple pattern outlined above and leave the listener to fill in the beats. You will have some assistance, though, beginning with John Coltrane's entrance, because drummer Jimmy Cobb starts using a wire brush to play ride rhythms on the ride cymbal. If you still have yet to figure out where the beats are by the time you are near the end of the selection, simply listen to Cobb's playing under the final Miles Davis solo. It is almost exclusively quarter notes, one note on each beat.

3. Remember that the tempo is very slow, and that you should therefore take care to not be counting twice as fast or four times as fast as the beats are passing.

4. If your mind wanders, let the sound of mode #4 refocus your attention. It has a Spanish flavor that differs noticeably from the flavors of the other modes. It has also attracted the longest improvisations from the musicians and can therefore give you the most time to get back with it. In fact, if you

lose your place and all of a sudden find yourself in the middle of that mode, you can restart your counting when that flavor disappears. The disappearance of that flavor will signal the beginning of mode #5.

5. Start counting anew when a different solo voice enters. Remember that the sequence is four measures of piano and bass introduction followed by these sounds each running five modes in sequence: muted trumpet, tenor sax, alto sax, piano, and muted trumpet.

6. Listen carefully for the bass notes that begin the measures. If a new mode is starting, this will often be signalled by the sound of a NEW bass note on the first beat of the measure.

7. To help you anticipate each new mode within a single musician's solo, keep in mind that *generally*
   a. Miles Davis lets bassist Paul Chambers lead him to each new mode. Chambers plays the important note of the mode while Davis is silent, then Davis enters with a new melodic idea to fit the mode.
   b. Coltrane tends to increase the number of notes played per beat just before beginning a new mode. In other words, if you hear Coltrane sound like he is going faster and faster, consider the likelihood that he is requesting the next mode.
   c. Adderley suggests the upcoming mode by a peculiar choice of notes in his line. The flavor of his melody line shifts when he is about to change modes.

8. Once you know where you are, if it is the beginning of a mode, count "1234   2234   3234   4234" in order to keep your place by tallying beats as they pass. Each group of four beats ("1234") accounts for one measure. You tag the measures by saying a number to yourself at the beginning of each one. If it is the first measure for the mode, you say, "ONE two three four." If it is the second measure of a given mode, you say, "TWO two three four." If it is the third measure, you say, "THREE two three four."

Eventually you should be able to follow the changing modes without referring to the guide. Your ears will tell you what mode is in effect at a given moment. The whole point of this exercise is to help you peek into what the jazz improviser is doing. By being able to identify the same sounds that the improviser is using as basis for his solos, you will lessen the mystery of how solos are put together and how musicians manage to play well together without having to discuss their parts or use prewritten themes. The more you recognize in the sounds, the better prepared you are to go on to an appreciation of the compositional beauties present in the improvised lines. Listening for modes to change at the slow pace used by these performers should better equip you for listening to chords changing in conventional jazz pieces. The better you get at accurately anticipating chord changes, the more you will realize how the improviser's lines reflect his own appreciation of how the chords are progressing in a given piece. To a great extent, the progress of a melody line mirrors the progression of harmonies that lies beneath it in the accompanying chord changes. The improvised line reflects the flavor of the underlying chord, and a line improvised in "Flamenco Sketches" often bears the same character as the mode that is implied in that moment's accompaniment harmonies. Once you begin confidently following the music in this piece, it will be as though you are peering through a microscope. But instead of tiny things being made to appear large, ordinarily quick-paced improvisational processes have been slowed down for your calm examination.

INTRODUCTION

Four measures of mode #1. The sound of this mode is indicated by bass notes and chord voicings set in a pattern previously used by Bill Evans for his "Peace Piece." What were originally left-hand parts for pianist Evans are given here to bassist Paul Chambers. The pattern has Chambers playing on only the first and the fourth beats of each measure. Pianist Evans plays chords whose harmonies flesh out the rest of the mode's flavor.

*Elapsed Time*

0'18"

MILES DAVIS MUTED TRUMPET IMPROVISATION
(with only piano and bass accompaniment)

| mode #1 | mode #2 | mode #3 | mode #4 |
|---|---|---|---|
| four measures | four measures | four measures | eight measures |

1' 44"

| mode #5 |
|---|
| four measures |

2' 03"

JOHN COLTRANE TENOR SAXOPHONE IMPROVISATION
(with piano, bass, and ride cymbal accompaniment)

| mode #1 | mode #2 | mode #3 | mode #4 |
|---|---|---|---|
| four measures | four measures | four measures | eight measures |

3' 25"

| mode #5 |
|---|
| four measures |

3' 42"

CANNONBALL ADDERLEY ALTO SAXOPHONE IMPROVISATION
(with piano, bass, and cymbals accompaniment)
Notice that Chambers plays less predictably during this solo.

| (one-measure introduction by piano and bass using mode #5) | mode #1 eight measures | mode #2 four measures | mode #3 eight measures |
|---|---|---|---|

5' 06"

| mode #4 eight measures | (Drummer Jimmy Cobb plays double-time and adds high-hat closings during the middle of Adderley's treatment of this mode.) | mode #5 four measures |
|---|---|---|

5' 54"

BILL EVANS PIANO IMPROVISATION
(with bass and ride cymbal accompaniment)

| mode #1 | mode #2 | mode #3 | mode #4 |
|---|---|---|---|
| eight measures | four measures | eight measures | four measures |

(See page 421 for musical notations and technical names of these modes.)

| Elapsed Time | |
| --- | --- |
| 7' 33" | mode #5<br>four measures |
| 7' 50" | **MILES DAVIS MUTED TRUMPET IMPROVISATION**<br>(with piano, bass, and ride cymbal accompaniment) |

| mode #1<br>four measures | mode #2<br>four measures | mode #3<br>four measures | mode #4<br>eight measures |
| --- | --- | --- | --- |

| 9' 11" | mode #5<br>two measures |
| --- | --- |

After *Kind of Blue* was released, many jazz musicians began using these formats instead of popular song formats. During the 1960s and 70s, numerous players rejected the bop custom of using chords that changed frequently and bore preset durations. Entire performances were based on a single chord instead of an elaborate progression of different chords. Some performances contained spontaneous chord changes instead of preset changes. In summary, **the historical significance of** *Kind of Blue* was three-fold: 1) it represented a set of inspired improvisations by an all-star band; 2) it was a highly palatable departure from bop-derived styles; and 3) it introduced a generation of improvisers to mode-based formats. Incidentally, it is the most frequently cited album in lists of musicians's and critics's favorites.

Further historical perspective can be gained for *Kind of Blue* when we consider that at the same time it arrived, considerable attention was also being given to Ornette Coleman, a saxophonist who specialized in improvising with no preset harmonies at all. Whereas Davis was substituting long stretches of modes for rapidly changing chords, Coleman's improvisations were neither mode-based nor chord-based. Coleman worked from shifting tone centers. His improvisations followed only the internal logic of his melodic inventions, instead of adhering to a single key, mode, or chord progression. Unlike Davis, Coleman almost never used a pianist. Improvisation using such approaches had been recorded by others before Coleman and Davis (see Lennie Tristano, Shorty Rogers, et al. in chapter 10). But only after this late-1950s work of Davis and Coleman did the approach catch on in the mainstream of jazz. And by the mid-1960s, free-form and modal approaches were mixed in the music of many bands. (Numerous improvisations that began without preset key or chords soon acquired tone centers and modal organizations.) These related approaches became so abundant that during the 1970s, more than half of all jazz and jazz-derived performances contained at least some modal or free-form improvisations. During that period, fewer than twenty prominent modern jazz combos played selections which fit neither modal nor free-form styles. An entire school of jazz styles embraced the practice of not presetting the harmonies for improvisation (see chapter 14). During the 1980s, the music of the so-called "new age" bands was largely modal. Many of the jazz-rock fusion bands of the 1970s and 80s combined passages of chord progression-based improvisation with passages of mode-based improvisation. Davis himself alternated among all these formats. The impact of *Kind of Blue* was immense. The complementary developments associated with Coleman combined with the Davis innovations and determined the way much jazz was structured in the succeeding two decades.

**The 1959–63 Rhythm Section**

The rhythm section Miles Davis used from 1959 to 1963 consisted of pianist Wynton Kelly (1931–1971), bassist Paul Chambers, and drummer Jimmy Cobb. Their work is documented in the albums *Miles Davis at Carnegie Hall, Friday Night at the Blackhawk, Saturday Night at the Blackhawk, Someday My Prince Will Come,* and in the selection "Freddie the Freeloader," on *Kind of Blue.* Their relaxed, even swing feeling, their lightness and bounce distinguished them from all others, except perhaps the Count Basie rhythm section of the 1930s. Modern musicians of the era considered this Davis rhythm section to be among the most desirable accompanying units in jazz. Paul Chambers was already discussed in the hard bop chapter, but we will examine Kelly and Cobb here.

Wynton Kelly was a bop pianist who played with a lighter, less complicated feeling than Bud Powell used. He swung infectiously, and his accompaniments followed the melodic and rhythmic flights of the Davis hornmen so well that Kelly's bandmates could hardly help but swing too. Kelly was one of Davis's all-time favorite accompanists, and Cannonball Adderley also praised him highly. Kelly combined influences ranging from Powell to Horace Silver, and, at least on *Someday My Prince Will Come,* the chord voicings of Bill Evans. In turn, Kelly himself was influential. Among the modern pianists who show his influence are Herbie Hancock, Warren Bernhardt, and Keith Jarrett.

**Jimmy Cobb** (b. 1929) was a steady and swinging drummer. More conservative in his accompanying style than Philly Joe Jones, Cobb nonetheless contributed a very significant characteristic to modern jazz of the 1960s and thereafter: **Cobb's ride rhythms were placed toward the front edge of the beat in a way that made them seem to pull the beat.** Though this aspect is subtle, it is quite significant because drummers before Cobb had traditionally played more toward the center of the beat. Tony Williams, who replaced Cobb in the Davis group, adopted Cobb's timekeeping technique and played consistently on the leading edge of the beat. Williams had a marked effect on the overall feeling of the Davis quintet because of that. Williams, in turn, influenced other drummers who became prominent in the 1970s and 80s, all of whom followed Cobb's tendency.

**The 1963–68 Rhythm Section**

In 1963, Miles Davis hired a new rhythm section comprised of pianist **Herbie Hancock,** bassist **Ron Carter,** and drummer **Tony Williams.**[13] This Davis rhythm section remained intact, at least on records, from 1963 until 1968. These musicians created a new jazz idiom. Though moments in their music resembled the sounds of

[13]By the summer of 1964, this rhythm section had joined Davis to make half of a studio album, *Seven Steps to Heaven,* and three concert albums: *Miles in Europe, My Funny Valentine,* and *Four and More.* For more details about personnel, concert dates, and recording sessions for Miles Davis bands of the 1960s, see the book *Milestones 2,* by Jack Chambers (Beech Tree, 1985). For an appraisal of the Davis career, see *Miles Davis* by Ian Carr (William Morrow, 1982).

Tony Williams, a prime force in the Miles Davis rhythm section of 1963–68. (*Photo by Charles Behnke*)

hard bop and free jazz, their music did not truly belong to either of those classifications. Hints of their new idiom were evident in some of their first recordings, for example *My Funny Valentine*, of 1964. Then by 1965 and 66, every album they produced was filled with new concepts. In addition, these concepts were packaged in performances whose quality was so finished that it belied its freshness. The innovations of this band were performed so smoothly that many listeners, especially journalists, failed to recognize the band's historical significance. Its innovations were at least as significant as those in Davis's better known styles. Moreover, this music disappointed so many jazz fans who expected extensive repetition of brief rhythms, recycled jazz phrases, and funky melodies that it ranked as one of the least popular phases in the Davis recording career. (For examples of this music, listen to their 1967 studio recording of Masqualero in the JAZZ CLASSICS CASSETTE.)

Herbie Hancock, Ron Carter, and Tony Williams all displayed stunning technical prowess on their respective instruments. Together they created what was probably the smoothest rhythm section sound jazz had experienced. The Hancock-Carter-Williams unit had excitement and power like the Garland-Chambers-Jones rhythm section and sensitivity and delicacy like the Bill Evans-Scott LaFaro-Paul Motian unit. (For a sample of Evans, LaFaro, and Motian, listen to "Solar" in the JAZZ CLASSICS CASSETTE.) These players had digested the work of their most impressive predecessors, combined it with in-depth knowledge and mastery of twentieth century classical music (Bartók, Hindemith, Debussy, etc.), and then built upon that foundation to create something newer and more sparkling than any other combinations. (Listen to "Masqualero" on the JAZZ CLASSICS CASSETTE, and focus your listening solely on the piano, bass, and drum parts.) This rhythm section could play persuasively in the bop manner if it wished. It could emulate the Wynton Kelly-Paul Chambers-Jimmy Cobb style. And it could work well in the quiet, reflective manner of the Evans-LaFaro-Motian unit. But it was freer, more flexible and daring than those other units, and it came up with music that sounded like no jazz ever heard before. This unit's collective originality and creativity remained unsurpassed decades after its monumental contributions to the 1967 Davis album *Sorcerer* (from which "Masqualero" is taken). Their consolidations were so startling and so well played that it took most of jazz about twenty years to catch up, as evidenced by the wave of similarly styled bands emerging in the 1980s, including those of Wynton Marsalis and Terence Blanchard.

Hancock, Carter, and Williams maintained an almost magical level of rapport. They were able to play cohesively at breakneck tempos[14] or, in the context of a slow piece, they could avoid explicitly stating tempo, and sound instead as though someone were conducting them through gradual accelerations and decelerations.[15] (Listen to the middle section of "Masqualero" on the JAZZ CLASSICS CASSETTE). Their rapport and high level of musicianship allowed them to change rhythms, textures, and moods spontaneously at any moment of a performance, at any tempo, and on any chord progression. Their versatility and lightning quick responsiveness were extraordinary. Because of this, **the Davis group of the 1960s was one of very few jazz bands that drastically varied its levels of loudness. It was also distinguished for creating a wide variety of distinctly different accompanying rhythms and chord patterns. A clear departure from bop traditions was evident in many of their performances.**

Pianist Herbie Hancock combined the best qualities of an improviser: a clear conception, fertile imagination, a highly developed sense of continuity, and excellent instrumental proficiency. He had a quick, precise touch and comped briskly. Like his colleagues in the Davis group, he was also a composer, and his improvisations revealed his acute sense of compositional balance and integrity. He was able consistently to devise coherent, well-structured solos, even for pieces that provided him with only a mode, a mood, a key, and a tempo. Hancock was able to devise and perform accompaniment patterns spontaneously during group improvisations that brought the performance a form, direction, and substance comparable to that of a symphonic piece which had been worked out in advance. Hancock contributed gracefully shifting rhythms and harmonies that were more advanced than the patterns used by bop pianists or by such contemporary pianists as Bill Evans and McCoy Tyner. What he invented as underpinning for the soloists often had the character of modern symphonic music. Incidentally, Hancock's superb mastery of the piano and his creative flexibility and taste as an accompanist put him in great demand as a recording pianist. Hancock appeared on more record dates than any

[14]"Walkin'" on *Four and More*.
[15]"My Funny Valentine" on *My Funny Valentine*, "Madness" on Nefertiti, and "Masqualero" on *Sorcerer*.

other jazz pianist of the 1960s. (For an outline of Hancock's career and contributions, see chapter 15.)

Bassist Ron Carter (b. 1937) had a slick, round tone. He walked with uncanny perfection and buoyancy. Both his tone and his sense of timing exhibited a uniformly high level of quality. Carter played more toward the front of the beat than Paul Chambers did, thereby meshing with the timekeeping manner introduced by drummer Jimmy Cobb in the previous Davis band. He provided a sturdy, yet responsive foundation for the quintet. Among musicians, Carter is often considered the most swinging accompanist after Ray Brown and Sam Jones. Yet despite his excellence as a timekeeper, Carter did not always restrict himself to walking. He incorporated other rhythmic figures, too. (Listen to his work at the beginning of "Masqualero.") He was continuously devising new ways both to underpin the group sound and to enrich the musical events that occurred around him.[16] This was no small achievement, either. Tony Williams was encircling Carter with exploding rhythmic ideas that had never been used before in jazz combos. And, at the same time, pianist Herbie Hancock was inventing new harmonies to fit these rhythms and moods, all of which had to be smoothly integrated almost at the moment they were conceived. Carter acquitted himself so well in these circumstances that Miles Davis was not the only leader who appreciated him. By the mid-1970s, Carter had been employed on more than four hundred records.

Drummer Tony Williams (b. 1945) represented the highest level of drum technique, and he was possibly the most influential jazz drummer of the 1960s. He was very fast, and his cymbal tones were separated with crystal clarity. Williams provided a model of light, sharp sounds. His ride cymbal sound was very crisp and distinctive, and, because he used a smaller bass drum than most pre-1960s drummers, the low register component of his sound was well articulated. Williams was an extremely sophisticated rhythm section player, looser and more of a risk taker than any of his predecessors. Williams did more than kick and prod the hornmen. By the time *Filles de Kilimanjaro* was recorded in 1968, he had assumed a role so prominent that his creations often overshadowed the other sounds in the group. His was a very assertive style.[17] Williams overflowed with imagination. He devised numerous ways to establish new moods and state the tempo. To name just two, as early as the 1964 *Four and More* album, he had played pieces without consistently snapping his high-hat shut on the second and fourth beats of each measure, thereby keeping time only with the ride cymbal and using the high-hat only for bursts of color. Then on "Freedom Jazz Dance" in the 1966 *Miles Smiles* album, he closed his high-hat sharply on every beat, a timekeeping practice later adopted by hundreds of jazz-rock drummers. He also colored the group sound with a seemingly endless variety of cymbal splashes, snare drum fills, and imaginative rhythmic patterns distributed over all his drums and cymbals (particularly evident at the beginning and the end of

---

[16]Listen to Carter's playing on "Pee Wee" and "Masqualero" (*Sorcerer*), "Freedom Jazz Dance" (*Miles Smiles*), and "Riot," "Fall," and "Nefertiti" (all on *Nefertiti*).

[17]Compare Kenny Clarke's performance on the records Miles Davis made during the early 1950s with Williams's playing on *Filles de Kilimanjaro* or *Miles Smiles*. You will hear a drastic difference between the two.

"Masqualero"). His work often departed from the dance band and marching band traditions of jazz drumming, and his methods were consistent with orchestral concepts in which percussion instruments perform melodic and texture-generating roles. Listening to the Davis recordings of this period will reveal why so many drummers were awed and inspired by Williams. Some musicians feel that, by his playing, Williams was the musician most responsible for instigating the florid constructions that came from the mid-1960s Miles Davis quintet. It was Williams who most often provoked the other musicians into their daring flights of nontraditional playing. (To study his contributions, listen to "Masqualero" on the JAZZ CLASSICS CASSETTE, and focus your listening solely on drums and cymbals.)[18]

**The 1964-68 Compositional Style**

After saxophonist-composer Wayne Shorter joined Miles Davis in 1964, Davis recorded very few conventionally constructed pieces. Most tunes Davis played during the 1950s fit conventional song forms.[19] **After 1964, Davis favored tunes which did not have bridges, complex turnarounds, or any section demarcations which can easily act as barriers to an unencumbered, free-flowing sound.** Most of his post-1964 recordings were made up of tunes which had fewer chord changes than those in pop

**Figure 12.1.** Wayne Shorter's melody lines often contain strings of notes separated by the interval of a fourth. Here is part of his "Masqualero." The notes of one phrase of the melody appear on this keyboard in numbered sequence.

[18]Though it took a long time to become common in jazz, the influence of the 1963–68 Davis rhythm section style was evident later in recordings by Joe Henderson (*Power to the People*, Milestone 9024, LP, 1969; *Tetragon*, Milestone 9017, LP, 1967–68; *In Pursuit of Blackness*, Milestone 9034, LP, 1971; *The Kicker*, Milestone 9008, LP, 1967; *If You're Not Part of the Solution, You're Part of the Problem*, Milestone 9028, LP; and Joe Farrell (*Joe Farrell Quartet*, CBS 40694 (CTI 6003), CD, 1970). The rhythm section style of *Miles In Europe* and *Four and More* was later heard in records by Freddie Hubbard, Jackie McLean (*Right Now*, Blue Note 84215, LP, 1965; and others. The Davis quintet approaches on *Miles Smiles*, *Miles in the Sky*, and *Nefertiti* influenced the Art Lande group of the 1970s (*Rubisa Patrol*, ECM 1081, LP, 1976); and the Wynton Marsalis/Branford Marsalis quintet of the early 1980s (*Wynton Marsalis*, CBS 37574, CD/LP, 1982; *Think of One*, CBS 38641, CD/LP, 1983; *Black Codes*, CBS 40009, CD/LP, 1985).

[19]An examination of the tunes on his 1961 *Someday My Prince Will Come* and *In Person at the Blackhawk*, his 1963 *Seven Steps to Heaven* and *Miles in Europe*, and his 1964 *Four and More* and *My Funny Valentine* reveals that, after the departure of Bill Evans and prior to his work with Wayne Shorter, Davis had not explored much new territory in the area of song forms.

Bassist Ron Carter and tenor saxophonist Wayne Shorter photographed here while with the mid-1960s Miles Davis group. (*Photo courtesy of Bill Smith*)

standards by Richard Rodgers or George Gershwin, or jazz standards by Charlie Parker, Dizzy Gillespie, or Thelonious Monk.[20]

Another trait which lent the 1965–68 recordings their distinctive flavor was **the use of space in tune construction.** Sometimes several measures of the melody were filled with silence. Quite often, trumpet and tenor would lay out while the rhythm section continued to play and generate a mood.[21] Incidentally, these differences in compositional form led to a drastic change not only in the sound of the Miles Davis bands then, but also in other groups of that period in which similar procedures were being used.

[20]A large number of post-1964 compositions are all A instead of A-A-B-A, A-B-A-B, or A-B-A-C. On the *E.S.P.* album is Shorter's "Iris," a sixteen-bar waltz, all A. On the *Sorcerer* album is Shorter's "Prince of Darkness," sixteen bars long with very few prearranged harmonies. On the *E.S.P.* album is his "E.S.P.," sixteen bars long, all A, with important and frequent chord changes. It is played twice, as twelve bars + four-bar turnaround, then twelve bars + four-bar conclusion. The four-bar sections differ, but the twelve-bar sections are identical.

[21]On the *Miles Smiles* album is Shorter's "Dolores," thirty-eight bars long, divided into phrases of two, two and one-half, three, and three and one-half measures. These phrases are separated by spaces in which the horns do not play. Only the rhythm section is heard, continuing and developing patterns they played underneath the horns.

One other important aspect of the group's compositional style was a significant lessening in the number of rapid, jumpy eighth-note figures which typified the highly syncopated lines of bop. The Davis repertory still contained pieces with some eighth notes and syncopation, but many of the post-1964 tunes were constructed of smoothly contoured lines with frequent sustained tones. By comparison with the compositional style of bop, the tunes this band played were usually less densely packed. They had fewer intricate figures. An airy feeling was more common than a crowded feeling. This, in turn, influenced the character of improvisations the band produced. More variety was possible because of the greater freedom implied by the openness in feeling. (To illustrate the difference between bop and this new style, compare "Shaw Nuff" with "Masqualero" in the JAZZ CLASSICS CASSETTE.)

The Davis quintet performance of Shorter's "Nefertiti," on the *Nefertiti* album of 1967, illustrates both these aspects. It is a sixteen-bar tune, all A. There is a new chord in every measure, but the motion always has a slow, floating quality. Nothing abrupt or jumpy happens in either the melody or the chord changes. This melody's silences and sustained tones produce an effect unlike that of bop melodies. In addition, the entire performance consists of the melody being repeated again and again, a device later employed extensively by post-1968 Davis groups and spin-offs from those bands. In fact, with no improvised solos by anyone else, this version of "Nefertiti" is practically a feature for Tony Williams. The lazy, expansive feeling evoked by the performance suggests the impressionistic classical music of Claude Debussy ("La Mer," "Prelude to the Afternoon of a Faun") and Maurice Ravel ("Daphnis and Chloe"). The style of this "Nefertiti" performance places the burden of complexity on the rhythm section, quite the reverse of bop tendencies. So not only does the style of the melody differ from bop, but the style of the accompaniment differs, too. It is a loose, highly active improvisation by piano, bass, and drums that alternates from walking bass and ride rhythms to moments with volatile drumming and very little internal repetition. Sometimes Carter is playing four times as many notes as a bassist would usually play. At other times, he is playing only a fourth as many as we would expect. Hancock does not always play conventional comping rhythms, either. This contrasts sharply with the almost unvarying sequences of walking bass, ride rhythms, and comping which typify bop accompaniment style. **The post-1964 Davis quintet evolved away from the bop formula of quick, jumpy melodic figures on top and stable, metronomic pulse patterns on the bottom. Shorter's writing brought stable simplicity to the top, and Williams's drumming brought super-charged rhythmic complexity to the bottom. This reversal of roles later became common in jazz-rock groups, especially in the band called Weather Report.**

The three characteristics outlined above all fit with the tremendously explorative attitude of drummer Tony Williams and the effect he had upon his fellow bandmates. He spurred them to use the new freedom that came from the nontraditional song forms and to contrive a fresh sound. This resulted in their creating phrases that were unlike those in previous jazz styles, and it nudged them to devise sound masses that evolved spontaneously and freely shifted. The result of this triumphed to carry the listener on an adventure filled with surprises.

In addition to their extraordinarily high instrumental proficiency, improvisatory freshness, and their unique contributions to the development of jazz accompaniment style, Hancock, Shorter, Carter, and Williams managed to ensure that the variety of moods and rhythmic styles employed in the 1964–68 Davis Quintet was vast. They recorded waltzes,[22] fast pieces,[23] slow-reflective pieces,[24] pieces in which a sequence of different rhythmic styles are created,[25] and pieces that anticipated the jazz-rock fusion styles (see chapter 16).

**Wayne Shorter**   Between summer of 1964 and winter of 1970, Miles Davis employed Wayne Shorter (b. 1933), one of the most outstanding tenor saxophonists in jazz of the 1960s, and possibly the most original tenor stylist to emerge after Coltrane and concurrent to Albert Ayler. Shorter was also a composer whose work provided a foundation for the new jazz idiom that was created by the Davis band of 1965–68. Some musicians consider Shorter to be the most important jazz composer of the 1960s and 70s. His highly original writing and playing had already been central to the Art Blakey bands of 1959–64, and they later became central to the work of Weather Report, an innovative jazz-rock fusion band of the 1970s and 80s.

Shorter's creativity had several sides to it. Some musicians and fans are impressed the most by the side he showed in his work with Art Blakey. They may prefer it because his improvisatory methods with Blakey represent the closest he came to hard bop and to using traditional ways of devising lines, such as basing phrases on strings of eighth notes, for example. His work was fluid and extremely intense, projecting a rawness that is common to hard bop. Some listeners find this work more emotionally compelling than his other work. Despite his links with tradition, however, Shorter's playing with Blakey was largely original, and its level of inspiration was consistently striking.

Many musicians and fans believe that Shorter's studio recordings of 1965–68 with Miles Davis constitute his most impressive work. Though similar in many ways to his work with Blakey, these performances highlighted an even more unconventional and exceedingly explorative side to his talents. A softness and introspective quality were exposed here that were not as evident in his work with Blakey. Though his playing in all contexts always exhibited a highly logical quality, his thinking here was more calmly logical, as though this new setting allowed him to be less hurried and more reflective. Perhaps that was why some listeners perceived this music as cool and abstract. Incidentally, the few rare recordings that are available of him playing with this band in concert and night club appearances reveal him wrestling passionately with dense swaths of color and rhythm that seem to be burning through the center of the band sound, not cool at all.

---

[22]Davis's "Circle" and Shorter's "Footprints" (both on the *Miles Smiles* album), Hancock's "Little One" and Carter's "Mood" (both on the *E.S.P.* album) and Williams's "Pee Wee" (on the *Sorcerer* album)

[23]Jimmy Heath's "Gingerbread Boy," Shorter's "Dolores" and "Orbits" (all on the *Miles Smiles* album), Williams's "Hand Jive" (on the *Nefertiti* album), Hancock's "The Sorcerer" (on the *Sorcerer* album), Carter's "R.J." and Shorter's "E.S.P." (both on the *E.S.P.* album)

[24]Shorter's "Fall" (on the *Nefertiti* album) and "Vonetta" (on the *Sorcerer* album)

[25]Davis's "Country Son" (on the *Miles in the Sky* album) and in the Davis-Carter "Eighty-One" (on the *E.S.P.* album)

### Listening Guide for "Masqualero"

Recorded in 1967 by trumpeter Miles Davis, tenor saxophonist Wayne Shorter, pianist Herbie Hancock, bassist Ron Carter, and drummer Tony Williams, first available on the album *Sorcerer* (Columbia CL 2732, reissued as CBS 9532).

The melody for "Masqualero" was composed by Wayne Shorter. Like his tunes "Nefertiti" and "E.S.P.," it also features a succession of notes that are separated by the interval of a fourth (see page 236). The second phrase of the melody has only ten notes—one pitch played three times, followed by a pitch one fourth lower that is played three times, followed by a pitch that is another fourth lower played three times, followed by a pitch that is a half step lower. Incidentally, this particular sequence of intervals contributes to the sense of mystery—that much of Shorter's music evokes.

The arrangement of "Masqualero" here is almost entirely spontaneous. Unissued live recordings of this piece by the same band only remotely resemble it. Unlike the arrangements discussed in previous listening guides, there is only a hint of preset organization here, often only the tempo and a few bass notes. The piano, bass, and drum parts were being devised while they were being performed. This recording presents pianist Herbie Hancock, bassist Ron Carter, and drummer Tony Williams in a cooperative improvisation of immense scope and invention. Played with impeccable musicianship, this performance is a stunning example of master improvisers confidently working at a high level of creativity. It is essential to remember that Hancock, Carter, and Williams are not merely accompanying trumpeter Davis and saxophonist Shorter. They are working as composers collaborating in the creation of a new piece of music. They are particularly sensitive to each other's playing, and they complement one another extremely well. This performance offers more examples of spontaneous interaction than any other piece on the JAZZ CLASSICS CASSETTE. The result is an extemporaneous work that takes the listener through significant changes in loudness, melody, texture, and rhythm, showing almost as much internal contrast and development as we might find in a prewritten symphonic piece. In some respects, it even evokes the drama we expect of an opera.

The musicians were free to invent melodies and transform them throughout the performance. Some solo passages are particularly melodic, as in the sax improvisation from about 5' 25" to 5' 50". The improvisers sometimes quote or paraphrase the original melody or the improvised line of a fellow band member. Occasionally they pass it around, each player echoing another's phrase (as in Hancock mimicking Davis at about 53" and at 1' 01" and Carter paraphrasing the melody at about 6' 35"). Sometimes they play the intact sequence of notes that define the mode (as in the sax solo at about 3' 43").

Many accompaniment harmonies in this performance were chosen spontaneously during the performance itself, not planned in advance. The musicians were free to create new melodies and harmonies guided loosely by the knowledge of what notes would be compatible with those provided by the bass part and the melody that occurred at the beginning of the piece. Basically, the harmonies here only give the music a start. They do not influence the course of improvised ideas as much as chord progressions in earlier styles did. Nor do the accompaniment rhythms under the melody constrain the rhythmic aspects of the music that evolves during the performance. Though steady tempo is maintained throughout the performance, the players are free to change melody, texture, and rhythmic style from moment to moment. Unlike pre–1960s jazz, central features of this piece's organization emerge and change spontaneously.

Over the course of the performance, soloists vary the extent to which they make their phrases swing. Sometimes they lock their rhythms tightly to the underlying pulse (as in the end of the trumpet solo, at about 2' 47"). The accompanists also vary in this respect. Tony Williams plays a continuous sequence of eighth notes on his ride cymbal through much of the piece, though he interrupts it sporadically to play rhythms on his snare drum and tom-toms that decorate the solo lines and change the mood of the performance. Ron Carter plays widely differing patterns on bass, never walking, though sometimes he plays the steady pattern that Wayne Shorter wrote for the piece.

Outstanding features of this performance include the remarkable freshness of the solo improvisations, the spontaneous changes in intensity (as in the steady increase from 5' 30" to 5' 50"), changes in rhythmic style (it changes most dramatically at 2' 37" and 3' 20"), and changes in texture. The music's texture thickens at about 1' 50" and thins at about 2' 12", then thickens again at about 2' 37" and thins at about 3' 20". Texture changes also occur at 6' 30" and 7'. It thickens considerably at 7' 52" and thins at 8' 18".

Probably the best way to begin appreciating this performance is to first make yourself comfortable in a place removed from anything you might find distracting. Use of a headset would be ideal. Close your eyes. Empty your mind of all thoughts and feelings except the intention to let the music take you wherever it can. Pretend that you are on an unhurried journey with trustworthy guides who promise to show you many new vistas. Then just listen. Don't be concerned with trying to identify all the sounds the first time you listen. Pursue those details in repeated listenings with this guide. The virtues of this performance are not only the beauty of the sounds themselves but also the success with which the players have improvised shifting lines and textures, as though their parts were strains of movement in a ballet with three or more dancers always in motion.

The form for most of this performance of "Masqualero" is A-B-A, sections of which are 8, 6, and 8 measures long, respectively. Though following repetitions of that form for most of the performance, the band makes a few departures from that organization. These are noted in the descriptions of the Wayne Shorter and Herbie Hancock solos.

OPTIONAL TECHNICAL INFORMATION: Musicians describe the harmonic basis of improvisations in this piece as "playing off a pedal point" and using a "modal flavor" or "modal color." This means that one note (usually in the bass register), "the pedal," dominates throughout that section, and atop it are played strings of notes that draw from one particular mode, though the musicians do not adhere exclusively to those notes.* Periodically a single chord abruptly occurs that differs significantly in flavor from the collection of chords that have maintained a given mode for a long passage. Musicians call the use of this chord "a cadence point," a moment of resolving tension and preparing for another stretch of music. Such a chord is used here to allow a few beats of separation between sections, particularly at the end of each B-section.

## INTRODUCTION  (8 measures)

*Instruments: piano, bass, and drums*

The proceedings begin loosely and then tighten as the horns's entrance approaches. Williams is playing complicated rhythms on the ride cymbal and rolls on his tom-toms. High-hat cymbals are vibrating against each other. Carter is playing pizzicato eighth notes and pauses, mostly irregular figures. Hancock is firmly sounding a string of chords that ascend like steps, each one ringing and separated from the next by a brief pause.

Rhythmic activity in the bass and drums is so complex that the down beat may be hard to detect. Hancock makes the rhythm clearer. His piano chords are grouped in three's; the first chord of each group is played on the downbeat.

---

* For details, study the phrygian mode on page 419 of this book, and see chapter 6 in *Creative Jazz Improvisation* by Scott Reeves. Some of Shorter's improvisation from this performance is transcribed and analyzed by Reeves.

*Elapsed Time*

## FIRST STATEMENT OF THE THEME (A-B-A)

0' 14"

*A-Section* (8 measures)

The opening statement can be interpreted as a dialog between the horns and the piano The composed melody starts with a two-bar phrase and alternates with two measures of silence. Hancock uses the silence to respond to the previous melodic statement.

Trumpet and sax play three notes slurred together in harmony. Hancock responds with two quick chords, then three chords that mirror the horns's opening notes.

0' 22"

Trumpet and sax play notes of the second phrase in octaves and unisons. The melody moves by the interval of a fourth.

Horns pause again for seven beats while the piano fills in with a brief melodic phrase of harp-like tones which complements the second hornlike phrase.

0' 29"

*B-section* (6 measures)

Horns return in harmony.

A brief trumpet phrase is answered by sax.

0' 36"

Trumpet plays harmony notes beneath sax.

This statement of the B-section concludes with horns, piano, and bass uniting on two chords, punctuated by drums. These two chords (termed a "cadence point") will be heard during the solos and can be used by the listener as indications for the form. Sax trails off at the end of this section.

0' 39"

*A-section* (8 measures)

Trumpet plays the first phrase alone. Hancock's chords, higher in pitch and more sharply articulated than before, lend more tension to this second statement of the A-section.

0' 47"

Sax joins trumpet to play the second phrase of the melody, but an octave higher than before.

Hancock plays a sequence of chords slurred together, echoing the rhythm of the previous two-measure melody.

## FIRST CHORUS OF MILES DAVIS TRUMPET SOLO (A-B-A)

0' 54"

*A-section* (8 measures)

Davis opens with a slow, three-note climb that is mimicked by Hancock on piano. (This follows the dialog format used in the melody statements.) Then Davis comes down from the high register with a more involved figure, and is pursued by a piano figure imitating the last few notes in that phrase.

1' 08"

*B-section* (6 measures)

Piano accompanies Davis with a slowly ascending, step-wise string of notes.

1' 15"

A transition occurs between 1' 15" and 1' 20". This is the "cadence point" (interruption in the harmony that has been sustaining underneath the first four measures of the B-section). Williams underscores the change in harmony with his drumming before the group begins the last A-section.

1' 19"

*A-section* (8 measures)

Activity lessens temporarily.

Bass is neither walking, nor playing a single repeating figure. It is playing fragmented patterns of eighth notes that do not emphasize the first beat of each measure. This lends the music a suspended feeling.

## SECOND SOLO CHORUS FOR MILES DAVIS  (A-B-A)

1' 33"

*A-section* (8 measures)

Hancock alternates between a pair of chords and a contrasting rhythmic pattern.

Williams has begun a pattern of steady eighth notes played by drum sticks striking the ride cymbal.

1' 48"

*B-section* (6 measures)

Exploding sounds from drums; temporary departure from steady rhythms on ride cymbal. Energy has increased accordingly, and Hancock's two chords which conclude the B-section struggle to be heard through the busy texture. This lasts until about 2' 15".

1' 58"

*A-section* (8 measures)

Williams plays a slow roll on the tom-tom followed by the arrival of a high note on the trumpet.

## THIRD CHORUS OF MILES DAVIS SOLO  (A-B-A)

2' 12"

*A-section* (8 measures)

Activity softens, the mood calms, as though to prepare for another barrage. Williams returns to steady eighth notes on ride cymbal.

2' 27"

*B-section* (6 measures)

Davis glosses a single tone over and over before ending his phrase.
Tom-tom roll and high-register trumpet phrase begin a new adventure.

2' 37"

*A-section* (8 measures)

Piano plays a repeating chorded figure in a staccato manner, which starts on the down-beat of the measure ("bump. .bump-bump. . . . .bump. .bump-bump . . . "). This rhythm persists through the next A-section, blurring the ending of this chorus and the beginning of the next (to about 3' 05"). Cymbals become louder, crashing amidst the timekeeping rhythms. These alterations in piano and percussion patterns dramatically change the music's character.

## FOURTH CHORUS OF MILES DAVIS SOLO  (A-B)

2' 51"

*A-section* (8 measures)

Trumpet goes into the high register, squealing doit-like. Davis emphasizes the beats very prominently.

3' 06"

*B-section* (6 measures)

Carter is playing fragmented figures of eighth notes in the upper register of his bass, serving as a transition between the end of the trumpet solo and the beginning of the saxophone solo. Drums and cymbals get softer, evoking a mood of anticipation.

| | |
|---|---|
| *Elapsed Time* | **DISCREPANCY IN FOLLOWING THE COMPOSITION'S FORM:** |

The band drops the final *A-section*.

**3' 16"**   *A-section* (8 measures)

This section is shared by Davis fading out and Shorter entering during the fourth measure. The music conjures a mysterious mood.

**3' 20"**   ## WAYNE SHORTER SAXOPHONE SOLO

Shorter paraphrases the tune's melody, stretching each note until it is almost behind the beat.

Shorter begins with rhythms that do not swing in a particularly obvious manner. The rhythm section is propelling the piece, and Shorter's lines are oozing over it. Notice the remarkable continuity in the construction of Shorter's improvisation.

**3' 31"**   *B-section* (6 measures)

Carter is sliding pitches on his bass and playing eighth note figures interspersed by silences. He also repeats and extensively develops a single idea, interesting by itself, apart from its accompaniment value.

**3' 39"**   Just prior to the beginning of the last A-section Shorter plays a long, mournful, high note on his tenor sax. (Shorter has said that the ultimate skill is achieved when a player can make a listener cry by playing just one note.)

**3' 42"**   *A-section* (8 measures)

Carter is accompanying with a bass figure that is three beats long, setting up a pattern of accents that contrasts with the piece's underlying four-beat pulse. He continues this into the next chorus.

## SECOND CHORUS OF WAYNE SHORTER SAXOPHONE SOLO   (A-B-A)

**3' 56"**   *A-section* (8 measures)
**4' 03"**   Sax is playing syncopated tones starkly separated from each other.

**4' 10"**   *B-section* (6 measures)

Shorter pauses at the end of this section.

**4' 21"**   *A-section* (8 measures)

Shorter returns with a low-pitched sustained tone. His line then slowly climbs out of the low register, seeming to float past the beats instead of closely aligning with them.

## THIRD CHORUS OF WAYNE SHORTER SAXOPHONE SOLO   (A-B-A)

**4' 35"**   *A-section* (8 measures)

Shorter creates a long melodic line that slides outside the harmonies of the accompaniment. Drums and cymbals are momentarily silent.

**4' 49"**   *B-section* (6 measures)

Sax line climbs into the higher register, each note a half step higher in pitch. Carter accompanies with a pizzicato tremolo on bass.

**5' 00"**   *A-section* (8 measures)

| | |
|---|---|
| *Elapsed Time* | **FOURTH CHORUS OF WAYNE SHORTER SAXOPHONE SOLO**   (A-B-A+2-A) |
| 5' 15" | *A-section* (8 measures) |
| | Piano ceases for the entire chorus. Notice the tension evoked by its absence. |
| 5' 29" | *B-section* (6 measures) |
| | Drumming is highly active, louder and more dense. |
| 5' 40" | *A-section* (8 measures plus an extra 2 measures) |

Shorter creates a new, more animated mood, collaborating only with bass and drums, mostly tom-toms. He selects high pitched sax tones and seems to be having a musical conversation with drums. Shorter invents ascending phrases that logically build upon each other, each separated by silence, each higher in tension until he reaches the climax note. This peak occurs later than the eighth measure. So Hancock waits two extra measures before he returns to complement the resolution of the tension and restart repetitions of the composition's 8–6–8 measure form.

Departure From Composition's Form: An Extra A-Section

5' 56"   *A-section* (8 measures)

Piano resumes. Hancock plays the down beat for the first of every group of eight beats.

Once again Shorter uses his device of constructing phrases which build upon each other. This time the phrases descend, and excitement descends accordingly.

The sounds of drums and cymbals soften in anticipation of the upcoming piano solo.

## HERBIE HANCOCK PIANO SOLO

This solo has very few bop characteristics. It often sounds more like the impressionistic piano music of twentieth century composers Claude Debussy and Maurice Ravel.

DEPARTURE FROM COMPOSITION'S FORM:

The band plays no B-section here.

6'11"   *Extra A-Section* (8 measures)

DEPARTURE FROM COMPOSITION'S FORM:

The band plays an extra *A-section* (8 measures)

6' 25"   *A-section* (8 measures)

Cascades of legato notes in harmony making a waterfall-like sound. It is accompanied by a roll played by drum sticks on the high-hat cymbal and very little bass activity. This creates the illusion that timekeeping has been suspended. Notice how this has dramatically changed the character of the music.

6' 39"   *B-section* (6 measures)

Hancock sounds the same piano note again and again, then a new one again and again. Each one is higher pitched than the last, giving direction to the solo line.

Bass is echoing the melody.

6' 50"   *A-section* (8 measures)

*Elapsed Time*

**DEPARTURE FROM COMPOSITION'S FORM:**

7' 03"  EXTRA *A-Section* (8 measures)

## SECOND CHORUS OF HERBIE HANCOCK PIANO SOLO (A-B-A)

7' 17"  *A-section* (8 measures)

Harp-like piano tones ringing, separated by silences; accompanied by steady eighth notes on ride cymbal.

7' 31"  *B-section* (6 measures)

Bass is echoing the melody.

7' 42"  *Last A-Section* (8 measures)

Hancock plays chords on the piano in a staccato rhythmic way, re-establishing swing feeling and preparing for return of the horns. Bass repeats same note again and again (termed a "pedal tone").

## FINAL MELODY STATEMENT (A-B)

7' 56"  *A-section* (8 measures)

Trumpet and tenor sax return in harmony. They are answered by piano.

Second phrase is played in octaves by trumpet and tenor sax. Piano answers by playing notes in pairs (intervals of a fourth) ascending the keyboard.

8' 10"  *B-section* (6 measures)

Trumpet and saxophone exchange the phrases of the B-section, after which the saxophone trails off.

## ENDING (A-B)

8' 21"  *A-section* (8 measures)

No horns.

8' 35"  *B-section* (6 measures)

Piano, bass, and drums use the accompaniment for the *B-section* to tack on a conclusion. Piano chords are played percussively with clashing voicings.

Williams is scattering strokes around his drum set.

The piece concludes with a roll on the tom-tom with the piano sustaining the same chord that has been used to end previous *B-sections* (the "cadence chord").

Despite the highly logical stance in Shorter's music, the lines were very fresh and rarely predictable. That lack of predictability intensely attracted some listeners, though it lost others. This work could be viewed within the avant-garde category because Shorter was severely stretching the boundaries of what a jazz improviser could do without totally ignoring steady pulse and preset accompaniment harmonies. By this time, he had evolved even further away from the bop approach to melody. His lines were formed from notes of many different durations, not primarily eighth notes. And his rhythms were not necessarily those associated with jazz. In this phase of his career, he did not routinely build solos from standard bop rhythmic figures that swing in obvious ways and busily fill every moment. Some of his phrases did not swing. They intentionally floated over and past the beat instead of getting down inside it. Shorter played lines of smoother contours than those of most hard bop saxophonists. His work did not have as many abrupt starts and stops, or the bobbing up and down that typified bop. His melodic approach often recalled the concise, floating themes, interspersed with long silences, that we find in music by nonjazz composers such as Maurice Ravel, Claude Debussy, and Erik Satie.

Though some listeners think they detect the influence of Sonny Rollins or John Coltrane in Shorter's earliest playing on record (1959 and 60), the bulk of Shorter's style is most accurately viewed as original and not derivative. Any evidence of stylistic debts to the giants who preceded him has been so thoroughly transformed in his playing that to dwell upon it is unwarranted. In his recordings with Davis, Shorter's tone quality, articulation, rhythmic conception, and melodic tendencies all differ significantly from every major saxophonist who preceded him. His playing was as free of clichés as any saxophone style yet devised. Shorter had such extraordinarily high standards for originality that he usually managed to improvise solos that were free of patterns. He tried to create something entirely new upon each opportunity to improvise, and he usually succeeded.[26]

Shorter's tone quality and manner made his playing easily distinguishable from other saxophonists. Shorter had a gray tone with a broad-textured surface and soft edges. It was a hard sound, but he could temper that hardness according to the mood of the music. Until the 1970s, his tone rarely had vibrato. Though most saxophonists depend partly on vibrato as an expressive device, Shorter cultivated so many other expressive devices that listeners tended to not miss the vibrato. He made masterful use of various attacks and releases. He could slide up into the pitch of a note or strike it head on. He could release a note by carefully tapering it or by bending its pitch up or down. The note might trail off and disappear, or it might fall and then slide up to another. Though his technique was primarily legato, he sometimes gave out stark announcements consisting of brief tones.

Wayne Shorter brought an outstanding gift for melody to his solos. Listening to him improvise is like looking over the shoulder of a composer as he invents and

[26]He could handle hard, raw playing, and yet his ballad work was tender. Among his most inspired and well formed improvisations are those he contributed to the 1965 *E.S.P.* and the 1967 *Sorcerer* albums of Miles Davis. Listen to his solo on "Eighty-One" from *E.S.P.* Note the middle section which is so melodic that it could be taken out of context and used as a tune. Yet in spite of its very deliberate construction, it carries searing emotional impact. Listen to his improvisation on "Pee Wee" on Davis's *Sorcerer*. It is haunting in its other-worldly beauty. Listen to his solo on "Limbo," in *Sorcerer*, in which he manages a very unusual construction that hangs together with tuneful integrity despite extremely turbulent drumming all around it, and no piano accompaniment.

Shorter's saxophone style influenced a number of players who became prominent during the 1980s, including Jane Ira Bloom, Branford Marsalis, Donald Harrison, Bill Kirchner, Tim Ries, and Bob Belden. Shorter's influence has also been acknowledged by David Liebman and Michael Brecker, two saxophonists who began receiving wide acclaim during the 1970s.

develops themes. Not only did he invent theme after new theme, often using unusual intervals as he improvised, but he tried to make something significant out of each kernal of melody that he invented. Shorter was a very intelligent improviser who brought a strong sense of continuity to his lines. (Listen to his solo on "Masqualero" in the JAZZ CLASSICS CASSETTE.) Almost every one of Shorter's solo choruses was a coherent and concise melodic statement. Moreover, he played them in a manner which was somehow graceful and ferocious at the same time. Some listeners find a bittersweet quality in his music.

Beginning in 1969, Shorter's style on studio recordings became extremely sparse. He rarely again played as fluidly or lyrically as in his 1965–68 collaborations with Davis. This was also the time he began playing soprano saxophone. Both these changes are evident on two Davis albums, *In a Silent Way* and *Bitches Brew*, made at a time when Davis was moving into jazz-rock. Shorter continued to play both soprano and tenor saxophones with Weather Report, the jazz-rock fusion band he joined a year after leaving Davis. Shorter changed his style drastically when he joined Weather Report. Instead of long, melodic phrases, he often played short bursts of notes alternating with long silences and sustained tones. This new style meshed well with the sound of a group which depended upon unusual percussion sounds, conversational bass figures, and crackling keyboard ideas. Often Shorter let many beats pass without playing at all. Then, after playing only a note or two, he became silent again. His was a very difficult role. Instead of creating melodic improvisations, he participated in a collective effort to create undulating textures. The delicate balance achieved in the collective improvisations of Weather Report's early years is due in part to Wayne Shorter's tasteful and very disciplined sense of musical discretion. **He artfully made the difficult transition from jazz soloist in the conventional sense to ensemble improviser in the new context created by Weather Report.** (Listen to Shorter on "Surucucu" in the JAZZ CLASSICS CASSETTE, taken from a 1972 concert performance available in Weather Report's *I Sing the Body Electric*.)[27]

**Wayne Shorter was one of the key composers of the 1960s and 70s.** He wrote extensively for albums of his own and contributed substantially to the repertories of three historically significant groups: Art Blakey's Jazz Messengers (1959–64), the Miles Davis Quintet (1964–69), and Weather Report (1971–85). Though the details are beyond the nontechnical scope of this book, **Shorter's historical significance is partly determined by the unusual ways that he makes chords move within his compositions.** Some of his tunes place chords in sequences which had never been common to jazz. His compositions are the subject of much study by musicians and scholars, and Shorter is one of the most respected of all post-bop jazz composers. His tunes are performed and recorded by hundreds of other musicians. Many feel that his writing is even a more important contribution to jazz than his saxophone playing.

Shorter was notable for supplying Weather Report with a style for one branch of its repertory: pieces conveying a pastoral feeling achieved by dreamy melodies

---

[27]Also listen to his work on "Umbrellas" and "Seventh Arrow" on their first album *Weather Report*, CBS 306611, LP, 1971.

containing many silences and sustained tones, performed at a relatively slow tempo. They often resulted in a sense of suspension.[28] An historic aspect in the performance of some of these pieces is the **reversal of character traditionally assumed by jazz melody and accompaniment, respectively.**[29] The melodies here are floating and simple, whereas the accompaniments are hard driving and complex, as in the Davis quintet recording of Shorter's "Nefertiti."

Another aspect of Weather Report's music linked to the 1967 studio recording of "Nefertiti" is the **extensive repetition of melodic lines within a single rendition while continuous variation of accompaniment figures occurs.** This was not Shorter's idea; it stemmed from the manner in which the music was organized by Miles Davis and Tony Williams at the original "Nefertiti" recording session. However, Shorter's composition provided the impetus for this approach, and both Shorter and Weather Report's leader Joe Zawinul capitalized upon the approach in constructing pieces for the band.[30]

The facets described here only scratch the surface of Shorter's compositional contributions. For example, he also wrote a number of engaging themes that are waltzes. And he wrote pieces for Weather Report that possess a funky, dance-like sound.[31] To begin exploring the world of Shorter's music, keep in mind that Shorter's work for Miles Davis and Weather Report is easy to find because it is on Columbia records that were sufficiently popular to stay in print. However, do not let the convenience of this Columbia documentation allow you to overlook the richness contained in the many albums he made as bandleader for Blue Note records[32] and those made with Art Blakey for Blue Note, Riverside, and other companies. Many of the compositions that have attracted the attention of musicians and scholars lie in the Blue Note material.

[28]Listen to "Three Clowns" on Weather Report's *Black Market* album (CBS 34099, LP, 1976) and "Harlequin" on their *Heavy Weather* album (CBS 34418, CD/LP, 1977).

[29]Such melodies as "Manolete" and "Non-Stop Home" on Weather Report's *Sweetnighter* album (CBS 32210, LP, 1977) possess clarity and simplicity, whereas the accompaniment is turbulent. (You might recall that, at least as early as the bop era, horn lines had traditionally been more complex than their accompaniments.) This practice continued the manner in which the Miles Davis Quintet had performed Shorter's "Nefertiti" on the 1967 Davis album called *Nefertiti*. The serene, floating quality of "Nefertiti" had also been present in co-leader Joe Zawinul's writing. This was evident at least as early as the 1969 Miles Davis recording of Zawinul's "In a Silent Way" and the 1970 Zawinul recording of "Dr. Honoris Causa" (Zawinul—*Zawinul*, Atlantic 1579, CD/LP, 1970). Zawinul had been attracted by the flavor of the Miles Davis "Nefertiti" performance, and Shorter and Zawinul extended this compositional flavor when they teamed up to co-lead Weather Report.

[30]Listen to "Boogie Woogie Waltz," "Manolete," and "Non-Stop Home" on Weather Report's *Sweetnighter* album.

[31]Listen to "Port of Entry" on Weather Report's *Night Passage* album (CBS 36793, CD/LP, 1980) and "Mysterious Traveler" on their *Mysterious Traveler* album (CBS 32494, CD/LP, 1974).

[32]Wayne Shorter—*Night Dreamer*, Blue Note 84173, CD/LP, 1964; *Speak No Evil*, Blue Note 46509 (84194), CD/LP, 1964. Sheet music for Shorter compositions is in *The World's Greatest Fakebook* (Sher, 1983), *The New Real Book* (Sher, 1988), and *Wayne Shorter Jazz Classics* (Jamey Aebersold, 1985), all available from Aebersold, 1211 Aebersold Drive, New Albany, IN 47150.

## CHAPTER SUMMARY

1) Miles Davis is an innovative trumpeter and bandleader.

2) He hired key innovators of the day at three different phases of jazz history and led them to outstanding recordings that remain landmarks to those styles—cool jazz, modal jazz, and jazz-rock fusion.

3) The Davis trumpet style is unmistakable for its tone quality, expressive variations in pitch and judicious timing of phrases. He is not afraid to play simply, and some of his most dramatic solos are constructed of very few notes.

4) Davis displayed a concern for smooth sound texture that was evident in his trumpet sound as well as his attraction to Claude Thornhill's band sound, and a particular interest in meshing with the chord voicings of his accompanists.

5) With the help of pianist Bill Evans on the *Kind of Blue* album, Davis popularized mode-based formats in modern jazz.

6) With arranger Gil Evans, Davis recorded three famous albums of third stream music: *Miles Ahead, Sketches of Spain*, and *Porgy and Bess*.

7) Tenor saxophonist Wayne Shorter contributed a fresh solo style to jazz.

8) Shorter's solos and compositions significantly affected the character of the Art Blakey band, the Miles Davis group, and Weather Report.

9) Shorter was influential in his compositional use of a) the interval of a fourth, b) sustained tones and silences in melody lines, c) melodic construction that suggests a dreamy, floating quality, and d) chord sequences previously unusual in jazz.

10) The Davis rhythm section of 1964–68 had pianist Herbie Hancock, bassist Ron Carter, and drummer Tony Williams.

11) The Hancock-Carter-Williams unit was among the most skilled, gifted, and explorative rhythm sections in jazz history.

*NOTE:* For more about Miles Davis, his groups, and sidemen, see the two-volume biography by Jack Chambers, *Milestones 1* (Beech Tree, 1983) and *Milestones 2* (Beech Tree, 1985), Ian Carr's *Miles Davis: A Biography* (William Morrow, 1982), and *Miles, The Autobiography* (Simon & Schuster, 1989).

**MILES DAVIS RECORDS**

Most of the Miles Davis career is documented by just two record companies: Prestige and Columbia. To help you obtain the music discussed in this chapter, the Miles Davis recordings made for Columbia that were cited in this chapter, the Bill Evans chapter, the John Coltrane chapter, and the jazz-rock fusion chapter are listed here in chronological order. For each entry, the current catalog number is listed first, and the original catalog number appears in parentheses. Other catalog numbers that have been assigned to these records over the years can be found in previous editions of *Jazz Styles* and its *Teachers Manual & Discography*. Cited albums made for Prestige whose catalog numbers are not footnoted in this chapter can be found in the teachers manual along with alternate catalog numbers.

*Round About Midnight*, CBS 40610 (CL 949), CD/LP, 1955–56
*Basic Miles*, CBS 32025, LP, 1955–58
*Miles Ahead*, CBS 40784 (CL 1041), CD/LP, 1957 with Gil Evans
*Milestones*, CBS 40837 (CL 1193), CD/LP, 1958
*Porgy & Bess*, CBS 40647 (CL 1274/CS 8085), CD/LP, 1958 with Gil Evans
*Jazz at the Plaza*, CBS 32470, LP, 1958
*Kind of Blue*, CBS 40579 (CL 1355/CS 8163), CD/LP, 1959
*Sketches of Spain*, CBS 40578 (CL 1480), CD/LP, 1959–60 with Gil Evans
*Someday My Prince Will Come*, CBS 40947 (CL 1656), CD/LP, 1961
*Friday Night at the Blackhawk*, CBS 44257 (CL 1669), CD/LP, 1961
*Saturday Night at the Blackhawk*, CBS 44425 (CL 1670), CD/LP, 1961
*Miles Davis at Carnegie Hall*, CBS 8612 (CL 1812), LP, 1961
*Seven Steps to Heaven*, CBS 8851 (CL 2051), LP, 1963
*Miles Davis in Europe*, CBS 8983 (CL 2183), LP, 1963
*My Funny Valentine*, CBS 9106 (CL 2306), LP, 1964
*"Four" and More*, CBS 9253 (CL 2453), LP 1964
*Heard Round the World*, CBS C2 38506, LP set, 1964
*E.S.P.*, CBS 9150 (CL 2350), LP, 1965
*Live at the Plugged Nickel*, CBS C2 38266, LP set, 1965
*Miles Smiles*, CBS 9401 (CL 2601), LP, 1966
*Sorcerer*, CBS 9532 (CL 2732), LP, 1967
*Nefertiti*, CBS 46113 (CS 9594), CD/LP, 1967
*Miles in the Sky*, CBS 9628, LP, 1968
*Filles de Kilimanjaro*, CBS 46116 (CS 9750), CD/LP, 1968
*In a Silent Way*, CBS 40580 (CS 9875), CD/LP, 1969
*Bitches Brew*, CBS 40577 (GP 26), CD/LP set, 1969
*Big Fun*, CBS 32866, LP set, 1969–72
*Live-Evil*, CBS 30954, LP set, 1970
*Miles Davis Live at the Fillmore*, CBS 30038, LP set, 1970
*Black Beauty*, CBS/Sony SOPJ 39–40 (Japan), 1970
*A Tribute to Jack Johnson*, CBS 30455, LP, 1970
*Get Up With It*, CBS 33236, LP set, 1970–74
*On the Corner*, CBS 31906, LP, 1972
*Miles Davis in Concert*, CBS 32092, 1972
*Agharta*, CBS 33967, 1975

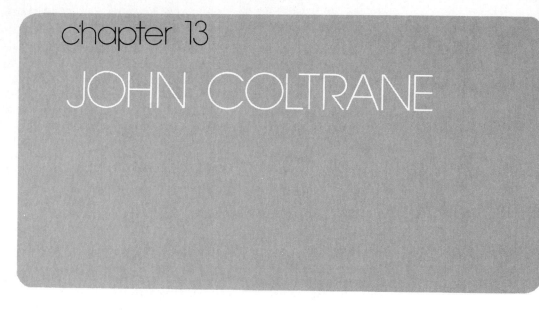

# chapter 13

# JOHN COLTRANE

John Coltrane is among the ten most important figures in jazz history. He has had profound impact as a tenor and soprano saxophonist, composer, and bandleader. Hundreds of Coltrane imitators could be found among saxophonists of the 1960s, 70s and 80s. His improvisational concepts and compositions were used not only by saxophonists but also by pianists, trumpeters, and guitarists. The combo sound that his quartet perfected was not only a major force during the few years the quartet toured, but has remained an influential model ever since the group disbanded. The immense force of Coltrane's music has inspired poetry, sculpture, and modern dance. Even a church was founded in Coltrane's name.

**COLTRANE'S PRE-1960 STYLES**  Though relatively unknown during the 1940s and early 50s, Coltrane performed in those years with a muscular style that drew upon the models of Lester Young, Dexter Gordon, and Sonny Stitt.[1] He could also be heard milking high notes in a very emotional way. This style of wailing into the high register, the "cry," became a Coltrane signature in the 1960s. Musicians who remember hearing him play during the 1940s comment that his style was already distinctive even then, and that it had

[1]Listen to Coltrane's solo on "We Love To Boogie" in Dizzy Gillespie's 1951 album *Dee Gee Days*, Savoy 10517 CD or ZDS 4426 (2209 LP), and compare it to Lester Young's solo on Count Basie's 1939 recording of "Pound Cake" (*The Essential Count Basie, Vol. 1*, CBS 40608, CD/LP) and Young's own 1945 recording of "D.B. Blues" on *Aladdin Sessions*, Blue Note 456 (Aladdin 801). Then compare the "We Love To Boogie" solo with Dexter Gordon's work from 1947 in Gordon's album *Long Tall Dexter*, Savoy 2211. To hear the similarities with Stitt, compare Coltrane's work on Miles Davis's recording of "Oleo" (*Relaxin'*, Fantasy/OJC-190 (Prestige 7129), CD/LP, 1956) with Stitt's work in "Eternal Triangle" on Dizzy Gillespie's *Sonny Side Up*, Verve 825674 (MGV 8262), CD, 1957. For more about Coltrane's career, see *Chasin' the Trane* by J. C. Thomas (Doubleday, 1975; reprinted by DaCapo) and *Coltrane: A Biography* by C. O. Simpkins (Herndon House, 1975).

an extraordinary urgency. On the few recordings in which he made brief appearances as a sideman between 1951 and 1954, his playing reveals a very serious, highly intense craftsman.

Coltrane had developed a very individual style by 1955, when he first recorded with Miles Davis and started becoming known to a larger audience. By then, his roots were far less evident than his own fresh ideas.[2] His approach was unusually vigorous. His tone was rough-textured and biting, huge and dark. Coltrane gave it a massive core and a searing intensity. It was full and penetrating in every register, from the lowest notes to the highest. He played with remarkable speed and agility, possibly as much as any other saxophonist in jazz history. His mastery of multiphonics also expanded the repertory of techniques to which other saxophonists aspired.[3] Coltrane's impressive command over the tenor saxophone inspired hundreds of other saxophonists to strive for exceedingly high levels of instrumental proficiency. Like Charlie Parker before him, Coltrane caused young players to cultivate a taste for rapid, densely-packed solo improvisations.

Coltrane's playing was not captured on record very often before he joined Miles Davis. Yet his leading contemporary, tenor saxophonist Sonny Rollins, had already made a mark in the world of jazz tenor with numerous recordings. By the time Coltrane began to record more and gain recognition of his own, Rollins was already a prominent figure, even though he was four years younger than Coltrane. This may partly explain the widespread misunderstanding that Rollins came first, and explain why when Coltrane became prominent—using a style drawn in part from the same sources Rollins used—some listeners thought Coltrane was influenced by Rollins. However, the two styles can be distinguished in several respects. Coltrane employed a tone that was larger, coarser, darker, and weightier than Rollins's. By comparison with Rollins, Coltrane played with a more searing quality, improvised in less of a stop-and-go manner, and made less use of silence. Coltrane also drew much less from Charlie Parker's style.[4] Also, Coltrane projected a less light-hearted and playful feeling than Rollins, he was less tuneful in his improvisations, and he used staccato less often than Rollins.

Coltrane's pre-1960s playing showed an infatuation with chord changes. He loved to add chords to a tune's existing chord progression. For instance, Coltrane took "Tune-Up," Eddie Vinson's sixteen-measure composition, almost doubled the

[2]Listen to the Miles Davis recording *The New Miles Davis Quintet*, OJC-006 (Prestige 7014), 1955, then *Steamin'*, Prestige 7580 (7200), *Cookin'*, OJC-128 (Prestige 7094), *Workin'*, OJC-296 (Prestige 7166) and *Relaxin'*, OJC-190 (Prestige 7129), 1956.

[3]Wind instruments such as saxophone and clarinet can be coaxed to produce two or more sounds at the same time. Some of these multiphonics, to give them their technical name, sound like chords. In his "Harmonique," on the 1959 album *Coltrane Jazz*, Atlantic 1354, Coltrane used the method to harmonize a melody note. During the mid-1960s, he frequently used multiphonics for controlled screeches that helped create peaks of musical excitement. An isolated example is his solo on the 1961 "Chasin' The Trane" in his *Live At The Village Vanguard*, MCA 39136 (Impulse 10), and there are many instances within his albums *Meditations*, MCA 29022 (Impulse 9110); *Expression*, MCA 29023 (Impulse 9120); and *Live In Seattle*, MCA 2-4134 (Impulse 9202).

[4]To hear the Parker roots in the Rollins style, listen to Parker play tenor sax on "Half Nelson," a 1947 recording, *Bird: Savoy Original Master Takes*, Savoy 8801 CD (2201 LP).

original number of chords in it, added a somewhat different melody, and called it "Countdown."[5] What is most significant here is not just that he added chords to an existing progression—others had often done this before—but the challenging manner in which he chose new chords and the way he improvised solos over them. Then, when he improvised solos, Coltrane devoured the chord changes, trying to acknowledge every note in every chord and every scale that might be compatible with it. This was a historically significant contribution to the evolution of jazz styles. Journalist Ira Gitler described Coltrane's furiously paced streams of notes as "sheets of sound."

A peak for Coltrane's infatuation with frequently changing chords and rapid playing was the title track on his *Giant Steps* album, recorded in 1959. As in "Countdown," the chords seldom last more than two fleeting beats, and each chord stakes out new territory. Coltrane originally wrote "Giant Steps" as an exercise to gain mastery over improvising through chord progressions in which few notes are held in common from one chord to another. In other words, the chords move so frequently that the improviser is given almost no chance to develop an idea on a given chord or to take an idea and stretch it across common tones of successive chords. In "Giant Steps," the chords change at the same pace as the melody notes. Its quick tempo and unusual construction place exceptional demands on the improviser. The piece met Coltrane's practice needs, and eventually it became a popular test piece for improvisers. It entered the ranks of other pieces possessing difficult chord changes, such as "All the Things You Are" and "Con Alma."

Many listeners are familiar only with the hard-driving style that Coltrane preferred when improvising on medium-tempo and up-tempo pieces. However, Coltrane was also one of jazz history's most outstanding players of slow, pretty melodies. When playing such pieces, Coltrane seemed to harness most of the energy he customarily released in his dense, multinoted passages and channel it into a few deep, full-bodied tones that seemed to glow. He blew through and past long tones and flawlessly slid from one interval to another, treating each with solemn respect. Like his early idol, alto saxophonist Johnny Hodges, he played ballads by maintaining an unusual depth and fullness of tone and an exquisite sense of timing for ornaments. For instance, Coltrane's frequent use of scale-wise lead-ins to dramatically-timed high notes might be likened to the long, drawn-out smears that marked the Hodges approach. Some musicians feel that by listening to Hodges, Coltrane

[5]"Countdown" is on Coltrane's *Giant Steps*, Atlantic 1311, CD/LP, 1959. The written music for the piece is available, with a recording of rhythm section accompaniment, as Volume 28 of Jamey Aebersold's *A New Approach to Jazz Improvisation*, available from Jamey Aebersold, 1211 Aebersold Drive, New Albany IN 47150. In his *Creative Jazz Improvisation* (Prentice-Hall, 1989), Scott Reeves discusses Coltrane's chord progression style along with a transcription of the solo on "Giant Steps," also available from Aebersold. More transcribed solos and analyses of this Coltrane period appear in Stuart Isacoff's *Solos for Jazz Tenor Saxophone* (Carl Fischer, 1985; available by mail from Carl Fischer Music Store, 62 Cooper Square, NY, NY 10003).

learned how to make the saxophone sing. (This aspect is demonstrated by Coltrane's solo in "Flamenco Sketches" on the JAZZ CLASSICS CASSETTE.)[6]

Coltrane popularized a number of different compositional devices in modern jazz. The pedal point is one of the best known. For example, on the *Giant Steps* album, his composition "Naima" has a single note, the *pedal point*, repeating continuously underneath the melody for the first eight measures. Then a new pedal point accompanies the second eight measures. This device achieves an effect like that of a drone sustained despite shifts in the tune's harmony. The effect on the listener is to build suspense, because the listener expects a chord to change, a progression to resolve. Repeated bass notes in the pattern of pedal points came to be strongly identified with Coltrane's sound, especially during the 1960s. They were commonly part of the accompaniment to improvisations in pieces with Spanish and Indian flavor, a character that came to be called "modal."

**NON-BOP FORMATS**    Though Coltrane never improvised pieces without planning the harmonies to be used, he did explore approaches which depended less on the preset movement of harmonies than bop did. These approaches can be grouped in two ways. Neither of these ways provides a truly accurate description of what is going on, but both ways acquired labels that found a permanent place in the vocabulary of musicians and jazz journalists. One is "free." The other is "modal."

**Free Jazz**    Coltrane was interested in the music of Ornette Coleman, the most prominent figure in the "free jazz" approach which evolved away from adhering to preset progressions of chords and sometimes also dispensed with distinctions between soloist and accompanist. (See next chapter.) In 1960, Coltrane recorded an album called *The Avant-Garde* with Coleman's group, minus Coleman. On the album, he performed three Coleman compositions. In 1965, Coltrane recorded an album called *Ascension*, in which he used an approach like Coleman's approach to the 1960 album *Free Jazz* (excerpted in SCCJ). *Ascension* employed collective improvisation with high-energy, high-density playing that departed from bop conventions of jazz phrasing and rhythmic feeling. As in *Free Jazz*, *Ascension* contained moments in which all the musicians improvised different lines at the same time. Coltrane took a cue from fellow saxophonist Albert Ayler and began improvising turbulent streams of notes, interspersed with saxophone sounds that resembled

---

[6]Almost every album that Coltrane made for the Prestige record company contains at least one ballad. The 1956 album *Mating Call*, OJC-212 (Prestige 7070), under Tadd Dameron's leadership, has several lush ballads. Coltrane's *Soultrane*, OJC-021 (Prestige 7142), CD/LP, features "Theme for Ernie" and "I Want To Talk About You." Slow tunes were the format for some of Coltrane's best compositions, too. Listen to "Naima" from *Giant Steps;* "After the Rain" from *Impressions*, MCA/Impulse 5887 (A-42), CD/LP; "Wise One" and "Lonnie's Lament" from *Crescent*, MCA/Impulse 5889 (A-66), CD/LP; "Dear Lord" from *Transition* MCA 29027 (Impulse 9195); and "Ogunde" from *Expression*, MCA 29023 (Impulse 9120). SCCJ has his "Alabama."

jangling cries and screams. (Ayler is discussed in the next chapter.)[7] This approach capitalized on the high register of the saxophone and mined the instrument's capacity for shrill, rasping sounds that often contained many different tones at once. These sequences of notes did not possess the melodic contours of conventional jazz improvisations, nor did they evoke the easy rise and fall of tension and the swing feeling of earlier styles. Instead they focused on the development of mood and texture, replacing the earlier priorities of tunefulness and swing feeling.[8]

Improvisation on *Ascension* was neither totally collective nor totally free of prearrangement, nor was it atonal (for explanation of scales, tone center, and atonality, see pages 365–369). Careful listening will reveal a few changes of chord (or tone center) because Coltrane preset four scales for the musicians to use. The changes do not occur often, but they do occur; so it is not totally free of form. Brief, loosely stated ensemble passages separate the solos, which in turn receive rhythm section accompaniment, as is traditional in conventional jazz. Collectively improvised sections are balanced in duration and texture. Coltrane used four other saxophonists, two trumpeters, and rhythm section. He preset the order for the solos so that no two similar instruments played back to back. This allowed a trumpet solo to follow a sax solo, for instance, rather than following another trumpet solo. Coltrane's use of preset scales and the separation of soloist and accompanist roles contradicts the "free jazz" label that frequently has been applied to this music.

During the 1960s and 70s, a number of other modern jazz musicians tried collective improvisation, with high-energy, high-density playing that contained no bop phrasing or swing feeling. Similar styles appeared sporadically during the 1970s and 1980s, for which some of the impetus could be attributed to Coltrane, because he was the most prominent bandleader to engage in this style. Note, however, that Coltrane recorded large-ensemble collective improvisation only once, otherwise limiting his use of this technique to quartet and quintet formats.

**Modal**  The mode-based pieces and long improvisations of John Coltrane and his 1965–67 associate, tenor saxophonist Pharoah Sanders, had a profound impact on the history of modern jazz. This format signaled a striking departure in the evolution of Coltrane's style because such a harmonic basis for improvisation is as undemanding as the chord progression for "Giant Steps" is demanding. During the late 1950s, Miles Davis recorded mode-based pieces that proved to be highly influential.[9] However, the pieces by Coltrane and his disciples were even more influential. But before we discuss the details of these famous recordings, let's examine some tricky terminology.[10] A mode is a scale containing a predetermined selection of notes.

[7]Compare Coltrane's playing in the beginning of his solo on "Expression" from his album of the same name, or on the middle of "Mars" on *Interstellar Space*, MCA-29029 (Impulse 9277), with Ayler's playing in the middle of "Ghosts" from his *Spiritual Unity*, ESP-DISK 1002.

[8]For other examples of this approach, listen to *Meditations*, MCA 29022 (Impulse 9110) and *Live In Seattle*, MCA2-4134 (Impulse 9202).

[9]"Milestones," CBS 40837 (Columbia CL 1193/CS 9428) and "So What," from *Kind of Blue*, CBS 40579 (CS 8163), also in SCCJ

[10]If you are not familiar with the concepts of scale, mode, chord progression, or song form, you may find it helpful to study pages 365–72 before going further in this chapter. Technically-inclined readers may also wish to examine pages 418–23.

Because his music was only loosely based on certain modes, Coltrane's 1960s playing was not always modal in the strictest sense of the word; only in the loose sense used by jazz musicians and journalists. In his "modal" work, Coltrane adhered to the overall harmonic orientation of certain modes, but he also employed notes outside the mode. Moreover, because much of Coltrane's and Sanders's work is simply based on repeating patterns of only two chords, it may be an unnecessary complication to use the word "modal" to describe their music. Instead, we could merely specify the two chords.

One of Coltrane's most famous "modal" performances can be heard on his 1960 album *My Favorite Things*.[11] The title track is based on a well-known melody from Rodgers and Hammerstein's Broadway show "The Sound of Music." This proved to be one of Coltrane's best-selling recordings, undoubtedly due in part to the great familiarity of the tune. The performance's popularity stems also from several musical components which collectively make it easy to listen to: the minor key, the simplicity in the accompaniment harmonies, waltz meter; and the extensive repetition of short patterns (these final two components lend a hypnotic, swaying feeling). As a result of the attraction musicians had to this particular record, the soothing, meditative mood of this performance was evoked by much jazz made by other groups during this period.

The strategies used to construct Coltrane's performance of "My Favorite Things" are important to understand because they became a model format. Pianist McCoy Tyner uses the tune's chord progression as a guide for accompanying Coltrane's rendition of the melody. However, the improvisations are accompanied by a two-chord repeated pattern of indefinite length in the key of E minor, later shifted to the key of E major. For constructing his soprano saxophone improvisation, Coltrane draws liberally from a single scale that is compatible with Tyner's accompaniment.[12] Such a basis for improvisation signalled a striking departure in Coltrane's style because it is so simple by comparison with the complexity of the chord progression for "Giant Steps." This new approach became very popular with improvising musicians. In fact, between the late 1960s and mid-1970s, very few prominent modern jazz combos played much else. But despite the prominence of Coltrane's "modal" style and his "free jazz," his 1960s output continued to contain popular songs and twelve-bar blues pieces.[13]

For a brief period during the early 1960s, much of Coltrane's work was less dense and intricate than it had been. Some of his work was quite simple and obvious in its

[11]Atlantic 1361, CD/LP, 1960

[12]Coltrane recorded several other improvisations that were based mostly on long stretches of repeating, two-chord patterns. In 1961, he recorded "Olé" on *Olé Coltrane*, Atlantic 1373, CD/LP, and "Impressions" on *Impressions*, MCA/Impulse 5887 (A-42), CD/LP. In 1962, he recorded *Coltrane*, MCA/Impulse 5883 (A-21), CD/LP, including "Tungi," "Miles Mode," and "Out of This World," all of which featured long passages of improvisation based on a single mode or a two-chord repeating figure.

[13]For example, in 1960, he recorded an entire album of blues tunes: *Coltrane Plays The Blues*, Atlantic 1382. In 1964, he recorded *Crescent*, MCA/Impulse 5889 (A-66), including "Bessie's Blues," and he recorded *A Love Supreme*, MCA/Impulse 5660 (A-77), CD/LP, with another twelve-bar blues titled "Pursuance." In concert performances, he frequently included standard tunes such as "Bye, Bye, Blackbird" and "Inchworm."

development. He had taken a cue from the style of fellow tenor saxophonist John Gilmore, who sometimes developed solos by repeating the same rhythm with different pitches, changing the notes without changing the rhythm, sometimes placing the same rhythm at different spots in the measure, occasionally inverting a phrase, as though peering at it from several different angles and sharing each view with the listener.[14] Coltrane also developed his solo improvisations in the logical manner he had learned from a famous book of practice patterns and compositional devices by Nicolas Slonimsky that demonstrates how to vary note choices in an enormous number of ways and still remain related to a fundamental chord or scale.[15] The effect of taking seriously Gilmore and Slonimsky was to slow down and clarify his improvisations.

Very soon Coltrane was back to producing high-density improvisations with very convoluted lines. But this time the twisting and turning did not reflect complex chord progressions as in his late-1950s "sheets of sound" period. Instead, these new patterns only *sounded* as complex. They were a speeded-up variant of the Gilmore and Slonimsky methods, and they were set atop relatively unchanging accompaniment harmonies. And, significantly for jazz history, those patterns and formulas that Coltrane refined became common vocabulary for an entire generation of improvisers. During the 1980s, more than twenty years after he introduced them, these patterns were still considered fundamental building blocks for jazz improvisations, not just among saxophonists, but also among trumpeters, guitarists, and pianists.

**THE CLASSIC QUARTET** Coltrane was a member of the Miles Davis groups on and off for almost six years, having made his earliest Davis recording in 1955, his last in 1961. During this period, Coltrane also recorded with a few other leaders. Though he also recorded under his own name, he did not lead a group of his own with a consistent personnel and a sound that was uniquely identifiable until 1960 when he was no longer touring with Davis. After several different combinations of musicians, he finally settled with pianist McCoy Tyner, bassist Steve Davis, and drummer Elvin Jones. He used a number of different bassists during the 1960s, but after Steve Davis had played with him on several albums in 1960 and 1961, Coltrane used Jimmy Garrison the most. Garrison was with Coltrane on most of the remaining recordings, and he stayed with the saxophonist even after Tyner left in 1965 and Jones left in 1966.

[14]The technically-inclined reader may wish to examine the mutual use of isorhythms that is demonstrated by Gilmore on his solo in "Jet Flight" (the Sun Ra album *The Futuristic Sounds of Sun Ra*, Savoy MG 12169, reissued as *We Are in the Future*, Savoy SJL 1141) and by Coltrane in the middle of his solo on "Impressions" (the November 5, 1961 recording in *Impressions*).

[15]The formula for Coltrane's and Gilmore's above-cited solos may be roughly likened to alternating word order and loudnesses in repetitions of a brief sentence ("Let's go get the truck.") in this way: "Let's go get truck the." "Let's go get THE truck." "Let's go GET the truck." "Let's go get truck THE." Then, perhaps changing to "Let's go get the CAR." "The CAR get." "Get the CAR." And so forth. If this analogy does not make sense to you, listen again to the musical passages cited in footnote 14, and note the ways both saxophonists develop solos by systematically reworking very brief, three to five note, melodic fragments.

*Left to right:* McCoy Tyner (piano), John Coltrane (tenor sax), Jimmy Garrison (bass), Elvin Jones (drums), 1962. (*Photo courtesy of Duncan Schiedt*)

**The Coltrane quartet was one of the most important groups in jazz history, and some historians consider it to have been the most influential of all jazz combos.** (Listen to them play "The Promise" on the JAZZ CLASSICS CASSETTE.)[16]

**Elvin Jones** As far as some listeners are concerned, Elvin Jones (b. 1927) has proven himself to be the most overwhelming drummer in jazz history. He has established a position on the drums that equals the power and innovation established by Charlie Parker and John Coltrane on the saxophone. Like Parker and Coltrane, Jones is a remarkably consistent performer. He seems to play every tune as though it is his last chance. An almost superhuman energy and endurance is associated with him. And his imagination seems to match his energy.

Jones avoids the relative simplicity and repetition of most pre-1960 drummers. He rarely plays the obvious. In fact, in his most adventuresome work, he even avoids directly stating the first beat of each measure. His conception of the beat is a wider unit in time than had been usual with previous drummers. His timekeeping is steady, but loose, filled with rhythmic subtleties. He roams through his drums and cymbals, distributing portions of triplets. He phrases in three's instead of two's and

[16]Its effect was particularly notable in records by Pharoah Sanders, the Bobby Hutcherson-Harold Land groups, and those of David Liebman, McCoy Tyner, Charles Lloyd (1966–69), John Handy (mid-1960s only), and Gato Barbieri.

·four's. He often begins his triplex division of time at the middle or end of a beat, and continues to juxtapose a staggered waltz feeling across the duration of several measures (for explanation of triplets and waltz meter, see pages 358–362). During all that time he would still be maintaining a basic meter of four and swinging infectiously.

With Coltrane's group, Jones was able to play many rhythms at once and have the entire sound swell and heave like an ocean of activity under Coltrane's playing. (This is particularly evident in his work on "The Promise" in the JAZZ CLASSICS CASSETTE.) Elvin Jones was one of the first drummers to play polyrhythmically and still swing hard in a loose, flowing way (for definition and explanation of polyrhythm, see page 364). Earlier drummers who attempted to use polyrhythms had sounded stiff and self-consciously calculating.

While listening to Elvin Jones, you might get the impression that he is juggling. Things seem forever in the air, never sharply defined in exact, predictable proportions. But the different rhythms played simultaneously were not just randomly different. They were constructed to complement each other. And, in a broad sense, they fit together. It might not be obvious unless you listen carefully to four- and eight-measure sequences in their entirety. Some of his figures purposely omit a stroke or two but let you feel the missing stroke in the overall pattern. He distributes the parts of his triplets so that perhaps the first third is silent and next two are sounded on snare drum. Or perhaps the middle member is omitted. Sometimes the first two members of a triplet will sound on the snare drum and the third on the high hat or the bass drum. It might be because of his complexity and lack of predictability that few drummers ever managed to sound like him.

Jones wove his parts around those of his bandmates in as important a way as any front-line hornman at a Dixieland jam session.[17] The whole character of the Coltrane quartet reflected the highly interactive style of Elvin Jones. Jones played with the surging power and imagination of two or three drummers combined, and his force was absorbed quite musically into the quartet concept. In fact, the style of Elvin Jones was possibly the most indispensable part of that ensemble concept.

After leaving Coltrane, Jones formed a sequence of high-quality groups which, during the late 1960s and throughout the 1970s, offered some of the rare jazz neither significantly influenced by rock or electric instruments nor predominantly modal in orientation. He usually employed two tenor saxophonists and a bassist, but no piano. He employed some of the best saxophonists playing at that time, and most of his tenor men were influenced by Coltrane.[18] The music in some of his groups almost achieved the solemn urgency that had been created by the Coltrane quartet.

**McCoy Tyner**     Coltrane's pianist from 1960 to the end of 1965 was McCoy Tyner (b. 1938). Creating an original approach from the linear style of Bud Powell, the block chording of Red Garland, and the voicings of Bill Evans and Horace Silver, he achieved a fresh approach to jazz piano. He already had been a distinctive and

[17]Listen to Elvin Jones in Coltrane's "Sun Ship" (*Sun Ship*) and "My Lady" (*Live at Birdland*, MCA/Impulse 33109, CD/LP, 1963).

[18]Joe Farrell, George Coleman, Frank Foster, Steve Grossman, David Liebman, and others.

aggressive stylist in the Art Farmer-Benny Golson Jazztet, but then he went on to carve a very personal style for himself within the Coltrane quartet. His was one of the most easily recognizable styles in all of jazz. He was a prime force in jazz piano styles of the 1960s and 70s. He was almost as influential as Evans and at least as influential as Herbie Hancock. Tyner's extensive use of chords voiced in fourths was widely adopted (see Figure 13.1). His extremely percussive, ringing style of comping became a model for pianists of the late 1960s and the 1970s, especially those pianists playing in Coltrane-inspired groups. His fast solo lines also inspired numerous pianists, though few could match his imagination. The five-note (pentatonic) patterns he perfected as basis for his lines soon became stock solo vocabulary for numerous pianists (see Table 13.1). His originality and influence was so extensive that he even affected pianists who already had well-established styles of their own.

McCoy Tyner's playing furnished a center for the Coltrane quartet sound. It was as though he established a pivot for the seesawing of sounds that were being generated around him in the quartet. His stability in this capacity was partly due to his frequent use of a loud, held note (technically called a pedal point) or a loud, held interval (usually a fifth) played with extreme force by his left hand while his right hand sounded chords that had a bell-like ring with very open quality derived from using intervals of a fourth. (See Figure 13.1, and try it out for yourself on the piano. If you strike the keys with tremendous force, you might approximate the sound of McCoy Tyner.) These clear, open-voiced chords represented more stability than was occurring in the saxophone and drum sounds surrounding them. In most groups of this period, the bass part was the simplest and steadiest. But in the Coltrane quartet, Tyner's piano part vied with the bass part in its steadiness. (See pages 417–418 for a technical explanation of these harmonies, and listen to Tyner play them on "The Promise" in the JAZZ CLASSICS CASSETTE.)

**Jimmy Garrison**    Jimmy Garrison (1934–1976) was an imaginative bass player who held his own within the fiercely active Coltrane quartet. He had a large, deep, rough tone quality and remarkable stamina. McCoy Tyner praised his timekeeping skill. In addition to walking, Garrison invented rhythms which countered and complemented those of Tyner and Jones. Of all the bassists Coltrane used, even those with more speed and polish than Garrison, Garrison seemed the perfect match because he intuitively understood the unorthodox directions that Coltrane and Jones were taking.

**Figure 13.1**  Piano keyboard illustration of fifths in left hand and fourths in right hand.

Left hand
(5th)

Right hand
(4ths)

**TABLE 13.1. A Few of the Many Pianists Influenced by McCoy Tyner**

| | |
|---|---|
| Chick Corea | Ronnie Mathews |
| Alice McLeod Coltrane | Stanley Cowell |
| Kenny Gill | Hilton Ruiz |
| Bobo Stinson | Michael Cochran |
| Joe Bonner | Joanne Brackeen |
| Bill Henderson | John Hicks |
| Lonnie Liston Smith | Hal Galper |
| Onaje Allan Gumbs | Gil Goldstein |
| Harold Mabern | |

Occasionally, Garrison took to strumming his bass almost as though it were a guitar. His use of double stops (two strings sounding together) and his strumming have been widely imitated. He was not the first to use such techniques, but his particular handling of them might have been the stimulus behind their popularity with jazz bassists of the 1960s and 70s. Some of Garrison's double stopping may have had its source in Coltrane's interest in drones and in music employing two tones sustained together, a fifth apart. In the modal music of their native cultures, bagpipes, sitars, and tambura achieve exactly that effect. Coltrane's use of two bassists on "Olé" (on his *Olé Coltrane* album) and "India" (on his *Impressions* album) might have also stemmed from that interest.

**The Sweep**  One of the most significant advances made by the 1960s Coltrane quartet was a pioneering move toward a sweeping, broadly paced organization of parts, a change in feeling that was partly due to **a departure from:**

1) explicit statement of the markers for each measure,
2) accompaniment style in which chords changed frequently,
3) dependence on simple ride rhythms and walking bass patterns,
4) bouncing solo lines of eighth-note sequences with few sustained tones.

This new, widely imitated approach produced music which seemed to breathe more deeply and build excitement more broadly and solemnly than earlier jazz styles usually did. (Listen for these aspects in "The Promise" on the JAZZ CLASSICS CASSETTE.) Phrases spanned larger units than the four- and eight-measure progressions that typified most jazz improvisation. There was more creation of a suspended feeling, which, each time it resolved, proved to be dramatic in its effect. Much of the new feeling was directly caused by **the particular collection of techniques** which the group refined:

1) Sustained and repeating sustained tones in the bass part (pianist's left hand, bassist's plucking) which are technically termed *pedal points*.

**TABLE 13.2. A Few of the Many Saxophonists Influenced by Coltrane**

| | |
|---|---|
| Pharoah Sanders | Pat LaBarbera |
| Charles Lloyd | Bob Berg |
| Joe Farrell | Sonny Fortune |
| Wayne Shorter | Jan Garbarek |
| Gato Barbieri | Michael Brecker |
| John Klemmer | Andrew White |
| Nathan Davis | James Spalding |
| Lew Tabackin | Ernie Krivda |
| Robin Kenyatta | Joe Lovano |
| Steve Grossman | Charles B. Owens |
| Billy Harper | Bob Mintzer |
| David Liebman | Manny Boyd |
| John Surman | Bill Evans |
| Bennie Maupin | Frank Foster |
| Carlos Garnett | Joe Henderson |
| Steve Marcus | David Young |
| Teddy Edwards | Harold Land |
| Cannonball Adderley | Frank Tiberi |
| Steve Lederer | Gregory Herbert |
| Rich Perry | |

2) Drum patterns whose basic unit occupied several measures instead of just a few beats.

3) Sustaining piano chords (sounding them loudly and letting them ring).

4) Using a single mode (or a two-chord pattern) for a long time, instead of using numerous changes in harmony.

5) Long saxophone glissandos which were carefully timed and spanned a large portion of the saxophone's pitch range:
   a) sometimes used to preface a dramatically placed high note.
   b) sometimes evoking a rhapsodic effect.
   c) sometimes snaking in and around a central idea. (These are evident in Coltrane's solo on "The Promise.")
   The rhythmic construction of these glissandos departed from swing feeling and approximated an orchestral concept reminiscent of music that is not as rigidly tied to the beat as are marching and dancing traditions.

6) Use of sustained tones in saxophone solos (allowing listeners a point of focus and relief from having to follow ever-changing melodic contours).

7) Long-term continuity of mood, as though the composition and lengthy improvisations were conceived in their entirety rather than being a sequence of tune and solos that merely strung together swinging phrases in jam session manner.

**COLTRANE'S IMPACT**

John Coltrane exerted a striking effect on his listeners. People who hated his music fought in print with those who were impressed by it. Some felt jazz history ended with Coltrane, whereas today many feel it only just started with him. Not long after Coltrane formed his own group, there were so many saxophonists imitating him that jazz journalists began complaining about a general lack of originality as vehemently as they had responded to the wave of Charlie Parker disciples that rose during the 1950s. Coltrane was the subject of numerous scholarly analyses, and the 1980s saw an increased flow of publications which evaluated Coltrane's work from a technical standpoint.[19] Saxophonist Andrew White was so inspired by Coltrane's music that he transcribed more than four hundred recorded Coltrane solos note for note. (White published the transcriptions, and he continues to make them available by mail order.)

Each of Coltrane's style periods caused many musicians to try out the techniques that Coltrane had popularized. First it was multi-noted playing and difficult chord progressions. Coltrane's manner for replacing the chord changes from standard tunes was adopted by many. Musicians began making their own chords move in the manner demonstrated by Coltrane in his "Giant Steps" and "Countdown" progressions. Then it was modal style and pedal points. After that, it was simultaneous collective improvisation and the creation of frantic turbulence that emphasized textures more than development of melodic improvised lines. Sometimes it appeared as though a large community of musicians had decided that Coltrane was their guide, and they postponed generating ideas of their own until they could see what he was going to do next. Even musicians who were already known for considerable originality felt the impact of Coltrane's work.[20]

[19] A few of the publications containing transcriptions and analyses of Coltrane's work: Don Sickler's *John Coltrane: Improvised Saxophone Solos* (Studio PR/Columbia Pictures Publications, 1979/1986), David Baker's *The Jazz Style of John Coltrane* (Studio PR/Columbia Pictures Publications, 1980), Stuart Isacoff's *Solos for Jazz Tenor Sax* (Carl Fischer, 1985), Scott Reeves's *Creative Jazz Improvisation*, (Prentice-Hall, 1989), Barry Kernfeld's "The Two Coltranes" (*Annual Review of Jazz Studies*, 1983), and Lewis Porter's "John Coltrane's 'A Love Supreme': Jazz Improvisation as Composition" (*Journal of the American Musicological Society*, volume 38, Fall 1985). The first four publications are available from Jamey Aebersold. The last two can frequently be found in the bound-journals section of most well-stocked college music libraries. If you cannot locate them, ask a reference librarian for assistance. Transcriptions for most of the Coltrane solos discussed in this book, including the solos on "Flamenco Sketches" and "The Promise," heard in the JAZZ CLASSICS CASSETTE, are available separately from Andrew White, 4830 South Dakota Ave, N.E., Washington, D.C. 20017. White publishes over 400 Coltrane solo transcriptions.

[20] Chick Corea credits Coltrane for inspiring the compositions "Litha" and "Straight Up and Down." He also cites Coltrane's *Meditations* and *Ascension* for influencing his own free-form approach used on the *Is* album. "A Love Supreme" was recorded by jazz-rock stars John McLaughlin and Carlos Santana. "Giant Steps" was standard repertory for jazz musicians of the 1970s and 80s.

Coltrane had a marked influence on saxophonists during the 1960s (see Table 13.2). Along with Ornette Coleman, Coltrane became the primary model for new saxophonists to study, and several older players also incorporated his techniques in mid-career. Such established players as Frank Foster, Harold Land, Teddy Edwards, and Cannonball Adderley all demonstrated the acquisition of Coltrane techniques. Adderley absorbed some of the Coltrane

John Coltrane playing soprano saxophone, the instrument he helped popularize during the 1960s. (*Photo supplied by Bill Smith*) Listen to the JAZZ CLASSICS CASSETTE, side 2 to hear Coltrane play this instrument on "The Promise."

**Soprano Saxophone**

About the time he formed his own groups (1960–61), Coltrane began playing soprano saxophone in addition to tenor. (Coltrane plays soprano on "The Promise" in the JAZZ CLASSICS CASSETTE.) Soprano saxophone had been previously used on recordings by Sidney Bechet, Johnny Hodges, Charlie Barnet, and Steve Lacy, though it had not caught on as a standard jazz instrument. But a few years after Coltrane first used it, the soprano saxophone had become quite popular with jazz saxophonists, and, by 1970, most tenor saxophonists were performing on it. By the early 1970s, even players who were not necessarily followers of Coltrane also used

approach while playing in the Miles Davis band with him during the late 1950s. (There are a few particularly Coltrane-like moments in Adderley's solo in "Fun" on Adderley's *Mercy, Mercy, Mercy* album.) Coltrane's influence even showed up in Woody Herman's big band, an unlikely context because its saxophone section had been identified with the sound of Stan Getz and cool jazz. Many of Herman's players of the 1970s and 80s have used Coltrane's methods, and the band recorded Coltrane's compositions "Naima" and "Giant Steps."

In tallying Coltrane's disciples, note that Coltrane was rarely the only influence these players had. Woody Herman's 1970s saxophonists, for example, drew from a variety of sources, and the most outstanding players who were affected by Coltrane have shown marked individuality as well as the influence of other sources. Joe Farrell, for example, also cited Charlie Parker as a primary influence. Michael Brecker cites Coltrane as a main influence but also cites King Curtis, Junior Walker, Wayne Shorter, and David Liebman.

soprano. Such men as alto saxophonist Cannonball Adderley and tenor saxophonist Sonny Rollins, who had established unique, well-known styles on their chosen saxes, also began recording with soprano sax. Some players adopted it almost to the exclusion of their tenors.[21] Coltrane's popularization of the instrument coincided with a practical problem that 1970s saxophonists encountered: trying to be heard over loud rhythm sections. The range and tone quality of the soprano saxophone helped saxophonists cut through the sound created by increasing numbers of drums and amplified instruments which comprised groups of the 1970s. The attraction to soprano saxophone can be attributed partly to the attraction of players to Coltrane, partly to the practical advantages of its sound, and partly to the search for fresh sounds that has always characterized jazz musicians.

### Listening Guide for "The Promise"

Composed by John Coltrane; Recorded October 8, 1963 at Birdland, in New York City, by John Coltrane (soprano sax), McCoy Tyner (piano), Jimmy Garrison (bass), and Elvin Jones (drums); available on the JAZZ CLASSICS CASSETTE, Side Two; originally on LP as *Live at Birdland* (Impulse A–50), reissued on CD (MCA 33109).

This performance is in the JAZZ CLASSICS CASSETTE for several reasons that are important both historically and esthetically. It offers a succinct and representative sample for the middle period of the classic Coltrane quartet. This recording conveys how the group sounded in a typical setting because it was recorded live during a performance at Birdland, a New York nightclub. This selection clearly demonstrates the unique accompanying style of this innovative rhythm section, using its polyrhythmic approach, solemn and broadly paced kind of swing feeling, Tyner's pedal points, and Jones's complex layers of sound. (Jones's triplet patterns are conspicuous throughout the performance.) The form of the composition is typical of many Coltrane pieces from this period because it has long stretches in which only two chords alternate (musicians call them "G minor and C seven"). This pattern became a preferred form during the 1960s, 70s, and 80s. This particular performance is also outstanding for its distinctly melodic, five-chorus piano solo by McCoy Tyner. It catalogs many of the much-imitated methods that Tyner developed. This selection also contains a Coltrane soprano sax solo in the style that became widely imitated during the 1970s and 80s. It features his climbing, scale-like runs, his expressive bends of pitch, and dramatically timed peaks of tension. Coltrane often prefaced high notes with a very deliberate climb, and ultimately sounded as though he were squeezing them out of his horn. As in the Johnny Hodges approach, the way Coltrane prefaced each important high note was almost as essential as the note itself. This is central to an impassioned effect we term "the cry." Coltrane's solo also shows his characteristic approach to working over brief figures from many different angles. This performance was also chosen because it provides many illustrations of "the sweep."

Listen for the flowing drum patterns that run throughout the accompaniment, especially the prominent use of tom-toms. The patterns used here differ considerably from the relatively

---

[21]On their post-1968 Miles Davis recordings, Coltrane disciples Steve Grossman and Dave Liebman played more soprano than tenor. Saxophonist Joe Farrell, another player who absorbed portions of the Coltrane style, recorded an entire album, *Moon Germs*, without using his tenor, and Wayne Shorter recorded *Super Nova* without his.

unadorned timekeeping patterns we heard in previous selections on the JAZZ CLASSICS CAS-SETTE. This is the style that Elvin Jones invented.

The piece is performed in a medium tempo. There is no introduction. The performance begins with Coltrane playing the melody and the rhythm section accompanying him. Bass and drums play more densely as the performance unfolds, and the peak of intensity occurs in Coltrane's last two solo choruses. Things wind down gradually from there, though the final melody statement is so liberally ornamented it sounds like Coltrane is unwilling to restrain his creative juices and return to the theme for an ending.

The first time you listen to this, just sit back and let the sounds wash over you. The music has a sure momentum that will carry you along with it. The next several times you listen, you may begin to notice that there is a rocking back and forth motion achieved by the combination of walking bass, drummer's timekeeping patterns, and the piano accompaniment's use of two chords alternating with each other. When McCoy Tyner accompanies himself in his solo, we can hear him playing the first chord two or three times in succession then the second chord once, sometimes twice. Then he repeats the cycle. This persists for long stretches and helps the band get into a groove. However, you will also notice that the groove is periodically interrupted by a bridge. You may begin to recognize its occurrence by the sound of a new chord (musicians call it "F seven"). It is often signalled by a loud, held bass note on piano that contrasts with the steady rocking motion that we have come to expect. The new bridge chord is in effect for eight beats, and then it begins alternating with another chord (musicians call it "D seven") that is also in effect for eight beats every time it comes along. The bridge lasts for eight measures, about 12 seconds. The drumming is more complicated and less predictable during these interruptions, though timekeeping is still maintained. Because the bridge departs from the repeating patterns, it serves to build tension that is ultimately resolved by a return to the repeating pattern. And if you lose your place, it can signal you.

Technical Note: For the accompaniment to the melody, the A-section has eight measures of a G minor chord alternating with a C seven chord (four beats each), then at 12 seconds into the piece, two measures of F seven, two measures of D seven, two of F seven again, two more of D seven. That sixteen-measure sequence repeats. Then beginning at 47 seconds into the piece, there are eight more measures of G minor alternating with C seven.

Accompaniment chords for all solo choruses follow a slightly different sequence of durations than under the melody statements. The form is 16–16–8(Bridge)–8, in which the accompaniment chords are the same for the first sixteen, second sixteen, and the final eight measures.

*Elapsed Time*

## FIRST CHORUS (A-B-A-B-C)

Melody Statement by Coltrane on Soprano Saxophone

Each section lasts 8 measures, and the C-section is accompanied by the same chords as the A-section.

Accompanying the sax, the piano plays resounding bass notes and sustained mid-range chords. They see-saw with a bass note on the first beat and a chord on the third beat of each measure.

| | |
|---|---|
| 0' 12" | B (8 measures) |
| 0' 23" | A (8 measures) |
| 0' 34" | B (8 measures) |
| 0' 46" | C (8 measures) |

| Elapsed Time | |
|---|---|
| *0' 57"* | **SECOND CHORUS** (A-A-B-A, 8 measures in each section) |
| | Piano Solo Improvisation by McCoy Tyner |
| | This is an exceedingly melodic improvisation based on brief phrases that often seem to answer each other. Tyner plays each note very forcefully. |
| *1' 10"* | *Second A-section* |
| | Piano, bass, and drums firmly establish what musicians call a "groove." This is a strong sense of swing feeling that makes you feel good. It is steady and unrushed, but not lazy. It is always going forward, as though strutting. |
| | The solid walking bass provides a firm frame of reference for the passage of beats. The drumming is simpler here than underneath the melody statment. |
| *1' 16"* | Tyner is quadruple-timing the rate of notes in the line played with his right hand while he comps at a normal rate with his left hand. |
| *1' 23"* | *Bridge* |
| | Drumming becomes more complex. |
| *1' 34"* | *Last A-section* |
| | Tyner improvises a funky melodic idea, played in harmony by his right hand while he comps in a lower register with his left hand. |
| *1' 47"* | **THIRD CHORUS** (A-A-B-A) |
| *1' 51"* | Tyner is quadruple-timing his melody line. |
| *2' 00"* | *Second A-section* |
| | Tyner improvises a funky, harmonized line. |
| *2' 12"* | *Bridge* |
| *2' 25"* | *Last A-section* |
| | Tyner improvises a funky, harmonized line. |
| *2' 37"* | **FOURTH CHORUS** (A-A-B-A) |
| | Tyner improvises a simple line in the high register that develops readily by continuously transforming a single idea. |
| *2' 50"* | *Second-A section* |
| | A cymbal crash begins this section. |
| *3' 02"* | *Bridge* |
| | Tyner uses locked hands-block chording to play an idea that includes an answer within the logic of his overall statement. Drumming activity increases. |
| *3' 14"* | *Last A-section* |
| | Tyner develops a funky, harmonized line from his first idea. Drumming returns to more conventional rhythms. |
| *3' 27"* | **FIFTH CHORUS** (A-A-B-A) |
| *3' 33"* | Tyner begins by quadruple-timing. |

| *Elapsed Time* | |
|---|---|
| 3' 40" | *Second A-section* |
| 3' 44" | Tyner trills. |
| 3' 52" | *Bridge* |
| | Tyner begins with a funky, repeated idea that is harmonized. |
| 4' 00" | Tyner ends this statement with quadruple-timing. |
| 4' 05" | *Last A-section* |
| | A cymbal crash begins this section. |
| | Tyner improvises a clear, simple melody line from another idea. |

### SIXTH CHORUS (A-A-B-A)

4' 17"

Tyner uses a pattern of offering resonant bass notes as a call and a block-chorded line as a response. Drumming is more active.

4' 30"

*Second A-section*

A cymbal crash begins this section.

4' 41"

A brief drum roll announces the beginning of the bridge.

4' 43"

*Bridge*

Cymbal crashes and tumultuous drumming occur throughout. Snare drum and tom-toms are prominent.

Bass drum sounds are conspicuous two measures before the last A-section.

4' 55"

*Last A-section*

Drumming is coordinated with the drama of the piano solo.

### SEVENTH CHORUS (A-A-B-A)

5' 07"

Coltrane Soprano Saxophone Solo

Notice how Coltrane rises into the pitch of his first note. Drumming activity increases.

5' 15"

Coltrane uses a scale-wise run to preface an important high note.

5' 20"

*Second A-section*

5' 26"

Coltrane is quadruple-timing to 5' 45". His playing is hot immediately, displaying the urgency for which he is distinguished.

5' 33"

*Bridge*

Coltrane is quadruple-timing. Drum sounds are churning underneath the sax sound. Loud, held bass tones are emanating from the piano.

5' 46"

*Last A-section*

The sax part is very forceful, and the cymbal crashes are timed as responses to Coltrane's high notes.

### EIGHTH CHORUS (A-A-B-A)

5' 57"

Sax is quadruple-timing until 6' 08".

6' 10"

*Second A-section*

Coltrane plays the same note again and again, coming at it from different angles.

| Elapsed Time | |
|---|---|
| 6′ 23″ | **Bridge** |
| | Coltrane prefaces his high note very emotionally, then plays as though he is squeezing it out of his horn. |
| 6′ 31″ | Coltrane often reiterates a note, each time coming at it from a different angle. |
| 6′ 36″ | **Last A-section** |
| | Coltrane quotes and paraphrases the original melody. |

**NINTH CHORUS** (A-B-A-B-C)    6′ 48″

*Final Theme Statement*

Oceans of percussion support Coltrane's melody line.

7′ 02″    *Bridge*

Coltrane is liberally ornamenting his original melody line. Many of his main melody notes are reiterated emphatically.

7′ 13″    *Second A-Section*

Coltrane makes more reiterations of selected notes in restating the melody.

Piano creates a rocking motion by repeating a pattern having a bass note on the first beat, a chord on the third beat.

7′ 26″    *Second Bridge*

7′ 38″    *C-Section*

7′ 49″    a long roll on cymbal

8′ 00″    Tension is resolved when the piano chord sustains, cymbals ring, and the bass improvises a finish.

A written transcription of this solo is available from Andrew White, 4830 South Dakota Ave. N.E., Washington, D.C. 20017.

## CHAPTER SUMMARY

1) John Coltrane was an innovative saxophonist, composer, and bandleader who had enormous impact on modern jazz, particularly in the 1960s.

2) He devised several original styles of saxophone playing, first inspired partly by Lester Young, Dexter Gordon, and Sonny Stitt during the 1940s, and then partly by Ornette Coleman, John Gilmore, and Albert Ayler during the 1960s.

3) Coltrane's first new style was evident in recordings he made in the Miles Davis bands of the 1950s.

4) Coltrane played such energetic, densely-packed solos that his late-1950s playing was described as "sheets of sound," though he was also a remarkably restrained player of lush ballads.

5) As a composer Coltrane was known for devising progressions of chords which change frequently and change in ways that severely challenge improvisers, as in his "Giant Steps."

6) Coltrane's compositions and arrangements popularized the use of pedal points and drone notes in jazz accompaniments, as in his "Naima."

7) Coltrane's "classic quartet" used pianist McCoy Tyner, bassist Jimmy Garrison, and drummer Elvin Jones from 1961 to 1965.

8) The quartet popularized "modal" styles of improvisation in which accompaniment harmonies do not change frequently.

9) The quartet refined methods of achieving a sweeping, broadly paced organization of parts which was more dramatic and orchestral than previous improvisational styles in jazz.

10) Coltrane's albums *Ascension* and *Meditations* were influential models in "free jazz" approaches where all musicians often improvised different lines at the same time with a high-energy, turbulent manner.

11) Elvin Jones was one of the first drummers to play very polyrhythmically and still swing hard.

12) McCoy Tyner popularized voicing chords in fourths and constructing lines from five-note patterns.

13) Coltrane popularized the soprano saxophone in modern jazz.

Elvin Jones. (*Photo by Mark Vinci*)

# chapter 14
# 1960s & 70s AVANT-GARDE & "FREE" JAZZ

The term **avant-garde** refers to the advance group in any field of endeavor. It designates individuals who are ahead of their peers in developing the newest, freshest creations. Although most of the style chapters in this book are concerned with innovators rather than imitators—Louis Armstrong and Earl Hines in the 1920s, Lester Young and Roy Eldridge in the 1930s, Charlie Parker and Dizzy Gillespie in the 1940s, and so on—in all fairness, all the chapters could have "avant-garde" in their title; yet this is the only chapter titled "avant-garde." There are two reasons for this. First, the term has been applied in recent writing about jazz history as though it were a style unto itself. New kinds of jazz in the 1960s and 70s were often grouped under a single umbrella term such as "avant-garde," "the new thing," "outside," or "out music," instead of original names such as Dixieland, swing, or bop. Second, this textbook needs a chapter to discuss several significant modern styles not given chapters of their own. The avant-garde creations of Miles Davis, John Coltrane, Elvin Jones, and Wayne Shorter, as well as the jazz-rock avant-garde of Joe Zawinul and John McLaughlin, are discussed elsewhere, as are the avant-garde creations of Lennie Tristano, Jimmy Giuffre, and Thelonious Monk, which coexisted with these styles. So when considering this chapter's title, remember that perhaps the full title ought to be "avant-garde jazz styles of the 1960s and 70s not treated in separate chapters." Also keep in mind that there were other fine avant-garde musicians and composers during this period who are not mentioned here due to space limitations.

"Free jazz" is another label attached to some of the avant-garde jazz styles of the 1960s. Most closely associated with **Ornette Coleman** and **Cecil Taylor, the term "free jazz" derives from the practice of improvising music that is free of preset chord progressions.** To a certain extent, the term has also been applied to improvisation that is free from observing conventional practices of any kind, not just preset chord progressions or tempos. A model for much of this music is a 1960 Coleman album called *Free Jazz*,[1] which contains simultaneous collective improvisation by two bands attempting to remain free of preset key, melody, chord progressions, and meter (the excerpt from this album in SCCJ displays some but not all of what is later described here).[2] But the term "free jazz" can be deceiving because very little of the music is entirely free of tempo, key, or traditional distinctions between soloists and accompanists. Moreover, a substantial portion of the music has preset melody, organization of themes, or other structure. We will examine more of that later.

**Most free jazz groups omitted piano because historically the jazz pianist had assumed a role of providing chord progressions, and the restrictions created by the organization that came with preset chord progressions were exactly what free players were trying to free themselves from.** Another reason for the scarcity of pianists in free jazz is that few pianists were comfortable improvising without the suggestion of chords or key. It was as though, having been the harmonic gatekeepers for so long, they could not function when such gates as chord progressions and song forms were removed. (For explanations of these traditions, see chapter 3 and the JAZZ STYLES CASSETTE.)

The next three characteristics of free jazz are incidental to the idea of freedom from preset chord progressions, but they happen to be identified more with free players than with bop or cool players. First, **many free players earned a reputation for more extensive manipulations of pitch and tone quality than had been used by players of any other style since early jazz.** Ultra-high-register (altissimo) playing was common, with the addition of shrieks, squawks, wails, gurgles, and squeals. Rough, hoarse tone qualities were also common. Second, **the improvisation of textures seemed to assume greater importance for some free players than the development of melodies. The "free jazz" label was often applied to music of high energy and dense textures which maintained turbulent activity for lengthy periods.** Some free players became so firmly identified with "energy playing" that the "free jazz" label often became applied to high-energy, nonelectronic music, even when preset keys and forms were present. Third, **the free players's conception of melody displayed a loosening of bop melodic and rhythmic practices.** Free jazz signaled an end to long, convoluted streams of eighth-note figures which reflected the movement of favorite chord progressions in conventional bop patterns. Phrasing was often more fragmented. Sustained tones were alternated with screeches and moans. There was an unfinished quality in many performances.

Another trend identified more with free jazz than with bop or cool was **the adoption of non-European musical approaches which neither rely extensively on chord progressions nor use much harmony. This includes some types of music from Africa, Indonesia, China, the Middle East, and India.** Because free jazz's rejection of piano and preset harmony was musically not too distant from these non-European forms of music that did not use chord progressions or chord instruments, it was

[1]Atlantic 1364, CD/LP, 1960

[2]During the 1960s, aspects of these methods were also incorporated into the styles of John Coltrane, Albert Ayler, and a few of the groups they influenced. Coltrane's name has become prominently associated with free jazz despite the relatively small representation of these kinds of approaches in his recorded output and the fact that almost none of his music is free of preset musical organization.

logical for such development to have occurred with free players. This interest led to an amalgamation of jazz with music of non-European cultures, sometimes termed **Third World music,** resulting in a form of music that is simpler than bop. It manifested itself in the use of non-Western instruments and the cultivation of non-Western approaches to playing European instruments. In this way, it considerably extended the range of sounds used by jazz musicians. Free jazz players were not the only jazz musicians who showed this interest, but the persistence of these elements in free music of this period marks one of the first such lasting blends since the periodic infatuations jazz had previously had with Latin American music.

**ORNETTE COLEMAN**

One of the most influential forces in jazz of the 1960s and 70s was Ornette Coleman. Some consider him to have been as historically significant as Charlie Parker.[3] Coleman is primarily an alto saxophonist, though he also plays trumpet and violin. On his 1958–59 recordings, he displayed a soft, pure tone, and he moved from note to note in legato fashion, as if smoothly sliding along small subdivisions of pitch. His tone did not have the edge of Charlie Parker's or the body of Cannonball Adderley's. Coleman began his notes more bluntly and used a slow vibrato. In later years, he made his tone somewhat brighter and gave it an edge. Though he seems able to play almost everything he attempts, he lacks the ultra-high-level command possessed by Parker, Adderley, and Lee Konitz. (Get SCCJ and listen to Coleman's sound on "Lonely Woman," then compare it with Parker's on "Embraceable You," Adderley's on the Miles Davis "So What," and Konitz's on Tristano's "Crosscurrent.")

Coleman is one of the freshest, most prolific post-bop composers; he has written every tune on more than twenty albums. His style is quite original, and he has an exceptional gift for melody. Some of his tunes are quite catchy, and, like those of

[3]There are numerous similarities between Parker and Coleman. A few suggest the influence of Parker on Coleman; others merely show that both men drew from similar sources. Though Coleman's timbre was unique, it resembled Parker's more than it resembled that of Johnny Hodges, Benny Carter, or Lee Konitz. Coleman's playing also had the soulfulness of Parker's and the explosions of slippery notes found in some Parker improvisations. Both had a gift for melody. Both used a lot of bluesy inflections of pitch and timbre (on his first few recordings, all for Contemporary, Coleman's inflections and their timing resemble Parker's). Like Parker, Coleman also liked to quote pop tunes briefly. For instance, themes from "If I Loved You," "Hawaiian War Chant," "Cherokee," and "Blues in the Night" ("My Mama Done Told Me") have all been interjected in his improvisations at various times. Coleman also used a few bop phrases in his improvisation and recorded Parker's tune, "Klactoveesedstene" (*Paul Bley at the Hillcrest Club*, Inner City 1007, LP, 1958).

Although I disagree with the statement, I have heard Coleman called "just another bebop alto player." The rhythmic complexity of bop, however, should make Coleman's less complex music easy to distinguish from bop. It is understandable how the occasional bop phrasing, steady tempo, and bluesy melodic figures in Coleman's playing might lead a listener to call him a bebop player. But what is remarkable about this view is that it coexists with a completely different response to Ornette Coleman's style: many people, after all, consider him a revolutionary figure. There are valid reasons for both reactions. Coleman was innovative, but he did not step out of thin air. For more about Coleman, see A. B. Spellman's *Black Music: Four Lives* (Schocken, 1966), pages 44–65 in Ekkehard Jost's *Free Jazz* (Universal Edition, 1975; reprinted by DaCapo, 1981), and pages 76–85 in Gunther Schuller's *Musings* (Oxford, 1986).

Ornette Coleman, alto saxophonist and the leading figure in free–form jazz. Pictured here at age 42 in 1972 with bassist Charlie Haden and drummer Eddie Blackwell. (*Photo by Bill Smith*)

Thelonious Monk, sound simple, despite their unusual rhythmic and harmonic qualities. The playfulness of Coleman's tunes is also reminiscent of Monk's work.[4]

Although often called free jazz, Coleman's music actually has quite a bit of self-imposed structure. Constant tempo is usually employed. Written and memorized tunes are usually used during some portion of his performances. And, of course, there is nothing haphazard about the freedoms with which he and his sidemen play. They are limited by their own decision to listen to each other carefully, and they plan their music while they improvise. Coleman's brand of free jazz

[4]A number of musicians have shown interest in Ornette Coleman's compositions. Coleman's impact has been especially notable in pianist Keith Jarrett, who has written and improvised in the style of Coleman as well as dedicating a tune to him, "Piece for Ornette." Further acknowledgment to Coleman has been given by fellow saxophonist Roscoe Mitchell, who titled one of his pieces "Ornette" and by bassist Charlie Haden, who wrote another called "O. C."

Though many of Coleman's pieces are simply springboards for improvisation, some have been arranged for ensembles. His "Forms and Sounds" was scored for flute, oboe, clarinet, bassoon, and French horn. His "Saints and Soldiers" and "Space Flight" were arranged for two violins, viola, and cello (*Forms and Sounds: The Music of Ornette Coleman*, RCA Bluebird 6561 (LSC 2982), CD, 1968). "Skies of America," which he considers one of his best works, was scored for symphony orchestra (*Skies of America*, CBS 31562, LP, 1972).

also uses instruments in conventional solo and accompaniment roles. In his trio, Coleman usually seems to be soloing while his bassist and drummer accompany. Though there is interaction, give-and-take, and mutual stimulation, there is little doubt that Coleman is the soloist. (Listen to "Congeniality" in SCCJ.)

For a trio performance to be truly free of role conventions, the three instruments would have to be undifferentiated in their roles: the absence of a solo voice would be as common as the presence of a solo voice; the drums would be accompanied by sax and bass just as often as the sax was accompanied by drums and bass. Actually, if "free" means freedom from conventional roles or forms, there would not even be any solos at all, since solos and accompaniment are just as much conventions as constant tempo, meter, key, and chord progressions. True musical freedom can indicate the ability to play whatever is in the musician's head, regardless of its adherence to musical conventions such as these. The problem is that this is not humanly possible. Musicians are not capable of being so "free." Musical conditioning—and the very process of learning to play an instrument—prevent so great an independence. Therefore this extreme definition of musical freedom is not too helpful in describing free jazz, and it is clearly not a description of Ornette Coleman's music.

In short, Coleman's music is free only in some respects: it is free of preset chord progressions and their chorus lengths. Some, but not most, of his work is also free of meter and constant tempo. The music does not lack a sense of key, it is not atonal, and it is certainly not random (see pages 365–369 for discussion of scales, modality, tonality, and atonality). Coleman freely changes keys, but he usually stays in each one long enough for us to hear that he is, indeed, in a particular key.[5] Also, his key changes are logical and obvious; they reflect the melodic integrity of his improvised lines.

Coleman attempts a difficult task when he rejects the use of preset chord changes. Without the rise and fall of musical tension indicated by chord changes, his music still has the rise and fall of tension generated by his bassist and drummer; but that is all he has to support and inspire his creations musically. Outside of that, every measure is taxing his imagination, calling upon him to fill it with an interesting and meaningful line. But because none of those measures are supplying any organizational ideas in the form of chord changes, Coleman's improvising cannot fall back on the underlying musical motion of chord changes or on the supportive sound of a pianist's comping. By foregoing preset chord changes, and their associated chorus lengths, turnarounds, and bridges, he has brought us an especially abstract—and challenging—form of musical experience.

Despite the freedom of his improvisational approach, Coleman's improvised lines often resembled chord progression-based lines. For Coleman, melody is primary and harmony secondary. It may sound as though he is inventing chord progressions as he improvises lines, but this is only because the harmonic logic of those lines resembles that of chord-progression-based lines we have heard elsewhere. The construction of his lines is ruled by his musical past in the same way that our perception as listeners is ruled by our past listening experiences. Coleman plays

[5]To be technically accurate, it must be said that Coleman works off shifting tone centers.

freely, but in his lines we can hear organization like that in more conventional improvisation. Some of this comes from the very melodic nature of much of his work. (In fact, Coleman has been called the supreme melodist.) The feeling of a definite key (tone center) is present in each portion of his solos, though he changes keys at will.[6] Also, part of the chord-progression feeling in Coleman's music stems from the approach taken by his bassists, especially Charlie Haden. Though Coleman's bassists follow the harmonic directions indicated by his improvisations, at times they also take the lead themselves. Coleman's line may suggest a chord progression which the bassist will complete, or vice versa. Coleman and his bassist remain alert to chord progressions that are suggested in each other's lines.

Modern jazz has been influenced by Ornette Coleman's tunes because they are so original and by his unique saxophone style because it is so emotional and melodic (see Table 14.1). But Coleman has had just as much impact through his decision to discard chord changes and his belief that an improviser can let the melody go its own way and not need to be directed by preset progressions of chords. Though it is not his best album, Coleman's 1960 *Free Jazz* paralleled Miles Davis's *Kind of Blue* in its historical impact on improvisational approaches. *Kind of Blue* popularized modal approaches; *Free Jazz* contributed to more frequent use of free-form approaches. On the album Coleman used two pianoless quartets. The personnel of the first included his regular quartet: trumpeter Don Cherry, bassist Charlie Haden, and drummer Eddie Blackwell. The second was made up of alto saxophonist/bass clarinetist Eric Dolphy, trumpeter Freddie Hubbard, bassist Scott LaFaro, and drummer Billy Higgins. (All these names are important because all these men are giants in post-bop jazz.) The eight musicians played together, sometimes improvising all at once, never using any preset arrangement of themes, chord changes, or chorus lengths. Tone centers were evident, though they were not agreed upon in advance. (Listen to the excerpt from this album that is in SCCJ.)

Despite the album title, the music on *Free Jazz* is not entirely free. There are prearranged ensemble passages and solos with rhythm section accompaniment, as well as a bass duet. Some of the solos, especially Freddie Hubbard's, sound as though they were based on a preset chord progression, though the progression is suggested

**TABLE 14.1. Some of the Many Musicians Influenced by Ornette Coleman**

| | | | |
|---|---|---|---|
| John Tchicai | Carlos Ward | John Coltrane | Pat Metheny |
| Marion Brown | Archie Shepp | John Carter | Joseph Jarman |
| Dewey Redman | Oliver Lake | Charles Brackeen | Paul Bley |
| Jimmy Lyons | Roscoe Mitchell | Keith Jarrett | James "Blood" Ulmer |
| Sonny Simmons | Jan Garbarek | Bobby Bradford | Ronald Shannon Jackson |
| Prince Lasha | Anthony Ortega | Don Cherry | Jamaaladeen Tacuma |
| Henry Threadgill | Albert Ayler | Charlie Haden | Saheb Sarbib |

[6]Coleman used nine different keys in improvising on "Dee Dee," in his album *Ornette Coleman At the Golden Circle, Vol. 1*, Blue Note 84224, CD/LP, 1965.

only by the resemblance of the improvised line to other progression-based lines, not by the sound of any chording instrument. Brief themes recur in the improvisation and are passed back and forth among group members (an aspect not evident in the SCCJ excerpt). Rarely are all eight players improvising at the same time. Both bassists and both drummers play throughout most of it, but usually a single horn (Coleman, Dolphy, Hubbard, or Cherry) surfaces while the others stay out. Occasionally all the horns return to embellish the prominent voice.

Other jazz groups had recorded collectively improvised free pieces at about the same time and even prior to Coleman's first recordings (see chapter 10 for Tristano, Giuffre, Rogers, et al.). But these were isolated efforts, and the approach did not catch on in the jazz mainstream. After Coleman's *Free Jazz*, however, a number of other musicians also recorded in a similar format; some of them are discussed in this chapter.

**DON CHERRY**  Don Cherry (b. 1936) is a trumpeter, composer, bandleader, and a leading figure in free jazz. He was a regular member of Ornette Coleman's groups in the late 1950s and early 60s, having played on all of Coleman's important early recordings, including *Something Else*,[7] *Change of the Century*,[8] and *Free Jazz*.

Though strongly influenced by Coleman, Cherry also cites bop trumpeters Fats Navarro and Clifford Brown as influences. Consistent with this bop connection, Cherry has recorded improvisations which closely follow preset chord progressions and contain phrasing and note choices that derive from bop methods.[9] However, like Coleman, most of Cherry's recorded improvisation goes its own way spontaneously instead of relying on a preset progression of accompanying chords. Cherry's improvisations are strikingly original, filled with lines and melodic fragments which draw little from standard jazz cliché. (Listen to Cherry on Coleman's "Congeniality" and "Lonely Woman" in SCCJ.) Cherry does not ordinarily use chord instruments in his bands, and he has devoted a considerable portion of his career to playing types of Oriental, Turkish, and Indian music that also omit chording instruments and chord-progression-based compositional forms.

Cherry is quite flexible as an improviser, capable of constructing logical solo lines as well as spontaneously constructing parts for collective improvisation.[10] In this way, he is a throwback to the earliest improvisers, for whom sensitivity and instantaneous flexibility were essential to making good collective music. He can successfully improvise lines which swing and stick close to the beat, but he can also play against meter, as though ignoring the beat and resisting swing. In this way, what Cherry does rhythmically is analogous to what he does harmonically. Musicians term the conventional playing as "inside" and the other approach as playing "outside." Because many modern players are comfortable with only one of the two approaches, it is notable that Cherry is adept at both.

[7] OJC-163 (C-7551), LP, 1958
[8] Atlantic 1327, LP, 1959
[9] Listen to "Jayne" on Coleman's *Something Else*.
[10] Listen to his work on Sonny Rollins's *Our Man in Jazz*, RCA LSC 2612, reissued as *Sonny Rollins, Vol. 3 & 4*, RCA (France) 741091/092, LP set, 1962. Also see pages 133–162 in Jost's *Free Jazz*.

Since the mid-1960s, Don Cherry has spent considerable time in Europe and has devoted much of his recording to music which is not closely related to the jazz tradition. This body of music is frequently dubbed "Third World music." Cherry's interests have led him to compose and perform extensively in groups using such instruments as the tamboura, sitar, finger cymbals, conch horn, African finger piano, and gong. Cherry learned to play flute, bamboo flute, and assorted percussion instruments at this time. This music makes much use of drones and extensively repeated accompaniment figures. Some pieces are based entirely on chants in which the same few notes are played over and over again. For the jazz listener, there is often little in this music which truly distinguishes it from its non-jazz sources.[11]

**CECIL TAYLOR**    Cecil Taylor (b. 1929) is a pianist, composer, and bandleader who developed a unique and specialized style of modern jazz during the late 1950s and early 60s. His style is not merely different, innovative, or unconventional; rather, it is **a major alternative to the mainstream of modern jazz styles.** (Listen to "Enter Evening" in SCCJ, but note that it is among the most tame of all Taylor's recordings. The vast majority of his recorded music sounds wild and extremely turbulent.)

Taylor does not play with modern jazz swing feeling, and he frequently emphasizes musical textures rather than musical lines. Although quite syncopated, his rhythms tend to be played slightly ahead of or on top of the beat, and they lack the lilt and buoyancy of conventional jazz rhythmic style. As jazz scholar Harvey Pekar has noted, Taylor does not try to swing: his music is too tense to swing.

Cecil Taylor, 1990, age 61. (*Photo by Grace Bell*)

[11]*Eternal Now*, Antilles 7034, LP, 1973.

The manner in which Taylor goes about making music does not resemble most jazz traditions. Taylor's notes often seem to be generated in layered groups, designed to create textures of sound and sound shapes instead of singable phrases that lope along. The textures are rich in internal movement; they seem to shimmer and explode. In fact, much of Taylor's music is comprised of quick, tightly packed, staccato figures played in a manner that is very percussive, with few moments of serenity. Some observers have commented that Taylor seems to "attack" the piano keyboard, and they are astounded because he has the skill to strike odd sequences of piano keys with tremendous force at a dizzying pace and not miss any. What almost universally impresses listeners is that most of his performances seem to draw on a continuous source of high energy and maintain a feverish intensity for long periods.

Though his earliest recordings show that Taylor once based his improvisations on familiar tunes and chord changes, and he employed bop-style bassists and drummers,[12] he began playing without preset chord progressions or constant tempo, and frequently without a bassist during the 1960s. He often played free of the harmonic restrictions imposed by a preset progression of chords, though he did preplan what he called "unit structures." These were specific phrases and overall concepts about the architecture that the piece should assume. His preparation for performance does involve extensive rehearsal, and he does provide his musicians with musical figures to play. However, his approach does not always involve dictating the exact synchronization of parts, their timing, or tempo. In addition, he requires his musicians to improvise some passages without the guidance of preset themes, chord progressions, or chorus lengths. They are freely improvised. In other words, Taylor's music is not entirely free-form, but it is free of the preset forms that most jazz musicians use.

Brief portions of some Taylor improvisations are genuinely atonal. This is unusual in jazz, and in Taylor's work as well, because even the most adventuresome free-form improvisations are usually organized around tone centers, keys, modes, or shifting tone centers.[13] More than any other jazz style, Taylor's resembles the music of mid-twentieth-century composers Karlheinz Stockhausen, Oliver Messiaen, and Luciano Berio. His improvisations have a hint of Thelonious Monk or Duke Ellington, but generally they sound more orchestral than jazz-like. (Listen to "Jitney #2" in the JAZZ CLASSICS CASSETTE.)

Some of Cecil Taylor's group performances begin with a theme loosely stated by horns and accompanied by his piano improvising in a florid, orchestral fashion. Then a collective improvisation begins in which nearly everyone participates. The emphasis is on creating textures. The style is not melodic in the pop-tune sense, the swing-era sense, or the bop sense. Some textures change gradually, others abruptly. Occasionally a preorganized ensemble portion erupts. Usually the group creates a whirlpool of sound and maintains a frantic pace.[14]

[12]*In Transition*, Blue Note 458, LP set, 1955 & 1959
[13]*Silent Tongues*, Arista 1005 (Freedom), LP, 1974
[14]*Live at the Cafe Montmartre*, Fantasy 86014, LP, 1962; or *Nefertiti*, Arista/Freedom 1905, LP set, 1962; Taylor's most widely discussed examples of this are *Unit Structures*, Blue Note 84237, CD/LP, 1966; and *Conquistador*, Blue Note 46535 (84260), CD/LP, 1966. For more about Taylor, see Spellman's *Black Music: Four Lives*, pages 66–83 in Jost's *Free Jazz*, pages 301–311 in Len Lyons's *The Great Jazz Pianists* (Quill, 1983), and pages 65–75 in Gunther Schuller's *Musings* (Oxford, 1986).

### Listening Guide for "Jitney #2"

Composed, arranged, and performed by pianist Cecil Taylor; recorded July 2, 1974 at the Montreux Jazz Festival in Switzerland; available on the JAZZ CLASSICS CASSETTE, side 2; originally on *Silent Tongues* (Arista-Freedom AL 1005), reissued on CD as Freedom FLP 41005.

Though many listeners report having difficulty with Cecil Taylor's music, this example should prove comprehensible to you if it is replayed several times. It is an exciting performance excerpted from one of Taylor's most widely hailed albums. His thinking on this is very clear, and we cannot be distracted or overwhelmed by the playing of additional musicians because Taylor is entirely alone here. Moreover, this performance will not require you to maintain concentration for long because Taylor plays for only three minutes and twenty-one seconds.

As in listening to most music, you might wish merely to let it wash over you the first time you hear it. Let it take you wherever it can. On successive replayings, you may become intrigued by the prospect of trying to follow Taylor's thinking as the performance unfolds. Note, however, that not all the listening strategies that you developed from previous listening guides will apply here. This music is not divided into 12-measure or 32-measure choruses with introductions, A-sections, and B-sections that you can latch onto. It does not usually follow set durations of modes or keep time, either. To make a distinction between the end of one section and beginning of another becomes impractical. Instead of following such recurring patterns, Taylor devises his own ideas and lets them recur and be transformed over the course of his performance. For instance, he uses one main statement, the first two notes, followed by a chordal answer. When Taylor reiterates that opening statement, he often repeats this pattern almost intact, though he occasionally adds one or two notes to its opening. Try to become familiar with that opening statement and then attempt to recognize recurrences among Taylor's more complicated inventions. You might be able to hear it recur in faster or slower form, and in a higher pitch range. Often Taylor will play for several seconds without referring to it in any obvious way. In fact, much of this performance is filled with cascading notes and jarring clusters of tones.

This music gives us an opportunity to ponder the way jazz can be defined. The piece contains a substantial amount of improvisation because, though it contains a few preconceived ideas, these ideas are arranged and developed spontaneously. Steady tempo is not used, however, and most listeners agree that Taylor's rhythms fail to swing in the jazz sense. The music resembles contemporary piano works by nonjazz composers such as Olivier Messiaen. Because of its nonswinging rhythmic feeling, some people do not refer to this music as jazz. They feel that "improvised concert music" is a more accurate description. On the other hand, Taylor has a history of playing within the jazz tradition, and he cites Duke Ellington, Thelonious Monk, and Lennie Tristano as important influences on his development. In fact, some people consider all of Taylor's music to be jazz because of its association with the jazz tradition.

| *Elapsed Time* | |
| --- | --- |
| | the opening statement, followed by variations |
| | bass notes followed by mid-register chords |
| 0' 10" | opening statement again, then echoed many times in various transformations |
| 0' 17" | opening statement followed by quasi-broken chords, turning into runs |
| | more variations of the opening idea, leading to rapidly played passages, and a return to that same idea |
| 0' 26" | opening idea again, followed by chords |
| 0' 30" to 50" | cascades of notes that paraphrase the opening idea |
| 0' 45" | first climax, as Taylor reaches the upper register of the keyboard |

| | |
|---|---|
| | series of repeated, broken chords played by two hands in the middle of the keyboard, tremolos scattered across the keyboard until about 56″ |
| 0′ 56″ | switch to single notes instead of chords |
| | Taylor introduces a new idea and then develops it. |
| 1′ 06″ | return to opening idea |
| 1′ 08″ | opening idea again |
| 1′ 09″ | opening idea again |
| 1′ 12″ | opening idea again |
| 1′ 15″ | a new idea and several repeats of it |
| 1′ 23″ | Intensity begins to increase. |
| | notes scattered all over the keyboard |
| 1′ 35″ | tremolos scattered across the keyboard |
| 1′ 47″ to 1′ 55″ | variations of the opening idea |
| 1′ 50″ | Intensity still increases as heavy chords are played at slower pace. |
| 1′ 57″ | a new idea |
| 2′ 05″ | very rapid sprinkling of notes, lasting until 2′ 39″ |
| | cascades of notes, variations of the idea, in different keys |
| 2′ 43″ | Intensity starts increasing again, in preparation for the last climax, with briefly repeated runs. High-pitched ideas occur with chorded responses in bass range. |
| 2′ 45″ | Taylor is briefly melody-like until 2′ 53″, then he resumes the turbulence. |
| 3′ 00″ | lots of scattered tremolos; faster pace |
| 3′ 07″ | Quick trills are exchanged. |
| 3′ 15″ | Taylor plays tone clusters alternately in low then high registers. |
| 3′ 17″ | Taylor pounds out a string of tone clusters, ending in the low register. |
| 3′ 21″ | Taylor concludes abruptly with a restatement of the opening idea. |

**ALBERT AYLER**   One of the most original saxophonists to emerge after Charlie Parker and Ornette Coleman was tenor saxophonist Albert Ayler (1936–1970). His style remains one of the most unusual in jazz history. He perfected an approach to improvisation that was technically very demanding. Ayler's lines ran the entire range of the tenor saxophone and through at least one additional octave beyond the conventional "highest note." He played throughout that range with swooping, swirling legato figures, and a light, slippery tone, at times reminiscent of the C-melody saxophone. Ayler made moans and wails an essential part of his musical vocabulary. Much of his music was strikingly voice-like. His vibrato was sometimes slow, at other times moderately fast, but always very natural, and delivered in a driven sort of way. In his extended high register, Ayler played with the ease that good players exhibit only in the conventional midrange of the tenor saxophone. His playing often sounded like rapid, legato violin playing. These elements created an otherworldly quality. There was never anything mechanical or academic about Ayler's playing. Whether listeners enjoyed his music or not, it provided an intensely emotional experience for them.

Ayler's rhythmic conception was not like bop rhythmic conceptions. In fact, it was unlike any swinging jazz style. Like his melodic approach, his rhythmic approach had more in common with classical and folk music than with jazz. (See chapter 2 for more about different types of swing feeling.) Ayler swung in a manner which only approximated conventional jazz swing feeling. Much of his work did not swing at all. The lack of swing feeling was often caused by a continuously high level of tension, in place of the alternation of tension and relaxation that typifies bop.

Like Ornette Coleman, Ayler followed preset harmonic and rhythmic structures only loosely, and he preferred bands with no chording instrument. Ayler's bassists were some of the same gifted musicians employed by Coleman and Bill Evans. His drummers were of the "free" school, concerned little with simple timekeeping, very interested in group interaction and the creation of varied sounds and textures.[15] Like Coleman, Ayler also used a Charlie Parker tune on one of his first recordings.[16] And, like Coleman, he followed its harmonies only loosely. In other words, he acknowledged bop but did not actually play in the bop style.[17]

Ayler triggered a major style change for John Coltrane in the mid-1960s, and he had a sustained impact on numerous other saxophonists who were considered avant-garde during the 1970s and 80s.[18] The close adherence to tempo that was central to bop and bop's offshoots largely disappeared in players who were affected by Ayler. His rhythmic elasticity was absorbed into the styles of many avant-garde players. A number of players drew from the combined influences of Ayler, Coleman, and Coltrane. These new players perpetuated the timbres and erratic contours associated with free jazz, even when performing pieces that followed preset chord changes and tempo.

**CHARLES MINGUS**    Charles Mingus (1922–1979) is historically significant as

1) one of the first virtuoso bass soloists to appear after Jimmy Blanton,
2) a bandleader who employed unorthodox techniques and all-star personnels; and
3) a prolific composer-arranger who
   a) created unique blends of premodern and modern jazz traditions, ranging from Jelly Roll Morton and Duke Ellington to bop and free jazz,

[15]*Spiritual Unity*, ESP Disk 1002, LP, 1964
[16]"Billie's Bounce," on *My Name Is Albert Ayler* Fantasy 86016, LP, 1963
[17]Ayler's style lived on in the playing of tenor saxophonist David Murray, whose first album, *Low Class Conspiracy* (Adelphi 5002, LP, 1976), demonstrated that he had learned the Ayler techniques and begun to use them masterfully. Murray further honored Ayler by composing "Flowers for Albert" (*Flowers for Albert*, India Navigation 1026, LP, 1976). In listening for the Ayler connection in Murray's playing, you must hear Murray's first two albums, not his later works. After those first albums, Murray's playing began to sound less and less like Ayler's.
[18]Ayler's effect on Coltrane is especially evident in Coltrane's *Meditations*, MCA 29022 (Impulse 9110), 1965, and *Interstellar Space*, MCA 29029 (Impulse 9277), 1967.

Charles Mingus, bassist-bandleader-composer, second only to Duke Ellington in achieving colorful integration of composition and improvisation. Pictured here at age 29, in 1951. (*Photo by Bob Parent, courtesy of Don Parent*)

b) drew from such diverse sources as Negro gospel music, Mexican folk music, and twentieth-century European concert music; and

c) wrote distinctive melodies.

Mingus did not become widely known until the late 1950s, though he had been making highly creative recordings as a bandleader since the mid-1940s. By the late 1950s, when his work began to be issued by major record companies, he had already recorded as bassist with such modern giants as Miles Davis, Charlie Parker, and Dizzy Gillespie (for discussion of his stature as a bassist, see chapter 9). Historically significant as a bassist, Mingus is at least as significant as a composer and bandleader. Like Ellington's, his name represents an entire idiom which, though rooted in other idioms, is uniquely his own.

Mingus wrote more than one hundred fifty pieces, many of which have been rearranged and recorded several times. He explored styles as diverse as:

1) program music ("Pithecanthropus Erectus," the story of man)[19]

2) funky, bluesy, gospel-oriented music, with shouting and hand clapping ("Better Git It in Your Soul")[20]

[19]*Pithecanthropus Erectus*, Atlantic 8809 (1237), CD/LP, 1956
[20]*Mingus Ah Um*, CBS 40648 (CL 1370), CD/LP, 1959

3)  Third Stream music ("Revelations")[21]

4)  bop (with Charlie Parker, Dizzy Gillespie, Bud Powell, and Max Roach)[22]

5)  free jazz (portions of "What Love")[23]

6)  music for film ("Shadows")

Mingus has employed diverse instrumentations, including the following:

1)  his own solo piano[24]

2)  jazz quintets of trumpet, tenor saxophone, piano, bass, and drums[25]

3)  pianoless quartet[26]

4)  five trumpets, four trombones, tuba, cello, oboe, flute, six saxophones, piano, bass, and three drummers[27]

5)  two trumpets, trombone, French horn, flute, bassoon, two saxophones, harp, piano, guitar, vibraharp, two basses, and drums (see footnote 21)

Throughout his career, Mingus displayed the influence of Ellington. The methods of Ellington are obvious in one of the earliest Mingus recordings, "Bedspread," made in 1946 as a 78 r.p.m. single for a company called Four Star. Even the style of improvisations on "Bedspread" shows a similarity to the Ellington approaches. Mingus has composed and recorded pieces dedicated to Ellington, such as "Duke's Choice" and "An Open Letter to Duke." Ellington-like use of plunger-muted brass playing has appeared in Mingus works. The Johnny Hodges alto saxophone style has, at the request of Mingus, been incorporated into the playing of such otherwise non-Hodges-styled saxophonists as Charlie Mariano, Jackie McLean, and John Handy. Mingus has also recorded several Ellington compositions.

Mingus is far better known for his combo recordings than for his big band material. The Mingus combo approaches are distinguished because they seldom resemble the jam session format adopted in most modern jazz concerts and recording sessions. Instead of being restricted to only a unison theme statement, a string of improvised solos with improvised accompaniments, and another theme statement, the Mingus approach relies heavily on the alternation of composed and improvised passages and on preset accompaniments. These sustain the listener's interest in a novel way and tend to relieve him from the necessity of extended concentration. Also to Mingus's credit is that, despite the amount of planning in his performances, a looseness prevails, and a feeling of naturalness is conveyed by his music. In many

[21]*Modern Jazz Concert*, Columbia 127, LP, 1957, reissued on *Jazz Compositions*, CBS 37012, LP
[22]*Jazz at Massey Hall*, OJC-044 (Debut 124), CD/LP, 1953
[23]*The Complete Candid Recordings of Charles Mingus*, Mosaic MD3-111, CD set/MR4-111, LP set, 1960–61
[24]*Mingus Plays Piano*, MCA 29067 (Impulse 60), LP, 1963
[25]*Mingus Moves*, Atlantic 1653, LP, 1973
[26]With Eric Dolphy, Ted Curson, and Dannie Richmond; see footnote 23
[27]"Half-Mast Inhibition" and "Bemoanable Lady" on *Mingus Revisited (Pre-Bird)*, Emarcy 826496 (Mercury 20627), CD, 1960

performances, Mingus rejected conventional bop accompaniment patterns in favor of preset statements which broke the flow of music by introducing stops and changes of style in mid-performance. Portions of some solos were accompanied by nothing more than hand clapping and shouting. Drumming might use a waltz pattern one moment and a conventional jazz pattern the next moment. Passages might contain many stop-time solo breaks. The tempo might be slow one moment and doubled the next. In fact, Mingus is one of the few bandleaders in jazz history to explore the gradual speeding and slowing of tempo. These procedures are similar to those used by Jelly Roll Morton and Duke Ellington. And, like the finished products of Morton and Ellington, the Mingus material rarely sounded anonymous or mistakable for an ordinary recording session run in a more conventional fashion.[28]

Mingus's unorthodox approaches to combo performance had several significant impacts. They forced improvisers away from producing purely bop-styled solos in an uninterrupted stream. They gave improvisers a varied background which elicited more varied solos than conventional settings would have elicited. They gave listeners brief, reassuring chunks of music in the form of figures that became familiar because they regularly recurred during the piece. This allowed listeners to latch onto something familiar amidst the flow of freshly improvised solos. This is an important observation because, in most bop performances, familiar material was offered only at the beginning and the end of a piece. The Mingus technique of placing recurring devices *within* the piece offered listeners something that they could not ordinarily expect from other kinds of modern jazz (though this approach later became associated with bands led by former Mingus sidemen Thad Jones and Ted Curson).

To achieve a successful integration of composed and improvised music, Mingus obtained a high degree of artistic cooperation from his musicians. As a bandleader and arranger, Mingus had a sense of what players to cast in what roles and how to pry out maximum distinctiveness in a performance. He colorfully mixed snips of improvisations with his prewritten ensemble sounds to weave unusual textures. Then, instead of thrusting their favorite phrases unthinkingly onto his music, the players were forced to appreciate his musical wishes and give those wishes higher priority than they gave their own. Players had to interpret his demands as well as contribute original twists of their own. Performance was often indistinct from rehearsal. The music amounted to a workshop endeavor in that Mingus gave his musicians sketchily written parts, dictated parts to them by playing phrases on the

---

[28]The first album Mingus made for Columbia, *Mingus Ah Um* (later reissued as *Better Git It in Your Soul*), contains examples of the varied accompaniment devices Mingus used. The version of "Fables of Faubus" in this collection switches accompanying style several times. It goes beyond the more subtle alterations in comping, bass lines, and drum fills which occur routinely in most modern jazz combo performances. "Bird Calls," from the same album, shows an integration of collective improvisation with more structured approaches. It is so well managed that, as with his 1957 "Ysabel's Table Dance" from the *TiaJuana Moods* album (RCA LSP 2533; reissued as *New Tijuana Moods*, RCA Bluebird 5644, CD/ 5635 LP, 1957), listeners are often unable to determine what elements are improvised and what elements are composed. For more about Mingus, see Brian Priestly's *Mingus: A Critical Biography* (Quartet, 1983; reprinted by DaCapo), and pages 35–43 in Jost's *Free Jazz*.

piano or the bass, and described in words the conceptions which he wanted converted to music. (Listen to "Hora Decubitus" in SCCJ.)[29]

**ERIC DOLPHY**    Modern jazz has known numerous virtuoso saxophonists, but Eric Dolphy (1928–1964) could be called virtuoso on three different instruments: flute, alto saxophone, and bass clarinet. Dolphy mastered the complete range of every instrument he played, and he capitalized on almost every sound it could produce. He even studied bird calls and mimicked them in his solos. Slides and smears connected Dolphy's notes. Sometimes his lines bounced and twittered exuberantly with animal cries interspersed with bop licks. Dolphy was also a composer whose pieces were as peculiar as Thelonious Monk's, but with odd intervals and syncopations even more jarring because they came at the listener much faster. Upon first hearing them, listeners often perceive Dolphy's compositions as erratic and unpredictable. Like his solo improvisations, they are so unusual that some listeners at first assumed the notes were not related to the chord changes in the accompaniment and that Dolphy either did not know what he was doing or was intentionally fooling people with random note choices. His style perfectly fit the "avant-garde" and "out" characterizations, and was even mistaken by some for free jazz. Contrary to what some thought, however, Dolphy was quite sincere and thoroughly schooled, knew exactly what he was doing, and purposely connected every note to preset progressions of chords in the accompaniment. The connections were far less obvious than in earlier jazz styles, but they were not so remote that Dolphy's playing could be considered free of form.

Dolphy's first well-known recordings were made with the Chico Hamilton quintet during the 1950s, he then recorded with Mingus from 1960 to 1964. Many musicians regard his collaborations with Mingus to be among the most outstanding recordings in this period of jazz history. In 1961 and 1962, Dolphy toured and recorded with fellow saxophonist John Coltrane.[30]

Dolphy's 1958–59 work with Chico Hamilton's group was rooted in bop phrasing and swing feeling.[31] His later work, however, was characterized by explosive tor-

[29]In the 1960 pianoless quartet of Mingus, Dolphy, trumpeter Ted Curson, and drummer Dannie Richmond, there was an exceptional level of empathy between Mingus and Dolphy. The two have an extended dialog on "What Love" that is filled with humor and flexible interaction. The conversation between Mingus's pizzicato bass and Dolphy's bass clarinet is so human that it almost makes you think words are being exchanged. It is very coherent and skillful. See footnote 23.

[30]Dolphy solos on Coltrane's "India" (*Impressions*, MCA 5887 (Impulse 42), CD/LP, 1961) and "Spiritual" ("*Live*" *at the Village Vanguard*, MCA 29009 (Impulse 10), LP, 1961). Coltrane's *The Other Vanguard Tapes* (MCA2-4137 (Impulse 9325)) has better solos from these sessions. Coltrane's *Olé Coltrane* album (Atlantic 1373, CD/LP, 1961) uses Dolphy, but lists him as "George Lane" on the album jacket. Before his death in 1964, Dolphy also made a number of albums as a leader, such as *Out to Lunch* (Blue Note 46524 (84163), CD/LP, 1964), but some of his best work was documented in Mingus recordings.

[31]Some of his alto saxophone playing of that period sounds like Charlie Parker and Cannonball Adderley, though his main influence was fellow Californian Sonny Criss, and he was also quite familiar with Johnny Hodges, as evidenced by Dolphy's unaccompanied alto saxophone solo on "Tenderly" (*Far Cry*, OJC 400 (NJ 8270), CD/LP, 1961) and his work on Hamilton's *Gongs East* (Discovery DS-831 (Warner Bros. 1271), LP, 1958).

rents of notes, with neither conventional melodic development nor bop phrasing. He could also play with swing era lushness, sometimes on the same piece in which he showed the wild and jumpy side of his style.[32]

Eric Dolphy's impact was not as extensive as Ornette Coleman's or John Coltrane's, but there were musicians after the mid-1960s who played his tunes, composed in his style, and drew upon his improvisational methods. Saxophonists and flutists were especially impressed by Dolphy's consummate mastery of his instruments and his courage to use that skill to invent and perform what often seemed outrageous sounds. He opened up a new horizon for modern jazz by showing that such an unorthodox manner of playing could be acceptable.

**FREE DRUMMERS**

Several highly imaginative drummers have been associated with free jazz (see Table 14.2). They developed a style which did not rely on repetitive ride rhythms, high-hat closings, and bass drum patterns. Though much of their work did imply tempo, the rhythms they invented only sporadically stated it. All four of the drummer's limbs in this "free drumming" style performed a function similar to the "chattering" done by bop drummers's left hands on snare drum (for explanation of bop techniques, listen to JAZZ STYLES CASSETTE, side 1). In other words, "chattering" came from the entire drum set, and free drummers were not relegating their right hands to stating a consistent timekeeping rhythm nor their high-hats to snapping shut sharply on every other beat. All four limbs were devoted to generating an undercurrent of activity that popped and crackled with changing sounds. **By comparison with swing era and bop methods of rhythm section drumming, free jazz style produced sound patterns that were less predictable, and they offered varieties of color and shading that were more extensive. This was a complete departure from the traditions of marching band and dance band. The style of free jazz drumming is closer to an orchestral concept of percussion because it emphasizes color and shading instead of timekeeping.**[33]

**FREE BASSISTS**

A number of fine bassists have been associated with free jazz (see Table 14.2). Most have played in more conventional settings, too. In this chapter we are singling out two of the best known, Charlie Haden and Dave Holland.

**Charlie Haden** (b. 1937) is the bassist most prominently associated with Ornette Coleman during the 1950s and 60s. He also received wide exposure as a member of

[32]In his long duet with bowed bass on the first half of "You Don't Know What Love Is" (*Last Date*, Fontana 822226 (Limelight 86013), CD, 1964), Dolphy's flute solo is so rich in tone quality, it sounds as though he savored the vibrations of each note before proceeding to the next.

[33]Listen to Sunny Murray's playing on Cecil Taylor's 1962 recording of "Trance" from *Live at the Cafe Monmartre* (Fantasy 86014) or on Albert Ayler's 1964 album *Spiritual Unity* (ESP DISK 1002). Or listen to later examples of a similar style in the drumming of Barry Altschul on "Q & A" and "Interception" on bassist Dave Holland's 1972 album *Conference of the Birds*, ECM 829373 (1027), or on "Thanatos" and "Vendana" with Holland in Chick Corea's 1971 album *A.R.C.*, ECM 833678 (1009), CD.

**TABLE 14.2.  Some of the Many Musicians Who Have Improvised Without Preset Chord Progressions**

| Saxophonists | Trumpeters | Bassists |
|---|---|---|
| Ornette Coleman | Bobby Bradford | Charlie Haden |
| Eric Dolphy | Freddie Hubbard | Dave Holland |
| Albert Ayler | Don Cherry | David Lee |
| Archie Shepp | Don Ayler | Malachi Favors |
| Bill Smith | Lester Bowie | Fred Hopkins |
| Henry Threadgill | Bill Dixon | Jimmy Garrison |
| Sam Rivers | Dewey Johnson | Scott LaFaro |
| David Murray | Eddie Gale Stevens | Charlie Mingus |
| Oliver Lake | Ted Curson | Buell Neidlinger |
| Anthony Braxton | Leo Smith | Bob Cranshaw |
| Roscoe Mitchell | | Henry Grimes |
| Joseph Jarman | | David Izenzon |
| John Coltrane | | Gary Peacock |
| Dewey Redman | | Richard Davis |
| John Gilmore | | Steve Swallow |
| Danny Davis | | Alan Silva |
| Marshall Allen | | |
| Pharoah Sanders | **Pianists** | **Drummers Associated with Free Jazz** |
| Sonny Rollins | Lennie Tristano | |
| Gato Barbieri | Keith Jarrett | Milford Graves |
| Marion Brown | Paul Bley | Sunny Murray |
| John Tchicai | Sam Rivers | Andrew Cyrille |
| Jimmy Lyons | Sun Ra | Rashied Ali |
| Ken McIntyre | Cecil Taylor | Beaver Harris |
| Steve Lacy | | Barry Altschul |
| Pat Patrick | | Charles Moffett |
| | | Don Moye |
| | | Steve McCall |
| | | Dennis Charles |
| | | Ed Blackwell |
| | | Billy Higgins |
| | | Paul Motian |

the Keith Jarrett Quartet during the 1970s, a band which drew considerable inspiration from Coleman's music. Though usually classed with free jazz musicians, Haden is known for playing that is firmly tied to the movement of harmonies fundamental to nonfree styles. In fact, his work is usually bound more closely to jazz traditions than is the work of those he accompanies. One of his greatest contributions was to translate what free hornmen were doing into a more conventional jazz time feeling. This helped unify the group sound by anchoring creations of the hornmen which were frequently without feeling of formal meter, and it also brought swing feeling to many musical ideas that probably would not have swung by themselves. (Listen to Haden on Coleman's "Congeniality" and "Lonely Woman" in SCCJ.)

As an accompanist, Haden constructs lines that move with unerring logic, no matter how quickly directions change in the solo lines. He manages to pick up direction that momentarily occurs in solo lines and instantaneously align himself with it. This is a skill he shares with the playing of fellow bassists Dave Holland (b. 1946) in Sam Rivers's groups and Malachi Favors (b. 1937) in the Art Ensemble of Chicago. All three bassists represent the strongest connection with conventional jazz that each of their respective groups displays. They are also distinguished by a higher level of instrumental facility than their horn-playing colleagues display. Haden, Holland, and Favors use very full and warm tones. They favor a clean, firm sound rather than the rough-hewn, explosive quality used by the hornmen they accompany. In fact, Haden makes the richness of his tone an element in his vocabulary of musical devices. He attaches more importance to single tones and the ways they can be manipulated than was the fashion with most bassists during the 1960s and 70s. He is concerned more with sound than speed, and he is not interested in improvising bass solos in the style of hornmen. Each of his notes reflects intense deliberation. Haden contrasts with most of his contemporaries in that he is not concerned with intricacy.

**Dave Holland** is known for music he played with such chord-progression-based musicians as Miles Davis and Chick Corea as well as for his playing in free-form settings. No matter what setting he is in, Holland always seems to choose the right notes and fit them together in a highly musical way that is complete and warm at the same time. He has a conception of broad scope, an imagination which rivals Scott La Faro's, and a swinging manner of timekeeping. Holland's playing exudes strength and confidence. His tone glows with a unique color and the vibrato he gives to many long tones. Naturalness is a pervasive feeling in his style. He can take racing tempos and still swing and sound pretty. Ballads are a joy for his approach. In addition to being present in many ground-breaking recordings of Miles Davis and Chick Corea, Holland was also leader on an important record session that has been associated with avant-garde jazz: *Conference of the Birds* (see footnote 33). His work with numerous groups led by saxophonist Sam Rivers parallels the work Charlie Haden did with Ornette Coleman and Keith Jarrett; but Holland has more speed and agility than Haden and uses those abilities in ways that are not part of Haden's style. Holland can play horn-like bass solos in the bop manner as well as create action-filled textures as accompaniment in free jazz contexts.

**CHICAGO AVANT-GARDE**   A number of stylistically related black musicians from Chicago began gaining attention during the late 1950s and early 60s and finally received wide critical recognition during the late 1970s. The music of these players helped define avant-

**Figure 14.1.** An instrument used in Sun Ra's band: kettledrum (two or more kettledrums are called timpani).

garde jazz for the 1960s and 70s.[34] This stream of Chicagoans can be considered as three groups: 1) the musicians associated with Sun Ra, beginning during the 1950s, 2) the Association for the Advancement of Creative Musicians (AACM), an alliance of black players spearheaded by pianist Richard Abrams in the mid-1960s, and 3) the most well publicized of all AACM members, the Art Ensemble of Chicago and saxophonist-composer Anthony Braxton, who became well known in the 1970s.

**SUN RA**  Sun Ra (b. 1915) is an immensely creative pianist, composer, arranger, and band-leader who has been active as a professional musician since the 1930s. He formed his own big band during the 1950s. Like Duke Ellington's, many of Ra's principal sidemen have stayed with him for twenty and thirty years at a stretch. He has written and performed in a kaleidoscopic range of musical styles. Sun Ra's output is uniquely his own music, but its diversity is most expediently characterized by comparison with similar work of better-known musicians in more familiar styles:

1)   Some pieces resemble the chant music of Africa.
2)   Some works suggest the mode-based work of John Coltrane in the 1960s.[35]
3)   Some of Sun Ra's mid-1950s music almost sounds like a modern jazz version of Duke Ellington's music in the 1940s.[36]
4)   Some of Sun Ra's work in the mid-1960s resembled contemporary classical music using electronically altered and synthesized sounds.[37]

[34]Much of this Chicago activity was occurring well before the first recordings of Ornette Coleman became available. We can therefore assume that much of it originated with the Chicagoans and was not derivative. However, the second wave of Chicagoans and their St. Louis relatives, the Black Artists Group, clearly derived some inspiration from Coleman and Albert Ayler. For more, see pages 163–199 in Jost's *Free Jazz*. Also see the interview with Sun Ra in Len Lyons's *The Great Jazz Pianists*.

[35]*Nubians of Plutonia*, Impulse 9242 (Saturn 406), LP, 1959

[36]*Sun Song*, Delmark 411 (Transition 10), LP, 1956; *Super-Sonic Sounds*, Impulse 9271 (Saturn 216), LP, 1956

[37]*Magic City*, Impulse 9243 (Saturn 711)

**Figure 14.2.** Instruments used in Sun Ra's band (left to right): Piccolo, flute, clarinet; bass clarinet lying in front.

Differences between Sun Ra's writing and that of conventional big bands can be summarized easily by saying that Sun Ra capitalizes on the diversity that is possible with big band instrumentation and overlooked by most other bandleaders. For instance Sun Ra

1) uses many different combinations of trumpets, trombones, saxophones, piano, bass, and drums;

2) extends the range of tone colors by adding electronic instruments (he employed electric piano and synthesizers long before rock groups made their use common);

3) makes imaginative use of timpani (see Figure 14.1), celeste, xylophone, bass marimba, bells, and chimes;

4) uses saxophonists who play instruments unusual in jazz, such as piccolo, oboe, bassoon, and bass clarinet (see Figures 14.2 and 14.3);

5) requires nearly all his sidemen to double on percussion instruments;

6) sometimes creates passages by means of simultaneous collective improvisation instead of composition;

7) gives performances in which pieces are not separated, where the entire evening is an uninterrupted sequence of unusual sounds.

**Figure 14.3.** English horn, oboe, and bassoon.

Sun Ra's use of synthesizers and the overall conception for many of his 1960s albums, especially *Heliocentric Worlds of Sun Ra, Vol. 1 and 2*,[38] suggest the work of twentieth-century classical composers Edgard Varèse and Krzysztof Penderecki. Central to the conception of such work is the notion that music can consist of sound by itself instead of sound in the conventional form of melody and harmony. Chunks of sound are sequenced in place of the standard ideas of melody and chord progression. When Sun Ra and his improvisers address themselves to this style, the result has a more natural and flowing character than similar music performed by symphony orchestra musicians.

[38]ESP DISK 1014 & 1017, LP, 1965

Sun Ra has also been active in the free jazz approach. Portions of his performances are collectively improvised with little apparent prearrangement (*Astro Black, Magic City, Heliocentric Worlds of Sun Ra Vol. 2*). His free jazz passages differ from those of Ornette Coleman and John Coltrane because they have more evident continuity and compositional organization. It is also important to recognize that Sun Ra has succeeded artistically with free-form collective improvisation in big band contexts—something other leaders have not attempted, probably for the reason that large ensembles pose great difficulty because of the problems musicians must overcome in considering so many other sounds that are being played at the same time as their own.

In many ways, Sun Ra is like Duke Ellington. His fascination with widely diverse textures and his unconventional arranging methods are one similarity. He also has the rare skill possessed by Ellington of being able to oversee combinations of improvisation and composition and blend them in a unified form. Like Ellington, Sun Ra brings out the best in his sidemen who, in turn, adapt their improvisatory styles to the varying moods within his compositions.

Saxophonists **Marshall Allen** (b. 1924) and John Gilmore are Sun Ra's strongest improvisers, and both have remained with the band for more than thirty years. Allen, who can play all the woodwind instruments, has contributed extremely imaginative oboe and piccolo solos to Sun Ra's recordings. He has also improvised free-form, high-energy alto saxophone solos that capitalize on the instrument's altissimo register and depart totally from conventional organization of pitches and jazz swing feeling. In his playing, long sequences of squeals and screeches are connected with tremendous intensity and developed organically to set the mood for Sun Ra's pieces.

**John Gilmore** (b. 1931) is almost totally unknown outside of Sun Ra's bands, though he is recognized and respected among knowledgeable jazz musicians, and has recorded with the noted bands of drummer Art Blakey and pianists Andrew Hill and Paul Bley (see page 258 for Gilmore's influence on Coltrane). Gilmore stands out among post-bop saxophonists for a distinctive, hard-hitting style, and is known for a very raw, hard bop approach. He has also devised an approach whereby individual notes are not as important as the overall contours and timbre of the sound. Like Albert Ayler, Gilmore has refined a high-energy style of swirling legato figures that are not melodic or rhythmic so much as they are like extended screams and growls that help generate a mood and a sound mass.

Apart from John Gilmore, few of Sun Ra's sidemen have recorded with better-known bands. One exception is trombonist Julian Priester, who worked with the band of drummer Max Roach and was part of an innovative septet led by pianist Herbie Hancock during the 1970s. Like Sun Ra's of the early 1960s, **Herbie Hancock's group of the early 1970s used synthesizer, varied percussion sounds, piccolo, and bass clarinet, and often produced music resembling that of twentieth-century composer Edgard Varèse. That Varèse-like style, as practiced by Hancock and Sun Ra, resembled background music for science fiction and space travel films, and it was popularly labeled "space music."**

Sun Ra's live performances are accompanied by singing, dancing, costumes, and unusual lighting. A Sun Ra concert is a multimedia experience. This has been unusual in modern jazz even though it has become common in rock. Though entertaining for some of Sun Ra's listeners, it has been distracting for others, and his reception has suffered among some musicians and critics. Listeners fail to take Sun Ra's music seriously also because Sun Ra attaches to his music a humorous emphasis on philosophy, astrology, space travel, and astronomy. Another factor explaining his failure to attract a wider audience is his diversity. It is possible, for instance, to hear five different Sun Ra approaches and still not be acquainted with all of his facets. Though it is unfair to judge Sun Ra's work on the basis of merely one album or a few live performances, many listeners dismiss his music in precisely this way, and Sun Ra remains the most controversial musician in this chapter.

Despite the unusual breadth, depth, and originality of his music, Sun Ra is relatively unknown. His recordings number over one hundred, but because he has made and distributed most of them himself, and because of the unorthodox sound of his music, few of his records have received much attention. Even though he has contributed major innovations in jazz composition as well as introducing synthesizers and big band free-form improvisation to jazz as early as the 1950s and 60s, Sun Ra was still little known during the 1970s and 80s. His obscurity has prevailed despite the reissue of many of his albums by the well-distributed Impulse label in the 1970s and new recording activity by foreign companies in the 1980s.

## THE ASSOCIATION FOR THE ADVANCEMENT OF CREATIVE MUSICIANS

The Association for the Advancement of Creative Musicians (AACM) is a Chicago-based collective of modern jazz musicians founded in the early 1960s by saxophonist Fred Anderson and pianist Muhal Richard Abrams. It organized concerts, recordings, training, and promotion for black musicians who had an affinity for jazz that was not squarely within the bop tradition. Their music was almost exclusively nonelectronic and separate from jazz-rock. Though generally possessing considerable originality, much of the AACM's music resembles Sun Ra's, Ornette Coleman's, and the work of Charles Mingus in several respects. First, its **rhythmic feeling lacks the flowing, easy character of conventional jazz and is more like the unpredictable nature of modern concert music.** Second, **solos are often freely improvised and inspired more by the mood of the piece than by standard bop patterns.** Third, **the music uses a larger assortment of accompaniment rhythms than was common to bop.** And fourth, **the proceedings display a rough quality** consistent with the Mingus concept that each performance is really a public workshop rather than a finished product.

## The Art Ensemble of Chicago; Roscoe Mitchell, Joseph Jarman, Lester Bowie, Malachi Favors

The Art Ensemble of Chicago emerged during the late 1960s. The group makes music which does not follow any strict set of rules. They choose styles freely, and they refuse to base their music on the expectations set by a particular idiom or a particular audience. They embrace the music of the whole world as their repertory. Though they have sometimes applied conventional jazz approaches, the group has performed in a broad range of styles, some of which, like Sun Ra's, have not been squarely within the jazz tradition. In their work they have:

1) mimicked street bands of foreign countries,
2) performed lighthearted dramatic sketches,

The Art Ensemble of Chicago (left to right): Roscoe Mitchell, Lester Bowie, and Joseph Jarman, 1973. The large instrument in the foreground is a bass sax. (*Photo by Bill Smith*)

3)  recited poetry,
4)  worn costumes and stage makeup,
5)  made sounds for sound's sake instead of making sounds that followed traditional concepts of melody and harmony,
6)  improvised without following preset progressions of chords.

Some of their music is similar to that of Ornette Coleman, Don Cherry, and Albert Ayler, especially in their large assortment of tone qualities and pitch bends. Their jazz solo conceptions owe much to Coleman. They do not use piano, and, although all group members play percussion instruments, many of their recordings dispense with the conventional jazz drum set. Timekeeping and a harmonic background are provided by bassist Malachi Favors, who has outstanding technique and distinctive improvisational flexibility. Without his strength and imagination much of the group's music would be weak.

The Art Ensemble members seem to play almost every instrument, including ones that most listeners have never seen before. They collect instruments from all over the world, and their stage setting looks like a museum. To simplify the task of identifying the players, we should note that **Lester Bowie** (b. 1941) is primarily a trumpeter, **Malachi Favors** concentrates on bass, and **Joseph Jarman** (b. 1937) and

**Roscoe Mitchell** (b. 1940) are primarily saxophonists. In addition to percussion instruments, Mitchell plays soprano, alto, tenor, and bass saxophones, clarinet, and flute. Joseph Jarman plays soprano, alto, tenor, and bass saxophones, clarinet, bassoon, flute, oboe, and vibraharp. Since 1970, drummer **Don Moye** (b. 1946) has also been recording with the group.

The Art Ensemble of Chicago uses musical elements that have been relatively neglected in the mainstream of modern jazz styles. The group has repackaged ideas that the originators of free jazz had pioneered, presenting them in a less frantic and more humorous way. A notable contribution is the group's practice of taking a brief melodic fragment and altering it over long stretches within a performance. Another feature is that, in place of rapidly flowing bop lines, the group offers unusual instruments and varied tonal inflections. Strict tempo is often rejected. The group stands out in their avoidance of traditional format in which improvised solos are strung together one after another, without a storytelling quality to unify the piece. During the 1980s, however, they did record several albums that imitated modern jazz approaches to timekeeping and solo improvisation.

In place of complex chord progressions and virtuoso displays of technical prowess, the Art Ensemble offers simplicity and careful use of silence. In fact, the group has made more use of silence and changes in loudness than most jazz-oriented groups since Jimmy Giuffre's in the 1950s and 60s. This puts them in direct contrast with John Coltrane's high-energy, dense-textured music of the 1960s and the loud, repetitive jazz-rock of the 1970s. The Art Ensemble is one of the first groups since the Modern Jazz Quartet to become known for exploration of soft and gentle sounds.[39]

**Anthony Braxton**

One of the most broadly talented figures to emerge during the prominence of the AACM is Anthony Braxton (b. 1945). If ever there was a jazz-oriented musician whose work resists categorization, it is Braxton. He performs on an enormous variety of flutes, clarinets, and saxophones, yet the tone color he extracts is unlike the accepted model for each. He sometimes improvises solos with conventional modern jazz accompaniment, yet his solo lines do not resemble standard modern jazz approaches of Charlie Parker or John Coltrane. Though he is usually classed within the jazz idiom, very little of Braxton's music swings in the jazz sense (see chapter 2 for explanation of swing feeling). Though sometimes suggesting atonality, Braxton's lines resemble less the truly atonal music of Arnold Schoenberg than an odd blend of Lee Konitz and Eric Dolphy. In addition, some of his unaccompanied work draws upon Oriental methods of tone alteration, timing, and motivic development. His large-scale work for symphony orchestra, however, clearly displays the influence of his favorite non-jazz composers Karlheinz Stockhausen, Krzysztof Penderecki, and John Cage.[40] Braxton organizes groups whose instrumentation is unusual, such as two unaccompanied saxophones or simply saxophone and trombone.

[39]*A Jackson in Your House*, Affinity AFF9 (Actuel BYG2), LP, 1969; *People in Sorrow*, Nessa 3, LP, 1969; *Nice Guys*, ECM 827876 (1126), CD/LP, 1978; *Urban Bushman*, ECM 829394 (1211), CD set, 1980

[40]*For 4 Orchestras*, Arista 8900, LP set, 1978

Yet when employing big band instrumentation, his orchestrations dance back and forth between parade music, snatches of jazz history, and twentieth-century concert music.[41] Braxton seems to be tireless and blessed with endless imagination, but because his music goes far beyond jazz idioms, he should not be viewed only as a jazz musician.[42]

**THE WORLD SAXOPHONE QUARTET**

The Black Artists Group was formed in St. Louis during 1968 along the same organizational lines and musical views that inspired the AACM in Chicago. Three saxophonists coming from this organization became prominent in the late 1970s and early 1980s: **Oliver Lake** (b. 1942), **Julius Hemphill** (b. 1940), and **Hamiet Bluiett** (b. 1940). These men recorded in numerous combinations and performed extensively on their own during that period, but their highest critical acclaim was earned when they performed in combination with saxophonist **David Murray** (b. 1955) within a group they had founded in 1976 called the World Saxophone Quartet (WSQ). Though flute and clarinets are also used, basically the WSQ consists of Lake and Hemphill on alto, Murray on tenor, and Hamiet Bluiett on baritone saxophone.

The WSQ drew from the approaches of Ornette Coleman and Albert Ayler, but they placed a greater emphasis on composition. The diversity of tone colors associated with free jazz players and such earlier bands as Duke Ellington's recurred and was extended. The free-form collective approaches of Coleman inspired the WSQ, but a greater balance of contrasts was achieved by WSQ because they carefully alternated prewritten parts with improvised solos and simultaneous collective improvisations. Greater clarity of sound was also achieved because the WSQ performed without piano, guitar, bass, or drums.

The music of the WSQ is especially distinctive because much of it is delivered in a light-hearted manner. Diversity and activity seem the key guidelines. Some passages recall Igor Stravinsky's writing for woodwinds, while others suggest Ellington's saxophone writing. Like the Art Ensemble of Chicago, the WSQ is significant for offering a unique refinement of free-form methods combined with numerous traditions of jazz and nonjazz sources.[43]

**POPULAR APPEAL**

The styles described in this chapter are the least popular jazz styles in history. During their earliest years, groups playing these styles were not wanted by jazz clubs, and few record companies showed any interest in recording them. The passage of thirty years has done little to change this. Most of the pivotal recordings by Don Cherry, Albert Ayler, Sun Ra, and Cecil Taylor are no longer in print, and many never sold sufficient copies to absorb production costs. No album by any musician discussed in this chapter ever penetrated the list of "top 200" best-selling

[41]*Creative Orchestra Music*, RCA Bluebird 6579 (Arista 4080), CD, 1976

[42]Examples of Braxton's work: *Three Compositions of New Jazz*, Delmark 415, LP, 1968; *For Alto*, Delmark 420, 1968, solo; *Five Pieces 1975*, Arista 4054, LP, 1975.

[43]SCCJ-R contains a version of "Steppin'" from WSQ's *Live in Zurich*, Black Saint 120056 (BSR0056), CD/LP, 1986. Of their many albums, fans often prefer the first, *Steppin'*, Black Saint 120027 (BSR 0027), CD/LP, 1978.

albums in any year. Not much modern jazz is played on the radio, but the situation is especially unfortunate for free jazz. Some major cities never heard more than a few samples of free jazz during the entire decade of the 1960s. There are jazz stations which have never played any of Sun Ra's music. Although musicians usually blame their fate on a lack of promotion, several other styles of modern jazz have managed to sell without much promotion. This suggests that even if the avant-garde styles had been promoted, their popularity would still have been limited. The problem is that most listeners find them unswinging, difficult to follow, chaotic, and nerve-wracking. So, ironically, this music of great innovation has also been a music that has received very little exposure.

## CHAPTER SUMMARY

1) Free jazz improvisation does not adhere to preset progressions of chords and sometimes also dispenses with preset melody and steady timekeeping.

2) Free jazz has a reputation for wider variation in pitch and tone quality than bop, and some free jazz involves lengthy collective improvisations that are loud and frenzied.

3) Prominent free saxophonists include Ornette Coleman and Albert Ayler.

4) Free jazz pianist Cecil Taylor is known for dense textures and much turbulence in his improvisations.

5) Prominent bassists in free jazz include Charlie Haden and Dave Holland.

6) Trumpeter Don Cherry was Ornette Coleman's sideman for the late 1950s and early 1960s, one of the most original improvisers to appear since bop, and one of the first to explore Third World music.

7) Free jazz drummers have perfected approaches which depart from marching band and dance band tradition by generating an ever-changing undercurrent of activity instead of standard timekeeping patterns.

8) Charles Mingus was an innovative modern bassist and a bandleader-composer who combined composition and improvisation while creatively altering accompaniment patterns.

9) Sun Ra and other avant-garde players from Chicago departed from bop practices of melody, chord progressions and swing feeling in addition to incorporating Third World music.

10) Beginning in the 1950s, pianist Sun Ra's big band methods demonstrated some of the most varied voicings since Duke Ellington's.

11) Sun Ra explored collective improvisation in big band music during the 1960s and 70s, and was one of the first jazz composer-arrangers to extensively use synthesizers and electric keyboard instruments.

12) The Association for the Advancement of Creative Musicians was a Chicago-based collective founded by Richard Abrams during the 1960s.

13) The Chicagoans stressed continuity between composition and improvisation.

14) The AACM's Art Ensemble of Chicago, which gained prominence during the 1970s, consisted of trumpeter Lester Bowie, saxophonists Roscoe Mitchell and Joseph Jarman, bassist Malachi Favors, and drummer Don Moye.

15) Multi-instrumentalist Anthony Braxton is a composer and improviser of sweeping scope who does not play in bop style and whose music draws from non-Western music, the styles of Eric Dolphy and Lee Konitz, and twentieth-century symphonic music.

16) The World Saxophone Quartet is made up of David Murray, Julius Hemphill, Oliver Lake, and Hamiet Bluiett. It has demonstrated a successful integration of prewritten passages and freely improvised parts without rhythm section accompaniment.

Ornette Coleman's band minus Coleman: Don Cherry (pocket trumpet), Charlie Haden (bass), Eddie Blackwell (drums), and Dewey Redman (tenor sax). During the mid-1970s this personnel went by the name of "Old and New Dreams." (*Photo by Bill Smith*)

# chapter 15
# BILL EVANS, HERBIE HANCOCK, CHICK COREA, & KEITH JARRETT

The most influential jazz pianist to emerge after Bud Powell was Bill Evans, and the combined influence of Powell and Evans is apparent in three of the most widely imitated pianists after Evans: Herbie Hancock, Chick Corea, and Keith Jarrett. Each of these players toured and recorded with Miles Davis, and each became an important composer and bandleader in his own right. These three pianists attracted large popular followings and had record sales and concert receipts that far exceeded those of both Powell and Evans. This chapter is devoted to the piano styles of Evans, Hancock, Corea, and Jarrett, their respective group styles, and the innovations in rhythm section playing that Evans pioneered.

**BILL EVANS**

Bill Evans (1929–1980)[1] played with Miles Davis for about nine months during 1958 and 1959. The exposure he received from playing with Davis and contributing to the classic Davis album *Kind of Blue* brought him to the attention of jazz musicians and fans. (Listen to *Kind of Blue's* "Flamenco Sketches" in the JAZZ CLASSICS CASSETTE.) Shortly before his involvement with *Kind of Blue*,[2] Evans had made a

[1]For more about Evans, see the book by Gene Lees, *Meet Me at Jim & Andy's* (Oxford, 1988), subscribe to the newsletter *Letter From Evans*, 2712 Cady Way, Winter Park, FL 32792-4856, or contact the Bill Evans Archives, P.O. Box 803, Southeastern Louisiana University, Hammond, LA 70402. For commentary about Evans, Herbie Hancock, Chick Corea, and Keith Jarrett, see *The Great Jazz Pianists*, by Len Lyons (Quill, 1983), and the booklet that accompanies *Jazz Piano*, the Smithsonian Press compilation of recordings. *Jazz Piano* also presents Evans-LaFaro-Motian on a 1959 recording of "Autumn Leaves" and a 1961 live recording of "Waltz for Debby," as well as a 1968 live solo recording by Evans of "I Loves You Porgy." A transcription and analysis of the Evans solo on "Nardis" (from *Explorations*, Riverside 351, reissued as OJC 37) is in John Rodby's *Solos for Jazz Piano* (Carl Fischer, 1989; order from Carl Fischer Music Store, 54 Cooper Square, NY, NY 10003). A transcription of "Peri's Scope" (*Portrait in Jazz*, Riverside 315, reissued as OJC 88) is in John Mehegan's *Jazz Improvisation, Vol. 4* (Watson-Guptill, 1965; reprinted by Amsco, 1973).

[2]Recordings with Miles Davis in 1958 include *Jazz at the Plaza* (CBS 32470, LP) and "Stella by Starlight," "Put Your Little Foot Out," and "On Green Dolphin Street" (*Basic Miles*, CBS PC 32025, LP).

**301**

Bill Evans, 1960, age 31. (*Photo by Chuck Stewart*)

trio record that had a lasting effect on many listeners. Evans himself considered the album to be one of his best. It was called *Everybody Digs Bill Evans*,[3] and its "Peace Piece" remains for many fans their favorite Evans performance. The chord voicings, bass part, and mood of "Peace Piece" provided the basis for "Flamenco Sketches" on *Kind of Blue*.

The Bill Evans style is unique in the history of jazz piano. His tone and conception are delicate without being fragile. On slow pieces, he sometimes creates a harp-like effect, by sounding single tones and letting them ring, as though to savor each vibration. (Listen to this in his solo on "Flamenco Sketches" in the JAZZ CLASSICS CASSETTE.) Though he possessed considerable dexterity, his work was never flashy. Though he was physically quite strong, he usually steered clear of an aggressively percussive manner. Evans crafted his improvisations with exacting deliberation. Often he would take a phrase, or just a kernel of its character, then develop and extend its rhythms, its melodic ideas, and accompanying harmonies. Within the same solo he would often return to it, transforming it each time. And while all this was happening, he would be considering ways of resolving the tension that was building. He would be considering rhythmic ways, melodic ways, and harmonies, all at the same time, long before the moment that he decided was best for resolving the idea.

During Bill Evans's improvisations, an unheard, continuous self-editing was going on. He spared the listener his false starts and discarded ideas. Though he had a creative imagination, Evans never improvised solos that merely strung together ideas at the same rate they popped into his head. The results of these deliberations could be a swinging and exhilarating experience for the listener, but they reflected less a carefree abandon, than the well-honed craftsmanship of a very serious per-

[3]OJC-068 (Riverside 1129), CD/LP, 1958; The first Evans trio record is *New Jazz Conception*, OJC-025 (R-223), CD/LP, 1956.

former working in the manner of a classical composer. The adjective most frequently applied to his music is "introspective."

Bill Evans refined an approach to rhythm in jazz improvisation that has been called "non-obvious pulse," "floating pulse," "phrasing across the bar line," and "de-emphasizing the beat." (If you are not familiar with concepts of beat, meter, and rhythm, study the "Elements of Music" appendix before continuing this chapter.) His work was rhythmically very involved. Essentially, it entailed constructing phrases without starting or stopping them on main beats, or otherwise accenting beats that indicate the meter of the piece—the first of every four beats, in meter of four, for example. His phrases do not necessarily accent beats in ways that jazz listeners had come to expect—the manner of march and dance rhythms. Though his melodic ideas are very rhythmic, they are not obvious in terms of the beat. Evans may, for instance, stagger a melodic figure across several measures, always accenting the upbeats, never squarely accenting a downbeat, but floating past it instead. This contrasts with the rhythmic tendencies of most pianists, because, unlike Evans, they frequently accent the beginning of the first beat of a measure. Evans *conceived* most of his improvisations in reference to the meter and tempo of the piece. Yet without walking bass or ride rhythms as a reference, listeners often could not gain a clear indication of this. Unlike most hard bop pianists, Evans evolved away from playing strings of bouncing eighth notes that explicitly delineated each beat and formed contours that evenly rose and fell. The architecture of his lines was more complex, and tension was resolved less often. He did swing. In fact, many of his admirers praised his quality of swing feeling. However, in the perceptions of listeners who were accustomed to hearing a very relaxed, easily rolling line with frequent and explicit references to the first beat of the measure, Evans was not swinging. Though these tendencies became far more pronounced later in his career, the character of this rhythmic approach is evident in his widely acclaimed work of June 25, 1961, the last recording he made with bassist Scott LaFaro. This session has come to be known as the "Village Vanguard session" because it was recorded live during his appearance at that New York nightclub and was originally issued on an album called *Sunday at the Village Vanguard* (excerpted in "Solar" on the JAZZ CLASSICS CASSETTE).[4]

Prior to 1959, Evans displayed considerable dexterity, and his style included elements from several sources. His long, fast, smoothly contoured eighth-note lines remind us of saxophonist Lee Konitz, one of his early favorites. Because Konitz derived his style from pianist Lennie Tristano, the Evans approach can be said to exhibit Tristano's influence. Evans's piano solos also borrowed elements from bop

[4]Because of this famous recording and his other work, Bill Evans influenced various stages in the careers of many modern jazz pianists, especially in the jazz use of chord voicings originally identified with French Impressionist composers Maurice Ravel and Claude Debussy. Listen to the second movement of Ravel's "Sonatina" to hear one source for the Evans chord voicings. To detect the influence of the Evans voicings and manner in others, listen to Herbie Hancock on "My Funny Valentine," especially the introduction (Miles Davis—*My Funny Valentine*, CBS 9106, LP, 1964), and "Pee Wee" (Miles Davis—*Sorcerer*, CBS 9532, LP, 1967); Chick Corea on the Stan Getz album *Sweet Rain*, Verve 815054 (V8693), CD, 1967; Keith Jarrett on "Pretty Ballad" from Jarrett's album *Somewhere Before*, Atlantic 8808 (Vortex 2012), CD/LP, 1968; or Jarrett on "Ellen David" in Charlie Haden's album *Closeness*, A&M CD-0808 (SP710), CD, 1976.

pianist Bud Powell. Occasionally, Evans also used some bluesy figures which might be traced to pianist-composer Horace Silver, a far-reaching force during the 1950s. The manner in which Evans developed his ideas across a solo improvisation also reflects his debt to Nat Cole, who had also influenced Powell and Silver. In addition, Evans cited George Shearing as having opened his ears to the beauties of tone.

After *Kind of Blue*, Evans made the first of four LPs with bassist Scott LaFaro.[5] He began ridding himself of bop clichés and devised an original, very personal style that offered an alternative to bop-based approaches. It departed from bop traditions to an extent almost as great as the departure made by Cecil Taylor. However, because Evans played tunes that listeners recognized and because his style was so subtle, Evans was not generally recognized as an avant-garde figure, even though his music—especially the Village Vanguard session—was undeniably avant-garde.

Most of Evans's lines were composed of smoothly connected notes. Rarely after 1959 did he play lines with disconnected or staccato notes, instead favoring a legato style. His left hand gained importance and was soon sustaining chords in almost every measure instead of merely punctuating right-hand lines. The melodies he improvised were frequently chorded, note for note, in the locked-hands style. He worked out methods for voicing his chorded lines in terms of modes and used tight clusters of notes. Evans drew from the harmonies of Debussy and Ravel, and he employed voicings that were frequently composed of the interval of a fourth. (Listen to his accompaniments for Miles Davis on "So What" in SCCJ.)

Evans often chose pretty melodies which were economical in their construction yet provided interesting chord progressions for the improviser. His best-known composition, "Waltz for Debby," embodies the essence of his style.[6] He liked waltzes, an unusual preference for a jazz musician. Among the waltzes to which he gave his tender treatment were "Someday My Prince Will Come," "Alice in Wonderland," "Tenderly," "Skating in Central Park," and "I'm All Smiles."

**Rhythm Section Innovations**    During 1961, **Scott LaFaro** (1936–1961) demonstrated advances that were as historically significant as those of Jimmy Blanton two decades earlier. **LaFaro demonstrated that the bass can contribute ensemble interplay that provides a feeling of grace and freedom for the underpinnings of a group sound, and he devised a fresh conception for improvising bass solos.** LaFaro is also influential for having pioneered using more than just one or two fingers to pluck the bass strings. Previously, bassists had primarily employed only one or two fingers instead of borrowing from the technique of classical guitarists as LaFaro did. LaFaro's new technique lent added speed and allowed greater intricacy and continuity in his lines.

[5]The best compilation of this music is *Bill Evans at the Village Vanguard*, Riverside 60-017, CD, 1961; or *Sunday at the Village Vanguard*, OJC-140 (Riverside 9376), CD/LP.
[6]in *Jazz Piano*, Smithsonian 039, CD, LP, or cassette sets

**Listening Guide for "Solar"**

Composed by Chuck Wayne; recorded June, 25, 1961 at the Village Vanguard in New York City by Bill Evans (piano), Scott LaFaro (bass), and Paul Motian (drums); available on the JAZZ CLASSICS CASSETTE, originally on *Sunday at the Village Vanguard* (Riverside 376), reissued on CD as *Bill Evans at the Village Vanguard* (Riverside 60–017).

Bill Evans had several different stylistic phases in his career. The JAZZ CLASSICS CASSETTE samples two of them. His piano voicings, modal thinking, and very spare solo style affected the sound of "Flamenco Sketches," a selection taken from the Miles Davis album *Kind of Blue* of 1959. "Solar" was selected to provide the clearest example of the unique approach that Evans and bassist Scott LaFaro developed for playing together. In this performance LaFaro does not walk. Moreover, his rhythms contain very little repetition. Unlike traditional bass playing that provides a very predictable foundation for the soloists, LaFaro's role here can be likened to an everchanging counteractivity. Sometimes in fact it is not clearly subordinate to Evans but instead seems to go its own way, as in the first few choruses. Some listeners have construed it as an almost continuous musical conversation with Evans. LaFaro's accompaniment does not resemble the ways bassists had traditionally accompanied jazz pianists.

This performance of "Solar" also illustrates subtle ways of phrasing that came to characterize more and more Evans solos after the 1950s. Termed "non-obvious pulse" or "phrasing across the bar line," these approaches are particularly evident in the fifth and the seventh choruses. In the fifth chorus, almost all the accents in Evans's line are on the off-beat, and all three of his phrases are staggered across several measures. They are rhythmically displaced, never starting or clearly resolving on a strong beat. Evans seems to stretch figures out so they sound half-time, yet he sometimes comes back to a feeling that is almost double-time. The rhythms that Evans uses are so subtle in their relationship to the underlying pulse that we may have difficulty verifying the passage of beats and the beginnings of choruses if we ignore the drummer's timekeeping rhythms. Evans intentionally blurs conventional landmarks in the composition so thoroughly that this recording represents a significant departure from a jazz tradition of rhythmic obviousness. This is a new kind of jazz piano style.

The composition was written by guitarist Chuck Wayne, though it has always been mistakenly credited to Miles Davis. It is twelve measures long, but it does not follow a typical blues chord progression.

## FIRST CHORUS

*Melody Statement*

Evans begins alone, playing the first phrase of the melody in octaves. Then he is joined by LaFaro and Motian, and he plays the second phrase in harmony and the remaining phrases in octaves. LaFaro improvises melody lines of his own in the character of the "Solar" melody. LaFaro's lines occasionally incorporate phrases from the original melody and mimic Evans's lines. They also contain figures that state the pulse and outline notes in the chords.

In the first five choruses two interweaving melodies are offered instead of the usual format in which piano melody is accompanied by walking bass. Both melodies come in and out of the foreground. Though LaFaro's lines are usually somewhat subordinate to Evans's, they are more dense, more varied, and closer to the foreground than bass parts had traditionally been.

*Elapsed Time*

0' 15"

**SECOND CHORUS**

*Evans Restates The Melody*

All piano phrases are harmonized. LaFaro rotates among roles as countermelody creator and beat decorator.

0' 28"

**THIRD CHORUS**

Evans begins his solo improvisation by voicing all his lines in octaves and not comping for himself. While Evans departs from the melody as he improvises, LaFaro paraphrases it. This amounts to a two-part invention with drums and cymbals accompaniment.

0' 41"

**FOURTH CHORUS**

Evans and LaFaro continue to improvise counterlines to each other, LaFaro occasionally quoting the melody.

0' 54"

**FIFTH CHORUS**

LaFaro moves to a less melodic and more rhythmic role. Evans phrases his own improvisational ideas in rhythmic ways that do not convey the pulse of the piece in a particularly obvious manner.

1' 07"

**SIXTH CHORUS**

1' 20"

**SEVENTH CHORUS**

1' 34"

**EIGHTH CHORUS**

1' 47"

**NINTH CHORUS**

Beginning in the fourth measure, Evans constructs about twelve measures worth of lines from quarter-note triplet figures.

1' 58"

**TENTH CHORUS**

2' 11"

**ELEVENTH CHORUS**

After the fourth measure, Evans stops voicing his lines in octaves and begins to play one note at a time instead. He generates solo lines with his right hand and comps for himself with his left hand. Note how soft, light, and infrequent his left hand chords are.
This pattern persists until the sixteenth chorus.

2' 25"

**TWELFTH CHORUS**

2' 36"

**THIRTEENTH CHORUS**

2' 48"

**FOURTEENTH CHORUS**

3' 02"

**FIFTEENTH CHORUS**

3' 15"

**SIXTEENTH CHORUS**

Evans paraphrases the melody, using locked-hands block chording.

The idea of pianists and bassists engaging in musical conversation had been explored by Duke Ellington and Jimmy Blanton in 1940.[7] Evans and LaFaro refined this idea with drummer Paul Motian in their last recording together, made June 25, 1961 (excerpted in "Solar" on the JAZZ CLASSICS CASSETTE). LaFaro sometimes walked and sometimes soloed. But more often he vigorously supplied nonrepetitive figures that pitted an extra counteractivity against the sounds of piano and drums. While Evans was playing melody or improvising, LaFaro contributed a great diversity of musical ideas. He would throw in melodic figures, mimic or answer Evans, and underscore the figures Evans and Motian played. In addition, LaFaro often fed ideas to Evans. **LaFaro was not merely a timekeeper capable of impressive solos. He was a melodic player as important to the Evans trio as a saxophonist or trumpeter was to the standard jazz quintet.** LaFaro set the pace for a whole school of modern jazz bassists who, like himself, possessed spectacular instrumental facility. And like LaFaro, they interacted with pianists and drummers in imaginative and highly active manners.[8]

It was partly the Evans piano style that made possible LaFaro's contributions to these new concepts of jazz trio playing. One crucial aspect was its leanness. By contrast, in a Bud Powell-style trio, the amount of melodic and rhythmic interaction between bassist and pianist is relatively limited because the pianist fills up most of the spaces with long lines of his own.[9] The bassist must focus on explicitly stating the beats, and he has little chance to do much else. Another aspect is the way Evans voiced chords. The notes he chose allowed bassists more latitude because their own notes were less likely to duplicate or clash with those in his chords. Incidentally, the ways Evans voiced chords for and reharmonized standard tunes became models for the playing of those tunes by many other musicians thereafter. **Evans provided the perfect context for the blossoming of LaFaro's new approach to bass improvisation because the Evans piano style left room for the bass in the forefront of the combo sound, and because Evans encouraged LaFaro to capitalize on the opportunity by taking chances and trying all sorts of nontraditional techniques.** This was also the manner in which Evans collaborated with LaFaro's most gifted successors, Eddie Gomez and Marc Johnson. This style allowed them more flexibility and room for creativity than they experienced with other bandleaders.[10] (Listen to demonstration and explanation of this style on the JAZZ STYLES CASSETTE, side 1.)

---

[7]"Pitter Panther Patter" and "Mr. J.B. Blues" in *Duke Ellington 1940*, Smithsonian 2013, LP set.

[8]The clearest example of this style is in "Solar," *Sunday at the Village Vanguard*, OJC-140 (Riverside 9376), CD/LP, 1961

[9]Compare the Evans-LaFaro recordings with work by the trios of Art Tatum, Bud Powell, Oscar Peterson, or Ramsey Lewis. Evans, Powell, and Peterson examples can be found in *Jazz Piano*, Smithsonian 039.

[10]In some passages, Evans's bassists do not emphasize all four beats of each measure, but instead concentrate only on the first and third. (Listen to "All of You" in *Bill Evans at the Village Vanguard*, Riverside 60-017, CD, 1961.) LaFaro's playing often seemed to decorate the first and third beats and let the second and fourth beats pass. Even though four beats are present, only two are emphasized; musicians would say the music is "in two" or "two-beat style." What LaFaro did here is called a "decorative two feel."

Drummer **Paul Motian** (b. 1931) contributed an approach of great imagination and discretion to the Evans trio recordings of 1961. He decorated the combo sound and played accents which complemented the rhythms of LaFaro and Evans. Motian masterfully used wire brushes to obtain light, crisp sounds from his snare drum and cymbals. (For demonstration, listen to the JAZZ STYLES CASSETTE.) His highly original drum style employed contrasting sound textures and tone colors as elements of musical interest in themselves. In addition, his pioneering use of rhythmic displacement allowed him to interact more sensitively and inventively than most previous jazz drummers had done. His style of interactive coloring in the intimate trio context became a model for drummers playing in similar settings, and it contributed to the emancipation of the rhythm section. Incidentally, Motian furthered these innovations when he played with the Keith Jarrett quartet during the 1970s. On selected pieces with this later group, he nearly eliminated repetitive timekeeping patterns from his playing and was somehow able to *sound* free of meter while still playing within it.

The Bill Evans trio recordings of 1961 involve a great deal more than piano playing accompanied by a walking bass and a timekeeping drummer. Instead, they are composed of three constantly shifting parts which sway together. The tempo is usually steady, but it is not always made obvious by every beat sounding loudly and clearly. Some listeners perceive the music as Evans, LaFaro, and Motian carrying on three-way musical conversations in tempo.[11] Their musical words and phrases are both long and short, fluid and abrupt; they are not necessarily strings of eighth notes organized in the convoluted fashion that typifies bop, nor the long, smoothly contoured, eighth-note lines that typify Lennie Tristano and Lee Konitz. In other words, the group offers much melodic variety as well as substantial rhythmic variety. Swing feeling is merely one of a number of different rhythmic possibilities they explored.

**The most historically significant contributions of the Evans-LaFaro-Motian trio recordings of 1961 were to loosen the common practices of the bop style rhythm section** which had become standard during the 1940s and 50s—walking bass, drummer playing ride rhythms and snapping shut high-hat cymbals on the second and fourth beats, pianist playing long strings of eighth notes. Though they occasionally played in conventional bop style—especially before the June, 1961 sessions—their impact was to help emancipate the piano, bass, and drum roles.[12] The calm thoughtfulness, subtlety, and delicate interaction among them provided an alternative to the more straight-ahead style of the Oscar Peterson trios, or the gospel-like orientation of other groups of the same period led by Ramsey Lewis, Les McCann, and Gene Harris (of the Three Sounds).

[11]An example of this is "Solar," *Bill Evans at the Village Vanguard.*

[12]A vivid illustration of this influence is provided by listening to the rhythm section style of pre-1963 Miles Davis records such as the 1958 *Milestones* or the 1961 *Miles Davis at Carnegie Hall*, then listening to the Bill Evans 1961 *Sunday at the Village Vanguard* before listening to the rhythm section on any 1963–67 Davis albums, particularly on "All of You" in the 1964 *My Funny Valentine*, "Circle" in the 1966 *Miles Smiles*, or "Pee Wee" in the 1967 *Sorcerer*. The difference between pre- and post-1963 styles reflects the influence of the 1961 Evans trio concepts.

Herbie Hancock, 1987, age 47. (*Photo by Ray Avery*)

**HERBIE HANCOCK**  Herbie Hancock (b. 1940) played with Miles Davis from 1963 to 69 and became the most sought-after band pianist of the 1960s. Many musicians feel that Hancock's freshest work is the playing he did with Davis. Hancock comped in a brisk manner and used a gentle, even touch. Somehow he managed to sound light and airy, yet muscular and firm, all at the same time. Hancock absorbed several influences while he was developing his style during the late 1950s and early 60s. Some of his playing has the funky, bluesy figures and the rhythmic bounce that typified Horace Silver and Wynton Kelly. He was also inspired by the chord voicings and movement of harmonies perfected in the music of Clare Fischer, a prominent pianist/composer/arranger. But Bill Evans was the most significant influence on Hancock. The Evans use of harp-like, ringing tones surrounded by silence surfaced in Hancock's playing, as did Evans's chord voicings and mode-based thinking. Other similarities to Evans include Hancock's smooth legato lines and locked-hands style. Like Evans, he also frequently improvised passages in which accents went against the meter and let his ideas float free of reference to the underlying beat. In such excursions, Hancock drew from the ideas of twentieth-century classical composers Maurice Ravel, Claude Debussy, and Paul Hindemith.[13] But he did not merely imitate the

[13]The Evans influence can be heard in Hancock's playing on the Miles Davis albums *"Four" and More* and *My Funny Valentine*. And, at times, the Tristano-like approach that Evans used in constructing lines is also evident in Hancock's work, as on solos with Davis in "The Sorcerer" (*Sorcerer*), "Agitation" (*E.S.P.*), and "Orbits" (*Miles Smiles*). The flexible and intelligent interaction between Hancock, Ron Carter, and Tony Williams on "Pee Wee" (*Sorcerer*) and between Hancock, Buster Williams, and Al Heath on "He Who Lives in Fear" (*The Prisoner*, Blue Note 46845 (84321), CD/LP, 1969) recalls the sensitive interactions in the 1961 recordings of Bill Evans, Scott LaFaro, and Paul Motian. For catalog numbers and recording dates of the Miles Davis recordings, see the end of chapter 12.

music of his models. There was a tremendous sense of flexibility and openness in his improvising, resulting in a great amount of freedom and variety in his music. He extended the methods of his models and added so many original ideas that his style is instantly recognizable. (Listen to and compare the Evans work on "Solar" with the Hancock work on "Masqualero" in the JAZZ CLASSICS CASSETTE.)

One of Hancock's greatest contributions was to help free the pianist from the accompanying patterns that had become relatively commonplace for hard bop pianists. In the Miles Davis quintet, where he had an almost magical rapport with his equally daring companions, Hancock mixed the impressionistic and mode-based approaches to harmony of Debussy and Ravel with the polyrhythmic approaches to accompaniment that were being devised by drummer Tony Williams. At times his work in the *Sorcerer* album is indistinguishable from modern classical piano, sprinkled with melodic fragments and suspensions. (Listen to his work in "Masqualero" from *Sorcerer* in the JAZZ CLASSICS CASSETTE.) He could give the listener the impression of movement even when chords were not actually moving—at least as they might be expected to move in the twelve-bar blues and the popular songs of earlier eras, in which chords were treated as though their "function" were to "resolve" to another chord. In essence, Hancock fulfilled the trends that were already occurring in the Davis group when he joined—basing improvisations on modes instead of chord changes, using chords more for their sound quality (musicians call it a chord's "color") than for their capacity to increase and decrease tension when they change. In these new contexts, there were long passages in which chords did not change, yet the amount of activity Hancock generated in these new ways made up for the absence of "functional" chord changes. In the Davis quintet, Hancock coordinated with Tony Williams and bassist Ron Carter to pinpoint a mood and go with it rather than be a slave to a progression of chords. His rapport with Carter and Williams was so remarkable that he could also change a mood abruptly and then instantaneously develop rhythms and harmonies to carry it. He also allowed his improvised melodies to dictate the harmonies, rather than the reverse, which had been the standard. This marked a significant freedom associated with the groundbreaking Hancock-Carter-Williams rhythm section. All this and more can be heard in "Masqualero" on the JAZZ CLASSICS CASSETTE. It was a reprise to *Kind of Blue.*

Hancock created consistently stimulating, swinging, and polished piano improvisations. His playing nearly always has a meticulous and finished quality. His execution is firm and swinging without being violent or insistent. Both his solo work and his accompanying project politeness and sensitivity.[14] Hancock has shown broad scope and versatility; his style is compatible with several different streams of modern jazz. He has contributed immeasurably to hundreds of records—not only those of the Miles Davis quintet. He was so impressive during the 1960s that many excellent pianists, including Kenny Kirkland, George Cables, Larry Willis, Warren Bernhardt, Jim McNeely, Marc Cohen, Joey Calderazzo, Billy Childs, Marcus Roberts, and Fred Hersh drew from his style in the process of devising their own approaches. Even Chick Corea showed Hancock's influence.

[14]Listen to his trio rendition of his composition "The Sorcerer" in *Jazz Piano*, Smithsonian 039.

Another side to Hancock's creativity is his productivity and originality as a composer and arranger. By the early 1970s, he had written every tune on eight of his own albums, and he had written or coauthored many of the tunes on seven more. His "Dolphin Dance" is one of the most revered of all modern jazz compositions. Musicians are unanimous in their praise of its beauty and the clever progression of chords and pedal points that are intertwined with its delightful melody. "Maiden Voyage" became a staple for young musicians of the 1960s and 70s, especially because of its modal construction (see page 422 for a technical analysis). His funky, bluesy piece "Watermelon Man" became very popular, especially in Mongo Santamaria's version, during the mid-1960s. The big bands of Woody Herman, Si Zentner, and Maynard Ferguson all played their own arrangements of it, and it was performed by almost every wedding band in America whenever a funk piece was requested. By the 1980s, Hancock had captured a slice of the dance music market with numerous albums of funk music.

To survey the first fifteen years of Hancock's compositional productivity on records, it may help to group his output by idiom: 1) the lush, classical music style of "Suite Revenge" on *Death Wish*,[15] background music for the Charles Bronson movie; 2) the rock-influenced *Fat Albert Rotunda*;[16] 3) the funky, hard bop approach of *Taking Off*;[17] 4) Gil Evans-like work on *The Prisoner*; 5) writing that recalls music of Sun Ra on *Sextant*[18] and *Crossings*;[19] 6) the style of the 1960s Miles Davis Quintet on *Maiden Voyage*[20] and *Empyrean Isles*;[21] 7) the Sly Stone-influenced style of *Head Hunters*[22] and *Thrust*.[23]

Hancock did much of his creative writing after he left Miles Davis and began leading his own groups.[24] The music of Hancock's first post-Davis group capitalized on some of the advances made in the Davis groups of the 1960s. For *The Prisoner*, Hancock wrote legato passages for trumpet, trombone, and tenor saxophone employing sustained tones which had few eighth-note figures or jumpy syncopations. In accompanying the horns, Hancock, his bassist and drummer generated considerable activity in the manner that he had done with Carter and Williams in the Miles Davis quintet.

Hancock's second post-Davis band recorded the albums *Mwandishi*, *Sextant*, and *Crossings*. For these works, Hancock developed concepts that had been apparent in the late-1960s Davis albums *Nefertiti*, *In a Silent Way*, and *Bitches Brew*. There was extensive use of synthesizers and exotic percussion effects. In place of the busy, lightning-quick phrases of bop, Hancock frequently substituted legato lines of sustained tones that conveyed a languorous feeling. The emphasis was more on developing moods than on developing conventional jazz swing feeling or complicated chord progressions and intricate solo lines. In place of the standard tone colors of sax, trumpet, piano, bass, and conventional drum set, each of Hancock's seven group

---

[15]CBS 36825 (33199), 1974    [16]Warner Bros. 1834, LP, 1969
[17]Blue Note 46506 (84109), CD/LP, 1962    [18]CBS 32212, LP, 1972
[19]Warner Bros. 2617, LP, 1971    [20]Blue Note 46339 (84195), CD/LP, 1965
[21]Blue Note 84175, CD/LP, 1964    [22]CBS 32731, CD/LP, 1974
[23]CBS 32965, LP, 1974
[24]Hancock had led groups in recording studios before and during his years with Davis, but they were not usually working bands. Most were put together solely for the recordings.

members was responsible for a larger assortment of sounds. His trumpeter doubled on fluegelhorn and percussion. His trombonist played tenor trombone, baritone trombone, and bass trombone. His saxophonist played alto flute, soprano saxophone, piccolo, bass clarinet, and percussion. And Hancock often played electric piano, with echo and fuzz effects to alter its tone. Also, in addition to bass and drums, Hancock carried one musician who played nothing but synthesizer. Though this became common in the 1980s, such a practice was unusual for the early 1970s. Partly because of his use of synthesizer and its association with science fiction films, Hancock's style on these albums was often referred to as "space music."

Despite the innovations and the high-level musicianship in Hancock's first two post-Davis bands, there was not enough demand for their music to pay its expenses. Partly for this reason and partly out of a stated desire to reach larger audiences, Hancock then embarked on a string of styles that were less jazz-like and more in the genre that young audiences of the period wanted for dance and party music. For more than twenty years after he was forced to disband his *Mwandishi/Crossings/Sextant* band, Hancock enjoyed immense success and popular acclaim for styles that he devised, in part, from models within a popular black genre known as *funk music*. His first big hit came when he imitated the style of Sly Stone by creating the *Head Hunters* album, which sold just under a million copies. Then, with the success of its follow-up, *Thrust*, and many albums of discotheque-type dance music, Hancock was assured of selling about 200,000 copies of each new album when it remained unusual for jazz albums to sell more than 15,000 copies. The music had less and less jazz improvisation in it, and more and more dance rhythms that were highly syncopated and repetitive. Melodies were simple and heavily rhythmic. Though much of the public routinely places it in the jazz category, Hancock himself has said that he does not consider this music to be jazz. As of this writing, his widest recognition has come from a 1983 work called "Rockit." The recording is a lighthearted construction of novel sound effects that are packaged with an engaging funk rhythm, all tightly arranged with the same sense of balance and completeness ordinarily associated with Hancock. It was originally included in *Future Shock*, an album that went gold and stayed on the popularity charts for more than a year.[25] As a single, "Rockit" remained in the popularity charts for nine weeks, and as a video it was one of the fifteen most popular of the year.

Funk music is not all that Hancock pursued after his innovative septet folded. Frequently he has regrouped the original rhythm section from the 1960s Miles Davis group to record and tour with other musicians who play in styles like the Davis quintet—Wynton and Branford Marsalis, for example. Though Hancock is no longer breaking new ground in that context as he did with Davis, these bands have consistently been of the highest quality, and they have generated considerable excitement. In summary, decades after first impressing the jazz world with his own original playing and composing, Herbie Hancock has continued to make that original style available. Furthermore, he has also expanded the breadth of his activities by adding a repertory that pleases the larger pop music audience.

[25]CBS 38814, CD/LP, 1983

**CHICK COREA**   Chick Corea (b. 1941) followed Herbie Hancock as pianist in the 1968 Miles Davis quintet. He performed with Davis from the fall of 1968 to the summer of 1970. Corea soon joined the ranks of Hancock, Bill Evans, and McCoy Tyner as the most prominent and most imitated pianist in jazz.[26] His style originated with aspects from the jazz piano approaches of Bud Powell, Horace Silver, Bill Evans, and McCoy Tyner and the classical pieces of twentieth-century composers Paul Hindemith and Béla Bartók.[27] Like Tyner, Corea voiced chords in fourths—musicians call it *quartal harmony*—and devised lines from five-note scales—musicians call them *pentatonics*. He went beyond Tyner, however, by using other advanced voicings in addition to fourths.[28] Corea may also have absorbed ideas for using fourths from Horace Silver.[29] These voicings proved especially effective for the electric piano, an instrument that was becoming popular when Corea's career was taking off. The overtones produced by the instrument make chords voiced in the manner of bop pianists sound muddy, whereas the open quality achieved by voicing in fourths is less easily muddied by the electric instrument.

Latin American music also inspired Corea's style. Early in his career, Corea had played in several bands that featured Latin American music.[30] Even in non-Latin

[26]Jan Hammer, Richard Beirach, Jeff Lorber, Andy LaVerne, and Mulgrew Miller were among the many who exhibited his influence.

[27]The mid-1960s recordings that Corea made with Blue Mitchell show the influence of Bud Powell and Horace Silver. His work with Herbie Mann and Cal Tjader points up his use of Evans and Tyner as sources. (See teachers's manual for discography of Mitchell, Mann, and Tjader records featuring Corea.) Though drawing from Tyner, Corea's style differs from Tyner in several respects. For example, in Tyner's reharmonization of popular-song chord progressions, his use of fourths simplifies the movement of harmonies, whereas Corea's delineates the movement of harmonies. Though both Tyner and Corea occasionally venture outside their harmonies, Corea's "outside" lines usually return to the harmonies in a more systematic way, whereas Tyner uses his outside playing more for its coloristic value alone. Though both improvisers use pentatonics, Tyner tends to use them more against pedal points, whereas Corea employs them as much in lines that are set atop moving chords.

Though similar in many ways to Bill Evans, Corea devotes a very large portion of his output to voicing in fourths, whereas Evans tends toward a balance of quartal and tertial harmonies. Though both Evans and Corea play notes in a very marked manner, Evans is more legato and Corea more staccato. To hear Corea's resemblance to Evans, listen to Evans on "Flamenco Sketches" in the Miles Davis album *Kind of Blue* or on "Peace Piece" in *Everybody Digs Bill Evans.* Then listen to the title track from Return to Forever's *Where Have I Known You Before* (Polydor 825206 (6509), CD/LP, 1974) or "Song for Lee Lee" on Corea's *Piano Improvisations Vol. 2* (ECM 829190 (1020), CD/LP, 1971). Also listen to other Evans solos on those albums, then to Corea's solos on the Stan Getz album *Sweet Rain* (Verve 815054 (V 8693), CD, 1967). Note that Corea's compositions "Tones for Joan's Bones" (on Corea's *Inner Space*, Atlantic 305 (Vortex 2004), CD, 1966) and "Windows" (on Getz's *Sweet Rain*) reflect the Evans style of chord voicing.

[28]See pages 376, 417–418 for greater coverage of sounds created by fourths. Fourths are used extensively in the melody line of his tune "Litha" and his left-hand comping on the album *Now He Sings, Now He Sobs.* The chord voicings in *Now He Sings, Now He Sobs* are reminiscent of music by Hindemith.

[29]Corea demonstrated a few of Silver's devices on Blue Mitchell's album *The Thing to Do* (Blue Note 84178, CD/LP, 1964), which was recorded by the Horace Silver quintet with Corea in Silver's place. Even Corea's compositions on the album are in Silver's style.

[30]The bands of Willie Bobo, Cal Tjader, Herbie Mann, and Mongo Santamaria.

Chick Corea, shown here in 1990, at age 49. (*Photo by Dan Morgan*)

jazz contexts, Corea's playing bears the double-time feeling that is characteristic of Latin American music. He plays his notes in a manner that is very even, with each one markedly emphasized. (For explanations of double-time and staccato, listen to JAZZ STYLES CASSETTE, side 2.) Corea's crisp, percussive touch enhances the Latin feeling. This is also consistent with his bright, very spirited style of comping.

In 1968, Corea summarized his vocabulary of melodic, rhythmic, and harmonic strategies in *Now He Sings, Now He Sobs*, an album of original compositions and improvisations with bassist Miroslav Vitous and drummer Roy Haynes. ("Steps" is excerpted from this album on the JAZZ CLASSICS CASSETTE.) This album inspired hundreds of pianists, and it became a staple in the record collections of modern jazz musicians.[31] In 1981, the trio regrouped and made two more albums together.[32]

[31]Blue Note 90055 (Solid State 18039), CD/LP, 1968. Some musicians learned to play its music note for note, and we are indebted to a few of them for transcriptions of his piano part. Bill Dobbins prepared *Chick Corea: Now He Sings, Now He Sobs* (Advance Music, 1988), and a number of observations about Corea's style that appear in this chapter were made originally by Dobbins in personal communication with the author. Scott Reeves transcribed and analyzed Corea's solo on "Matrix" in his book *Creative Jazz Improvisation* (Prentice-Hall, 1988), and a few of his ideas are presented in this chapter. Both these books are available from Jamey Aebersold, P.O. Box 1244, New Albany, IN 47150; phone 1-800-456-1388. The recording of "Matrix" is in *Jazz Piano*, Smithsonian 039, LP, CD, and cassette sets.

[32]*Trio Music* (ECM 827702 (ECM2-1232), CD/LP set, 1981) and *Trio Music Live in Europe* (ECM 827769 (1310), CD, 1986). Other selections from the *Now He Sings, Now He Sobs* session that were not issued with the album are in *Circling In* (Blue Note-LA 472-H2), which also has Corea-Braxton-Holland-Altschul material. These other selections are also on the CD reissue of *Now He Sings, Now He Sobs* (Blue Note 90055).

**314**

## Listening Guide for "Steps"

Composed by Chick Corea; recorded in March, 1968 by Chick Corea (piano), Miroslav Vitous (bass), and Roy Haynes (drums); available on the JAZZ CLASSICS CASSETTE, Side Two; originally on *Now He Sings, Now He Sobs* (Solid State 18039), reissued on LP as Blue Note 90055, on CD as B 27-90055-2 .

This selection is taken from the most revered Chick Corea album, *Now He Sings, Now He Sobs*. The music represents the earliest summary of Corea's compositional and improvisational vocabulary, and it offers some of the best playing on record for drummer Roy Haynes. This album is as historically significant to Corea followers as *Sunday at the Village Vanguard* is to fans of Bill Evans.

When this recording was made, drummer **Roy Haynes** (b. 1926) had already been a favorite of jazz musicians since the 1940s. Though neglected by jazz journalists and historians, he is ranked by musicians as a peer of Max Roach and "Philly Joe" Jones. He preceded Tony Williams by decades in several of the ways he emancipated the drummer from the role of mere timekeeper. Some feel that he outshines Roach and Jones and is unsurpassed as the most creative and tasteful of modern drummers. Many would make Haynes their first choice as accompanist. *Now He Sings, Now He Sobs* contains possibly his best and most well-recorded work on record, though few listeners knew he was on it because the manufacturer failed to list personnel on the album jacket. At the time the album was recorded, bassist **Miroslav Vitous** (b. 1947) was just becoming known among musicians and had yet to attain the stature he later gained as cofounder of Weather Report, the pioneering jazz-rock fusion group. Vitous possesses phenomenal technique and a fertile imagination. (Listen to "Surucucu" at the end of the JAZZ CLASSICS CASSETTE for examples of Vitous performing in a freer role and using arco technique.)

*Now He Sings, Now He Sobs* is pivotal not just because the music is so well played and swinging, but also because its style is not really bop or hard bop. The manner of choosing notes for the lines is fresh, and so is the manner of relating the lines to the chord voicings. They are not necessarily all bop-derived.[33] By comparison with Bud Powell, Corea places his left-hand jabs in a higher pitch range, constructs them out of different intervals, and does not phrase his

[33]Even though "Matrix" and "Steps" are 12-bar blues tunes, listeners do not usually recognize them as blues because of the fresh way Corea treats their form. Portions of his solos steer clear of traditional ways for announcing the significant chord changes that earlier pianists would make at the fifth, ninth, and eleventh measures. For some of Corea's solo passages, the arrival points are determined exclusively by the direction of the melodic line. Sometimes he leaves out those moves, other times he stretches the traditional time before playing them. In other words, he restructures the tension points. The ways bop pianists favored for adding chords to make more movement within the twelve-measure progression are also missing. And when Corea does add chords, their identity is not as pronounced, because voicing in fourths makes the origin of the chord ambiguous. Moreover, sometimes Corea phrases in ways that do not neatly fit the three four-measure phrase organization his predecessors were inclined to use when playing the blues. He starts and stops his lines in nontraditional places, but the result does not sound odd. Incidentally, it is precisely the fact that it does not sound odd, coupled with the smoothness and finished quality of his constructions that mask the music's adventuresome construction in the ears of some listeners. Many have failed to appreciate the newness of Corea's ideas because the presentation was so smooth that it failed to jar them.

The second to last piece on the album, "Now He Beats the Drum, Now He Stops," also begins with a traditional foundation, the chord progression to "How Deep Is the Ocean?" But Corea takes that set of chords, combines it with a few ideas from a Bill Evans rendition, and composes a fresh and original piece that sounds like nothing ever heard before.

right-hand lines in the legato manner of a jazz saxophonist. Instead, Corea plays as though every note has a little point on it. The rhythms in the compositions and the improvised lines differ considerably from bop, too. They do not bear the same patterns of accents that typify bop style. Some of this playing also has the ring of classical music, especially that of Bartók and Hindemith. Though classical music does not swing, some of its compositional strategies and flavor were embraced by Corea. The sparkling touch of Corea and the bright tone quality he extracts from the piano also remind us of classical music. Corea's higher pitch range and staccato tendencies seem to make the music dance with a snap and lightness that are not often conveyed by bop piano styles. Despite these differences, however, the music has a few bop characteristics. Most of the music keeps a steady tempo and follows chord progressions. The bassist walks, and the drummer plays ride rhythms. The pianist plays long strings of eighth-notes with his right hand and syncopated jabs of comping with his left hand. Moreover, most of the music swings with an easy rise and fall of tensions.

The JAZZ CLASSICS CASSETTE version of "Steps" includes the introduction, two renditions of the theme in an up-tempo, twelve-bar blues form, twenty-two choruses of piano improvisation, two more renditions of the theme, and a coda. On the original album version, a drum solo smoothly evolves from the coda and introduces a new piece, "What Was." The fade-out on the JAZZ CLASSICS CASSETTE version does not exclude any part of the trio performance or the form of the "Steps" composition. It merely stops before the drum solo and "What Was."

*Elapsed Time*

## INTRODUCTION

Corea's notes here, though fast and spirited, are relatively free of steady tempo, and the ideas roam loosely through the waves of sound that comprise this section. Initially the introduction may seem confusing. However, after you have listened to the entire piece several times, you may begin to recognize fragments of ideas in the introduction that recur in Corea's solo choruses. The bass is silent, but Roy Haynes accompanies the piano with light, clicking sounds made by striking the rims and shells of his drums with his sticks, and he makes faint "ching" sounds by operating his high-hat with its foot pedal.

0' 43"

Tempo begins.

0' 47"

## FIRST STATEMENT OF THEME

The beginning of the twelve-bar form occurs when piano and bass sound an interval of two low-pitched notes (a fifth apart) three times in succession (bum. . . . . .bum. . bummmmmmm. .). Then the mid-register melody line begins. The piano rhythms are underscored by very light cymbal and snare drum sounds.

If you try to use the melody to help you identify the piece's 12-bar blues form, you may become confused because the melody line does not begin until the third measure of the form.

0' 57"

## SECOND STATEMENT OF THEME

1' 06"

## FIRST SOLO CHORUS

You should have less difficulty determining the beginning of the solo improvisation than the beginning of the theme. The solo starts on the first beat of the first measure of the form, when walking bass and ride rhythms commence. To keep your place by counting measures, remember that the tempo is fast. Then synchronize your counting with the bass: "1234 2234 3234 . . . 11 234 12 234."

Corea comps for himself by playing three-note chords in jabbing, often syncopated ways with his left hand. Frequently he lets his right hand rest, and all we hear is the sound made by his left hand.

1' 15"

### SECOND SOLO CHORUS

In this and most subsequent choruses, Corea's lines are generally played in the piano's upper register.

1' 25"

### THIRD SOLO CHORUS

Notice how Haynes continuously varies the timekeeping rhythm that he plays on the ride cymbal.

2' 49"

### TWELFTH CHORUS

Corea plays the first six measures with both hands locked together in block chord fashion. The seventh measure is played by his left hand alone, then he returns to his pattern of staccato three-note chords (usually voiced in fourths) in the left hand and long strings of eighth notes in the right hand.

3' 46"

### EIGHTEENTH CHORUS

Corea plays long strings of eighth notes near the center of the piano keyboard.

3' 56"

### NINETEENTH CHORUS

Corea does not play any eighth notes in this chorus, but instead plays syncopated 1 1/2- and 2-beat chords for the first six measures. Then he plays block chords directly on the beat for the remainder of the chorus. This departure from the relatively steady pattern of previous choruses inspires Roy Haynes to respond with a considerable amount of crackling sounds on the drums.

4' 13"

### TWENTY-FIRST CHORUS

The last four measures are filled with chords played by both hands locked together.

4' 24"

### TWENTY-SECOND SOLO CHORUS

The first six measures are filled with chords played by both hands locked together. The remaining measures are filled with low pitched chords providing a transition to the return of the theme.

4' 36"

### THEME STATEMENT

4' 43"

### THEME STATEMENT

4' 55"

### CODA

On and off between 1969 and 1972, Corea led a trio with bassist Dave Holland and drummer Barry Altschul. Free-form improvisation was featured on two of their albums, *The Song of Singing* and *A.R.C.* In some settings, they were joined by saxophonist Anthony Braxton, with whom their group name became Circle.[34] This

[34]*Song of Singing*, originally on Solid State, later on Blue Note 46401 (84353), CD, 1970; *A.R.C.*, ECM 833678 (1009), CD, 1971; During this time, Corea also appeared on the Miles Davis albums *In a Silent Way, Bitches Brew, Live at the Fillmore,* and *Black Beauty* (CBS Sony SOPJ 39/40 (Japan), 1970). *Black Beauty* is the only Davis album in which Corea solos at length, and, though available only as an import, it is well worth having because it constitutes some of the best work of his career.

period of Corea's output reflects the influence of pianist Paul Bley, bassist Gary Peacock, and saxophonists John Coltrane, Albert Ayler, and Ornette Coleman. The music also drew from twentieth-century composers John Cage and Karlheinz Stockhausen. Corea's use of the free-form approach resulted not only in the turbulent music found on *A.R.C.* and *The Song of Singing*, but also in the serene pieces he freely improvised in his *Piano Improvisations Vols. I & II*.[35]

After Circle disbanded, Corea formed a new group with himself on Fender Rhodes electric piano (an instrument that produces a light, vibraharp-like tone), bassist Stanley Clarke, Airto Moreira—a Brazilian drummer who had played with Miles Davis together with Corea—and singer Flora Purim, Airto's wife. Airto had played auxiliary percussion with Davis, but he used a conventional drum set with Corea. The group's sound was light and happy, full of Latin American rhythms and Spanish themes. The name of the group and its first album was *Return to Forever*. Their second LP was titled *Light as a Feather*.[36]

These two albums became favorites among musicians, especially young players who were active during the 1970s. With this band, two of Corea's most popular tunes became known: "Spain" and "La Fiesta." Within a few years, the influence of this sound was evident in a number of jazz-rock fusion bands, including Spyro Gyra.

The group Chick Corea carried through the middle 1970s was strongly influenced by rock and funk music, often displaying the insistent, machine-like sound of hard rock. Corea employed rock-influenced electric guitarists—first Bill Connors, then Al Dimeola. Corea retained bassist Stanley Clarke, now playing electric bass guitar more than acoustic bass. Drummer Lenny White rounded out the group. White's style was a very full, active approach which combined aspects of the Tony Williams techniques with those of modern rock and funk drummers and Latin American percussion ensembles. Some of the group's material was orchestral, very involved, and highly imaginative, moving between rock, classical, and jazz idioms. The records made during this period sold well, and independent recording careers soon resulted for Clarke and Dimeola.[37] White and Dimeola left Corea during the summer of 1976, though the Return to Forever group name was retained for a number of Corea's subsequent projects. Thereafter, Corea appeared in a wide assortment of contexts. Al Dimeola, Stanley Clarke, and Lenny White went on to lead bands of their own, occasionally regrouping with Corea to tour and record.

Corea was a prominent composer during the 1960s and 70s. His "Windows" and "Crystal Silence" became jazz standards. Al Jarreau's vocal rendition of Corea's "Spain" was a hit record. Like much of Horace Silver's work, many of Corea's compositions are more than merely a melody and a chord progression for improvisation. Some pieces have different sections, each with a distinctive rhythmic and

[35]All selections there were spontaneously conceived and performed, with the exceptions of "Song for Sally," "Song of the Wind," "Some Time Ago," "Trinkle Tinkle," and "Masqualero."

[36]ECM 811978 (ECM 1022) CD/LP, 1972; Polydor 827148 (PD 5525), CD/LP, 1972. See John Rodby's transcription and analysis of Corea's solo on "Spain" from *Light as a Feather*, in *Solos for Jazz Piano* (Carl Fischer, 1989). Order from Carl Fischer Music Store, 54 Cooper Square, NY, NY 10003.

[37]Stanley Clarke's *School Days* was a hit, as were Al Dimeola's *Elegant Gypsy* and *Casino*.

tonal flavor. For example, "Windows," "Spain," and "Litha" are melodies and arrangements all rolled into a single package.[38] Also like Silver, Corea writes pieces that make good use of preset bass lines in the accompaniment, particulary those with a Latin American flavor.[39] In addition, many Corea compositions feature bass doubling the melody of the piano and horn parts, no matter how rapid and intricate the line. This arranging practice took advantage of the high-level instrumental proficiency of jazz bassists during the 1970s and 80s.[40] It was widely imitated in jazz-rock groups of the 1970s and 80s.

Corea's acoustic jazz of the 1960s and 70s did not gain a particularly wide audience. For instance, albums such as *Now He Sings, Now He Sobs, A.R.C.,* and *The Song of Singing* were frequently out of print for years at a time. On the other hand, his jazz-rock fusion music acquired a wide following, he became known for his use of synthesizers, and the Chick Corea Elektric Band of the 1980s managed to be among the few jazz groups known to a large audience.

**KEITH JARRETT**   When Chick Corea left Miles Davis, pianist Keith Jarrett (b. 1945) took his place and performed with Davis until the winter of 1971. Like a few other Davis sidemen, Jarrett had also played with Art Blakey. But Jarrett's widest pre-Davis exposure had come as a member of saxophonist Charles Lloyd's quartet, beginning in 1966. In recordings with Lloyd, Jarrett had proven himself a powerful improviser whose talents and stature paralleled Herbie Hancock and Chick Corea. Jarrett had as much or more command of the piano as they, but more important, he had his own distinctive approach: He was a piano original. Jarrett's playing demonstrated imagination of enormous scope, and he seemed able to draw from any musical idiom and incorporate its elements in a convincing way. In Jarrett's playing were bits of Bill Evans,[41] twentieth-century classical composers Béla Bartók, Alban Berg, and Maurice Ravel, American gospel music,[42] country music, and Ornette Coleman.

Often Jarrett's lines project a singing quality (and sometimes you can hear Jarrett humming the lines as he plays them). These lines have the sweep of an inspired

[38] Listen to "Windows" and "Litha" in the Stan Getz album *Sweet Rain*, Verve 815054 (V8693), CD, 1967.

[39] For example, the bass lines that accompany his "Señor Mouse" (*Crystal Silence*, ECM 831331 (1024), CD/LP, 1972) are central to the composition. Without them, the melody would not convey the same flavor.

[40] John Patitucci's playing of the rapid melody line to Corea's "Got A Match" dazzled listeners of the 1980s.

[41] To detect Jarrett's debt to Evans, listen to "Shades of Jazz" on Jarrett's *Shades*, Impulse 9322, LP 1975; and "Ellen David" on Charlie Haden's *Closeness*, A&M CD-0808 (SP710), CD, 1976.

[42] Jarrett's style is a curious blend of influences. There is a hint of Wynton Kelly in his playing on Art Blakey's *Buttercorn Lady*, Emarcy 822471 (Limelight 82034), CD, 1966. Bill Evans and Ornette Coleman are obvious. Jarrett's piano style and quartet sound of the 1970s were modeled by pianist Paul Bley and his group that included saxophonist John Gilmore, bassist Gary Peacock, and future Jarrett drummer Paul Motian, documented on recordings made in 1964, originally issued as *Turning Point* (Improvising Artists 373841) and *New Music: The Second Wave* (Savoy 2235), reissued as *Turns* (Savoy 1192, LP).

A combination of influences converged in a musical friendship that Jarrett began with

Keith Jarrett, 1968, age 23. (*Photo by Chuck Stewart*)

human voice or a surging saxophone improvisation. In fact, Jarrett plays soprano saxophone in some of his concerts, and he is quite accomplished on the instrument. The long, legato sax lines he creates are mirrored by his long, legato, sax-like piano lines.

Jarrett is also a prolific and original composer. He has written mounds of material for his own albums and contributed significantly to the records of Charles Lloyd and Norwegian saxophonist Jan Garbarek. Some of his albums contain extended performances with little or no improvisation; in these pieces, the line between classical music and jazz is blurred.[43]

Keith Jarrett devised a distinctive quartet sound from 1971 to 1976 with tenor saxophonist Dewey Redman, bassist Charlie Haden (both from Ornette Coleman's

---

pianist John Coates around 1957. Jarrett listened extensively to Coates in person as well as becoming interested in a few of Coates's favorites: Paul Bley, Ornette Coleman, black gospel music, and early white American music. Jarrett later displayed some of the same amalgam of these styles that Coates was perfecting in the early 1960s. Both Coates and Jarrett were making albums during the 1970s that reflected those influences, and the music of the two men is very similar. (Listen to *The Piano Sound of John Coates*, Omnisound 1004, LP.)

[43]*In The Light*, ECM 835011 (1033/34), CD set, 1973

band), and drummer Paul Motian, formerly of the Bill Evans trio. Jarrett's group arranged a unique combination of:

1)  elements from the Coleman approach[44]
2)  elements of the Bill Evans style[45]
3)  extension and development of rubato style
4)  long, vamp-based improvisations which were funky in Jarrett's unique way
5)  Third World approaches (Redman playing musette, the group using several unusual instruments such as steel drums, finger cymbals, etc.)
6)  unique, non-bop timekeeping techniques used by Motian and Haden
7)  group improvisations which use rubato.

During the 1970s and 80s, Jarrett made many albums and concert appearances as an unaccompanied solo pianist. It is notable that Jarrett was one of the few pianists of that time who did not regularly play electric piano. It is also noteworthy that Jarrett's improvisations were more spontaneous than those of most jazz pianists because he rarely used prewritten melodies or preset chord progressions. His playing could be funky, earthy, and gospelish,[46] or pretty and orchestrally lush.[47] Sometimes he clearly stated a tempo. Other times he implied only a momentum. Jarrett is one of the few pianists to improvise free jazz and to show the influence of Ornette Coleman's melodic style.[48] Like Coleman, he stays away from staccato phrasing,

---

[44]Jarrett wrote melodies in Coleman's style as well as soloing in it. Redman soloed in the Coleman style, and Haden's unique approach was central to both the Coleman and the Jarrett groups. (See photo of Haden and Redman on page 300.)

[45]Listen to Jarrett's up-tempo piano lines on "Shades of Jazz" in Jarrett's *Shades* (Impulse 9322, LP) and the slow playing, with its sustained tones and chord voicings on "Rainbow" in Jarrett's *Byablue* album MCA 29047 (Impulse 9331), LP, 1976. Compare this with *Bill Evans at the Village Vanguard* or *Everybody Digs Bill Evans*.

[46]Listen to his "In Front" in *Jazz Piano*, Smithsonian 039, LP, CD and cassette; also on *Facing You*, ECM 827132 (1017), CD/LP, 1971.

[47]*Staircase*, ECM 827337 (1090), CD, 1976

[48]It helps us hear Jarrett's debt to Coleman when Jarrett omits left-hand playing and improvises lengthy, saxophone-like solos with his right hand. In fact, when accompanied only by drums and bass (especially Coleman's own Charlie Haden), and not playing in a two-handed pianistic style, Jarrett often sounds like Coleman transferred to the piano. For more comparisons between Coleman and Jarrett, listen to Jarrett's soprano saxophone playing on "Pocket Full of Cherry" in his *Bop-Be*, MCA 29048 (Impulse 9334), 1976; and "Part a" of "Encore (a-b-c)" in his *Eyes of the Heart*, ECM 825476 (1150), CD, 1976. Jarrett's stylistic debt to Coleman is particularly evident in his solos on Jan Garbarek's *Belonging*, ECM 829115 (1050), CD/LP, 1974. Despite all the similarities between styles, even to employing the same sidemen (Dewey Redman and Charlie Haden), at least three differences between Coleman's and Jarrett's approaches immediately come to mind: 1) Coleman is more complex than Jarrett, is more varied and unpredictable in his improvised lines, and draws upon a wider selection of moods and tempos; 2) Jarrett possesses very high-level technique, and because of the uniformity in touch this affords, he plays more smoothly than Coleman and his music is less jarring; and 3) the notes in Jarrett's lines seem more loyal to the original key that a given piece is in, and Coleman shifts tone centers more often.

works from shifting tone centers, has a way of bursting forth with slippery streams of notes, and occasionally gives his playing a twangy flavor that is reminiscent of country music.

As an unaccompanied solo pianist, Keith Jarrett has created one of the first jazz sounds since the Modern Jazz Quartet's whose appeal crossed the line from jazz audiences to audiences customarily more fond of symphonic music. He is one of the first solo jazz musicians to consistently pack auditoriums throughout the United States and Europe and earn a satisfactory living as an improviser. Jarrett attracted audiences comparable to those of a nonimprovising classical virtuoso. The best illustration of the music behind this phenomenon is in his *Staircase* album. Among the explanations for its appeal are:

1) a rhapsodic style evoking a warm, sweeping mood
2) Jarrett's seemingly effortless control of the keyboard
3) his vamp-based passages in which brief accompaniment figures repeat again and again and are relatively easy to listen to
4) the clarity of his thinking
5) the music's classical rather than jazz feeling[49]

Jarrett's influence on jazz pianists has been slower to take hold than Herbie Hancock's and Chick Corea's. However, there are several players worth noting who recall Jarrett's sound, including Art Lande[50], Richard Beirach[51], and Lyle Mays (who played on numerous albums with Pat Metheny's group during the 1970s and 80s). Other pianists, less gifted than Lande, Beirach, and Mays, have begun imitating the simplest aspects of Jarrett's style, particularly the lengthy, vamp-based improvisations which seem soothing. They have become central to a popular kind of music known as "new age," which is frequently confused with jazz because it is improvised and many of its practicioners have previously played jazz. The improvisations of these latter imitators can be distinguished from those of Jarrett because the lines are far less rich with melodic ideas, and the rhythms are much simpler. Rarely do Jarrett's imitators attain the sweeping feeling that Jarrett can elicit in the listener, nor do they play with quite the smoothness and vitality that Jarrett displays.

[49]In a substantial portion of his unaccompanied solo improvisations, the musical vocabulary is classical. Much of this work sounds like piano sonatas by Maurice Ravel. This sound might provide a bridge for listeners who are not accustomed to jazz but are acquainted with symphonic music, especially the familiar works of French composers Ravel and Debussy. For many such listeners, the only aspect that separates Jarrett's work from classical music is that Jarrett's is largely improvised.

[50]Lande's affinity for Jarrett is particularly evident in Lande's album *Red Lanta*, ECM 829383 (1038), CD, 1973.

[51]Beirach's affinity for Jarrett is most noticeable on David Liebman's album *Forgotten Fantasies*, A&M Horizon SP-709, 1975. Note that his style has more resemblance to Chick Corea and Herbie Hancock and their mutual influence of Bill Evans.

## CHAPTER SUMMARY

1) Pianist Bill Evans came to attention during the late 1950s and became the most influential pianist since Bud Powell.

2) Though derived partly from the Tristano approach, Evans's style was original, especially in his voicings and his modal thinking.

3) With bassist Scott LaFaro and drummer Paul Motian, Evans devised a fresh approach to trio playing in which explicit statement of every beat was replaced by a highly flexible and varied group style, and the roles of soloist and accompanist were often blurred.

4) LaFaro's remarkable speed and imagination pushed jazz bass styles ahead as Jimmy Blanton's had twenty years earlier.

5) Evans influenced Herbie Hancock, Chick Corea, and Keith Jarrett, all of whom, in turn, led innovative bands and influenced many other pianists.

6) Hancock refined the Evans style, added the influence of Wynton Kelly, and raised accompanying techniques to a high level of imagination and variety while with Miles Davis.

7) Hancock led several groups of his own that played his many original compositions, including "Maiden Voyage" and "Watermelon Man."

8) Hancock's mid-seventies group, the Head Hunters, became a model jazz-rock-funk band and enjoyed very high record sales.

9) Chick Corea looked to Bill Evans as only one of many sources for his original piano style. Horace Silver, Thelonious Monk, Bud Powell, McCoy Tyner, and several classical composers also influenced Corea. His playing is more crisp and staccato than that of Hancock or Evans, and he favors Spanish themes and Latin American rhythms.

10) Corea popularized the use of fourths in compositions and piano voicings, and used them in ways that Evans and Tyner had not.

11) Corea's tunes were very popular. "Spain" and "Windows" became jazz standards.

12) Keith Jarrett showed the influence of Bill Evans and Ornette Coleman in developing his own piano style.

13) Jarrett was one of the most original composer-pianist-bandleaders of the 1970s, combining free jazz, funk, and a rhapsodic classical piano style that made him the most successful solo concert pianist in jazz history.

14) Jarrett's quartet of the 1970s mixed the methods and musicians associated with Ornette Coleman and Bill Evans and added country music, Third World music, and funk music in original combinations.

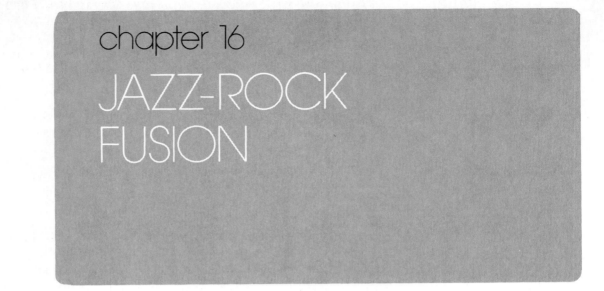

# chapter 16
# JAZZ-ROCK FUSION

Jazz-rock fusion was a dominant stream of styles during the 1970s and 80s, and it was the first group of jazz styles to attain widespread popularity since the swing era. The first few pages of this chapter are intended to help clarify what is included in the category of jazz-rock fusion. The rest of the chapter then discusses the major contributions of key figures: **Miles Davis, Larry Coryell, John McLaughlin, Joe Zawinul, Jaco Pastorius,** and **Pat Metheny.** The fusion styles of **Herbie Hancock** and **Chick Corea** have already been examined in chapter 15. The fusion music of **Wayne Shorter** has already been examined in chapter 12. The group called **Weather Report** receives lengthy treatment here not just because it was the leading and longest-lived fusion band, but also because it demonstrated fresh methods of simultaneous collective improvisation, and it investigated an enormous range of unusual rhythms and tone colors. **New Age** music, though it is only peripherally related to jazz, is also treated here because often it has been marketed in the jazz category as though it were a subcategory of jazz-rock fusion.

Jazz, rock, and funk music share similar roots in gospel music, work songs, and the blues, but they represent the products of two divergent lines of musical evolution (see Figure 16.1). For example, jazz employs aspects of formal European concert music and steers away from vocals; it is primarily instrumental music with an intricacy comparable to that of twentieth-century symphonic music. Rock and funk music, on the other hand, emphasize vocals and stick largely to elementary compositional forms such as the four-chord, twelve-bar blues and other brief chord progressions that repeat extensively. While the line of evolution leading to rock and funk music became a part of the popular music mainstream, jazz acquired a status like that of classical chamber music because its audience was small and specialized. While it is true that blues singers from the first part of the twentieth century such as Leadbelly and Bessie Smith are routinely cited in jazz history texts, they are usually mentioned in discussions of the origins of jazz rather than the dominant course of jazz itself. The stream of stylistic evolution that runs from Leadbelly through B. B. King to Jimi Hendrix was already essentially separate from jazz by the 1920s. Though the religious music that had influenced Bessie Smith continued to influence popular music, as seen in singers of the 1960s and 70s such as Aretha Franklin and James Brown, it only occasionally influenced jazz.[1]

Prior to the 1950s, blues and gospel music were especially influential in the popular music made by black performers who were marketed to black audiences. Ranging from Bessie Smith in the 1920s to Louis Jordan in the 40s, these performers made music that comprised the category called "race records." In 1949, this category acquired a new name—rhythm and blues (R & B)—and it strongly influenced another style of popular music called rock and roll (see Figure 16.1). In addition to showing these R & B roots, much rock also reflects the predominantly white musical streams of country music or hillbilly music (one early form of rock being termed rockabilly, early Elvis Presley exemplifying this style) and western swing (a form that combines hillbilly music and jazz with a diversity of ethnic traditions ranging from the dance music of Cajuns and Czechs to that of Mexicans, Germans, and Poles). Rock is distinctly removed from jazz, being significantly less like jazz than R & B had been. Note, however, that despite differences of players's race, rock and R & B remain similar because of such Afro-American traits as extremely simple melody lines, extensive pitch bending, reliance upon ostinato, and strict adherence to steady tempo.

Some R & B in the 1960s contained accompaniment rhythms more complicated than those in rock. During the late 1960s, some black styles which extended R & B became the source for intricately syncopated drum patterns and complementary bass figures. Some of the rhythm section musicians working for Motown recording artists[2] and for singer James Brown,[3] for example, devised accompaniment patterns which were more complicated than those being used at the time by rock groups. The work of accompanists for Sly Stone[4] during the early 1970s was especially complex, having built upon the Motown and James Brown techniques. By this time, the labels "funk" and "soul" had begun replacing the R & B label. However, this new pair of labels still served the same purpose their predecessors had served:

[1]What little impact gospel music made on modern jazz was usually felt in only the simplest styles, those containing characteristics similar to the black popular music known as rhythm and blues. These jazz styles were created by commercially successful players who, although possessing jazz skills, remained on the periphery of important jazz developments: the Earl Bostic and Eddie Vinson bands of the 1940s and 50s; organ and saxophone combinations such as those of Jimmy Smith and Stanley Turrentine, beginning in the late 1950s; the piano trios of Les McCann, Ramsey Lewis, and the Three Sounds; the combos led by King Curtis; pianist Ray Charles and the saxophonists he employed, including Hank Crawford and James Clay.

[2]Listen to the bass figures and drum patterns on the 1967 "Reflections" or the 1968 "Love Child" by Motown's Supremes. Or listen to the 1967 "I Heard It Through the Grapevine" by Motown's Gladys Knight or the 1968 "Cloud Nine" by Motown's Temptations, available on *The Motown Story*, Motown 6048 (726), CD/LP set; or see various *Hits* compilations of Motown/Tamla artists.

[3]Pay close attention to the rhythm section style on James Brown's 1967 "Cold Sweat," available on James Brown—*The CD of JB II*, Polydor 831700 (King), CD, 1959–1976.

[4]Listen to Sly Stone's "In Time," Sly & the Family Stone—*Fresh*, Epic 32134; see page 431 for a transcription of the drum part.

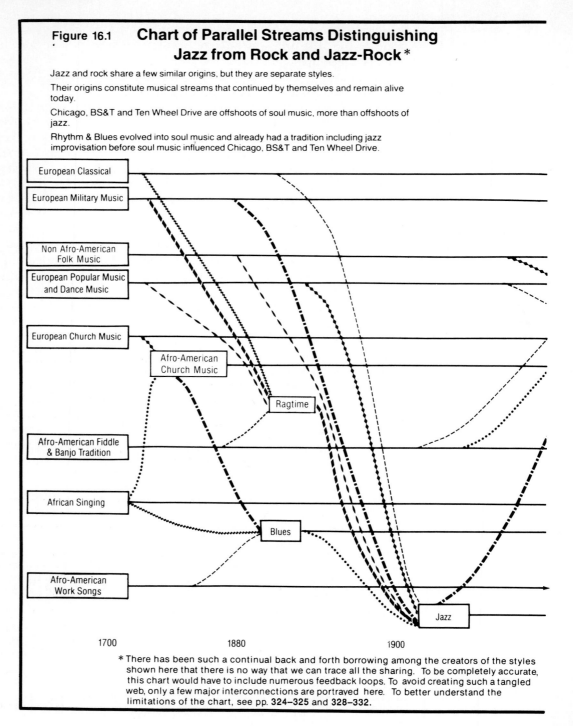

**Figure 16.1**    **Chart of Parallel Streams Distinguishing Jazz from Rock and Jazz-Rock** *

Jazz and rock share a few similar origins, but they are separate styles.

Their origins constitute musical streams that continued by themselves and remain alive today.

Chicago, BS&T and Ten Wheel Drive are offshoots of soul music, more than offshoots of jazz.

Rhythm & Blues evolved into soul music and already had a tradition including jazz improvisation before soul music influenced Chicago, BS&T and Ten Wheel Drive.

European Classical

European Military Music

Non Afro-American Folk Music

European Popular Music and Dance Music

European Church Music

Afro-American Church Music

Ragtime

Afro-American Fiddle & Banjo Tradition

African Singing

Blues

Afro-American Work Songs

Jazz

1700      1880      1900

* There has been such a continual back and forth borrowing among the creators of the styles shown here that there is no way that we can trace all the sharing. To be completely accurate, this chart would have to include numerous feedback loops. To avoid creating such a tangled web, only a few major interconnections are portrayed here. To better understand the limitations of the chart, see pp. **324–325** and **328–332**.

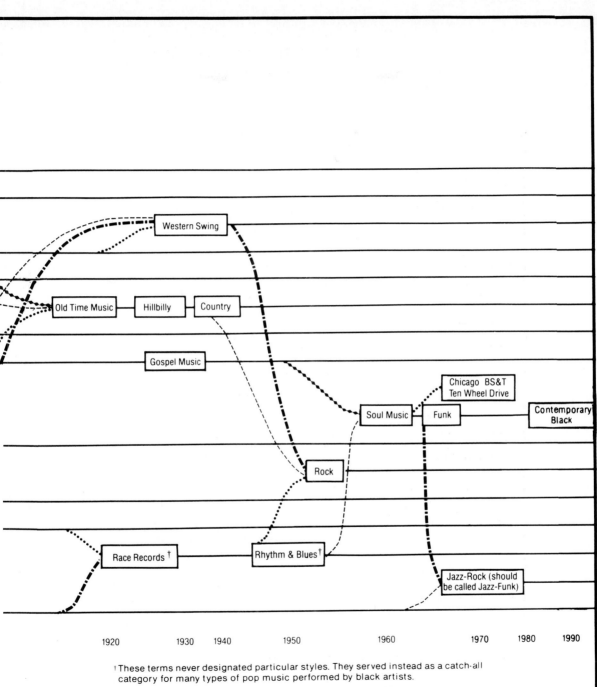

† These terms never designated particular styles. They served instead as a catch-all category for many types of pop music performed by black artists.

identifying a primarily black form of American popular music. It was this funk-soul category, not rock, which influenced a number of jazz musicians during the 1970s. Therefore **the jazz-rock label itself is not appropriate for the music that it identifies.** The music ordinarily signified by the term jazz-rock would more accurately be termed jazz-funk.[5]

By the mid-1960s, the dominant jazz and rock styles had evolved into uniquely separate idioms with little in common. Then, during the late 1960s, a partial blending of the soul-funk stream and the jazz stream occurred and was labeled "jazz-rock" (see Figure 16.1). Some jazz musicians remained unaffected by funk, and many funk groups continued unaffected by jazz. But much of the music produced by jazz groups during the 1970s and 80s demonstrated a larger number of funk characteristics than had previously been used in modern jazz, and some funk groups attempted to incorporate more of the improvisation and advanced harmonies found in jazz.

## DISTINGUISHING JAZZ FROM ROCK AND FUNK

Jazz of almost any period can be distinguished from rock and funk music in that rock and funk typically have:

1)  shorter phrase lengths
2)  less frequent chord changes
3)  less complexity of melody
4)  less complexity of harmony
5)  less use of improvisation, especially in accompaniments
6)  much more repetition of melodic phrases
7)  more repetition of brief chord progressions
8)  simpler, more repetitive drumming patterns
9)  more pronounced repetition of bass figures

More is preset in rock and funk performances than in jazz performances. Not only does jazz ordinarily require solos to be improvised fresh each time they occur, but it also requires that the accompaniments for the solos be improvised. Even the accompaniments for the theme statements are often different in each performance of a given tune.

Rhythmic feeling provides another means for distinguishing jazz from rock and funk music. Where jazz places emphasis on flexibility and relaxation, rock stresses intensity and firmness. Jazz projects a shuffling or loping kind of feeling. Where jazz attempts to project a lilting, bouncy feeling that seems to pull each beat along,

[5]The style which during the late 1970s and early 1980s was called disco is a blend of funk and Latin American rhythms played at the tempos most conducive for dancing (most commonly 120 beats per minute, the standard march tempo). It refers mostly to an accompaniment style which has been heard under almost every kind of solo line, from the singing of Donna Summer to swing era melodies to excerpts from Beethoven compositions. This style of music should also be removed from the umbrella category of rock.

rock and funk music seem to sit on each beat. Jazz musicians characterize the time sense of rock and funk musicians as "straight up and down."

Instrumentation preferred by jazz musicians is often different from that preferred by rock and funk musicians. Jazz musicians usually place far less emphasis than their rock and funk counterparts on using electronic instruments and high amplification of ordinary instruments.

**FORERUNNERS OF JAZZ-ROCK**

Mid-1960s forerunners of the "jazz-rock" approaches include the 1966 band called the Free Spirits[6] with guitarist Larry Coryell, the 1967 quartet of vibraharpist Gary Burton and Coryell,[7] and the Fourth Way, a 1968–71 band with pianist Mike Nock and violinist Michael White.[8] The greatest popular acclaim did not go to these groups, however. It went instead to a group, first recorded in 1967, called Blood, Sweat & Tears,[9] an eight-piece band featuring vocals in a James Brown and Ray Charles style with horn work similar to that of Brown and Charles. Next was the 1968 group called Chicago,[10] a seven-piece pop band featuring singing (solo voice as well as four- and five-part harmony) and late-1960s Motown-style ensemble figures voiced for trumpet, trombone, and saxophone. After them was the 1969 group called Ten Wheel Drive,[11] a ten-piece band whose style was similar to that of the first two. These three groups were identified by music journalists as "jazz-rock" bands, and they were phenomenally successful with the record-buying public.

When Ten Wheel Drive, Chicago, and Blood, Sweat & Tears emerged, they received much attention for their use of horns and improvisation. Listeners and journalists assumed that such elements lent jazz character to the music, that this was innovative, and that it justified the "jazz" part of the label "jazz-rock." Yet R & B bands, including those of soul singer James Brown for example, had been using horns and improvisation since the 1950s. In other words, some elements many journalists presumed were contributed to "jazz-rock" by Chicago and Blood, Sweat & Tears really reflected other traditions within popular music more than they reflected jazz (see Figure 16.1). Almost the only element these three popular "jazz-rock" bands had in common with jazz was the occasional presence of a brief, improvised solo, something that R & B had long been known for. Their ensemble playing was modeled after the James Brown and Motown brass style rather than jazz. And their singing style was patterned after soul singing. Admittedly, the harmonies written for their horns were more advanced than Motown's and James

[6]*Free Spirits*, ABC 593, 1966

[7]Gary Burton—*Duster*, RCA LSP 3835, 1967; *Lofty Fake Anagram*, RCA LSP 3901, 1967; selections from these LPs are reissued on *Artists' Choice*, RCA Bluebird 6280, CD/LP, 1966–68.

[8]The Fourth Way—*Sun and Moon Have Come Together*, Capitol/Harvest SKAO 423, 1969

[9]*Blood, Sweat & Tears*, Columbia 9720, CD/LP, 1969

[10]*Chicago Transit Authority*, Columbia 8, CD/LP, 1968; *Chicago's Greatest Hits*, Columbia 33900, CD/LP

[11]Ten Wheel Drive—*Construction No. 1*, Polydor 24-4008, 1969; *Brief Replies*, Polydor 24-4024, 1970

Brown's, but such sophistication had already been common in pop music and was not exclusive to jazz, either.

Another line of reasoning used in applying the jazz label to the most popular "jazz-rock" groups followed the knowledge that some members of the groups had played jazz or had jazz aspirations. This colored the thinking of journalists who overlooked the connections with James Brown and Motown and instead assumed a primary connection with jazz. These journalists ignored the fact that jazz musicians had frequently toured and recorded with popular non-jazz groups for decades prior to this, and their presence had not made those groups into jazz groups any more than the presence of jazz hornmen in Blood, Sweat & Tears made that group into a jazz band. Blood, Sweat & Tears was a highly professional and creative group of musicians who performed several different styles of popular music; but, they did not necessarily demonstrate a fusion of jazz with rock. The groups which genuinely developed a new kind of music by fusing jazz with rock and funk were those of Larry Coryell, Gary Burton, and Mike Nock. The most original fusions were made in the bands of trumpeter Miles Davis and those of some former Davis sidemen during the period between 1968 and 1975.[12]

**CHARACTERISTICS OF FUSION MUSIC**

Jazz-rock fusion mixed jazz improvisation with the instrumentation and rhythmic conception of R & B. The compositions, tone colors, and rhythms were adopted not only by musicians who were just then developing their own styles, but also by older, established players. Rhythm sections changed instrumentation by replacing piano with electric piano and synthesizer and by replacing acoustic bass viol ("string bass") with electric bass guitar ("Fender"). Pianists and guitarists often adopted repeating accompanying riffs in place of the spontaneous comping which had been customary since the 1940s. Bassists began accumulating the syncopated and staccato figures that drew upon late-1960s players in the Motown bands and the backup groups for James Brown and Sly Stone of the early 1970s. (See chapter 3 for instrument photos and page 427 for notations of rock bass figures.) Much as the early swing era bassists often had to play brass bass (tuba) as well as string bass viol, early fusion bassists often had to play bass guitar ("Fender") as well as string bass viol ("acoustic"), and many eventually abandoned bass viol for bass guitar.

Drummers learned new timekeeping patterns which resembled those of R & B as well as Latin American styles. (See page 431 for notations of drumming figures used in recordings by Sly Stone and Herbie Hancock.) Jazz-rock drumming style was very full and active. Following the lead of Tony Williams, the high-hat was snapped shut sharply on every beat instead of every other beat. There was an increase in the use of drums, particularly the bass drum, and a decrease in the use of cymbals for

[12]Miles Davis—*Bitches Brew*, CBS 40577 (GP 26), CD/LP, 1969; Weather Report (Joe Zawinul & Wayne Shorter)—*Weather Report*, CBS 30661, LP, 1971; Tony Williams/John McLaughlin/Larry Young—*Once in a Lifetime*, Verve 833563 (Polydor 25-3001), LP set, 1969–70; Mahavishnu Orchestra (John McLaughlin)—*The Inner Mounting Flame*, CBS 31067, CD/LP, 1971; and *Birds of Fire*, CBS 31996, CD/LP, 1972; Return to Forever (Chick Corea)—*Hymn to the Seventh Galaxy*, Polydor 825336 (5536), CD/LP, 1973; Herbie Hancock—*Head Hunters*, CBS 32731, CD/LP, 1974

**TABLE 16.1. A Few of the Many Jazz-Rock Musicians and Bands**

| Singer-Based Bands | Trumpet | Piano | Bass |
|---|---|---|---|
| Blood, Sweat & Tears | Randy Brecker | Herbie Hancock | Michael Henderson |
| Chicago | Tom Browne | Chick Corea | Stanley Clarke |
| Ten Wheel Drive | Michael Lawrence | Joe Zawinul | Jaco Pastorius |
| Chase | Lew Soloff | Jan Hammer | Rick Laird |
| | Miles Davis | Jeff Lorber | Jeff Berlin |
| | | Milcho Leviev | Jamaaladeen Tacuma |
| **Instrumental Groups and** | **Saxophone** | George Duke | John Patitucci |
| **Their Leaders** | | Bob James | Victor Bailey |
| | Michael Brecker | Lyle Mays | Marcus Miller |
| Lifetime (Tony Williams) | Wayne Shorter | | |
| The Head Hunters | David Liebman | | |
| (Herbie Hancock) | Steve Grossman | | **Vibraharp** |
| Return to Forever (Chick Corea) | Grover Washington | | Gary Burton |
| Mahavishnu Orchestra | Eddie Harris | **Guitar** | Roy Ayers |
| (John McLaughlin) | Ronnie Laws | | |
| Free Spirits (Larry Coryell) | David Sanborn | Pat Metheny | **Drums** |
| Fourth Way (Mike Nock) | John Klemmer | Al Dimeola | |
| Eleventh House (Larry Coryell) | Kenny G | John McLaughlin | Tony Williams |
| Blackbyrds (Donald Byrd) | Najee | Larry Coryell | Billy Cobham |
| Prime Time (Ornette Coleman) | | Steve Khan | Steve Gadd |
| Spyro Gyra | | Blood Ulmer | Lenny White |
| Word of Mouth (Jaco Pastorius) | | Mike Stern | Alphonse Mouzon |
| The Decoding Society | | John Scofield | Leon Chancler |
| (Ronald Shannon Jackson) | **Violin** | Bill Frisell | Harvey Mason |
| Caldera | | Alan Holdsworth | Ronald Shannon |
| Oracle | Michael White | George Benson | Jackson |
| Soft Machine | Jerry Goodman | | Peter Erskine |
| Jeff Lorber Fusion | Jean-Luc Ponty | | Al Foster |
| The Crusaders | Michael Urbaniak | | David Weckl |
| Weather Report (Joe Zawinul | | | Omar Hakim |
| and Wayne Shorter) | | | |
| Miles Davis | | | |
| Bob James | | | |
| Hiroshima | | | |
| Steps Ahead | | | |
| Yellow Jackets | | | |

timekeeping. The rhythms were stated insistently and not in a manner that alternated tension with relaxation as much as in jazz styles. The jazz-rock style maintained a high level of tension for long periods. There was considerably less bounce and lilt than in jazz of the 1950s, and timekeeping was more strictly stated than during the exploratory years of jazz in the 1960s. The first models for jazz-rock drummers were Tony Williams and Billy Cobham; then, after the mid-1970s, Steve Gadd, and after the mid-1980s, Dave Weckl.

The more jazz-oriented soloists in jazz-rock fusion tended to draw upon John

Coltrane's early-1960s style as a model if they were saxophonists, Freddie Hubbard if they were trumpeters, and Herbie Hancock, McCoy Tyner, and Chick Corea if they were pianists. Bop melodic rhythms were not compatible with most jazz-rock accompaniment patterns, but the 1960s Coltrane and Tyner lines were. Pianists and guitarists often adopted repeating accompaniment riffs in place of the spontaneous comping that had been customary in jazz since the 1940s. The more adventuresome accompanists played spontaneously and responsively, but the development of repeating patterns that could create a funk music feeling usually took higher priority than comping. The less jazz-oriented saxophonists in fusion used models from R & B and R & B-oriented jazz such as King Curtis, Junior Walker, Wilton Felder, and Hank Crawford, then during the 1980s Dave Sanborn and Michael Brecker. The less jazz-oriented pianists in fusion devised their own simpler styles or imitated players who leaned more toward the rock side of the jazz-rock mix.

**MILES DAVIS**   In addition to developing many highly creative extensions of existing jazz styles, the 1964–68 Miles Davis Quintet was one of the first established jazz groups to experiment with mixing the musical devices of rock and funk music with those of jazz. Rhythmic styles other than bouncy, swinging jazz patterns appear throughout their records. Drummer Tony Williams sometimes played straight, repeating eighth notes on the ride cymbal, and occasionally stated each beat by sharply snapping closed the high-hat. Bassist Ron Carter sometimes complemented those drumming patterns with simple, repeating bass figures that did not fit traditional walking bass rhythms. All of this bore a marked similarity to the rhythmic feeling of rock.[13] One album in particular, the 1968 *Filles de Kilimanjaro* (coming directly after *Miles in the Sky)*, clearly signaled a trend away from jazz sound. It not only used electric piano and bass, it also contained the extensive use of military-like drumming patterns that resembled the insistent playing of rock drummers more than the relaxed and lilting playing of modern jazz drummers.

The next two LPs that Davis recorded became significant in directing modern jazz of the 1970s.[14] These records were *In a Silent Way* and *Bitches Brew*, both made in 1969. They contained a variety of musical approaches, but their dominant style was a combination of jazz and rock. Many melodies were reminiscent of the floating, almost motionless feeling of Wayne Shorter's "Nefertiti;" and Shorter's tune "Sanctuary" was included on *Bitches Brew*.

---

[13]Listen to these hints of rock in the accompanying patterns on "Eighty-One" on the *E.S.P.* album, "Freedom Jazz Dance" on the *Miles Smiles* album, "Masqualero" on the *Sorcerer* album (and the JAZZ CLASSICS CASSETTE), and "Frelon Brun," "Tout de Suite," and "Filles de Kilimanjaro" on the *Filles de Kilimanjaro* album. See page 251 for catalog numbers of all Miles Davis albums, LP and CD format, cited in this chapter.

[14]For these sessions, Miles Davis drew from a pool of drummers—Tony Williams, Jack DeJohnette, Lenny White, Charles Alias, and Jim Riley. His pool of keyboard players included Herbie Hancock, Chick Corea, Joe Zawinul, and Larry Young. Wayne Shorter played tenor and soprano saxophones, Bennie Maupin played bass clarinet, John McLaughlin played guitar, and the bassists included Dave Holland and Harvey Brooks.

Miles Davis Band, the jazz-funk group with which Davis ended a five-year retirement in 1981. This photo was taken by Mark Vinci at a 1982 concert with (left to right): soprano saxophonist Bill Evans (his tenor sax is sitting to his right), electric bassist Marcus Miller, Miles Davis (wearing hat, holding trumpet), Mino Cinelu (playing conga drum), Al Foster (drums). Guitarist Mike Stern, a regular member of this group, is not shown.

**Partnership with Joe Zawinul**

*In a Silent Way* marked the beginning of Davis's **partnership with pianist-composer Joe Zawinul,** who had been with the Cannonball Adderley quintet during the 1960s. Davis's relationship with Zawinul was similar to those he had with Gil Evans in the late 1940s and late 50s, with Bill Evans on *Kind of Blue*, and with Shorter from 1964 to 69. Davis recorded Zawinul pieces of the "Nefertiti" style: "In a Silent Way" *(In a Silent Way)* and "Pharaoh's Dance" *(Bitches Brew)*. Davis continued to use Zawinul's compositions on later LPs but did not always credit Zawinul on the album labels.[15]

**Instrumentation**

The post-1968 music of Davis differed in several respects from his 1963–68 style. For example, instrumentation was altered as follows:

1) Electric piano and organ replaced conventional piano; and Davis often employed two or more electric keyboard instruments at once.
2) Electric bass guitar replaced acoustic bass viol (see chapter 3 for illustration).
3) Electric guitarists were more frequently employed; at one time, he had three in a single band.
4) The Davis saxophonists of this period spent more time on soprano sax than on any other instrument. The soprano had the potential for penetrating and

---

[15]Most Davis recordings made after 1969 list Davis as sole composer despite the fact that usually he was performing the compositions of others. Zawinul's "Orange Lady," which is the last third of "Great Expectations" on the *Big Fun* album, is wrongly credited to Davis. Hermeto Pascoal's "Little Church" and "Selim" are wrongly credited to Davis on the *Live-Evil* album.

carrying its sound over drums and electric instruments, where a tenor might not cut through.

·5) Davis usually employed two or more drummers. By the early 1970s, he had settled into the pattern of using one player on conventional drum set and another on auxiliary percussion such as conga drums, shakers, rattles, gongs, whistles, and a large number of instruments native to Africa, South America, and India. On several LPs, Davis used Indian musicians playing the sitar (a stringed instrument) and tabla (drums).

**Rhythm Section Concept**

The rhythm section concept was another way in which Davis's post-1968 groups differed from his 1963–68 groups. The later groups featured elaborate configurations of colors and textures, and rhythm section members played with a very high level of activity. The beat was easily detectable, but it was surrounded by a mass of constantly changing sounds, sometimes delicate and gentle, sometimes turbulent. Textures often seemed to be created for their own sake rather than as accompaniments. The textures on *In a Silent Way* and *Bitches Brew* were as much in the forefront as the written melodies and improvised solo lines. The textures were generated by several electric keyboard instruments (piano and organ), guitar, basses, and several drummers. Bass lines blended rock formulas, a freely improvised nonwalking style, and figures borrowed from Latin American music (see notated rock and Latin bass figures on pages 427 and 428).

Most post-1968 Davis music centered on a few repeated chords, a repeating bass figure, or a mode, rather than a sequence of frequently changing chords. The tunes reflected Wayne Shorter's composing style and the departures he had made from bop. Complexity was now concentrated in the rhythm section figures rather than in the melodies. Performance format differed as well. Instead of improvising on a single tune for five to ten minutes, everyone taking a turn soloing, with the entire band stopping before going on to the next tune, this new format made use of medleys. Davis conducted the transitions between tunes, and his bassists led the way by changing the patterns of their repeating figures. The bass was the pivot in this music; **bass figures were as essential to the 1970s and 80s style as complex chord changes had been to bop and hard bop.** *Live-Evil*, *Black Beauty*, and *Agharta* are albums providing representative examples of this music.

Davis often set up a new mood and the harmonies for it by playing chords in a rhythmic fashion on an electric keyboard instrument. In this way he often dictated the tempo and rhythm that was to persist throughout the next passage. Davis used this scheme to make transitions gracefully between moods within the medleys, sometimes continuing to reinforce the mood by comping on the keyboard.

Despite the marked simplification of rhythm section harmonies, improvising soloists tended to retain considerable harmonic complexity. John Coltrane had perfected techniques for spontaneously superimposing sequential patterns atop relatively static accompaniments. Such patterns were devised in ways that made them sound as though they possessed the direction that one ordinarily detects in a progression of chords. The listener would hear a coherence that is normally associated with melody lines that closely mirror an underlying set of chord progressions, yet that coherence did not necessarily derive from any progression of chords. These devices provided harmonic interest without depending on the movement of chords we ordinarily require to attain a similar effect. Coltrane and his pianist McCoy Tyner had developed these approaches for improvising on mode-based forms and repeating bass figures. The saxophonists and guitar soloists who worked with Miles Davis during the 1970s and 80s used these same techniques. It is important to note that these techniques replaced the bop concepts of jazz phrasing; none of Charlie Parker's or Dizzy Gillespie's pet phrases were used. In fact, much of the lyricism that had been associated with bop was not evident in this new style. Improvisers seemed more intent on creating moods than melodies.

**Personnel**

After 1968, Miles Davis led groups whose personnel was not as stable as his late 1950s and mid-1960s bands. During the 1968–73 period, each new LP had new personnel, and the musicians on tour were not always the same as those on the album. John Coltrane had been with Davis on and off for five years; Wayne Shorter had also stayed approximately five years. But after Shorter left, Davis employed more than five different saxophonists in five years.

The Davis rhythm sections were more stable, however. After various combinations of pianists, bassists, and drummers, he settled for several years on bass guitarist Michael Henderson and drummers Al Foster (conventional set) and M'Tume Heath (conga drums and auxiliary percussion). Between the 1971 departure of pianist Keith Jarrett and the mid-1980s, Davis often played without a keyboard instrument, except to begin pieces himself by setting up a mood with chords and rhythms that would establish a repeating figure, upon which the next passage would be based. After 1971 he almost always carried at least one guitarist, sometimes using three at the same time.[16] Beginning in the mid-1980s, Davis again carried two keyboardists, as he had done briefly during the early 1970s. And to that, he added a guitarist and saxophonist.

**Trumpet Style**

For the new jazz-rock idiom, Davis added new dimensions to his trumpet style. As he had done on many live recordings of the 1960s, he again played fast, sweeping runs in and out of his extreme high register. He wired his instrument to an amplifier and connected electronic attachments which simulated echo (by means of a tape loop device called Echoplex, evident on the title track from *Bitches Brew*) or created alterations of tone color previously achieved by rubber plunger mutes (by means of the wah-wah pedal, evident on "Sivad" in *Live-Evil*). He could be quite violent and sound much like a rock guitarist, or he could play in the tender, mournful manner he had displayed on *Porgy and Bess* and *Sketches of Spain*.

Sometimes most of the band would become silent while he quietly played with only one other musician, but that was rare. Usually the mood was very outgoing and full of unrelenting tension. The level of musicianship was very high, and the complexity of the music set it apart from rock, but it was often quite similar to the loud turbulence of many rock bands of the late 1960s and 70s. Admiration for such non-jazz musicians as Jimi Hendrix and Billy Preston was evident in Davis's music.

---

[16]For details on the personnel and instrumentation changes in this period, see the book by Jack Chambers, *Milestones 2* (Beech Tree, 1985).

The post-1968 Davis recordings displayed a blend of the jazz tradition, 1960s and 70s funk music, and the music of India and South America. It was infused with the spirit of Coltrane, but the tone colors were those of rock.

**1980s Formula**  The mid- and late-1980s recordings of Davis emphasized preset accompaniments that were produced for him partly by Robert Irving III and Marcus Miller. Davis added his trumpet sound to funk vamps that had been prepared for him, sometimes by computerized synthesizers. His formula for much of the 1980s was to employ a Hendrix disciple on guitar and a Coltrane disciple on saxophone, both of whom could play hot, funky solos on demand. This was placed atop thick layers of sounds produced by electronic keyboards, a drummer playing in a funk style that had been devised for the Davis bands by Al Foster, and a bassist playing in the funk style of Marcus Miller. Davis rarely allowed his keyboardists to solo. His music of this period was highly arranged and not as freewheeling and explosively daring as in the period immediately following *Bitches Brew*, exemplified by *Live-Evil*, *Black Beauty*, and *Agharta*. It was energetic, however, and its sound usually remained distinguishable from most pop music of the period.

**JOHN McLAUGHLIN**  John McLaughlin (b. 1942) is a British guitarist who had been active in British rock bands[17] and jazz groups since the late 1950s. He first became known to American musicians during the period 1969–71 when he began playing with Lifetime, the fusion band of drummer Tony Williams, and started recording with Miles Davis (see footnote 12).

McLaughlin is notable for his phenomenally high level of instrumental proficiency, and he has become one of the most prominent jazz guitarists since Wes Montgomery. Despite his being considered a jazz musician, McLaughlin used a tone which was unlike traditional jazz guitar quality. It was hard, not soft, cutting, not smooth, and metallic, not warm. In short, it had the color and texture preferred by rock guitarists, not jazz guitarists. Also, he frequently altered the size and shape of his tone by use of a wah-wah pedal and a phase shifter. (The phase shifter produces a subtle swirling of the sound.) Another point of contrast between McLaughlin and more traditional jazz guitarists is that most of his improvisations contain far less of the pronounced syncopation and the easy, relaxed, swing feeling that had previously typified jazz. Improvisations in McLaughlin performances were unlike the bouncy conception which was part of the Charlie Christian, Wes Montgomery, and Kenny Burrell styles. McLaughlin performances also lacked the gentle lyricism so characteristic of improvisations by Jim Hall.

The syncopations in John McLaughlin's lines were more typical of rock than of jazz. And his solos were often composed of long strings of sixteenth notes periodically interrupted by held tones which McLaughlin expressively distorted in waveform and in pitch. The inflections he preferred were refinements of those customary in rock and in blues guitar playing. McLaughlin's rhythmic conception and his

[17]McLaughlin had collaborated in 1963 with bassist Jack Bruce and drummer Ginger Baker, who later joined Eric Clapton in the well-known rock group called Cream.

melodic conception had more in common with classical music and the 1960s improvisations of John Coltrane than with standard bop practice. In his long lines of sixteenth notes, he often chose sequences reminiscent of the patterns used by Coltrane. Both McLaughlin and Coltrane had studied the music of India and were fond of basing their solos on modes learned from this study.

During the early 1970s, McLaughlin played a custom-made electric guitar having two necks, one with six and the other with twelve strings. He also worked with the vina, a seven-string Indian instrument that has four playing strings and three accompanying strings. During the late 1970s, he played another specially built instrument inspired by the vina, with a form like an autoharp's, having a scalloped fingerboard and accompanying strings.

McLaughlin's work in Lifetime and in his own Mahavishnu Orchestra projected unusually high intensity, partly due to high amplifier settings and a stress on rapid-fire, multinoted themes with extremely busy accompaniment. The interaction and determination displayed by such Mahavishnu albums as his 1971 *Inner Mounting Flame* and his 1972 *Birds of Fire* come from a high level of cooperation and mutual inspiration between drummer Billy Cobham, electric bass guitarist Rick Laird, and electric pianist/synthesist Jan Hammer. Many listeners feel that these recordings remain benchmarks for ensemble cohesion and inspired jazz-rock improvisation. Feeling for this music was so high that *Birds of Fire* in 1973 reached the very high position of number 15 on *Billboard's* record sales chart in the popular album category, in which most jazz albums never even reach position number 200. These two Mahavishnu albums are also distinctive for their use of irregular meters—time signatures which, though common to Indian music, had previously been rare in jazz and rock.[18] Many listeners consider this to have been the greatest of all fusion bands.

Not all of McLaughlin's 1970s output consisted of high-intensity electronic music. He also recorded on acoustic guitar in his 1970 *My Goal's Beyond*,[19] an album which McLaughlin personally lists among his favorite works. It contains one side of overdubbed, self-accompanying, solo guitar improvisations and one side with saxophone, violin, acoustic bass, and drums. There is an expansive and exhilarated feeling in the solo side, especially in McLaughlin's rendering of his original composition "Follow Your Heart." Though leaving the nonelectric approach for a few years right after this album, McLaughlin returned to it when touring and recording with Shakti, an Indian music ensemble comprised of violin, tabla, mrindagam, and ghatam. His fondness for the nonelectronic sound also emerged in what many fans consider to contain his best solo: "Rene's Theme," a duet with fellow guitarist Larry Coryell on Coryell's 1970 *Spaces*[20] album. This pairing with Coryell recurred during the 1980s when McLaughlin toured in duo and trio with several other guitar giants, all playing hollow-body guitar: Coryell, Al Dimeola, Christian Escoude, and Spanish flamenco guitarist Paco de Lucia.

[18]Over the years, McLaughlin's groups also offered fine examples of jazz-rock violin playing, first through Jerry Goodman, then, beginning in 1974, with Jean-Luc Ponty, whose recordings with his own bands have been among the best selling in all of jazz-rock.

[19]John McLaughlin—*My Goal's Beyond*, Rykodisc 10051 (Douglas 9), CD/LP, 1970

[20]Larry Coryell—*Spaces*, Vanguard 6558 (79345), CD, 1970.

Jazz-Rock guitarists-composers-bandleaders John McLaughlin (left) and Larry Coryell (below). (*Photos by Bill Smith*)

**LARRY CORYELL**

Guitarist Larry Coryell (b. 1943) is especially significant in jazz history because he was one of the first to blend the styles of country music, blues guitar, and rock with established jazz styles. He did this during the mid-1960s while playing in the bands of drummer Chico Hamilton and vibraharpist Gary Burton. Coryell's own group, the Free Spirits, was also active in 1966, well before the major onslaught of rock-influenced jazz groups in 1969 and 1970 (see footnote 6). Burton had been attracted to Coryell's work with the Free Spirits and the possibilities that it suggested for jazz. The 1967 *Duster* album contains several passages in which Coryell solos in a style clearly drawn from rock (see footnote 7). Burton and his other sidemen follow Coryell's lead and manage to approximate the flavor and intensity of Coryell's work. Burton further pursued this avenue with guitarist Jerry Hahn on a 1968 album called *Country Roads and Other Places*, and then continued to employ excellent guitarists who were interested in combining country music, rock, and jazz, along the way introducing Mick Goodrick and Pat Metheny.[21]

The Free Spirits, Foreplay (Coryell's 1969–72 band), and the Eleventh House (a later band) were all jazz-rock groups, but Coryell was not strictly a rock guitarist. As early as his time with Chico Hamilton, Coryell had proven himself to be an unusually imaginative and technically proficient improviser of jazz lines. His playing could be distinguished from McLaughlin's because Coryell's note beginnings were more percussive; they had more "pop." In addition, he was given to greater variety in his solos than McLaughlin. The twists and turns in Coryell's lines suggested more jazz roots. All these comparisons are easy to make because McLaughlin performed on Coryell's *Spaces* album, which documents a time when both guitarists were at a peak in their creativity and technical prowess.[22]

**JOSEF ZAWINUL**

Joe Zawinul (b. 1932) is a pianist and composer who moved from his native Vienna, Austria, to the United States in 1959. His first great impact was made with the bands of saxophonist Cannonball Adderley between 1961 and 1970, during which time he authored two of the band's most popular funk hits, "Mercy, Mercy, Mercy"[23] and "Walk Tall." His next great success came with Miles Davis's use of Zawinul's "In a Silent Way" as the title track for a 1969 album which pioneered the fusion of jazz improvisation with rock instruments and rock accompaniment practices. Davis also included Zawinul's "Pharaoh's Dance" on *Bitches Brew*, as well as using Zawinul as chief arranger for *In a Silent Way* and *Bitches Brew*.

In 1971 Zawinul founded an innovative jazz-rock band called Weather Report, and it was with this band's 1977 *Heavy Weather*[24] album that he enjoyed his greatest sales since "Mercy, Mercy, Mercy." The album sold more than 500,000

[21]Gary Burton features Goodrick and Metheny on his albums *Ring*, ECM 829191 (1051), CD, 1974; and *Dreams So Real*, ECM 833329 (1072), CD, 1975.

[22]Like McLaughlin, Coryell also demonstrated considerable interest in non-rock playing during the late 1970s and early 1980s. He performed as an unaccompanied solo guitarist, and he played duets with guitarists Philip Catherine, Steve Khan, McLaughlin, and violinist Michael Urbaniak.

[23]Cannonball Adderley—*Mercy, Mercy, Mercy*, Capitol 16153 (ST 2663), LP, 1966

[24]Weather Report—*Heavy Weather*, CBS 34418, CD/LP, 1977

copies (a certified "gold" album) and contained Zawinul's "Birdland," an arrangement of catchy, syncopated phrases in extended repetition, inspired by the composer's memories of hearing the Count Basie band at the New York nightclub called Birdland. (Listen to "Birdland" at the beginning of the JAZZ CLASSICS CASSETTE, immediately following Count Basie's "One O'Clock Jump.") The piece epitomizes the danceable, riff-band style favored by Basie, though translated here into jazz-rock. It received wide exposure in discotheques and in recordings by the Maynard Ferguson big band and the vocal group Manhattan Transfer.

Zawinul has made significant contributions in the use of electronic instruments for jazz. He had used the Wurlitzer electric piano on Adderley's 1966 recording of "Mercy, Mercy, Mercy," and he subsequently employed a Fender Rhodes electric piano on tour. Singer-bandleader Ray Charles had previously carried electric piano, as had Sun Ra, but it was not common in jazz until Zawinul began using it. Miles Davis was so taken with the Fender Rhodes when he heard Zawinul playing it in Adderley's band that he required its use by three successive pianists in his own bands—Herbie Hancock, Chick Corea, and Keith Jarrett—thereby influencing subsequent work by those men with their own groups. The Rhodes became the most common keyboard instrument in jazz groups of the 1970s; even such nonfusion pianists as Bill Evans and Oscar Peterson recorded with it. Zawinul was also one of the first musicians to master the Oberheim Polyphonic[25] and the Arp and Prophet synthesizers, as well as the ring modulator.[26]

One of the leading composers of the 1970s, Zawinul demonstrated a creativity which parallels that of Charles Mingus in the 1950s and Duke Ellington in the 1940s. He generated a broader variety of melodic and accompaniment rhythms than possibly any other jazz composer of the 1970s. Zawinul wrote numerous pieces that touched highly diverse tone colors and moods. Throughout his albums with Weather Report run playful melodies with highly imaginative accompaniments.[27] His "In a Silent Way" and "Arrival in New York" are impressionistic tone poems.[28]

Zawinul encouraged the use of a wide assortment of exotic percussion instruments by his musicians. He himself produced unusual timbres and rhythms by playing clay drum, tambura, xylophone, steel drums, and African thumb piano. Gentle sounds are conjured by ocarina, hollow-body guitar, thumb piano, and tambura on his "Jungle Book."[29] And like Ellington, Zawinul arranged wordless

[25]This is exemplified on side one of Weather Report's *Heavy Weather*.

[26] Zawinul first recorded with ring modulator in 1971 on "Seventh Arrow" in Weather Report's first album, *Weather Report*, CBS 30661, LP, 1971.

[27]"Man in the Green Shirt" (Tale Spinnin', CBS 33417, LP, 1975) and "The Juggler" (*Heavy Weather*)

[28]Both are on *Zawinul*, Atlantic 1579, CD/LP, 1970.

[29]"Jungle Book" is on *Mysterious Traveler*, CBS 32494, CD/LP, 1974. During a period of jazz history when electric instruments dominated the sound of most albums, Zawinul used strains of unamplified piano on the recording of Wayne Shorter's "Blackthorn Rose" (*Mysterious Traveler*), precisely sounding each tone, paced as though to savor its every vibration. He also used it in combination with sustained organ tones in his "Five Short Stories" (*Tale Spinnin'*).

vocals.[30] The breadth of timbral spectra in Weather Report's work might explain how Zawinul's music found its way onto the turntables of demonstration units in stereo equipment stores. Weather Report's creations had joined symphonic music as a vast source of varied timbres and loudnesses by which to judge the quality of sound systems.

**WEATHER**
**REPORT**

When Joe Zawinul left Cannonball Adderley's quintet in 1971 and joined saxophonist Wayne Shorter and bassist Miroslav Vitous, they were to create a remarkable new concept in improvisatory music embodied in the group called Weather Report, which would outlast all other jazz-rock fusion bands. Zawinul, Shorter, and Vitous were joined by two drummers, one on conventional drum set and one playing exotic percussion instruments and creating sound effects for which Airto Moreira had become known in the bands of Miles Davis. It should be noted that Weather Report performed in a broad range of original fusions of jazz with non-jazz styles. Only a

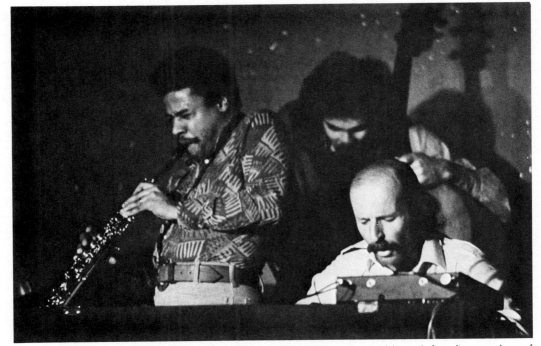

Wayne Shorter (soprano sax), Miroslav Vitous (bass), and Joe Zawinul (piano), founding members of Weather Report and masters of collective improvisation. Pictured here in the early 1970s. (*Photo supplied by Bill Smith*) Listen to these musicians play "Surucucu" on the JAZZ CLASSICS CASSETTE, side 2.

[30]Zawinul used his own voice in this capacity on his "Badia" (*Tale Spinnin'*) and "Jungle Book" (*Mysterious Traveler*), and that of bassist Jaco Pastorius on "Birdland" (from *Heavy Weather*, excerpted on the JAZZ CLASSICS CASSETTE). On "The Orphan" (*8:30*, CBS PC2-36030, LP set, 1979), Zawinul combined Wayne Shorter's tenor saxophone tone with the soft texture of a children's choir.

### Listening Guide for "Surucucu"

Composed by Wayne Shorter; recorded January 13, 1972 in Tokyo, Japan by Weather Report: Wayne Shorter (soprano sax), Joe Zawinul (piano), Miroslav Vitous (bass), Dom Um Romao (auxiliary percussion and vocal), and Eric Gravatt (drums); available on the JAZZ CLASSICS CASSETTE, Side Two; originally on *I Sing the Body Electric* (Columbia KC 31352).

Weather Report originated numerous approaches in their fifteen-year career. (An excerpt from their biggest hit concludes the Afro-American retentions sequence at the beginning of Side One on the JAZZ CLASSICS CASSETTE.) Though most famous for their funk music performed with electric instruments and their role as the premier jazz-rock fusion band, they are also historically significant for the way they loosened the roles of the rhythm section instruments and spontaneously devised collective interplay that was smoother and pleased more listeners than similar "free" jazz of the 1960s. Aside from the music on the band's first album (*Weather Report,* Columbia PC 30661), little of this loosely organized work is demonstrated in their studio recordings. We are therefore fortunate to have this concert recording available as documentation.

This performance draws partly upon a composed theme, Wayne Shorter's "Surucucu." But the musicians do not neatly divide their improvisations into a set number of beats that parallel the theme, nor do they use the theme to provide a chord progression that strictly prescribes the motion of harmonies for improvisation. The arrangement is spontaneous, and the theme is represented only in very fragmented form, a phrase here and there being played out of tempo by Shorter. Moreover, the sequence of sections here does not follow the traditional pattern of introduction, theme, solo choruses, theme, end.

Most of the sounds in this performance will be unfamiliar. The first sound was made by Dom Um Romao slapping his face and changing the shape of his mouth while making vocal sounds articulated by quick tongue movements. The zither-like sounds that accompany Romao's voice are produced by Joe Zawinul playing what is technically termed "prepared piano." Before the performance, he had prepared the piano strings by laying weights on top of some, wedging pieces of rubber between others, attaching clothes pins to others. Zawinul caused the piano strings to vibrate sometimes by plucking them himself and sometimes by depressing the piano keys in the conventional manner.

To appreciate how the music of Weather Report is unique, it is helpful to notice what is not heard: walking bass, ride rhythms, comping, and bop style horn solos. (Compare the "Surucucu" performance, for instance, with the playing of Chick Corea, Miroslav Vitous, and Roy Haynes on "Steps" in the JAZZ CLASSICS CASSETTE.) It is also important to recognize that the piece hangs together and has its own momentum without depending on many of the devices that propel standard jazz performances. There are exceptions. Vitous does briefly play repeating patterns on bass, as at 1' 25" into the piece, and Gravatt sometimes maintains long strings of repeated eighth notes distributed across different cymbals and drums, for example at 1' 33". Their most common practice, however, is to invent variations on steady rhythmic figures rather than strict repetitions of them.

| *Elapsed Time* | |
|---|---|
| | voice, accompanied by prepared piano and the sounds of Romao slapping his own face |
| 0' 27" | chords on prepared piano (to 39") |
| 0' 34" | the tinkling of a triangle |
| 0' 45" | trills played on a wooden flute |
| 0' 53" | Percussion enters; bass sustains deep-pitched tones. |
| 1' 07" | wire brushes playing snare drum and cymbals (to 1' 15") |

| | |
|---|---|
| 1' 10" | slide whistle |
| 1' 18" | Bass interjects sporadic comments. |
| 1' 20" | Timekeeping rhythms begin on cymbals struck with drum sticks. |
| 1' 25" | resonant, low pitched tones of highly amplified bass viol, played pizzicato in a timekeeping manner, accompanied by cymbals |
| 1' 27" | Zawinul strumming the strings inside the piano (to 1' 50") |
| 1' 33" | a single squawk from Shorter's soprano sax |
| | steadily repeating eighth notes on drums and cymbals |
| 1' 39" | chords played on prepared piano |
| 1' 50" | a sequence of sustained sax tones (to 2' 32") (a paraphrase of the "Surucucu" melody) accompanied by acoustic piano |
| 2' 17" | Zawinul strumming the strings inside the piano |
| 2' 20" | "Surucucu" melody in ascending sax tones which are detached from each other, ending with a high, scream-like sound and fall-off at 2' 30" |
| 2' 34" | Rhythm section unwinds, then resumes its pace. |
| 2' 40" | strumming inside piano (to 2' 50") |
| 2' 55" | high-pitched descending arpeggios on piano |
| 3' 05" | stop-time |
| 3' 07" | Zawinul plays highly-amplified Fender Rhodes electric piano and makes it sound like the distorted tone of an rock musician's electric guitar (to 3' 35"). |
| 3' 30" | Sax and electric piano improvise against each other, accompanied by bass and percussion (to 3' 53"). |
| 3' 53" | Shorter acts as though a member of the rhythm section by producing an unaccompanied, repeating figure in a fast staccato manner. |
| 4' 01" | Shorter's staccato figure accompanies Vitous, who has abandoned an accompanying role in favor of a melodic line played by bowing highly amplified upright bass. |
| 4' 04" | duet between legato sax and bass (to 4' 36") |
| 4' 15' | fade out |

small portion of their output truly qualifies for the jazz-rock category. The **collective improvisation of musical textures and the emancipation of rhythm section instruments from conventional roles were significant aspects of Weather Report's approach.**

**Miroslav Vitous** was a bassist uniquely able to improvise melodies as well as the average horn player, and he had already demonstrated his ability to alternate roles when he abandoned the timekeeping role in several selections on his own *Infinite Search* LP.[31] Vitous had a sophisticated melodic sense that put him in a class with such outstanding bass soloists as Paul Chambers and Scott LaFaro. He was also very

[31]Miroslav Vitous—*Infinite Search*, Embryo 524, LP, 1969

capable with bowed bass. Vitous had a keen sense of what to play for the sake of creating interesting rhythmic textures and how to keep his instrument's voice in sensitive musical conversations with other group members. Vitous did not simply break up walking bass lines or play in a decorative two feeling. **The Vitous contributions to Weather Report included fragmented melody statements, bowed sustained tones, and syncopated interjections.** He could just as easily bow melody in unison with a sax line as feed rock-style bass figures into the group texture. Vitous could play a unison with a rhythm the drummer was stating on ride cymbal or underscore a pattern being played on piano. Or he could quickly go back and forth. Vitous had cast off the restraints of traditional bass playing and become a textural improviser in the Weather Report context. Moreover, his work made sense, too. It was not just the flashy playing of a gifted showoff. (Listen to Vitous on "Surucucu" in the JAZZ CLASSICS CASSETTE.)

For Weather Report's first album, Airto Moreira overdubbed percussion parts in the recording studio. Though he never performed with the band, his imaginative, highly original use of Latin American percussion instruments provided a model for the unique combination of sounds that Weather Report refined. Dom Um Romao, another outstanding Brazilian percussionist, was the band's regular percussionist. Within a few weeks of the band's inception, Eric Gravatt became the band's regular drummer. The band then underwent numerous personnel changes, and, by the mid-1970s, bassist Miroslav Vitous was gone and the only founding members who remained were Shorter and Zawinul. After 1985, they were leading separate groups.

Weather Report came on the scene with the standard instrumentation of saxophone, piano, bass, and drums. They also had an auxiliary percussionist, but that was not unusual; many 1950s and 60s jazz groups had employed conga drummers or other auxiliary percussionists to add a Latin American flavor to their sound. What was unusual is that in its earliest albums, **Weather Report did not use its conventional instrumentation in conventional ways.** It was rare for bassist Miroslav Vitous to play walking lines, or for the drummer to play standard ride rhythms or close the high-hat sharply on the second and fourth beats of each measure. Zawinul usually did not comp for Shorter, and the auxiliary percussionist was not restricted to the conga drum.[32]

---

[32]"Eurydice," on Weather Report's first LP (*Weather Report*, CBS 30661, LP, 1971) is one of the few pieces which contains walking bass, drummer playing ride rhythms and closing high-hat on second and fourth beats, sax solo followed by piano solo, etc. And even in such a conventionally formatted performance, there are portions which deviate from the standard bop roles. For example, drummer Alphonse Mouzon often closed his high-hat on all four beats, and interjected musical comments to the point where instead of just keeping time and coloring the sound, he is heard in the forefront of the group. Bassist Miroslav Vitous often abandoned the walking role and instead contributed embellishments to the ensemble. Pianist Zawinul did not always comp behind saxophonist Shorter, either. He set up delicate flourishes, played counter-melodies, and sometimes laid out. Airto Moreira overdubbed interjections of colorful, speech-like sounds throughout the proceedings with his cuica, an instrument in which the player gently slides his fingers along a stick which in turn alters the tension of a specially connected drumhead and causes it to vibrate.

roots in Coleman, make Metheny's style especially compatible with that of his pianist, Lyle Mays, a Jarrett disciple. Together, Mays and Metheny have pioneered lush combinations of electronic alterations of keyboard and guitar sounds and integrated them rhythmically into an original quartet concept.[43] Their group sound is remarkably spacious and uncluttered. The music conveys a clear sense of openness. Though some of his music from the late 1980s falls into the "new age" category, Metheny might best be viewed as a fusion player who is sufficiently versatile and creative to play well in a number of different jazz styles. In fact he even recorded an extremely turbulent album of free jazz with Ornette Coleman.[44]

**NEW AGE**   During the 1980s a new idiom of popular music surfaced. Record stores initially did not have bins for displaying it. So they placed it in the jazz bins because to them it sounded more like jazz than like classical music or rock. Even after this music earned a bin of its own, a significant portion of the public continued to call it jazz. Record store clerks sometimes described it as a mixture of jazz and classical music, or "classical jazz," and it was found in the jazz bins of many stores even at the end of the decade. Though the music does employ improvisation as one of its methods, that is about all it has in common with most jazz. It does not swing. In fact its rhythms are purposely designed to avoid creating any of the tension that jazz swing feeling requires. The methods for creating this music prevent evoking tension in other ways, too. Tone qualities are soft and smooth. Changes in tone color and harmony are made only in the most gradual ways. Often the same chord or mode remains in effect for an entire performance. Loudness levels are usually low and remain that way for long stretches. Changes in loudness are rarely sudden. Models for this music were provided by modern classical composers Lamonte Young, Philip Glass, and Steve Reich. Those composers, in turn, had been influenced by Gregorian chant music as well as the sounds of nature—wind and waves, for example—and such continuous industrial sounds as an air conditioner's steady hum. Since these composers reduced music to a bare minimum of materials and activity, their musical approach was called "minimalism." Some of their music superficially resembled some of the unaccompanied piano improvisations of Keith Jarrett during the 1970s, as well as the solo piano pieces of French impressionist composers Claude Debussy

---

chorusing and echo are all time-delay techniques. Flanging is very small delay, 30–40 milliseconds. Chorusing is from 40 ms to where the human ear can detect it, 90 ms. Where the ear can discern between original signal and the delay is called an echo. In chorusing, you increase the feedback (the number of repeats); typically the repeats will tend to fade in intensity, the more there are. This makes it sound like many players, nonsynchronized, because of the slight imperfections in timing and pitch, thereby increasing the harmonics. The device will modulate the time delay slightly. It sweeps the time back and forth, from 1 or 2 ms away from 60 ms delay to 20 ms away from 60 ms—this is called the depth of modulation. It also adjusts for speed of modulation. The device mixes the direct signal with the repeated signal. Chorusing was originally devised to synthesize the Leslie organ effect. Digital delay converts the signal to a code via sampling, whereas an analog system will color the sound and degrade it.

[43]*The Pat Metheny Group*, ECM 825593 (1114), CD/LP, 1978; *Offramp*, ECM 817138 (1216), CD/LP, 1981

[44]*Song X*, Geffen 24096, CD/LP, 1985

and Maurice Ravel that had inspired some of Jarrett's work. Both products were calm and soothing. Neither projected jazz swing feeling. Much of it explored the sonorities of a single chord or brief chord progression.[45] The Paul Winter Consort and its spin-off group, Oregon, made music like this. Harpist Andreas Vollenweider promoted a similar sound and gained considerable popularity for it during the 1980s. Pianist George Winston imitated Jarrett's long, vamp-based improvisations that meander and seem soothing. Winston's records sold millions of copies, his concerts packed auditoriums, and his style was dubbed "new age."[46]

There is a subcategory of jazz-rock fusion music that is often enjoyed by new age music fans that has more pronounced rhythm and is often simply a refined and quieted style of funk music. During the 1980s, radio stations characterized this fare as "light jazz and soft rock." It employs jazz improvisation, saxophones, guitars, and the standard fusion rhythm section style with electric instruments and drums. However, it does not have the raw quality that previous jazz styles conveyed. It particularly lacks the intensity that characterizes hard bop. It is consistently smooth, without the rough edges we associate with most jazz. Though often played by jazz musicians who are capable of more exciting work—Grover Washington, Chuck Mangione, for example—this music and its improvised solos are very stylized rather than adventuresome. Saxophone improvisations recorded by Kenny G in the mid-1980s fall into this category. Many listeners choose to have this music around them because they find it pleasant and just as easy to ignore as to hear. In other words, it is background music with a beat. During the late 1980s, this music acquired the name "fuzak." This label combined the meaning of jazz-rock "fusion" with Muzak, a term for light, smooth background music, piped into doctor's offices and elevators. Most styles of jazz have had their easy-listening variants, and this is fusion's.

**POPULAR APPEAL**

By 1990, rock had been popular twice as long as swing in the mainstream of American music, and jazz-rock fusion itself had been popular for more than two decades. Fusion became the first jazz style since the swing era to gain popular acceptance anywhere near the level accorded to swing, and it lasted at least as long as the swing era. By incorporating elements of R & B and rock into their music, several established jazz figures achieved popular success that rivaled all the peaks of recognition accorded to jazz players since the end of the swing era's wide appreciation of jazz-oriented band music.[47] Though jazz instrumentals ordinarily sold fewer

---

[45]Jarrett's unaccompanied solo improvisations are far more varied, far more dynamic and should not be confused with either minimalism or the popular idiom it spawned. And his jazz work is not related at all to this movement.

[46]George Winston—*December*, Windham Hill 1025, CD/LP, 1982

[47]It had been unusual for jazz instrumentals to be within the top hundred best-selling albums for any given year, yet Herbie Hancock's Sly Stone-influenced *Head Hunters* album at one time managed to occupy position number 13 on the *Billboard* chart of popular albums, and Miles Davis, who had been one of the few in the past whose albums ever penetrated "the top 100," produced the greatest success of his career when he recorded the rock-flavored *Bitches Brew*, an album that once managed to occupy position number 35, far outselling his other four albums that had penetrated "the top 100."

than 10,000 to 20,000 copies, jazz-rock albums of the 1970s and 80s frequently sold more than 100,000 copies.[48]

This new success for jazz musicians did not depend so much on jazz character as on jazz-rock character. As with swing era big band recordings, those pieces presenting the least improvisation tended to enjoy the most popular acclaim. And, as with the hits of the swing era, jazz-rock hits were identifiable by simple, repeating riffs syncopated in a catchy way. Much of what went by the jazz-rock label consisted of little more than funky rhythm vamps, elementary chord progressions, and an improvised solo riding on top of it.[49] This music was so popular that, in addition to the "jazz-rock" and "jazz fusion" labels, it also acquired the label of "crossover" music because sales of the records crossed over from the jazz market into the popular market.

There are several possible explanations for the new popularity of jazz and jazz-rock in particular. First, rock had already been popular for more than fifteen years by the time that Herbie Hancock's *Head Hunters* was released. So perhaps when **jazz adopted the electric instruments and the accompaniment rhythms associated with rock** that was so familiar already, it was providing a bridge of similarity for listeners that eased them into a music that had otherwise been strange and difficult to listen to. A second possibility is that the **increased prominence of drums was more inviting to dancers.** Third is the **relative simplicity of chord progressions** found in jazz-rock. The new music was more involved than rock had previously been, but it was harmonically less complex than other jazz styles. A fourth explanation involves the **extensive use of repetition for a single accompaniment pattern.** Technically it is known as ostinato, which means that a particular rhythm or brief melodic figure is repeated continuously. It was fundamental to most of the jazz-rock hits of the 1970s, and its use might explain the enormous popularity for the boogie woogie style of jazz piano playing during the 1940s. Many of the largest-selling recordings in any category of music are distinguished by their simplicity, rhythmic vitality, and extensive use of repetition. This combination of features could also account for much of jazz-rock's commercial success.

[48]Trumpeter Chuck Mangione's rock-flavored *Feels So Good* (A&M 3219 (4658), CD/LP; 1977) sold about 2.2 million copies. Spyro Gyra's "Morning Dance" (MCA-37148 (Infinity 9004), CD/LP, 1979) sold over a million copies. Kenny G's *Duotones* (Arista 84427, LP/CD, 1986) sold over 6 million copies, as did George Benson's *Breezin'* (Warner Bros. 3111 (2919), CD/LP, 1976). And, after the Jazz Crusaders dropped "jazz" from their group name and began playing rock-oriented material, "The Crusaders" enjoyed hit after hit. Their *Southern Comfort*, *Images*, and *Street Life* albums each sold over 500,000 copies.

[49]This was the formula for several hits by saxophonists Grover Washington (*Mr. Magic*, Motown 5175 (Kudu 20), CD/LP, 1974), and Kenny G ("Songbird"), guitarist Earl Klugh (*Living Inside Your Love*, Capitol 48385 (Liberty 667), CD/LP, 1976), and the bands of Jeff Lorber (*Soft Space*, Inner City 1058, LP, 1978) and Spyro Gyra (*Spyro Gyra*, MCA 1651 (Amherst 1014), LP, 1977).

## CHAPTER SUMMARY

1) Jazz and rock represent different streams in Afro-American music, but they have occasionally overlapped.

2) Jazz differs from rock in its smaller amount of repetition, larger amount of improvisation, greater complexity, and higher level of musicianship.

3) Chicago, Blood, Sweat & Tears, and Ten Wheel Drive ought not to be called jazz-rock because they used little improvisation and had more roots in soul music than in rock and roll.

4) These three groups represent amalgamations of existing trends rather than a fresh style.

5) The most genuine fusions of funk and jazz occurred in bands of Larry Coryell, Gary Burton, Miles Davis, and the bands launched by their sidemen.

6) The most prominent jazz-rock guitarists were John McLaughlin, Larry Coryell, and Pat Metheny.

7) Their tone color and rhythmic conception departed from jazz guitar tradition and drew more from urban blues and rock practices.

8) John McLaughlin plays with phenomenal speed and precision, and draws from the music of India and John Coltrane.

9) McLaughlin led several innovative bands containing musicians who were themselves important jazz-rock bandleaders.

10) Pianist Joe Zawinul wrote the funk hits "Mercy, Mercy, Mercy" and "Walk Tall" while with Cannonball Adderley's band.

11) Zawinul's composition "In a Silent Way" and his arrangements formed the basis for the important 1969 Miles Davis jazz-rock albums *Bitches Brew* and *In a Silent Way*.

12) In 1971, Zawinul founded Weather Report, an innovative fusion band which lasted until 1985.

13) Weather Report featured compositions of Zawinul and saxophonist Wayne Shorter, touching French impressionist, African, Latin American, and classical European traditions.

14) Weather Report originally began with much collective improvisation.

15) Weather Report eventually adopted approaches employing extensive preset repetition and the feeling of soul music, culminating in Zawinul's riff-based hit "Birdland."

16) Roles for the bassists in Weather Report include walking, funk bass, soloing, and the interactive-nonrepetitive style.

17) Jaco Pastorius was the bass guitarist with Weather Report from 1976 to 1982, and his sound became an important model for bassists.

18) Pastorius was also a composer-arranger, combining such unusual tone colors as harmonica, steel drums, and children's voices in addition to integrating classical music and funk style for his own band, Word of Mouth.

19) The post-1968 work of Miles Davis displayed a blend of the jazz tradition, funk music, and the music of India and South America.

Herbie Hancock's first fusion band: Hancock (Fender Rhodes electric piano), Buster Williams (electric bass guitar), Bennie Maupin (bass clarinet), Billy Hart (drums), Eddie Henderson (fluegelhorn), and Julian Priester (trombone). (*Photo courtesy of the Cleveland Press Collection/Cleveland State University Archives*)

**BOOKS ABOUT ROCK AND JAZZ-ROCK**

For more information about rock and jazz-rock, see *The Rolling Stone Illustrated History of Rock and Roll*, edited by Jim Miller (Random House, 1980); *Jazz-Rock Fusion: The People and the Music* by Julie Coryell and Laura Friedman (Dell, 1978); *The Illustrated Encyclopaedia of Black Music*, edited by Mike Clifford (Harmony Books, 1982); *The Sound of the City* by Charlie Gillett (Outerbridge and Dienstfrey, 1970); *The Story of Rock* by Carl Belz (Oxford University Press, 1969); *The Art of Rock and Roll*, 2nd ed., by Charles Brown (Prentice-Hall, 1987); *The New Grove Dictionary of American Music*, edited by H. Wiley Hitchcock and Stanley Sadie (Macmillan [London], 1986). *Big Road Blues* by David Evans (University of California Press, 1982) gives an excellent background on blues style and its history. The following reference works are all compiled by Joel Whitburn and are available from Record Research Inc., P.O. Box 200, Menomonee Falls, Wisconsin 53051. In addition to cataloging popularities, they contain brief biographies of artists: *Top Pop Singles: 1955–1986; Top Pop Albums: 1955–1985; Bubbling Under the Hot 100: 1959–1981; Top Black: 1942–1986; Billboard's Top Videocassettes: 1979–1986.*

# appendix

**A Very Abbreviated Outline of Jazz Styles—Not strictly chronological; many styles overlap the same time periods, and most have continued long after their inception. Many innovators continued playing for decades after their style emerged.**

| Time | Style | Hornmen | Pianists | Composers-Arrangers | Rhythm Section Musicians |
|---|---|---|---|---|---|
| 1920s | Early Jazz | Louis Armstrong<br>Sidney Bechet<br>Bix Beiderbecke | James P. Johnson<br>Earl Hines | Jelly Roll Morton | Baby Dodds<br>Zutty Singleton<br>Pops Foster |
| 1930s | Swing | Coleman Hawkins<br>Roy Eldridge<br>Johnny Hodges<br>Benny Carter | Art Tatum<br>Teddy Wilson | Duke Ellington<br>Fletcher Henderson<br>Sy Oliver | Chick Webb<br>Dave Tough<br>Sid Catlett<br>Walter Page<br>Gene Krupa |
| Late 1930s | Transition to Bop | Lester Young<br>Don Byas | Nat Cole | | Count Basie Rhythm Section 1937–43<br>Jimmy Blanton |
| 1940s | Bop | Charlie Parker<br>Dizzy Gillespie<br>Dexter Gordon<br>Stan Getz | Thelonious Monk<br>Bud Powell<br>Al Haig | Thelonious Monk<br>Tadd Dameron<br>Dizzy Gillespie | Kenny Clarke<br>Max Roach<br>Oscar Pettiford |
| Late 1940s | Transition to Cool & West Coast | Lee Konitz<br>Miles Davis | Lennie Tristano | Claude Thornhill<br>Gil Evans | |
| 1950s | West Coast | Gerry Mulligan<br>Chet Baker<br>Art Pepper | Dave Brubeck | Gerry Mulligan<br>Shorty Rogers<br>Jimmy Giuffre | Chico Hamilton |

| Period | Style | | | | |
|---|---|---|---|---|---|
| 1950s | Hard Bop | Clifford Brown<br>Sonny Rollins<br>Thad Jones<br>John Coltrane<br>Cannonball Adderley<br>Miles Davis | Tommy Flanagan<br>Horace Silver<br>Red Garland | Horace Silver<br>Benny Golson<br>Cannonball Adderley<br>Jackie McLean<br>Gigi Gryce | Art Blakey<br>Philly Joe Jones<br>Paul Chambers<br>Sam Jones<br>Wilbur Ware |
| Late 1950s | Transition to Modal Jazz and Free Jazz | Miles Davis<br>John Coltrane<br>Ornette Coleman | Bill Evans<br>Cecil Taylor | Charles Mingus<br>Miles Davis | |
| Early 1960s | Coexistence of Hard Bop, Free Jazz, and Modal Jazz | Eric Dolphy | Bill Evans<br>McCoy Tyner<br>Cecil Taylor | John Coltrane<br>Ornette Coleman<br>Wayne Shorter<br>Charles Mingus<br>Don Cherry | Elvin Jones<br>Bill Evans Trio<br>with Scott LaFaro<br>Cecil Taylor<br>with Sunny Murray |
| Mid-1960s | | Freddie Hubbard<br>Joe Henderson<br>Wayne Shorter<br>Don Cherry | Herbie Hancock | Wayne Shorter<br>John Coltrane<br>Herbie Hancock | Miles Davis's 1963–68 rhythm section |
| Late 1960s | Transition to Jazz-Rock | Miles Davis | Joe Zawinul | Joe Zawinul | Tony Williams |
| 1970s | Coexistence of AACM, Jazz-Rock, and Modal Jazz | AACM players | Keith Jarrett<br>Herbie Hancock<br>Chick Corea<br>Joe Zawinul | Chick Corea<br>AACM<br>Joe Zawinul<br>John McLaughlin | Miroslav Vitous<br>Airto Moreira<br>Jaco Pastorius |

# ELEMENTS OF MUSIC

In describing the nature of jazz and the characteristics of different styles, several basic musical terms are quite helpful. This chapter is devoted to defining some of these terms, and I urge all readers, including those who are musically knowledgeable, to examine them carefully.

When people think of jazz, they usually think of rhythm first. But because the word rhythm is often used to describe a large variety of musical characteristics, some uses convey inaccurate or contradictory meanings. Much of the confusion can be avoided by first understanding three related terms for which rhythm is often mistaken: beat, tempo, and meter.

**Beat**   Music is often said to have a pulse. The unit of pulse is called a beat. When you tap your foot to music, you are usually tapping with the beat. Here is a visualization of the pulse sequences we call beats.

**Tempo**   Tempo refers to the speed or rate at which the beats pass. If you describe a piece of music as fast, you probably mean it has a rapid tempo, not that it occupies a short time span. When the beats continue at a regular rate, we say the tempo is constant. A clock's ticking is a good example of constant tempo. If the passage of beats is rapid, the speed is called up tempo. Medium tempo means medium fast.

**Meter**   The beats in music are rarely undifferentiated. They are usually heard as being grouped. Meter describes the type of grouping. Our perception of grouping results when sequences of beats are set off from each other. This occurs in several ways. Every third or fourth beat may be louder or longer than the others. It may be distinctive because it has a different pitch or tone quality. Those differences are perceived as emphasis or accent. If we hear a sequence of beats grouped in fours, it may be due to a pattern of accents which creates this effect: **ONE** two three four **ONE** two three four. That pattern represents a meter which musicians simply call "four."

If the beats fall into the pattern, **ONE** two three, **ONE** two three, **ONE** two three, musicians say that the music "is in three" or in waltz time.

Meters of four and three are quite common, but there are also meters of five, six, seven, and others. A meter of five might sound like **ONE** two three four five **ONE** two three four five, **ONE** two three four five, with a large accent on the first beat and no other accents. Or there may be a strong accent on the first beat and a smaller accent on the fourth: **ONE** two three **FOUR** five **ONE** two three **FOUR** five **ONE** two three **FOUR** five; or a smaller accent on the third beat: **ONE** two **THREE** four five **ONE** two **THREE** four five **ONE** two **THREE** four five. A meter of six usually feels like **ONE** two three **FOUR** five six **ONE** two three **FOUR** five six.

Each group of beats is called a **measure.** When the meter is three, there are three beats in a measure; when the meter is four there are four beats in a measure.

**Rhythm**   In the broadest sense, rhythm simply refers to the arrangement of sounds in time, and therefore encompasses beat, tempo, and meter. But rhythm has come to mean something more specific than these features. In fact, beat, tempo, and meter furnish the framework in which rhythm is described.

Imagine a continuous sequence of beats occurring at a constant tempo, with four beats to a measure. The steady beat which in musical notation is represented by a string of quarter notes can also be visualized as a series of boxes, representing equal amounts of time. Our meter would be called "four." Each beat is called a quarter note, and each unit of four beats constitutes a measure.

The sound within a measure can be distributed in an infinite number of ways, one of which includes "filling" the measure with silence. Rhythm is the description of how that measure or a sequence of measures is filled with sound.

Let us take a few examples, numbering the four parts of the measure one, two, three, and four, respectively. We shall create rhythms by using a single sound mixed with silence. First, divide a measure into four equal parts, filling only the first and third with sound.

We have a rhythm. It is not complex, but it does what a rhythm is supposed to do: it describes the distribution of sound over time. In fact, this is the bass drum part in numerous marches, and it is the string bass part in many slow dance pieces.

Now, instead of taking just one measure, take two measures as a unit of repetition. In other words, the rhythm is two measures long.

Finally, repeat a one measure rhythm to fill two measures worth of time. This might be heard as a two measure rhythm or as two one measure rhythms.

Rhythm is the distribution of sound over time, but rhythm also refers to the way sounds are accented. Usually, the first beat of a measure is accented. An example would be the typical OOM pah pah accompaniment for a waltz. In a measure of four, the first and third beats are often accented, as in the BOOM chick BOOM chick drum pattern used in much popular music.

Examining our use of accents can lend understanding to a rhythmic element called *syncopation*, a crucial aspect of jazz feeling. For example, if we expect to hear a sound on every beat but only hear it in a few odd places, the upset we feel is the result of syncopation. This upset can be very stimulating and contribute a prime component of jazz feeling.

Examine this manner of filling two measures.

Note that the sounds which occur, bordered by silence, in positions other than on the first and third beats seem to stand out. They seem to be self accenting. If we additionally stress these odd positions by making the sounds in those positions louder than the sounds in other positions, syncopation is enhanced: one TWO three four ONE two three FOUR.

The concept of syncopation partly depends on a listener's expectations. For example, if we are expecting to hear *ONE* two THREE four, but we actually hear one *TWO* three FOUR, we are experiencing syncopation. Jazz drummers often keep time by playing boom CHICK boom CHICK (one TWO three FOUR) instead of BOOM chick BOOM chick. This syncopation is part of what makes a performance sound like jazz. Another frequently used syncopation occurs when we hear one two three FOUR when we are expecting to hear ONE two three four. So you see that rhythm involves the arrangement of stresses in addition to just describing the arrangement of sound over time. We have also seen that a phenomenon called syncopation results when the sounds are arranged or stressed in unexpected ways. Of course, what is expected depends on what the listener is accustomed to hearing. Therefore the statement that syncopation consists of unexpected accent is inadequate. Perhaps a more useful definition involves the accent of beats other than the first and, in measure of four beats, also the third beat. Silence can also be syncopating. For example, if we encounter silence at a time when we are expecting to hear ONE, the feeling of syncopation results.

To understand more complex syncopations and another essential element of jazz feeling, the swing eighth note, requires an acquaintance with ways in which beats are divided into smaller units. Here is a measure in four, with four quarter notes to the measure. We can divide each quarter note in half to produce eighth notes.

There are two eighth notes for every quarter note. If we place accents on the eighth notes according to the way we previously accented the measure of quarter notes, we have *ONE* two three four

FIVE six seven eight. The time span for a measure of eight eighth notes is identical to that in a measure of four quarter notes, but keeping track of eight eighth notes is cumbersome. So we express the eighth notes in terms of subdivided quarter notes, saying "and" for the second half of each quarter note (every other eighth note): one and two and three and four and. Each word, whether it is the name of a number or the word "and," represents an eighth note.

Syncopation occurs when any of the "and's" receives more emphasis than the numbered units. Accenting the "and's" is essential to rhythms frequently employed in jazz. The final two beats in a measure are often divided into eighth notes with the last one accented the most: three **and four AND** (for notations of this and other syncopations, see page 428). Many notes which appear in written form on the first beat of a measure are played on the and of the fourth beat in the preceding measure when given a jazz interpretation. The practice of playing a note slightly before or slightly after it is supposed to be played is a syncopating device which jazz musicians apply to pop tunes in order to lend jazz feeling to a performance.

The quarter note can also be divided into three equal parts to produce what are called eighth-note triplets.

Here, each quarter note is divided into four equal parts, called sixteenth notes.

So far we have examined equal divisions of the quarter note. But it is also possible to divide it into notes of unequal value, for instance, a long note and a short note. One such pattern consists of a dotted eighth note followed by a sixteenth note. A dot after a note means that the note receives one and a half times its usual value; therefore the dotted eighth note has the combined value of an eighth note and a sixteenth note.

Another long-short pattern is based on the triplet division of the quarter note. The pattern is called a tied triplet figure. Here, the first note has the value of two-thirds of a quarter note, and the second has the value of one-third.

Jazz has one rhythmic quality which, to my knowledge, is not found in any other kind of music: jazz swing feeling. A discussion of it appears in the "What Is Jazz?" chapter, but that discussion hinges on the swing eighth note which is examined next.

Having heard the term swing eighth note, you might wonder how, if an eighth note is simply half the duration of a quarter note, we can have different types of eighth note, swing eighth note being one of them. Strictly speaking, you cannot have different types. An eighth note is an eighth note. Our descriptive language is loose enough, however, that we can use the term to label notes of slightly more or less duration than the eighth note is understood to receive.

(demonstrated in JAZZ STYLES CASSETTE, side 2)

This looseness in applying the term eighth note is not exclusive to jazz musicians. Nonjazz musicians often use terms such as **legato,** which means long or slurred together or connected. They use the term **staccato,** which means short, abruptly separated. A legato eighth note equals a full-value eighth note. A staccato eighth note, on the other hand, has variable duration. Its length depends on the style of performance, and its value may actually be less than half that of a legato eighth note. It can be called an eighth note only because it is immediately followed by silence which fills up the remaining time that a full-value eighth note requires. Perhaps a staccato eighth note should be called a sixteenth note, or it should bear some designation that is more precise than the label of "staccato eighth note."

*legato: slurred together*

*staccato: short*

|  |  |  |  |
|---|---|---|---|

Quarter notes

Eighth notes

Eighth note triplets

Tied eighth note triplet figures

Dotted eighth— sixteenth note figures

A wide assortment of eighth note durations and stresses are found in jazz styles. There are no jazz musicians who divide the beat in only one way. But there is a pattern that is more common than any other. It is a long-short sequence which is close, but not identical, to the pattern of durations found in the tied-triplet figures. The tied-triplet figure, you may remember, consists first of a long sound, then a shorter sound which is half the duration of the first sound. The two sounds together fit the duration of a single beat in the manner of a quarter-note triplet. The duration pattern most commonly employed by jazz musicians the **swing eighth-note pattern,** falls somewhere between the tied-triplet figure and a sequence of eighth notes having identical durations. In other words, the first member of the pair is shorter than the first member of a tied-triplet pattern, and the second member is somewhat longer than a triplet eighth note. But neither member's duration is truly equal to an even eighth note, what musicians call "a straight eighth."

(demonstrated in JAZZ STYLES CASSETTE, side 2)

The stress patterns for swing eighth-note patterns are distributed differently from player to player. Sometimes within the work of a given player, the stresses are distributed differently from performance to performance, sometimes from passage to passage. Basically, however, the first in a group of such swing eighth notes is louder than subsequent notes which occur on upbeats.

There is considerable confusion about notation of swing eighth notes. Such lack of uniformity exists in this regard that about the only accurate statement is that when reading eighth notes, the desired choice of duration patterns usually depends upon the particular band and the style of arrangement being played. A little history might make this point a bit clearer. In countless written arrangements of jazz-oriented pieces which were published before the 1960s, dotted-eighth sixteenth figures appeared whenever the arranger wanted a swing eighth sound. (The arranger did *not* want true dotted-eighth sixteenth note patterns in which long-short meant the long member sounded three times the duration of the short one.) The notation appeared as even eighths thereafter in most arrangements, but the intention was for those notes to also be played as swing eighths. (If an arranger of this period wanted *truly even* durations, a written message appeared above the notes: "even 8ths." The musician's assumption was to otherwise play all the written eighth notes in a swing rhythm.)

To appreciate the rhythms which typify jazz, we should keep in mind the fact that several rhythms are usually played simultaneously. *Polyrhythm* (meaning *many rhythms*) is very important to jazz. When you listen carefully to a modern jazz performance, you should be able to hear several different rhythms at the same time. These include the rhythm in the melodic line, that of the bassist, the rhythm played by each of the drummer's four limbs, and each of the pianist's two hands.

Polyrhythms are often created by patterns which pit a feeling of four against a feeling of three. In other words, two measures can be played at the same time, with one being divided by multiples of two and the other being divided by multiples of three. In addition to that, the onset of one pattern is often staggered in a way which results in something less than perfect superimposition atop another pattern. Pitting three against four and staggering the placement of rhythms can project the feeling that the rhythms are tugging at each other. The resulting combination of stresses can be extremely provocative, and it can produce new syncopations in addition to those already contained in the separate patterns.

You can now understand why to say that jazz is quite rhythmic is to make an almost meaningless statement. All music has rhythm, and most music has syncopated rhythms. What sets jazz apart from many other types of music is the preponderance of syncopated rhythms, the swing eighth note sequences, and the constant presence of polyrhythm.

**SCALES, KEYS, TONALITY, AND MODALITY**

Understanding scales is basic to appreciating chord progressions, and an acquaintance with scales and chord progressions aids our knowledge of the rules which guide jazz improvisation. Everyone is familiar with musical scales. No one has been able to live very long without hearing a friend, neighbor, or family member practice "his scales."

Scales comprise the rudiments of beginning practice routines for singers and instrumentalists alike. Even people who cannot read music are familiar with the sequence *do* (pronounced dough), *re* (pronounced ray), *mi* (pronounced mee), *fa, sol, la, ti* (pronounced tee), *do*. Those eight syllables do not represent exact pitches as C, D, E, F, G, A, B, C; they are only the names of acoustic relationships. (Do not let that term, acoustic relationships, scare you. It is one of the simplest concepts in music. It means only that no matter what frequency of so many vibrations per second is assigned to *do*, the remaining seven pitches are determined by set multiples of it, for example twice the frequency, 1½ the frequency, and so forth.)

"*Do re mi fa sol la ti do*" numbers eight elements, the eighth element carrying the same name as the first, *do*. Its relationship to the first is exactly double the frequency of the first. For example, if the first *do* were 440 vibrations per second, the next higher *do* would be 880. It is no more complicated than that. That last *do* ends one sequence and begins another. The relationship between the bottom *do* and the top *do*, the first and eighth steps of the scale, is called an *octave*. The sound of two notes an octave apart is so similar that if they are played simultaneously, you can easily mistake the pair for a single tone. Most naturally produced tones contain an octave as one component of all the frequencies that combine to give a tone its own characteristic color or quality. The octave is called a harmonic or an overtone of the tone's fundamental pitch. That is the reason two tones an octave apart sound like one when they are played at the same time.

Since the interval of an eighth, from *do* to *do,* represents a doubling of frequency, you have probably guessed that those intervals between the first and the eighth must be fractions. You guessed correctly. The ratio of the fifth step (*sol*) to the first step (*do*) is $\frac{3}{2}$, that of the third (*mi*) to the first (*do*) is $\frac{5}{4}$, etc.

The seven note scale has many labeling systems. We have already used three of them: a) do, re, mi, fa, sol, la, ti, do; b) first, second, third, fourth, fifth, sixth, seventh; and c) the frequency ratios: re/do $= \frac{9}{8}$; mi/do $= \frac{5}{4}$; fa/do $= \frac{4}{3}$; sol/do $= \frac{3}{2}$; la/do $= \frac{5}{3}$; ti/do $= \frac{15}{8}$. Next is the system which uses alphabet letters A, B, C, D, E, F and G.

Look at the diagram of the piano keyboard printed here.

It is constructed so that the pattern of eight white keys and five black keys recurs again and again. The distance, or interval, between the beginning of one pattern and the beginning of the next is called an octave. The scale which beginners usually learn first is the C scale; the C scale is obtained by playing eight of the white keys in succession, starting with the one labeled C. That scale, C, D, E, F, G, A, B, C, contains the same note relationships which we know as do, re, mi, fa, sol, la ti, do. Play the notes of the C major scale in the order in which they are numbered in the diagram.

Look again at the piano keyboard.

The black keys are known as sharps and flats. Sharp is symbolized ♯ (like the number sign on a typewriter) and flat is symbolized ♭ (like the lower case b on the typewriter). The black keys derive their names from the white keys which are next to them. The black key to the right of A is called A-sharp because it is slightly higher than A. But it is also referred to as B-flat because it is slightly lower than B. If we want only a C scale, going up an octave from C to C, we use none of the black keys. But if we want scales which begin on any note other than C, we have to employ at least one (and sometimes all) of the black keys. For instance, to play a major scale on D, it is necessary to make use of two sharps, F-sharp and C-sharp.

D major scale

A scale may be played starting from any black or white key. Altogether there are twelve such scales. Going up (moving left to right) from C, they are the scales of C, C-sharp, D, D-sharp, E, F, F-sharp, G, G-sharp, A, A-sharp, and B. Or, naming them in descending order, C, B, B-flat, A, A-flat, G, G-flat, F, E, E-flat, D, and D-flat.

When musicians say that a tune is in a certain key, for instance, the key of C, they mean that the song is played with the notes of the major scale beginning on C.

The relationship of the notes of the major scale gives a song a particular kind of sound and structure which is called **tonality.** Although tonality is a complicated idea, it can be understood as the feeling that a song must end on a particular note or chord. A key defines a scale which, in turn, defines that key. If a piece of music has the feeling of reaching for the same note, the key note, or it seems loyal to some note more than to any other, the overall harmonic character of the piece is called *tonal*.

There is another term like the term scale that is not interchangeable with key. The term is **mode.** Like a scale, a mode describes a sequence of acoustic relationships. Some modes even have the same number of elements as the scales we just explored. In fact, the C scale has a mode name: Ionian. But if we use the notes in the C scale and start the sequence on D, we produce another mode, Dorian. In other words, if we go from D to D in the key of C, we have constructed the Dorian mode.

For each of the seven scale steps in a key, there is a corresponding mode. The major scale itself has a mode name: Ionian; beginning on the second step produces the Dorian mode; the third step, the Phrygian mode; fourth, the Lydian mode; fifth, the Mixolydian mode; sixth, the Aeolian mode; and seventh, the Locrian mode. Each has different sound because each has a different sequence of acoustic relationships which results from starting on different steps of the scale. I urge you to find a keyboard and play these modes. The concepts outlined here mean little without the sounds they describe.

We have seen that there are twelve keys, C, C♯ (or D♭), D and so forth. We also know that for each key there is a corresponding seven note scale starting on the note which bears the name of the key (C D E F G A B for the C scale). Within each key there are modes, one mode beginning on each of the seven steps. The mode constitutes an octave of its own. Scales (modes) of fewer than seven notes and greater than seven notes also exist (see page 418). The most common scale constructed of more than seven notes is the *chromatic,* simply that sequence of all the piano keys in an octave, white ones and black ones. Scale is a poor name because **the chromatic scale is actually just another way of dividing an octave into twelve equal parts.** It does not indicate a key as the C scale and the B♭ scale do. **The chromatic scale is only a sequence of very small intervals called half steps.**

The chromatic scale has twelve steps: C, C♯ D, D♯ E, F, F♯, G, G♯, A, A♯ and B. Unlike the modes, which have to be started on certain scale steps to guarantee their unique qualities, the chromatic scale can be started on any note, proceed through an octave and create the same identifiable chromatic quality no matter what note is chosen for its starting position. That means the C chromatic scale is identical to the C♯ chromatic scale (and all others). Perhaps it should be called "chromatic scale starting on C" or "chromatic scale starting on C♯," specifying exactly what tone is to be the reference note.

The chromatic scale is very important because it expands the number of acoustic relations possible. Given twelve different tones in place of only seven, we have the option of raising and lowering (sharping and flatting) virtually any note we wish. Most Western European music of the past two centuries uses the chromatic scale instead of limiting itself exclusively to notes within one key at a time or, what is even more restrictive, only one mode at a time. Music was produced during the twentieth century which used all twelve tones equally and discarded the feeling of particular keys. Tonal music, you remember, is simply music which seems to be loyal to a certain note, always reaching for that note. Music without tone center is called *atonal*.

Most music has key feeling even when employing all twelve tones in the chromatic scale. This is just another way of saying that most music has tonality. During improvised music, tone centers might shift, but they usually remain long enough for their effect to be perceived. Most jazz employs tone center. It is extremely difficult to improvise without at least implying temporary tone centers and key feelings. The twelve tones are usually employed to enrich the conventional do re mi tonal orientation instead of providing a harmonic orientation all their own, one of atonality. Keep in mind that some music employs more than one key at once, but this type of music is not generally termed atonal. It is called *polytonal* which means many keys.

If you play within the do re mi scale and enrich your melody with chromatic tones, the character of your playing can be partly described by how often you employ certain chromatic tones. Many people consider *bluesy quality* essential to jazz. A central component of bluesy quality is the frequent use of chromatics, three chromatics in particular: the *flat third, flat fifth* and *flat seventh* notes of the scale. In other words, chromatic scale tones are employed to enrich the seven tones already available.

In the key to C, the blue notes are E-flat, G-flat, and B-flat. Remember the C scale consists of C, D, E. F, G, A, and B; there are no sharps or flats (none of the piano's black keys). To create a blue note we lower the third step of the scale. In the key of C this means changing E (a white key) to E-flat (a black key). We use both E *and*

E-flat in constructing jazz lines, but the E-flat stands out because it is not one of the notes in the C major scale.

C scale without any blue notes          C scale with the flat third blue note

**(Listen to the JAZZ STYLES CASSETTE to hear these sequences.)**

The second most common blue note is achieved by lowering the seventh step of the scale. In the key of C, this means changing B (a white key) to B-flat (a black key). Again we use both B *and* B-flat for our lines, but the B-flat is more distinctive because it is not in the key of C.

C scale with the flat seventh blue note (B-flat)

Note that the concepts of regular third step and blue third step are like the concepts of major chord and minor chord (the sounds of which you can demonstrate for yourself, using the following keyboard diagram as a guide to positioning your first, third, and fifth fingers).

Major chord                    Minor chord

The third most used blue note is the lowered fifth. Its use was not frequent until modern jazz began in the 1940s, but thereafter it became a standard device to convey a bluesy feeling, much as the lowered third and seventh had been in early jazz. In the key of C, a flat fifth is achieved by lowering G (a white key) to G-flat (a black key).

Going up to the flat fifth (G-flat)    Coming down to the flat fifth (G-flat)

**BLUE NOTES**    The term "blue note" does not have a single, universally accepted use. Some writers use it to designate the flat third and flat seventh that were discussed above. These sounds might best be termed "chromatically lowered" pitches because they are lowered by one step of the chromatic scale, the interval known as a "half step," or a "chromatic semitone." Some writers use the term "blue note" to designate any pitch that is not completely a half step below another, making its classification "indeterminate" because, instead of being a clearly identifiable pitch of the chromatic scale, these are pitches we might find in the cracks between the keys, so to speak. Musicologists variously call them "neutral thirds," "heptatonically equidistant," or "indeterminate pitches" (see "Blue Notes and Blue Tonality" by William Tallmadge, *The Black Perspective in Music*, 1984, Volume 12, Number 2, pages 155–165). These pitches cannot be produced on the piano, but that does not mean that pianists have not wanted to produce them. The recent proliferation of synthesizers in the hands of jazz pianists saw the molding of numerous solos employing this second kind of blue note, apparently because synthesizers are capable of generating pitches that represent fine gradations between those found on the piano. Playing with pitches is termed "pitch bending." (Listen to side 2 of the JAZZ STYLES CASSETTE for examples.) With the advent of portable synthesizers, jazz keyboard players were no longer handicapped in this regard. Pitch bending had been a favored technique in the work of rock guitarists, and, when jazz synthesists used this technique, they often sounded like rock guitarists.

The attraction that jazz musicians have for out-of-tune thirds and sevenths might be the result of differences between European and African preferences for tuning. One origin is suggested here. The European seven-tone scale (do, re, mi, fa, sol, la, ti, do) is not based on equal divisions of the octave. It is a sequence of whole steps and half steps, each half step representing about one twelfth of an octave. (The interval between C and D or that between E flat and F is a whole step. The interval between B and C or that between E flat and E is a half step.) A mix might have resulted between the European approach and a West African approach which uses a heptatonic (seven-tone) scale in which the interval separating each successive tone is equal, not the unequal pattern we find in whole steps and half steps. This "equidistant heptatonic" has pitches which coincide fairly closely to those in the European seven-tone ("diatonic") scale, but with the third and seventh steps being flat, relative to their counterparts in the European scale. This means that if an African sang his own pitch in a European piece, the third and seventh would sound "blue," or not perfectly in tune. Note that the heptatonically equidistant scale only sounds blue by comparison to the set of expectations a listener has with the aural frame of reference of the diatonic scale.

**CHORDS AND CHORD PROGRESSIONS**

Familiarity with the concept of scales allows us to explore the concept of chords and chord progressions, which, in turn, is essential to appreciating the harmony that jazz improvisers follow. These concepts are quite simple, but they have far-reaching applications, not only in jazz, but in all music which uses harmony.

**A chord is obtained by sounding three or more notes simultaneously.** It does not matter what notes are chosen. Any notes will do. Try these:

Although chords can be constructed from any tones, they are usually described in terms of scale notes and given Roman numeral names. The most common chord, one alternately described as a tonic chord, a major triad, the key chord, or a I (Roman numeral for 1) chord, employs the first, third, and fifth notes of the scale: *do, mi,* and *sol.* In other words, this chord is produced by simultaneously sounding do, mi, and sol in any key, any register, with any loudness or tone color.

I chord in key of C

I chord in key of F-sharp

I chord in key of B-flat

(demonstrated in
JAZZ STYLES
CASSETTE,
side 1)

Chords are named for the scale step on which they are based. A I chord is based on the first step of the scale, do; a II chord is based on the second step, re; a III chord on the third step, mi; a IV chord on fa; a V chord on sol; a VI chord on la; and a VII chord on ti. This system of naming is very handy for describing chord progressions (see page 415 for notations of chord progressions).

A chord change is simply what it says, changing a chord. If we move from one chord to another, we have executed a **chord change.** We have moved forward, progressed, from one chord to another. In other words, a **chord progression** has been made. If the chords involved are those based on the first and second steps of the scale, respectively, we could describe the chord change as a I-II progression. If we move from a chord based on the first step to a chord based on the fourth, we create a I-IV progression. The reverse of that is a IV-I. If we move from the I chord to the V chord, and then back to the I chord, we create a I-V-I progression.

To hear the sound of a very common chord progression, the I-IV-I-V-I blues progression, find a piano, an organ, an accordion, or any other keyboard instrument and strike all the keys simultaneously, the number of counts (1234, 2234, etc.) indicated in the diagram on page **375.** You need not worry about what fingers to place on what keys. In fact, go ahead and use fingers from both hands if necessary. Try to keep a steady rate for striking the keys. If you can keep a steady rate, you may find that you are sounding like you have heard pianists and guitarists in rhythm and blues bands sound.

**Chord Voicing**    Most music uses chords which have been **voiced.** (For notated examples see page 417). The concept of voicing is a very simple concept. It involves the fact that the keyboard is a succession of repeating octaves.

With the resulting repetition of notes available, we can pull each chord note away from the position it holds within a single octave and spread the chord over the range of the keyboard. We can also include additional notes and/or omit some of the original notes. All these manipulations fall under the heading of voicing.

1234 2234 3234 4234 (I chord for 4 measures)

1234 2234 (IV chord for 2 measures)

(demonstrated in
**JAZZ STYLES
CASSETTE,**
side 1)

1234 2234 (I chord for 2 measures)

1234 2234 (V chord for 2 measures)

1234 2234 (I chord for 2 measures)

The same chord (three notes) arranged in different positions across the keyboard.

Jazz pianists can often be identified by the way they voice chords, and characteristic preferences in piano voicing are important components of the style in almost every period of jazz. In recent jazz, for example in the work of pianists McCoy Tyner and Chick Corea, **voicing in fourths** is quite common. Voicing in fourths means that chords are made up of notes four steps away from each other. In other words, a chord voiced in fourths might contain do, fa and ti instead of do, mi and sol. (The interval between do and fa is called a perfect fourth. To create a perfect fourth between fa and ti, the ti must be flatted. In building a chord composed of perfect fourths, each successive note is considered do of a new scale and the fourth note, fa, in that scale is used.) You can hear the sound of a chord voiced in fourths by playing this:

(demonstrated in
JAZZ STYLES
CASSETTE,
side 1)

The term voicing also refers to how the notes of a chord are assigned to instruments in an orchestra or band. The ranges of the instruments as well as their tone colors are taken into consideration in voicing chords. Characteristic voicings serve to identify the work of different arrangers. Duke Ellington, for instance, voices chords in a manner distinguishable from Stan Kenton. Both Ellington's chords and his choice of instruments differ.

Voicing is also a term used to identify the instruments playing a melody. For example, we might say Duke Ellington voiced the lead (the melody) for clarinet, trumpet, and tenor sax, meaning that those instruments played a unison passage in a particular Ellington arrangement.

**The Blues**  The term "the blues" has several meanings. It can describe

1) a sad feeling, or music which projects a sad feeling;
2) a rhymed poetic form;
3) a slow, funky, earthy type of music;
4) a type of chord progression, usually contained in twelve measures, which has certain predictable chord movements in the fifth, seventh, ninth, and eleventh measures;
5) any combination of the above.

Blues poetry is so common in popular music, that a technical description of the positions of accent and rhyme is not necessary in order for you to recognize the form. A single, very characteristic example, can serve to illustrate the structure of blues poetry:

My man don't love me, treats me awful mean. (pause)
My man don't love me, treats me awful mean. (pause)
He is the lowest man I've ever seen.            (pause)

The I, IV, and V chords are basic elements of harmony used in the blues. In the twelve-bar blues, which is the most common blues form, these chords are distributed over twelve measures in a particular way. Although many variations are possible, the basic form is always the same. The chords and their respective durations are shown in the following chart. Each slash (/) indicates one beat. Perhaps it is helpful for you to think of a chord played on each beat by a rhythm guitarist. Note that the principal chord changes occur in the fifth, seventh, ninth and eleventh measures.

I                    IV        I        V        I
//// //// //// //// //// //// //// //// //// //// //// ////

Although the chord relationships of the fifth, seventh, ninth, and eleventh measures usually hold, the remaining measures are the scene of countless alterations. Modern jazz blues progressions often employ more than one chord in a single measure and at least one change every measure. It is not unusual to have ten to twenty chord changes in the space of twelve measures. Sometimes the principal chords of the fifth, seventh, ninth, and eleventh measures are also altered (see page 416 for typical modern jazz blues progressions). When the blues is sung, the words are often distributed in a standard way over the twelve-bar progression (see page 379).

A blues can be fast or slow, happy or sad. It may have lyrics or it may be a purely instrumental piece, and its chord progressions may be simple or complex. For a piece to be a blues, the only requirement is that the I-IV-I-V-I chord progression or a variant of it be presented in a twelve-measure form.

**The Thirty-Two Bar AABA Tune**

Another form on which jazz musicians often improvise is the thirty-two-bar AABA tune. The thirty-two bar tune is made up of four eight-measure sections. The opening eight measures, called the A section, is repeated in the second section. The third part is the B section, sometimes referred to as the bridge, release, inside, or channel. The last eight bars bring back the material of the first eight. So the tune falls into what is called AABA form. Thousands of pop tunes composed during the 1920s, 30s, 40s, and 50s were thirty-two bars long in AABA form.

**Listening for the Twelve Bar Blues and Thirty Two Bar Forms**

To gain a practical familiarity with chord progressions, glance at the list of tunes on page 380. These are categorized as twelve-bar blues or thirty-two-bar tunes in AABA form. Go to a record collection and find performances of tunes on the list, and choose one of them. Listen to approximately the first thirty seconds to determine whether this rendition has an introduction or begins immediately with the tune itself. Also determine how fast the beats are passing. A clue can often be found in the bass playing. If the bass is walking, there is a bass note for every beat, four beats to the measure. Listening to that sound, you should be able to hear the pulse as though the bassist were a metronome. The sound of the drummer's ride cymbal may also be a good indication of where the beats lie.

Having listened long enough to determine the tempo, you will also have discovered whether or not there is an introduction, and the point at which it ends and the tune begins. If you are not sure whether the beginning of the piece is an introduction or part of the tune itself, wait a while and listen for it to recur. If it does not recur it is probably an

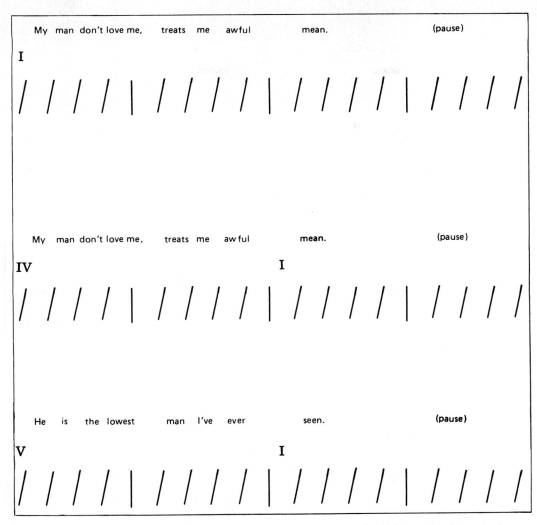

Blues poetic form in relation to the 12-bar blues chord progression.
The lyrics shown are from Billie Holiday's "Fine and Mellow." Copyright:
*Edward B. Marks Music Corporation. Used by permission.*

## Compositions in Twelve-Bar Blues and Thirty-Two Bar A-A-B-A Forms

### Twelve-Bar Blues Compositions

"Bags' Groove"
"Barbados"
"Billie's Bounce"
"Bloomdido"
"Bluesology"
"Blue Monk"
"Blues in the Closet"
"Blue 'n' Boogie"
"Blue Trane"
"Cheryl"
"Cool Blues"
"Cousin Mary"

"Footprints"
"Freddie the Freeloader"
"Goodbye Porkpie Hat"
"Jumpin' with Symphony Sid"
"Mr. P. C."
"Now's the Time"
"One O'Clock Jump"
"Sid's Ahead"
"Soft Winds"
"Straight, No Chaser"
"Walkin' "
"Woodchopper's Ball"

### Compositions with Thirty-Two Bar A-A-B-A Construction

"Ain't Misbehavin' "
"Angel Eyes"
"Anthropology"
"Birth of the Blues"
"Blue Moon"
"Body and Soul"
"Budo" ("Hallucinations")
"Darn That Dream"
"Don't Blame Me"
"Don't Get Around Much Anymore"
"Easy Living"
"52nd Street Theme"
"Flamingo"
"Four Brothers"
"Good Bait"
"Have You Met Miss Jones"
"I Can't Get Started"
"I Cover the Waterfront"
"I Love You"
"I'm Beginning to See the Light"
"It's Only a Paper Moon"
"I Want to Talk About You"
"Jordu"

"Lady Be Good"
"Lover Man"
"Lullaby of Birdland"
"Makin' Whoopee"
"The Man I Love"
"Midnight Sun"
"Misty"
"The More I See You"
"Moten Swing"
"Move"
"Oleo"
"Over the Rainbow"
"Perdido"
"Robin's Nest"
"Rosetta"
" 'Round Midnight"
"Ruby, My Dear"
"Satin Doll"
"September Song"
"Take the 'A' Train"
"Well, You Needn't"
"What's New?"
"What Is This Thing Called Love?"

introduction. In AABA form the first part, A, is immediately repeated, AA, before a new section, B, occurs. The routine for most twelve-bar blues tunes consists of repeating the entire twelve bars before beginning improvisation. Musicians occasionally use the same music for an ending that they used for the introduction. So if you hear something familiar at the end which does not seem to fit exactly in twelve or thirty-two bars, it may be the introduction attached for use as an ending.

By now you should know both the tempo at which to count beats and the moment to begin counting. Start when the tune itself starts (right after the introduction, in most cases). For a twelve-bar blues count: "1234, 2234, 3234, 4234, 5234, 6234, 7234, 8234, 9234, 10 234, 11 234, 12 234." Listen and count until you can detect the chord changes in measures five, seven, nine, and eleven:

$^{\text{I}}$//// | //// | //// | //// |$^{\text{IV}}$ //// | //// |$^{\text{I}}$ //// | //// |$^{\text{V}}$ //// |
//// |$^{\text{I}}$ //// | //// |

If your counting is accurate, you will eventually be able to anticipate these important chord changes. That should provide some insight into harmonies that the jazz musician uses in his improvisation.

Count like this for a thirty-two-bar AABA tune:

|  |  |
|---|---|
| (demonstrated in JAZZ STYLES CASSETTE, side 1) | "1234, 2234, 3234, 4234, 5234, 6234, 7234, 8234, |
| repeat | 234, 2234, 3234, 4234, 5234, 6234, 7234, 8234, |
| bridge | 234, 2234, 3234, 4234, 5234, 6234, 7234, 8234, |
| back to A | 234, 2234, 3234, 4234, 5234, 6234, 7234, 8234." |

Listen and count over and over until you cannot only hear the bridge and the repeated sections, A-A, when they occur, but anticipate them. Do not become discouraged if you find it necessary to start and stop many times. Counting beats and measures requires practice. It is very important because it may be your only clue to the tune's form once a soloist has begun improvising. Learning to count accurately may take a few minutes, a few hours, or even a few days, but it is essential to an understanding of jazz improvisation. It will be well worth the effort. You might get especially good at anticipating the B section. If you know the tune, or can learn it by listening a few times, try humming it while listening to the soloists improvise on its chord changes. This will help clarify the relationship between the improvisation and the original tune. It will also help you keep your place.

**Detecting Other Forms**

Not all tunes fit into the twelve-bar blues form or the thirty-two-bar AABA form. "I'll Remember April" is a forty-eight-bar ABCDAB form. "I've Got You Under My Skin" is a fifty-six-bar ABACDEF form. Together, the twelve-bar blues form and the thirty-two-bar AABA form probably describe more tunes than any other single form, but they actually describe less than forty percent of all tunes written between 1910 and 1960. Let us examine a few other forms.

The twelve-bar blues is a particular set of chord progressions (I-IV-I-V-I) in a twelve measure package. There are twelve-bar forms which are not blues simply because they do not follow the I-IV-I-V-I progression or any variation of it. For example, Richard Rodgers' "Little Girl Blue" is an AAB form in which each section is twelve bars long, but it is not a blues. It is also not uncommon in pop tunes to find a twelve-bar section which is actually an eight-bar progression with an extra four-bar progression connected to it.

The word "blues" in a song title does not necessarily signify the twelve-bar blues form. Both musicians and nonmusicians use the term "blues" to describe any slow, sad tune regardless of its chord progression. "Birth of the Blues" is a thirty-two bar AABA tune and "Sugar Blues" is an eighteen-bar tune. The "St. Louis Blues" is actually a twelve-bar blues plus an eight-bar bridge and an additional twelve-bar blues. Performers sometimes choose to repeat, delete, and reorder sections of "St. Louis Blues" when they play it.

Some people use the terms "eight-bar blues" and "sixteen-bar blues." Usually the tune they are describing has the I-IV movement in the first five bars and deviates from the twelve-bar I-IV-I-V-I progression thereafter. Some tunes of lengths other than twelve bars sound very much like twelve-bar blues simply because they contain the I-IV-I-V-I progression, but the durations of a few chords may be changed, and certain sections may be repeated. Herbie Hancock's "Watermelon Man," for example, has been called a "sixteen-bar blues."

Unlike the twelve-bar blues the thirty-two bar AABA form is not always based on the same basic chord progression. Many different chord progressions have been used in the AABA form. Fats Waller's "Honeysuckle Rose" and Erroll Garner's "Misty" are both thirty-two-bar AABA tunes, yet they have almost completely different chord progressions.

The form AABA does not always contain thirty-two bars nor does each section necessarily have the same number of measures. In "Girl from Ipanema," which is AABA, the A section has eight bars while the bridge has sixteen. In "Secret Love," another AABA tune, the A section has sixteen bars while the bridge has only eight.

There are also elongated versions of the basic twelve-bar blues and thirty-two-bar AABA forms. Lee Morgan's "Sidewinder" is a twenty-four-bar blues: each chord lasts twice as long as it would in a twelve-bar blues. Another example is the sixty-four-bar AABA form in which each section is sixteen bars long instead of eight. Ray Noble's "Cherokee" and Lerner and Loewe's "On the Street Where You Live" are both sixty-four bar AABA tunes. Charlie Parker's "Ko Ko," is based on the chord changes of "Cherokee"; consequently it is also a sixty-four-bar AABA tune. There are shortened versions of the thirty-two-bar AABA, too. Sonny Rollins's "Doxy" is a sixteen-bar AABA tune; each section is only four bars long.

AABA is not the only common thirty-two bar form for pop tunes. Numerous tunes fit an ABAC form (both the C section and the B section differ from the A section). "My Romance," "On Green Dolphin Street," "Indiana," "Sweet Georgia Brown," and "Out of Nowhere" all fall into a thirty-two bar ABAC form. In addition to the thirty-two bar AABA and ABAC, there is also the thirty-two bar ABAB. "How High the Moon" is an example. There are shortened versions of these, also. "Summertime" is a sixteen-bar ABAC tune. "Autumn Leaves" is a sixteen-bar AABC tune. Each section is four bars long in those tunes.

Hundreds of tunes fit into sixteen measures. "Peg o' My Heart" is a sixteen-bar pop tune. Horace Silver based his "The Preacher" on the sixteen-bar pop tune "Show Me the Way to Go Home." Wayne Shorter has written many sixteen-bar tunes, including "E.S.P.," "Nefertiti," "Prince of Darkness," etc. Some chord progressions are used in sixteen-bar tunes almost as often as the I-IV-I-V-I progression appears in the twelve-bar blues. Certain sixteen-bar progressions have become standard.

*Verse and Chorus.* It is important to note that the forms we have been examining refer only to chorus length. A large number of tunes consist of two major parts, a verse followed by a chorus. The verse traditionally differs from the chorus in tempo, mood, and harmony:

1) The chorus might be played at a faster tempo than the verse.
2) Verses are often performed freely, with accelerations and decelerations of tempo.
3) The verse might feel as though it is leading up to something, whereas the chorus usually has the stamp of finality to it.
4) There may be little similarity between chord progressions used in the verse and those in the chorus.
5) The key of the verse is sometimes different from that of the chorus.
6) Choruses are repeated, but once a verse is played, it is usually over for the entire performance.
7) The chorus is the section of the tune jazz musicians usually choose as basis for improvisation.

*Breaking into Multiples of Two.* When you are listening to performances and trying to detect forms, be aware that arrangements of thirty-two-bar AABA, ABAC, and ABAB tunes sometimes depart from strict repetition of those thirty-two bars. Arrangements sometimes contain four-, eight-, and sixteen-bar sections, formed by omitting or adding to portions of the original thirty-two-bar tune. Note also that many tunes, especially pre-1930s Dixieland tunes, have long, elaborate forms similar to those of marches and of nineteenth-century European dance music (such as the quadrille). Forms for many tunes in pre-1920s jazz were derived from march music. A piece might have a series of sections consisting of multiples of eight bars. Designating each section by a letter of the alphabet, a piece might conceivably follow a pattern like this:

$$A-A-B-B-C-D-E-F-C-D-E-F$$
$$16-16-16-16-16-16-24-32-16-16-24-32.$$

When listening for form, keep in mind that even in the most intricate pieces, forms can usually be broken down into two-bar segments. So if you are unable to divide a piece neatly into either four-bar or eight-bar sections, try using a few two-bar sections. "Sugar Blues" can be heard as 18 or as 8+10 or as 8+8+2. That form poses problems for the improviser because it tends to break the flow of ideas conceived in four- and eight-bar melodic units. It is like being forced to walk left, right, left, right, left, left, right. The form of the original "I Got Rhythm" is

$$A - A - B - A + \text{tag}$$
$$8 - 8 - 8 - 8 + 2 \text{ or}$$
$$8 - 8 - 8 - 10.$$

When jazz musicians improvise on its chord progression, they omit the two-bar tag. If included, the tag would interrupt the flow of the improvisations and again be like having to take two steps with your left foot before going back to an alternation of right with left. Another popular tune that has an unusual structure is "Moonlight In Vermont." It follows the form:

$$A - A - B - A + \text{tag}$$
$$6 - 6 - 8 - 6 + 2.$$

**Modal Forms**

During the late 1950s and especially during the 60s and 70s, modal forms practically eliminated the "change" part of "chord change." In modal music, improvisations are based on the extended repetition of one or two chords. Those chords contain so many notes that they either include or are compatible with all the notes in a scale. The term mode is synonymous with scale, hence the term "modal music." Although this is not the definition of modal employed by classical composers and in textbooks on classical music, it is what jazz musicians and jazz journalists have come to mean by "modal" (see page 418 for further discussion of modes). In most instances, jazz musicians also employ notes which are not contained in the mode or in the repeated chords. Some of John Coltrane's work, for example, is not strictly modal, but has the flavor of music which is.

In modal music the entire improvised portion of the performance is often based on a single chord and scale. Usually the chord and its scale are minor, Indian, Middle Eastern, or in some way more exotic-sounding than the chords used in most pop tune progressions. Because it is based on a single scale, the music has no real chord changes, just a drone.

Sometimes a melody containing chord changes of its own precedes the improvised section of a modal performance. John Coltrane's recordings of the Rodgers and Hammerstein tune "My Favorite Things" are a good example. Coltrane played the original melody while his rhythm section played the appropriate chord changes. Then the entire group improvised only on the primary chord of the tune (and of course, the scale compatible with that chord). Near the end of their improvisations, they switched to another chord, which lent the piece a slightly different character. Coltrane could have retained the chord progressions of the tune and used them as the basis for improvisation, but he chose not to.

Some modal music does have chord changes, or "mode changes." One rich chord (or scale, depending on how one cares to conceive it) is the basis for four, eight, or perhaps sixteen measures. Then a different chord is in effect for another similar duration. The Miles Davis tune "Milestones" is based on one mode for the first sixteen bars, a different mode for the second sixteen bars, and a return to the original mode for the final eight bars. The melody has the form AABBA, and each section is eight bars long. Herbie Hancock's "Maiden Voyage" has a thirty-two bar AABA construction; here each mode lasts for four bars. The A section is based on two different modes, each lasting only four bars. The B section makes use of another two modes also lasting four bars each. If each mode were labeled by letter name, "Maiden Voyage" could be described as X-Y-X-Y-Z-W-X-Y. "So What" (on the Miles Davis album *Kind of Blue*) has a melody in thirty-two bar AABA form, and the use of modes corresponds to that form: there are sixteen bars of one mode, eight of another, and a return to the original mode for the last eight bars. John Coltrane's "Impressions" not only takes the same form as "So What" but also uses exactly the same modes. (See page 422 for the modes used in "Milestones," "Maiden Voyage," and "So What.")

Much jazz of the 1960s and 70s was based on infrequent chord changes (another way of saying modal) instead of the frequent chord changes found in most twelve-bar blues and thirty-two-bar forms. Many groups abandoned both the blues form and the thirty-two-bar forms. Some groups used complex melodies and intricate rhythm section figures, yet their improvisations were based almost exclusively on one or a small number of chords ("Freedom Jazz Dance," for example).

## The Effects of Form on Improvisation

Song forms of four and eight bar sections tend to break improvisations into small segments of similar length. Divisions of form, in other words, can influence the flow of improvised lines. This is not necessarily a disadvantage, however. The divisions in form can frame well-chosen melodic figures, and they can provide a means of transition from one figure to another. This creates more continuity than a solo might contain without chord progressions. Forms based on single modes sounding indefinitely tend to free the improviser, enabling him to create lines that are as long or short, tense or relaxed as he desires. No preset tension-relaxation devices in the form of chord progressions are there to suggest construction patterns for his improvised lines.

*Bridges.* The B section of an AABA tune is called the bridge. It bridges the gap between repetition of A sections, and it usually provides a contrast to the material in the A sections. The bridge can break up or lift the mood established by repeated A sections. Many bridges are placed a few keys higher than the A section. A key change can be a boost in any situation, but is especially effective after the repeated A sections.

The bridge is important to improvisers because a good improviser can capitalize on the bridge's natural capacity to provide contrast. Some of the greatest solo segments in jazz are those improvised over the chord progressions of a tune's bridge. The rhythm section also takes advantage of the bridge and is often especially active just before the bridge is entered and just before it is exited. Heightened rhythmic activity can announce the arrival or departure of the bridge.

Combos often use the bridge as a container for solo spots. Sometimes a tune's melody will be played for the final time in the performance, and when the bridge occurs, everyone stops playing except the drummer. It becomes his feature. Then the entire band returns precisely on the first beat of the final A section.

In some jazz tunes the bridge consists only of chord changes. Such pieces require improvisation during the bridge but return to the written melody when the final A section is reached. Sonny Rollins's tune "Oleo" is an example. Many groups also use that approach on "The

Theme," a popular up-tempo number for jazz combos of the late 1950s and early 60s.

*Turnarounds.* Another important part in the construction of standard tunes is the turnaround (also known as the turnabout or turnback). In many, perhaps in most songs, the seventh and eighth measures of each section are occupied by a single sustained tone or two long tones (see below). That part of the tune might be considered dead space due to the lack of melodic movement, but the jazz musician uses that space. (See page 417 for common turnaround chord progressions.) He fills it with chord changes which lead directly to the beginning of the next section. Jazz musicians are expected to know a variety of chord progressions common to turnarounds. The manner in which they fill that space with chord changes and improvised lines is the art of the turnaround.

Turnarounds in 32-bar A-A-B-A and 12-bar blues.

In 32-bar A-A-B-A form:

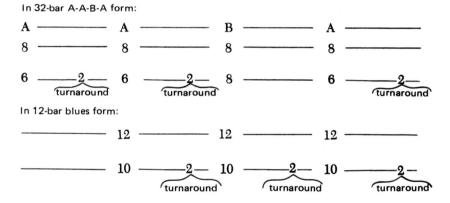

In 12-bar blues form:

The whole combo digs in when a turnaround comes up. Drummers tend to kick more and, thus, tie together the musical statements of one section and bring in the next. Those bassists who almost invariably walk are more likely to vary this pattern in a turnaround. Tension can be built during a turnaround and resolved by the onset of the next section of the piece.

**Phrasing in Relation to Form**

Jazz musicians prior to the mid-1940s tended to improvise phrases which coincided with the tune structure. Most progressions consist of two- and four-bar units, and improvised solos often proceeded in phrases of similar length. Furthermore, soloists tended to make larger silences at or near the end of an A section or B section. They rarely connected tune sections by continuing phrases through the turnarounds. They stopped at or before the turnarounds, and then started anew at the beginning of the next section. They treated the eighth bar line as a barrier. Twelve-bar blues solos often contained phrases which started at the beginning of each chorus regardless of what happened at the end of a previous chorus, thus treating the twelfth bar line as a barrier.

One characteristic of modern jazz (beginning in the 1940s) and the music of the players who most influenced it, was the use of phrases which began somewhere within an eight-bar section and continued into the next section without a pause. There was no lull during the turnaround.

A characteristic of some modern jazz during the 1960s and 70s was the absence of preset chord progressions. That free approach significantly loosened the tendencies of jazz phrasing. Although players retained patterns common to preceding jazz eras, they were free to phrase with greater variety due to the lack of underlying chord movements. Some jazz of this type projects a feeling of expansiveness quite unlike the crowded feeling often projected by modern jazz of the 1940s and 50s.

Some tunes which appeared during the 1960s, especially those of Wayne Shorter, were sixteen or more bars without any repeated sections. The A section was not repeated, there was no bridge, no turnaround. These tunes were "all A." That form enabled improvisers to play with great continuity yet without the crowded, segmented feeling which sometimes characterizes improvisations based on standard AABA and ABAC forms with the usual turnarounds and bridges. Sometimes a free, floating feeling could be projected by improvisers using these "all A" forms.

## TONE COLOR

An important element of music, usually the first to be perceived, is tone quality or tone color. The term tone *color* is preferable because quality can imply that a tone is good or bad. But because musical beauty is a subjective perception, the term quality is less appropriate than that of color, a neutral term. This element is also known as timbre (pronounced tamm'burr).

How can you tell the difference between the sound of a flute and the sound of a trumpet if they each play only one note, and it is the same note? The difference is tone color. What is tone color? It is traditionally defined as the spectrum of frequencies generated by each instrument in its own unique way.

This definition is an oversimplification of a complex situation in which many factors come into play.

The spectrum of frequencies produced by an instrument is not fixed. The spectrum varies depending on the pitch and the forcefulness with which it is played. The ways in which a player starts and stops a note, the attack and release, also are important in determining tone color. The attack and release are accompanied by temporary changes in a tone's frequency spectrum.

Another complication arises from our tendency to associate an instrument's tone color with the aggregate effects of all the notes being played on it rather than the spectrum of frequencies present in a single note.

Finally, when sounds come to our ears, they are modified by room acoustics and by recording and playback techniques. The way our ears deal with that variability is quite involved.

Tone color varies greatly from one instrument to another, and there are also especially discernible differences in tone color among jazz musicians playing the same instrument. For example, to speak of the tenor sax tone color of John Coltrane or Stan Getz is to describe sounds so unique that some inexperienced listeners could differentiate them as easily as they could distinguish flute from trumpet. The evolution of jazz tenor saxophone playing reflects not only changes in the phrasing and rhythms, but also changes in tone color.

Tone color is a very personal characteristic of a player's style. Jazz musicians place great emphasis on creating the particular tone colors they want. A jazz musician's attention to tone color is comparable to an actor's concern for costume, make-up, and voice quality combined. Tone color is so important to saxophonists that many spend lifetimes searching for the perfect mouthpiece. They also experiment with different methods of blowing and different ways of altering the vibrating surface of the cane reeds that are attached to their mouthpieces.

Because the tenor saxophone is capable of producing an exceptionally wide variety of tone colors, it is easier to differentiate jazz tenor saxophonists by tone color alone than it is to recognize a particular trumpeter or pianist. That is not to say that differences are absent from trumpeter to trumpeter or from pianist to pianist. The differences are just more subtle.

Two pianists can play the same piece on the same piano and produce quite different sounds. No two pianos have the same tone color, and one piano can produce distinctly different tone colors, depending on how hard the keys are struck. The use of the pedals and a pianist's timing in releasing one key and striking the next are crucial to the sound. A key may be released before, after, or at the same time as the next is struck. When a note is short and ends well before the next note begins, we call it a staccato note. If one key is released after the next is struck, the two sounds overlap in time. Notes played smoothly one after the other are said to be legato. The amount of overlap influences the clarity of attack and the dimension of legato-staccato. Our ears hear sounds in combined form rather than as single tones. Whatever is left in the air from a preceding sound mixes and colors the subsequent sound. The relationship between consecutive sounds, ranging from complete separation to extreme overlapping, are resources which contribute to the personal character of a pianist's style. Count Basie's touch and tone color differ remarkably from Duke Ellington's. Perhaps you will perceive Basie's touch as lighter than Ellington's. No matter how you describe the sound, you will notice a difference if you listen carefully.

Guitarists' interest in tone color is manifested by their search for different types of picks, guitar strings, and amplifiers. Guitar amplifier dial settings are essential to the control of tone color. Bass players are also concerned with many of the same factors.

Trumpeters and trombonists explore available tone colors by experimenting with mouthpiece changes, methods of blowing, mutes, and instruments which represent different manufacturers and models.

Straight          Cup          Harmon          Stem for
                               without stem     Harmon

Mutes. (Listen to the JAZZ STYLES CASETTE, side 2, for the sound of each.)

**Intonation** is also an important aspect of tone. Intonation refers to playing in tune, playing sharp or flat. Playing sharp means playing at a pitch level somewhat higher than the average pitch of the ensemble. Playing flat refers to playing a pitch somewhat lower than that of the ensemble. Do not confuse the terms sharp and flat with words describing actual note names such as C-sharp and B-flat. These notes are raised (sharped) and lowered (flatted) by a larger amount than is usually the case in out-of-tune playing. That is, the interval between C and C-sharp is greater than the interval between C and that of a performer playing C a bit sharper than his fellow ensemble members. Small deviations of pitch occur all the time even in the best ensembles, but larger deviations lead listeners to comment "someone is playing out of tune."

Why is intonation described in this section on tone color? Intonation affects the tone color of both the soloist and the ensemble as a whole. If a group of musicians played the same piece twice, once without listening or adjusting to each other's pitch (perhaps by pre-tuning their instruments and then wearing ear plugs for the performance), and then a second time, listening carefully to each other's pitch and continuously adjusting accordingly, you would hear two performances, each having distinctly different tone colors. Ensembles which lack precision tuning have a thicker, rougher sound than precisely tuned ensembles. One element of a slick ensemble sound is careful and consistent tuning.

For tone color reasons, some soloists systematically play a little "high," meaning a bit sharp. Intonation is a musical resource for them. This is common in most types of music, including symphonic, but it is especially true for jazz soloists. A tone cuts through an ensemble if it is a bit sharper than the average pitch of that ensemble. Some jazz soloists seem to play at the average pitch. Others tend to different degrees of sharpness. That is another component of tone color which helps us identify a particular player's work.

Miles Davis playing trumpet using Harmon mute.

# GUIDE TO RECORD BUYING

One key to being a happy jazz fan is finding the right albums. This section of the book is directed at explaining numerous short cuts to help you.

**Minimizing Risk in Selecting Albums**

In seeking record-buying advice, try not to assume that a newspaper, book, or magazine is an authority in itself. We may think their endorsements represent knowledge and understanding somehow greater than that of a single individual. Usually, however, a record review or list of recommended listening reflects only one individual's preferences and his own understanding or lack of understanding.

You may perhaps feel that it is impossible to make good choices without extensive previous knowledge. But the situation is not quite that desperate. Listening to records before you buy them is always a wise practice. Friends, libraries, jazz courses, and radio programs can often help here.

Try to avoid record buying as an impulse purchase. Unless you want a record purely for academic reasons or historical perspective, you might realize too late that you have spent your money on something you do not enjoy. That point might seem elementary, but, unless you can afford to experiment expensively, it is worth keeping in mind. Many albums list musicians and tunes which look great but turn out sounding less than great. Since advance listening will be impossible for many albums, you will have to collect opinions from friends, music teachers, and jazz journalists. If there is a jazz radio station near you, do not hesitate to phone and ask them to play a particular album. (College radio stations not only broadcast more jazz than commercial stations, but they are also more likely to be interested in your requests.) Another strategy is to phone the station just after it has broadcast something you enjoyed, and ask for the album title and record company name. Then decide what records you really want, write down their titles, labels, catalog numbers, and carry that list with you. Then prepare yourself for the frustration, common to jazz fans, of rarely seeing a desired album in the record racks. (Most current jazz albums must be special-ordered, and all out-of-print albums must be obtained through very special sources.)

Those strategies are not guaranteed to always bring records you like. Even if you follow all this advice, you may end up with a record you do not enjoy just because jazz represents an enormous variety of styles, and you may dislike at least one of them. In fact, you may dislike several entire styles plus many players within additional styles. You should also remember that many players had several different periods during their careers. You may enjoy their playing from one period but not from another. (If you do not have access to a comprehensive record collection, your opinion of a particular style or player may be based on only one recording. If that single example is either not stylistically representative or not typical of the quality of improvisation for a given musician, and you dislike what you hear, you run the risk of unintentionally dismissing a larger area of music. Beware!)

**Confusing Album Titles** Buying albums with which you are unfamiliar often raises a general problem: Taking album titles seriously. This applies especially to the category of albums bearing titles such as "The Best of ———," "The Indispensable ———," "The Essential ———," and "——— at His Very Best." The biggest drawback is that such a set usually contains only a single record company's recordings, and that particular company may not have recorded the artist during his creative peak. Another company may have. And, of course, both companies may have released LPs called "The Best of ———." We must remember that many artists have had several different styles during their careers and a creative peak for each. They may have been recording for a different company during each important period.

John Coltrane is a case in point. He made important recordings as a bandleader for three different companies (Prestige, Atlantic, and Impulse), and each company documented a different stage in his career. Additionally, some of his best work was recorded under the leadership of Miles Davis for Columbia, a fourth record company. One implication of all this is that an Atlantic record called *The Best of John Coltrane* cannot contain the best Coltrane work from all three periods—although it could sample some of his best Atlantic sessions.

Another point to consider is that many players made some, or perhaps all, of their best recordings as sidemen in other men's bands, not as leaders on their own record dates. Lester Young probably did his best work as a sideman with the 1936–41 combos and big bands associated with Count Basie (reissued by Columbia-Epic and Decca-MCA). His own subsequent combo dates as leader sound unlike the Lester Young of the 1936–41 Basie groups. An Emarcy LP of some 1943–44 sessions called *Pres At His Very Best* is probably not his very best. A Verve LP of 1950s sessions called *The Essential Lester Young* is probably "essential" only to those Lester Young collectors who already have much of his earlier work. Both those LPs contain good playing, but if you are limited to a single album of Lester Young, neither of them would be appropriate. Their titles are misleading.

There are other examples of the confusion arising from album titles and varied careers. In the 1960s, pianist Herbie Hancock and saxophonist Wayne Shorter both made records for Blue Note as leaders of their own recording groups. During much of that time they were also recording for Columbia in the Miles Davis Quintet. Most of their playing on the Davis recordings is superior to that on their own records. But since they were leaders on the Blue Note sessions, those sessions, instead of the Columbia ones, provide the pool for albums titled "The Best of ————." I am not saying that Hancock's or Shorter's Blue Note work is poor. On the contrary, it is excellent music and it also features the beautiful composing that Hancock and Shorter are known for. The point is that, when heard strictly as piano and saxophone improvising, the Hancock and Shorter Blue Note work may not truly represent the absolute best of either man as claimed by an album title. Incidentally, a Columbia album called *The Best of Herbie Hancock* (JC 36309) contains neither his great playing with the 1963–69 Miles Davis groups nor his excellent music and beautiful composing found in his Blue Note work. The album samples yet another facet of Hancock: his jazz-rock material.

Another problem is that the choice of selections usually represents only an opinion, and that opinion is limited by the taste and knowledge of the person in charge, in addition to the dictates of the company. Therefore, even if an artist recorded solely for one company throughout his creative peak, a "Best of ————" album might leave out that artist's best work simply because the person in charge was ignorant of the music.

Another confusing album title is "Greatest Hits." It is usually misleading because, in addition to all the previously mentioned problems, a player's greatest hits measured by sales figures alone may not even appear on an LP titled "————'s Greatest Hits." For example, the largest-selling Miles Davis Columbia recording, his 1969 *Bitches Brew* (GP 26), is not represented on the Columbia album *Miles Davis' Greatest Hits* (PC 9808). Again, by sales figures alone, the 1964 Verve recording of "Girl From Ipanema" was Stan Getz's greatest hit. Yet there is a Prestige LP titled *Stan Getz' Greatest Hits* (Prestige 7337) drawn from 1949 and 1950 sessions. The Prestige material is excellent, perhaps better than the Verve material, yet it does not include his largest selling hits as the album title deceptively implies.

In summary, superlatives are rarely applied accurately in naming jazz records. You might be able to avoid confusion by reading album liner notes, carefully looking for recording dates and personnel, and consulting authorities to determine what companies were recording the artist during critical portions of his career.

**How to Locate Records**    Many people think certain records are available only in big city stores. But actually, no matter where you live, most records can be obtained by mail. It might be more practical to get records by mail even if you live in or near a big city which is full of record stores, such as New York or Los Angeles. Bus fare, or the price of gas and parking, could amount to a substantial fraction of the price of a record. Even then, a record store often orders your request by mail anyway, which leads to the main point: most of the jazz records mentioned in this book will not be found in average record stores. If they are available to a store, they will probably require a special order. You therefore ought to phone ahead to determine whether traveling an inconvenient distance will be worthwhile. Some stores accept special orders over the phone. You then have only to call the store periodically, and find out whether your order has arrived. (Note that most stores are not interested in your special order business. It is an unprofitable hassle for them. However they will often fail to admit this to you. They will simply take forever or never bother to notify you when they give up trying to find a particular item.) My advice is to forget the stores, and go mail order. Several jazz magazines whose addresses are listed on page 408 will supply you with any currently available jazz record. Out-of-print records can be obtained by getting your name on the mailing lists for jazz record auctions. (Scan the fliers they send, and bid, by mail, on what you want.) The addresses for jazz magazines and specialty record stores on page 399 should be used to begin this process.

**About Reissues**    Many jazz recordings which have disappeared from catalog listings return later in altered form. This includes the category known as reissues, re-releases, and repackages. Before I discuss them, here is a bit of relevant history. Prior to the widespread use of twelve-inch, 33⅓ rpm (revolutions per minute) LP (long play) records, most jazz was issued on ten-inch, 78 rpm records. (Remember those heavy black discs which almost invariably broke into pieces when you dropped them?) Twelve-inch 33s were not common until the 1950s, so many bop and West Coast style bands—in addition to Dixieland and swing bands—were initially presented on 78s. Several forms of recording material exist including paper, wire, tape, and plastic disc. (In addition to the ten-inch 78s and twelve-inch 33s, there have been twelve-inch 78s, ten-inch 33s, seven-inch 45s, twelve-inch 16s, etc.)

Due to the size of the record and the speed of rotation, most 78s could accommodate only about three minutes of music per side. An album consisted of several records packaged much like a book or a photo album, each record having a separate pocket or sleeve. The set was often bound in leather or cardboard. Then when the LP arrived, many of the three-minute jazz instrumentals originally on 78 were issued again (reissued) on 33⅓ rpm albums. This time, the word album meant a single record containing many selections. All the records in this book's premodern section and a few modern records are to be found in this kind of "reissue." Later on, LPs themselves began to be reissued, re-released, and repackaged. This is the altered form in which you can often find music originally available on records which have "disappeared" from the catalog.

Many albums that are no longer available in the United States are available in foreign countries under the same titles they carried before they went out of print in the United States. During the 1970s, for instance, Japanese distributors began repackaging out-of-print American albums with the album jacket art and liner notes intact. However, relying on imports is not usually that convenient. You ordinarily must match tune titles, personnel, and dates to determine whether a foreign release is the same as the American original you are seeking. A list of importers and their addresses appears on page 399.

Note that jazz groups have frequently recorded several versions of the same tunes, and many players did certain tunes with several different groups. Since you are a jazz fan, your interest lies not necessarily in listening to the tunes themselves but to particular improvisations. You must find the actual performances you want. The improvisation on other versions might not even resemble what you want.

The most common reissue situation is that not only are album titles changed, but material from certain recording sessions is scattered over several different albums. Another common problem is that the original recordings may have belonged to companies which later sold their material. (For instance, one reissue of Charlie Parker recordings originally made for Dial is called *The Dial Masters.*) The original company's name helps you identify reissued material. However, when record companies are bought and sold, sometimes the music is reissued intact, causing you no headaches. (For example, Impulse was bought by ABC, then by MCA, but the 1960s Coltrane classics originally made for Impulse continued to be distributed intact. They have to be sought from MCA, however, not from Impulse.) Another key to locating material in reissued form is that it is often identified by where it was recorded. (For example, the famous Bill Evans–Scott LaFaro music originally made at the Village Vanguard for Riverside record company has been reissued by Fantasy-Prestige-Milestone as *The Village Vanguard Sessions.* Charles Mingus's frequently reissued material from a famous concert at Toronto's Massey Hall, featuring Charlie Parker and Dizzy Gillespie, is sometimes labeled *The Massey Hall Concert.*)

When seeking music that you think is out-of-print, you need complete listing of the musicians on the record date, the tune titles, original album title and record company name, the recording dates, and the original catalog numbers. Personnel listings can be especially useful because material is sometimes reissued under the name of a musician who was a sideman on the original recording session but has now become important enough to warrant a reissue of his work that is packaged as though he were leader at that original session. (For example, a 1956 Tadd Dameron album called *Mating Call* has been reissued under John Coltrane's name and called *On A Misty Night* because Coltrane was a sideman on it but is now in much demand in his own right. Several reissues of Joe Oliver's Creole Jazz Band have come out under Louis Armstrong's name even though Armstrong was a sideman, not the leader, on Oliver's recordings. Much pre-1940 Lester Young is now available in reissues under Young's name despite its having been recorded under Count Basie's leadership.)

You can keep up with what is being reissued by reading jazz magazines and visiting record stores. If you do not want to wait for a particular out-of-print record to be reissued (and some never are), contact importers, rare record stores, and record auctioneers. If you are a serious jazz fan, you will probably have to subscribe to at least one or two of the standard jazz magazines listed on page 408. This will allow you to keep up with material that you will never hear on the radio or see in your local record store. When this book went to press, the magazines that attempted to announce, if not review, most new records and reissues were *Cadence* and *Jazz Times*. Subscription prices were very reasonable, and the magazines' information was indispensable. (It is an enormous job to identify all the albums that come out, but *Cadence* managed to do it, while other magazines only highlighted samples of current product.) If you do not have the patience to wade through hundreds of record listings month after month, but you still want a particular hard-to-find or out-of-print album, write one of the specialty stores. The staffs of these firms are jazz fans who perform location services primarily because they want to share their love for jazz with others and because they know how to help fans who lack the necessary information and contacts. Addresses for these services appear on page 399.

**Many Versions of the Same Tune**

The problem of a single tune recorded many times by the same artist increased substantially during the 1960s and 70s. This was due to increases in: (1) legitimate reissue programs by major firms, (2) illegitimate releases (called bootleg or pirate records) by numerous small firms, and (3) the discovery, or, in many cases, rediscovery, of a seemingly endless variety of broadcast performances, called air shots or air checks. (Music of the 1930s and 40s, unlike that of the 50s and 60s, is well documented by air checks because most jazz groups made live radio broadcasts in those days.)

Beginning in the 1960s, record companies began massive distribution of repackaged material. Hundreds of albums with new titles were introduced. Many contained music originally on 78s. Other albums had music originally available on LPs. Some of the albums featured alternate, but originally rejected, versions of tunes. These are called alternate takes. (Some are labeled as alternate takes, but for others, you have to hear both versions to know whether they differ. They sometimes have improvisation equal or superior to the versions originally issued.)

Albums flooded the market from companies, both American and foreign, which operated without the consent of the recorded artists (or of their estates, in the case of deceased artists). Those albums constitute the illegitimate releases mentioned earlier. The companies were small and disappeared quickly. Some of their material had appeared previously on other records, but much of it had never been available before. A lot of it presumably came from homemade recordings of night club appearances and radio broadcasts. Many albums have incorrect tune titles. Few contain complete personnel listings and recording dates. Many display poor sound fidelity. But if you can tolerate all those weaknesses, you might be well rewarded by the music itself. It also may be worthwhile knowing about bootleg recordings because the appearance and distribution of them is a very common phenomenon and likely to continue.

With the bootleg material added to the legitimate releases and reissues, it became possible to own more than eighty albums of Charlie Parker, more than one hundred of Duke Ellington, etc. The record collector might be confronted with five to ten Parker versions of "Confirmation" and "Ornithology" and just as many Ellington versions of "Mood Indigo" and "Sophisticated Lady." Keeping track of recording dates and personnel became essential to discussing particular performances of these frequently recorded tunes.

A few Charlie Parker classics illustrate the usefulness of having personnel, tune titles, recording dates, and original record company name before you begin seeking a particular recording. The much praised music that Parker originally made in the form of 78s for Dial Record Company has been sold in numerous forms, some of them offered by tiny, obscure record companies that worked without the consent of Parker's estate. Take "Embraceable You," for example. Parker recorded many different versions of it. But if you want his famous Dial recording of it, you must remember that he made two different versions at the same session, and you must remember the 1947 recording date, and that the pianist was Duke Jordan, the bassist was Tommy Potter, and the drummer was Max Roach. Any deviation from that particular combination of identifiers signals that you are holding another version of the tune instead of the famous classic version. It is also essential to note the record company name and recording date if you want to locate Parker's famous 1945 "Now's the Time," that was made for Savoy record company with the Miles Davis trumpet solo that was later adapted and recorded by pianist Red Garland on the Miles Davis *Milestones* album. It is especially easy to become confused in this instance because another version of the same tune was also recorded by Parker without Davis in 1953 and released on a Verve album called *Now's the Time*. There are instances in which historic figures recorded only one version of a given tune, but the more you study jazz, the more you will find it beneficial to **keep track of details to ensure you're buying what you originally set out to buy.**

One final example is offered to illustrate the usefulness of having complete information about an improvisation you seek. If you have a transcription of a Miles Davis trumpet solo from a performance of "Joshua," and you want to hear the original or play along with it, you cannot simply run out and buy the correct album, even if you already have the personnel listing and the year of recording. Miles Davis recorded "Joshua" at least three times with saxophonist George Coleman, pianist Herbie Hancock, bassist Ron Carter, and drummer Tony Williams. Two out of the three times were in the same year, 1963. One version was released on *Seven Steps to Heaven*, an album which was issued with two different catalog numbers: Columbia CS 8851 and CL 2051. Another version was released on *Miles Davis in Europe* (Columbia CL 2183 and CS 8983). Then Davis recorded another version in 1964 that was released in *Four and More* (Columbia 9253 and CL 2453).

**Rare Record Dealers, Importers, and Auctioneers**

Rare Records
417 East Broadway
Glendale, Ca. 91205

Jazz Etc.
P.O. Box 393
Bergenfield, N.J. 07621

The Jazz and Blues
  Record Center
Box 87 Station J
Toronto, Ontario
M4J 4X8 Canada

Cadence Record Sales
Box 345 Route 1
Redwood, N.Y. 13679

Daybreak Express Records
P.O. Box 150250 Van Brunt Station
Brooklyn, N.Y. 11215-0005

International Association of
  Jazz Record Collectors
1917 Schwier Drive
Indianapolis, Indiana 46229
(Write for a membership listing,
then determine who specializes
in the style you seek, and write
that member.)

Import Record Service
P.O. Box 166
Roselle Park, N.J. 07204

Oaklawn
Box 2663
Providence, R.I. 02907

World Records
P.O. Box 2613
San Rafael, CA 94912-2613

The Smithsonian Institution keeps hard-to-find jazz items in print long after private companies have deleted them from their catalogs. As this book went to press, Smithsonian was carrying rare items by Joe Oliver, Sidney Bechet, Louis Armstrong, Duke Ellington, Art Tatum, Teddy Wilson, Henry "Red" Allen, John Kirby, Freddie Keppard, Fletcher Henderson, and Dizzy Gillespie. When searching for recordings cited in this book, it would be wise to first check the most current Smithsonian listings. You can get a catalog by writing Smithsonian Press, Washington, D.C. 20560. If you already know what you want, you can order it by phone with their toll-free number 1-800-336-5221.

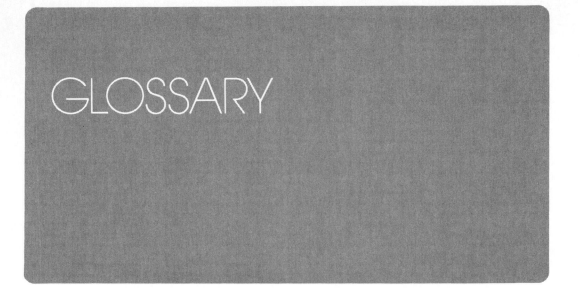

# GLOSSARY

**antiphonal**   an adjective describing a common pattern of interaction between improvisers or between sections of a band, taking the form of a question and answer or a call and response.

**arco**   the technique of playing a stringed instrument with a bow.

**atonal**   the character and organization possessed by music that has no key (see page 369 for further explanations and illustrations).

**attack**   the very beginning of a sound (opposite of release).

**back beat**   strong accent on the second and fourth beats of every four-beat measure; a term usually applied to the work of a band's drummer.

**ballad**   a slow piece

**big band**   an ensemble of ten or more players.

**blue note**   1) a pitch somewhere between a major third and minor third or between a major seventh and minor seventh step of the scale (see page 371).
2) minor third or seventh scale step (see page 370).

**blues**   1) a simple, funky style of black music separate from but coexistent with jazz; beginning at least as early as the turn of the century, probably much earlier; exemplified by such

performers as Blind Lemon Jefferson, Leadbelly, Lightnin' Hopkins, Muddy Waters, T-Bone Walker and Robert Johnson. It has been and continues to be an influence on jazz and rock. The majority of blues compositions employ the I-IV-I-V-I chord progression or a variation of it.
2) a piece characterized by any one or any combination of the following—
a) the I-IV-I-V-I chord progression or some variation of it in a twelve-measure package
b) a sad feeling
c) a slow pace
d) poetry in the form of paired couplets in iambic pentameter
e) many lowered third, fifth, or seventh intervals
(see page 369 for further explanation)

**bomb**   a pronounced accent played by the drummer.

**boogie woogie**   a premodern jazz piano style associated with Meade Lux Lewis and Albert Ammons. It is characterized by a repetitive left-hand bass figure that states almost every beat by dividing it into dotted-eighth sixteenth-note patterns.

**bop (bebop)**   the style associated with Charlie Parker, Dizzy Gillespie, Thelonious Monk,

Bud Powell, Dexter Gordon, and Sonny Stitt (see pages 139–151).

**break**   1) the portion of a piece in which all band members stop playing except the one who improvises a solo. The tempo and chord progressions are maintained by the soloist, but, because the band has stopped, it is called a stop-time. Rarely do such breaks last longer than two or four measures (listen to JAZZ STYLES CASSETTE, end of side 1).
2) the solo itself.

**bridge**   the B part of an A-A-B-A composition; also known as the channel, the release, or the inside (listen to JAZZ STYLES CASSETTE, end of side 1).

**broken time**   1) a style of rhythm section playing in which explicit statement of every beat is replaced by broken patterns which only imply the underlying tempo, exemplified by the 1961 Bill Evans trio with Scott LaFaro and Paul Motian.
2) the manner of playing bass or drums in which strict repetition of timekeeping patterns is not maintained, but constant tempo is; exemplified by the 1960s and 70s playing of Elvin Jones.

**chart**   the jazz musician's term for what is written as musical arrangement. This is distinguished from the classical musician's "score" because not all the notes are present. Many spaces in the chart are filled only by symbols indicating the chord progression that guides improvisation. Often the drum "parts" are almost blank.

**chops**   instrumental facility

**chord progression**   1) when one chord changes or "progresses" to another chord.
2) a set of harmonies in a particular order with specified durations; for example, the twelve measure I-IV-I-V-I blues progression (see pages 377–379 and 416).
3) the sequence of accompaniment chords intended for a song but used instead as the basis of a jazz improvisation.

**chorus**   1) a single playing through of the structure being used to organize the music in an improvisation.
2) a jazz solo, regardless of its length.
3) the part of a pop tune performed in constant tempo and repeated several times after the

verse has been played, usually the only portion of a tune's original form used by the jazz musician (see page 14 for further explanation).

**collective improvisation**   simultaneous improvisation by all members of a group together.

**comping**   syncopated chording which provides improvised accompaniment for simultaneously improvised solos, flexibly complementing the rhythms and implied harmonies of the solo line (listen to JAZZ STYLES CASSETTE and see pages 424, 425, and 429).

**cool**   1) an adjective often applied to describe the subdued feeling projected by the music of Bix Beiderbecke, Lester Young, Claude Thornhill, Gil Evans, Miles Davis, The Modern Jazz Quartet, Gerry Mulligan, Lee Konitz, and Jimmy Giuffre (see page 174).
2) sometimes used as a synonym for West Coast style.
3) sometimes used to denote modern jazz after bop.

**counterpoint**   two or more lines of approximately equal importance sounding together.

**Creole-**   1) French- or Spanish-speaking individual born in the New World.
2) a person who has mixed French and African ancestry and was born in the New World (also known as "Creole of Color," as opposed to the white-skinned Creole defined above).

**decay**   the very end of a sound; also known as a release. Opposite of attack (see page 46 for discussion).

**Dixieland style**   1) Chicago combo style that was prominent during the 1920s.
2) a synonym for all preswing-era combo jazz.

**double stop**   sounding two bass strings at the same time.

**double-time**   the feeling that a piece of music or a player is going twice as fast as the tempo, although the chord progressions continue at the original rate.

**Fender bass**   electric bass guitar, used to play bass lines instead of chords; common in jazz rhythm sections after 1970.

**fill**   in general, anything a drummer plays in addition to basic timekeeping patterns; in particular, a rhythmic figure played by a drummer to—

1) fill a silence

2) underscore a rhythm played by other instruments

3) announce the entrance or punctuate the exit of a soloist or other section of the music

4) stimulate the other players and make a performance more interesting.

**free jazz** an approach associated with Ornette Coleman and Cecil Taylor, in which the music contains improvised solos which are free of preset chord progressions, and sometimes also free of preset meter (see pages 272–283).

**front line** musicians appearing directly in front of the audience, not blocked from view by another row of musicians. This designation is sometimes used to separate hornmen (because they stand in the front of a combo) from accompanists (who usually appear to the rear of the hornmen).

**funky** 1) earthy or dirty

2) mean, "low down," evil, or sexy

3) bluesy

4) gospel-flavored

5) containing a predominance of lowered third, fifth, and seventh steps of the scale.

(*Note: During the 1970s this adjective was applied to describe rhythms as well as melody, harmony, and tone color characteristics.*)

**fusion** a synonym for jazz-rock style (see pages 324–354).

**fuzak** music that blends the characteristics of jazz-rock fusion styles with the characteristics of Muzak. It tends to stress electric instruments, steady funk rhythms, smooth textures, without many surprises. Used as background music during the 1980s and 90s by listeners who liked the softer variants of fusion and funk. Often applied to music of Kenny G, Grover Washington, Earl Klugh, and Najee.

**growl style** a method used by some trumpeters and trombonists in which by unorthodox use of mutes, lips, mouth and blowing techniques a sound is produced that resembles the growl of an animal. Despite the odd assortment of sounds that the growl includes, recognizable melodic figures can be played with this alteration of tone quality. (See Bubber Miley, Cootie Williams, and Joe "Trickey Sam" Nanton).

**hard bop** the jazz style associated with Horace Silver, Art Blakey, and Cannonball Adderly (see page 195–218 for further explanation).

**head** the melody or prewritten theme for a piece.

**head arrangement** a band arrangement that was created extemporaneously by the musicians and is not written down.

**high-hat (sock cymbal)** an instrument in the drum set which brings two cymbals together by means of a foot pedal (see page 24 for illustration).

**horn** general label for any wind instrument; sometimes includes stringed and percussion instruments as well (the most general term for all instruments is ax).

**jam session** a musical get-together where improvisation is stressed and prewritten music is rare (jam means to improvise); may refer to a performance which is formally organized or casual, public or private, for profit or just for fun.

**jazz-rock** a variety of styles beginning in the late 1960s that use electric instruments, funk rhythm accompaniments and jazz improvisation; also known as fusion music; often applied to the post-1968 music of Miles Davis, Spyro Gyra, Weather Report, the Crusaders, John McLaughlin, the electric music of Herbie Hancock and Chick Corea (see chapter 16).

**laid back** an adjective used to describe a feeling of relaxation, laziness, or slowness; often describes the feeling that a performer is playing his rhythms a little later than they are expected, almost after the beat or "behind" the beat.

**lay out** to stop playing while other players continue.

**legato** a style of playing in which the notes are smoothly connected with no silences between them (opposite of staccato).

**lick** a phrase or melodic fragment.

**locked-hands style** a style of piano playing in which a separate chord parallels each note of the melody because both hands are used as though they are locked together, all fingers striking the keyboard together; also known as block chording, playing the chord notes as a block instead of one at a time. (See sections on Milt Buckner, Lennie Tristano, George Shearing, Ahmad Jamal, Red Garland, and Bill Evans.)

**modal**  music in which the melody and/or harmony is based on an arrangement of modes. In jazz, the term can mean music based on the extensive repetition of one or two chords or music based on modes instead of chord progressions (see page 418 for further explanation).

**mode**  1) the manner of organizing a sequence of tones, usually an ascending sequence of an octave.
2) the arrangement of whole steps and half steps common to scales.
(See pages 226–231 for further explanation.)

**mute**  an attachment which reduces an instrument's loudness and alters its tone color (see page 390 for illustrations).

**new age**  music that is soft and soothing, lacks variety in rhythm, loudness and chords. Often applied to the work of George Winston, selected works of Pat Metheny and others who recorded for Windham Hill, Narada, and ECM record companies.

**pedal point**  low-pitched, repeated, and/or sustained tone. It usually retains its pitch despite changes in chords and improvisations occurring around it; common in the 1960s work of John Coltrane and McCoy Tyner.

**pitch bending**  purposeful raising or lowering of a tone's pitch; usually done for coloration or expressive purposes (see pages 45–47 for illustrations and explanation).

**pizzicato**  the method of playing a stringed instrument by plucking instead of bowing.

**polyrhythm**  several different rhythms sounding at the same time (see page 364).

**progressive jazz**  music associated with Stan Kenton (see page 182).

**ragtime**  1) a popular turn-of-the-century style of written piano music involving pronounced syncopation.
2) a label often applied to much pre-1920 jazz and pop music, unaccompanied solo piano styles as well as band styles, improvised as well as written music.

3) the style of music associated with composers Scott Joplin and Tom Turpin.

**release**  1) the manner in which a sound ends or decays (opposite of attack).
2) the bridge of a tune.

**rhythm section**  the group of players whose band function is accompanying. This role is particularly common for pianists, bassists, and drummers, but it is not exclusive to them (see pages 20–27 for explanations and illustrations, see pages 424–430 for musical notations).

**ride cymbal**  the cymbal suspended over a drum set, usually to the player's right, struck by a stick held in the drummer's right hand; used for playing timekeeping patterns called ride rhythms (see page 23 for illustration).

**ride rhythm**  the pattern a drummer plays on the ride cymbal to keep time, the most common being ching-chick-a-ching-chick-a (see notations on page 430).

**riff**  1) phrase
2) melodic fragment
3) theme.

**rim shot**  the drum stick striking the rim of the snare drum at the same time as it strikes the drum head.

**rip**  an onset ornament in the form of a quick rise in pitch directly preceding a tone. (Listen to Bix Beiderbecke or Louis Armstrong.)

**rubato**  free of strict adherence to constant tempo.

**scat singing**  jazz improvisation using the human voice as an instrument, with nonsense syllables (dwee, ool, ya, bop, bam, etc.) instead of words.

**sideman**  a designation for each musician in a band except the leader.

**sock cymbal**  see **high-hat.**

**staccato**  brief and separated (opposite of legato).

**stride**  1) left-hand style used by early jazz pianists. It usually employs a bass note on the first and third beats of each measure and a chord on the second and fourth.
2) the piano style of James P. Johnson and Willie "The Lion" Smith.

**swing** 1) a word denoting approval—"It swings" can mean it pleases me; "to swing" can mean to enjoy oneself; "he's a swinging guy" can mean he is an enjoyable person.

2) the noun indicating the feeling projected by an uplifting performance of any kind of music, especially that which employs constant tempo (see pages 5–6 for further explanation).

3) the feeling projected by a jazz performance which successfully combines constant tempo, syncopation, swing eighth notes, rhythmic lilt, liveliness and rhythmically cohesive group playing (see pages 6–7 for further explanation).

4) the jazz style associated with Count Basie, Duke Ellington, Jimmie Lunceford, Benny Goodman, Art Tatum, Roy Eldridge, and Coleman Hawkins, as in the "swing era" (see pages 86–138).

**syncopation** 1) stress on any portion of the measure other than the first part of the first beat (and, in meter of four, other than the first part of the third beat), i.e. the second half of the first beat, the second half of the second beat, the fourth beat, the second half of the fourth beat, the second beat, etc.

2) stress on a portion of the measure least expected to receive stress (see page 360 for further explanation).

**synthesizer** any one of a general category of electronic devices (Moog and Arp, for example) which produces sounds or alters the sounds created by other instruments.

**Third Stream** a style which combines jazz improvisation with the instrumentation and compositional forms of classical music (see page 153 for further explanation).

**tone color (timbre, tone quality)** the characteristic of sound which enables the listener to differentiate one instrument from another, and, in many cases, one player from another.

**tremolo** 1) fluctuation in the loudness of a sound, usually an even alternation of loud and soft.

2) a manner of playing a chord by rapidly sounding its different notes in alternation so that the chord retains its character, but also sustains and trembles.

3) the means of sustaining the sound of a vibraharp (see page 152).

4) an expressive technique for use by instruments in which vibrato is very difficult (flute, for example) or in which the variation of pitch necessary for vibrato may not be wanted (some styles of oboe playing, for example).

5) the rapid reiteration of the same note.

**turnaround (turnback, turnabout)** a short progression within a chord progression that occurs just prior to the point at which the player must "turn around" to begin another repetition of the larger progression (see page 387 for further explanation and page 417 for musical notation).

**two-beat style** a rhythm section style which emphasizes the first and third beats of each four-beat measure, often leaving the second and fourth beats silent in the bass; sometimes called boom-chick style.

**vamp** a short chord progression (usually only one, two, or four measures long) which is repeated many times in sequence. Often used for introductions and endings. Much jazz and pop music of the 1960s and 70s used vamps instead of more involved chord progressions as accompaniment for melody and improvisation.

**vibrato** the slight fluctuation of a tone's pitch, alternating above and below its basic pitch; used as an expressive device, varied in speed and amplitude by the performer to fit the style and feeling of the music (see page 46 for further explanation).

**voicing** 1) the manner of organizing, doubling, omitting, or adding to the notes of a chord (see pages 374–376).

2) the assignment of notes to each instrument (see page 377 for further explanation).

**walking bass** a style of bass line in which each beat of each measure receives a separate tone, thus creating a moving sequence of quarter notes in the bass range.

**West Coast style** the jazz style associated with Gerry Mulligan and Chet Baker during the 1950s (see **cool** and pages 180–194 for further explanation).

# SUPPLEMENTARY READING

## Biographies

ARMSTRONG, LOUIS. *Satchmo: My Life in New Orleans.* Englewood Cliffs, N.J.: Prentice-Hall, 1954.
Louis Armstrong's autobiography.

CARR, IAN, *Miles Davis: A Biography.* New York: William Morrow, 1982.
An intelligently written and knowledgeable biography of Davis by fellow jazz trumpeter Carr. Contains discography as well as transcriptions of solo improvisations.

CARR, IAN, FAIRWEATHER, DIGBY, and PRIESTLEY, BRIAN. *Jazz: The Essential Companion.* New York: Prentice Hall Press, 1988.
The single most intelligently written biographical reference work to be published during the 1980s. Contains hundreds of biographies of jazz musicians written by jazz musicians.

CARNER, GARY. *Jazz Performers: An Annotated Bibliography of Biographical Materials.* Greenwood Press, 1990.

CASE, BRIAN, and BRITT, STAN. *The Illustrated Encyclopedia of Jazz.* New York: Harmony Books, 1978.
Over 400 biographical entries.

CHARTERS, SAMUEL B. *Jazz: New Orleans 1885–1963, An Index to the Negro Musicians of New Orleans.* New York: Oak Publications, 1963. (Also Da Capo.)
A valuable source of biographical and musical information on the first jazz musicians.

CHILTON, JOHN. *Who's Who of Jazz: Storyville to Swing Street.* London: Chilton Book Co., 1972.
Available from the Bloomsbury Book Shop, 31–35 Great Ormond Street, London, W.C. 1, England. Biographies of hundreds of musicians born before 1920.

DANCE, STANLEY. *The World of Count Basie.* New York: Charles Scribner's Sons, 1981.
Covers Basie and his sidemen in profile and interview formats.

DANCE, STANLEY. *The World of Duke Ellington.* New York: Charles Scribner's Sons, 1970. Also Da Capo paperback.

DANCE, STANLEY. *The World of Earl Hines.* New York: Charles Scribner's Sons, 1977 (hard cover). Da Capo (paperback).
Includes reminiscences by numerous Hines associates, an exclusive chronology of Hines's life, excellent bibliography and discography, plus historical accounts in Hines's own words.

DANCE, STANLEY. *The World of Swing.* New York: Charles Scribner's Sons, 1975. Also Da Capo.
Vignettes of swing era figures, an emphasis on interview material.

ELLINGTON, DUKE. *Music Is My Mistress.* Garden City, N.Y.: Doubleday, 1973. In Da Capo paperback.
Duke Ellington's autobiography.

ELLINGTON, MERCER. *Duke Ellington In Person*. Boston: Houghton-Mifflin, 1978. Also Da Capo paperback.
A biography by Duke Ellington's son, sideman, and road manager.

FEATHER, LEONARD. *The New Encyclopedia of Jazz*. New York: Bonanza, 1960.
Leonard Feather and Ira Gitler's monumental compilation with over two thousand biographies from A to Z.

FEATHER, LEONARD. *The Encyclopedia of Jazz in the Sixties*. New York: Horizon, 1966.
A follow-up to the above, this one including 1400 biographies.

FEATHER, LEONARD, and GITLER, IRA. *The Encyclopedia of Jazz in the Seventies*. New York: Bonanza, 1976.
A follow-up to the above.

FEATHER, LEONARD. *From Satchmo to Miles*. New York: Stein and Day, 1972.
Chapters on Louis Armstrong, Duke Ellington, Count Basie, Lester Young, Charlie Parker, Dizzy Gillespie, Miles Davis and others.

FOSTER, GEORGE MURPHY "POPS." *Pops Foster: The Autobiography of a New Orleans Jazzman*. Berkeley, Calif.: University of California Press, 1971.
Contains numerous details of New Orleans jazz history from the turn of the century plus much on the history of jazz in Chicago. The musical information in the book is indispensable to understanding the history of jazz rhythm section playing, and is not limited to the bass style of its author.

GARA, LARRY. *The Baby Dodds Story*. Los Angeles: Contemporary Press, 1959.
Contains a peek into the techniques used by early jazz drummers. Also has much on New Orleans and Chicago jazz history.

GILLESPIE, DIZZY. *To Be or Not to Bop*. Garden City, N.Y.: Doubleday, 1979.
Reminiscences by Gillespie plus interviews with his colleagues done by Al Fraser.

GITLER, IRA. *Jazz Masters of the Forties*. New York: Macmillan, 1966. Reprinted by Da Capo.
One of the most intelligently conceived jazz history books, it includes musical and biographical discussions of Charlie Parker and the alto and baritone saxophonists, Dizzy Gillespie and the trumpeters, Bud Powell and the pianists, J. J. Johnson and the trombonists, Oscar Pettiford and the bassists, Kenny Clarke, Max Roach, and the drummers, Dexter Gordon and the tenor saxophonists, Lennie Tristano and Lee Konitz, Tadd Dameron and the arrangers.

GOLDBERG, JOE. *Jazz Masters of the Fifties*. New York: Macmillan, 1965. In Collier paperback. Also Da Capo hard cover.
A chapter each on Miles Davis, Thelonious Monk, Gerry Mulligan, Charlie Mingus, John Coltrane, Sonny Rollins, Ornette Coleman, and Cecil Taylor.

HADLOCK, RICHARD. *Jazz Masters of the Twenties*. New York: Macmillan, 1965. In Collier paperback.
A chapter each on Armstrong, Beiderbecke, Earl Hines, Fats Waller, James P. Johnson, Fletcher Henderson, Eddie Lang, and The Chicagoans.

HITCHCOCK, H. WILEY (Ed.). *The New Grove Dictionary of American Music*. London: Macmillan, 1986.
Contains numerous biographies as well as different jazz styles summaries.

JEWELL, DEREK. *Duke: A Portrait of Duke Ellington*. New York: Norton, 1977.
Biography by a British jazz critic who knew Ellington.

PORTER, LEWIS. *Lester Young*. Boston: G. K. Hall, 1985.
A scholarly and technical study of Young done by a fellow saxophonist and jazz historian.

REISNER, ROBERT. *Bird: The Legend of Charlie Parker*. New York: Citadel, 1962. Reprinted by Da Capo Press.
Charlie Parker biography in the form of documents.

RUSSELL, ROSS. *Bird Lives: The High Life and Hard Times of Charlie Parker*. New York: Charterhouse, 1973. In Popular Library paperback.
Charlie Parker biography in the style of a novel.

SHAPIRO, NAT, and HENTOFF, NAT. *Hear Me Talkin' to Ya.* New York: Dover, 1955. Also Peter Smith. Also Greenwood.
Interviews with famous jazz musicians.

SHAPIRO, NAT, and HENTOFF, NAT. *Jazz Makers.* New York: Rinehart, 1957. Also Grove Press, Greenwood, and Da Capo Press.
A chapter each on Jelly Roll Morton, Baby Dodds, Louis Armstrong, Jack Teagarden, Earl Hines, Bix Beiderbecke, Pee Wee Russell, Fats Waller, Art Tatum, Coleman Hawkins, Benny Goodman, Duke Ellington, Charlie Parker, Fletcher Henderson, Count Basie, Lester Young, Roy Eldridge, Charlie Christian, and Dizzy Gillespie.

SIMPKINS, C. O. *Coltrane: A Biography.* New York: Herndon House, 1975.
Contains transcriptions, work sheets, interviews, and analyses in addition to biographical details.

SPELLMAN, A. B. *Black Music: Four Lives.* New York: Schocken, 1966.
Biographical interviews with Ornette Coleman, Cecil Taylor, Jackie McLean, and Herbie Nichols.

STEWART, REX. *Jazz Masters of the Thirties.* New York: Macmillan, 1972. In Collier paperback. Also Da Capo hard cover.
A chapter each on Ellington, Hawkins, Henderson, Basie, Art Tatum, and Benny Carter.

SUDHALTER, R. M., EVANS, P. R., and MYATT, W. D. *Bix: Man and Legend.* New York: Schirmer Books, 1974.
An exhaustive biography of Bix Beiderbecke. Written by fellow trumpeter Sudhalter, this book includes technical analyses, an excellent discography, an almost day-by-day chronology of Beiderbecke's life with explanations for almost every mystery surrounding it. Also contains transcriptions of excerpts from solos.

SUMMERFIELD, MAURICE J. *The Jazz Guitar.* Gateshead, Tyne and Wear, England: Ashley Mark Publishing Company, 1978.
Biographies of almost all the prominent guitarists in jazz history.

TAYLOR, ARTHUR (Ed.). *Notes and Tones.* New York: Perigree, 1982.
Interviews with Miles Davis, Randy Weston, Ornette Coleman, Philly Joe Jones, Don Byas, Ron Carter, Johnny Griffin, Charles Tolliver, Eddie Lockjaw Davis, Leon Thomas, Max Roach, Erroll Garner, Dizzy Gillespie, Carmen McRae, Nina Simone, Tony Williams, Sonny Rollins, Don Cherry, Hampton Hawes, Kenny Clarke, Freddie Hubbard, Richard Davis, Elvin Jones, Kenny Dorham, Art Blakey, Hazel Scott, and Betty Carter.

THOMAS, J. C. *Chasin' the Trane: The Music and Mystique of John Coltrane.* Garden City, N.Y.: Doubleday, 1975. In Da Capo paperback.
Impressionistic biography with quotes from Coltrane's colleagues interwoven. Excellent discography. Includes poetry inspired by Coltrane's music.

ULANOV, BARRY. *Duke Ellington.* New York: Creative Age, 1946. In Da Capo paperback.

WILLIAMS, MARTIN. *Jazz Masters of New Orleans.* New York: Macmillan, 1970. In Collier paperback. Also reprinted by Da Capo.
A chapter each on King Oliver, Jelly Roll Morton, Sidney Bechet, Louis Armstrong, and Original Dixieland Jazz Band.

## Jazz Magazines

*Coda*
Box 87 Station J
Toronto, Ontario
M4J 4X8 Canada

*Down Beat*
180 W. Park Ave.
Elmhurst, IL 60126

*Crescendo*
122 Wardour St.
London W1V 3LA
England

*Jazz Educators Journal*
Box 724
Manhattan, Kans. 66502

*Cadence*
Cadence Building
Redwood, N.Y. 13679

*Jazz Journal International*
35 Great Russell Street
London WC1B3PP
England

*Jazz Times*
8055 13th Street Suite 312
Silver Spring, Md. 20910-9968

*Jazziz*
P.O. Box 8309
Gainesville, FL 32605-8309

*The Wire*
Units G & H
115 Cleveland Street
London W1P 5PN
England

## Sources for Information About Jazz Records

*Bibliography of Discographies—Volume 2–Jazz* (1981) by Daniel Allen
R. R. Bowker Company
1180 Avenue of the Americas
New York, N.Y. 10036

International Association of Jazz Record Collectors
P.O. Box 800
Grand Central Station
NY, NY 10163
(Become a member, then correspond with others who share your interests.)

Bibliography of Discographies—Journal of the Association for Recorded Sound Collections
Box 1643
Manassas, Vir. 22110

International Association of Sound Archives
Open University Library
Walton Hall
Milton Keynes MK7 6AA
England

*Jazz Bibliography* (1981) by Bernhard Hefele
K. G. Saur Publishers
Munich, West Germany

## Basic Jazz Record Resource Materials

These are discographies, books that tally such things as personnel for particular recording sessions, listings of all the recording sessions for a particular player, listings of all the recording sessions done by a particular company, all the different catalog numbers under which a particular performance has been issued, how many versions were made of a given tune at a given recording session, the day and place of recording, etc.

*Jazz Records 1897–1942* by Brian Rust
Storyville Publications and Co. Ltd.
66, Fairview Drive
Chigwell, Essex IG7 6HS
England
(Also available from Oaklawn Books, Box 2663, Providence, R.I. 02907)

*Jazz Records 1942–* by Jorgen Grunnet Jepsen
(Available from Oaklawn Books; see address above)

*Sixty Years of Recorded Jazz 1917–1977* by Walter Bruyninckx
Lange Nieuwstraat 121
2800 Mechelen
Belgium
(Also available from *Cadence*, Cadence Building, Redwood, N.Y. 13679, and from Oaklawn Books, see address above)

*Note:* Oaklawn Books carries hundreds of discographies, rare jazz books, and imported jazz books. Write them to get on their mailing list.

## Texts for Readers Familiar with Musical Notation

HODEIR, ANDRÉ. *Jazz: Its Evolution And Essence.* New York: Grove Press, 1956. In Da Capo paperback.
Technical analyses of various styles and recordings including an essay on trombonist Dicky Wells and one on Ellington's "Concerto for Cootie."

JOST, EKKEHARD. *Free Jazz.* New York: Da Capo Press. Or Vienna, Austria: Universal Edition.
First published in 1975, this text contains technical analyses and notations of work by John Coltrane and Miles Davis (*Kind of Blue*), Charles Mingus, Ornette Coleman, Cecil Taylor, Archie Shepp, Albert Ayler, Don Cherry, The Association for the Advancement of Creative Musicians, Sun Ra, and The Art Ensemble of Chicago.

OSTRANSKY, LEROY. *The Anatomy of Jazz.* Seattle, Washington: University of Washington Press, 1960. Also Greenwood.

SCHULLER, GUNTHER. *Early Jazz: Its Roots and Musical Development.* New York: Oxford University Press, 1968.
Scholarly and quite technical examination of the earliest jazz known, its possible sources in African music and nineteenth-century American popular music. Detailed analysis of Louis Armstrong, Jelly Roll Morton, assorted pre-swing players, Fletcher Henderson, Ellington's earliest recordings, Bennie Moten and bands of Kansas and Missouri during the 1920s and early 1930s.

TAYLOR, BILLY. *Jazz Piano: A Jazz History.* Dubuque, Iowa: William C. Brown, 1983. Reminiscences by a well-known jazz pianist and teacher. Interspersed with musical notations and technical discussion, although the book should be understandable to nonmusicians who wish to ignore them.

## Technical References

BAKER, DAVID. *Jazz Improvisation: A Comprehensive Study for All Players.* Chicago: Maher, 1969.

A helpful instruction manual for intermediate and advanced as well as beginning jazz improvisers.

COKER, JERRY. *Improvising Jazz.* Englewood Cliffs, N.J.: Prentice-Hall, 1964.
Excellent explanation of chords, chord progressions, how to swing, and how to improvise melodically.

MEHEGAN, JOHN. *Jazz Improvisation 1. Tonal and Rhythmic Principles.* New York: Watson-Guptill Publications, 1959.

MEHEGAN, JOHN. *Jazz Improvisation 2. Jazz Rhythm and the Improvised Line.* New York: Watson-Guptill Publications, 1962.

MEHEGAN, JOHN. *Jazz Improvisation 3. Swing and Early Progressive Piano Styles.* New York: Watson-Guptill Publications, 1964.
These textbooks by Mehegan provide a scholarly instruction series for the serious jazz student who has solid knowledge of the piano. The series is not exclusively for pianists, but any hornmen using it must have some acquaintance with the keyboard. Distributed by Music Sales, P.O. Box 572, Chester, N.Y. 10918; and Songbooks Unlimited, 352 Evelyn St., Paramus, N.J. 07653-0908.

MOST, SAM. *Metamorphosis: Transformation of the Jazz Solo.* Tustin, Calif.: Professional Music Products, 1980.
A very practical guide for the advanced music student who is learning how to develop improvised solo lines.

RIZZO, PHIL. *Creative Melodic Techniques Used in Jazz Improvisation.* Modern Music School, 101 Northfield Road, Bedford, Ohio 44146.
Manual for the beginning improviser.

SUDNOW, DAVID. *Ways of the Hand: The Organization of Improvised Conduct.* Cambridge, Mass.: Harvard University Press, 1978.
A difficult-to-read narrative on how one man learned how to play jazz piano. Filled with useful photographs and drawings of hand positions on the keyboard.

ZINN, DAVID. *The Structure and Analysis of the Modern Improvised Line.* New York: Excelsior Music Publishing Company, 1981.

Available through Theodore Presser Company in Bryn Mawr, Pennsylvania 19010. A very formal, technical instruction manual for musicians. It should also interest music theorists because it represents an intelligent analysis for the construction of melodic lines from rhythmic and harmonic perspectives.

*Note:* To keep up with the currently available technical references, you might find it helpful to be on the mailing list of Jamey Aebersold, who distributes hundreds of such publications and tests their usefulness at the clinics he runs. Write Jamey Aebersold, 1211-D Aebersold Drive, New Albany, Ind. 47150.

## General References

BASCOM, WILLIAM R., and HERSKOVITS, MELVILLE J. (Eds.) *Continuity and Change in African Cultures.* Chicago: University of Chicago Press, 1959.

Contains an excellent chapter on African music by Alan Merriam and several other studies of African art and culture that should be helpful for readers interested in the roots of jazz.

BERLIN, EDWARD A. *Ragtime: A Musical and Cultural History.* Berkeley, Calif.: University of California Press, 1980.

Scholarly evaluation of ragtime. Includes musical notations.

COKER, JERRY. *Listening to Jazz.* Englewood Cliffs, N.J.: Prentice-Hall, 1978.

One of the best guides to appreciating the playing of jazz improvisers. Loaded with insights about how musicians develop solos. Keyed to the *Smithsonian.* Contains numerous, detailed analyses that often require musical background from the reader.

COLLIER, JAMES LINCOLN. *The Making of Jazz.* Boston: Houghton-Mifflin, 1978.

If you can get past the author's attempts at psychoanalyzing musicians, you will find some interesting musical analyses here. This is probably the longest American history of jazz, and it integrates a large assortment of styles in an easy to read manner.

FEATHER, LEONARD. *The Book of Jazz.* New York: Horizon, 1957, 1965, 1976 (hard cover). Dell (paperback).

An instrument by instrument history of jazz plus discussions of the origins of jazz and the nature of jazz improvisation. This book, in all its revisions, remains the best compact guide to jazz and summary of the perspectives of the world's foremost jazz journalist.

SOUTHERN, EILEEN. *The Music of Black Americans: A History.* New York: W. W. Norton, 1971, 1983.

Covers popular music, classical music, folk music, religious music, and jazz.

## Women in Jazz

PLACKSIN, SALLY, *American Women in Jazz.* Available from the author, 300 Henry Hudson Parkway, Riverdale, NY 10463.

HANDY, ANTOINETTE, *Black Women in American Bands and Orchestras.* Metuchen, New Jersey: Scarecrow Press, 1981.

DAHL, LINDA, *Stormy Weather: The Music and Lives of a Century of Jazzwomen.* New York: Pantheon Books, 1984.

LEDER, JAN, *Women in Jazz: A Discography of Instrumentalists,* 1913–68. Greenwood Press, Box 5007, Westport, Connecticut 06881.

UNTERBRINK, MARY, *Jazz Women at the Keyboard.* Available from McFarland and Company, P.O. Box 611, Jefferson, North Carolina 28640 (phone 919-246-4460).

MCCORD, KIMBERLEY, "History of Women in Jazz," *Jazz Educators Journal*°, 1986, Vol. 18, No. 2, pages 15–19, 65, 79.

MCCORD, KIMBERLEY, "All-Women Jazz Groups," in Charles Brown (Ed.), *Jazz Research Papers*°, 1986, pages 134–40.

MCCORD, KIMBERLEY, "The Conceptualization of Women in Jazz," in Charles Brown (Ed.), *Jazz Research Papers*°, 1985, pages 93–105.

KOENIG, KARL, "Women Pianists in Early New Orleans Jazz," in Charles Brown (Ed.), *Jazz Research Papers*°, 1986, pages 115–21.

° *Jazz Educators Journals* and *Jazz Research Papers* are available from **The National Association of Jazz Educators**, Box 724, Manhattan, Kansas 66502 (phone 913-776-8744).

# SOURCES FOR NOTATED JAZZ SOLOS

There are hundreds of books filled with transcriptions of famous jazz improvisations. Catalogs and ordering information for them are available in *Jazz Educators Journal,* the official journal of the National Association of Jazz Educators. You can get back issues from school band directors who belong to the organization. Or you can join the organization yourself by sending them your check. It is only a small fee, and the information they distribute is well worth it. Just write National Association of Jazz Educators, P.O. Box 724, Manhattan, Kans. 66502.

Many jazz books and magazines include notations of jazz improvisations. The Mehegan books, listed here under "Technical References," contain numerous solo transcriptions. *Down Beat* magazine, listed on page 408 under "Jazz Magazines," includes transcriptions or instructional aids in almost every issue. Going through back issues of *Down Beat* can reveal a treasure house of notations.

James DaPogny has transcribed several Jelly Roll Morton piano solos and added them to published works and music from the rolls of player pianos for a total of 40 numbers in *Ferdinand "Jelly Roll" Morton: The Collected Piano Music,* published by Smithsonian Institution Press/G. Schirmer.

The most dedicated of all solo transcribers is Andrew White. From him, you can order more than 400 John Coltrane solos, more than 300 Charlie Parker solos, and several Eric Dolphy solos. Just write Andrew's Music at 4830 South Dakota Avenue, N.E., Washington, D.C. 20017.

Jamey Aebersold distributes numerous books of solo transcriptions. One series is by David Baker, and it includes one book each for Clifford Brown, Miles Davis, John Coltrane, Sonny Rollins, Cannonball Adderley, and Fats Navarro. Aebersold also distributes transcription books by Ken Slone and Don Sickler. Slone has prepared a book of Clifford Brown solos. Sickler has one of Joe Henderson's solos. There are also some fairly elaborate transcription books from a series originally published under the auspices of *Down Beat* magazine. It includes *Jazz Styles and Analysis: Guitar* by Jack Petersen (74 solos from 64 guitarists), *Jazz Styles and Analysis: Alto Sax* by Harry Miedema (125 solos from 103 saxophonists), and *Jazz Styles and Analysis: Trombone* by David Baker

(157 solos). Aebersold distributes so many more such books, you ought to just send him a letter listing the soloists you seek. Then, with your letter, include a stamped post card addressed to you, and ask Aebersold to return the postcard with the availability and price written on it so that you can order what you want that he has. When this book went to press, Aebersold was carrying books of solos by Stan Getz, Chick Corea, Louis Armstrong, Bill Evans, Horace Silver, Benny Goodman, Art Tatum, J. J. Johnson, Charlie Parker, Thelonious Monk, Bud Powell, Paul Chambers, Dexter Gordon, and others. Simply write Jamey Aebersold at 1211X Aebersold Drive, New Albany, Ind. 47150. (The same advice about the post card applies to dealing with Andrew White. In fact, White has been known to transcribe solos on demand. So if you want to pay for something that is not already in his catalog, consider commissioning it from him.)

Many solo transcriptions can be found in doctoral dissertations. These are books written to earn a doctor's degree. Most are never commercially published. However, when the doctor's degree is granted, most dissertations are automatically deposited with a company called University Microfilms, which permanently retains one copy and then makes and sells additional copies on demand. This has been occurring only since 1956, so do not contact University Microfilms for work completed before then. University of Chicago, Harvard University, and Massachusetts Institute of Technology are among the few institutions that do not contribute to this repository.

To get a dissertation, write University Microfilms International, 300 Zeeb Road, Ann Arbor, Michigan 48106. Tell them the author's name (it helps to have the middle initial), the first two words of the title, the college where the dissertation was done, and the year it was completed. This information, or at least the first two parts of it, help them identify the dissertation when you lack the catalog number.

When you correspond with them, tell them your college affiliation because they extend a discount to students and faculty. If you do not want to write them, you can phone them at their toll-free number (1-800-521-3042; from Michigan, Alaska, and Hawaii: 313-761-4700; from Canada: 1-800-268-6090) and you can even order them to bill your credit card.

You will probably come across many titles of books, articles, and dissertations that you just want to glance at and not necessarily own (most cost more than 20 dollars). For that reason, it is handy to know about interlibrary loan services. If you have never used such a service, ask the staff at your college library reference desk. The staff should have a computer that will tell what nearby library is holding the book, article, or dissertation you want. The staff can put in a request, then you need wait only a few days or weeks before your library receives it for you. Then you can check it out just as you would check out one of your own library's holdings. Note that if you want only a single article from a periodical, your interlibrary loan staff can sometimes arrange for a distant library to copy the article and send it for you to keep. (This can be quite convenient when you want a particularly good transcription that lies in an old jazz magazine that no one in town seems to have.)

To keep up with new dissertations that are being added to the literature about jazz, you could scan the music listings in your library's current copies of *Dissertation Abstracts*. This is a periodical that publishes summaries of dissertations that have just been completed.

Here are a few dissertations that have many transcriptions in them:

*Charlie Parker: Techniques of Improvisation*, by Thomas Owens, 1974, University of California
Catalog Number 75-1992
(Contains about 250 Parker solos)

*A History and Analysis of Jazz Drumming to 1942,* by Theodore Dennis Brown, 1976, University of Michigan
Catalog Number 77-7881
(Contains numerous drum solos and timekeeping rhythms as well as analyses.)

*The Improvisational Techniques of Art Tatum,* by Joseph A. Howard, 1978, Case Western Reserve University
Catalog Number 78-16468

Carl Fischer Music, Inc. (62 Cooper Square, NY, NY 10003) has published several books by Stuart Isacoff that contain solo transcriptions, accompanied by useful analyses and comments about the styles of major players. *Solos for Tenor Sax* contains analyses of improvisations by John Coltrane, Stan Getz, Coleman Hawkins, Oliver Nelson, and Sonny Rollins. *Solos for Jazz Trumpet* contains analyses of improvisations by Louis Armstrong, Dizzy Gillespie, Miles Davis, Lee Morgan, and Freddie Hubbard. *Solos for Jazz Alto Sax* contains analyses of improvisations by Cannonball Adderley, Paul Desmond, Eric Dolphy, Johnny Hodges, Charlie Parker, and Phil Woods.

*Structural Development in the Jazz Improvisational Technique of Clifford Brown,* by Milton Lee Stewart, 1973, University of Michigan
Catalog Number 73-24692

*John Coltrane's Music of 1960 Through 1967,* by Lewis R. Porter, 1983, Brandeis University
Catalog Number 83-18239

*Jazz, 1920 to 1927: An Analytical Study,* by Launcelot Allen Pyke, II, 1962, State University of Iowa
Catalog Number 62-4988
(Contains transcriptions of 1926 "Perdido Street Blues" with Kid Ory, Johnny Dodds and Baby Dodds, 1923 "Snake Rag" by King Oliver's Creole Jazz Band, 1942 "Down By the Riverside" by Bunk Johnson's Original Superior Band, 1927 "Keyhole Blues" by Louis Armstrong and His Hot Seven, the 1923 Gennett recording of "Dippermouth Blues" by King Oliver's Creole Jazz Band, 1924 "Cake Walkin' Babies" by Armstrong and Bechet, 1926 "Big Butter and Egg Man From The West" by Louis Armstrong and His Hot Five, 1923 "Sweet Lovin' Man" by King Oliver's Creole Jazz Band minus Oliver, 1925 "Papa De-Da-Da" by Armstrong and Bechet, and 1923 "Southern Stomps" by Oliver's Creole Jazz Band.)

# FOR MUSICIANS

This section is designed to give musically literate readers a chance to experience some of the musical elements discussed in the text. It is possible to learn more by playing the examples at the piano than by simply reading the attached explanations. After you have played these figures yourself, they will be easier to hear in jazz recordings.

**Chords and Chord Progressions**

We can imagine chords as being built by tones in major scales (Bb C D Eb F G A Bb or C D E F G A B C or D E F# G A B C# D). Beginning with a single tone, the chord is made by adding every other tone in the scale. In other words, the first, third, and fifth tones are used when the beginning tone is the key note (first tone of major scale). The second, fourth, and sixth tones are used when the chord is based on the second step of the scale. The third, fifth, and seventh tones are used when the chord begins on the third step of the scale.

If a chord is based on the first tone of the major scale, it is called the "one chord," symbolized by the Roman numeral for one, I. (Roman numerals are used for chord names.) The chord based on the second step of the major scale is a II chord. The labeling system continues through the VII chord.

**415**

Of course, there is more to it than that. Before you can apply chord knowledge to studying improvisation, you must become acquainted with the construction of many types of chords: dominant sevenths and major sevenths; major, minor, diminished, and augmented chords; chords with added ninths, elevenths, and thirteenths; chords with added fourths and sixths, flat fifths, raised ninths, etc. And there is a collection of different chord labeling systems which also must be confronted.

**Twelve-Bar Blues Progressions**  Though basically a I-IV-I-V-I progression, the twelve-bar blues may contain a huge assortment of chord progressions. Here are three possibilities for a blues in the key of C.

**Turnarounds**  Turnarounds are the chord progressions occurring in the seventh and eighth, fifteenth and sixteenth, thirty-first and thirty-second bars of a thirty-two-bar chord progression, and in the eleventh and twelfth bars of a twelve-bar blues progression. Some turnarounds occupy more or less than two measures, however. Turnarounds provide an opportunity for numerous variations, which depend on the preferences and era of soloist and rhythm section.

G7                C
/ / / / | / / / / :‖

Dm7              G7                C
/ / / / | / / / / | / / / / :‖

Dm7              A♭m9   D♭7      C
/ / / / | / / / / | / / / / :‖

Dm7              Fm7              C
/ / / / | / / / / | / / / / :‖

Fm7              B♭7              C
/ / / / | / / / / | / / / / :‖

Dm    E♭7      A♭     B7      E     G7      C
/ / / / | / / / / | / / / / | / / / / :‖

**Voicing**   Rarely is a chord played with its tones contained in a single octave, the root on the bottom, the third in the middle, and the fifth on the top.

Usually chords are voiced. This means that the positions of a chord's tones are scattered over the keyboard; the tones may be altered, doubled, added to, missing, and so forth. Instead of having the root on the bottom and the fifth on the top, a chord might have its root on top and fifth on the bottom.

Or perhaps the third is on the bottom with the fifth next and the root on top.

In some voicings, the root is doubled by being duplicated in different octaves.

Quite frequently the sixth is added to enrich major triads.

Instead of being voiced in thirds (every other step in a major scale), some chords are voiced in fourths.

There are a great variety of possibilities available in voicing chords. Only a few simple examples have been cited as an introduction. In addition to striking force, phrasing, speed, and precision, an important characteristic of a jazz pianist's style is his preference in voicings. For instance, McCoy Tyner often uses an interval of a fifth in the left hand together with a chord voiced in fourths in the right hand.

**Modes**   Though used for centuries in classical music, modes just recently became popular harmonic bases for jazz improvisation. Modes are constructed using the tones for the major scale, and different modes are produced by starting on different notes of the scale. Each mode's unique sound is the result of its particular arrangement of whole steps and half steps. For example, in the Ionian mode (also known as the major scale), half steps occur only between the third and fourth tones and the seventh and eighth (an octave up from the first) tones.

The Dorian mode is constructed from the same tones as the Ionian, but it begins on the second tone of the major scale. The Dorian mode has half steps between its second and third and its sixth and seventh tones.

There is a mode for each step of the major scale. Each mode has a distinct musical personality because its half steps fall in different places.

Examine the following modes, play them and listen carefully. Find the position of the half steps in each mode. Once you know a mode's pattern of whole and half steps, you should be able to begin it on other notes. Remember that the interval between B♭ and C is defined as a whole step as is that between E and F♯. Remember also that the interval between B and C is a half step as is that between E and F.

**Ahavoh Rabboh (Jewish)**

**Pentatonic**

**Whole Tone**

**Diminished**

**Inverted Diminished**

**Modal Construction of "Flamenco Sketches"**

The piece "Flamenco Sketches" on the Miles Davis album *Kind of Blue* follows the modal construction illustrated below. (Note that the piece was labeled "All Blues" on many copies.)

mode 1  C Ionian

mode 2  A flat Ionian

mode 3  B flat Ionian

mode 4  D Phrygian

mode 5  G Aeolian

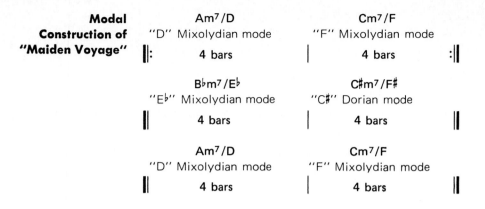

**Modal Construction of "Maiden Voyage"**

| Am⁷/D | Cm⁷/F |
|-------|-------|
| "D" Mixolydian mode | "F" Mixolydian mode |
| ‖: 4 bars | 4 bars :‖ |

| B♭m⁷/E♭ | C♯m⁷/F♯ |
|---------|---------|
| "E♭" Mixolydian mode | "C♯" Dorian mode |
| 4 bars | 4 bars |

| Am⁷/D | Cm⁷/F |
|-------|-------|
| "D" Mixolydian mode | "F" Mixolydian mode |
| 4 bars | 4 bars |

"D" Mixolydian, first mode for A section of "Maiden Voyage" Am⁷/D

"F" Mixolydian, second mode for A section of "Maiden Voyage" Cm⁷/F

"E♭" Mixolydian, first mode for bridge of "Maiden Voyage" B♭m⁷/E♭

"C♯" Dorian, second mode for bridge of "Maiden Voyage" C♯m⁷/F♯

**Modal Construction for "So What" and "Impressions"**

**Dm⁷**  
"D" Dorian mode  
‖: 8 bars :‖

**E♭m⁷**  
"E♭" Dorian mode  
‖ 8 bars ‖

**Dm⁷**  
"D" Dorian mode  
‖ 8 bars ‖

"D" Dorian mode for first sixteen bars of "So What" and "Impressions"

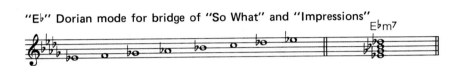

"E♭" Dorian mode for bridge of "So What" and "Impressions"

**Modal Construction of "Milestones"**

**Gm⁷/C**  
"G" Dorian mode  
‖: 8 bars :‖

**Dm⁷/E**  
"A" Aeolian mode  
‖: 8 bars :‖

**Gm⁷/C**  
"G" Dorian mode  
‖ 8 bars ‖

"G" Dorian mode for first sixteen bars of "Milestones"

"A" Aeolian mode for bridge of "Milestones"

(notated by David Berger).

"Boston" or Two-handed Stride-style Comping
(notated by David Berger)

**Comping**　Here are two examples of piano accompaniments, or comping, for a jazz twelve-bar blues solo. Comping is accompaniment simultaneously composed and performed to fit the style of a piece, and harmonic and rhythmic directions of the solo line. Comping usually contains pronounced syncopation.

Note that these chords have been voiced. Comping involves countless ways to voice chords, alter chord progressions, and design rhythms. But basically, comping is meant to accompany and complement the solo line by producing syncopated, unpatterned bursts of chords. Patterned chording, by definition, cannot flexibly enhance a spontaneously conceived solo line. Prewritten patterns (and accompanying figures (notated by David Berger).

Bebop-Style Comping
(notated by David Berger)

which sound prewritten) cannot sensitively interact with solo improvisation. The improvising soloist might just as well be playing with a big band using written arrangements. (For examples of comping which sensitively interact with and enhance improvised solos, listen to Tommy Flanagan and Herbie Hancock. For examples of accompanying which are not comping in the sense used above but are more like prewritten material, listen to post-1960 Horace Silver and to John Lewis's work with the Modern Jazz Quartet.)

**Walking Bass Lines**  Walking is meant to provide timekeeping in the form of tones chosen for their compatibility with the harmonies of the piece and style of the performance. Ideally, the walking bass complements the solo line.

Three choruses of walking bass are shown here. They display three levels of complexity.

Walking bass lines for the 12-bar blues in the key of C (conceived and notated by Willis Lyman).

**Rock Bass Lines**    Jazz bassists of the 1970s incorporated many devices which were previously used mainly by rock bassists. A number of rock bass figures are notated here to illustrate the material from which many 1970s jazz bassists drew.

Rock bass figures (notated by Richard Straub).

**Latin American Bass Line**   During performances of many jazz pieces of the 1950s and 60s, including the first eight bars of "On Green Dolphin Street" and "I'll Remember April," bassists employed a figure like the one below which was called a "Latin bass figure."

**Syncopations**   The rhythms common to jazz contain many syncopations. Here is a collection of examples.

Comping Figures for "Rhythm Changes" (notated by Jerry Sheer). This is a typical example of piano comping for improvisations that follow the chord changes used by George Gershwin to accompany his melody "I Got Rhythm." This would also fit "Cottontail," "Shaw Nuff," "Lester Leaps In," and "(Meet the) Flintstones."

**Ride Rhythms**   Ride rhythms are used by drummers to keep time and propel a performance. These rhythms contribute to jazz swing feeling, accomplishing in the high register (cymbals) what the walking bass does in the low register.

Basic Jazz Ride Rhythm Common in Slow and Medium Tempos (4-Beat Feel)*

Basic Jazz Ride Rhythm Common in Fast Tempos (4-Beat Feel)

VARIATIONS:
Medium Tempos — Elvin Jones

Medium Tempos — Roy Haynes

Fast Tempos — Billy Higgins

Fast Tempos — Roy Haynes

Basic Jazz Ride Rhythm Used to Imply 2-Beat Feel

*NOTE: The 12/8 figures are notated from 4/4 tunes. (Transcribed by Chuck Braman.)

**Jazz-Rock Drumming**  Drummers since the late 1960s learned new timekeeping patterns which resembled the materials of r & b as well as Latin American styles.

Andy Newmark — "In Time" from Sly Stone's *Fresh* 1973

Mike Clarke — "Butterfly" from Herbie Hancock's *Thrust* 1974

KEY (for this page only):

CLOSED HIGH HAT STRUCK WITH STICK    OPEN HIGH HAT STRUCK WITH STICK    SNARE DRUM    BASS DRUM    HIGH HAT SHARPLY CLOSED WITH FOOT

(Transcribed by Chuck Braman.)

## A Small Basic Collection of Jazz Videos

*Trumpet Kings* (VIA) 60 minutes; narrated by Wynton Marsalis; includes Louis Armstrong, Bunny Berigan, Roy Eldridge, Red Allen, Dizzy Gillespie, Miles Davis, Freddie Hubbard and others.

*Piano Legends* (VIA) 63 minutes; narrated by Chick Corea; includes Earl Hines, Fats Waller, Art Tatum, Thelonious Monk, Bill Evans, Cecil Taylor and others.

*One Night With Blue Note, Vol. 1* (SVS) 55 minutes; Bobby Hutcherson, Herbie Hancock, Ron Carter, Freddie Hubbard, Joe Henderson, Tony Williams, Stanley Jordan, Art Blakey, Curtis Fuller, Johnny Griffin, Walter Davis and Reggie Workman.

*One Night With Blue Note, Vol. 2* (SVS) 60 minutes; Kenny Burrell, Grover Washington, Grady Tate, Reggie Workman, McCoy Tyner, Jackie McLean, Woody Shaw, Cecil McBee, Jack DeJohnette, Charles Lloyd, Michel Petrucciani, Lou Donaldson, Jimmy Smith and Cecil Taylor.

*Sun Ra: A Joyful Noise* (RHAP) 60 minutes; documentary and much live music.

*Satchmo* (CBS); documentary on career of Louis Armstrong.

*Duke Ellington and his Orchestra* (JCVC-101) film clips of the Ellington band, 1929–52.

*After Hours* (RHAP) 27 minutes; 1961 short featuring Coleman Hawkins, Roy Eldridge and Cozy Cole.

*Thelonious Monk: Straight, No Chaser* (WB); performances and recording session, some dialog.

*Bill Evans on the Creative Process* (RHAP); 20 minutes; Evans talks and plays.

*The Coltrane Legacy* (VAI); 61 minutes; John Coltrane, Eric Dolphy, Elvin Jones, McCoy Tyner, Reggie Workman, Jimmy Garrison performances; interviews with Jimmy Cobb, Elvin Jones, Roy Haynes, Reggie Workman.

*A Different Drummer: Elvin Jones* (RHAP); 30 minutes; documentary of Jones demonstrating his drum technique, performing with his 1979 quartet and rare footage with John Coltrane quartet.

**Distributors to contact for the above and for additional jazz videos:**

Video Arts International (VAI)
Box 153, Ansonia Station, Dept. J.
NY, NY 10023

Rhapsody Films (RHAP)
P.O. Box 179
NY, NY 10014
(212) 243–0152

CBS Music Video Enterprises (CBS)

JCVC Jazz Classics—Videofidelity

Warner Brothers Films (WB)

Jamey Aebersold
P.O. Box 1244C
New Albany, IN 47150
1–800–456–1388

Original Music
R.D. 1, Box 190
Lasher Road
Tivoli, NY 12583
(914) 756–2767

Jazzland
Box 366
Dayton, Ohio 45401
(513) 222–2413

The Jazz Store
333 Beech Avenue
Garwood, NJ 07027

## *Jazz Classics* **Cassette Contents**

Side One:

*Street Cries of Charleston* (Afro-American male street vendor)
*Fishermen, Strawberry, Devil Crab* (Miles Davis-Gil Evans)
*Hunter's Dance* (West African field recording: Guinea)
*One Day* (Angelic Gospel Singers/Dixie Hummingbirds)   1951
*One O'Clock Jump* (Count Basie)   1942
*Birdland* (Weather Report)   1977
*Dixie Jazz Band One-Step* (Original Dixieland Jazz Band)   1917
*West End Blues* (Louis Armstrong and Earl Hines) 1928
*You've Got To Be Modernistic* (James P. Johnson)   1930
*Cottontail* (Duke Ellington big band featuring Ben Webster)   1940
*Harlem Airshaft* (Ellington band featuring Cootie Williams, Barney Bigard)   1940
*Transblucency* (Duke Ellington and Lawrence Brown)   1946
*Prelude to a Kiss* (Duke Ellington and Johnny Hodges) 1957
*Taxi War Dance* (Count Basie big band featuring Lester Young)   1939
*Lester Leaps In* (Lester Young and Count Basie)   1939
*Shaw Nuff* (Charlie Parker and Dizzy Gillespie)   1945
*Four Brothers* (Woody Herman big band)   1947
*No Figs* (Lennie Tristano, Lee Konitz, Stan Getz)   1950
*Frame for the Blues* (Maynard Ferguson big band) 1958

Side Two:

*Flamenco Sketches* (Miles Davis, John Coltrane, Cannonball Adderley, Bill Evans)   1959
*Solar* (Bill Evans, Scott LaFaro, Paul Motian)   1961
*The Promise* (John Coltrane, McCoy Tyner, Jimmy Garrison, Elvin Jones)   1963
*Jitney #2* (Cecil Taylor)   1974
*Masqualero* (Miles Davis, Wayne Shorter, Herbie Hancock, Ron Carter, Tony Williams)   1967
*Steps* (Chick Corea, Miroslav Vitous, Roy Haynes) 1968
*Surucucu* (Weather Report: Joe Zawinul, Wayne Shorter, Miroslav Vitous, Dom Um      Eric Gravatt)   1972

## *Jazz Styles* **Cassette Contents**

Side One:

Jazz Drum Set
Chords and Chord Progressions
I-IV-I-V-I Blues Progression
Chord Voicing
Comping and Syncopation
Bass Styles
Rhythm Section Roles
32-Bar A-A-B-A *I Got Rhythm*/*Flintstones*
Stop-Time Solo Break

Side Two:

Double-Time
Half-Time
Pianist's Left Hand vs. Right Hand
Stride Style Left Hand Piano Playing
Walking Tenths
Horn-Like Piano Lines
Octave-Voiced Piano Lines
Piano Tremolo
Swing Eighth Note Pattern
Legato
Staccato
Vibrato
Drop/Fall-Off
Scoop
Smear
Dolt
Blue Notes
Trumpet, Fluegelhorn and Mute Timbres
Clarinet
Soprano Sax
Clarinet vs. Soprano Sax
Alto Sax
Tenor Sax
Baritone Sax
Flute
Flute vs. Clarinet
Tenor Sax vs. Soprano Sax
Trombone and Mute Timbres
Timbre Reviews
Guitar and Banjo
Guitar/Banjo Timbre Review
Vibraharp
Instrument Identification Quiz

# INDEX

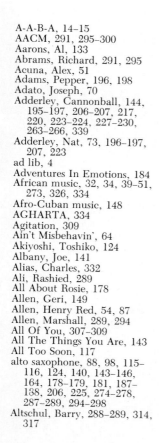